Plot Guide to 100 American and British Novels

Plot Guide to 100 American and British Novels

- Plot Outlines
- Character Analyses
- Critical Evaluations

with a Special Introduction
on
How to Read a Novel

Edited by Abraham H. Lass

Boston   THE WRITER, INC.   Publishers

To Betty and Janet

Preface

In presenting this new edition of *A Student's Guide to 50 American Novels* and *A Student's Guide to 50 British Novels* in this one-volume, hardcover edition under the title, *Plot Guide to 100 American and British Novels,* the editor hopes to provide a convenient, permanent reference book for three kinds of readers. First, for the reader who is not yet the reader he wishes to be—who knows there is much in store for him, who has not tasted more than a portion of the feast. For him, this will be an overview. He will *know about* these novels (characters, plots, themes, styles) before he goes on to *know* them. The second kind of reader has sampled many of these novels and may need little more than a review of what he has already enjoyed or a reference guide for further study. And third, for the reader who may himself be a writer of fiction.

"Find writers who write as you would like to and study them" is the sound advice of a well-known novelist. With this reference book, the writer has a practical gazetteer, a guide to the novelist's world.

For each of the 100 novels covered in this book there is:

1) an annotated list of the main characters
2) a full, clear, comprehensible summary of the significant incidents and themes
3) a biographical sketch of the author
4) a digest of present-day critical opinion of the novel, placing it in its proper context in the development of the novel and indicating how contemporary readers and critics evaluate it

While no selection of titles could please everyone, we believe that the novels chosen for this book will challenge the intelligent person to make his own rich and varied reading program. Here are the masterpieces and the milestones, the "classics and commercials," the great books and the near-great. Here are the seed books, the novels from which have sprung new novels and new ideas. All of them are still widely read and discussed. They are part of every reader's heritage.

If these novels have one thing in common despite differences in age and manners, it is that they have all (in Wordsworth's phrase) "kept watch o'er man's mortality." They have something everlasting to report to us about ourselves, and they report it in the syllables of art.

To read or to reread these novels—and this book will have achieved its purpose if it sends you back to the originals—is to take part in a magnificent adventure of the spirit: to understand what made D. H. Lawrence say, with an artist's pardonable license, "Being a novelist, I consider myself superior to the saint, the scientist, the philosopher, and the poet. The novel is the one bright book of life."

A. H. L.

Contents

Contents

How to Read a Novel

Why do people read novels? Perhaps for the moment the world is *too much* with them—or *not enough*. They may be seeking relief or discovery; they may wish to be comforted, uplifted, amused, stimulated, or even provoked—but *always* to be entertained. And so they turn a page and step into another man's world.

In one novel we may find what Graham Greene calls "an entertainment," a tale unfolded for our enjoyment; we shall not even mind a few tears in the telling of it. In another novel perhaps we find a few of the answers. What we have only half suspected of human experience is blindingly clear in the author's searchlight; a facet of man has been illuminated.

Often a novel offers us both adventure and insight. Herman Melville in *Moby Dick,* for example, takes us on a heroic whaling voyage; from the moment we ship out of Nantucket with Ishmael and Queequeg and the harpooners, we are exploring strange waters on a mad quest. And, again, in *Lord Jim,* Joseph Conrad takes us on an exciting voyage to such seaports as Bombay, Calcutta, Rangoon, Penang, Batavia; to the deck of the steamer *Patna* in the Arabian Sea, and to the Malaysian jungle of Patusan. Yet, these voyages are the means of exploring ourselves. When we are home again, we are richer for understanding certain profound ambiguities in Captain Ahab's, in Jim's, in all men's nature.

Whatever the novel, it is well to look sharp in the writer's world. For each novel is the individual vision of an artist, his direct impression of reality. To share his discoveries we must look at the view he sees from his personal porthole. If every prospect immediately displeases and every man seems vile, we may be allowing our prejudices to come between us and the writer's sights. (Tom Sawyer so troubled the good ladies of nineteenth-century Brooklyn that they had him banished from the public library; Huckleberry Finn was condemned as subversive of the morals of youth, as indeed he is, if youth are bound to such widely accepted principles as the sanctity of law, property, and public opinion over the sanctity of man. And in England, Tess and Jude once scandalized Thomas Hardy's public so much that after the hostile reception of *Jude the Obscure* he stopped writing novels entirely; the Rector of Broxton in *Adam Bede* was "little more than a pagan" to George Eliot's readers; Heathcliff apparently struck the first readers of *Wuthering Heights* with such unpleasant force that Charlotte Brontë felt it necessary to come to her sister's defense in the famous statement which begins, "Whether it is right or advisable to create beings like Heathcliff, I do not know; I scarcely think it is.") Before we complain to the novelist that we find his country uninhabitable, we should be humble and permit him to show us its "manners, climates, councils, governments."

The Novelist's View of Reality

Very well, says the reader with humility to the novelist, show me a slice of life.

Novelist A may choose to cut his slice horizontally; Novelist B, vertically. The method calls for close attention.

A, following a straight chronological line, begins at the beginning of his hero's story, goes on through the middle until he comes to the end, and stops. Pete Prentiss is born, attends school, falls in love with Lucille Lambent, serves in the army, and (after a suitable number of interesting complications linked by character and motive) marries or dies.

B, on the other hand, is going to ignore chronology and cut Pete down the middle for our examination; like Macbeth, he'll "unseam" him from the nave to the chaps. He will disclose his memories, joys, agonies, reveries—with no respect to time. There will be a flashback to Kitten Huxley's cocktail party, when Lucille first met that awful Mike Ebsen, and Pete had the strange talk with the Swami Vitrananda. If Novelist B is quite modern, he will not end his novel, but will leave his hero (who is not a hero at all) in the middle of a moment of consciousness which can be traced backward or forward in time, as the reader wishes.

The meaning of reality, the nature of the real, has been a point of dispute among novelists, as between philosophers and physicists, for more than half a century. One of the most illuminating quarrels was carried on between Virginia Woolf and a group of novelists—Arnold Bennett, H. G. Wells, John Galsworthy—whose "materialism" seemed to Mrs. Woolf to be the negation of life. In *Mr. Bennett and Mrs. Brown,* she pointed out how these novelists had crowded out reality with the furniture of their novels; they had laid so much dull stress on environment, social setting, the fabric instead of the substance, that the essence of being had escaped them.

In a famous statement in her essay "Modern Fiction" in *The Common Reader,* Mrs. Woolf puts the case for all the novelists of sensibility, the "stream of consciousness" stylists, who were to follow. "Life is not a series of gig-lamps symmetrically arranged," said Mrs. Woolf (demolishing Novelist A); life is *"a luminous halo, a semi-transparent envelope"* which surrounds man from the beginning of consciousness to the end.

Mrs. Woolf developed her own luminous style—a delicate and subtle handling of those currents of consciousness where she believed the truth of "reality" lay—in her novels *Mrs. Dalloway, To the Lighthouse,* and *The Waves.* In the work of many of our contemporaries, as in Mrs. Woolf's and in Joyce's work, the stream of consciousness has become an almost lyrical flow.

For one of Mrs. Woolf's characters, Mrs. Ramsay in *To the Lighthouse,* when life sinks down for a moment and there is no need to act, the range of implicit experience seems limitless. In the depth of being herself, "a wedge-shaped core of darkness," she triumphs over life; things come together in "this peace, this rest, this eternity."

This is a very different kind of reality, of course, from that in many novels, or for that matter in many people's experience. Meeting it in prose fiction today, the reader does well to approach it as he approaches the reality of a poem: with a response to its rhythms, its imagery, its timeless flow of memories and impressions.

Character in the Novel

Mr. Bennett and Mrs. Woolf were agreed on one point at least: The essential concern of the novelist is with "character in itself"; only if the characters are real has the novel any chance of surviving. "The only classification of the novel that I can understand," wrote Henry James in *The Art of Fiction,* "is into that which has life and that which has it not."

The characters above all in a novel can *solace* us, in E. M. Forster's words. We who can hardly understand ourselves, much less one another, in our imperfect world, meet in the novelist's world "a more comprehensible and thus a more manageable human race" and we have the enormously comforting illusion of understanding, at last, the secret, invisible truth of people.

When the reader puts together all the clues to character that the novelist has included in his book, when he perceives the truth of Ahab in *Moby Dick,* or Reverend Dimmesdale in *The Scarlet Letter,* or Isabel Archer in *The Portrait of a Lady,* or Heathcliff in *Wuthering Heights;* or of Philip Carey in *Of Human Bondage,* or Pecksniff in *Martin Chuzzlewit* or Becky Sharp in *Vanity Fair*—even though none of these may know it of himself, he is almost like the Creator in all-knowing wisdom.

Yet, according to Elizabeth Bowen, a subtle novelist and, in her "Notes on Writing a Novel," a most illuminating critic, characters are not *created* by the novelist at all. They are *found;* they pre-exist in his consciousness and reveal themselves slowly to his perception as he is writing, as might "fellow-travellers seated opposite one in a dimly lit railway carriage."

What the novelist is inviting the reader to do, then, is to *recognize* the people of the novel as they play their roles in the story.

We use the word *play* advisedly. The people of the novelist's world are very busy every moment. They are making choices of alternative behavior; they are speaking or not speaking in a certain way; when they are not around, they are being discussed by other characters.

To recognize Sister Carrie in Dreiser's novel or Eustacia Vye in Hardy's *The Return of the Native,* the reader might well imagine that he is watching her in a drama literally played upon a stage. He may ask himself the same questions about the people in a novel that he subconsciously asks about the figures in grease paint who move before footlights:

What is the effect on these people of the *setting* they
  are in?
What do I know of the *antecedent action?*
What signs of *motive* do I perceive?
Where are the evidences of *conflict* (within and without)?
How does this person see himself? How does he wish
  others to see him? How is he seen by others?
How does he give himself away—in gesture, inflection,
  choice of words?
Where is the *climax* of this person's conflict? Is it in-
  evitable in terms of what has gone before?

And so on. It is a game only a little different from the one
the reader plays every day. Listening to his neighbor protest,
"I am the last person in the world to gossip," he knows her
for a talebearer; trying to solve the riddle of the face opposite him in the subway (eyes full of pain, slack mouth,
shaving-cut on chin), he wonders what the combination of all
these features means. In novels, however, the characters are
explicable; the writer has willed it so. If the reader is perceptive enough, he can pluck out the heart of each man's
mystery.

Sometimes the clues are tiny. Every reader understands the
significant event, the major decision. But it is also a revealing
incident, says Henry James, when a woman stands up with
her hand resting on a table and looks at you in a certain way.
A chance word or sigh, Forster reminds us, is just as much
evidence as a speech or a murder.

The playwright, of course, has always understood this, and
that is why we urge the novel reader to behave as if he were
watching a play.

Chekhov, in whose dramas there is no melodrama, only the
reverberation of the thousand small shocks that make life
palpable, said in one of his letters that the things that happen
onstage should be as complex and yet as simple as they are
in daily reality. "For instance, people are having a meal at
a table, just having a meal, but at the same time their happiness is being created, or their lives are being smashed up."

How many meals are eaten in novels! And every one of them
is "evidence." In *Pride and Prejudice*, the ineffable Mr. Collins,
enjoying a repast with his noble patroness, the Lady Catherine
de Bourgh, is condemned by Jane Austen with words from

his own mouth as a small-souled snob. As Edith Wharton shows Ethan Frome having supper alone with Mattie Silver after his wife, Zeena, has gone to Bettsbridge, he inarticulately expresses his love in a dozen ways. Wang Lung in *The Good Earth,* because it is his wedding day, sprinkles a dozen curled, dried leaves of tea into the boiling water in his father's breakfast bowl; the old man protests that it is like eating silver, but drinks greedily, and we understand the poverty of the good earth and the hunger of the age, so like a child's eagerness for its feeding. Little Pip, in Dickens's *Great Expectations,* is judged "naterally wicious" by all the company at Mrs. Joe Gargery's Christmas dinner, but we know that he is eating his heart out, along with his dinner.

(In Dickens, by the way, there are few characters, and many caricatures: The people are the same each time they appear. They never surprise us. They are readily identifiable by tag lines and stock reactions. Mr. Micawber is predictably optimistic; Uriah Heep consistently 'umble. According to E. M. Forster's terminology, useful in modern fiction also, such "flat" characters, or static figures, are in contrast to "round" characters, who develop and behave unpredictably, though always inevitably. Elizabeth Bowen believes that ideal novels should contain only "round" characters—yet what a pity to lose Dickens's people on a literary technicality! Genius, having created and populated a world, can also animate it with "flats.")

Living characters in novels, once fully perceived, are life-stretchers for us all. We love, hate, suffer, comprehend with them vicariously. They satisfy our hunger to share the news about the human condition. Real people have a way of keeping themselves to themselves; characters in books open their hearts. We know what Robinson Crusoe felt and thought on that lonely island, and Defoe has us hear from Moll Flanders herself about all the husbands she married. We share every minute of Henry Fleming's first experience of battle in Stephen Crane's *The Red Badge of Courage.*

Sharing is a two-way journey. What is the reader's part? Empathy, imaginative sympathy, understanding of human values. As the characters grow larger in our imagination and in our sympathy, they take on meanings larger than themselves, possibly larger than life. Ahab is no longer the captain of the *Pequod,* but the symbol of all obsessive pursuit of the unattainable. Sydney Carton in *A Tale of Two Cities* is no longer an

eighteenth-century lawyer; he is a symbol of all charming
wastrels and self-sacrificing romanticists.

At the very least, the reader of novels will have, as Thoreau
did at Walden, a great deal of company in his house, especially in the morning, when nobody calls.

The Novelist at Work

"Why should a story not be told in the most irregular fashion that the author's idiosyncrasy may prompt, provided that
he gives us what we can enjoy?" asked George Eliot, in her
Leaves from a Notebook. "The dear public would do well to
reflect that they are often bored from the want of flexibility in
their own minds. They are like the topers of 'one liquor.'"

No two novelists are alike; there are as many kinds of novel
today—there have always been as many kinds of novel—as
there are readers to discover them. Without too much literary
analysis, it is possible to satisfy one's curiosity about the way
in which a novelist has set about making us enjoy his book.

Here is a brief list of checkpoints. Each novelist will have
approached a checkpoint in his own way.

Description of the Characters

The story-teller is no painter, but he must leave images in
the reader's mind.

Here, for example, is Billy Budd as Melville first pictures him
for us:

> He was young; and despite his all but fully developed
> frame, in aspect looked even younger than he really was.
> This was owing to a lingering adolescent expression in
> the as yet smooth face, all but feminine in purity of natu-
> ral complexion, but where, thanks to his seagoing, the lily
> was quite suppressed and the rose had some ado visibly to
> flush through the tan.

Obvious? But more will be demanded from the reader before
he will be able to see Billy. The young foretopman, says the
novelist,

showed in face that humane look of reposeful good nature which the Greek sculptor in some instances gave to his heroic strong man, Hercules.

That sentence calls for background. Melville will set his picture up for you only if you will collaborate with him.

Again, in *The Old Man and the Sea*, Hemingway recreates reality—his reality—with such precision of vivid detail that the whole world seems to be his own invention. For example, here is his description of the old man catching a dolphin:

> Just before it was dark, as they passed a great island of Sargasso weed that heaved and swung in the light sea as though the ocean were making love with something under a yellow blanket, his small line was taken by a dolphin. He saw it first when it jumped in the air, true gold in the last of the sun and bending and flapping wildly in the air. It jumped again and again in the acrobatics of its fear and he worked his way back to the stern and crouching and holding the big line with his right hand and arm, he pulled the dolphin in with his left hand, stepping on the gained line each time with his bare left foot. When the fish was at the stern, plunging and cutting from side to side in desperation, the old man leaned over the stern and lifted the burnished gold fish with its purple spots over the stern. Its jaws were working convulsively in quick bites against the hook and it pounded the bottom of the skiff with its long flat body, its tail and its head until he clubbed it across the shining golden head until it shivered and was still.

To experience this passage is to know not only fish and man but the novelist as well. Who but Hemingway could have written this?

The English novel furnishes equally graphic illustrations, as may be seen in the following example from *Pride and Prejudice,* in which Jane Austen sketches Mr. and Mrs. Bennet with rapid brilliance:

> Mr. Bennet was so odd a mixture of quick parts, sarcastic humour, reserve, and caprice, that the experience of three and twenty years had been insufficient to make

his wife understand his character. *Her* mind was less difficult to develop. She was a woman of mean understanding, little information, and uncertain temper. When she was discontented she fancied herself nervous. The business of her life was to get her daughters married; its solace was visiting and news.

Doesn't the fun of the passage increase if you collaborate with Miss Austen?

In *Great Expectations,* Dickens re-creates people with such a wealth of sensuous and vivid detail that the whole world seems to be his own invention. For example, here is his description of Pip's visit to Mr. Trabb to be measured for a new suit:

> Mr. Trabb had sliced his hot roll into three feather beds, and was slipping butter in between the blankets, and covering it up . . . When I had entered, [Mr. Trabb's boy] was sweeping the shop, and he had sweetened his labors by sweeping over me . . . Mr. Trabb, taking down a roll of cloth, and tiding it out in a flowing manner over the counter, preparatory to getting his hand under it to show the gloss. . . .

And so forth—to be enjoyed by the reader with the novelist's own gusto in the simplest acts of living.

Point of View

"The whole intricate question of method, in the craft of fiction, I take to be governed by the question of the *point of view*—the question of the relation in which the narrator stands to the story." And Percy Lubbock goes on to say (in *The Craft of Fiction*) that the novelist can describe his characters from the outside, as an impartial or partial observer; or from the inside, as a presumably omniscient force. He can also take the viewpoint of one character who does not know the motives of the others.

Although Henry James felt that the novelist should stick to one point of view in a story and not shift arbitrarily, E. M. Forster has been able to cite a number of instances where a novelist has been able to manage more than one shift rather well. For our part it matters very little how the novelist manages his camera-eye just so he puts in focus for us a world that is both plausible and lasting. What he shows us will depend on his *moral* lens.

Stendhal, writing to Balzac says: "I see but one rule, *to be clear*. If I am not clear, all my world crumbles to nothing."

Plot, Story, Theme

These are words to play with. When they are well handled by a writer, the reader does not have to notice them at all. But if you lift an eyebrow at such cavalier treatment of textbook terms, here are some definitions:

> The *story* is the answer to "And then what happened?"
> The *plot* tells us why it happened just so.
> The *theme* explains why the writer had to tell this particular story.

Or, in the delightful simplicity of *Aspects of a Novel*: "The King died and then the Queen died" is a story. "The King died and then the Queen died of grief" is a plot. (We do not have a theme for this yet.)

Causality is everything. Well, nearly everything. In his introduction to Henry James's *The Princess Casamassima,* Lionel Trilling outlines a story which has run through a number of nineteenth-century English, continental, and American novels, the story of The Young Man from the Provinces. Of humble and often mysterious birth, intelligent and proud, he moves into society, making great demands on life.

In one way or another, this is the skeleton of Stendhal's *The Red and the Black,* of Dickens's *Great Expectations,* and later of Scott Fitzgerald's *The Great Gatsby.* Yet plot, story, theme are nothing without the essence of all, which is the novelist's personal idiom, his statement outside logic or causality, a statement poetic in that it is always its own excuse for being.

And that brings us to the question of style.

Style

In Leo Tolstoi's *Talks with Tolstoi,* we have the following description of a writer's approach to his art:

Sophia Andreevna said: "It was the last time Turgenev stayed at Yasnaya, not long before his death. I asked him: 'Ivan Sergeevich, why don't you write now?' He answered: 'In order to write I had always to be a little in love. Now I am old I can't fall in love any more, and that is why I have stopped writing.'"

And Tolstoi himself, speaking in exasperation:

One ought only to write when one leaves a piece of one's flesh in the ink-pot each time one dips one's pen.

Lest you think, "Ah well, the Russians . . .!", here is another novelist's statement of what it means to write—Arnold Bennett, in his *Journals*:

The novelist should cherish and burnish this faculty of seeing crudely, simply, artlessly, ignorantly; of seeing like a baby or a lunatic, who lives each moment by itself and tarnishes by the present no remembrance of the past.

On every page of his novel, the writer has left his signature for us to read. The oldest quotation of all, Buffon's "The style is the man," is still the most accurate.

Here, then, is "another man's world."

American Novels

The Nineteenth Century

The Last of the Mohicans

by

JAMES FENIMORE COOPER (1789–1851)

Main Characters

Natty Bumppo—(known, too, as Leatherstocking, "La Longue Carabine" or Long Rifle, Hawkeye, and at other times in his career, as Deerslayer and Pathfinder): Tall, lean, hard, a supreme woodsman and a natural moralist. Proud and loyal, he speaks sometimes like a backwoodsman and sometimes like a philosopher.

Chingachgook—The "noble savage"—a Mohican of the Delaware family, silent, a fierce enemy and devoted friend, the soul of honor and a master of woodsman's lore.

Uncas—His son, an even nobler savage, the "last of the Mohicans," an Indian Adonis, without fear and without deceit.

Magua—The wicked Indian, handsome, eloquent, but treacherous. The inheritor of the most fearsome qualities of the Hurons (or Mingoes, in the language of the Delawares), he has also developed the most reprehensible characteristics of the whites.

Colonel Munro—Commander of the besieged Fort William Henry, an affectionate father, a resolute soldier, now a gallant old man despite military and personal misfortunes.

Cora—His eldest daughter, beautiful, high-spirited, indomitable, in her early twenties. Her "charged color" betokens the "dark" half of her origin.

3

Alice—Cora's blonde half sister, four or five years younger than Cora, dazzling to look at, but timid and easily overwhelmed by circumstances.

Major Duncan Heyward—A colonial officer, brave, honorable, forthright, a bit pompous, ignorant of Indian ways and warfare. He loves Alice Munro.

David Gamut—The lank, awkward, ingenious psalmodist whose main ambition is to sing and teach the songs of David (in very poor translations) and who is capable of remarkable fortitude.

The Story

The year is 1757. Fort William Henry, near Lake Champlain in upper New York, commanded by Colonel Munro, is under siege by the French and by the Huron Indians (Mingoes). Cora and Alice Munro set out from Fort Edward along the Hudson to join their father. In their party are an ungainly and eccentric teacher of psalmody, David Gamut; a gallant young officer, Major Duncan Heyward; and a fierce, cunning Indian guide, Magua. Magua misleads them. Pretending to have lost the way, he takes them into Huron territory. Luckily their path crosses that of Natty Bumppo, the intrepid scout, and his two Indian companions, Chingachgook and his brave son Uncas, the "last of the Mohicans." Quickly they agree to seize Magua. But before they can act, Magua escapes into the forest.

Realizing that the hostile Mingoes surround the party, the scout makes the party wait till dark. Then, while his Indian companions hide the horses, he leads the others to a canoe that he has hidden among the bushes, and ferries them to an island. Here there is a cavern where they can rest in relative safety. But the horses, set upon by wolves, scream in terror, and the Mingoes discover and attack their enemies. The scout, an infallible shot (nicknamed "La Longue Carabine"), picks off the boldest Mingoes on the opposite shore.

Natty and his friends have run out of ammunition. Resolutely the fugitives wait, determined to meet death bravely. Cora, the elder and more spirited of the sisters, urges them to escape. Somewhat unwillingly, the scout, Uncas, and Chingachgook

cast themselves into the current to emerge at a distant point in the forest opposite. Major Heyward, David Gamut, and the ladies are captured and hurried along a trail by the Hurons. Cora breaks branches to mark their path till one of the Indian rear guard stops her, pointing significantly to his tomahawk. During a pause in the march, Magua offers to release Alice if Cora will come to his wigwam as his wife. Cora rejects him. Maddened, Magua hurls his tomahawk at Alice. It misses and quivers above her head. Heyward bursts his bonds, hurling himself at one of the savages. The savage slips from his grasp, raises his knife—when suddenly a rifle cracks and the Indian falls dead.

Natty, Chingachgook, and Uncas have come to the rescue. A fierce battle follows, in which the captors are overcome but Magua escapes. Natty then explains that he and his Indian comrades have been following their trail all along.

Once again the party sets out for Fort Henry which is surrounded by Montcalm's forces. Luckily a dense fog has settled over the Fort, obscuring them from the enemy, but causing them to lose their way. The keen-eyed Uncas, however, lights upon the furrow of a cannon ball fired from the Fort and gives them their bearings.

The reunion between Colonel Munro and his daughters is affecting. Nevertheless, since the Fort is threatened, Natty and Heyward must go about their separate duties. Natty, back from a mission to Fort Edward to deliver the Colonel's plea to Webb, the British commander, is captured. General Montcalm releases him, after taking from him the letter from Webb, and invites Munro to a personal interview. In his place, Munro sends Heyward, who cannot get any relevant information from Montcalm. Upon Heyward's return, Munro insists that he disclose his feelings before reporting on his mission. Heyward then confesses his love for Alice—much to Munro's disapproval, since he thinks that Cora, the daughter of his mulatto first wife, has been rejected because of her mixed blood. After Heyward, with less than complete candor, reassures him, the Colonel listens to Heyward's report and decides to go with him to Montcalm.

Montcalm shows them the letter from Webb who declares that he cannot send reinforcements to the Fort and counsels surrender. Shattered, the Colonel determines to resist despite the odds. He is dissuaded by Montcalm, who offers him honorable terms of surrender. Munro accepts.

But Montcalm cannot control the savagery of his Indian followers. They attack a party of women and children leaving the Fort and slaughter them without mercy. Magua, their leader, again captures Cora and Alice, along with Gamut, who does his futile best to protect them. Magua leads his prisoners to the camp of the Hurons, among whom he is a chief (though in disgrace for his addiction to firewater). He gives Alice into their custody, leading Cora to the camp of the nearby Delaware tribe.

But Natty and his Indian friends are on the trail, with Munro and Heyward. They arrive at the Huron camp where they see Gamut who has escaped confinement because the Hurons think he is mad. Heyward decides to enter the Huron camp, disguised as a healer. He is tentatively accepted by the Indians, and one even requests his services for his stricken daughter-in-law. But before Heyward can oblige, Uncas is captured and the Hurons hold a council to decide his fate.

On the way to the sick woman, Heyward and the Huron are followed by a bear. The Huron knows that the bear is a local magician, but Heyward does not and is understandably nervous. Left alone to perform his ministrations, Heyward sees the bear remove his head: Natty Bumppo is revealed! The two now make their way to the chamber of the cave where Alice is imprisoned. Magua surprises them but is subdued by Natty. Heyward and Natty escape, carrying Alice to the Delaware camp. Natty then returns to the Hurons and in his bear outfit rescues Uncas.

The party reach the Delaware camp again, but Magua follows them, demanding the sisters and denouncing Natty. When Heyward pretends to be "La Longue Carabine," Natty displays his unbelievable prowess as a marksman to establish his identity. The ancient Delaware chief Tamemund comes forward to listen to Magua's argument that he be given all the English prisoners. Tamemund agrees, but Cora pleads that Uncas be allowed to speak. Uncas's brave demeanor impresses the Delawares, but Tamemund nevertheless pronounces his doom. One of the Delawares rips Uncas's hunting shirt and leaps back astonished, for beautifully tattooed on Uncas's breast is the figure of a small tortoise, the totem of the Mohicans, the race from which the Delawares spring.

Tamemund welcomes Uncas as the chief who will succeed him. Magua, however, demands Cora, since she is his hostage according to Delaware law. Though Hawkeye offers to take her place, Magua's demand is granted. Uncas warns Magua that he will pursue him as soon as sundown arrives. Magua laughs scornfully and leaves.

At sundown the Delawares pursue, aided by Heyward and Natty. There is a devastating fire fight. The battle seems to be going against the Delawares when the Colonel and Chingachgook, who have remained hidden in a nearby beaver dam, appear and turn the tide. The Hurons are destroyed or scattered—all except Magua, who with two of his men seizes Cora and escapes. But Uncas follows—to his doom. Magua buries his knife in the Mohican, while another Indian kills Cora. Magua bounds over the rocks and almost eludes his pursuers—but Natty's rifle finds its mark and Magua falls from a precipice to his death.

At the Delaware camp there is deep mourning. Chingachgook laments the death of his noble son, the Colonel his courageous daughter. After solemn burial ceremonies, the whites return to their civilization—all except Natty, who remains with Chingachgook.

Critical Opinion

Cooper's *Leatherstocking Tales* have firmly imprinted on the minds of Americans and Europeans an image of the Indian and the frontiersman. That the image is violently distorted may be regrettable. It is apparently ineradicable as well. The novels, published at different times in Cooper's long career, create a powerful myth of early America—its brave and incredibly capable frontiersmen, its wicked and noble savages, its wide, beautiful virgin forests, its gradual and reluctant acceptance of civilization. Listed according to *Leatherstocking's* chronology, they are *The Deerslayer* (1841), in which Natty is a young man; *The Last of the Mohicans* (1826) and *The Pathfinder* (1840), Natty from age thirty-five to thirty-nine;

The Pioneers (1823), which finds Natty in his seventies; and *The Prairie* (1827), in which Natty is an old man past eighty.

Of all the novels, *The Last of the Mohicans* is the most attractive. Here we find the noble Chingachgook and his nobler son Uncas, the exciting chases, pursuits, and rescues, the splendid panorama of the fresh and vital American land. The novel is marked by Cooper's faults, too: the wooden speech of the characters, the incidents that exceed not only belief but possibility, the plot endlessly coiling back upon itself. Mark Twain has summarized all the negative criticisms in his hilarious attempt to prove that Cooper simply could not manage to tell a story.

Yet Cooper still holds his readers. The breathless action of *The Last of the Mohicans,* the continuous excitement it generates, the animated pictures it paints of woods, camps, and settlements ("some of the loveliest, most glamorous pictures in all literature," D. H. Lawrence says), its poetic, pastoral vision of a frontier life, justify its great and continuing popularity. It is one of the supreme narratives of adventure in American literature.

The Author

James Fenimore Cooper was born in 1789 in Burlington, New Jersey. When Cooper was a year old, his father settled in Lake Otsego, in southern New York, where he owned a vast tract of land (now Cooperstown). In this semi-frontier area (from which the Indians had departed much earlier), Cooper was brought up to be an active country gentleman. After being tutored privately, he entered Yale College, from which he was expelled for setting off a small explosion in another student's room. In 1806, at his father's suggestion, Cooper shipped to England as a common sailor on a merchant vessel; later, however, he was commissioned and served three years in the U.S. Navy, resigning after his father's death to take over the management of the family estate. In 1811, he married Susan Augusta DeLancey, daughter of a wealthy Westchester landowner whose family had been staunchly Tory during the Revolution.

It seemed hardly likely that Cooper would become an

author. He hated even to write a letter. But in 1819, he boasted to his unbelieving wife that he could write a better novel than the one they were reading together. She challenged him. The result was *Precaution* (1820), a polite and moralistic tale laid in England. *The Spy* (1821) was a far more significant work, employing American backgrounds and characters and enjoying an enormous success.

From the age of thirty-one to his death, Cooper wrote thirty-three novels, besides a number of volumes of travel, social commentary, and naval history. The most important are of course the *Leatherstocking Tales,* the saga of Natty Bumppo and America's receding frontier: *The Pioneers* (1823), *The Last of the Mohicans* (1826), *The Prairie* (1827), *The Pathfinder* (1840), and *The Deerslayer* (1841). Cooper's sea stories, too, especially *The Pilot* (1823), *The Red Rover* (1828), and *The Two Admirals* (1842), are brisk and vigorous fiction, and nautically authentic besides.

For seven years (from 1826 to 1833), Cooper lived in Europe both to improve his health and to protect the European rights to his books. While he was there, Cooper's ardent patriotism was aroused by unfair British attacks on America, and he attempted to answer them in *Notions of the Americans* (1828). However, when he returned to America he was severely critical of the changes effected by Jacksonian democracy in the years he had been abroad. In *The American Democrat* (1838), he incorporated his objections which were considered thoroughly objectionable by the majority of his countrymen.

The last seventeen years of Cooper's life were spent in a series of battles for aristocratic social principles coupled (as his enemies generally failed to observe) with democratic political principles. The lawsuits—for libelous assaults upon him, and for infringements on his property—to which he devoted his energies (successfully, as a rule) made his final years troubled ones. He died at Cooperstown in 1851, recognized throughout the world as America's first great novelist.

Billy Budd—Foretopman

by

HERMAN MELVILLE (1819–1891)

Main Characters

Billy Budd—Foretopman of the *Indomitable*, a handsome, innocent, cheerful sailor who generates good will and who is falsely accused by Claggart.

Claggart—Master-at-arms on the *Indomitable*, an intelligent, smooth-spoken, malignant petty officer.

Captain Vere—Captain of the *Indomitable*, a stern but fair intellectual for whom the good of the British Navy takes precedence over all other considerations.

The Story

Billy Budd, foretopman of the H.M.S. *Indomitable* in the year 1797, is extraordinarily genial and good-looking. But more, he generates the kind of amiability and good will that turns even a surly and disgruntled crew into a cheerful and united one. Admired by officers and men alike, Billy is the model of "the handsome sailor." He has been impressed from an English merchantman, *Rights-of-Man*, aboard the *Indomitable*, and he accepts his new status gracefully.

Billy, however, incurs the enmity of Claggart, the master-at-arms, a petty officer who functions as a sort of police chief. Claggart, a spare, apparently balanced man of superior intel-

10

ligence, hates Billy for reasons that may not be easily fathomed
—perhaps simply the natural antagonism that evil feels for
innocence. He torments Billy in a number of underhanded
ways that Billy does not at all suspect. Even when he is told
by a grizzled old seaman that Claggart is down on him, that
Claggart has been disarranging his gear and is thus responsible
for the dressing down that Billy has been receiving from other
petty officers—even then Billy can scarcely believe that Claggart could be so hostile to him.

Soon Claggart attempts a more vicious tactic. He directs
one of his minions to approach Billy and offer him a bribe
if he will join in a plot against the ship's officers. Billy rejects
the tempter, but he does not divulge the offer to anyone.

Claggart, progressively maddened by Billy's innocence and
goodness, finally takes overt action. He approaches the commanding officer of the *Indomitable,* Captain Vere. Vere has
proved his value to the Navy more than once. An intrepid
officer, strict but fair, dedicated to his task and remarkably
efficient, Vere is subject to criticism only on the grounds of
his intellectual, almost scholarly temperament. To him, Claggart makes an astonishing accusation: that Billy Budd has
been fomenting disaffection aboard the *Indomitable,* very
likely mustering the men for mutiny. Despite his dislike of
Claggart and his doubts about the truth of the accusation, Vere
has Billy summoned.

Billy has one flaw. Under emotional stress, he stammers and
gurgles, and can speak only with the greatest difficulty. This
proves to be tragic. For when Claggart repeats his accusation
before Billy, the latter is stricken dumb. Urged by Vere to
speak, Billy strikes out instead. His right arm shoots forward,
and Claggart, who receives the blow full upon the forehead,
falls to the deck. Though Vere, Billy, and then the ship's
surgeon try to revive him, their efforts are fruitless. Claggart
is dead.

The Captain calls a drumhead court composed of three
officers. He will not wait till the ship reaches shore because
the late mutinies make immediate disciplinary action im-
perative. Billy testifies that he had not intended to kill Claggart—that could he have spoken he would not have struck
the blow. The court believes him and seems inclined to
leniency. But Captain Vere insists that the court has one

matter to consider and only one: not the motives or the provocation but simply the consequences of the blow, the deed itself. It is to be concerned not with speculative natural justice but with rigorous martial law. Billy may be acquitted by God, not by the court-martial proceeding under the law of the Mutiny Act. There is no arguing against the Captain's brief. Billy is sentenced to be hanged at the yardarm next morning.

Billy spends the night in an agony proceeding less from fear than from realization of the diabolical in some men. Captain Vere visits him, but what passes between them remains unknown. Next morning, after a brief session with the Chaplain, Billy speaks his last sentence, "God bless Captain Vere!"

A singular event occurs when Billy's body reaches the end of the yardarm. No muscular spasm is discerned, a singularity that the officers discuss without arriving at an explanation. The sailors' reaction to Billy's death is evidenced by the legends and stories and ballads that soon spring up. Billy becomes a kind of folk hero to them. As for Captain Vere, not long after, he falls in battle when the *Indomitable* engages the *Atheiste*. His last words are "Billy Budd, Billy Budd."

Critical Opinion

Billy Budd—Foretopman, written in the last decade of Melville's life, was not published until 1924, thirty years after the author's death. It is now generally considered one of his major works, his final statement about man's condition on earth. What the statement means, however, has been argued vigorously. Most critics regard it as Melville's "testament of acceptance." Billy Budd, symbol of innocence, of natural virtue, is disgraced. Following a natural impulse, he strikes and accidentally kills his false accuser. As a result, he is condemned to be hanged.

And rightly, for this world is a battleship of sorts. A battleship has one reason for being: to fulfill a mission—the destruction of an enemy. But to accomplish the mission, it must be rigorously governed—by martial rules, by discipline, by rank. Billy breaks the chain of command and so must be punished. However, it is only in this battleship world—where right and wrong are pragmatic by necessity, where justice is keyed to mission—that Billy's sentence is "right" and "just." Before God's great judgment seat—where absolute right prevails, where justice is keyed to motive and intent—Billy will be rewarded. Billy, who at times resembles Adam in his innocence and Christ in his agony, perhaps represents virtuous man, whose purposes a diabolical force (Claggart) distorts, while God (Vere) looks unhappily on—bound by His own laws.

On the other hand, a few critics regard *Billy Budd* as another chapter in Melville's long pessimistic commentary on man, God, and destiny. They insist that it is not different from *Moby Dick* or *Pierre* in essence, that it extends Melville's rejection of the world as it is. Thus the short novel must be read with a continuous awareness of its ironies, and Billy's final cry, "God bless Captain Vere," masks Melville's real meaning. In any event, *Billy Budd* has a fascinating surface. Its subsurface interpretation will continue to excite critics for a long time to come.

Moby Dick

by

HERMAN MELVILLE

Main Characters

Ishmael—The narrator, a young man who goes to sea whenever life on land makes him feel desperate.

Queequeg—A tattooed cannibal, Starbuck's harpooner, who is a brave and generous comrade to Ishmael.

Ahab—Captain of the *Pequod*, a blighted man whose relentless pursuit of the great white whale, Moby Dick, strips him of human sympathies.

Starbuck—First mate of the *Pequod*, a courageous and rational man who tries ineffectively to turn Ahab from his obsession.

Stubb—Second mate of the *Pequod,* a man whose function in life is killing whales and who consequently has become more of an instrument than a human being.

Flask—Third mate of the *Pequod,* careless, mindless, fearless.

Tashtego—A Gay Head Indian, harpooner for Stubb.

Daggoo—A gigantic Negro savage, harpooner for Flask.

Fedallah—A mysterious Parsee, Ahab's harpooner, possessed of occult powers and, it may be, in league with diabolical ones.

Father Mapple—The eloquent preacher of the Whaleman's Chapel at New Bedford.

The Story

Ishmael, the narrator, having little money and finding life on shore grim, decides to go to sea. Quitting Manhattan, he journeys to New Bedford and puts up at the Spouter Inn. To his consternation, he discovers that his roommate is a tattooed cannibal named Queequeg who prays to a Congo idol and is armed with a tomahawk that does double duty as a pipe. Queequeg, however, proves to be a really amiable young man. After sharing the same bed for a night, he and Ishmael become firm friends. Next morning being Sunday, Ishmael goes to the Whaleman's Chapel where he hears an eloquent sermon preached by Father Mapple, once a whaler himself. His subject is Jonah; his theme (of central importance): "If we obey God, we must disobey ourselves."

Ishmael joins forces with Queequeg whose essential nobility he comes to realize. They take passage to Nantucket where they hope to sign aboard a whaling ship. On the way Queequeg first chastens a bumpkin who mimics him, then rescues him when he falls overboard. At Nantucket, the pair find the *Pequod* and Queequeg's remarkable skill with the harpoon quickly gets them berths aboard her. The Quaker owners, however, promise Ishmael a very small portion of the proceeds to accrue from the voyage. Though Ishmael and Queequeg are warned by a ragged old sailor named Elijah not to sail on the *Pequod,* they disregard his dire prophecies.

Not till the *Pequod* is well under way does Ahab, captain of the vessel, appear. A tall, broad man seemingly made of bronze, Ahab is blighted. A livid white scar, superstitiously attributed to his strife with the elements, threads its way down from his gray hair. He has a white leg, made from the jaw of a sperm whale. His own leg was snapped off by Moby Dick, a huge white whale, the source of terrifying stories. Before long, Ahab's relentless mission becomes clear: he is determined tò pursue Moby Dick and kill him.

Ahab soon summons the entire ship's company and nailing a Spanish gold coin to the mainmast, promises that it shall belong to the man who first raises the white whale. Then, his passionate eloquence overriding all resistance, he pledges the crew to his purpose in flagons of rum. By force of his will, he compels the mates to cross their lances while he grasps them at their center—a kind of diabolical communion. Finally he fills the hollow sockets of the harpooners' harpoons with rum and bids them drink to the death of Moby Dick.

The three mates provide intriguing contrasts. Starbuck, the first mate, is a brave but rational man who hunts whales simply to make his living. Only he opposes Ahab's monomaniacal drive, albeit futilely, since he does not have Ahab's intensity or power. Stubb, the second mate, is a human instrument for the destruction of whales. Flask, the third mate, is careless, mindless, fearless. For the whaleboat he commands, each mate has the harpooner corresponding to his temperament—Starbuck has Queequeg; Stubb has Tashtego, a Gay Head Indian; Flask has Daggoo, a gigantic Negro savage.

As the *Pequod* cruises, she encounters other ships and stops for gams (gossip). There is the *Bachelor*, homeward bound, laden with whale oil, manned by a crew pleasantly occupied with the Polynesian girls who have eloped with them. There is the *Jeroboam*, which has suffered from closing with Moby Dick and which carries a mad prophet, Gabriel, who warns that the white whale is God. And most disheartening, there is the *Rachel*, which has lost a whaleboat among whose crew was the Captain's twelve-year-old son. Though the Captain has long been a comrade of Ahab's, Ahab will not join in the search for the missing boy.

Ahab alienates himself more and more from the human condition. He throws his pipe overboard, an act that points up his rejection of such homely pleasures as might be afforded by his home, his young wife, his child. He broods, curses, despairs—but he persists in his quest for Moby Dick. Starbuck attempts to bring him back to some consideration for his men, but he rejects the mate's persuasions. Only to Pip, the small Negro boy, half-crazed from narrowly escaping death by water, does Ahab show even the remotest kindliness.

A symbol of Ahab's progressive dehumanization is Fedallah, the leader of the group of Parsees (Persian fire-worshipers) whom Ahab has smuggled on board. Fedallah serves as Ahab's harpooner, perhaps his evil spirit as well, for he is almost always present when Ahab performs any of his defiant, diabolical acts. Ahab baptizes the lance fashioned by the ship's blacksmith, using the blood of the three pagan harpooners as the baptismal fluid, not in the name of the Father but in the name of the devil. With the Parsee watching, Ahab destroys the ship's quadrant. Again, during a great storm in which corposants (glowing balls of flame) tip all the yardarms, Ahab places his foot on the Parsee, grasps the mainmast links, and defies the lightning. After the thunder reverses the compasses, Ahab constructs others with the sailmaker's needles.

It is Fedallah, too, who issues the strange prophecy that heartens Ahab because he misconstrues it. Fedallah declares that Ahab can have neither hearse nor coffin; before he dies he must see two hearses at sea, the first not made by mortal hands, the wood of the second grown in America. Moreover, Ahab can be killed only by hemp and, at the last, Fedallah will precede him—be his pilot.

After wearying months of pursuit, the crew sight Moby Dick, his dazzling hump high above his slightly projecting head. He is surrounded by hundreds of sea fowl. Tall broken spears are embedded in his huge back. The whaleboats are lowered for the encounter. Moby Dick eludes his pursuers, dives deep, then surfaces and snaps Ahab's boat, hurling Ahab and his Parsee crew into the water. Aboard the *Pequod* once more, Ahab scornfully rejects Starbuck's interpretation that the wrecked boat constitutes an omen.

The next day, Moby Dick is again sighted and again the chase is on. The monstrous whale wreaks more havoc this time, swamping all three whaleboats, tangling all the harpoon lines, and breaking Captain Ahab's ivory leg. In the melee,

Fedallah is drowned. For the second time, Ahab turns a deaf ear to Starbuck's plea that he abandon his pursuit of the white whale.

On the third day, the spout that signals the white whale's presence is seen for the third time. Ahab again leads the chase. Maddened by the harpoon wounds inflicted on the two previous days, Moby Dick flails the mates' boats apart, churns the water, and swims away—revealing as he does the body of Fedallah, lashed to the white whale by the lines of the irons that had pierced him on the preceding day. Part of the Parsee's prediction is fulfilled: Fedallah has gone before Ahab to be his pilot. Suddenly the enraged white whale sees the black hull of the *Pequod* and, turning, bears down upon it and strikes it with monstrous force. The ship reels, settles, and begins to sink. The second part of the prophecy comes to pass: The *Pequod* is the second hearse, its wood grown in America. Ahab's boat comes alongside the white whale, and he hurls his harpoon into Moby Dick. The line, however, runs foul and, as Ahab stoops to clear it, the flying turn catches him round the neck, and he is shot out of the boat and instantly strangled. The Parsee's prophecy is now fully realized: Ahab is killed by hemp.

Only Ishmael escapes. He crawls atop a coffin built by Queequeg. The coffin had been shot from the *Pequod*. On the closed coffin Ishmael floats till the *Rachel*, still in search of her Captain's son, finds him.

Throughout Ishmael's story, from the sailing of the *Pequod* on, are interspersed chapters on whaling. While they do not further the story, they comment upon it obliquely, supplying the background and pointing up the symbolism. The ubiquity of whales, whaling as a pattern of life, the kinds of whales, the parts of the whale, the habits of whales—these matters continually interrupt and simultaneously deepen the narrative.

Critical Opinion

Moby Dick is a towering book—and a profound one. The narrative has a surging movement, exciting episodes, and dramatic confrontations. The style is by turns poetic, humorous, romantic, and factual. But *Moby Dick* has depths that "make a man swim for his life."

Melville wrote *Moby Dick* at the height of his powers. "Until I was twenty-five," he wrote Hawthorne, "I had no development at all. From my twenty-fifth year I date my life. Three weeks have scarcely passed at any time between then and now that I have not unfolded within myself. But I feel that I am now come to the inmost leaf of the bulb, and that shortly the flower must fall to the mould." He derided the novels he had published because they did not "dive," because they were not charged with "the powers of darkness," because they did not draw to exhaustion on his creative potential.

He apparently began *Moby Dick* as another realistic, broadly comic whaling adventure, but after the twenty-second chapter revised his purpose. The *Pequod* became more than a whaling vessel; it became a small, contained world. The monomaniacal captain and the huge whale he pursued, though they remained realistic beings, became symbolic figures as well—great and complex creations that each reader must interpret for himself. Is Ahab evil man trying to destroy good, hurling himself futilely against God or attempting to become God? Is Ahab heroic man striving to wrest the secret of creation, or protesting against the evil of the universe or against evil fate? Is Ahab simply mad, or irresponsible, or mistaken in his quest? These are only a few of the innumerable questions that have been asked and "answered." But, as one critic points out, "To set down an 'approved' answer, as to a problem in algebra, would be presumptuous—and besides, some problems have no approved answer."

But if *Moby Dick* is a challenging book, if it forces its reader to "depth-dive," it is also, as more than one critic has affirmed, "the best sea story ever written," at once "the epic and the encyclopedia of whaling." And it is as well the epic of man refusing against all reason to submit to things as they are.

The Author

Herman Melville was born in 1819 in New York City, of Scotch-English and Dutch ancestry. When he was eleven, his family moved to Albany, where he attended the Albany

Academy for two years. Then, after his father died deep in debt, the thirteen-year-old boy embarked on a variety of occupations. For five years he worked as a clerk, a farm hand, even a teacher, despite his own scanty schooling.

At eighteen, perhaps because no better alternatives offered themselves, Melville became a sailor, signing aboard as a cabin boy on a trading vessel bound for Liverpool. The brutalities he witnessed on ship and on shore in the Liverpool slums destroyed his romantic notions of a sailor's life. Four years after his return, however, finding nothing to keep him on land, he sailed again, this time on the *Acushnet*, a whaler bound for the South Seas. Conditions aboard were intolerable. With a companion Melville jumped ship at one of the Marquesas Islands, where for a month he was a guest of the Typees, a cannibal tribe. Though he enjoyed the experience for the most part, he was glad to accept a berth aboard the Australian whaler that rescued him. But once again, after participating in a mutiny and being jailed briefly, he deserted at Eimeo, near Tahiti, and wandered among the natives, vastly preferring them to the missionaries. He made his way to Hawaii aboard a whaling ship cruising the South Pacific, worked for fourteen weeks in Honolulu spotting pins in a bowling alley, and then enlisted in the U.S. Navy for a homeward cruise. He landed in Boston nearly three years after his departure on the *Acushnet*, his sailing career ended.

No other career beckoning him, Melville began to write, drawing freely on his seagoing experiences for his first four novels: *Typee* (1846) describes his cannibal experiences; *Omoo* (1847), his wanderings in Tahiti; *Redburn* (1849), his maiden voyage to Liverpool; and *White-Jacket* (1850), his last voyage on a United States warship. *Mardi* (1849) is an allegory rather than a novel, confused but intermittently fascinating in its satiric comments. Unlike his autobiographical novels, it failed disastrously.

Melville's great novel, *Moby Dick*, was (like *Mardi*) an attempt to break away from the romantic semi-autobiographical narratives which pleased the public but not the author. Its critical reception was mixed and it sold badly. *Pierre* (1852), subtitled *The Ambiguities*, a tortured, perverse, deeply pessimistic book, was greeted with unmixed and uncomprehending attacks. From this point on Melville's productivity declined. *Israel Potter* (1855), *The Piazza Tales* (1856), *The Confidence Man* (1857), a volume of poems, *Battle Pieces and Aspects of the War* (1866), a long narrative poem, *Clarel* (1876), and the posthumously published *Billy Budd* (1924) did not increase his contemporary reputation.

Melville had married in 1847, and the need to support his family forced him to try magazine writing and lecturing. In 1866 he became an inspector in the New York Customs House, a position he retained until 1886. He died, almost forgotten, in 1891.

Since then his fame has skyrocketed. He is one of the two most widely read and written-about authors of nineteenth-century America. Mark Twain is the other. Melville's poems, stories, and novels, long out of print, have been republished in a variety of editions. Once virtually ignored, he is today almost universally hailed as America's greatest novelist.

The Scarlet Letter

by

NATHANIEL HAWTHORNE (1804–1864)

Main Characters

Hester Prynne—The adulterous wife of an elderly English scholar, beautiful, passionate, loyal, and noble in enduring her penance—the embroidered scarlet "A" (for "Adultery") that she is condemned to wear.

Roger Chillingworth—The name assumed by Hester's husband to conceal his identity so that he may more easily discover the partner of her sin. Short, thin, pale, dim-eyed from poring over books, he becomes progressively more distorted in his relentless pursuit of the wrongdoer.

Arthur Dimmesdale—The minister who is Hester's "fellow sinner and fellow sufferer." Deeply religious, eloquent, intellectually gifted, he suffers because of his inability to confess his sin.

Pearl—The illegitimate daughter of Hester and the minister, radiantly lovely, yet perverse and defiant.

The Story

The introductory essay describes the author's term as Surveyor of the Salem Custom House, his antiquated colleagues and subordinates, and his politically motivated "decapitation," or discharge. Examining old records one day,

he comes across a faded, gold-embroidered "A" and a small
roll of dingy paper. Recorded there by an ancient predecessor
is the dark, dramatic tale that, suitably edited, Hawthorne
pretends to give us in *The Scarlet Letter*.

The narrative opens with the chorus-like denunciation by
the women of Boston—the Puritan Boston of the mid-seven-
teenth century. Their anger is directed against Hester Prynne
who leaves the jail carrying her three-month-old baby and is
guided to the platform of the pillory. Hester, whose husband
has not been heard from for two years, has borne an illegitimate child and refuses to divulge the identity of the father.
For her crime she has been sentenced to stand for three
hours on the platform of the pillory and for the rest of her
life to wear the mark of shame on her bosom—the scarlet
"A." An aged clergyman exhorts her to reveal the identity of
the father. She refuses, even when the Reverend Arthur
Dimmesdale adds his heartfelt, compassionate plea.

In the crowd, watching curiously, is a small, slightly
deformed man whom Hester recognizes with dread. After
returning to prison, Hester and the child need a physician
and are visited by the observer, who has learned the arts of
medicine from books and from the Indians among whom
he has sojourned. He calls himself Roger Chillingworth; he is
in reality Hester's husband. Having administered a soothing
medication to his patients, he declares that by a kind of
intuitive, sympathetic penetration, he will discover Hester's
fellow sinner. Before leaving, he makes Hester promise to
keep his own secret as she has her lover's.

Hester leaves prison and establishes herself in an abandoned
cottage on the outskirts of the town, earning her scant livelihood by the expert work of her needle—the same needle that
embroidered the beautiful and baleful scarlet "A" which she
must always wear. Her daughter, Pearl, grows into an exquisite, elfin child. Not the least of Hester's tortures are Pearl's
frequent questions as to where she came from and her refusal
to accept the answer that her Heavenly Father sent her.

The minister, Arthur Dimmesdale, has meanwhile been
declining. He grows daily paler and thinner, and often suffers
heart pains. He accepts the proffered medical aid of Roger
Chillingworth who becomes his regular companion. Chillingworth has another purpose besides curing the minister. He

penetrates deeply beneath the surface spirituality of the minister and detects a secret sin working there. In the process of searching, Chillingworth becomes more evil and ugly. Indeed, many people in Boston whisper that Arthur Dimmesdale is haunted by Satan or Satan's emissary.

One day, when the minister has fallen into a deep sleep, Roger Chillingworth enters, lays aside the vestment that covers his patient's bosom, and sees—what? We are not told, but the sight seems to please him immensely.

On an obscure night in May, the minister, as if in the shadow of a dream, walks to the scaffold where Hester underwent her public shame. Sunk in misery, he stands in her place. Hester, who has been watching at the bed of the dying Governor Winthrop, comes to the scaffold, accompanied by Pearl, and stands beside the minister. Pearl asks him if he will stand with her mother and her at noon tomorrow. Not tomorrow, he replies, but at the final judgment. Pearl's laugh is interrupted by an immense "A" which seems to flare across the sky. Or perhaps it is merely a meteor that the guilty imagination of the Reverend Dimmesdale construes as an "A," the symbol of Hester's sin. At the same moment Pearl points to the dim figure of Roger Chillingworth who has suddenly appeared and who with apparent concern leads the minister home.

The minister's illness continues—and his physician seems to grow more devilish. Hester, however, develops the hidden resources of good within her. She cannot achieve peace, though, because of her anxiety about Pearl and the minister. On a chill afternoon, she meets her pastor in the forest. She is again filled with tenderness for him as she sees him ill and suffering. He tells her of Chillingworth's probing. His own sin, grave as it is, nevertheless is not so black as that of the physician who has violated the sanctity of a human heart. Hester insists that their deed of passion had a consecration of its own. Though he does not accept her justification, neither does he repudiate it. And soon they determine (at her strong suggestion) to escape together to another place where his talents can be fulfilled. She discards her scarlet "A"—but Pearl, who has been playing elsewhere during the passionate interlude, refuses to rejoin her mother till Hester replaces it.

The third great scene of the novel also unfolds on the

scaffold. The minister has delivered the election sermon for the new governor. It is an eloquent and moving address. The minister's suffering, though stemming from sin, appears now to make him spiritual. Ironically, as his spirit clouds through concealment, his power as minister increases.

But his sermon seems to have deprived him of vital force. Leaving the church, he almost falls, yet refuses support. He sees Pearl and Hester in the audience, calls them to him, and embraces them—in spite of the protests of Roger Chilling-worth who thrusts himself forward. With Hester's help, Dim-mesdale ascends the platform to declare that he is a polluted priest who has compounded his sin of adultery by hiding it cunningly, hypocritically. He bares his breast to reveal what has been engraved upon it. As he does, Roger Chillingworth mutters, "Thou hast escaped me!" The minister acknowledges Pearl as well as Hester, then expires.

What was the revelation? Most spectators testified that it was a scarlet letter like Hester's but imprinted in flesh. Some contended that Chillingworth's magic had produced it, others that it had been the operation of spiritual guilt upon the flesh. Certain of the witnesses, nevertheless, maintained that the minister's breast had borne no mark whatever.

Deprived of the object of his revenge, Roger Chillingworth dies within a year. It is believed that Pearl, redeemed by the minister's confession, grew into a softened and subdued woman who married well and happy. As for Hester, after some absence, she returns to Boston to live out her life comforting and counseling the sorrowful and erring. At her death she is buried near the minister, one tombstone serving both and bearing the legend: "On a Field, Sable, the Letter A, Gules."

Critical Opinion

Almost unanimously, critics agree that *The Scarlet Letter* is Hawthorne's one faultless book. Elsewhere, Hawthorne's symbolism and allegory may be intrusive, his intensity too great for the story, his characters bloodless, his humor forced. But in *The Scarlet Letter* the "representation is as imaginatively real as its meaning." Hawthorne's characters fully embody the dark drama that he conceived.

From Hawthorne's day, when Melville (who learned much from him) praised "the great power of blackness in him" and his deep tragic sense, to the present, when Harry Levin notes the "vivid particularity" with which Hawthorne projects his "general vision of evil," commentators have focused on his brooding moral insight. Hawthorne felt in every fiber of his being that current notions of "the perfectibility of man" were illusory; worse, they were comfortable lies. He believed that the imaginings of man's heart were wicked and that original sin was a reality. Thus he could perceive psychological depths where other novelists merely skimmed surfaces.

The "moral" of *The Scarlet Letter* is that adultery is sinful and that those who sin must suffer. But penance is not enough; it must be fused with penitence. Dimmesdale's pride, his egotism, his fear of social ostracism render his suffering fruitless because he conceals his sin, shrinks from joining Hester in her disgrace. Hester grows spiritually as the minister declines.

Yet the sin of Hester and Dimmesdale is not the most dehumanizing one: it is a sin of passion, of the heart. Chillingworth, however, has sinned through calculation, through the deliberate misuse of intelligence. "He has violated, in cold blood, the sanctity of the human heart."

Pearl, who has been called the scarlet letter endowed with life, is perhaps the only character in the book who deserves (and has received) adverse criticism. She never is more than an allegorical figure, never is assimilated into the story itself. Hawthorne needed her as the emblem of the sin that the romance analyzes. But readers wish they could accept her as real. She is the only imperfection in a tale that powerfully and poetically exploits the discordant motives and destructive passions deep within us.

The House of the Seven Gables

by

NATHANIEL HAWTHORNE

Main Characters

Colonel Pyncheon—The ruthless Puritan who seizes Matthew Maule's land.

Matthew Maule—The "Wizard" condemned for witchcraft through Colonel Pyncheon's zeal.

Thomas Maule—Matthew's son, who builds the "House of the Seven Gables."

Hepzibah Pyncheon—The sweet-natured but sour-faced maiden lady who in 1850 inhabits the house.

Clifford Pyncheon—Hepzibah's beloved brother, a handsome and sensitive man, intellectually torpid from his long imprisonment.

Phoebe Pyncheon—The pretty, sprightly niece of Hepzibah and Clifford, who brings some cheerfulness into the gloomy old house.

Holgrave—The young daguerreotypist, a reformer who lives in one of the gables and who falls in love with Phoebe.

Uncle Venner—The aged odd-job man of the town, a homely philosopher who helps cheer Hepzibah and Clifford.

Judge Jaffrey Pyncheon—The cousin of Hepzibah and Clifford, an apparently benevolent man, rich and respected, but really a vicious hypocrite.

The Story

Almost two centuries before the story opens, Matthew Maule built a small thatched house in one of the pleasantest locations of old Salem. With the growth of the town during the next thiry or forty years, the site became very desirable to Colonel Pyncheon, a strong-willed Puritan who put forward a substantial legal claim to it. Maule, however, was obstinate in defending his rights and the Colonel's claim was unsuccess-ful.

Those were the days when even. the soberest men and women believed in witchcraft, and Maule was accused of its practice. No one was more zealous in bringing about his condemnation than Colonel Pyncheon. At the moment of execution, Maule cursed his enemy. Pointing to the Colonel, grimly watching, he said, "God will give him blood to drink."

The Colonel paid no attention to the curse. After Maule's death, he took over his land and on the very place where Maule's small house had stood built a mansion with seven peaked gables. Strangely, the Colonel offered the job of architect to Thomas Maule, the son of the man he had helped hound to death; and strangely, too, Thomas Maule accepted the job and performed it faithfully.

But "Wizard" Maule's curse proved effective. The Colonel, like more than one of his descendants, died of apoplexy, choking on his own blood. Though he left his son a large fortune, the deeds or other documents supporting his son's claim to a great tract of land in Maine could not be found.

In the middle of the nineteenth century, the time of our story, the "House of the Seven Gables" on Pyncheon Street (once Maule's Lane) is occupied by Hepzibah Pyncheon, a descendant of the Puritan Colonel. She is a kind-hearted woman, but so cross-looking that she either frightens children or excites them to mockery. She decides to eke out her income by opening a penny-shop and selling soap, candles, brown sugar, etc. Unfortunately, her vinegary looks discourage customers and her business seems likely to fail.

Quite unexpectedly, Hepzibah receives a visit from a country cousin, Phoebe Pyncheon, a pretty, cheerful young woman. Her visit is to be short or long, depending on how she and Hepzibah suit each other. Hepzibah welcomes Phoebe reluctantly, for her brother Clifford is to come home soon and Hepzibah is uncertain how he will accept Phoebe. Clifford has been in prison for thirty years, convicted, on the basis of a long chain of circumstantial evidence, of having killed his uncle, old Jaffrey Pyncheon.

Phoebe soon proves that she suits Hepzibah very well indeed. She takes over the penny-shop, and her energy and her bright personality make it a profitable enterprise. More-

over, she pleases Clifford immensely. His loving but forbid-
ding-looking sister oppresses him. Hepzibah bravely turns to
Phoebe, and she agrees to take care of Clifford. It is no easy
task. An extraordinarily handsome and sensitive man, Clifford
has been blighted by his prison years and is now lacking in
physical or mental energy. Nevertheless, Phoebe's attentive-
ness as well as her gaiety and youthful beauty rouse Clifford
and frequently lift the wretchedness that has descended on
him.

Phoebe also charms another resident of the old house, a
young daguerreotypist named Holgrave who inhabits one of
the gables. In spite of Holgrave's tendency to join a variety
of reform movements, Hepzibah has grown rather fond of him.
And Phoebe, who often works with him in the little garden
kept for Clifford's pleasure, also begins to trust and rely on
him.

With the occasional exception of Uncle Venner, who lives
at the farm maintained for old folk by the town and who does
odd jobs for the townspeople, Clifford, Phoebe, and Hepzibah
are the only people who ever enter the parlor of the house,
a forbidding room dominated by the green portrait of Colonel
Pyncheon. Once, Judge Jaffrey Pyncheon, the cousin of
Hepzibah and Clifford, tries to force his way into it to speak
to Clifford, but Hepzibah's agitation and Clifford's wails of
alarm—perhaps, too, the presence of Phoebe—cause the
Judge to abandon his attempt. The Judge is the great man of
the town, rich and respected, though not very much liked
despite his studied benevolence and ingratiating manners.
Clifford obviously is terrified of him, and Hepzibah despises
and fears him.

After staying with the brother and sister a number of weeks,
Phoebe decides to go home for a few days to make arrangements for moving permanently to the house of the seven
gables. She says an affectionate goodbye to Clifford and
Hepzibah, and a cordial one to Holgrave whose statements
and, even more, reticences puzzle and disquiet her. She is
not gone very long when Judge Pyncheon arrives at the
house determined to speak to Clifford about his happiness
and well-being. Hepzibah resists the Judge firmly but tremu-
lously.

The Judge abandons all pretense, threatening to have Clifford committed to an asylum for the insane if Hepzibah continues her resistance. Boldly Jaffrey Pyncheon puts forth his reason: he is convinced that the uncle whose fortune he inherited—the uncle whom Clifford is alleged to have murdered —left an estate two or three times as large as appeared after his death and that Clifford can give him a clue to the recovery of the remainder. Hepzibah knows that the Judge means to carry out his threat. She has no choice except to summon her brother. Judge Pyncheon enters the parlor and sits beneath Colonel Pyncheon's portrait, on the very chair in which the old Puritan was found dead more than a century and a half earlier. Hepzibah goes in search of Clifford. He is nowhere to be found. Frantically Hepzibah returns to the parlor to ask the Judge's help. The Judge is sitting motionless. Just then Clifford appears, laughing wildly. He points to the Judge. He is dead! Clifford insists that they leave the house at once. He and Hepzibah take a train ride during which Clifford talks freely and even fearlessly to complete strangers. Formerly he shunned everyone except the inmates of the house of the seven gables.

Meanwhile Phoebe has returned from her visit home. She is admitted by Holgrave who tells her that the Judge is dead. He has suffered a stroke of apoplexy just as his ancestor, the Colonel, had. The uncle whom Clifford was accused of killing undoubtedly suffered the same fate. Phoebe wishes to throw open the doors and make the secret known, but Holgrave prevents her. He tells her that he loves her, that she is his only hope for happiness. She protests that it seems wrong to speak of love at such a time, but nevertheless confesses that she loves him, too.

In the midst of Phoebe and Holgrave's avowals, Clifford and Hepzibah return. The Judge is declared by the authorities to have died from natural causes, the hereditary illness of his family. It is clear as well that the uncle, allegedly murdered, must have died in the same manner and that Jaffrey Pyncheon, to gain the inheritance, planted the fraudulent evidence that convicted Clifford.

Clifford, his mind far less troubled now, recalls that as a boy he discovered a secret spring that caused the portrait of Colonel Pyncheon to swing forward and reveal a compartment in which important documents were hidden, but he has forgotten the location of the spring. Holgrave, though, says he can find it. He presses the spring, the portrait falls to the floor, and behind it is a recess holding the deeds to a vast tract of land—Colonel Pyncheon's missing property. The Judge supposed, erroneously, that Clifford knew of lands belonging to their uncle, not of these lands, which are worthless after the lapse of so many years.

Phoebe asks Holgrave how he came to know about the secret spring, and Holgrave reveals his identity. He is a descendant of "Wizard" Matthew Maule and of Thomas Maule who had built the house of the seven gables. The secret of the spring and the documents had been passed from father to son through the Maule generations. The marriage of a Maule and a Pyncheon—which shortly takes place—at last dissipates the curse.

Clifford and Hepzibah inherit the Judge's estate and, with Holgrave, Phoebe, and Uncle Venner leave the house of the seven gables to live in the Judge's mansion.

Critical Opinion

The House of the Seven Gables appeared in 1851 when Hawthorne was living near Lenox in the Berkshire Hills of Massachusetts. It was written when Hawthorne's "situation was as close to ideal as it gets for a writer." He liked his new home; the success of *The Scarlet Letter*, published a year earlier, had brought him fame and relieved him of financial worries; his family was flourishing. Consequently *The House of the Seven Gables*, though it traces the same pattern of guilt and expiation as *The Scarlet Letter* and points up as grim a moral—that "the wrongdoing of one generation lives into the successive ones"—is a less intense and far less gloomy book.

Hawthorne, indeed, believed that it was "a more natural book for him to write" and preferred it to *The Scarlet Letter*. Most of his contemporaries agreed; few modern readers do. *The House of the Seven Gables* is light, charming, and fanciful, but it lacks the dark power of the earlier tale. It is more relaxed, more diffuse, more digressive. Some episodes—the frantic train trip of Hepzibah and Clifford, for example—seem irrelevant to the plot. Moreover, Hawthorne hurries the events of his story and resolves too many of its complications too easily.

The House of the Seven Gables, Hawthorne insisted, was not a novel but a romance. Fidelity to the truth—except "the truth of the human heart"—was not a requirement for the romance: the author could alter and arrange facts, even introduce the marvelous if he chose to. The figures of the romance, too, need not be real; and Hawthorne's, as Henry James comments, are "figures rather than characters, . . . pictures rather than people." Yet they are perfectly in harmony with the story, perfectly capable of carrying its weight, perfectly at home among its lights and shadows. If *The House of the Seven Gables* is not Hawthorne's most moving work, it is his most graceful and most pictorial.

The Author

Born in Salem of a distinguished Puritan family, *Nathaniel Hawthorne* seems early to have been destined for suffering. His father, a sea captain, died of yellow fever in Guiana when Nathaniel was four. His mother entered upon a long period of mourning, secluding herself in her home, even taking her meals alone. Between the ages of nine and twelve, Hawthorne was invalided by a leg injury sustained while playing ball. A three-year stay in the Maine woods, which he thoroughly enjoyed, helped his recovery.

Hawthorne enrolled in Bowdoin College and graduated in 1825. Then he, too, embraced solitude, spending the next twelve years in his mother's house, reading, writing, and thinking. A juvenile novel and some excellent short stories and sketches are the products of these lonely years.

Partly with the help of Sophia Peabody, whom he married in 1842, he escaped from his self-imprisonment. During the next eight years, he wrote much, became Measurer at the Boston Customs House (1839-40), joined the Utopian Community of Brook Farm for six months (1840-41), and accepted the position of surveyor of the Salem Customs House (1846-49). Discharged from the last position when the Democrats fell from power, he again devoted himself to writing. During the early 1840s he had composed his first distinctive tales

which were distinguished by a heightened Puritan consciousness of sin and suffering. Now, freed from his Surveyorship,
Hawthorne experienced a release of creative energy. In 1850
he wrote his greatest study of Puritan sensibility, *The Scarlet
Letter*. The next year saw the publication of *The House of the
Seven Gables,* a novel of ancestral guilt, and the year following, the story of his disillusionment with the Brook Farm
adventure, *The Blithedale Romance.*

As a reward for a presidential campaign biography he wrote
for his Bowdoin classmate Franklin Pierce, Hawthorne was
appointed consul at Liverpool and later Manchester (1853–56).
He stayed abroad for seven years in England and in Italy,
where he began *The Marble Faun* (1860). He returned to
America in 1860, settling in Concord.

In spite of such diversions as politics, consular service, and
travel, Hawthorne dedicated his life to writing the tales and
novels that make him the first American who truly merits a
place in world literature.

Uncle Tom's Cabin

by

HARRIET BEECHER STOWE (1811–1896)

Main Characters

Uncle Tom—A Negro slave, gentle, devout, humble, but resolute in cleaving to the good.

Aunt Chloe—A famous cook, a devoted servant, Tom's self-sacrificing wife.

Arthur Shelby—Tom's master in Kentucky, a "fair average kind of man," good-natured and self-indulgent.

Emily Shelby—His wife, an excellent mistress but powerless to aid Tom when he needs her most.

George Shelby—Their son, high-spirited, generous, deeply loyal.

Dan Haley—A slave trader immune to human decency.

Tom Loker—A slave hunter, but potentially redeemable.

Marks—His shrewd, self-serving ally.

Eliza Harris—A sweet, brave, loving slave.

George Harris—Her proud and intelligent husband.

Harry—Their captivating child.

Senator John Bird—An essentially good man whose human sympathies are briefly obscured by false principles and opportunistic politics.

Rachel Halliday—A kindly, sweet-tempered Quaker lady, who serves the cause of anti-slavery.

Simeon Halliday—Her husband.

Phineas Fletcher—A fighting Quaker.

33

Aunt Dorcas—Tom Loker's Quaker nurse who helps restore him to health and to humanity.

Augustine St. Clare—Tom's New Orleans master; on the surface, clever, cynical; at heart, idealistic, tormented.

Marie St. Clare—His selfish, egotistic wife.

Ophelia St. Clare—His Vermont cousin, an epitome of New England merits and faults, strait-laced, honest, conscientious, truly religious.

Evangeline (Eva)—St. Clare's saintly young daughter, moved by more than human love, faith, goodness.

Topsy—The mischievous black sprite who disorders the St. Clare household until Eva's love reforms her.

Simon Legree—Tom's last master, sadistic and bestial.

Cassy—The unhappy quadroon whom Legree forces to serve his base requirements but who nevertheless retains compassion and dignity.

Quimbo and *Sambo*—Two Negro slaves whom Legree has debased but who are saved by Tom's heroic example.

Emmeline—The lovely hopeless and terror-stricken girl whom Legree purchases to replace Cassy.

The Story

During the years before the Civil War, the Shelby plantation in Kentucky seems a happy place. Its master, Arthur Shelby, is open-handed and good-natured; his wife, Emily, benevolent and sincerely religious; their young son George, warm and affectionate—the plantation favorite. The slaves are treated kindly—almost like human beings instead of property. Uncle Tom, a devout and devoted Negro, is Mr. Shelby's trusted agent. His wife, Aunt Chloe, is regarded as more than a superb cook; she is practically one of the Shelby family. And their children give promise of walking in the upright ways of their parents.

But Mr. Shelby is improvident, and his debts force him to sell Uncle Tom to a gross slave trader, Dan Haley. With Tom, he must also sell Harry, the five-year-old son of Eliza and George Harris, the former a beautiful young quadroon whom he owns, the latter an intelligent and manly mulatto who is the chattel of an unfeeling slaveholder. Fearing to be sold down the Mississippi River and unable to endure his master any longer, George determines to escape to Canada and freedom. He takes sorrowful leave of his son and wife. Soon after his departure, she discovers that Shelby has agreed to sell Harry and, unable to endure that prospect, she too plans to escape.

Carrying the child, Eliza trudges wearily to a village on the banks of the Ohio River. Here she finds refuge at an inn and waits for a boat that will carry her across the ice-caked river. The abysmal Haley, however, has followed her though he has been delayed by the false directions of the Shelby slaves who accompany him. Eliza sees him and fears capture. Frantically she vaults from the bank of the river to a cake of ice, then to another, and still another. Leaping, slipping, bleeding, she somehow miraculously reaches the Ohio side.

There she is directed to the house of Senator Bird, a good man imprisoned by his "principles." He has voted for the law forbidding shelter or aid to escaped slaves. But when he sees poor Eliza and Harry, pity stirs in him and he takes them to the farm house of a Southerner who, convinced that slavery is sin, has freed his own slaves and aids others to escape. He conducts Eliza and Harry to the home of Rachel and Simeon Halliday, members of a Quaker settlement. They both hate slavery. There Eliza finds warmth and hope. The Hallidays make possible a reunion between her and her husband George who, fierce for freedom, has armed himself and has passed as a Spaniard.

Meanwhile Haley has enlisted the services of two slave hunters, the brutal Loker and his vicious assistant Marks, who follow the trail of the refugees. Accompanied by Phineas Fletcher, another valiant Quaker, George, Eliza, and Harry flee once again. They are overtaken at a narrow pass, but George puts up a spirited defense and Phineas hurls Tom Loker into a chasm. The fugitives proceed by boat to Canada, a free country.

Uncle Tom's progress is not so happy. His departure from the Shelby plantation is dismal: Aunt Chloe despairs, the children sob, George Shelby rages, vowing that he will have Tom back when he is a man. Haley takes Tom on a steamboat down the Mississippi to New Orleans. Along the way he sees the dreadful sights of slavery—the suffering in squalid quarters, families torn apart, a woman ending her miseries in the river when separated from her child. Tom reads his Bible and sings his hymns, but is nonetheless forlorn. He makes friends with a lovely golden-haired girl, little Evangeline (Eva) who is traveling with her father. When she falls overboard, Tom jumps in to rescue her. After this, Eva easily prevails upon her father, Augustine St. Clare, to buy Tom.

St. Clare is returning from Vermont where he has recruited his spinster cousin, Ophelia St. Clare, to act as his housekeeper and to keep the St. Clare household in order. Its master is indolent, its mistress lost in hypochondria, self-pity, and selfishness. Tom's existence there, however, is relatively pleasant. He idolizes Eva, and she responds lovingly. Love is her central quality—one she lavishes on all, even on Topsy, the mischievous little black sprite whose training has made lying and stealing as familiar to her as being whipped. She can remember nothing of her family or origins. "I spect I grow'd. Don't think nobody never made me," she says. Topsy is redeemed, finally, but far more by Eva's love than by Miss Ophelia's severities and moralities.

Eva is doomed. She grows paler and more languid each day, though her bright spiritual light does not fade. Tom, whom St. Clare at Eva's urging has promised to free, feels that her end is near. Even Marie emerges from the miasma of self-pity. Eva's dying is an ascent to glory, to the Christ whom she adores.

After Eva's death, the household is desolate. St. Clare, deeply skeptical, struggles for a faith in the divine purpose, a faith that eludes him. He puts off giving Tom his freedom, though he firmly intends to. Then one day at a café he tries to separate two brawling men and is fatally wounded. He dies, not before he, too, is vouchsafed a vision of infinite pity.

Disregarding her husband's wish, Marie decides to sell her slaves, Tom among them. Auctioned at a slave warehouse, he is purchased, along with Emmeline, a beautiful fifteen-year-old girl, by Simon Legree, a bestial plantation owner. Legree hates Tom, piles the cruelest labors on him. Emmeline he reserves for his own pleasures, displacing for her his handsome quadroon mistress, Cassy. Tom suffers but his Bible and his faith help him to endure—even when, because he will not whip a sick woman, Legree has him whipped by his two degenerate slaves Quimbo and Sambo, till he is nearly dead.

Emmeline and Cassy become friends. Cassy, who has had two children taken from her and sold, tries to protect Emmeline from Legree's bestialities. They fervently wish to escape, but the thought of Legree's savage dogs, trained to pursue escaping slaves, deters them. At last Cassy hits on a plan. She works on Legree's ignorant and superstitious fears, convincing him that the attic (where he has performed barbarous acts) is haunted. Then, making it appear they have fled for the swamps, she and Emmeline hide in the attic, knowing he will not dare venture there.

Uncle Tom has been told of their stratagem. Though tortured by Legree and beaten by his two henchmen, he refuses to divulge their hiding place. This final punishment is fatal. On his deathbed, sustained by his ardent faith, he is visited by George Shelby, a young man now, who has come too late to ransom him. Forgiving Legree with his last breath and blessing George, Tom dies.

George has the small satisfaction of knocking Legree down and of burying Tom. Unhappy, he boards the steamboat that will take him back to Kentucky. On the boat he meets and protects Emmeline and Cassy who have made their escape amid the excitement. During the journey they meet a French lady, Madame de Thoux. Having learned that he is a Kentuckian, she questions him eagerly about George Harris, her brother, separated from her in childhood. Now the wealthy widow of a West Indian planter, she is in search of George. Cassy, hearing of George's wife, Eliza, and discovering the details of her history, realizes that Eliza is the daughter so long ago snatched from her. All except young Shelby journey to Canada and there find George and Eliza, living modestly but comfortably. It is a tearful and joyful reunion.

Except for Simon Legree, most of the people who have suffered so much woe arrive at something near happiness, as much happiness at least as their sufferings allow them to experience. Legree dies insane. Quimbo and Sambo, however, moved by the force of Tom's heroic example, become regenerate Christians. George Harris, in order to help his race with all his powers, migrates to Nigeria along with Eliza and Harry. With them, of course, goes Cassy. The other child of which she has been deprived, a son, is located after intensive

search and will shortly join her in Nigeria. Topsy returns to
Vermont with Ophelia St. Clare, is later baptized, and becomes a missionary in Africa. George Shelby returns to his
plantation and frees his slaves, allowing them, if they choose,
to remain as paid workingmen.

Critical Opinion

The publication of *Uncle Tom's Cabin* has been called "the
most sensational event in the world history of the novel."
Translated into dozens of languages, it has sold millions of
copies. Dramatized in 1852 by George L. Aiken, it has held
the stage for a hundred years. It made Harriet Beecher Stowe
the most loved and the most hated woman in America. When
Lincoln met her during the Civil War, he commented, "So
you're the little lady who wrote the book that caused the great
war."

Actually, Harriet Beecher Stowe had not intended to beat
any war drums; and the war would certainly have arrived had
her book never been published. She hoped to make men
abominate slavery by presenting an imaginative account of its
cruelties—an account she documented laboriously in *A Key to
Uncle Tom's Cabin* (1853). But her great book, she maintained, was not a willed composition at all. "God wrote it,"
she said. "I merely did His dictation."

Uncle Tom's Cabin has a hundred faults of sentimentality,
artificiality, obviousness. Its construction is bad and its characterization worse. It is filled with errors and distortions. None
of these, however, lessens the profound effect the book creates.
It is passionate and powerful. Even reading it today, one experiences shock, pity, horror—in spite of the melodrama, the
stereotypes, the bathos.

The Author

Harriet Beecher, born in Litchfield, Connecticut, in 1811,
spent her first twenty-one years in New England. The seventh
child of the Reverend Lyman Beecher, a severe Calvinist, she
had a rigid Puritan upbringing. Her early life was colored by

religious tracts and religious schools. Had she been born a boy, she would certainly have become a preacher, like six of her brothers—one of them the renowned Henry Ward Beecher. But since that career was closed to her, she did the next best thing. She became a teacher when she was fourteen.

When she was twenty-one, she moved with her family to Cincinnati, and taught for a time in the Lane Theological Seminary, of which her father was president. At twenty-four, she married a fellow teacher, Professor Calvin E. Stowe, already a distinguished Biblical scholar.

In 1850, Harriet moved East again with her husband and seven children. Calvin Stowe had been called to a professorship at Bowdoin, then at Andover. In spite of her family and religious duties, Harriet started to write, releasing the imagination that since childhood had been directed into other channels.

She began writing *Uncle Tom's Cabin* in 1851 for serial publication in an abolitionist journal, *The National Era*, of Washington, D.C. The phenomenal success of the novel has obscured the worth of her other writings, which many scholars regard as superior to *Uncle Tom's Cabin*: *The Minister's Wooing* (1859), *Oldtown Folks* (1869), *Sam Lawson's Fireside Stories* (1871), *Poganuc People* (1878). This group of New England fiction—set between Maine and Connecticut—is, despite didacticism, an important and influential contribution to regional literature.

Harriet Beecher Stowe's novels and stories, which she continued to write for fifty years till her death in 1896, run to sixteen volumes. Some of the "yarns" are dated, but more than a handful, "in addition to being authentic, . . . are charming and comic—the mature creations of a great writer."

Tom Sawyer

by

SAMUEL LANGHORNE CLEMENS (1835–1910)
(MARK TWAIN)

Main Characters

Tom Sawyer—A twelve-year-old boy, endowed with a wildly
romantic imagination and an inordinate love of mischief.
Sid—Tom's priggish, tattling brother.
Aunt Polly—Tom's kind-hearted, devout, and fussy aunt and
guardian.
Becky Thatcher—The lovely blonde, blue-eyed girl whom
Tom chooses for his sweetheart.
Joe Harper—Tom's bosom friend.
Huck Finn—The homeless, ragged, but self-sufficient son of
the town drunkard.
Injun Joe—The vicious halfbreed who terrorizes Tom and
Huck.
Muff Potter—The town drunk and scapegoat.

The Story

Tom Sawyer of St. Petersburg, Missouri, has a talent for
mischief and none at all for school. He plays hooky one day
and his righteous brother Sid tells their Aunt Polly. Tom is
sentenced to whitewash the fence, an unpleasant chore, but he
pretends to be fascinated by it. Shortly, several of his cronies
offer to relieve him. Tom allows them to whitewash—at a

price, and thus becomes possessor of the richest boys' treasure in town.

Tom manages to get into all kinds of trouble. He accumulates yellow tickets by trade, not by memorizing the Bible verses for which they are awarded. When he is asked, as an informal test of his knowledge, who were the first two apostles, he replies, "David and Goliath." In church he finds the sermon much less intriguing than watching the pinch bug he has released fasten onto a dog which runs howling out of church. He challenges the overdressed, sissified new boy in town to combat and defeats him.

Another newcomer, Becky Thatcher, captures Tom's youthful fancy with her blue eyes and blonde hair. At the cost of a whipping from the schoolmaster, Tom contrives to sit next to her in class. Working very rapidly, he declares his love for her, forces a similar declaration from her, and becomes her accepted fiancé. But when he inadvertently lets slip that he has been engaged at least once before, Becky spurns him and Tom leaves full of self-pity and anger.

Playing Robin Hood with his friends, racing ticks, fighting mock battles, planning a career as a pirate, and taking part in whatever adventures come along are far more attractive to Tom than going to school. One adventure has dire consequences. Eluding the vigilance of Aunt Polly and Sid, Tom sneaks out with Huck Finn, the town ragamuffin, to make a midnight visit to the graveyard. They plan to visit the grave of someone wicked, wait for a devil to emerge, then swing a dead cat (Huck has procured one) after them, saying, "Devil follow corpse, cat follow devil, wart follow cat, I'm done with ye!" Instead of the devil, though, the boys come upon three grave robbers: young Dr. Robinson, Injun Joe, a malevolent halfbreed, and Muff Potter, the local drunk. Out of sight, they hear Injun Joe demand more money, Muff Potter second the demand, and Dr. Robinson refuse. The doctor strikes Muff, knocking him out. Injun Joe, furious, drives his knife into the doctor. Then he puts the knife into the hand of the still-unconscious Muff, and when Muff awakens, convinces him that he jumped the doctor and knifed him. But Injun Joe magnanimously promises to be silent. Frightened, the boys run off and take a bloody oath never to tell what they have seen. They are sure that if they do, Injun Joe will exact some kind of dreadful revenge.

Tom and Huck try their best to forget, even when Muff Potter is arrested for murder. In this they are aided by a pirate interlude. Feeling much put upon by Aunt Polly, who makes him swallow evil-tasting medicine, Tom escapes to nearby Jackson's Island in the company of Huck and Joe Harper. The boys have a glorious time fishing, swimming, and learning to smoke a pipe. Meanwhile they see boats go by searching for their bodies, and they finally realize that their folks must be worried. Besides, the boys are getting bored. Tom swims back to town at night to discover what he can. He finds his Aunt Polly and Mrs. Harper and their neighbors dissolved in tears. Everyone is recalling Tom and Joe fondly. Tom is tempted to show himself when he hears about the funeral service being planned for him and his companions on Sunday. He sneaks out of the house and returns to the island. On Sunday, just at the height of the congregation's wailing and in the midst of the preacher's eulogy, Tom, Joe, and Huck walk down the aisle. Joy, tears, and thanksgiving are their reward.

Tom and Becky make up. The normal round of St. Petersburg life proceeds until the trial of Muff Potter. Evidence against him is overwhelming; conviction seems sure. Then Tom is called to the witness stand. He bravely tells how Injun Joe killed the doctor and framed Muff. Injun Joe jumps out the window and escapes. Muff goes free, and Tom is the hero.

But time again weighs heavily on Tom. With Huck he decides to dig for treasure. (Robber bands had frequented the area near St. Petersburg not long before.) After some fruitless digging, the boys take pick and shovel to a haunted house. While they explore the upper story of the house, they hear voices, and peering through knotholes, see a ragged creature and a Spaniard. The Spaniard turns out to be Injun Joe, come to bury $650. While digging, Injun Joe strikes a box filled with a few thousand dollars in gold coins—presumably robbers' treasure. But Joe has grown suspicious. He decides to remove the treasure, he tells his crony, to "Number Two—under the cross."

The boys decide to watch for the false Spaniard and his friend, and to trail them if they appear. They finally locate Injun Joe, drunk at a tavern. Since Tom is to go on a picnic given by Becky for her friends, Huck agrees to stand guard and see if he can follow the Indian to the treasure hoard. One night he and his partner emerge, and Huck pursues. Hidden, he overhears their plan to rob the Widow Douglas and to mark her up with a knife. Injun Joe still bears a grudge against her late husband. Though terrified, Huck summons aid. The villains are routed but escape.

Meanwhile, at the picnic, Becky and Tom have entered a cave and become separated from the other picnickers. For three terrible days they are imprisoned in the cave without food or light. One day Tom sees a hand holding a lighted candle! It is Injun Joe hiding out! Luckily Injun Joe does not recognize Tom, and flees. At last Tom sees a gleam of light. With Becky he follows it to an opening in the cave, and together they return to their rejoicing families. Becky's father closes up the cave to prevent further accidents. Injun Joe is trapped inside. Tom tells Huck he is convinced the treasure must be in the cave. He and Huck enter the cave through the opening Tom and Becky used, and in one of the chambers find a cross made with candle smoke, and under it the treasure!

Tom and Huck transfer the gold coins to small bags and carry them to St. Petersburg. They are stopped at the Widow Douglas's and invited in. There Huck's heroism in rescuing the widow is revealed, and Tom tops the revelation by displaying the treasure. The boys are wealthy now with an income of a dollar a day. But Huck, who has been taken in by the widow and made to dress in civilized fashion and even to attend school and church, is not happy. He leaves the widow. Only Tom's inducement, that he will form a robber band and Huck will be a member, moves Huck, reluctantly, to give the thing another chance.

Critical Opinion

If the reader chooses not to commit himself to *The Adventures of Tom Sawyer,* he can advance reasons enough for his restraint. The plot is as melodramatic as a dime novel's. The sequence of events is casual, even wayward—or, as Howells puts it, Mark Twain "sets down the thing that comes into his mind without fear or favor of the thing that went before or the

thing that may be about to follow." The adult characters are
sticklike figures, conventionally conceived supernumeraries.
The sentimentality engendered by nostalgia sometimes over-
flows to drown out the reality.

Such reasons, nevertheless, miss their mark. *Tom Sawyer* is
American myth, not realistic record—despite its "acute minor
realisms." To read it otherwise is to misread it and so to miss
the magical experience that several generations of boys—and
their fathers—have found it.

For if the reader gives himself to it, *Tom Sawyer* is a steady
delight. The book has been called an "American idyl," "a
romantic remembrance of things past," and by the author,
"simply a hymn, put into prose form to give it a worldly air."
Mark Twain said that he recalled, not invented it. "Most of
the adventures recorded in the book really occurred," he wrote
in the preface.

Tom Sawyer is rich in pastoral scenes that have become
American classics: Tom's whitewashing of the fence (with
collaboration), his releasing of the pinch bug in church, his
gallant blame-taking for Becky's misdemeanor in school. And
darker scenes, too: Tom's frightened glimpse of Injun Joe in
the cave, his graveyard visit with Huck, his testimony for Muff
Potter.

Moreover, the talk in the book—its idiom and syntax—is a
triumphant achievement (as well as a model for the writers
who followed Twain). The boys whose conversation we over-
hear are sometimes "splashed by caricature," but their actions
"turn on the hard hinges of true boy-psychology." Finally the
lines of the plot, though far-flung, all converge satisfyingly at
the climax. Had Mark Twain not written *The Adventures of
Huckleberry Finn*, says Dixon Wecter, this would be his finest
novel.

The Adventures of Huckleberry Finn

by

SAMUEL LANGHORNE CLEMENS

(MARK TWAIN)

Main Characters

Huckleberry Finn—The narrator, a thirteen-year-old boy who hates all the restraints of "civilization."

Tom Sawyer—Huck's bosom companion, a highly imaginative and romantic boy.

"Pap" Finn—Huck's disreputable father, a drunken bully.

Widow Douglas—The kind, well-meaning lady who attempts to "civilize" Huck.

Miss Watson—Her spinster sister.

Judge Thatcher—Guardian of Huck's fortune.

Jim—A Negro slave, illiterate and superstitious but brave, generous, and good.

Colonel Grangerford—The head of an aristocratic family engaged in a blood feud with the neighbors, the Shepherdsons.

Buck—His good-natured son, about Huck's age.

The King—A confidence man befriended by Huck and Jim.

The Duke—Another confidence man, who proves as untrustworthy as his companion, the king.

Mary Jane—The innocent and very gullible niece of the dead Peter Wilks, an easy prey for the confidence men.

Sally Phelps—Tom Sawyer's good-hearted aunt.

Silas Phelps—Tom Sawyer's equally good-hearted uncle.

The Story

Huckleberry Finn, a thirteen-year-old boy living in St. Petersburg, Missouri, has been taken in hand by the Widow Douglas, who with the overzealous help of her spinster sister,

Miss Watson, undertakes to civilize him. Huck is chided when he attempts to smoke or even fidget. He is introduced to spelling and compelled to say his prayers—projects he wholeheartedly opposes. Only his adventures with Tom Sawyer, his bosom friend and a complete romantic, make his captivity bearable. Huck and Tom have discovered a buried treasure,* and Huck fears that his blackguard father will take the money from him. Consequently he "sells" his fortune—$6,000—to Judge Thatcher, a fiction that will prevent the senior Finn from getting his hands on it.

"Pap" Finn, a dirty, fish-belly-white, regularly drunk villain, catches Huck and keeps him prisoner in an abandoned cabin on the Illinois side of the Mississippi. Although Huck enjoys fishing and hunting, he is periodically terrified by his father's drunken, maniacal rages—often accompanied by beatings. So he decides to escape. Once, when Finn (old at fifty) goes to town for whiskey, Huck tunnels his way out and shoots a pig. Then he smashes the door, hacks the pig's throat, bloodies the ax and the cabin generally—all to make it appear that he has been murdered by a burglar or other intruder. After this fevered activity, he puts some provisions into a canoe and makes for Jackson's Island near Hannibal.

There, when he hears the boom of cannon, he knows that his strategy has been successful, that a searching party on a ferryboat is firing cannon to make his body surface. Having had a smoke, he proceeds to explore the island. He comes upon a campfire and recognizes Miss Watson's Negro slave Jim sleeping there. Jim confesses that he has run away because Miss Watson was about to sell him down the river. Huck and Jim join forces, fish, paddle round the island, and wander over it. One morning, after a violent storm, they see a farm house floating on the river. They paddle out to examine it and find a dead man in the house. Jim looks closely, covers the face with rags, but won't let Huck look at it.

Huck feels things are getting dull, so he slips on one of the dresses salvaged from the floating house and goes to the Illinois shore. He makes an unconvincing girl. The answers he invents when a shrewd farm woman questions him, though admirably quick, are contradictory. She exposes him easily by dropping a lump of lead into his lap and watching him clap

---

* See *The Adventures of Tom Sawyer*.

his legs together. A girl would have reacted by spreading them, she points out. However, Huck quickly shifts his line and tells the woman that he's a runaway apprentice. He learns that people are out looking for Jim—and for the $300 reward offered for his capture. Many think that Jim killed Huck. Pap is also suspected. There is a $200 reward offered for him— since he has gone off with a couple of hard-faced characters and hasn't been seen since.

Returning to the island, Huck rouses Jim, telling him that they must shove off if they are to elude capture. Piling their possessions on a raft they have salvaged, and trailing the canoe, they set out along the Mississippi for Cairo, Illinois where they can enter the mouth of the Ohio River. They run at night and rest during the day, sometimes "borrowing" a watermelon or a chicken from the farms they pass.

Now follow a series of turbulent adventures on the river. The earliest is almost the last. Below St. Louis, Huck and Jim encounter a steamboat, apparently foundered on a rock. They board her and find two bandits who have bound a third and are about to leave him, knowing that he will drown when the boat cracks. Huck and Jim are almost caught when their raft breaks loose, but they grab the bandits' skiff, leaving the would-be abandoners themselves abandoned.

Jim proves to be a devoted comrade. He shields, protects, and even instructs Huck. Once, after Huck's canoe is separated from the raft, Jim agonizes about Huck's safety, worries himself sick because he thinks Huck is lost. Huck suddenly appears, however, and pretends that Jim has been sleeping and has dreamed the whole episode. Jim, at first almost convinced, realizes when he sees the evidence of leaves and rubbish on the raft, that Huck has been fooling him. He rebukes Huck for his callous behavior. Huck apologizes.

On another occasion, just after Huck has suffered pangs of conscience at helping a slave escape, some men approach the raft, searching for escaped slaves. Huck tricks them into believing that his father is on the raft, sick with smallpox. The men gingerly leave some money for him and hastily push off.

Matters become worse. Huck and Jim bypass Cairo—Jim's great hope—in the night, and their raft is cut in two by a steamboat. Huck dives and escapes the wheel, but he can't find Jim. He goes to shore and is at once taken in by the

Grangerfords, a "mighty nice family": the aristocratic and benevolent Colonel Grangerford and his wife, two daughters, and three sons, one of them, Buck, a boy of Huck's age. The Grangerfords are engaged in a senseless blood feud with the Shepherdsons, another family whom they rather admire but persist in killing (and being killed by). The origins of the feud have become somewhat vague to both sides. A Grangerford girl and a Shepherdson boy fall in love and elope, precipitating a murderous ambush in which Buck, his father, two brothers, and a cousin are killed—along with some Shepherdsons. Huck feels the worse about this episode since unwittingly he has helped trigger this phase of the feud by delivering a message in which the two lovers arranged their elopement. Huck learns more about the cruelty that obsesses even "good" people.

Jim has escaped, too, and makes contact with Huck through the assistance of some of the Grangerford slaves. Together they return to the river, board their raft, and slide along the river. But their peace does not endure for long. Huck takes aboard two fugitives who are being chased by a mob, and they shortly reveal themselves to be two complete rogues— confidence men, each of whom has escaped a crowd eager to tar and feather him. One of them, about thirty, sells patent medicines, acts, teaches singing, "slings" lectures—does "most anything that comes handy, so it ain't work." The other— "about seventy," Huck says, perhaps inaccurately—doctors, cures by laying on of hands, tells fortunes, but thinks preaching is his special vocation. Soon each begins to demonstrate his talents. The younger asserts that he's the Duke of Bridgewater, falsely deprived of his high estate; the elder identifies himself as "the pore disappeared Dauphin, Looy the Seventeen." Huck and Jim, of course, feel it necessary to wait upon them hand and foot, a service they accept as their aristocratic due.

In one town a camp meeting is in process and the king passes himself off tearfully as a pirate converted by the preacher at the meeting and eager to leave for the Indian Ocean to convert other pirates—a statement of intention that proves very profitable, since the audience contributes generously to the project. In another town the pair of mountebanks put on a bizarre version of the balcony scene from *Romeo and*

Juliet, and almost get themselves run out of town for following it with *The King's Cameleopard* ("Ladies and children not admitted"). The latter performance consists solely of the king capering about the stage naked except for being painted in rainbow fashion. The pair might have been run out of town on a rail if one of the audience hadn't suggested that the same trick be played the next night on the rest of the townfolk. The audience accepts the suggestion and waits for revenge the next night. But the duke and king make their getaway after collecting the receipts for the second performance.

Huck sees another frightening instance of pride and cruelty. In one river town a harmless drunk named Boggs hurls dire but meaningless threats at a Southern aristocrat, Colonel Sherburn. The Colonel, after warning him to stop, shoots him. An aroused mob goes to the Colonel's house to lynch him—but he turns them away, scornfully telling them it needs a man to lynch someone, not a mob—unless the lynching is done Southern fashion, in the dark and with masks.

The two rapscallions (Jim's characterization of the royal pair) next try their most odious gambit. Waiting for a steamboat near a small town, they learn from a departing resident that his fellow townsman, Peter Wilks, has died, leaving behind three nieces and considerable property. The king learns further that Peter's two brothers, Harvey and William, are expected from England but haven't arrived. Immediately the king's plan is formed: he will be Harvey, the duke will be William (deaf and dumb), and Huck their servant. They easily deceive the innocent girls and gullible townspeople. Mary Jane, the eldest, whom Huck is attracted to, in order to show her faith in her "uncle," turns over the inheritance to the king. But Huck tells her the truth, and the king, despite his eloquence, doesn't get away with the scheme. The real brothers appear and identify themselves. Again only an expeditious retreat saves the two from a lynching party.

The most monstrous act of the charlatans is to turn Jim in as an escaped slave for forty dollars. Huck discovers Jim's whereabouts. His conscience has been troubling him. He believes it wrong to help a slave escape—almost an abolitionist act. Now he writes Miss Watson, informing her that a Silas Phelps has Jim and will give him up for the posted reward. Then, after writing the letter, he thinks of how good Jim has been to him, how steadfast through all their adventures. He says to himself, "All right, then, I'll *go* to hell," and he tears the letter up.

Arriving at the Phelps farm, Huck—much to his amazement —is enthusiastically greeted as Tom Sawyer, the nephew of Aunt Sally Phelps and Uncle Silas Phelps. He accepts the identification, hoping it will help him to engineer Jim's escape, and is able to answer all questions about the Sawyer family. The reason for Huck's being mistaken for Tom Sawyer is cleared up by Tom's sudden arrival. The Phelpses were expecting Tom, their nephew, whom they had never seen. Tom sizes up the situation with his customary acuteness and declares himself to be Sid Sawyer, Tom's brother. To Huck's astonishment, Tom eagerly enters into the "immoral" scheme of freeing Jim—but insists that the freeing has to be done in style, the style he has learned from his avid reading of the literature of escape. Tom's plan involves saws, chains, journals, magic, and some anonymous letters of warning. When finally the boys help Jim escape, the letters of warning that Tom has lavishly distributed, alert the neighbors who gather at the Phelps farm. Tom receives a bullet in the leg from one of them. Jim again displays his heroism by refusing to escape while Huck goes for a doctor. Instead he stays to nurse Tom tenderly and is captured. But Tom now springs his surprise: Old Miss Watson is dead, and she has set Jim free in her will. All of Tom's rigmarole and stratagems have been put on for sheer fun and adventure.

At this juncture, Aunt Polly appears. She has been puzzled about the letters she has received referring to Sid who has remained at home with her. She soon clears up the identities of Tom and Huck. Jim, now a free man, tells Huck that "Pap" Finn is dead: he was the man in the floating house, the man whose face Jim would not let Huck see. As for Huck, he thinks he must light out for the "territory" because Aunt Sally wants to adopt him and civilize him, and he's "been there before."

Critical Opinion

"All modern American literature," Ernest Hemingway wrote,

"comes from one book by Mark Twain called *Huckleberry Finn* . . . it's the best book we've had." Hemingway's comment stretches things a little, but *The Adventures of Huckleberry Finn* is, in fact, a marvelous book—"a joy forever," to quote Dixon Wecter, and "unquestionably one of the masterpieces of American and of world literature."

A sequel to *Tom Sawyer*, it is a much better book because Huck is far more interesting and complex than Tom; because Huck, who tells the story in his own wonderful vernacular, almost never strikes a false note; because Huck's experiences are deeper-going and his moral travails more meaningful. "A great-spirited boy among mean-spirited men," one critic observes, "Huck stands alone and ponders a decision usually left to those much older and more experienced—the reconciliation of piety with human decency." And his decision—to follow his own moral impulse rather than village morality—amounts almost to a vindication of what Mark Twain called "the damned human race," damned for its comfortable hypocrisies, its thoroughgoing dishonesties, and its pervasive cruelties, all of which Huck plentifully observes on his river odyssey with Jim.

Jim is as great a creation as Huck. Bernard De Voto calls Jim the only heroic character Mark Twain ever drew in his novels. Jim's heroism lies in his kindness, endurance, courage, and essential humanity. He contrasts dramatically with the scoundrels of the Mississippi frontier, with Pap Finn, the "Duke," and the "Dauphin," as well as with its aristocracy, Colonel Sherburn, the Grangerfords, and the Shepherdsons.

The Mississippi itself functions as a character in the novel, its greatest character some readers feel. The river gives form to the wanderings of Huck and Jim and from it arise the fun and the horror, the beauty and the color, of the book. To it Huck and Jim return gratefully after each unhappy adventure on shore, to move with it peacefully and freely once more.

The entrance of Tom Sawyer toward the end of the novel is perhaps a blight on an otherwise perfect book. The uproar and intrigue that Tom introduces shatter the tone of the story, shift it from high comedy to low farce.

Huckleberry Finn, however, is so great that it rises above even Tom and his shenanigans.

The Author

Samuel Langhorne Clemens was born in Florida, Missouri, in
1835. Four years later his family settled in Hannibal, Missouri,
a sleepy river town where he led the romantic boy's life described in *Tom Sawyer* and *Huckleberry Finn*. His father, an
unsuccessful lawyer turned unlucky merchant, died in 1846.
Before Sam was twelve, his schooling was over, and he became
a printer's apprentice and, not long after, the author of occasional newspaper pieces.

At eighteen he set out on his travels. He worked as a jour-
neyman printer in a number of large cities from St. Louis eastward to New York. In 1857 he took passage at New Orleans,
intending to proceed to South America. But luckily he met
Horace Bixby, a river pilot, who agreed to teach him piloting,
fulfilling Sam's boyhood ambition. As Bixby's apprentice, he
learned to navigate every inch of the 1,200-mile Mississippi
River. This was the happiest period of his life, he recalled in
Life on the Mississippi. In his four years on the river, he acquired "his richest store of literary material." Here, he derived,
too, the name "Mark Twain," from a river cry signifying two
fathoms (or twelve feet).

With the advent of the railroad, the demand for river pilots
declined. So Clemens went westward in 1861 to Nevada.
There he tried his hand at mining, worked as a journalist on
the Virginia City *Enterprise*, and engaged in some unsuccessful speculation. Here he also met the first of several literary
advisers, "Artemus Ward" (Charles Farrar Browne), a famous
humorist. When Clemens pushed on to San Francisco to work
on the *Morning Call*, he submitted a story to Ward for a collection the latter was editing. It arrived too late, and the "villainous backwoods sketch"—"Jim Smiley and His Jumping
Frog" (1865)—appeared in the *Saturday Press*. Widely cir-
culated, it gave Samuel Clemens his first recognition.

Clemens' reputation grew substantially during the next
decade. In 1865 he went to the Hawaiian Islands as a newspaper correspondent. The humorous lectures he delivered upon
his return were enormously popular. In 1867 he traveled in
Europe and the Holy Land. His hilarious if philistine record of
the trip in *The Innocents Abroad* (1869) swelled his reputa-

tion and bank account. Following his romantic courtship of and marriage to Olivia Langdon, daughter of a wealthy coal dealer in Elmira, New York, Clemens moved to Hartford. There he produced his three most memorable books: *The Adventures of Tom Sawyer* (1876), *Life on the Mississippi* (1883), and *The Adventures of Huckleberry Finn* (1885).

Royalties from his books and proceeds from his lectures made Clemens an extremely rich man. His unfortunate investments, however, left him bankrupt. In 1895, at the age of sixty, he set out to pay his creditors and recoup his fortune. Through a triumphal lecture tour and the continued success of his books, he managed to do this.

Clemens built a magnificent home at Redding, Connecticut, and lived there in princely style. But, despite the adulation of his multitude of readers, the honors showered upon him at home and abroad, and the warm friendship of some notable men, his last years were melancholy, sometimes desperately unhappy. The death of his wife and all but one of his children left him lonely and deepened the pessimism that underlay his humor. He died in 1910. A number of his books have appeared posthumously; the most important of them, *The Mysterious Stranger* (1916), is also his bleakest and most despairing view of man.

Samuel Clemens was a matchless humorist. But he was also a gifted creator of memorable characters like Huckleberry Finn and Tom Sawyer. "Increasingly," writes Walter Blair, "Clemens' countrymen appreciate the charm of his personality, the breadth and depth of his richly native experiences, the unostentatious artistry revealed by his best writings." He is, William Dean Howells adds, "sole and incomparable, the Lincoln of our literature."

The Rise of Silas Lapham

by

WILLIAM DEAN HOWELLS (1837–1920)

Main Characters

Silas Lapham—A self-made man, an American go-getter, fundamentally sound, honest, and brave.

Persis Lapham—His wife, loyal, loving, and a moral prod to Lapham.

Irene Lapham—Their beautiful, efficient, but not especially intelligent younger daughter.

Penelope Lapham—Their droll, perceptive, humorous, though not particularly pretty elder daughter.

Tom Corey—Member of a wealthy upper-class Boston family who seeks employment in Lapham's paint business.

Mr. Corey—Tom's father, a charming dilettante.

Mrs. Corey—Tom's mother, conventional, aristocratic, good-natured.

Jim Rogers—The unscrupulous businessman whom Silas has once taken advantage of.

Mr. Sewell—The intelligent minister, foe of cant and sentimental humbug, who advises Silas and his wife at a critical period.

The Story

Silas Lapham, as he appears to a journalist who interviews him, is a solid, self-made man, perhaps a bit smug but none-

54

theless shrewd and enterprising. Though the journalist is right, there is more to Silas Lapham. He has every reason to be satisfied with himself. He is wealthy because he aggressively and proudly sells a superior paint, manufactured from minerals he has discovered on the Vermont farm inherited from his father. He has married a schoolteacher, Persis, who has proved a loyal and loving wife as well as a moral guide—almost a conscience. Lapham has two affectionate daughters: Irene, the younger, is not only a beauty but also a capable "manager" about the house; Penelope, the elder, is a droll and perceptive young lady. Finally, Lapham has served his country, becoming a colonel during the Civil War.

Lapham suffers from a secret shame, though he never admits it, despite his wife's prodding. He once took on a partner, Jim Rogers, whose money helped him exploit the paint. Then, partly because Rogers was a drag on the business and partly because Lapham could not stand sharing the ownership of his beloved paint with anyone, he crowded Rogers out. The maneuver, while perfectly legal, was morally suspect, as his wife and occasionally his conscience remind him.

Since Lapham and his family have moved to Boston, he has developed social ambitions. Three Boston Brahmins—Mrs. Corey and her two daughters—come to call in belated acknowledgment of the kindness that Mrs. Lapham had shown them at a resort where they had met. While perfectly polite, Mrs. Corey had intimated that none of their friends lived in Lapham's part of town. The hint is enough. Silas determines to build on a lot he owns in the fashionable Back Bay area. He is mildly supported by his wife, Persis, but not by Irene or Penelope whose education for fashionable society has been neglected.

Silas intends to build a big house. His excellent architect helps him. One day, as they visit the site of the construction, they see Rogers. Persis is deflated and declares that she will not live in the house, but Silas grimly denies having wronged Rogers and persists in his project.

On another occasion, Irene accompanies her parents to the site. They are surprised by the appearance of Tom Corey, a young Brahmin whom Irene finds extremely pleasant. After some casual talk, during which Silas brags a good deal, as is his habit, Corey leaves and the Laphams return home. Irene

confides to her sister, though indirectly, that she is smitten
with Tom Corey.

As for Tom, he tells his father—a charming and cultivated
dilettante who has refrained from work all his life—that he
would like to get a job, preferably with Lapham. Having
received his father's quizzical blessing, Tom applies to Silas
directly, much to the latter's gratification since his wife
regards young Corey as belonging to another social sphere.
Tom's plan is to serve as foreign representative after he has
learned the business.

Silas takes Tom to his summer home at Nantasket to discuss
the matter. It is the first of many visits, for even after Tom's
proposition has been accepted, he returns frequently. All the
Laphams, including Irene, suppose that he admires Irene—
although it is Penelope whom he always talks about and to
whom he listens delightedly.

After a while the Coreys feel obliged to invite the Laphams
to dinner. Penelope, who has disliked Mrs. Corey from the
start, refuses to go, but the others accept eagerly, though they
are uneasy about their social ineptitude. The dinner is a
fiasco. Silas, unused to wine, drinks to excess and begins to
brag obnoxiously. The next day, of course, Silas is desperately
unhappy. He is not comforted by Tom's assurances that everyone at the party understood the reasons for his unseemly
behavior. Silas offers Tom an opportunity to resign, but he
refuses it and will not listen to Silas's self-abasement.

Some hours later Tom comes to the conclusion that he has
not shown Silas enough sympathy, and sets off to visit him.
Silas is not home—but Penelope is. She greets him amiably
and, as always, chatters amusingly. Before very long, Tom
finds himself telling Penelope that he loves her. She is amazed,
bewildered, but not altogether unhappy. Like all the Laphams
(and the Coreys, too), she supposed that Tom was paying
court to her far more beautiful sister. She sends him away.
Next morning Penelope conveys the news of Tom's preference
to her mother who tells Silas. Puzzled about the course they
ought to take and deeply unhappy about the necessity of
inflicting pain on one of their daughters, they recall a minister,
Mr. Sewell, whom they met at the Coreys' dinner party. His
commonsense denunciation of sentimental novels and their
false solutions to human problems especially impressed Silas.

They call on him, and his advice immediately appeals to them. One must suffer rather than three, he says, if none is to blame. The principle of the economy of pain would be obvious if false tradition did not prevail.

To Persis falls the duty of telling her daughter Irene that Tom loves Penelope. She performs it bluntly. Irene takes it without tears, presents to Penelope the mementos of Tom that she has cherished, and returns to her room. She cannot respond to Penelope's compassionate attempts at reconciliation or her parents' either. As soon as she can, she leaves for their Vermont farm.

Silas runs into serious financial troubles. To please Persis and perhaps to ease his own conscience, he has lent Rogers $20,000 on securities worth only a fraction of that amount. Moreover, Rogers has involved him in disastrous financial speculations. Especially disheartening to Silas has been his discovery that some mills given to him by Rogers as collateral for the loan are on the line of a railroad that has been purchased by a powerful combine that can force sale of the mills whenever it chooses, at whatever price it sets. Tom offers to lend Silas $30,000, but Silas gallantly refuses.

Silas hopes to get some money to buy out a new company that can produce paint as good as his but at a lower cost. He decides to sell the elegant house he has been building. But luck has turned against him. Because of his own carelessness, the house—on which he has allowed the insurance to lapse—burns down. Rogers meanwhile has located some Englishmen who are willing to buy the mills even when they are informed (as Silas insists they must be informed) that the railroad controls the value of the property. Silas discovers that the Englishmen are acting as agents for wealthy men who would be cheated if he sold them the mills. He rises to the moral challenge, rejects the deal, and goes bankrupt.

The affair between Tom and Penelope is happily resolved. Tom persists in his proposal even after Silas's bankruptcy, and Penelope ultimately consents to marry him. Irene, who has returned from Vermont upon hearing of her father's misfortunes, gives the lovers her blessing. After their marriage, Tom and Penelope leave for Mexico, a move that will minimize family friction (for the Coreys cannot wholly approve of Penelope nor she of them) and further Tom's busi-

ness career. And Silas, much poorer but not poverty-stricken,
retires to his Vermont farm. He finally sells his mines and
works to the firm he had once hoped to purchase—but he
still produces a special high-grade paint, the Persis brand.
Both he and his wife are content with the moral choice that
he so courageously made.

Critical Opinion

The Rise of Silas Lapham has not been exempt from the
attacks commonly launched against Howells' fiction. Critics
have deplored its lack of passion, its unvarying restraint, its
refusal to explore the depths. Some have assailed it for its
"unfavorable picture of the modern industrial and financial
order" and others for its superficial analysis of the predatory
nature of big business. Nevertheless, it has been said that "it
has every appearance of being an American classic."

The reasons are plain. Howells' double plot—the temptations of Silas Lapham and the winning of Penelope—is
expertly constructed. The characters, especially Silas Lapham
—the self-made American businessman, honest, awkward,
innocent in social relations despite his shrewdness in business
affairs, fundamentally moral despite his single lapse from
probity—are thoroughly realized. The style is graceful,
flexible, tinged with humor.

It is Howells' ethical theme, however, that is most important. More than one critic has thought the title ironic,
supposing that *rise* implied "social ascent." And at least one
critic thought it misleading, supposing that *rise* alluded to
Silas's business success. Howells himself, though, specifically
declared that he conceived the rise to be a moral one. Silas,
having learned from sad experience, rejects expedient solutions, refusing to wear moral blinders, to cheat even through
a substitute. There are, Howells seems to insist, no substitutes
for honesty—nor anything so valuable.

The commonsense formula of Mr. Sewell, the minister,
underlines the same principle in a different context: If none
is to blame, one must suffer rather than three. This lucid
doctrine—"the economy of pain"—illustrates Howells' stand
against romantic illusion and for truth, in life as in literature.

The Author

William Dean Howells, who was born in Ohio and died in New York, wrote about eighty books. He was, one commentator says, "in himself almost an entire literary movement." He early developed a love of books, and working in the office of his printer-father, educated himself intensively by a long course of reading. Beginning his career as a journalist in Ohio, he soon developed a reputation for competence. As a reward for writing a campaign biography of Lincoln, he was given a consulship in Venice. Returning to the United States in 1865, he joined the staff of the *Nation* and later the *Atlantic.* In 1871 he attained the highest editorial post in the country as editor of the *Atlantic,* where he remained until 1881. In 1885 he left Boston for New York, the new literary capital, and wrote "at large" for *Harper's.*

Meanwhile Howells had been pouring forth a stream of books—essays, criticisms, autobiographies, short plays, poetry, and novels. He became the acknowledged "dean of American letters," a position that nobody has quite filled since. He deserved his eminence for introducing Americans to foreign writers—about everyone of real importance, from Goldoni to Tolstoi—and for advancing the careers of such writers as Frank Norris, Stephen Crane, and Hamlin Garland. Moreover, he fought the good fight for realism in American literature, and opposed the cult of sentimentality that was restricting the growth of American letters.

Howells' own novels are not thrilling productions. In all forty of them, O. W. Firkins writes, "adultery is never pictured; seduction never; divorce once and sparingly . . . ; marriage discordant to the point of cleavage, only once and in the same novel with the divorce; crime only once with any fullness . . . ; politics never; religion passingly and superficially; science only in crepuscular psychology; mechanics, athletics, bodily exploits or collisions very rarely." Because so many of the basic themes that intrigue us are missing from Howells, his influence and popularity have declined. Yet in *A Hazard of New Fortunes* (1890), *A Modern Instance* (1882), and above all in *The Rise of Silas Lapham,* he has explored lucidly and attractively aspects of American life seldom touched on earlier and never in quite the same way.

These novels have been read for three-quarters of a century, and they still are engrossing documents. They go far to justify Carl Van Doren's observation that Howells "produced in his fourscore books the most considerable transcript of American life yet made by one man."

The Portrait of a Lady

by

HENRY JAMES (1843–1916)

Main Characters

Isabel Archer—A twenty-three-year-old American girl, pretty, confident, and determined to discover for herself the limits of freedom and responsibility.

Gilbert Osmond—Isabel's husband, dilettante expatriate, cruel and vain, who tests Isabel's psychic endurance.

Mme. Serena Merle—Osmond's former mistress and mother of their illegitimate child, Pansy. A deeply emotional woman, Serena is sympathetic, yet wholly unscrupulous where her daughter's interests are involved.

Ralph Touchett—Isabel's gentle English cousin, an invalid who tries to live vicariously through her. Mature and knowledgeable, he prepares Isabel for the world she must face.

Henrietta Stackpole—A brash American journalist, sure she can outwit and outmaneuver any "foreigner."

Lord Warburton—An affable but ineffectual young nobleman who would like to marry Isabel.

Caspar Goodwood—A forthright, vigorous American who pursues Isabel before her marriage and again after it founders, an ideal hero who never wins the heroine.

The Story

In the summer of 1872, Isabel Archer, a young, beautiful American from Albany, New York, is a guest at the country home of her wealthy English cousins, the Touchetts. In accepting her aunt's invitation to make her first trip abroad, Isabel explains that being abroad will deepen, not alter, her fundamental purpose in life—to live fully and independently. "I always wanted to know the things one shouldn't do. . . . So as to choose," Isabel remarks. During the first stage of her European experience, Isabel acquires the knowledge she needs to make her ultimate choice. Before the novel ends four years later, she understands what her invalid cousin Ralph Touchett said in the beginning about her fund of worldly knowledge, "Yes, of happy knowledge—of pleasant knowledge. But you haven't suffered, and you're not made to suffer."

Isabel's experiences at Gardencourt, the Touchett estate, cause her little suffering. Old Mr. Touchett enjoys her freshness and forthrightness. A liberal young aristocrat, Lord Warburton, falls in love with her and unsuccessfully proposes marriage. Her cousin Ralph, who also loves her deeply but vainly, instructs her in the nuances of European custom. Isabel also has on hand two old American friends, Henrietta Stackpole, a journalist who is wholly insensitive to subtleties in human relationships and disapproves of Americans living abroad, and Caspar Goodwood, Isabel's indomitable suitor. Rejected by Isabel before her trip, Caspar pursues her to Gardencourt. She dismisses him again, insisting he leave her for at least two years, until she probes the limits of her freedom.

Ralph persuades his dying father to leave Isabel a fortune of £60,000 to enable her to test her theories of independence. Just at this point Isabel meets Mme. Merle, an American-born cosmopolite who attracts and disarms Isabel by candidly confessing that she is a parasite. The worst of her type— as well as the most fascinating and delightful—Mme. Merle assures Isabel, is Gilbert Osmond: "No career, no name, no position, no fortune, no past, no future, no anything." Yet he is, Mme. Merle adds, "a man made to be distinguished" and a man Isabel must meet.

In Italy, six months after she has become an heiress, Isabel meets Osmond, as Mme. Merle has intended. Mme. Merle's purpose in bringing the two together is simple. As the mother of Osmond's illegitimate fifteen-year-old daughter, Pansy (who lives with Osmond), Merle hopes to assure the child of economic security. Isabel, however, knows only that Osmond appears to be mature, intellectual, and suave. She sharply denies the criticism of Osmond's superficiality and selfishness offered by Ralph, Caspar, and Mrs. Touchett. A few months later she marries Osmond.

Three years later the results of Isabel's marriage begin to emerge indirectly. Osmond and Mme. Merle have been trying to prevent young Ned Rosier from wooing Pansy. Rosier is not poor, but Merle and Osmond hope for a better match. When Lord Warburton comes to visit, they see the perfect suitor, titled and wealthy. Because Isabel is unaware that Pansy prefers Rosier, she agrees to Osmond's demand that she encourage Warburton's suit, even if she has to use as leverage Warburton's still warm affection for her.

At this point Isabel engages in a long internal monologue, sitting before the fire and reviewing the events of her past three years. Only vaguely conscious of some link between Osmond and Mme. Merle, she is profoundly aware of disappointment and anguish in her own life with Osmond: "Suffering, with Isabel, was an active condition . . . it was a passion of thought, of speculation, of response to every pressure." She knows that Osmond desired her once as an addition to his art collection. Because she has displayed a mind of her own, Isabel realizes, this complete egoist's hatred "has become the occupation and comfort of his life."

When Isabel realizes that Pansy does not love Warburton, she tries to break up the relationship. Though Osmond's fury is cool and controlled, Isabel has wrecked his plan completely. He retaliates by forbidding Pansy's marriage to Ned Rosier and shipping her off to a convent. Although Mme. Merle is disappointed, she cannot be so cruel. She, too, manages to wound Isabel by making it clear that she has engineered Isabel's fate from the outset. To Osmond, Mme. Merle makes yet more explicit her estimate of his viciousness ("Have I been so vile all for nothing?").

From England comes word that Ralph Touchett is dying

and wishes to see Isabel. Osmond refuses to let her go, but when Isabel learns from Osmond's sister, Countess Gemini, that Mme. Merle and Osmond were once lovers, she feels no guilt about disobeying Osmond. In her final talk with Ralph, Isabel admits that she has been used, and apologizes for having disappointed him. Ever generous, Ralph reassures her: ". . . if you've been hated you've also been loved." Soon Caspar Goodwood proves that such love can still be hers. Like the others, Caspar has suspected her unhappiness but has been powerless to interfere. Now he demands that she admit her affection for him. Guardedly she does so, and Caspar embraces her passionately. Isabel nevertheless leaves him and returns to Osmond. As the novel closes, Henrietta Stackpole says to Caspar, ". . . just you wait!" But Caspar recoils from such optimism "shining at him with that cheap comfort." Henrietta's "key to patience" opens no door to a happy ending.

Critical Opinion

Henry James regarded *The Portrait of a Lady* as his first "big" novel. His critics have generally agreed, and some believe James never surpassed his achievement in this work of his "middle period." Certainly, in plot, characterization, and technique, *The Portrait* deserves high praise. This masterly sketch of a young woman determined to choose her fate rather than have it thrust upon her stirs compassion without sentimentality. The focus remains sharply and objectively on Isabel's inward imagination and her preparation for the ordeal she must endure.

The stages that precede Isabel's becoming an heiress and choosing Osmond have been carefully plotted to reveal the possibilities before her: the gentle but colorless charm of Lord Warburton, and the attractive but frightening virility of Caspar Goodwood. Because she is, as James notes, still "too young, too impatient to live, too unacquainted with pain," there is also Ralph Touchett to serve as guide and commentator. Thus James mounts a subtle setting of American and European taste, culture, and morality against which his young heroine stands in sharp relief. Together scene and character operate to shed brilliant light and ominous shadow on Isabel as she in turn casts her own luminous glow.

Though few critics disagree about the psychological implications of the first half of the novel, they are often in conflict about the latter half, especially about such questions as these: Why does Isabel choose Osmond? Why, after her disillusionment, does she reject Caspar and return to Osmond? About her original choice, some critics say it represents her proud rejection of those who would too rigidly direct her destiny. Leon Edel argues that Osmond represents a "safe" choice between the social commitments posed by Warburton's aristocratic world and the personal commitment demanded by Caspar Goodwood.

Isabel's determination to stay with her loathesome husband poses a more difficult problem. The range of theories here is great: Isabel has too much respect for the marital vow to abandon it; her sense of duty, especially to Pansy, is overpowering; her dread of an intense emotional involvement with Caspar makes even Osmond endurable; her moral values demand that she pay full retribution for her error. Whatever conclusion the reader reaches, he will find it difficult not to respect this young heiress whose integrity never falters even when her intelligence and imagination seem to waver. Surely no reader can forget her remarkable internal monologue (one of the first in modern fiction) as she sits alone before the fire and inwardly confronts the knowledge her freedom has purchased. It is a passage of surpassing beauty and tragic awareness.

The Turn of the Screw

by

HENRY JAMES

Main Characters

Governess—The spinster whose diary recounts the strange experiences of the children, the adults, and the ghosts.

Miles and Flora—The charming, precocious children in the governess' charge.

Mrs. Grose—The earthly, simple housekeeper who tries unsuccessfully to maintain a balance between the real and the spectral.

Peter Quint (a ghost)—Redheaded, sensual, evil, the deceased ex-steward of the estate.

Miss Jessel (a ghost)—Former governess of Miles and Flora and mistress of Quint.

Douglas—Reader of the tale and owner of the governess' diary. He knew her when she was his sister's governess and he was a college student.

Narrator—A liberal-minded fellow now in possession of the original manuscript.

The Story

On a Christmas Eve, long after the event, Douglas reads to an assembled group of friends the governess' diary, a meticulously written narrative of macabre events.

The governess, twenty-year-old daughter of a country parson, is hired by a handsome gentleman (her diary suggests that she is infatuated with him) to attend to the education of his late brother's two children. At Bly, a country estate, the youngsters live with a plain, motherly housekeeper, Mrs. Grose, and a large staff of servants. The governess is wholly enchanted with eight-year-old Flora—"the most beautiful child I had ever seen"—and looks forward to meeting

66

ten-year-old Miles who is away at school. Two days later she meets him unexpectedly, for he has been expelled from his boarding school as a bad influence. Can one so young corrupt others? she wonders. Mrs. Grose defends the boy vigorously and positively. The governess swiftly surrenders to his charm and beauty: "Everything but a sort of passion of tenderness was swept away by his presence."

She has already shown some curiosity about her predecessor, Miss Jessel, learning from Mrs. Grose only that she was pretty and that she is dead. Now the governess immerses herself in the joys of teaching her bright and lovable charges. They fill her present as nothing has filled her "small, smothered" past.

Strolling on the lawn one afternoon, enjoying a reverie about meeting a handsome man on the grounds of Bly, she looks up and sees—beyond the lawn, atop a tower—a strange man, his gaze fixed upon her, his appearance neither familiar nor agreeable. Troubled but determined not to worry Mrs. Grose or the children, she keeps silent. A few days later, when the same face appears at the dining-room window, she is horrified because the face seems to be searching for someone. She rushes outside but discovers no one. Suddenly she encounters the startled Mrs. Grose, who asks what has happened. The governess describes her two visions of the man who is "a horror"—red-haired, pale-faced, tall, well-dressed, but ghastly. Shaken, Mrs. Grose groans that the figure is that of Peter Quint, the master's valet, and adds, "Mr. Quint is dead."

Mrs. Grose now tells the governess that Quint is probably seeking the children, particularly little Miles, with whom he was friendly, too friendly and too free, as Quint was with everybody before he was found dead in a ditch one wintry morning. The governess determines to protect Miles at any cost, keeping him indoors yet telling him nothing to arouse his fears. With Flora, however, she continues to walk about the estate. A few day later, standing beside Flora at the edge of the lake, the governess senses another presence. Across the lake she sees staring at them "a woman in black, pale and dreadful." More terrible than the vision is the governess' sense that Flora has also seen the figure but pretends not to. The governess tells poor Mrs. Grose of her latest experience. By persistent questioning she elicits from Mrs. Grose the admission that the woman in black may be Miss Jessel, the former governess—and the mistress of Quint—who died while giving birth to his illegitimate child. What horrifies the governess most is her inner conviction that Miles and Flora are in league with the ghosts.

Meanwhile the children behave as winningly as ever. Their gaiety and sweetness are in utter contrast to the corruption the governess senses everywhere. A night later, hearing a rustling on the stair, the governess rushes out and confronts Quint on the stairwell. She rushes to Flora's room and discovers her bed empty. The child, unharmed, is at the window. She explains that she thought someone, possibly the governess, was walking about the grounds and had merely come to look. The governess does not challenge the explanation. A fortnight later, however, the governess, awakening shortly after midnight, steals to a window and sees an incredibly eerie sight: Flora gazing down from her terrace upon the moonlit lawn where Miles stands, transfixed, staring at the tall tower where Quint stares back at him.

Despite Miles's insistence that he and Flora have made up this "game" to show her how, for a change, they can be "bad," the governess remains certain that her charges are thoroughly infected with evil. Though Mrs. Grose urges her to tell her employer about the situation, she insists it is her duty not to bother him. She must save them herself. During the succeeding weeks she tries to keep the children as close to her as possible. Each conversation convinces her that their damnation is near. When Miles protests that she has become too possessive, she takes his complaint as further evidence of his attachment to Miss Jessel and Quint.

Completely distraught, the governess resolves to leave her post, but when she sees Miss Jessel seated in the children's schoolroom one afternoon, her determination is renewed. She writes to her employer, inquiring why Miles was expelled from school. As she sits writing the letter, Miles joins her. They talk for a while, pleasantly (almost like "honeymooners," James suggests), and suddenly she embraces the boy passionately, pleading with him to let her save him. At that moment, though the windows are shut, a shrill gust sweeps the room and the single candle is snuffed out. Miles shrieks, but insists he has blown it out himself.

Influenced by the governess' suggestions, Mrs. Grose also believes that the children are possessed by the infernal presences. The governess' letter to her employer, for example, has disappeared, apparently stolen by Miles. At the lake, Mrs. Grose's terror deepens when the governess suddenly asks Flora where Miss Jessel is, grasps the child's arm, and points to where Miss Jessel is standing across the lake. Mrs. Grose does not admit she sees Miss Jessel, and neither does Flora. Instead, the child demands to be taken away from the governess. The next day Mrs. Grose reports to the governess that Flora, sick in bed and feverish, has spoken "horrors," using bad language about the governess. The governess persuades Mrs. Grose to take Flora away to her uncle for the time being.

Alone now with Miles, the governess resolves to make him confess so that she can save him. She asks him why he stole her letter. Would that also explain his expulsion from school? He admits taking the letter ("To see what you said about me"), but denies that he stole at school. Rather, he admits, though evasively, to saying "things" to a few friends who then repeated them. As the governess presses Miles to reveal the nature of those "things," the face of Quint appears to her at the window. Hysterically, she clasps the boy to her. Miles whispers, "Is she *here*?" and then, "Miss Jessel, Miss Jessel." The governess cries that it is not Miss Jessel. "It's *he*?" the boy asks, and the governess flashes back at him, "Whom do you mean by 'he'?"

"Peter Quint—you devil!" Miles exclaims, demanding to know where the vision is. Hearing the boy speak the name convinces the governess that she has wrung the confession she needs to save him. Triumphantly she points to the window. Miles cries out and seems to fall, but she catches him and holds him close to her. Only her final sentence remains: "We were alone with the quiet day, and his little heart, dispossessed, had stopped."

Critical Opinion

One may read *The Turn of the Screw* on a number of levels. James, for example, said it was "a piece of ingenuity pure and simple, of cold, artistic calculation . . . to catch those not easily caught." Thus a reader may appreciate the story as sheer entertainment, enjoying it as a tour de force of suspense and horror, without ever knowing what the horror really is. The details are always wholly realistic and yet the effect is thoroughly romantic, because James writes about those things that, as he said, "we cannot possibly ever directly know."

Many critics insist, however, that the story's artistry is felt only when the reader recognizes the psychological aberration implicit in the governess' behavior. As Edmund Wilson and others argue, she is a sexually frustrated woman suffering from delusions and able, with fatal effect, to persuade others to share her delusion. Leon Edel adds that James's own disappointment as a dramatist is reflected in the haunted anguish of the governess.

Beyond the Freudian analysis lie other plausible interpretations. For example, the story has overtones of religious import: innocent children in a country Eden corrupted by evil (Quint in red and Miss Jessel in black—devil and death). The governess becomes, in this theory, a savior who fails because the force of evil is too great.

Readers must decide for themselves whether Quint and Miss Jessel really appear or are hallucinations. Are the children as innocent as they seem? Whatever the answer, most readers, like most critics, will find *The Turn of the Screw*, whether simple ghost story or complex psychological or theological narrative, a superbly wrought, absorbing tale.

The Author

Henry James was less than a year old when his wealthy parents first took him abroad. Of the seventy-three years that remained to him, James would spend fifty in Europe, and shortly before his death, he would become a British subject. It was not that James despised America, but rather that as an artist he decided that Europe, and especially London, held "the biggest aggregation of human life—the most complete compendium in the world." Out of that decision came some of the finest fiction of an age: *The Portrait of a Lady* (1881), *The Wings of the Dove* (1902), *The Ambassadors* (1903), and *The Golden Bowl* (1904).

James's boyhood and youth were years of rich intellectual ferment. His father, a friend of Emerson's, delighted in stirring debate between Henry and his brother William (later the famous psychologist). Throughout their lives a kind of lively competition animated their relationship.

Since James's back injury disqualified him for service in the Civil War, he was free to turn his attention exclusively to writing. After several early efforts, he won his first real fame with *Daisy Miller* (1878), a short novel about an American girl abroad. Working with great ardor at his craft, he found no time for marriage. His biographer, Leon Edel, recently published evidence of a close liaison between James and an American woman writer, Constance Fenimore Woolson, who later committed suicide.

As James's art matured, it became subtler, more complex, and more intricate. Although readers grew less receptive, James worked determinedly (despite profound depression) to penetrate the surface of reality and to disclose the core of the human heart.

James's productivity staggers the imagination: more than one hundred novels and stories, as well as plays, biography, travel books, and criticism. For the twenty-four volumes that comprise the New York edition of his novels, he prepared prefaces that rank with the finest critical essays about his work. An artist of great sensitivity, James paved the way for some of the major psychological novelists of the twentieth century.

The Red Badge of Courage

by

STEPHEN CRANE (1871–1900)

Main Characters

Henry Fleming—A young Union volunteer ("the youth") who loses his illusions about the glory of war and matures into manhood after his first experience in combat.

Jim Conklin—An older soldier ("the tall soldier"), knowing and patient, from whose death Henry learns much.

Wilson—"The loud soldier," a terrified braggart who helps Fleming understand the nature of courage.

The Tattered Man—A wounded soldier whose concern for Fleming increases the youth's sense of guilt.

The Story

On the day before initiation into battle, a company of Union soldiers conceal their fear underneath their cocky bragging. The boasts of Wilson, "the loud soldier," and the more reasonable observations of Jim Conklin, "the tall soldier," lead young Henry Fleming to wonder how he himself will respond to combat. Will he prove himself a hero, or will he run in terror? "He was an unknown quantity," Crane observes.

As a yellow sun blots out the red eyes of the night fires, the first day's battle begins. Fleming's imagination never has a chance to function during the skirmish. Curiosity, rage, and above all, the momentum of the mob carry him along. During those early hours, Fleming sees his first corpse and watches the boastful Wilson break down in fear. But because Fleming was "not a man but a member," part of a "subtle battle brotherhood . . . a mysterious fraternity born of the smoke and danger of death," he passes safely through his initial encounter.

His joy in his triumph over terror is, however, short-lived. Minutes after it has been repulsed, the Rebel army regroups for a counterattack. Now, for the first time, Fleming's imagination stirs and he begins "to exaggerate the endurance, the skill, and the valor of the onrushing enemy." He envisages them as dragons, machines of steel—unconquerable. Suddenly the soldier beside him howls and flees. Frenzied, abandoning cap and rifle, Fleming runs away, too. Ironically, the enemy attack is unsuccessful.

Ashamed and resentful, Fleming plunges into a forest, "going from obscurity into promises of a greater obscurity." Deep in the forest, "where the high arching boughs made a chapel," Fleming discovers that nature offers no real solace. For there, propped against a tree, mouth agape, eyes sightlessly staring upward, is a corpse.

Awed and horrified, Fleming flees the appalling spectacle. The stillness about him is shattered by the violent sounds of men in flight. A host of wounded soldiers join him in retreat, but he takes little comfort from the contrast between their wounds and his wholeness. "He wished that he, too, had a wound," Crane writes, "a red badge of courage." But before he can succumb to self-pity, he is catapulted into his first personal experience with death. He has seen men die, but never any who have been intimate friends. Now he watches the mortally wounded Jim Conklin stagger toward some isolated place where he may die without being run over by passing artillery wagons. Jim's grotesque dance of death awes him and adds to his growing sense of guilt. Unwittingly a tattered soldier who expresses concern for Fleming's welfare adds to his anguish.

At the deepest level of his inward torment, Fleming wins some respite. The regiment, now in full flight, overtakes him. Fleming seizes one soldier to ask what has happened. Hysteri-

cal, the man smashes his rifle butt into Fleming's skull. When
Fleming recovers consciousness, he has a "red badge." Led
back to his own company by a soldier with a cheery voice,
Fleming is greeted by all as a wounded veteran. Inwardly,
however, he remains disconsolate, aware that more struggle,
more suffering lie ahead.

In the final battle, Fleming wins his real red badge. This
time he fights neither as a member of a mob nor as an enemy
of the universe. Rather he is an angry man, devoured by a
vengeful fury directed against the living men who are trying to
destroy him. He fights, as his officer notes, like a wildcat, a
war devil. He leads a futile charge, wholly unconscious of any
purpose except the need to destroy. When a color sergeant
is shot, he plunges into murderous fire to retrieve the flag
from the enemy. At the end of the battle—which the North-
erners have neither won nor lost—Fleming discovers that the
true significance of his badge has nothing to do with courage.
It is not a blow on the head or a sacrifice to patriotic frenzy,
but a freedom from illusion about great deeds or chances for
survival. It is an acceptance of the simple fact that death, after
all, is only death. Knowing this, Fleming, as the novel ends,
has attained his maturity and become a man.

Critical Opinion

When it was first published in 1895, *The Red Badge of Courage* won praise from many reviewers, especially in England
where H. G. Wells and Joseph Conrad admired its profound
sensibility and fertile imagination. More recently, critics have
disagreed about its theme and its art, though most acknowledge that it is a masterpiece.

Many early critics argued that Crane's war novel is domi-
nantly naturalistic, i.e., as Crane had written of his earlier
Maggie, "it tries to show that environment is a tremendous
thing in the world and frequently shapes lives regardless."
Today critics believe that Fleming is not merely a wisp in a
turbulent universe. At least he does not sink in ignoble defeat.
He learns much about himself and the universe during the
novel, and most important, he manages to achieve maturity
and a kind of dignity by asserting his will. The novel seems,

then, to be closer to realism—an objective study of the conflict between man's will and his fate.

Crane's wealth of colorful imagery (suggested by the paintings of the French impressionists) has also aroused wide discussion. Are Crane's images merely the extravagant excesses of a gifted amateur? Or are they related organically to Crane's theme? Thus, the color red, which dominates the novel ("red cheers," "red sun," "red eyes," "crimson roar"), is linked to themes of terror and guilt, rage and heroism. Similarly, innumerable *animal* and *machine* images suggest the bestiality and impersonality of war. Some critics have analyzed the imagery even further, hinting that Christian themes of sacrifice and redemption or ritual patterns of initiation lie embedded in such symbols as the death of Jim Conklin or Fleming's journey to the forest.

The Red Badge of Courage is, as Ernest Hemingway observed, "all as much one piece as a great poem is." In a great poem, the synthesis of the parts adds up to an inescapable truth. Although Crane's novel challenges one with its broad range of possibilities, the perceptive reader never loses sight of its core: the emerging character of Henry Fleming. Structure, imagery, character contrasts—all contribute to the vivid portrait of a young man discovering himself under the most trying of all human conditions—war.

The Author

"I decided that the nearer a writer gets to life, the greater he becomes as an artist," *Stephen Crane* once wrote. Ironically Crane, born six years after the close of the Civil War, drew upon imagination rather than experience to write his great novel of that war, *The Red Badge of Courage*. His brief life was not, however, without excitement. Crane grew up in a literary environment. Both of his parents were writers. But the boy rebelled against the restrictions imposed by his stern Methodist parents. He read novels and plays and, worse, he played baseball. Indeed, Crane's ambition was to be a professional ballplayer.

Crane's dedication to sports rather than to studies cut short his college career. In his early twenties he turned to journalism, which was to be his life work. From his newspaper assignments emerged some of his most notable fiction. While covering the Bowery, he lived briefly as a derelict and gathered material for his moving story, *Maggie: A Girl of the Streets* (1893). In the Far West he studied lonely frontier men and produced two memorable short stories, "Blue Hotel" and "The Bride Comes to Yellow Sky." During the Spanish-American War, as a correspondent on a gun-running boat, Crane was shipwrecked. Soon afterward, he wrote his great short story about men against nature, "The Open Boat."

Crane's life was filled with action. It was also, unhappily, filled with much sadness and frustration. His war experiences undermined his health and left him with incurable tuberculosis. His love for Cora Taylor, who had once run a sporting house, earned him much ridicule and social censure. For a short time, he and Cora found refuge and happiness in England, but it was too late for the ailing Crane. At twenty-eight he died. His work, however—vigorous, realistic, poetically imaginative—helped open the way to modern American fiction.

Looking Backward

by

EDWARD BELLAMY (1850–1898)

Main Characters

Julian West—A conventional young Bostonian of 1887 who is precipitated 113 years into the future.
Edith Bartlett—His fiancée.
Dr. Leete—The patient physician who explains carefully to Julian the social organization of America in the year 2000.
Edith Leete—Dr. Leete's kind and sympathetic daughter, a source of comfort and stability to Julian West.
Mrs. Leete—The doctor's amiable wife.

The Story

Julian West, in 1887, when the story opens, is an upper-class Bostonian, engaged to the charming Edith Bartlett. Save for his occasional concern about industrial unrest, he is a quite ordinary American who shares the ideals and prejudices of his time and class. Plagued by insomnia, he builds beneath his house a soundproof sleeping chamber hermetically sealed with stone slabs. Occasionally he summons a hypnotist who effectively puts him into a deep sleep. He has instructed his Negro servant in the technique of waking him.

After visiting his fiancée one night, Julian returns home and, unable to sleep, has resort to his hypnotist. When he awakens, he is surprised to see a man and two women near his bed. He makes inquiries—and to his utter disbelief, at least initially, discovers that he has been asleep for 113 years. Presumably his house burned down and his servants died in the flames. Julian, in his secret subterranean room, was untouched by the fire and continued to sleep right through the century. Then, in the year 2000, Dr. Leete, the gentleman at his bedside, a retired physician, while excavating in order to build an underground laboratory, discovered the chamber and revived the sleeper.

Julian slowly accepts his situation, the more easily because of the presence of Edith Leete, the doctor's lovely and sympathetic daughter. In the society to which he has awakened, the state owns all the means of production and distribution. The change was effected without violence. The absorption of business into ever-larger monopolies, a tendency already apparent in the nineteenth century, resulted in one huge syndicate that consolidated the entire capital of the nation. The nation took over the syndicate, thus becoming one great business corporation. All citizens, whatever their work, now share equally in the profits and economies of the new society. Though money as such has been abolished, each citizen receives an amount of credit in the government storehouse. The title to such equality is simply the worker's humanity. Moreover, each worker can live in luxury because the elimination of competition has brought shoddy or useless production to an end.

It is no longer necessary to maintain a vast army. Other nations have followed America's lead, and cooperation among nations is now the universal rule. The police force is greatly diminished. Since the economic motives for crime have largely disappeared, so has crime. Of course, there are instances of "atavism" or regression. These people are treated in hospitals, not jails.

Julian's bewilderment and disorientation, especially when he sets out alone to explore the new Boston, almost shatter him. But the kindness and sympathetic understanding of Edith and her mother and father save him.

The explanation of the new society continues, Dr. Leete serving as the chief expositor. Education, broadly based and liberal, is the same for everyone. All men go to school till they are twenty-one. Then for three years they engage in menial service, to which no onus is attached. Dr. Leete, for example, served as waiter in one of the enormous, superbly constructed and expertly managed restaurants where the citizens generally take at least one of their meals daily. When a man is twenty-four, ability and inclination determine his career. Some citizens receive further education to prepare them for a profession. Others enter the industrial army, rising as high as their skills and talents permit. If anyone chooses to change his vocation, he is given every opportunity to do so. If a man, for example, thinks that he would like to become a physician, his way is smoothed, provided he can meet the severe academic qualifications. As a rule, such shifts in vocation are discouraged after a man becomes thirty-five. The reason is obvious. Except for judges and some administrative officers, all men retire at forty-five.

How are the disagreeable jobs filled? By lowering hours and improving conditions to the point at which enough men will volunteer for them—even if this entails an hour a day (or less, conceivably) of tedious labor. And what makes men strive to attain superiority when it brings them no monetary rewards? Their commitment to their society: service to the nation, patriotism, passion for humanity—all fostered and encouraged by their education and training.

The President of the United States is chosen by a method that ensures his qualifications. He is elected by the chiefs of the ten grand divisions of the industrial army. These, in turn, are chosen by the chiefs of each trade or guild. And to prevent intrigue, the chiefs of each guild are elevated not by its active members but by its retired or honorary members. The President is usually about fifty when he assumes office, an honorable exception to the rule of retirement at forty-five. He serves for five years and is responsible to a national Congress which may approve him for another five years or, as seldom happens, refuse to approve. The latter circumstance is rare because the President has risen through the ranks, amply demonstrating his fitness and devotion all along the way.

Women participate fully in the new society's benefits and contribute fully to its wealth. Only while they bear and rear children do they leave active service. Most serve from five to fifteen years; those without children fill out the full term.

Relieved from a servile or degrading dependence, women are more cultivated, more vigorous, freer than ever before. They even have a representative in the Cabinet, chosen on the same principle as the chiefs of the industrial army. The representative may veto measures respecting women's work, pending appeals to Congress. There are no lawyers in this society. Instead, three judges—sober, intelligent, acute people who are also an exception to the practice of retirement at forty-five—investigate thoroughly and dispassionately the merits of the cases before them and render their decisions. If the cases involve women, the judges are women. If they involve a man and a woman, a man and a woman judge must consent to the verdict.

Edith Leete seems to Julian West to prove the virtues of the new society. Intelligent, sensitive, deeply understanding, she arouses his love. He wants to confess it, but the thought of his deficiencies as a man from an inferior, antiquated world prevent him. After he listens to a sermon over the telephone-radio, on the principles of the new Christianity, in which love is the touchstone and guiding principle, his feelings of inadequacy deepen. But Edith's gentleness and compassion break through his reservations. He tells her of his love and she responds gladly. She has always loved him, she says. She is the great-granddaughter of his nineteenth-century fiancée, Edith Bartlett. The letters he had written to Edith have been passed down to her; and even before meeting him, she had determined to marry only another Julian West. Dr. and Mrs. Leete cheerfully give their formal consent. Julian, however, will be no drone in the twenty-first century. He will assume a position for which he has the most valid credentials of any man in the new century: professor of nineteenth-century history.

Critical Opinion

During the first year of its publication, *Looking Backward* sold slowly; then it began to catch on sensationally. In 1890 the *Literary Bulletin* of Houghton Mifflin, its publishers, declared: "*Looking Backward* holds in American literature an almost unique place in character and popularity. Of only one other book [*Uncle Tom's Cabin*] have 300,000 copies been printed within two years of its publication." And since 1890 it has sold millions of copies here and abroad. It is a required text for many courses in American literature. It ranks high among the most influential American books. By most literary critics and historians it is regarded as "the most important Utopian novel in American literature."

Bellamy wrote *Looking Backward* when industrial strife seemed to be the new way of life in America, when the memories of the Haymarket Riot were still fresh in the minds of his readers, when accounts of unemployment, unrest, and bloody strikes were familiar newspaper reading. Bellamy's practically perfect society, to be achieved without class war or even minor disturbances, appealed deeply to millions of people. Moreover, Bellamy's calm—even conservative—prose, embellished with attractive but not startling metaphors and parables, contributed enormously to the book's success.

Looking Backward has been called "a fairy tale of social felicity." Its solutions to difficult social problems, especially its description of society's facile transition from laissez-faire capitalism to nationalism, have been described as oversimple. Its basic analogy, between a military army and a social army, has been judged psychologically false. Nevertheless, Bellamy's vividly realized picture of "a technology organized for production rather than for profit" is certainly the most famous of American Utopias and easily takes its place as one of the best projections of an ideal society in all literature.

The Author

Edward Bellamy, the son of a Baptist minister, was born in Chicopee Falls, Massachusetts, in 1850. After attending school in his native town and failing to be admitted to West Point because he could not meet its physical requirements, he attended Union College for one year. At eighteen he traveled abroad for a year as companion to a wealthy cousin, becoming aware of "the extent and consequences of man's inhumanity to man." Coming home, he declared, he saw "even in his own comparatively prosperous village, the same conditions in course of progressive developments." He studied law, was admitted to the bar, and abandoned his legal career after one case, repelled by the law's prejudice in favor of the rich. For the next nine years, Bellamy worked as a newspaperman on the New York *Evening Post,* the Springfield *Union,* and the *Springfield Daily News,* the last founded in 1880 by him and his brothers.

In 1877 Bellamy began to publish novels that won the admiration and praise of William Dean Howells, the leading American critic of the time: *Six to One: A Nantucket Idyl* (1878), a romance without social content; *The Duke of Stockbridge* (serialized in part in 1879, but not published till 1900), an interesting fictional study of Shays' Rebellion that reveals Bellamy's Populist sympathies; *Dr. Heidenhoff's Process* (1880), a remarkable foreshadowing of the modern "psychiatric novel."

Looking Backward: 2000–1887 (1888), after a relatively quiet initial reception, brought Bellamy fame and a mission. He refused to exploit his success commercially but entered on a ten-year period of controversy and polemics. With the royalties from *Looking Backward* he started his own publication, *The New Nation* (1891), to campaign for his social program. He lectured extensively, and also began a sequel to *Looking Backward.* This was *Equality* (1897), a bolder and more vigorous work. In writing it, Bellamy exhausted his energies. A trip to Colorado failed to restore his health, and he died in 1898 of tuberculosis.

The Twentieth
Century

The Octopus

by

FRANK NORRIS (1870–1902)

Main Characters

Presley—A thirty-year-old poet settled in California to write a romantic epic of the West, graduate of an Eastern college, sensitive, hopefully committed to beauty as an alternative to evil.

Vanamee—Presley's friend, a shepherd, a wanderer, and a mystic with "an almost abnormal capacity for great happiness and great sorrow." He tries desperately to evoke the spirit of his brutally ravished dead sweetheart, Angele.

Annixter—A young rancher, college-educated but rough-hewn, a stanch and courageous fighter for his cause.

Hilma Tree—A pretty nineteen-year-old working girl at Annixter's Quien Sabe Ranch. Fresh, unassuming, and generous, she is a perfect foil and mate for Annixter.

Magnus Derrick—Called "Governor" since he long ago ran unsuccessfully for that office. Owner of the Los Muertos Ranch, an honest, earnest man lacking the decisiveness needed to guide the community that looks to him for leadership.

Mrs. Derrick—His wife, a handsome woman, hopelessly out of place in the harsh world of the West and willfully isolated in her private realm of decadent poetry and fiction.

Harran Derrick—The youngest son, Magnus' favorite, and manager of Los Muertos, eager to fight for the farmers' rights.

Lyman Derrick—The eldest son, a corporation lawyer, ambitious, unscrupulous, ready to cooperate with any power that will lead him toward his goal—the governorship his father failed to attain.

S. Behrman—President of the Loan and Savings Bank of Tulare County, leading real estate and mortgage broker in town, fat, oily, and ruthlessly effective as the chief local agent of the railroad.

Shelgrim—President of the Pacific and Southwestern Railroad, the "octopus" company whose tentacles crush the wheat ranchers. An elderly but articulate and powerful man who believes himself wholly innocent of malice and sees the struggle between railroad and farmer as one of natural forces.

Dyke—A former railroad engineer, now a hops grower caught in the vise of freight costs.

Hooven—A German wheat farmer, vigorously and openly antagonistic to the railroad powers, and willing to fight to the death to protect his interests.

Osterman, Broderson, Dabney—Wheat farmers.

Ruggbag, Delaney, Christian—Agents of the railroad.

Genslinger—Editor of the local newspaper, a hireling of the railroad.

The Story

In late September, toward the close of the nineteenth century, Presley walks along the sun-baked farm land of Bonneville in California's San Joaquin Valley. The grimy farmers seem brutish to him, hardly the sort of people he hopes to include in his proposed poem about the romance of the West. And their problems, too—surviving increases in freight rates, mortgage commitments, and land grabs—seem alien to his vision of the beautiful countryside. He listens with barely controlled impatience to the complaints of farmer Hooven, fired after seven years from Magnus Derrick's ranch because Derrick can no longer afford outside help, and to those of Dyke, released after ten years as a railroad engineer because he has refused to accept a sharp paycut. Presley finds more comfort with his old friend Vanamee, working as a shepherd on Buck

Annixter's ranch, who urges him to put his hexameters to work
on an epic of the West in which problems of the present will
recede into a panorama of the land and of all nature. But
even as Presley dreams, a train hurtles by and massacres a
group of Vanamee's sheep that have stumbled onto the tracks.
This grim, bloody episode adds to Presley's imagination a less
tender but more compelling image: ". . . the iron-hearted
Power, the monster, the Colossus, the Octopus."

Of the railroad's many tentacles, the one most threatening
to the farmers is a proposed regrading of their land. Years
earlier, farmers had taken advantage of the Government's invitation to settle and develop the rich valley land. They were
aware even then that not all of the land was legally theirs,
but the possibility of making a quick fortune in wheat over-
came their fears. What now keeps them from absolute ownership of their ranches is the bonus the Government had given
the railroad for constructing the road: vast tracts of land over-
lapping the farmers' holdings. Originally the Government had
intended that the farmers ultimately repurchase the railroad's
holdings at about two dollars and a half per acre. The railroad, however, conscious of the improvements wrought by the
farmers, shrewdly plans no such modest price. Doggedly and
unrealistically, the farmers cling to their slender hope that the
announced price will not exceed five dollars an acre.

To assure themselves a fair chance of winning their battle,
the farmers determine to place one of their own men on the
powerful railroad commission that sets freight rates and approves land-regrading plans. However, as one of them, Osterman, points out, the only way to obtain that post is to bribe
the appropriate officials in San Francisco. Magnus Derrick
vehemently opposes such underhanded actions; his wife, less
from scruple than from fear, encourages Magnus to submit
rather than fight the railroad. Caught between the arguments
of his fellow ranchers, his own integrity, and his wife's importuning, Magnus vacillates.

Meanwhile the seeding goes on; the farmers hope for rain
and try to order their private lives. The brusque Annixter has
the most difficult time. Apart from his difficulties as a farmer
(the bank has already refused his offer to repurchase all of its
holdings on his ranch at the original price), Annixter finds
himself emotionally disturbed by the presence of Hilma Tree.

Her pleasant exchanges with Delaney, one of Annixter's
hands, goad him to jealous fury, and he angrily fires Delaney.
Clumsily and boorishly, he makes a befuddled and unsuccessful attempt to embrace Hilma, managing only to frighten her.
But during the great barn dance he holds for everyone in the
neighborhood, Annixter learns that Hilma returns his affection. At the height of the party, Delaney, drunk and belliger-
ent, rides into the barn, gun in hand, and threatens Annixter
who until that moment has been dancing with Hilma. As
Annixter starts to thrust Hilma toward safety, they exchange
a brief but significant glance that assures Annixter of her affection. Then he shoves her away and, while the guests cringe,
shoots Delaney in the hand and emerges as the local hero.

At the very climax of the gaiety, however, the tentacles of
the railroad reach in to destroy the farmers' good cheer. Word
arrives that the railroad has set the price for repurchase of the
land at between $22 and $30 per acre, and has expressed willingness to sell it to anyone who will pay the price. Momentarily struck dumb by the horror of their situation, the farmers decide to establish a "League," with Magnus Derrick as
president, to battle the railroad and keep it from taking over
the land. All of the members except Magnus sign, but this
time, as his wife once more tries to dissuade him, the men
crowd about him, sweep his wife away, and Magnus affixes
his signature. As the first book ends, Vanamee says to Presley,
"I think that there was a dance in Brussels the night before
Waterloo."

By this time, too, Presley's romantic notions about the West
have begun to disappear. Increasingly he has come to sympathize with the farmers and to hate the inequities that cripple them. At the same time he knows that the farmers have
also been opportunists and have loved profits more than they
have loved the land. In conversation with Cedarquist, a
wealthy manufacturer, he learns that the great struggle in
American life is against exploitation, and that the struggle
must continue so long as no way is found to rouse the public
from apathy or to quell the aggressiveness of the monopolistic
trusts. Above all, Presley now realizes that his poem must be
about the people he has hitherto ignored, not just a vague
tribute to the land.

To press their interests, the farmers manage to place

Lyman Derrick on the commission. This feat is accomplished by a sizable bribe arranged and paid for by Magnus. The railroad, using dummy buyers (like Delaney, who bids on Annixter's ranch), has already instituted eviction proceedings against the farmers and has won its initial test cases in both the local and circuit courts. Dyke, the ex-engineer, believes himself fortunate in having begun as a hops farmer, thus avoiding the predicament of his friends. Thinking that he will avail himself of the cheap freight rate quoted by the railroad, Dyke has mortgaged his home to S. Behrman to raise money for seeds and supplies, and contracted with several dealers for delivery of his crop at a low but profitable price. But when Dyke comes to Behrman to arrange final details for shipping his crop, he discovers that the freight rate has more than doubled, wiping out not only his profits but also any remote chance of financial survival. What, he demands of Behrman, does the railroad base its rates on? Emphasizing each word with a tap of his finger, Behrman replies, "All the traffic will bear."

In the midst of all the turmoil, Annixter carries on his amorous pursuit of Hilma. Although, in a tender scene she admits her love for him, he tells her that what he has in mind is an affair, not marriage. Astonished and hurt, she leaves his ranch with her parents to go to San Francisco. Alone in the fields that night, Annixter suddenly realizes that he, too, is in love. At the moment of his awareness, he notes that the wheat has just broken through the ground. In another part of the dark wheatfield, Vanamee, seeking mystically to recall his dead beloved, calls forth her daughter who sleepwalks across the field toward him.

Annixter follows Hilma to San Francisco and persuades her to marry him. After a brief and happy honeymoon, they entrain for Bonneville and the ranch. En route, the train is stopped and the mail train held up, a brakeman fatally wounded, and $5,000 stolen. The dying brakeman identifies the holdup man as a former employee of the railroad, and Annixter knows at once that Dyke is the culprit. After his experience with Behrman, Dyke talks with everyone in town about his misery, but it is while listening to Caraher, the local bartender and anarchist, that Dyke settles upon his foolhardy plan to take his revenge on the railroad. While Dyke hides in the mountains, where Behrman's deputies search for him, Annixter and Hilma take his mother and child to Quien Sabe Ranch.

Presley completes his poem, now entitled "The Toilers," and at Vanamee's urging, publishes it in the daily press rather than in a literary magazine so that the masses may read it. The poem wins national acclaim as a cry of the downtrodden, but Presley still finds himself personally apart from the people he has come to admire, unable to join them in any specific action in their cause.

Some weeks pass, during which the farmers learn to use the rifles Annixter has had shipped to his ranch, and then Lyman Derrick arrives to announce the new freight rates. He assures the farmers that the commission has managed to obtain an average 10-per-cent decrease in rates, but a quick examination of the freight charts reveals that all of the major decreases are assigned to those points from which almost no shipments are made. No changes of any kind have been made in Bonneville's rates or in those of any other community where trade is active. Even Magnus recognizes that his son has sold out the farmers and when Annixter punches Lyman, the disillusioned father cannot bring himself to intervene.

Later that same evening, the newspaper editor, Genslinger, confronts Magnus with evidence of the bribery that gained Lyman his post and demands $10,000 not to print the story. To make the barb even more painful, he tells Magnus that Lyman had been pledged to the railroad long before the bribery. Alone in his desperation, Magnus decides to send the money to Genslinger. Ironically he gives it to Presley to deliver at the same time the poet is sending off the manuscript of "The Toilers" to his publishers.

The next day, Hilma's birthday, as Annixter tells Presley how his love for her has enriched his life, Dyke rides wildly onto the ranch begging for a fresh horse. Annixter provides one and Dyke dashes off, pursued by Delaney, Behrman, and others. At the rail depot, Dyke leaps aboard an engine and tries to escape with it, but the railroad men signal ahead for a derailment. Seeing what they have done, he backs up, exchanges shots with his antagonists, is wounded, and leaps from the train, running to hide in the tall wheat of Annixter's farm. Trapped when he falls from a stolen horse, Dyke finds himself only a few feet from Behrman and feels elated that at least he can kill this monster. But his gun misfires, and though he struggles valiantly and savagely, he is subdued. Some months later Dyke is sentenced to life imprisonment.

With the wheat at its summer-ripe fullness (Hilma, incidentally, is now pregnant), the farmers take time out from their worries to have a jack-rabbit hunt and barbecue. After they have flushed out tens of thousands of rabbits and corralled them, they allow the Portuguese laborers to slaughter them brutally. Again, however, as earlier at Annixter's barn dance, the railroad interrupts the festivities. A messenger tells Annixter that Delaney has moved into his house and thrown out all of Annixter's possessions, and that another group of railroad men is heading toward Magnus Derrick's Los Muertos Ranch for the same purpose. The railroad has simply decided not to bother waiting for the Supreme Court decision, convinced that it will win and has the right to proceed as it wishes.

Aroused and determined to prevent the intrusion, Annixter and Derrick try to call the men together to fight the interlopers. But instead of the 600 Leaguers they had counted on, they can rally only nine men to go with them. The men intercept the marshal, accompanied by Behrman, Delaney, and several other railroad hirelings. A heated argument takes place between Magnus and the railroaders, and a shot fired by Hooven sets off an exchange of volleys. When the smoke clears, Delaney and another railroad agent lie dead. Among the five dead farmers are Annixter, Harran Derrick, Hooven, and Osterman.

That night Hilma suffers a miscarriage. That same night Presley enters in his journal his sense of horror at what the people of America have allowed to take place. ". . . it is Lexington," he writes. "God rouse us from our lethargy. . . ." To himself he vows revenge on Behrman and Shelgrim, the president of the railroad.

At a protest meeting the next evening, the Leaguers ironically blame Magnus for not having avoided violence by gathering all 600 men to face the railroaders. Presley harangues the crowd about the need to overwhelm their oppressors, but as he finishes amid their wild applause, he realizes that their response has been but an emotional outburst of

momentary conviction, that an hour later they will once more
subside into apathy. Taking full advantage of the farmers' indecisiveness, some railroad agents in the audience distribute
hundreds of copies of the Genslinger newspaper telling the full
story of Magnus' bribery in behalf of Lyman. Again Magnus
has been sold out. The beaten old man is left abandoned by
those who had hitherto looked to him as their leader. Later
that night Presley acts for the first time as he has always hoped
he would. He hurls a bomb through the window of Behrman's
dining room. The room is totally wrecked, but Behrman
miraculously escapes unharmed.

What remains of the novel is for the most part a tying together of the shreds and tatters of human aspiration. The Supreme Court finds in favor of the railroad, and the farmers are
either dispossessed or reduced to leasing their own land from
the railroad. Magnus Derrick, almost senile, accepts from
Behrman a job as assistant freight manager at fifty dollars a
week. Hooven's wife and daughters try to survive in San Francisco, but the elder daughter is swiftly reduced to prostitution,
and the mother, accidentally separated from her, dies in the
streets of starvation, her younger daughter beside her. Lyman
Derrick, enjoying a happier fate, has become the railroad's
candidate for governor of California.

Presley, too, is in San Francisco, waiting for a ship to take
him to India. Before sailing, he calls on Shelgrim and discovers that the tycoon is not at all the monster he has anticipated.
Intelligent and even charitable, Shelgrim points out to Presley
that the wheat and the railroad are forces governed not by
men but by the laws of supply and demand. "Blame conditions," he argues, "not men." S. Behrman is also in San Francisco, paradoxically to supervise the loading of wheat aboard
the ship that will carry Presley to India. As he watches the
wheat pour into the hold, Behrman loses his footing and falls
into the hold. What ensues is a hysterical dance of death as
Behrman claws and crawls trying to avoid sinking beneath the
dusty cargo. The dance ends as the wheat runs into his gaping
mouth, suffocates and buries him.

As the boat sails, Presley asks whether anything is left and
finds his answer in a recollection of Vanamee's mystical faith
in the ultimate triumph of good and truth. The individual may
die, but the race lives on.

Critical Opinion

Despite its extravagant melodrama, *The Octopus* has its base in solid fact—the historical event known as the Mussell Slough affair of 1878, during which almost all of the catastrophic events cited in Norris' story did in fact occur. Had Norris rigorously followed the disciplines of naturalistic fiction laid down by Emile Zola, *The Octopus* would have emerged as a purely scientific sociological document. But though critics continue to disagree about the novel, they are in accord on one point—that Norris is not detached about the people or the events that fill his broad canvas.

Presley's slow but inevitable development into conscious sympathy with the downtrodden farmers is evidence of Norris' own compassion. It is not, however, an uncritical sympathy, for Presley (whose real-life counterpart, incidentally, is Edwin Markham, "The Toilers" being the counterpart of Markham's "Man with the Hoe") recognizes the economic opportunism of the farmers, too. What confuses the issue and diminishes the impact of the novel is the intrusion of the quasi-mystical thesis about pervasive forces in nature that move man despite his will. On the surface, such an approach seems conventionally naturalistic, but Norris refuses to see the forces as indifferent, insisting through both Vanamee and Presley that nature ultimately works for good and for truth. If nature is all good, then it is man—both railroader and farmer—who has interrupted the perfection of the world. Thus, Norris fuses his philosophic idealism with his sociological sympathy for the underdog and achieves a fundamentally distorted and unconvincing outlook.

However illogical Norris' thinking, his narrative force compels the reader to continue without loss of enthusiasm to the very last page of the long novel. *The Octopus* is rich in memorable episodes—the dance at Annixter's barn, the jack-rabbit hunt, the pitched battle between the farmers and the railroad men, and the death of S. Behrman—and in a host of unforgettable, if often overdrawn, characters. Its greatest weakness is the overly long, rhapsodic passages about Vanamee and his dead love, Angele. Yet even these have at times a lyric tenderness.

Norris spent four months in the library researching the facts for *The Octopus*. Whatever the weaknesses of the book, it easily transcends mere reportage. William Dean Howells admired it when it was published, H. L. Mencken and Theodore Dreiser in the years that followed. Today it continues to merit the attention of anyone interested in man's greed and compassion, inhumanity and idealism, struggles, defeats, and aspirations.

The Author

Frank Norris' mother was a well-known actress, his father a successful jewelry man. In 1884, when Norris was fourteen, the family moved from his birthplace, Chicago, to San Francisco where he attended preparatory school before going to Paris to study art. In Paris he became a dilettante, more fascinated with atmosphere than with his studies. He nevertheless began to write romantic stories and sketches that were published in California newspapers. Norris' father, alarmed that his son might become a writer rather than a businessman, brought him home to enroll at the University of California. Norris managed to pass nothing during his four years there and earned no degree. But he did discover the writings of Emile Zola (as well as those of Kipling and Richard Harding Davis) and begin work on one of his finest naturalistic studies, *McTeague*, published in 1899. During a year at Harvard, he came under the influence of Lewis Gates, a teacher of creative writing, and wrote *Vandover and the Brute* (published posthumously in 1914) while continuing his work on *McTeague*.

For a year Norris covered the Boer War for the San Francisco *Chronicle*, writing several articles and a few stories and, unhappily, falling victim to a fever that undermined his health. For the next few years he worked again as a journalist in California but also completed another novel, *Moran of the Lady Letty* (1898). In 1898, while covering the Spanish-American War, he met Stephen Crane whose writing he admired but whose callous attitude toward war he despised.

Back in America, Norris found himself becoming increasingly conscious of social and economic problems. While working as an editor for Doubleday, Page, he conceived the idea of an "epic of the wheat," a trilogy of which he completed both *The Octopus* (1901) and *The Pit* (1903) before his death, which followed an attack of appendicitis. The last novel of the trilogy, to be called *The Wolf*, was never written.

Norris wrote enough during his short life to fill a ten-volume edition of collected writings, including critical essays and short fiction as well as novels. As an editor, too, he left a memorable heritage, for it was through his efforts that Theodore Dreiser's novel *Sister Carrie* was published.

The Call of the Wild

by

JACK LONDON (1876–1916)

Main Characters

Buck—The 140-pound dog, powerful, loyal, endowed with
almost human intelligence, who reverts to savagery.
François—A French-Canadian dog-sled driver.
Perrault—His companion on the trail.
Spitz—A huge, crafty Spitzberger dog, Buck's deadly rival.
John Thornton—The kind master, wise in the ways of dogs,
whom Buck loves.

The Story

Buck, a powerful 140-pound dog, a cross between a St.
Bernard and a Scotch shepherd, is the trusted and valued
companion of Judge Miller and his family. He roams the Miller
acres in the Santa Clara Valley of California, an aristocrat rejecting all attempts to make him a pampered kennel dog. It is
the year when the Klondike strike makes dogs like Buck valuable as never before. One of Judge Miller's gardeners, a gambler sorely in need of money to pay his debts, sells Buck to a
man who specializes in procuring dogs able to survive in
Alaska. Trusting at first, Buck soon protests against the in-
dignity of a rope around his neck. But he is choked into in-

sensibility, caged, hurled into a train, and arriving at Seattle, taken by wagon to a trainer.

Hungry and parched, Buck by this time is a demon. Released from the cage, he furiously hurls himself at the trainer. He never reaches him. The man hits him hard with a club. As often as Buck charges, he is struck. Finally he loses consciousness. He has learned his first great lesson: a man with a club is master.

Before long he is sold to two French-Canadians, Perrault and François, and suffers through a terrifying voyage to Alaska. The ferocity of the huskies is beyond his comprehension. One attacks and kills a large, friendly Newfoundland dog who had been on the boat with Buck and who is torn to pieces by the fierce pack that gathers. Another dog, a snow-white Spitzberger who has had some arctic experience, incurs Buck's enduring hatred by enjoying the savage spectacle.

One morning Buck is harnessed and set to work hauling a sled. Shocked, he knows enough not to rebel. François, the driver, and the other dogs soon teach Buck how to pull the sled and stay clear of the traces, how to dig in the snow for shelter when sleeping, how to steal without being caught.

Perrault and François carry mail to the prospectors in distant areas. The team must traverse difficult and dangerous trails, often running forty miles a day on a pound or a pound and a half of sun-dried salmon. From the beginning Buck resents Spitz's leadership, though he tolerates it. But Spitz's sly malignance infuriates him. Attacked by a group of starving huskies from some Indian village, Spitz seizes the opportunity to spring on Buck. Only by bracing himself to withstand the charge and then fleeing does Buck save himself. His hatred grows. He does all he can to undermine Spitz's leadership. The two must fight, and fight to the death. When Spitz kills a rabbit Buck has been chasing, the time arrives. Spitz is a clever and practiced fighter, but Buck crunches his forelegs with his teeth and topples his enemy. After the battle the other dogs tear Spitz apart.

Buck silently demands the leadership of the team, refusing to enter harness until he receives it. The drivers capitulate, and Buck becomes a severe taskmaster, literally whipping the dogs to a new solidarity.

At Skaguay, after three days of rest—hardly enough, considering that the dogs had made a record run of 560 miles in fourteen days—the team is turned over to a Scotch halfbreed. The new run is to Dawson, and the sled carries a heavy load of mail. Buck has developed pride in his leadership, and his task, arduous as it is, gives him satisfaction. But often a strange atavistic dream comes to him: visions of a primitive world and of primitive men with whom his ancestors had hunted.

After only two days' rest at Dawson, the dogs are back on the trail to Skaguay. Arriving there thirty days after they had left it, they are sold so that fresh batches may take the place of the overtired dogs. Buck and his mates are purchased by two men and a woman who know nothing of the frozen country or of dogs. They overload the sled, mistreat the dogs, overfeed them at first—and then, when provisions run short, nearly starve them. Many of the dogs die, others become so weak that they can hardly draw the sled. By sheer luck the party arrives at the camp of John Thornton who advises them not to continue because the ice over the river is too thin. But the men do not listen to Thornton. One of them whips Buck, whose mistreatment has reduced him to a virtual skeleton. Buck refuses to respond, and his tormentor trades his whip for a club. Thornton can no longer bear to witness this cruelty and springs on the man, pushing him away from Buck. Then he cuts Buck's traces. The group continues on its way. Before they are quite out of sight, a section of ice gives way; both dogs and human beings disappear under water.

John Thornton nurses Buck back to strength. Buck conceives for the man a deep and abiding love, greater than he has ever felt before. Only Buck's adoration prevents him from answering "the call of the wild," to return to the primitive life that now beckons him insistently. After Thornton's partners arrive, the men break camp and Buck goes with them. While poling a stretch of rapids, Thornton falls overboard. Following Thornton's orders, Buck swims to shore where a rope is fastened to his shoulders and neck. Despite the current, which threatens to submerge him, he swims back to Thornton who grabs him. Together they make their way to shore, nearly smashed by the rocks and half-drowned.

Thornton's pride in Buck grows. In town he boasts that Buck can "break" a sledge loaded with a thousand pounds from ice, start it, and walk with it for a hundred yards. Challenged, he accepts a wager of $1,200 on Buck's ability to perform a task suitable for a team, not a single dog. Nevertheless, by a tremendous effort, Buck accomplishes the incredible feat.

With the money, Thornton and his two partners go in search of a fabled mine. They never find it, but their wanderings lead them to a broad valley where, in a shallow place, gold lies like butter. The men take thousands of dollars in gold each day. While they work, Buck answers the call of the wild. He absents himself from the camp for days, runs with a wolf, hunts as his remote ancestors once did—and with all their cunning. Returning after a long absence, he finds Thornton and his friends murdered. The Indians who killed them are still in the camp, dancing their victory. Filled with frenzy, Buck hurls himself on one of the Indians, ripping his throat open. Without a pause, he plunges at the rest until panic seizes them, and, convinced that an evil spirit is attacking them, they flee in terror.

Buck now joins the wolf pack. Proving his right by combat, he becomes their leader, crafty and strong beyond any of his fellows. The pack prospers. The Indians are certain that Buck is a Ghost Dog, a demon come to torment them. But on one day each summer, Buck comes across the valley to the stream where John Thornton lies. Here he sits musing for a time. Before he departs, he howls once, long and mournfully.

Critical Opinion

His compassion and his intelligence may have prompted Jack London to enlist on the side of the underdog. But emotionally, he seems to have been drawn to the raw, primitive power and the figure of the superman. This idealized creation of the German philosopher, Friedrich Nietzsche, became for London the peak of the evolutionary process and the hero of his novel *The Call of the Wild.*

This saga of Buck, the "civilized" dog who reverts to the savagery of his wolf ancestors, has been abundantly criticized. It has been described as a callow and brutal romance, as an icebound pulp story, and as an extreme expression of the "cult of raw meat and red blood."

Not many defenders of *The Call of the Wild* would be

likely to deny that the novel is generally sensational, often incredible, and sometimes even a bit ludicrous. Why, then, is it the most widely read, most fondly remembered of Jack London's fifty books? The answer is: Buck, the heroic dog who embodies all the virtues we most admire—courage, loyalty, endurance, determination, and intelligence. Against a strange and intriguing background, he moves through a series of rousing, blood-tingling adventures, and emerges from them in a way that gratifies and delights us. Like the heroes of the great novels of the Western world, Buck develops an acute and sure knowledge of his powers and his defects.

After we have read the novel, we may balk at the lack of realism and logic in Buck's brooding introspectiveness, his long memory (not only of his own life but of the "life of his race" as well), and his extraordinary strength. But while we are reading—while we strain with Buck as he attempts to pull the sled held fast by ice and loaded with a thousand pounds of flour, or circle with him as he seeks an opening in the defenses of the sly and malignant Spitz—neither realism nor logic seems relevant to us. It is here in the directness and immediacy of our irresistible response to *The Call of the Wild* that we see the triumph of Jack London's storytelling art.

The Author

Jack London's life was as turbulent as any described in his fifty books. Born in San Francisco in 1876, he was the illegitimate son of Flora Wellman and Professor W. H. Chaney. His father, an itinerant astrologer, deserted Flora Wellman while she was pregnant. Eight months after the birth of her son, she married John London, a kind man whose commercial activities were doomed to failure. Jack London's early life was passed in dire poverty along the waterfronts of San Francisco and Oakland. He sold newspapers in saloons, worked in canneries, set up pins in a bowling alley.

By the time he was eighteen, London had been a hobo, an oyster pirate, a longshoreman and (as he said of himself) "a drunken bum." At the urging of his family, he set out to sea on a whaling vessel. He returned from the cruise determined to "live by his brain," and at nineteen began high school. At some point in his brief career, he had been converted to socialism. During his studies he made speeches for the cause, one of which landed him in jail. He entered the University of California but left before completing his first year, partly because he wanted to help support his mother, partly because he detested college. In 1896 he set out for the Klondike to prospect for gold, but scurvy forced him to return before he had washed a trace of metal.

By this time Jack London had developed into a kind of intellectual. He had read Marx, Darwin, Spencer, Nietzsche, and out of their works had forged his own private philosophy. He began writing and was successful nearly from the beginning, his Alaskan stories appearing in the *Overland Monthly,* the *Black Cat,* and in 1899, *The Atlantic Monthly.* His first book, a collection of stories entitled *The Son of the Wolf,* was published in 1900. Soon others followed: *A Daughter of the Snows* (1902), *The Call of the Wild* (1903), *The Sea Wolf* (1904), *White Fang* (1906)—all extremely popular works.

London wrote too much, however, to maintain a high level of craftsmanship. He drove himself to produce in order to earn the money to support his extravagant style of living. Moreover, personal crises interfered with his art. In 1900 he married Bessie Maddern, and divorced her three years later to marry Charmian Kittredge. He continued to drink too much, despite his novelistic tract (drawn from experience), *John Barleycorn* (1913). In 1916, following the lead of his fictional hero in *Martin Eden,* another autobiographical novel, he committed suicide.

Of his many books, only a handful continue to be widely read in the United States. Abroad, especially in the Soviet Union, though he abjured socialism in his later years, London ranks much higher than in his own country. However, his remarkable anticipation of fascism, *The Iron Heel* (1907), his socially conscious *The People of the Abyss* (1903), and the Klondike takes—particularly *The Call of the Wild*—are still very much alive.

Ethan Frome

by

EDITH WHARTON (1862–1937)

Main Characters

Ethan Frome—At fifty-two, a man with the look of one who has long lived in a special hell of his own.

Zenobia (Zeena)—His querulous, demanding, shrewish wife (seven years older than he) whose hypochondria enables her to control her husband.

Mattie—Zeena's graceful, pretty cousin whose coming to the farm provides the only bit of brightness in Ethan's existence.

The Narrator—An engineer working for a time near Starkfield, Massachusetts, who pieces together the story of Ethan Frome.

Denis Eady—The well-to-do Irish owner of the Starkfield livery stable, once Mattie's admirer.

Ruth Hale—Mattie's friend from whom the narrator gleans the hints that help him reconstruct the story.

The Story

The setting of *Ethan Frome* is Starkfield, Massachusetts. The narrator, an engineer, is for a time working in Corbury Junction and living in Starkfield (the nearest habitable place). In that town one day he sees a striking figure, the magnificent ruin of a man, tall and powerful, but stiff-jointed and maimed.

Curious, the narrator inquires about him, but gets only bits of information. The man's name is Ethan Frome. He lives on his farm with his wife Zeena (Zenobia), "the greatest hand at doctoring in the country," and his cousin Mattie. He had a smash-up twenty-four years ago.

Chance helps the narrator learn more. The horses that he has been hiring to take him to the train for Corbury Junction fall ill. The Irish stable owner, Denis Eady, suggests that Ethan Frome's bay still has legs and that its owner will be glad to earn a dollar. The narrator approaches Frome who agrees to drive him to the train daily. One stormy day the train is stalled, and Frome takes his passenger to Corbury Junction, a considerable distance away. Returning in a blizzard, Frome invites him to spend the night at the farm which is nearer than Starkfield. He gladly accepts the invitation. That night he finds the clue to, and gradually reconstructs, Ethan Frome's story.

It begins on Ethan's starved farm and sawmill, from which he barely ekes out a living. He is trapped by circumstances he cannot control. First his father, then his mother, fall ill. He cares for them. Ethan, a native says, "always done the caring." During his mother's illness, his cousin Zenobia Pierce comes over from the next valley to help nurse her. Seven years older than Ethan, gaunt and angular, she nevertheless brings a touch of femininity into the house, and she manages it efficiently. Ethan, who began a technical course before his father's illness, still wants to be an engineer. He feels sure that with Zeena's help he can leave the farm to live in a town where there are lectures and libraries and where people do things. Moved partly by this hope and partly by gratitude, he marries Zeena.

The dream vanishes soon. Zeena has an affinity for sickness. Whining, utterly self-centered, she renders Ethan's existence bleaker than ever. Into this cheerless household some brightness penetrates when Ethan's wife's cousin Mattie comes to live with them and to aid Zeena. Mattie's father has died after appropriating (perhaps misappropriating) his relatives' money, and she has been left nearly destitute. Her grace and sweetness, so different from his wife's chill rigidity, captivate him. He calls for Mattie on the rare occasions of a Starkfield dance or other festivity. He assists her with the chores that sometimes overwhelm her. He suffers agonies of jealousy when smart Denis Eady, the Irish grocer's son, flirts with her.

When Ethan walks her home from a dance one night, his arm encircles her. He promises her that on the next moonlit night he will take her coasting down the steep Starkfield hill. Zeena is waiting up for them and receives them more sullenly than ever. She informs Ethan that she is going to town to consult a new doctor. Though he dreads the thought of the expense—for Zeena is unrestrained in her hypochondria— he consents because it will give him his first opportunity to be alone with Mattie. He arranges for the hired man to drive Zeena to the train, pretending that he must collect a debt from the local builder.

With Mattie, his innocent companion in the house, Ethan experiences a strange new joy. But bad luck mars it. The cat breaks Zeena's treasured pickle dish which Mattie has taken down from its high place in the cupboard. Ethan puts the pieces together carefully and replaces the dish. The rest of the evening passes delightfully, though Ethan approaches Mattie no closer than to kiss the edge of something she is sewing.

Back from town, Zeena tells Ethan that the doctor says she must have someone in to "do" for her; she may not work at all about the house. Ethan is dismayed. He can't afford a hired girl. Zeena tells him that Mattie, of course, must go. That ought to save something at least; and besides, she intimates significantly, Mattie has been with them too long. Ethan tries to plead for Mattie, but Zeena is adamant, especially after she discovers the broken pickle dish. Ethan desperately tries to run away with Mattie, but is brought up sharply by the hard realities. How will they live? He hasn't even enough money to pay their fare out West. And how will Zeena manage? The farm and the mill are so heavily mortgaged as to be worth next to nothing.

Over Zeena's querulous objections, Ethan drives Mattie to the train. Both are in despair: he, because with Mattie goes all that makes life endurable for him, and she, because she loves Ethan and because she is utterly without resources. Their embraces are interrupted by tears. When the horse reaches School House Hill, Ethan determines that he and Mattie will have their long-delayed coast. In a nearby sled, they make their descent, Ethan easily avoiding the great elm that looms at the foot of the hill and that has worried Mattie. Ascending with Ethan, she is mastered by a fresh hope. She has before tearfully exclaimed that she wished she were dead. Now she suggests that they coast down the hill again—and never come up any more. Ethan hesitates, then agrees. But their fate is grimmer than death. They crash into the elm; Mattie and Ethan survive despite their terrible injuries but remain invalids for the rest of their lives. Zeena emerges from her self-imposed illness to care for them—complainingly but resolutely.

The narrator sees the three tragic victims of life together: Mattie as fretful and shrill as Zeena ever was, Ethan's face showing the pain that racks his body and spirit, Zeena cranky but enduring. "I don't see there's much difference," says Mrs. Hale, an old friend of Mattie's, "between the Fromes up at the farm and the Fromes in the graveyard; 'cept that down there they're all quiet, and the women have got to hold their tongues."

Critical Opinion

Ethan Frome is widely regarded as "securely on the level with the few great tragic novels in English," as a New England tragedy of greater "power and elevation" than any novel since Hawthorne's *The Scarlet Letter*. But there are those who differ sharply with this view. While acknowledging the technical expertness of the novel, Bernard De Voto insists that it is not "a transcript of human experience" or "an exploration of or comment on genuine emotion." Alfred Kazin, too, feels that *Ethan Frome* fails ultimately because its world is abstract. Edith Wharton "never knew how the poor lived in Paris or London; she knew even less of how they lived in the New England villages where she spent an occasional summer." Others have criticized the "literary" quality of the villagers, the "contrived" plot, the "synthetic" New England dialect.

It is true, of course, that *Ethan Frome* departs from the norm of Edith Wharton's fiction, which usually involves meticulous analysis of the crumbling of fashionable society as a result of its own inner corruption and of the onslaught of vulgar "new riches." Whether she is accurate in her description of life in a small New England town may be questioned. Literary sociologists have presented evidence to show that she is not. But such evidence hardly touches the heart of the novel. The doom that hangs over men, the dark force that threatens them always and that may at any time descend—this is the true center of the novel. The New England scene is the backdrop, not the meaning of the novel. As an ironic tragedy of love, *Ethan Frome* transcends particular places and people.

The Author

Edith Wharton was born in New York in 1862, the daughter of wealthy and socially prominent parents. She was brought up in New York, receiving her early education from private tutors and governesses. It was a life, she recalled much later, "safe, guarded, and monotonous," its pattern broken by frequent journeys abroad and summer holidays in Newport.

Her life after her marriage to Edward Wharton in 1885 seemed likely to follow the same pattern. A Bostonian, descendant of an aristocratic Virginia family, he was independently wealthy. Together they spent a good deal of time traveling in Europe. But from 1900 on, Edward Wharton suffered from mental illness, and in 1906 his condition was judged hopeless.

Edith Wharton had attempted some writing earlier—some criticism of current modes of interior decorating and several stories. Now, perhaps on the advice of physicians, she started writing seriously. In 1902 she published her first novel, *The Valley of Decision*, a re-creation of the Italian courts on the eve of the French Revolution. Her first really important novel was *The House of Mirth* (1905), an affecting portrait of a woman in fashionable society that created something of a furor in its day. The years of her greatest achievement were 1911, when she published her grim New England study, *Ethan Frome*, and 1920, when she completed her Pulitzer Prize-winning *The Age of Innocence*, another of her "inside" portraits of New York society.

After her great period, her creative powers declined, though there were occasional evidences of her earlier talents in *The*

Writing of Fiction (1925), a fascinating discussion of her literary credo, and A *Backward Glance* (1934), an interesting but too reticent biography.

Edith Wharton's efforts for the Allies during World War I brought her the Legion of Honor and other awards. For the most part, she lived her last years quietly in France, years rendered tolerable by her intimate friendship with Walter Berry, an American international lawyer, and her friendship with other writers. She died in France and was buried in the Protestant Cemetery at Versailles.

My Antonia

by

WILLA CATHER (1876–1947)

Main Characters

Jim Burden—The narrator, a successful railroad lawyer who looks back nostalgically to the golden years of his youth on the Nebraska prairies.

Antonia Shimerda—A Bohemian girl, vital, strong, warm, who accepts adversity as a condition of life and triumphs over it.

Mr. Shimerda—Ántonia's father, a frail, sensitive man, incapable of surviving the harsh realities of pioneer life.

Mrs. Shimerda—Ántonia's mother, a greedy, ungrateful, shrewd woman.

Ambrosch Shimerda—Ántonia's brother, surly, suspicious, sullen.

Marek Shimerda—Antonia's imbecilic brother.

Krajiek—A Bohemian, greedy and unscrupulous, who cheats the Shimerdas.

Mrs. Herling—The amiable and musical next-door neighbor of Jim's grandparents in Black Hawk.

Lena Lingard—A pretty Norwegian farm girl who opens a successful dressmaker's shop in Lincoln and with whom Jim has a love affair.

Mr. Cutter—A lecherous, avaricious, unscrupulous money-lender.

Mrs. Cutter—His aggressive, masculine wife with whom he is continually at war.

Larry Donovan—A ne'er-do-well who seduces Ántonia and deserts her.

Mr. Cuzak—Ántonia's husband, a strong, lively, good-natured farmer.

Jim's Grandparents—Good, kind, religious folk.

Jake Marpole—One of Jim's grandfather's hands, a friend and ally to Jim.

Otto Fuchs—Another hired man, who instructs Jim in the ways of prairie life.

The Story

Jim Burden, a successful railway lawyer married to an unsympathetic wife, tells the story of his youth on the Nebraska prairies and of the vital Bohemian girl whom he has never ceased to love. At ten, after the death of his parents in Virginia, he travels to Nebraska to live with his grandparents. Accompanying him on the long train journey is Jake Marpole, one of his father's hired hands, who is going to work for Jim's grandfather. They hear of a Bohemian family, their train companions, who are going to settle on a Nebraska farm, but not until they arrive at Black Hawk do they actually catch a glimpse of them.

Jim's grandparents are active people, kind and religious, and Jim speedily comes to love the brilliantly colored, ever-moving, limitless prairie lands. Before long his grandmother suggests that they visit their new Bohemian neighbors, the Shimerdas. They are driven there by their hired man, Otto Fuchs, an Austrian who teaches Jim much about prairie life. The Shimerda family consists of the father, frail, melancholy, elderly, and dignified, obviously unused to farm work; the mother, shrewd, grasping, sharp; two sons—Ambrosch, a suspicious and surly youth of nineteen, and Marek, an imbecilic boy; a small girl, Yalka, mild and obedient; and the fourteen-year-old Ántonia, vibrant, warm, joyous. The Shimerdas have been duped by a countryman, Krajiek, who has overcharged them for their farm, equipment, and animals. They are living in a sod dugout in the utmost poverty and eagerly welcome the Americans and the food they bring. None of the Shimerdas knows more than a few words of English. The father asks Jim to teach Ántonia his language.

Through glorious afternoons of their first autumn, they explore the prairie, seeing the prairie-dog villages, once killing a snake, but mostly reveling in the magnificence of the country. Winter does not wholly cut them off, except when the snowfall is too heavy. Mr. Shimerda cannot adjust to the rough life of the new land. He makes two friends, Russian bachelors who speak something of his language. But one of them leaves Nebraska after the other dies seeing terrifying visions of wolves: once, driving the lead sled in a wedding party, he had thrown the bride and groom to the pursuing wolves in order to lighten the load and ensure his escape. His only friends gone, Mr. Shimerda's desolation deepens until, able to bear it no longer, he shoots himself. He is buried on the farthest southwest corner of the Shimerda acres, where eventually two roads would cross, in accordance with Bohemian custom.

Following her father's death, Ántonia works in the fields with her brother Ambrosch, doing a man's work, reveling in her strength. Jim's lessons stop, especially after the ingratitude and boorishness of Ambrosch lead to a fight with Jake. Jake knocks him off his feet and pays a fine in town for breaking the peace.

Soon after, Jim moves to the town of Black Hawk with his grandparents who are getting too old to work the farm. He makes friends with the Herlings, their next-door neighbors, a gay and intimate family. Though Jim likes town, he misses the prairie and Ántonia. When the Herlings' cook leaves, his grandmother suggests they try Ántonia. She soon becomes one of the Herling family, enjoying their talk and music and doting on their children. Other farm girls migrate to town, too. With Lena Lingard, a pretty Norwegian girl who works for the town's dressmaker, Ántonia becomes especially chummy. When a dance pavilion is set up in town, the girls become wildly excited, eager to finish their chores and go dancing—Ántonia most eager of all.

One night Mr. Herling catches Ántonia slapping a young man who has escorted her home and has attempted to kiss her. The fresh, vivid country girls always seemed a threat to their languid town sisters, and Mr. Herling insists that Ántonia stop attending the dances or seek another job. Ántonia does not hesitate. She leaves, to accept a place with the Cutters, a couple in a continual state of matrimonial discord. Mr. Cutter is a lecherous, greedy moneylender. On one occasion Jim saves Ántonia from being attacked by him.

Jim graduates from school as class valedictorian, studies hard during the summer, and in the fall goes to Lincoln to attend the state university. Here he comes under the influence of Gaston Cleric, a brilliant, dedicated scholar who opens up vistas of classical learning for Jim, though he knows that he himself can never become a scholar. Jim's devotion to his studies is interrupted when Lena Lingard moves to Nebraska to open her own dressmaking establishment. Jim forms a deep attachment for her, taking her to the theater, breakfasting with her Sundays, relaxing in her company. Parting is a wrench for both of them, but Jim—nineteen now—has decided to follow Cleric to Harvard and complete his education there.

For the next two years, Jim remains at Cambridge. Before entering law school, he returns to Black Hawk for a visit. There he hears what has happened to Ántonia. She fell in love with the ne'er-do-well Larry Donovan, who promised to marry her, but delayed, living on her money till it was gone, and then deserted her while she was pregnant. Ántonia returned to the Shimerda farm and worked hard in the fields until her baby was born. Now her life is centered on her daughter, though she still labors as hard as a man on the farm. Jim visits her briefly and their deep friendship for each other reasserts itself. He promises to see her again.

It is twenty years before Jim keeps the promise. During those years he has become a successful, if perhaps spiritually unfulfilled, railway lawyer. On his way East from California, he interrupts his journey to visit Ántonia. She has married and raised a swarm of children. She greets him joyfully, proud of her family, happy in her life. She has worked with her husband, a Bohemian, encouraged him, persevered with him. They are not rich, but they have enough to make them happy. Jim enters fully into the family life during his three-day stay, enjoying Ántonia's radiant delight in her lot. He leaves,

promising to return next summer to take the boys hunting. He
stops for a while at Black Hawk and gazes at the prairie (now
highway and plowed land), musing—with some sadness but
with acceptance—about his destiny and Ántonia's and the
past they had possessed together.

Critical Opinion

My Ántonia is representative of Willa Cather's interest, early
and late, in the theme of the immigrant pioneers—the Swedes,
Norwegians, Poles, Slavs, Bohemians, and French who bravely
make "a new settlement of the frontier." *My Ántonia* glosses
over none of the unpleasantness of pioneer life, nor does it fail
to recognize that there were many unpleasant pioneer folk—
the greedy, repellent Krajiek, for example; or the sullen, ungrateful Ambrosch; or the wheedling, crafty, and foolish Mrs.
Shimerda. But Willa Cather writes from a depth of affection
and understanding that converts the bleak and often deadly
pioneer experience into something rich and warm. Surely
every reader comes increasingly to admire Ántonia, the strong,
brave, enduring woman who suffers and triumphs, who loses
her teeth but keeps "the fire of life."

The flaw in the novel, critics point out, is that its center
of gravity shifts from Ántonia to Jim. Thus in the third section
of the book, Ántonia nearly disappears and Jim emerges as
the focal figure. However, we should be aware of the significance of the *My* of the title: Ántonia is central to the novel
only when she is central to Jim. When Jim leaves Black Hawk
for the university, Ántonia recedes—in the story as in Jim's
life. She returns at the end because she evokes Jim's past,
because her battered yet vital person makes him recall how
much he has lost through his "success."

With some exceptions, critics concede that Willa Cather's
My Ántonia is "the most masterly of her novels and one of the
classics of our literature." It is, says Henry Seidel Canby, "the
story of a great woman ennobling common things and a common struggle by elemental passion." T. K. Whipple more suc-
cinctly calls it an instance of "the victory of mind over
Nebraska."

The Author

Willa Sibert Cather was born in Winchester, Virginia, in 1876, but her formative years were spent in Nebraska where her father owned a ranch. She at once fell in love with the country, still a pioneer territory, and its people. "I have never found any intellectual excitement more intense than I used to feel when I spent a morning with one of these pioneer women at her baking or buttermaking. I used to ride home in the most unreasonable state of excitement; I always felt as if they told me so much more than they said—as if I had actually got inside another person's skin."

Her elementary schooling was presided over by her mother. Not till the family moved to Red Cloud, Nebraska, did she have any formal education. But her mother's teaching, based on the English classics and on Latin, was sound enough to enable her to perform excellently at high school and at the University of Nebraska.

Because of her passion for music, which she retained all her life, Willa Cather determined to move to a city where she could hear it. She chose Pittsburgh and there found employment as editor and theater critic for the *Leader*. Newspaper work proving insufficiently attractive, she taught English at Allegheny High School from 1901 to 1906. Then the publication of a book of poems, *April Twilights* (1903), and a collection of stories, *The Troll Garden* (1905), both well reviewed, led to her obtaining an editorial position on *McClure's* magazine in New York. From 1906 to 1912, she was its managing editor.

The success of her novels made it possible for her to quit her magazine work and devote herself exclusively to writing. She continued to live in New York but took frequent trips abroad, to the prairies, and finally to the Southwest desert country (which almost replaced the prairies in her affections). She remained Miss Cather till her death in 1947.

Except for *One of Ours* (a Pulitzer Prize winner in 1922) and *The Professor's House* (1925), Willa Cather's novels characteristically are devoted to the themes of the immigrant who pioneers in a new and hard land—*O Pioneers!* (1913) and *My Ántonia* (1918); and of the quest for stability as represented by the Catholic Church—*Death Comes for the Archbishop* (1927) and *Shadows on the Rock* (1931).

Winesburg, Ohio

by

SHERWOOD ANDERSON (1876–1941)

Main Characters

George Willard—A young reporter, eager to set forth from Winesburg to encounter the world. His sensitivity and receptivity make him the confidant of most of the characters in the book.

Elizabeth Willard—His mother, once ebullient and vibrant, now, at forty-five, physically and psychically shriveled.

Tom Willard—His father, an ambitious hotelkeeper, passionate about politics but almost wholly indifferent to his wife.

Dr. Reefy—A doctor, sympathetic and compassionate, the only adult love in Mrs. Willard's life.

Wing Biddlebaum—A berry picker, once a gifted schoolteacher, gentle, timid, lovable, and the possessor of extraordinarily expressive hands. His real name is Adolph Myers.

Dr. Parcival—A doctor no longer in practice, who has retreated in terror and guilt from all experience.

Jesse Bentley—A farmer, obsessed by God and money, determined to use his grandson, David, to open a path between himself and God.

Kate Swift—A schoolteacher, stern, but deeply aware of promise in the young and dedicated to encouraging any sign of genius.

Alice Hindman—A spinster oft disappointed in love and bursting with unsatisfied passion.

Wash Williams—The telegraph operator, a violent anti-feminist and a hater of life.

The Rev. Curtis Hartman—Pastor of the Presbyterian Church, quiet and devout but also filled with soul-shattering carnal urges.

Enoch Robinson—A would-be artist and *bon vivant* who has failed in both roles and finds himself frighteningly alone and embittered.

Louise Trunnion—The serving girl at the Willards' who initiates George into sex.

Belle Carpenter—The flirtatious daughter of a bookkeeper and George's second conquest.

Helen White—Daughter of the town banker, educated and sophisticated, who gives George his last and most significant sexual experience.

The Story

(Note: Because *Winesburg, Ohio* comprises several connected short stories, the relevant story titles have been supplied in parentheses at appropriate points.)

Although Elizabeth Willard's girlhood dreams of becoming an actress and living an excitingly romantic life have been pulverized by the drab routine of her marriage to an insensitive husband, she refuses to abandon her hopes for her only son, George. Above all, she dreads the possibility that her husband will force George into a career that will keep him in Winesburg and suffocate his will and his imagination ("Mother"). Only once in her married life does Mrs. Willard know release from the stultifying world of Tom. With Dr. Reefy (whose own marriage, though happy, ended after a year with the death of his wife—"Paper Pills"), she finds herself able to speak of her early dreams and aspirations, and of the marriage she foolishly allowed herself to make. For a brief moment, in Dr. Reefy's arms, she finds respite. But the moment—interrupted by the noise of a clerk dumping rubbish outside the door—is short-lived and the two are never to meet again, for Mrs. Willard dies a few years later.

Ironically the $800 she has hidden in the wall behind her bed, money intended to help George get away from Winesburg, remains there unknown to all ("Death").

Mrs. Willard's fears that George will remain in Winesburg were not well founded. Even as she fretted about what her husband might insist upon, George was telling his father that he did not want an ordinary "successful" career. Above all, he knows that when he comes of age, he wants to go away, to "look at people and think." Only sixteen when he tells his father of his intention, George has already begun work on the local newspaper. His assignments bring him in touch with everyone in town, and from them he learns the poignant lessons of loneliness and frustration that lead him toward maturity and the day when he must leave Winesburg.

Wing Biddlebaum ("Hands"), the best berry picker in Winesburg, urges George to forget the routine world and learn how to dream. He reaches out and touches the young man's shoulders, almost caresses him, then, with a look of horror on his face, leaves. George cannot wholly understand the old man's terror and anxiety but suspects Wing's problems have something to do with his hands, "the piston rods of his machinery of expression." What George does not know is that years earlier Wing, as Adolph Myers, had been an inspired and inspiring teacher. Boys loved his gentleness, accepted his warm and friendly touch, and under his tutelage learned to dream. Unhappily, one half-witted boy who also loved Wing dreamed that his relationship with his teacher was sexual and told his parents about his dream as if it were true. As a result, Wing was accused of immorality and driven out of town, barely escaping hanging.

Other men in Winesburg have turned their backs on life, too, each for a different reason. Dr. Parcival ("The Philosopher") fills George with stories of his unhappy boyhood: a lunatic father, a drunken brother, an impoverished mother. "I want to fill you with hatred and contempt so that you will be a superior being," he tells George. So complete is Parcival's withdrawal from life that when a child is killed by a runaway horse, he refuses the pleas of the townsfolk to examine her. Yet he expects retribution, perhaps (he suggests) by lynching. Frightened as he is at the prospect, Parcival is convinced that the outcome will support his vision of life—"that everyone in the world is Christ and they are all crucified."

Enoch Robinson ("Loneliness") confides to George his life-long determination to be admired by all for his talents as an artist and a conversationalist. He went to New York and joined bohemian art circles, but neither his painting nor his talk held anyone's interest. He tried marriage but found it stifling, and at last sank into a self-pitying isolation in his Greenwich Village room. Into that room came a woman, a violinist, who often sat in silence with Enoch. At first Enoch believed that he might be able to lose his identity in her presence, but suddenly one night he felt compelled to make her understand who he was and how important his existence was. As he raved on about himself to the woman, he sensed that she understood him, but ironically, her understanding became a threat to his independence and impelled him to a frenzied verbal assault upon her. When he drove her from the room, however, Enoch realized that he was forever alone. And thus he returned again to Winesburg, the town he had many years before tried to escape.

Wash Williams, the old telegraph operator ("Respectability"), had loved his wife with a jealous passion which turned to bitter loathing when he discovered that she had several lovers. Yet even after he dispatched her home to her mother, he continued to send almost every cent he earned or saved. A few years later the girl's mother sent for Wash to visit. Lonely, he was determined to accept his faithless wife once more. As he waited in the living room, Wash heard mother and daughter conversing, and knew that if the girl were simply to enter and touch his hand, he would forgive and forget. What he had not expected, however, was that the girl would enter the room stark naked, pushed across the threshold by her mother. As the chilled George listens, Wash says he wanted to kill the mother, but succeeded only in hitting her with a chair before the neighbors intervened. Now, he moans, he can never get to kill her because she died of a fever only a month later.

Bitterness and frustration afflict many of the women of Winesburg, too. Alice Hindman ("Adventure") was a lonely woman in her late twenties, in love with the young man who had seduced her many years before, left town, and never returned. When her mother remarried, Alice became even more deeply aware of her isolation, clasped a pillow to her breast and even arranged the bedclothes to resemble a human form. One rainy night, desperate with longing, Alice rushed into the street naked, calling to a passer-by to wait for her. The passer-by proved to be an old man, deaf, who shouted back asking her what she wanted. Alice collapsed on the ground, then crawled on hands and knees back to her house. In bed, she turned her face to the wall and "began trying to force herself to face bravely the fact that many people must live and die alone, even in Winesburg."

Kate Swift ("The Teacher") had been George's teacher and he had often as a boy dreamed of making love to her. Neither pretty nor very young, Kate, despite a forbidding exterior, was "the most eagerly passionate soul among them." She had recognized in George's writing the possibilities of genius and had tried to make him conscious of the challenge and responsibilities of the artist. One evening when George, now a young reporter, came to her room to borrow a book, she began anew her impassioned appeal about art. Suddenly she kissed the embarrassed youth, then dismissed him by telling him it would be ten years before he understood what she was saying to him. The next evening, however, she came to George's office at the *Winesburg Eagle* and allowed him to embrace her. Almost ready to yield to him, Kate could not and struck George repeatedly in the face until he released her and she ran home.

Later that same evening, as George paced his office angrily after his rejection by Kate, the Reverend Curtis Hartman burst in, his hand dripping blood, and shouted at George that God had manifested Himself to him in the shape of a naked woman. Unhappily married to a frigid wife, unable to win his battle with his sensual yearnings, Hartman had some time earlier broken off a bit of stained glass in his church-office window and was thus able to peep across the walk into Kate Swift's bedroom. He struggled with his temptation, but on several occasions yielded and watched the teacher reading in her bed, yearning to see her body naked. On the night that Kate fled from George's arms, however, Hartman's desires were fulfilled. In her room, Kate flung herself naked upon the bed and, in tears, beat her fists upon the pillows. As Hartman watched, she suddenly rose and began to pray. Convinced that her gesture was a symbolic signal from God, Hartman smashed his fist through his window, knowing that now he would have to replace it and thus no longer be able to peep ("The Strength of God").

George's initiation into sex is achieved callously and unemotionally with Louise Trunnion, the Willards' maid ("Nobody Knows"). He makes merely a casual gesture of interest, and the girl easily though dispassionately gives herself to him. When she leaves, George laughs self-assuredly to himself that nobody knows what has happened and thus Louise cannot really cause him any trouble. In his succeeding affairs, however, George learns that love is more than a minor carnal episode. With Belle Carpenter ("An Awakening"), he senses a deeper, almost mystical, sense of being in "touch with something orderly and big that swings through the night like a star." But he experiences humiliation in his affair with Belle, too, for even as he holds Belle in his arms, her other lover, Ed Handby, the local bartender, comes by, pushes George into the bushes, and marches Belle off.

At eighteen, shortly after his mother's death and just before he leaves Winesburg, George knows that he is ready to share his brief but already rich past with another person. He has now come into sharp contact with love and death and has acquired knowledge about the joy and pain of human experience. He is, in brief, nearly mature, and ready for an experience that is tender and gentle. With Helen White ("Sophistication") he has that consummate experience. Helen is bored by her college-teacher suitor's pompous verbosity. She runs from him to find George and together, thoroughly conscious of their oneness though unable to express or explain it, they wrest from "their silent evening together the thing needed."

Early one morning in April, George takes the train that will carry him to the world beyond Winesburg ("Departure"). His mind filled with memories of the past and dreams of the future, George strays from the present momentarily, just long enough so that when he looks at the real world outside the train window, he has left Winesburg.

Critical Opinion

"I am a child, a confused child in a confused world . . . ,"
Sherwood Anderson wrote in his *Notebook* in 1916. In *Winesburg, Ohio* he translated that sense of isolation and alienation,
the confusion between self and society that has long been the
hallmark of American literature, into a high artistic achievement. The stories of *Winesburg* tell of the failure of both
emotional and intellectual communication, not merely in a
small town but among all men. All of the characters strive
toward that maturity that is the high-water mark of psychological development, but only George Willard can possibly
achieve it in the future. And Anderson provides no sentimental
assurance that George will fulfill his promise.

All of the other characters are, as Anderson called them,
"grotesques." In the prologue to the book, Anderson explains
that a "grotesque" is a person who has falsely shaped his life
about an assumed and all-embracing truth. Actually what
cripples these people is not so much their addiction to a particular truth as their failure to communicate to others their
most deeply felt emotions. As a result they drift in a terrible
void of aloneness, helpless by themselves, unable to be helped
by others. They inhabit a kind of twilight world where they
can neither see nor be seen.

Readers of *Winesburg, Ohio* will, of course, recognize that
Anderson knew Edgar Lee Masters' *Spoon River Anthology*,
the poetic rendering of the sterility and blighted hopes of small
towners. But Anderson gave to his tales a kind of narrative
unity lacking in Masters' poem. Certainly the form of *Winesburg, Ohio* is loose, hardly what one normally expects in a
novel. Yet, as Anderson has written: "Life is a loose, flowing
thing . . . but the whole . . . leaves a definite impression. . . ."
Thus, for Anderson and for most readers, the diverse stories
of *Winesburg, Ohio* form a cohesive unit, and the separate
lives fall together into an unmistakable pattern of human
sadness.

The Author

With almost no formal education, *Sherwood Anderson* became one of America's finest storytellers. Born in Camden, Ohio, he wandered restlessly from job to job, starting at the age of fourteen. After serving for a short time in the Spanish-American War, he returned to Elyria, Ohio, married, and briefly settled down as manager of a paint factory. But he was already planning a literary career, and, when he had enough money, he left the factory to try his luck in Chicago. There, working as an advertising writer and meeting major literary figures like Carl Sandburg and Floyd Dell who encouraged him, Anderson finished his first novel, *Windy McPherson's Son* (1916). But neither this initial venture nor its two successors won him the fame that came with the publication of *Winesburg, Ohio* in 1919.

In *Poor White* (1920), another successful novel, he studied the effects of industrialism on small-town life, and in a superb volume of short stories, *The Triumph of the Egg* (1921), he exploited still further the Freudian implications of personal frustration. Although he wrote and published many more books before his death (he choked on a toothpick), none matched the power and insight of these earlier works. Nevertheless, several of his writings merit attention, especially his autobiograp'.cal works: *Tar: A Midwest Childhood* (1926) and *A Story-Teller's Story* (1924). Also of interest for their comments about contemporary writers (he was a good friend of Gertrude Stein's and gave much help to young writers like Ernest Hemingway and William Faulkner) are his critical volumes: *Sherwood Anderson's Notebook* (1926) and *The Modern Writer* (1925).

After four marriages (his novel *Many Marriages*, 1923, depicts some of the difficulties he encountered) he settled near Marion, Virginia, to edit two newspapers, one Republican, the other Democratic.

Jurgen

by

JAMES BRANCH CABELL (1879–1958)

Main Characters

Jurgen—A pawnbroker and "the remnant of a poet"; witty, learned (especially in the lore he invents), skeptical. His three favorite sayings: "I am willing to try any drink once"; "Of course you may be right; and certainly I cannot go so far as to say you are wrong; but still, at the same time—"; and "I shall deal fairly with you."

Dame Lisa—Jurgen's shrewish yet fond wife.

Koshchei the Deathless—The Supreme Being (as far as we know) "who made things as they are."

Mother Sereda—Earth Goddess—also known as Aesred and Aderes (all anagrams for *Dea Res*, "the thing Goddess")—who has all Wednesdays in her keeping, the middle of working days and of all middles. Her function is to bleach all the colors of life; she is Gray Conformity.

The Centaur Nessus—A creature from Greek mythology, who takes Jurgen to the Garden between Dawn and Sunrise and gives him a magic shirt to wear.

Dorothy la Désirée—The first love of Jurgen, who deserted him to marry a nobleman whom she now regularly deceives with younger lovers.

Guenevere—The wife of Arthur, later the mistress of Lancelot, once the innocent if slightly obtuse beloved of Jurgen.

123

Anaitis—The Lady of the Lake, embodying the principle of desire and fulfillment.

Chloris—A Hamadryad whom Jurgen marries and lives with placidly.

Helen of Troy—The avatar of beauty, dream of the poet realized.

Florimel—A vampire on vacation in Hell, whom Jurgen meets while sojourning there.

The Story

The scene is Poictesme (a land of Cabell's creation) during the middle ages. Jurgen, a middle-aged pawnbroker who still retains something of his gift for poetry, passes a monk who has tripped over a stone and is roundly cursing the devil who placed it there. Jurgen defends the devil's industry and energy and walks on. Shortly he meets a black gentleman who thanks him for his good word and promises to reward him.

Returning home, Jurgen is unable to find his wife, Lisa, a lady "with no especial gift for silence." Though he bears her disappearance manfully, he is finally persuaded by his sister-in-law to seek Lisa who has been seen walking on a local heath. He follows her into a cave, and there sees not Lisa but the centaur Nessus, who gives him a bright shirt (perhaps the emblem of imagination or fantasy) and offers to carry him to the Garden between Dawn and Sunrise. It is a place of romantic illusions bred in youth. There Jurgen encounters Dorothy la Désirée—not as she is now, the faithless wife of the rich Heitman Michael, but as she was at eighteen, tender, vivid, and loving. Unhappily, though, Jurgen is no longer twenty and she does not respond to the poetry of a middle-aged pawnbroker.

The radiance of the garden vanishes, and Nessus changes into an ordinary riding horse. Jurgen mounts and rides until he comes to a great stone house where he sees an old woman bleaching. She is Sereda whose function. is to turn all color or beauty gray. Jurgen makes a song for her and in exchange she gives him a Wednesday of his twenty-first year to relive, for she is the mistress of all Wednesdays, "Time's middles."

She also gives him a shadow—her shadow—which accompanies him everywhere.

The bygone Wednesday to which Jurgen returns is again presided over by Dorothy, his beloved, who is being courted by Heitman Michael. This time, however, Jurgen is not defeated; three times he drives his dagger into the undefended back of his rival and then disposes of the body. He embraces his sweetheart just as Wednesday passes. The middle-aged Countess Dorothea is in his arms. Jurgen draws away with a shiver, reads her a brief lecture on morality, and resumes his journey.

Fortunately, Jurgen keeps his youth, and fortune stays with him. He comes upon a lovely young woman in a trance and awakens her with a long kiss. She proves to be Guenevere, not yet the bride of King Arthur or the mistress of Lancelot. With exceptional bravery he conducts her to Camelard, where her father, Gogyrvan Gawr, reigns. The king is a remarkably tolerant father. Though Guenevere is engaged to Arthur, Gogyrvan is willing to allow her to have an affair with Jurgen, who now calls himself Duke of Logreus, since he has certain rights as a champion. Gogyrvan insists on a promise, nevertheless: in all matters concerning his daughter's honor, he expects Jurgen to lie like a gentleman. Jurgen agrees, and nightly in the deserted Hall of Judgment Guenevere and he converse lovingly. Still, when Arthur arrives to claim his bride, Jurgen does not mourn. Guenevere, while charming, is a bit obtuse. (And even when most committed to her, Jurgen does not reject the love of Dame Yolande, another lady whom he has befriended.)

In the wedding party is the Lady of the Lake, Anaitis, enchanting and perverse. She is Queen of Cocaigne and directs erotic rituals throughout the world. She and Jurgen marry (despite the fact that he is theoretically still married to Dame Lisa) and they experiment continually. At first Jurgen is intrigued, but he becomes progressively less enthusiastic.

Consequently, when he has to leave Cocaigne at the Equinox, Jurgen is quite prepared "to taste a new drink." He chooses the country of Leukê, where Helen of Troy, the poet's ideal of beauty, reigns with Achilles in their palace at Pseudopolis. Before he sees the Queen, however, he quickly establishes a relationship with a tree nymph, the comfortable, plump and pretty Hamadryad Chloris to whom he identifies himself as King Jurgen. Since she desires it and no local legislation prohibits it, he marries her, living in her tree house. When conjugal happiness palls a little, he searches out Helen, but she is perfectly mated to Achilles. Jurgen sadly realizes that she must always remain an ideal for him, a perfection not to be attained, for once attained, she would make all other beauty seem flat and insipid.

But the forces of Philistia, the enemies of Romance, have no high illusions of beauty. They invade and burn Pseudopolis as a sacrifice to their god Vel-Tyno. Though Helen, Achilles and their retinue rise gleaming from the ground to escape their Philistine foes, the latter burn the tree of Chloris and kill her. Jurgen may still manage to survive in Philistia, for he has caught the fancy of its queen and has delighted her in his fashion, but he will strike no compromise with dull conformity. And two days before Christmas he is dispatched to the Hell of his fathers.

Jurgen adjusts quickly—this time as Emperor of Noumaria. He learns that Hell has been created by Koshchei the Deathless to satisfy the demands of ancestral conscience. His own particular father, Coth, is present, too, tormenting the devils with his insatiable demands for punishment. Coth conjures into existence—through his heated imaginings—a vampire, Florimel, whom Jurgen takes as his mistress. In short, he suffers not at all, except from the religion of Hell, which is patriotism, and from the government, which is an enlightened democracy.

Yet Jurgen wants to visit Heaven, giving as his unconvincing reason his desire to seek out Dame Lisa. With the aid of Jacob's ladder, he ascends to Heaven as Pope John XX. The boy angel who procures the ladder from one of Heaven's storerooms is—Jurgen himself, as he was. The affection of his grandmother, Steinvor, who visualized him as an angelic boy, is responsible for his being in Heaven. For Heaven, as the God of Jurgen's grandmother informs him, has been created by Koshchei according to the specifications of Steinvor. But none of the illusions that formed Heaven are Jurgen's, and so he departs to the heath from which he began his journeyings.

On the heath Mother Sereda is waiting. She takes back her shadow and takes away Jurgen's youth, leaving him as he was—which is what he wanted; familiar reality appeals more than glamorous illusion, for a youthful body and a middle-aged mind go poorly together. Nor does Koshchei, whom Jurgen stumbles upon immediately after, change his mind. And Koshchei does try, producing in turn Guenevere, the distillation of romantic faith; Anaitis, the emblem of desire; and Helen, the supreme embodiment of beauty. Jurgen longs for his termagant wife, Lisa. She appears, scolding furiously—overwhelming Jurgen and astonishing even Koshchei. Yet Jurgen is firm and Koshchei releases him to Lisa. As he enters his snug home, where she has preceded him, he is nearly content with domesticity, though he sighs a little.

Critical Opinion

When *Jurgen* was published in 1919, it met with three divergent responses. Critics like Carl Van Vechten, V. L. Parrington, Burton Roscoe, H. L. Mencken, and Sinclair Lewis hailed the book rapturously. Benjamin de Casseres called the author "the Watteau of ironists, the Debussy of prose, the Spinoza of word-magic, the Prometheus of an American Renaissance." And even so temperate a scholar as Carl Van Doren found the book to be "a progression full of beauty and pity and mirth, as if a huge organ should burst into laughter."

Another group of readers was less enthusiastic for varying reasons. Clifton Fadiman observed that the world of Poictesme has "the beauty and formal perfection of a well-known soap bubble." Others denounced it as veiled obscenity, as obsessively preoccupied with sex, as archaic in style and trivial in philosophy. William Summer brought suit against *Jurgen* for the New York Society for the Suppression of Vice, an action that failed after two years and triggered the enormous success of the book.

A very few perceived Cabell's *Comedy of Justice*, as the subtitle had it, for what it was: a witty, suggestive, and fundamentally moral tale. For though the hero is sufficiently libertine in his progress, he does finally prefer his wife and the dullness mingled with the delight of domesticity. *"Jurgen,"* says Joe Lee Davis, the most recent and scholarly of Cabell's critics, was ". . . as convincing a defense of monogamy as Homer's *Odyssey*."

The reputation of Jurgen has suffered through the years, partly because it was originally so overinflated, partly because the years themselves, years of depression and devastation, have been ruinous to witty fantasy. Contemporary historians of literature tend to dismiss the novel casually. Yet in the past decade Edmund Wilson has lauded it for its grace and imagination; there has been a spate of critical studies and re-evaluations of Cabell. Though it hardly seems likely that *Jurgen* will again be so generally and so generously praised as in the twenties, it surely will long be admired as a commentary, at once mordant and gay, on our impossible dreams and inevitable compromises.

The Author

James Branch Cabell once noted that his last name rhymed with "rabble." The observation was perhaps to be expected from the scion of one of the First Families of Virginia, an aristocrat reared in the ante-bellum tradition and always conscious of his distinguished lineage. This consciousness may indeed account for his long professional labors (from 1901 to 1911, and periodically throughout his career) as a genealogist—labors that produced three volumes on the Branch family and its connections. It accounts, too, for Cabell's lifelong interest in Virginia history and his appointment as editor for the Virginia War History Commission (1919–26).

After graduating from the College of William and Mary with high honors (as an upperclassman he was hired to teach other undergraduates French and Greek), Cabell worked for newspapers in Virginia and New York, engaged in genealogical researches, and began his career as a writer with some graceful but sentimental romances. In 1913 he married a widow four years his senior. Though his wife was less than fascinated by his writing, she proved a superb helpmate. Cabell partly repaid her by establishing her notable ancestry in *The Majors and Their Marriages* (1915). When she died in 1949, he was shattered. But the next year he married another, much younger

Virginia lady with literary aspirations, Margaret Waller Freeman.

Since Cabell wrote more than fifty books, clearly his dedication to literature is the most important fact in his long life. Though some of these books—his memoirs and his trilogy (*Smirt, Smith,* and *Smire,* 1934–37)—are remarkable achievements of wit and style, his huge epic of Poictesme in eighteen volumes is his enduring monument. Conceived as the "Biography of the Life of Manuel," the volumes trace the history of that mythical dignitary and of his descendants from 1234 to 1750. Cabell called on his vast knowledge of myth, story, folklore, legend, and history to fill in the imaginary terrain of Poictesme. Where knowledge failed, invention came to his rescue. Cabell never hesitated to invent myths, any more than personages or places. His expertness in genealogy and his predilection for anagram are also evident in his epic.

Of all of Cabell's work, *Jurgen* (1919) has achieved the greatest fame, not only because of its delightful satire but also because of the attempt by the New York Society for the Suppression of Vice to ban the book. It was triumphantly cleared in court, and its erudition and subtle eroticism have since delighted all but the most prudish readers.

Sister Carrie

by

THEODORE DREISER (1871–1945)

Main Characters

Caroline Meeber—"Sister" Carrie, a young country girl whose single, compelling drive is to possess whatever lies beyond her reach. She longs for love, fame, and wealth. She gets all of these, but at the end she is still yearning for the unattained and the unattainable.

George Hurstwood—Carrie's lover and "husband," a man of average sensibilities and passions trapped by hostile forces that undermine his will and turn him toward self-destruction.

Charles Drouet—Carrie's first lover, a stereotype of the traveling salesman: elegant, suave, sensual, shallow.

Mr. and *Mrs. Vance*—High-living neighbors of Carrie and Hurstwood in New York, who first expose Carrie to the temptations of New York's night life.

Robert Ames—A genial young man-about-town, with excellent taste in food, entertainment, and women—qualities that make him increasingly attractive to Carrie.

Julia, George, and *Jessica Hurstwood*—Hurstwood's wife, son, and daughter. Each is spoiled, selfish, and vindictive.

The Story

Aboard a train en route to Chicago, Caroline Meeber, aged eighteen, excitedly conjures up a romantic vision of the dynamic metropolis where she hopes to discover romance and wealth. She takes her first hesitant step toward fulfillment when she promises a train acquaintance, Charles Drouet, a young traveling salesman, to let him show her the city.

But Carrie's excursion with Drouet is temporarily postponed, as are her hopes for swift success. Living with her married sister in a tiny, drab apartment, Carrie feels too ashamed to have Drouet call and writes to put him off. Shocked by the grim drudgery of her sister's lot, Carrie is determined to shape a happier life for herself. Her initial efforts bring her little reward. In 1889 Chicago boasts an expanding economy for its half million inhabitants but has few jobs for inexperienced or unskilled girls. After days of jarring refusals, Carrie gets a job as an assembly-line worker in a shoe plant. Ill-paid, harshly overworked, she despairs of achieving the glamorous life she had envisioned. But she struggles on until she falls ill for a few days. Fired, she loses even the tenuous hold on economic security her job afforded.

A chance meeting with Drouet shortly thereafter measurably brightens Carrie's prospects. With his flair for ostentation (to Carrie, he seems at first a shining knight), Drouet takes her to dinner, to the theater, buys her clothes—and offers pointedly to take care of her. Thus, as Drouet's mistress, Carrie takes her first significant step toward reaching her goal. As a lover, Drouet is kind and thoughtful, but Carrie soon ignores his virtues and fixes upon his obvious shortcomings—lack of wit, showy taste, and a basic mediocrity.

Ironically, Drouet paves the way for his own defeat and for the progress of his successor, George Hurstwood. Hurstwood, manager of Fitzgerald and Moy's fashionable bar, is a reserved but personable man just short of forty. Married to a hostile, unlovable wife, and father of two grasping and disagreeable children, Hurstwood finds refuge among his friends and clients at the saloon. There Drouet lightheartedly and proudly introduces Carrie to Hurstwood. Occasionally, thereafter, Hurstwood visits Carrie and Drouet, joins them at the theater, and soon impresses Carrie as far superior to Drouet. One afternoon when Drouet has been called away on business, Hurstwood makes his first gentlemanly advance; Carrie's rebuff is ladylike but not sufficient to discourage Hurstwood.

In the months that follow, Hurstwood's passion increases. His aim is to have an affair, Carrie's to win marital status. (She is ignorant of Hurstwood's family life.) Meanwhile both Drouet and Mrs. Hurstwood grow suspicious of their respective partners. Mrs. Hurstwood boldly locks her husband out and institutes a lawsuit. Drouet tries to win back his mistress by informing her of Hurstwood's marital problem. Even after Drouet and Carrie have argued violently, he offers to allow her to use the apartment for which he pays rent. Carrie remains curiously unmoved by either Drouet's anger or gallantry: "It was not for her," Dreiser observes, "to see the wellspring of human passion."

A quick series of accidents thrusts the plot toward its turning point. First, Drouet returns to patch up his quarrel with Carrie, but finding her gone (she is out seeking a job), he leaves in anger. Then Hurstwood, seeing Drouet register at a hotel, concludes that Carrie and Drouet have broken, leaving the way open for him. Finally, Hurstwood, alone in his employer's office, discovers that the safe has been left open, and $10,000 in receipts is readily at hand. As he vacillates, now holding the money in his hand, now replacing it, a chance gust of wind swings the safe door shut, leaving him with the money.

Stirred into almost hysterical action now, Hurstwood seeks Carrie and deceives her into believing that Drouet has been hurt. Supposedly in search of Drouet, he takes her aboard a train headed for Montreal. At first irritated at the deception, Carrie yields to the lure of a new life in New York. Then she relents and consents to marry Hurstwood, each of them conveniently ignoring the obvious bigamy. Hurstwood's love for Carrie is sincere, but she knows only "a semblance of affection" created by "the drift of things and this man's proximity."

The two embark on a new life in a new metropolis. Carrie does not know, however, that detectives have already trapped Hurstwood in Montreal and compelled him to return all but a thousand dollars of his loot. Hurstwood must, therefore, begin life in New York without the essential ingredients of his success in Chicago: money and reputation. Like Carrie when she first walked the alien streets of Chicago, Hurstwood feels trapped by an environment in which "the great create an atmosphere which reacts badly upon the small." He tries earnestly but unsuccessfully to find a place in this new society. An investment in a new bar turns out disastrously, the income from various jobs disappears in extensive gambling bouts, the periods of unemployment grow longer and longer. As Hurstwood's fortunes dwindle, his manhood also declines. Once proud of his appearance, he now neglects to shave regularly, and he makes no protest when Carrie has him sleep in a separate room. Gradually he abandons even his quest for work, and rocks silently in a chair near a window. Once, humiliated, he serves as a scab during a trolley strike.

Carrie, meanwhile, flourishes. Fascinated by the city and by her lively neighbors, the Vances, she demands more and more of the material pleasures she dreamed of during her girlhood. When Hurstwood fails to provide more than a marginal living, her mild affection turns to contempt. Determined to make her own way, she becomes a chorus girl, advances rapidly to speaking parts and, at last, achieves stardom as a comedienne. By this time, she has decided to leave Hurstwood who sits pitiably in his rocker muttering, "I tried, didn't I?"

As Carrie's fortunes soar, Hurstwood's sink. Reduced to beggary in Stuyvesant Park, he thinks of suicide but lacks the fifteen cents for the gas jet in a Bowery flophouse. One snowy evening as Carrie leaves the theater surrounded by a throng of admirers, Hurstwood tries to push through to see her. He is summarily cast aside and tumbled headlong in the snow. Later that night he obtains the money he needs to carry out his suicide plans. Ironically, as the novel ends Carrie sits alone in a rocking chair, surveying her success, thinking of her lover, Bob Ames. Apparently successful, she remains discontented, yearning still for something elusive, something that, as Dreiser suggests, will forever remain just beyond her grasp.

Critical Opinion

Literary naturalism—as derived from the theory and practice of Emile Zola—commonly assigns to the novelist the role of dispassionate observer, of scientific recorder of the impact upon men of heredity and environment. To many critics, Theodore Dreiser remains the first and greatest of America's naturalists. His novels do record the effect of "chemisms," inner forces that enslave the will (for example, Carrie's "rudimentary mind" and Hurstwood's bodily "poisons" generated by remorse). Similarly, he describes the powerful impact of natural surroundings that produce "desperate results in the soul of man."

Had Dreiser been absolutely loyal to such a theory, however, he would probably not occupy his present place in American letters. For one thing, despite the massive—usually too massive—documentation with which he burdens his reader, Dreiser cannot suffocate his own passion or compassion. More than a scientist, he is a man of feeling. As he details Hurstwood's decline, Dreiser himself feels and communicates the pathos of human degradation. His own youthful ambitions for success and power are mirrored in Carrie's surge upward. But though he cannot resist admiring her rise, he understands the spiritual emptiness accompanying her triumph. Thus Dreiser humanizes the mechanistic thesis and makes memorable in his fiction the deeper, more lasting tones of humanity.

H. L. Mencken called *Sister Carrie* a "broken-backed" novel because the second half—for many readers the more interesting—concentrates upon Hurstwood, as the first does upon Carrie. This criticism has never been satisfactorily answered in literary terms. But then Dreiser cannot effectively be judged on purely esthetic grounds. The novel's structure is certainly faulty, and even more painful are its lumbering sentences, bad grammar, and ornately rhetorical images. For a few critics, these defects diminish Dreiser's stature as a great novelist. To many others, Dreiser's blunders contribute to his titanic force. Tragic reality beckons the creative writer to approach however he may. Dreiser plods and plunges, striking here at social and economic inequity, blasting there at false gentility and timidity. Relentlessly, however, he presses inward toward the inevitable center of experience, the human heart, driven by illusion, maimed by reality. Few American writers before or since have dramatized that tragic dichotomy more movingly.

An American Tragedy

by

THEODORE DREISER

Main Characters

Clyde Griffiths—The protagonist, a weak-willed materialist who awakens tragically from dreams of lavish economic and social success.

Roberta Alden—Clyde's gentle mistress, an innocent caught and destroyed in Clyde's tragedy.

Sondra Finchley—Clyde's ideal woman. Fascinated by her beauty and wealth, Clyde is utterly blind to her vanity, silliness, and irresponsibility.

Elvira and *Asa Griffiths*—Clyde's parents, poverty-ridden evangelists whose naïveté and unworldliness spur his desires for material things.

Esta Griffiths—Clyde's sister, whose seduction and abandonment foreshadow his own tragic future.

Samuel Griffiths—Clyde's wealthy uncle in Lycurgus. Shrewd and conservative, he is also more compassionate than his counterparts in high society.

Gilbert Griffiths—Samuel's son, young, aggressive, vain, a successful businessman and a snob.

Hortense Briggs—Clyde's first girl, a rapacious tease.

Orville Mason—The prosecuting attorney at Clyde's trial. Frustrated in his own life, he resents Clyde's amorous conquest.

Alvin Belknap—Clyde's defense attorney. With no special sympathy for Clyde, he recognizes Clyde's situation as one he himself experienced in youth, and thus brings a mildly ironic compassion to the case.

The Rev. Duncan McMillan—A dedicated zealot who tries to bring solace to Clyde in his last hours.

The Story

At dusk on a summer evening in Kansas City, homeward-bound office workers pause in the street to observe a strange family group. The father announces a hymn, the mother sings, a fifteen-year-old daughter plays the organ, and three younger children stand about. Only one of them, Clyde Griffiths, seems restless and ill at ease. At twelve, Clyde already feels out of place, his vanity and pride offended by his parents' poverty. Everywhere the boy senses the excitement of the city and yearns to share its wealth and beauty.

At sixteen, an attractive, well-mannered but ill-educated youth, Clyde is a bellhop at the Green-Davidson Hotel, goggling at men and women of the world and aspiring to their grace and mobility. With several of his fellow bellhops, he imitates them in the rites of liquor and sex. At a party he meets a rapacious young woman, Hortense Briggs, who brazenly teases him. Though Clyde thinks of Hortense romantically, she sees him as a source of cash. To give Hortense the price of a fur coat, Clyde must deny his sister Esta the money she needs for medical care. (She has been abandoned, pregnant, by her lover.) The climax of Clyde's adolescence occurs during a wild ride with Hortense and some other irresponsible youths. Their stolen car kills a child and crashes into a lumber pile. Clyde, concerned chiefly for his own safety, crawls away and escapes to Chicago.

Three years later, Clyde's mild sense of guilt disturbs him far less than his failure to make progress toward his social and economic goals. A chance meeting, however, with his uncle Samuel Griffiths sets him on his path. At his uncle's suggestion, Clyde leaves Chicago and journeys to Lycurgus, New York, where Samuel Griffiths' Collar and Shirt Company has won the family a solid place in the community. Given a virtually menial job in the factory, Clyde determines to forge his way upward. His prospects are less happy than he suspects, for the caste-conscious Griffiths clan looks upon him as a poor relative and dispenses condescension along with charity. Clyde's promotion to an assistant foremanship, for example, results less from recognition of his ability than from familial concern about outward appearances.

Few of the local people appeal to Clyde's yearning for high life, and he avoids the easy advances of the factory girls. His longing for society grows after the Griffithses (to fulfill a family obligation) invite him to dinner. There he meets Sondra Finchley, the "most adorable feminine thing he had seen in all his days," and he leaves determined to invade at any cost this world of luxury and beauty. For a time his determination is sidetracked by a chance encounter with one of the less aggressive factory girls, Roberta Alden, an attractive and gentle young woman. Drawn together by their mutual loneliness, Clyde and Roberta drift into a love affair. Roberta yields to Clyde hesitantly, her strong moral training urging her to caution. When at last she does accept him as her lover, however, her passion is sincere, her love profound. Clyde, though fond of Roberta, is chiefly proud of the amorous conquest he has made.

Lacking any real depth of feeling for Roberta, Clyde is easily drawn from her by Sondra who decides to "take him up . . . just for fun." Sondra's attentions reawaken Clyde's dream "to be lifted from the lowly state in which he now dwelt." Clyde continues to see Roberta, though Sondra, now charmed by her suitor, shows him warm affection. The double amour comes to its inevitable crisis when Roberta tells Clyde she is pregnant.

Failing to persuade Roberta to have an abortion and loath to marry her (especially since marriage with Sondra now seems a strong likelihood), Clyde grudgingly agrees to a "secret" marriage, suggesting that for the time being they live apart. Clyde promises to give Roberta the details of his proposal during a day's outing they are to share. By this time Clyde has determined never to marry Roberta. He tries—unsuccessfully—to thrust aside recurrent dreams and thoughts of murder. A newspaper account of a tragic lake drowning is too suggestive for Clyde's comfort as he contemplates his proposed rendezvous with Roberta at Big Bittern Lake. During their journey to Big Bittern, the water, the cries of the birds overhead, all echo dark thoughts of death. As he and Roberta row on the lake, his agony contorts his face. Frightened, Roberta beseeches him to speak, then crawls toward him to take his hand. Half in shock, he twists from her, swinging his camera-laden hand so that it strikes her across the face. Then, standing, half-prompted to help, half to apologize, he capsizes the boat. As they flounder in the water, the wale of the boat strikes Roberta in the head. She cries to Clyde for help. An inner voice also cries out to him to leave her; her death will seem accidental; he will be free. As he struggles to decide what to do, Roberta drowns. Once ashore, Clyde hastily and ineffectually hides the evidence of their visit, then heads back toward Lycurgus.

The third book (nearly half the length of the novel) concerns itself with Clyde's arrest, trial, and doom. At first confident that he has covered his tracks with masterly skill, Clyde feels safe. But once Roberta's body is discovered, mounting evidence points to Clyde's guilt. Arrested at a beach party with Sondra, Clyde insists that what occurred at Big Bittern was an accident, not murder. But since both the coroner and the district attorney, Orville Mason, scent political gain in a strong indictment, they decide to ignore truth and justice to pursue a conviction. Ironically, Clyde's defense attorney, Alvin Belknap, similarly hopes to benefit from a powerful exhibition of his skill. The trial degenerates into a travesty. The jury reaches its conclusion before the case begins. The press sensationalizes everyone, especially the mysterious "other" woman, Sondra, whose name both sides agree not to reveal. The lawyers match bravura performances.

Mason argues that Clyde at best willfully let his pregnant sweetheart drown. Belknap argues that Clyde is not a criminal but "a mental as well as a moral coward." In his carefully rehearsed testimony, Clyde gets little chance to search inwardly for the truth. His sole preoccupation is survival, and he lies witlessly, pitiably, and futilely. He is found guilty and condemned to death.

While Clyde is in jail, his mother preaches and writes to raise money for an appeal, even though she, too, has begun to doubt his innocence. She enlists the aid of the Rev. Duncan McMillan who volunteers to try to bring solace to Clyde during his last days. It is during his long conversation with

McMillan that Clyde gains some insight into his deepest mo-
tivations and learns that beneath his shabby protest of innocence lies a hard core of guilt. True, he did not murder
Roberta, but he did wish her dead. And worse, his sorrow
since has been less for her death than for the loss of his dream.
Clyde never achieves a clear understanding of himself. He
is never able to get the whole thing straightened out in his
own mind.

Clyde goes to his death urging all young men to lead good
Christian lives, but a hesitant, skeptical note jars the sentimental harmony of his appeal. A like note of bitterness pervades the closing scene as the Griffiths family gathers once
more to sing hymns in the street. The youngest among them
—Esta's illegitimate son—begs to be allowed a dime for ice
cream—and the terrible cycle seems about to begin anew.

Critical Opinion

Dreiser's *An American Tragedy* is not a tragedy in the conventional sense. Although Clyde is ambitious, his ambition
lacks the comprehensive force and energy to make it a "tragic
flaw" in the same sense as, for example, Macbeth's ambition.
Furthermore, Clyde lacks the tragic hero's nobility of mind
and strength of will. Though he enlists sympathy, Clyde fails
to win respect, for he is both weak and shallow. Nevertheless,
most readers will share F. O. Matthiessen's judgment that in
An American Tragedy, Dreiser has "written out of a profoundly tragic sense of man's fate."

That fate, as Dreiser expresses it, involves not only Clyde
Griffiths but also the nation whose youth he represents. The
sources of Clyde's failure are many, but chief among them is
the fatal illusion of success through wealth. Blinded to more
substantial values, Clyde sacrifices his single real possession—
personal identity—to the god of money. Nothing in his society encourages or recognizes anything more worthwhile than
the pursuit of material gain. The family unit collapses; religion
fails because of its narrow extremism; and even the law, during the trial, perverts truth. Nor are there among Clyde's peers
any who offer him a better way of life. They seem incapable
of love. They sink into a nameless ooze of impersonality, "ab-

sorbed," as Robert Penn Warren has observed, "by the great
machine of modern industrial secularized society." The tragedy
thus extends beyond the failure of the hero. It is the social
and moral tragedy of an age, a people, and a nation—an
American tragedy.

Dreiser's novel is bulky and at times tedious. Especially in
the account of the crime and the trial (which he took from
newspaper stories of an actual murder), Dreiser piles up
indigestible chunks of data and dialogue. Despite this, the
reader finds himself propelled by the novelist's intensity and
dramatic urgency. Dreiser possesses "a Balzacian grip on the
machinery of money and power," and as he moves in on a
scene or withdraws to survey it, he sweeps the reader along
with him. Action and imagery catapult the reader along with
Clyde toward the abyss lying beneath a world of shattered
illusions and false dreams.

The Author

As a child in Terre Haute, Indiana, *Theodore Dreiser* knew
almost daily hunger and poverty. Once he was even sent home
from school because he had no shoes. The roots of Dreiser's
passion for material success grew out of this arid soil. At sixteen, after the family had broken up several times, Dreiser
set out for Chicago alone, hoping to discover a career for
himself. It was a false start, for although he was, like Sister
Carrie, fascinated by the metropolis, he could find only a
succession of menial jobs.

After a year back in Indiana at the university, Dreiser
ventured once more toward the city, this time to try his luck
at journalism. For the next twenty years he worked at various
journalistic tasks—from reporting to editorial work—in the
Midwest and in New York. In 1898, shortly after he had begun work as a reporter, he married a woman he did not love,
and for the next forty years she refused him the divorce he
pleaded for. Not until her death in 1942 could Dreiser marry
the woman he had really loved during this period.

The publication of *Sister Carrie*, his first novel, in 1900,
did little to buoy Dreiser's hopes or fortunes. Because the
publisher's wife was shocked by Dreiser's portrait of an Ameri-

can girl, she persuaded her husband not to distribute the novel. For nearly a dozen years, the novel went without an American reading public. Not until he had achieved a national reputation as the editor of the famous Butterick fashion magazines did Dreiser gain an audience for his novel. By that time, however, he had survived his misfortunes and had achieved the wealth and fame he had yearned for since boyhood.

Beginning in 1911, Dreiser wrote four novels in as many years: *Jennie Gerhardt, The Financier, The Titan,* and *The Genius.* These, too, encountered resistance from publishers and self-appointed censors, but Dreiser, aided by distinguished critics like H. L. Mencken, fought the oppressive forces. Disgusted with the narrowness of the society of his time, he published only one more novel during the remaining thirty years of his life. That one, however, was his masterpiece, *An American Tragedy* (1925). Two of his novels were published posthumously.

At the height of his fame in the twenties, Dreiser dressed like a dandy, affecting a cane and leading a Russian wolfhound on a leash. He praised American rugged individualism and attacked the Soviet system after he returned from a trip to Russia. But during the 1930s, Dreiser grew increasingly disenchanted with American capitalism and began to support left-wing causes. In his social and political essays ("Tragic America"), he attacked the inequities created by the same individualism he had supported all his life. Just before his death, Dreiser joined the Communist Party, apparently convinced that the hope for economic and spiritual salvation no longer could be left to the will of the individual. His dream of material success turned at last into a nightmare.

Babbitt

by

SINCLAIR LEWIS (1885–1951)

Main Characters

George F. Babbitt—Prototype of the American bourgeois in
his comfortable mid-forties, solidly anchored to the standardized virtues of work, duty, and morality—yet somehow
restless, with a romantic urge to rebel.

Myra Babbitt—Babbitt's wife, "as sexless as an anemic nun,"
bursting with maternal instincts toward her husband as
well as toward her three children.

Verona, Ted, and *Tinka Babbitt*—Babbitt's brood. Verona,
twenty-two, a recent Bryn Mawr graduate dedicated to advanced notions about literature, sex, and social reform;
Ted (christened Theodore Roosevelt), a teen-age fraternity
man dedicated to the advance of school spirit and the re-
tardation of intellectual growth; Tinka, at ten, dedicated to
ice-cream sodas and candy.

Paul Riesling—Babbitt's best friend and alter ego. A would-
be artist (violinist), crushed by the twin molds of business
and marriage, Paul rebels, briefly but violently.

Tanis Judique—A widow, lonely, attractive, and liberated,
who helps Babbitt strip away a few layers of his hidebound
conventionality.

Vergil Gunch, Chum Frink, Orville Jones—Luminaries of the
Zenith Athletic Club and the Boosters' Club, outstanding

examples of what Lewis calls the "Standardized American Citizen."

Charles and *Lucille McKelvey*—Members of the aristocratic Union Club, a niche above and forever beyond the reach of the Boosters. McKelvey owns a construction company. His wife has elevated notions about art. Neither suffers from moral scruples.

Sir Gerald Doak—A visiting businessman, the British equivalent of Babbitt.

Seneca Doane—The radical idealist, a lawyer who challenges Zenith reactionaries but wins few adherents.

The Story

Just beyond the urban limits of Zenith (a thriving Midwestern metropolis of nearly a half-million people) lies Floral Heights, the home of George Follansbee Babbitt. Like the streets and skyscrapers of Zenith, the houses of Floral Heights are smugly the same, utterly devoid of individuality. To Babbitt, however, his house (in no sense a home) symbolizes the world of progress. His possessions—porcelain bathtub, fancy alarm clock, electric fan, percolator, toaster, and most sublime, his automobile—attest to his elevated status in Zenith.

To achieve his place as a solid citizen of Zenith (including membership in the Athletic Club and the Boosters' Club), Babbitt has worked diligently and aggressively as a real estate salesman, raised a reputable if undistinguished brood, and espoused the right causes. Whether in politics, art, or education, Babbitt detests socialists, foreigners, and reformers. (To be one of these, he feels, is probably to be the others as well.) Babbitt supports efficiency and laissez-faire, a "business Administration" like Warren G. Harding's. He favors but does not observe Prohibition, believes in the sanctity of marriage but yearns after his secretary. In brief, when forty-six-year-old George F. Babbitt wakes early one morning in April, 1920, his pink and pudgy countenance expresses the zesty energy, uncritical optimism, and innocent hypocrisy of the typical American bourgeois.

But a rebellious scowl lurks behind Babbitt's serene mask, a rejection of domesticity and a doubt about the worth of ma-

terial success. Outwardly, Babbitt observes the forms. He
urges his reluctant son toward college, nags his daughter toward social conformity, invites the snobbish McKelveys to dinner in a vain attempt to climb the social ladder, and ingratiates
himself sufficiently with his peers to win a vice-presidency in
the Boosters' Club. The seed of discontent, nevertheless, bur-
geons; rebellion threatens to sprout. The catalyst, strangely, is
Paul Riesling, Babbitt's college classmate and closest friend.

Once an aspiring concert violinist, Paul has descended to
selling tar roofing during the day and battling nightly with his
wife, Zilla, who despises but will not divorce or desert him. A
kind of mirror-image of Babbitt, Paul reflects an extreme form
of Babbitt's own marital dissatisfaction. Moreover, Paul's
refuge from the horror of his marriage—the clandestine love
affair—rouses Babbitt's latent passions. From the outset of the
novel, Babbitt has cherished a recurrent dream of a lovely
girl, a "fairy child" who will love him gently and deeply.

Babbitt's revolt begins simply. He turns on Zilla sharply
and denounces her for nagging Paul. To his own wife, Myra,
he says he is "sick of everybody and everything" and wants to
be left alone for a while. Shocked by his own audacity and
by the readiness with which Zilla and Myra yield to him,
Babbitt feels reduced to "primitive terror . . . wondering what
he could do with anything so unknown and so embarrassing
as freedom." What he does with his new freedom is merely to
go off with Paul for a joyous week of fishing and talk before
their wives join them.

His rebelliousness momentarily quenched, Babbitt bows
once more to middle-class convention. But when, during a trip
to Chicago, he encounters Paul with one of his mistresses,
Babbitt again grows restive. Two unexpected events convince
him he must make "a terrifying, thrilling break with everything that was decent and normal." Paul shoots Zilla and is
sentenced to three years in jail. Myra goes East for a visit,
leaving Babbitt entirely alone. Isolated, deprived of his alter
ego, Babbitt must face himself. The confrontation convinces
him that "perhaps all life as he knew it and vigorously practiced it was futile." When he wakes the next morning, Babbitt
is a conscious rebel.

At a party a few nights later, he makes his first ineffectual
pass at a neighbor's wife. Some days later he takes a young

manicurist to dinner and makes a fumbling, unsuccessful attempt to seduce her. With Tanis Judique, a widow approaching middle age, Babbitt at last discovers his "fairy child" in the flesh. Lonely and compassionate, Tanis brings to Babbitt an interlude of fulfillment. Even after Myra returns, he finds reasons to stay away from home to be with Tanis alone or with her bohemian friends. Boldly, Babbitt dares to dine with Tanis publicly within the sight of shocked Boosters.

Babbitt's revolt assumes a socio-political guise as well when he supports the town radical, Seneca Doane, during a workers' strike. To his fellow Boosters, Babbitt seems increasingly a "crank," and they apply intense pressure upon him to return to the fold. In fact, Babbitt has already found freedom most uncomfortable, but is too proud to yield to social pressure. Gallantly, Tanis releases him from his sexual adventure and returns him to his marital bondage. His friends, however, lack her delicacy and press him to acknowledge the social and political rightness of conventional thinking. Ironically, Myra's sudden illness provides the avenue for Babbitt's escape back to the "paralyzed contentment of middle age." As his old friends rally to his side during his siege of worry about Myra, Babbitt swears renewed allegiance "to his wife . . . to Zenith . . . to business efficiency . . . to the Boosters' Club . . . to every faith of the Clan of Good Fellows." To prove himself a worthy prodigal, Babbitt now campaigns vigorously against Doane.

Outwardly, the ending is happy. Myra recovers. The children marry. Business is booming. Inwardly, Babbitt keenly feels a sense of loss. To his son Ted, who has left college to marry the girl next door, Babbitt confides: "I've never done a single thing I've wanted to do in my whole life. . . . But I do get a kind of sneaking pleasure out of the fact that you knew what you wanted to do and did it." Perhaps, Babbitt tacitly suggests, another generation may discover a way to crash the barrier of "sound citizenship."

Critical Opinion

E. M. Forster, the distinguished British novelist and critic, once wrote about Sinclair Lewis that he was neither poet nor preacher, "but a fellow with a camera a few yards away." The candid photography in *Babbitt* captures unforgettably the banal and the absurd in Midwestern American life: the Babbitts' living room and the main street in Zenith; the boys at the club and the Babbitts at breakfast—all enlargements of false heartiness and empty-souled optimism. At the center of the group stands the man whose name has become an American byword for the essentially decent fellow who believes so deeply and uncritically in the values of his society that he forgets his own individuality.

The weakness of Lewis' novel lies in Babbitt's achieving a dimension beyond our expectation by undertaking to rebel. No one would have expected Vergil Gunch or Chum Frink to rebel, or George Babbitt either. Because he does, the reader may become confused. Is Lewis satirizing Babbitt as a conformist or as a rebel? Is he satirizing him as both? Or is he sympathizing with him as both? Most critics believe that Lewis never truly resolved his attitude toward Babbitt—that he simultaneously admired and despised Babbitt's bourgeois soul, approved and censured his brief revolt. That such indecision affected Lewis is not difficult to understand, for in many ways Babbitt and his creator are one and the same—a combination of philistine and rebel.

Babbitt does not, as H. L. Mencken claims, represent all there is to tell about the real America. Rather it shows us what Lewis' biographer, Mark Schorer, significantly describes as a half-truth. Lewis' vision is narrow, his emotion shallow. He shows us that we are spiritually sterile and to some extent even suggests why. What *Babbitt* achieves is a shrewd criticism of the surface of American experience, but the depths remain unplumbed.

Arrowsmith

by

SINCLAIR LEWIS

Main Characters

Martin Arrowsmith—The protagonist, a young medical researcher, torn between commitment to his ideal—the lonely path of pure science—and the worldly goal of science for profit.

Leora Tozer—Martin's wife, unsophisticated, utterly feminine, forthright and unaffected, warm and unswervingly loyal.

Dr. Max Gottlieb—Martin's scientific mentor and idol. A refugee German-Jew, he is shy, austere, dedicated, an "authentic scientist" and a decent human being.

Dr. Gustaf Sondelius—Another of Arrowsmith's heroes, a crusty but kindly Swede, a pioneer in battling disease epidemics and an indefatigable fund raiser.

Terry Wickett—Arrowsmith's closest friend, an uncomplicated man and a doggedly honest research worker.

Almus Pickerbaugh—The Babbitt of the medical world. Director of Public Health in Nautilus, Iowa, later U.S. Congressman, a preposterous but exuberant booster of good health and good business for wholesome, respectable Americans.

Ross McGurk—Millionaire founder of the McGurk Institute for Medical Research, unscrupulous in business but absolutely pure in his support of science and of Dr. Gottlieb.

Capitola McGurk—His wife, "a complete controller of virtuous affairs," including insufferable dinner parties, a dispenser of "cooing staleness."

Dr. A. DeWitt Tubbs—Director of the McGurk Institute when Arrowsmith arrives there, a man of little scientific knowledge but of considerable talent for high-level medical politics.

Dr. Rippleton Holabird—Head of the department of physi-

ology at McGurk, a youthful, charming, tweedy protégé of
Dr. Tubbs, destined for mediocrity and success.
Madeline Fox, Orchid Pickerbaugh, Joyce Lanyon—The
other women in Arrowsmith's life. Their roles, respectively:
Martin's college girlfriend; his first post-marital flirtation
("She's no orchid," Leora observes, "she's a bachelor's but-
ton"); Martin's second wife. All are more attractive physically than Leora, but also more superficial, less understanding.

The Story

From early adolescence, Martin Arrowsmith worships science and those who pursue its truths. As a fourteen-year-old,
he idolizes and is inspired by Doc Vickerson, a brilliant, alcoholic village physician. Seven years later, as a medical student
at the University of Winnemac, Zenith's proud education factory (its students are "beautifully standardized, with perfectly
interchangeable parts"), Martin discovers a new idol, Dr. Max
Gottlieb, a crotchety genius and professor of bacteriology and
immunology. Gottlieb's implacable insistence upon patience
and skepticism as the only paths to scientific truth challenges
Arrowsmith's youthful arrogance and agonized sense of in-
feriority. Doggedly he struggles to rise to Gottlieb's demands,
sloughing off the many temptations of the "men of measured
merriment"—the facile, graceful, empty-headed and hollow-
souled seekers after easy success. To win from Gottlieb an encouraging smile spurs Martin to renewed and enthusiastic
effort.

During his junior year, when he is Gottlieb's assistant, Martin becomes entangled with two fiancées: Madeline Fox, a glib
graduate student in English, and Leora Tozer, an unsophisticated student nurse. Absurdly he brings them together, hoping they will understand his plight. Madeline does not and
stalks off, leaving Martin to Leora, who accepts her triumph
with unaffected delight. Their marriage plans are temporarily
postponed when family illness compels Leora to return to her
home in Wheatsylvania. Lonely and irritable, Martin grows
careless at his work, defies Gottlieb and the dean, and is fired.
In anger and despair he turns for a time to the road, drifting

and drinking, but before he hits bottom, he flees to Leora. Despite the opposition of her limited and provincial family, they marry.

Determined now to earn a living, Martin returns to the university, apologizes to the dean (but not to Gottlieb), and works to complete his medical degree. Though he yearns above all to work with Gottlieb, he is too proud to apologize, and rationalizes about the superiority of his country medical practice in Leora's hometown in North Dakota. His year there proves frustrating and infuriating. Neither his patients nor his fellow-practitioners respect truth, preferring epidemics to preventive injections. The only significant event all year is his meeting with a visiting lecturer, Gustaf Sondelius, a famous epidemiologist, who reawakens Martin's dormant love for research. At the end of the year, encouraged by Leora, Martin writes to Sondelius, and, with his help, wins a post as an assistant director of public health in Nautilus, Iowa, a small-scale Zenith.

Martin's superior, Dr. Almus Pickerbaugh, is a "man of measured merriment." He never talks. ("He either bubbled or made orations.") Though he thwarts Martin's attempts to establish citywide pasteurization or the elimination of tenements where tuberculosis is breeding, Pickerbaugh does initiate several projects of his own, such as "Swat the Fly Week" and an "Open Your Window Parade." His "Eugenics Week" narrowly escapes disaster when members of the "model" family turn out to be epileptic, illegitimate, and wanted by the police. For a time Martin tries to fight Pickerbaugh, but at last he succumbs and learns how he too may smile with measured merriment. Part of the reason for his surrender may be his infatuation with Pickerbaugh's night-blooming nineteen-year-old daughter, Orchid. Pickerbaugh's election to Congress (his platform: "Just elect him for a term and all through the nation he'll swat the germ") solves the problem of Orchid but catapults Martin into a new challenge by making him the director of public health.

Martin meets the challenge honestly and energetically. He undertakes research once more and writes and delivers a learned paper. But whenever his plans endanger business, the politicians and churchmen of Nautilus block his efforts to improve public health. At last they force his resignation. Beaten

and dismayed, Martin accepts a routine testing assignment at a clinic in Chicago. His idealism seems atrophied, his
hopes diminished. Only his relationship with Leora thrives.
Out of the gloom and chaos, however, comes an invitation
from Gottlieb (who has read Martin's recently published paper) to join him at the distinguished McGurk Institute of Research in New York.

Gottlieb himself has experienced reverses. An impassioned
but tactless appeal to the administration at Winnemac in behalf of a research institute lost Gottlieb his post. A drug company hired him, but he left when they tried to commercialize
a vaccine he had discovered but not yet fully tested. Family
problems have also beset the old man: his wife died and his son
turned wastrel. But the offer from McGurk brought Gottlieb
economic and scientific security, both of which he now eagerly
offers to share with the protégé he has always most admired
and loved.

From the moment of his arrival at McGurk (nearly two-
thirds of the way through the novel), Martin is the kind of man
he always wanted to be. "I've found my work, I've found my
work," he exults, forgetting even to ask about his salary. For
months—serenely oblivious of the cliques and factions seething about him—he works feverishly on an experiment that
promises to prove revolutionary: the discovery of a virus that
destroys other viruses. When word of his progress leaks to Dr.
Tubbs, the director, Martin is pressured to publish his findings
before he has administered all the tests Gottlieb has urged him
to employ. Choosing integrity rather than fame, he plods on
with his work, only to have a scientist in France publish a
paper anticipating his findings.

Deflated but undismayed, Martin turns next to testing his
"phage" (as he calls the anti-bacterial serum) as a possible
weapon against specific disease. Now, because Gottlieb assumes the directorship of the Institute (Tubbs, a man of
measured merriment, goes on to a more glamorous post), Sondelius, Martin's idol of earlier years, arrives to become his
noisy but dedicated co-worker. Together they study the startlingly destructive effect of phage upon the bacilli of bubonic
plague.

The outbreak of plague on the island of St. Hubert in the
British West Indies provides the occasion for a large-scale test

of Martin's vaccine. Martin agrees to test the serum provided that rigid experimental conditions are observed: only half of the natives will be inoculated; the others, as controls, will receive no protective inoculation. Sondelius objects to these terms on humane grounds, but agrees to go along on the expedition to exterminate rats, one of his specialties. What he categorically refuses is to allow himself to be inoculated against plague until Martin promises to drop his system of controls. One last problem remains before the expedition leaves: What to do about Leora? She solves the difficulty swiftly and efficiently; she will go wherever Martin goes.

On the island of St. Hubert, bureaucracy rages as devastatingly as the plague. Once the reluctant governor admits the reality of the situation, he must fight all those who want tourist and export "business as usual." By cajolery and sheer lung power, Sondelius wins the right to exterminate rats. Martin, however, encounters stiffer opposition when he demands the right to inoculate only half the population. "I'm not a sentimentalist; I'm a scientist," he argues, and gets his way. Aided by a local native physician, he administers the serum and keeps meticulous account of the results, turning aside all pleas of those who must die because of his determination to be scientifically accurate. He withstands even the shock of Sondelius's death. But when Leora dies as a result of a careless infection through a cigarette, Martin's courage fails, and he inoculates everyone. Acclaimed as the hero of the island, he regards himself as a failure.

Back in New York, Martin is shocked and saddened to find Gottlieb lost in the shadowy mists of senile dementia. The man whose censure Martin most dreaded cannot even recognize him. Alone now, except for Terry Wickett, Martin plunges into research with an ardor that would have cheered Gottlieb. Almost whole again, Martin encounters another temptation: Joyce Lanyon, a wealthy, beautiful, socially important widow he meets at St. Hubert. Martin cannot resist Joyce, and for a year their marriage seems a possible way for him to survive the loss of Leora. Joyce gives Martin a son, but in return she takes from him his independence and individuality. His work suffers. He rebels, leaves her, and goes off to the Vermont hills to continue his research. With Terry Wickett as his only companion, Martin rededicates himself to the ardors

and rewards of pure research, freed at last from men and the
women of measured merriment.

Critical Opinion

Arrowsmith, some critics agree, is Sinclair Lewis' best novel.
A long novel, it lacks the concentration *Babbitt* achieves by
focusing upon a single region of the Midwest. In *Arrowsmith*,
Lewis hunts quarry that lurk in no single lair, for Zenith does
not contain all of the evils that beset the dedicated scientist.
The entire nation, as Lewis shows, abounds in commercialism,
quackery, political chicanery, social snobbism. Universities,
medical schools, hospitals, all tempt young idealists to abandon honesty in exchange for money or fame. Lewis lances his
prey with septic wit and irony. The Pickerbaughs and the
Tubbs, Holabirds and Capitola McGurks have all been inoculated against sincerity and idealism, but they are no match for
Lewis' satire.

The novel is not, however, merely a broadside attack. Nor
does it suffer from the ambivalence in attitude that under-
mines *Babbitt*. Martin Arrowsmith, like Babbitt, is drawn to
material success, but Martin "succumbs to his own integrity"
and forces himself to continue his struggle. In his delineation
of Martin, Lewis etches not only the true scientist's passionate
devotion to research, but also the growth of a gifted man with
very human weaknesses. Many people contribute to Martin's
development, none, of course, more selflessly than Leora, one
of the most luminous creations in American fiction. Through
Leora's death, Martin learns to face reality on his own. Until
her death, she had always been beside him at critical moments
to share his burdens. Similarly, Max Gottlieb, high priest
among Arrowsmith's demigods, must leave his protégé to find
his own way. The scientist, like all men, must learn that his
path is lonely.

Only occasionally does the novel falter. Sometimes, for example, Lewis digresses too long in his denunciation of social
villains; the plot calls him back long before he is ready to return. Sometimes, too, the butts of his ridicule lack dimension
and credibility.

Another weakness of Lewis' grows, ironically, from a source

of his strength. For his almost Zolaesque accuracy in scientific detail, Lewis turned to Dr. Paul de Kruif, the famous author of *Microbe Hunters*. What de Kruif provides is, of course, valid information, and for the most part it creates the suspense of research. But insistence upon rigid controls during the epidemic results almost in a caricature of the "inhumane" scientist. Such incidental failures do not really diminish the stature of the novel. It has, as Lewis Mumford has rightly observed, "that additional quality which belongs only to the higher levels of literature, the sense of facing the issues of life and death, and creating, in the very face of defeat, an inner assurance."

The Author

Sinclair Lewis was born in Sauk Center, Minnesota, the son of a country doctor and a consumptive mother who died when he was six. Tall and spindling, ugly, his face ravaged by acne, Lewis led a lonely, introverted youth. At Yale he refused to fit into conventional molds, tramping off one summer to Panama, another to Upton Sinclair's socialist community, Helicon Hall. He seemed alternately to burst with coarse, inexhaustible energy, and to withdraw into agonized moodiness. The cycle was to persist throughout his life.

After his graduation from Yale (1908), Lewis worked for several years variously as reporter, editor, advertising manager, and even as an idea man, selling plots for novels to Jack London and Albert Payson Terhune. His first novel, *Our Mr. Wrenn* (1914), won him enough praise to convince him that his future lay in fiction. Just married, he pressed on to write more fiction, but success and fame did not come until 1920. With *Main Street*, Lewis exploded upon the literary scene. His satirical account of Carol Kennicott's revolt against Gopher Prairie, the universal small town, brought him almost unanimous acclaim, abroad as well as at home. Within the next five years, Lewis added two more figures to his chronicle of the American middle class caught in the stultifying net of conformity: the protagonist of *Babbitt* (1922) and *Arrowsmith* (1925).

These three works rank as Lewis' finest. His later work— nearly a dozen novels, all financially successful—deteriorated in quality, though it never lost its vigor. Descending sometimes to caricature, sometimes to sentimentality, occasionally to both, Lewis nevertheless created memorable characters like Elmer Gantry, the rapacious preacher, and Sam Dodsworth, the henpecked automobile manufacturer. But Lewis himself became trapped by the success myth he had satirized and found it difficult at last to detach himself from the values of Gopher Prairie.

Outward success—the Nobel Prize, travel, marriage to famous journalist Dorothy Thompson, wealth—all these seemed increasingly empty as the years passed. Lewis' second marriage failed, his drinking got out of control, his friendships disintegrated. What remained was the early conflict between his enormous zest for life and his inward despair. Unfortunately, his fiction reflects little of the torment he felt when, shortly before he died, he said, "Oh God, no man has ever been so miserable." Ironically, Lewis' life, even more than his fiction, testified to the cruel gap between happiness and material success.

The Great Gatsby

by

F. SCOTT FITZGERALD (1896–1940)

Main Characters

Nick Carraway—The critical but compassionate narrator.

Jay Gatsby—Born James Gatz, he is the tragic hero who, para-doxically, is also a bootlegger and peddler of phony stocks. Reckless and romantic, he suggests the emptiness of the American success myth.

Daisy Buchanan—Nick's cousin. Once about to marry Gatsby, now wed to Tom Buchanan, she is lovely, exciting, and shallow. But for Gatsby she represents the fulfillment of his false dreams.

Tom Buchanan—Handsome, wealthy, and athletic, but also in-sensitive to the point of stupidity and cruelty.

Jordan Baker—Friend of Daisy and occasional girl friend of Nick; petulant, spoiled, and an incorrigible liar.

Myrtle Wilson—Tom's mistress. Wife of a garage owner, she is attractive, tasteless, and dismally vulgar.

George Wilson—Myrtle's browbeaten husband. Devoid of will and purpose, he becomes, ironically, the agent of the tragic climax.

The Story

The year is 1922, the setting Long Island, New York. At West Egg live Jay Gatsby and his neighbor, the narrator Nick

Carraway; Gatsby in a staggeringly elegant mansion, Nick in a small cramped cottage. Across the Sound in more fashionable East Egg live Daisy and Tom Buchanan. Midway between West Egg and New York City lies a vast ash dump near which are the garage and home of George and Myrtle Wilson. Significantly, all of the characters pass through this "valley of ashes," symbol of the barren spiritual wasteland they inhabit. It is here, too, that the terrible climax of the novel occurs. Upon this bleak setting stare the sightless blue eyes of Dr. T. J. Eckleburg—a grotesque billboard advertisement placed in the ash dump by an oculist. These blank eyes mirror unfeelingly the tragic events that pass before them.

After serving in World War I and getting an education at Yale, Nick begins work as a bond salesman. Settled in West Egg, he renews his acquaintance with his cousin Daisy and her husband Tom. From Daisy's friend, Jordan Baker, Nick learns that Tom is unfaithful and that Daisy is agonizingly aware of his infidelity. Tom boldly insists that Nick meet his mistress, Myrtle Wilson. Reluctantly, Nick joins Tom and Myrtle for a noisy party at their private New York apartment. The climax of the party occurs when Tom breaks Myrtle's nose for daring to mention Daisy's name.

Caught up in the bitterness of the Buchanans' turmoil, Nick finds himself almost immediately trapped as well in Gatsby's turbulent life. Gatsby's is a lavish world of weekend parties attended by guests who rarely meet their host, yet speculate freely upon the shady sources of his wealth. Gatsby's showy parties fail to satisfy his central, all-consuming passion—to reclaim Daisy whom he won and then lost while he was abroad during the war. To this purpose he enlists the aid of both Jordan and Nick who both know Daisy. A meeting is arranged at Nick's and soon Daisy is again Gatsby's mistress. For a short time Gatsby and Daisy share a happiness neither has known since their first encounter.

Gatsby's innocent assumption that he can sustain this idyl is short-lived. Reality intrudes as both Tom Buchanan and George Wilson discover almost simultaneously that their wives are unfaithful. Though Wilson has learned of Myrtle's trespasses, he does not know that Tom has deceived him. To Wilson, Tom is merely a customer at the garage and a potential source of used cars. Tom, however, suffers the "hot whips of panic" as he confronts the possible loss of a wife and a mistress. In a suffocatingly hot hotel room in New York, Gatsby demands—in the presence of Tom, Daisy, Nick, and Jordan— that Daisy leave her husband and admit that she has never loved him. Willing to acknowledge that she loves Gatsby and that she no longer loves Tom, Daisy cannot say that she has never loved her husband. Tom uses this wedge to expose and denounce Gatsby as an underworld creature. Daisy's silence before Tom's attack and her refusal to deny having loved Tom shatter Gatsby and wreck his illusions.

Earlier, when the five set out for New York, Tom's jealousy rages, inflamed by Daisy's insisting upon riding with Gatsby in the Buchanans' car while Tom and the others follow in Gatsby's. Now, triumphant and scornful, Tom encourages Gatsby to use his own car to drive Daisy back to West Egg. They leave together. Catastrophe awaits them on the road.

Beaten by her husband and locked in her room, Myrtle Wilson forces her way out and dashes into the road. Seeking refuge, she encounters violent death under the wheels of Gatsby's car which careens on without stopping. Soon after, Tom, Nick, and Jordan arrive at the now crowded garage where Tom discovers his mistress dead, her husband distraught. Tom's whispered words to Wilson (unreported until the closing pages of the novel) provoke a swift and terrible climax. First, however, Nick learns from Gatsby that Daisy, not he, drove the car that killed Myrtle. Gatsby announces his intention to assume all responsibility for Daisy's action. He never gets the chance. As he leaves Gatsby, Nick shouts to him across the lawn: "They're a rotten crowd. You're worth the whole damn bunch put together." The compliment wins from Gatsby a radiant smile—his last. A few hours later he is dead of a gun wound inflicted by George Wilson who then takes his own life.

Only Gatsby's aged father and a few servants join Nick at Gatsby's funeral. No other friends or former guests attend, despite Nick's earnest pleas. And Daisy and Tom have already left on a trip. Several months later Nick meets Tom and forces him to admit the truth: that he told Wilson that Gatsby was driving the death car. Obviously Daisy has never contradicted the lie. Furious, then compassionate, Nick realizes that it was "all very careless and confused. They were careless people,

Tom and Daisy—they smashed up things and creatures and
then retreated back into their money or their vast carelessness,
or whatever it was that kept them together, and let other people clean up the mess they had made. . . ."

Soon after, Nick breaks off his relationship with Jordan, conscious that she resembles Daisy too closely to share a vital
human relationship. His last gesture, however, reaches beyond
denial to awareness. Returning for a last look at Gatsby's mansion, Nick stands at the shore and recalls that centuries earlier
Dutch sailors had looked upon this island, their eyes and hearts
filled with illusions that prepared the way for Gatsby's hopeless dream, a dream whose doom had already been foretold
long ago.

Critical Opinion

The Great Gatsby was published in April, 1925, enjoyed enthusiastic reviews, and won Fitzgerald warm praise from writers he deeply admired. T. S. Eliot, for example, wrote Fitzgerald that *Gatsby* "has interested and excited me more than
any new novel I have seen, either English or American, for a
number of years . . . it seems to me to be the first step that
American fiction has taken since Henry James. . . ." But sales
failed to match critical acclaim. From a disappointingly modest beginning, *The Great Gatsby* reached fewer and fewer
readers until, by 1937, Fitzgerald reported that he could not
find a bookstore that stocked even a single copy. Today, nearly forty years after its initial publication, *Gatsby* sells about
50,000 copies a year, more than twice its original sale.

What has assured *Gatsby* its command of a larger audience
is a clearer understanding of Fitzgerald's achievement. *Gatsby*
is not—as many earlier critics wrongly assumed—an uncritical
study of manners during the Jazz Age. It is a penetrating
analysis of the failure of the Jazz Age to produce significant
or lasting values. Despite his personal ambivalence toward
wealth, Fitzgerald achieved in *Gatsby* enough detachment to
expose the disease corrupting the social and moral fiber of the
American spirit. That disease lay deep in the distorted imagination of Jay Gatsby. Duped by the dream of material success, Gatsby succumbed to warped fantasies, equating present

with past and love with wealth. Gatsby symbolizes America enslaved, as Fitzgerald writes, in "the service of a vast, vulgar, and meretricious beauty." In Gatsby's pitiable disillusion and defeat, Fitzgerald illustrates the fever that burns away the spiritual strength of so many Americans.

Although it attacks conventional values, *Gatsby* opens rather than shuts the door to change. Nick's growing awareness of the Buchanans' destructiveness and Gatsby's blindness offers hope. As the novel ends, Nick achieves maturity: he stands free of illusion yet capable of compassion. He can never become a Jay Gatsby or, far worse, a Tom or Daisy Buchanan. If then, as one critic has observed, *The Great Gatsby* dramatizes "the withering of the American dream," it offers also a more substantial alternative to it.

A brief note on the craft of Fitzgerald's finest novel: neither plot nor characterization is outstanding; elements of melodrama mar the narrative, and the characters are too foreshortened to possess depth. Nevertheless, Fitzgerald uses his selective technique creatively. From Joseph Conrad and Henry James he learned to employ an outside observer (Nick) to vivify portraiture and to create suspense. But above all, *Gatsby* is a triumph of mood and tone. Character, symbol, and image blend uniformly to produce a quality of lyric sadness that pervades the whole work. For its moral criticism and technical artistry, then, *The Great Gatsby* emerges, as Malcolm Cowley has observed, as "a fable of the 1920s that will survive as a legend for other times."

The Author

Great-grandnephew of Francis Scott Key, *F. Scott Fitzgerald* was born in St. Paul, Minnesota, to Catholic parents of Irish and Maryland-English stock. After completing a parochial education with indifferent success, Fitzgerald entered Princeton (1913), where his grades continued to suffer as he pursued extracurricular rather than academic interests, writing plays for the Triangle Club and poems and stories for the college literary magazines. A timely illness followed by enlistment in the Army saved him from failing out of college, but Fitzgerald's love for Princeton lasted throughout his life.

As a second lieutenant, Fitzgerald never served abroad, spending most of his time at training camps. With ample leisure but small funds at his disposal, he wrote his first novel and courted Zelda Sayre, the woman who proved one of the most powerful influences in his life. Not until his novel, *This Side of Paradise*, was published in 1920 did Zelda consent to marry her no longer impoverished suitor. *This Side of Paradise* established Fitzgerald as the voice of the Jazz Age and brought him, at the age of twenty-four, the wealth and fame he hungered after. For several years he and Zelda lived abroad, chiefly in Paris and on the French Riviera, luxuriously, extravagantly, and always hopelessly beyond their means. Many of his short stories were potboilers written to meet expenses. Some of them, however ("The Diamond as Big as the Ritz" and "Babylon Revisited"), rank with the finest short fiction of the century and compare favorably with his best novels.

From 1927 on, Zelda's mental health deteriorated and Fitzgerald's drinking habits worsened. By the mid-thirties he had become an alcoholic. His productivity had diminished, his debts had risen, and his reputation had faded. The final years, dramatically recorded in *The Crack Up* (1945), testify to Fitzgerald's courage as well as to his despair. With Zelda institutionalized (she died in a fire a few years after Fitzgerald's death), he struggled to support their daughter, Scottie, by writing scripts for Hollywood. But the machine had worn down. At the age of forty-four Fitzgerald died in Los Angeles of a heart attack. In his last incomplete novel, *The Last Tycoon*, Fitzgerald reveals that despite many failures, he retained both the integrity and the penetrating vision of a true artist.

The Sun Also Rises

by

ERNEST HEMINGWAY (1899–1961)

Main Characters

Jake Barnes—The hero, a journalist, made impotent by a war wound, in love with the beautiful, promiscuous Brett Ashley. A defensive cynicism, drinking, the outdoor life, and friendship help him live with his inner torment.

Brett Ashley—A cultivated Englishwoman, in love with Jake, but compulsively involved in a series of sterile love affairs.

Robert Cohn—A novelist and a doggedly persistent, briefly successful suitor of Brett, once a boxer and intellectual at Princeton, now a brooding moralist (despite his mistresses), and as a Jew, a defensive outsider in Brett's coterie.

Bill Gorton—Jake's friend, fellow journalist, and confidant, good-natured, tolerant, and humorous.

Mike Campbell—Brett's fiancé after her divorce from Lord Ashley, a heavy drinker and an economic and spiritual bankrupt infected with a vengeful anti-Semitism.

Pedro Romero—A young bullfighter in love with Brett. A brave and honorable matador, he narrowly escapes corruption of the traditions he most values.

Montoya—Proprietor of the Pamplona hotel where Jake and the others stay during the fiesta, a true *aficionado* of the traditions and tragic grandeur of the bullfight.

Count Mippipopolous—Worldly, wealthy friend and would-be lover of Brett. A veteran of seven wars and four revolutions, he believes in nothing but love.

The Story

Paris after World War I is the scene of the first of three sections of the novel, each narrated from the point of view of Jake Barnes. Despite a minimum of action, the opening section communicates the disillusion and discontinuity pervading the lives of a group of American and British expatriates who drift from bar to bedroom.

Jake and Robert Cohn represent irreconcilably opposed philosophies. The thirty-four-year-old Cohn, divorced, afflicted with a petulant, hysterical mistress, Frances Clyne, yearns for a happier existence. Inspired by W. H. Hudson's romance, *The Purple Land,* he dreams vaguely of starting afresh in South America. Cohn has money, talent, and intelligence (a moderate amount of each), but he cannot bring them simultaneously to bear upon reality. Foolishly he demands that life conform to his dream, making Brett Ashley his epitome of the dream woman who will share with him a better, more ennobling life.

Jake, on the other hand, elects to live with what is. When Cohn urges him to share the trip to South America, Jake replies: "You can't get away from yourself by moving from one place to another." Despite his seeming detachment, it is Jake who feels the agony of life more deeply and perceives it more sharply. Alone at night, the worst time for him, he lies awake and weeps despite his efforts "not to think about it." His inability to make love to Brett shatters him. When he is not alone, he endures his fate sardonically, as when he puts off a prostitute with the admonition that he is "sick"; stoically, as when he embraces Brett but insists that she simply not think about the absurdity of their love. Unlike Count Mippipopolous, Brett's epicurean admirer, Jake cannot compensate for the denial of his love by enjoying other women. Yet Jake and the Count are alike in their love for food, wine, adventure, and above all, in their determination not to complain about inescapable reality.

As the second section of the novel opens, others join Jake, Brett, and Cohn in Paris to plan a journey to Pamplona, Spain, for the annual July fiesta and bullfight. Before they leave, however, Jake learns with dismay that Brett has had a brief affair with Robert Cohn because "it would be good for him." Since Brett's drunken and abusive fiancé, Mike Campbell, will accompany them on the excursion, Jake tries unsuccessfully to dissuade Cohn from coming along. Cohn not only refuses to be put off, but even cancels a scheduled fishing trip with Jake to remain near Brett. That nobody wants him around fails to deter him. Silent, sober, and dour, he hangs on—watching and hoping.

Planning a reunion with the group in Pamplona, Jake goes off with his friend Bill Gorton (a fancier, when drunk, of stuffed animals) for five days of trout fishing in the Spanish hill country. Free of the tensions induced by Paris, Jake exults in the masculine out-of-door pleasures he shares with Bill. With almost total abandon, they fish, drink, and banter. Only when Bill tentatively probes his feelings about Brett or about his dormant Catholicism does Jake become evasive and withdrawn. Sensitive to Jake's pain, Bill quickly stops. Their affection for one another is deep, their brief holiday a success.

Soon thereafter Jake must forsake the ease of a world of men without women. At Pamplona, at the Hotel Montoya, the group once more gathers a few days before the opening of the fiesta. As they watch the unloading of the bulls, Jake, knowledgeable about such matters, explains how the docile steers quiet the angry bulls and guide them to the corral. The episode stirs Mike Campbell to bait Cohn by comparing him with a steer: "They never say anything and they're always hanging about so." Relentlessly and viciously, Mike taunts Cohn about his sobriety, his Jewishness, his affair with Brett. Only Brett can silence Mike. Bill Gorton leads Cohn off to calm him. Bill's good nature helps to restore some kind of harmony to the tense group.

That night, alone in his room with the light on, Jake lies in bed thinking about Brett, the others, and his own place among them. He concludes that despite the bitterness of his draught, it is worth drinking. Life is worth living if only for its occasional good moments. What one must do is learn to recognize and appreciate them. Universal truths are neither possible nor even necessary. "All I wanted to know," he tells himself, "was how to live in it."

A few days later the fiesta bursts into life and rockets noisily and violently for the next week. As the crowds throng into the street, one group dances about Brett, presses her into a bar and enshrines her atop a wine cask. Cohn, like Homer's Elpenor, falls asleep and is laid among the wine casks in the rear of the shop. Later, the friends watch the bulls chase the mob through the streets and even see one reveler gored to death. The great moments, however, occur in the arena. There, tutored by Jake in the nuances of bullfighting, they marvel at the skill and courage of Pedro Romero, a handsome young *torero*. Even Cohn, who had expected to be bored, admits his interest in the spectacle. Brett exceeds them all in her ardor. She confesses her desire for Romero to Jake and begs him to help her win him. Jake arranges a meeting and leaves the youth with Brett.

Hours later, seated with Mike and Bill, Jake faces an enraged Cohn. Horrified by his guess about Brett and Romero, which is confirmed by the complaisant Mike Campbell, Cohn calls Jake a pimp and knocks him out. Cohn discovers Brett in Romero's room, Jake learns later, and proceeds to beat the bullfighter mercilessly. When Brett denounces Cohn, he turns pitiably to Romero and offers to shake hands. Romero smashes Cohn's face. Cohn apologizes to Jake, and says goodbye, giving up all hope of winning Brett.

On the final day of the fiesta, Romero, his face battered, nevertheless performs magnificently in the arena, his grace and assurance inspiring the crowd to prolonged applause. The judges award him the coveted ear of the dead bull. That evening he and Brett leave Pamplona together. Jake, Mike, and Bill remain, drinking absinthe, Jake drunker and more depressed than ever.

The final, and briefest, section of the novel opens the day after the fiesta. In the anticlimactic stillness of Pamplona, the friends separate. Jakes goes off to San Sebastian to swim, catch up with the newspapers, and drink. Again, however, his respite is brief, for he receives a telegram from Brett urging him to join her in Madrid at once. When they meet, Brett tells him that she has left Romero. She has decided not to destroy his decency and innocence and, more important, weaken his power as a *torero*. Lacking Jake's formal religion, Brett believes that her gesture of renunciation brings her as near to religion as she can come. Jake merely urges her not to spoil the power of her emotion by discussing it.

The two ill-starred lovers ride together in a cab and sit tormentingly near one another. Brett exclaims in despair that she and Jake might have been wonderful for each other. Jake's rejoinder closes the novel: "Yes. Isn't it pretty to think so?"

Critical Opinion

The title of Hemingway's novel comes from a passage in the Old Testament, *Ecclesiastes*: ". . . vanity of vanities; all is vanity. . . . The sun also ariseth, and the sun goeth down, and hasteneth to his place where he arose . . . and that which is done is that which shall be done: and there is no new thing under the sun."

Like the Preacher of *Ecclesiastes*, Hemingway addressed a generation socially and morally disillusioned, and also like the Preacher, he seems at first glance to urge men to eat, drink, and be merry. Some critics of *The Sun Also Rises* consider it a defense of hedonism. Others, however, have found a truer, deeper meaning, a meaning clued by Hemingway's own statement that he did not regard his generation as lost or his novel as a hollow satire of his fellow man.

Stunned but not downed by adversity, Hemingway's heroes must learn the "code": to live and, if necessary, to die with courage and with dignity. Those who master the mystique of the code become Hemingway's elect, the initiated. Some, like Romero for example, are born initiates; they have inherited a tradition that enables them to confront the world bravely. Others, like Robert Cohn and Mike Campbell, fail because they cling, like Cohn, to false ideals, or like Mike, to sheer self-indulgence. Brett, some critics argue, belongs in the same category as Mike; others insist that her final renunciation of Romero lends her a kind of grandeur. Jake Barnes is the "code" hero in the making. His castration—a symbol of the sterility of the age—prevents his achieving fulfillment. But he can and does attain the self-knowledge that enables him to endure the frustration of his life with dignity.

The structure and style of *The Sun Also Rises* serve its theme very effectively. "Prose," Hemingway once wrote, is "architecture, not interior decoration." And Hemingway builds simply but soundly. Thus the apparent rambling of the early parts of the novel reflects the lack of direction in the characters' lives. As they discover purpose, the structure tightens and the plot surges ahead vigorously. At the end an aimless pattern follows the chaos of shattered dreams. Sentence style and language are part of Hemingway's purpose. The simple sentence and the monosyllabic word help him re-create the "feel" of the experience in all its immediacy. Hemingway's world is a violent world; to reproduce it poignantly and memorably, he uses staccato rhythms and unadorned language. At its best, his style is superb; at its worst, it parodies itself. In *The Sun Also Rises,* Hemingway is very much at his best.

A Farewell to Arms

by

ERNEST HEMINGWAY

Main Characters

Frederic Henry—An American lieutenant serving in the Italian ambulance corps during World War I. Uprooted, haunted by life's emptiness, disheartened by his own cynical escapism, he searches—at first indifferently, then desperately—for a truth to sustain his spirit.

Catherine Barkley—Frederic's love, a beautiful English volunteer nurse on duty in Italy. Serenely selfless, incapable of cynicism, she focuses every facet of her profoundly feminine sensibility upon her lover.

Rinaldi—An Italian Army surgeon and Frederic's best friend. Disillusioned, like Frederic, he has settled for the supreme beauty of successful surgery and the lesser joys of liquor and sex.

Priest—An Italian Army chaplain, devout, patient and gentle, unmoved by the gibes of his irreverent fellow officers.

Count Greffi—An aged aristocrat, wise in the ways of a brutal world, but firm in his conviction that love, not cynicism, sustains the human spirit.

Ettore Moretti—A young Californian enlisted in the Italian
Army. Brash, boastful, and a bore, his highest goal is military promotion.

Helen Ferguson—Catherine's friend, a dour Scottish nurse,
much concerned about the morality of Frederic's liaison
with Catherine.

Bonello, Piani, Aymo—Enlisted Italians under Frederic's command, all socialists, all without illusions about the war they
are trapped in, and all ready to spring themselves from the
trap at the first opportunity.

The Story

Awaiting an Alpine thaw that will permit an offensive
against the Austrians, a company of Italian troops in the Udine
Valley of northeastern Italy passes its time drinking and
wenching. Among the officers, an additional pastime is baiting the chaplain, an earnest young Abruzzi priest. Frederic
Henry, the American officer and narrator, respects the priest
for his untroubled faith and his quiet love for the clean, cold
country of his birth. Yet when Frederic goes on leave, he fails
to visit the priest's home. Instead, he wanders about Italy,
drifting into bars and brothels. The priest, he realizes, "had
always known what I did not know . . . although I learned it
later."

A few days after his return to his post, Frederic meets
Catherine Barkley whom he at first regards merely as a
beautiful and available woman. When, at their second meeting, she sharply rejects his advances, then a moment later
accepts his embrace and speaks prophetically of their future
love, he decides that she is "probably a little crazy"—perhaps
out of remorse for the war death of her fiancé. Frederic's
interest remains detached, yet he feels "lonely and hollow"
when he is away from Catherine.

Less than a week after their first meeting, Frederic is
ordered to the front. During a mortar attack, he and his
ambulance drivers crouch in a shallow dugout munching
cheese and macaroni. A shell explodes nearby, killing one
of the men and seriously wounding Henry in the head and
legs. En route to the field hospital in an ambulance, the

soldier in the stretcher above Frederic begins to hemorrhage, the blood dripping steadily down on him. When the ambulance arrives at the hospital, the soldier is dead.

Before he is shipped to the general hospital in Milan, Frederic receives visits from his surgeon friend, Rinaldi, and from the priest. Rinaldi teases him about sex. The priest urges him to seek a nobler kind of love, preferably of God but at least beyond lust. At the hospital in Milan, where Catherine is a nurse, she comes to him and he realizes that he is really in love with her. They consummate their love in Frederic's hospital bed.

The next morning a trio of windy, ineffectual doctors consult about Frederic's leg and agree that he must wait six months before his mutilated knee can be operated on. When Frederic protests, another doctor, Valentini, decides to operate the next morning. Like Rinaldi, Valentini is brisk, witty, and efficient. He needs no consultation. As Rinaldi says, "I don't think; I operate."

During the long summer of his successful convalescence, Frederic and Catherine are lovers. He wants to marry her, but she sees no need: "We are married privately," she says, and adds, "It would mean everything to me if I had any religion. But I haven't any religion." In contrast to the purity of their relationship is the tainted materialism of the world symbolized in Ettore who wants glory and recognition as a hero, and the crooked horse races, rigged for profit but devoid of any excitement.

Before Frederic returns to the front, Catherine tells him she is pregnant. Momentarily disturbed, he soon agrees that he, too, wants the child. Knowing the depth of her love as well as her fears about death, he is awed by her courage when she assures him during their last meeting that all will go well with her while he is away.

Frederic returns to the front and to the terrible retreat from Caporetto. He finds Rinaldi despondent because he has too few patients for surgery. Only when he is at work does Rinaldi's life take on meaning. Otherwise there is only sex and with it the dread of venereal disease. The priest, too, is depressed by the interminable war, his hope for peace growing dim. Soon, however, there is no time for talk, for the Germans break through the Italian lines and force a general retreat.

Columns of peasants join the troops along the jammed, muddy highways. When Frederic's truck gets stuck, he orders two sergeants to cut brush to support the wheels. When they ignore him and walk off as deserters, he shoots and wounds one of them, and Bonello, his sergeant, finishes off the other man. Afoot, Frederic and his three loyal noncoms try to avoid encounters with the Germans. Ironically, they are fired upon by Italians, and Aymo is killed. Bonello leaves, determined to save his life by surrendering.

Alone on the road with Piani, Frederic encounters throngs of Italians joyously deserting to return home. At a bridge across the river Tagliamento, he is arrested by Italian battle police assigned to capture and shoot deserting officers. As he awaits questioning, Frederic suddenly ducks away and plunges into the river. In the line of fire, he swims to safety, throws away his uniform, and rides to freedom beneath the canvas-covered guns on a gun train. "You were out of it now," Frederic thinks. "You had no more obligation." He has made his farewell to arms and a "separate peace."

In Milan, Frederic learns that Catherine and Helen Ferguson have gone to Stresa in the Italian lake country. He follows them and when he is reunited with Catherine, knows that only with her does the world seem real. He realizes, too, that the world will not abide such happiness. "If people bring so much courage to this world the world has to kill them to break them, so of course it kills them."

Their few days at Stresa are happy. One evening Frederic plays billiards with Count Greffi and listens to the aged philosopher distinguish between wisdom and cynicism. Like Catherine, Greffi lacks orthodox faith, but he believes firmly in life and in living it as well and as honestly as possible. The same evening Frederic is warned by the hotelkeeper of his imminent arrest as a deserter. A boat is provided for Frederic and Catherine and in the rain and wind they row across Lake Maggiore to Switzerland. Briefly detained by the Swiss customs, they persuade the officers that they are cousins traveling to enjoy the winter sports. Released, they find refuge in a lovely chalet overlooking Montreux.

Their winter is idyllic. But with the spring rain, the time arrives for Catherine's delivery and they leave for Lausanne. At the hospital Catherine's labor is slow and intense. As her strength wanes, the doctor suggests a Caesarean delivery. The child is stillborn and Catherine lies at the threshold of death. Terrified that she will die, Frederic tries to pray. In despair he recalls once having watched some ants atop a burning log. As the log burned, the ants fled—some to the fire, some to the end where they fell off into the fire below. For a moment Frederic knew the sensation of playing God. He thought briefly of lifting the log from the fire and saving the ants. Instead, he threw a cup of water on the log and merely steamed the ants. "You never had time to learn," he thinks. "They threw you in and told you the rules and the first time they caught you off base they killed you."

When he returns to Catherine, she knows she is dying. Denying that she is afraid, she admits only that she hates death. Then she dies. Frederic pushes the nurses out of the room. He wants his farewell to be private. But the parting seems senseless, like saying goodbye to a statue. Frederic leaves and walks back to his hotel in the rain.

Critical Opinion

For many readers, *A Farewell to Arms* is Hemingway's most appealing and affecting novel. The courage of Frederic and Catherine and the tragic consequences of their love, the atmosphere of the Italian war front and the powerful scenes of the debacle at Caporetto—these remain etched in memory long after other details have slipped away. Some critics have objected that Catherine is too idealized, too romantically compliant, too sentimentally a "code" heroine. As a result, they believe, Frederic's development proceeds with a slick, movie-script glibness different from the rough-edged force of *The Sun Also Rises*. For other critics, the emotional force of the novel as a whole transcends its several weaknesses.

Like most of Hemingway's novels, *A Farewell to Arms* is about love and death and the kind of courage one needs to experience them. In the beginning, Frederic lacks commitment of any kind. He cannot find in love of man, woman, or God any compelling reason for existence. Until he meets Catherine, he drifts with the moment. Afterward he moves inevitably toward an understanding of the fullness as well as the emptiness of life. He learns about the hollowness of abstractions: medals do not prove valor; a wedding need not signify a true marriage. He learns from Catherine—and from Rinaldi and Greffi as well—the potential force of the individual spirit. And he learns, above all, that those who undertake a "separate peace" win no lasting victory. By deserting the army to be with Catherine, Frederic symbolically bids farewell to military arms. Ironically, when she dies, he must bid yet another farewell—to the arms of his love.

The novel is rich in symbols. For example, the rain that opens and closes the book symbolizes death as well as life. What Frederic learns, then, is that a "code" hero must accept the truth that all stories end in death. That truth understood, life has moments of beauty and significance well worth the living.

The Old Man and the Sea

by

ERNEST HEMINGWAY

Main Characters

Santiago—A Cuban fisherman, old yet still rugged in body, young and indomitable in spirit.

Manolin—A Cuban boy, Santiago's companion. Too young to comprehend fully either the joy or the anguish of experience, he is sensitive enough to recognize the old man's wisdom.

The Story

Luckless but undaunted, old Santiago has fished the Gulf Stream off Havana for eighty-four days without catching a fish. For the first forty days, the boy Manolin went with him, but now his parents have sent Manolin to another boat. Still the boy serves the old man, bringing him food, beer, bait, and helping him carry his tackle to the skiff. In the old man's shack, they discuss baseball, the great Di Maggio, the splendid hauls they have made in the past. Alone, the old man sleeps and dreams of his youth in Africa and of the lions who played on the beaches.

At dawn on the eighty-fifth day, Santiago sets sail again, confident that somewhere in the sea he loves like a woman is the big fish he must catch. He sails far out into the Stream, baits and sets his lines, and drops them into deep water. Waiting, he watches a school of dolphin pursue flying fish and he curses a malevolent Portuguese man-of-war that drifts near by. He catches a small tuna and waits hopefully for the big strike. When it comes, it is deceptively gentle, the merest tug, but Santiago knows that it is a marlin nibbling his bait 600 feet below. Speaking aloud, the old man urges the marlin to sample more of the bait. When he senses the right moment, Santiago pulls hard and settles the hook. The long battle has begun.

With the noon sun high and hot, Santiago feeds his marlin the line it needs as it swims off towing the skiff northwest, away from land. Santiago can do nothing except wait for the fish to tire. Meanwhile, he grips the heavy line in his callused hands and braces it across his naked shoulders. All afternoon the fish tows the boat, then after sunset and into the chill night. Although he wishes he had Manolin with him to help, the old man is determined to conquer the fish alone. At the same time he begins to think about the fish at the end of his line and about other great fish he has caught. During the night the fish lurches, pulling Santiago down on his face and cutting his cheek. But the old man never relaxes his vigil.

By morning the old man is stiff as well as hungry. Still he cannot exert tension on the line lest the fish break it. As Santiago talks to the birds overhead, the fish suddenly surges and the line cuts through the old man's hand. Despite his pain, the old man is pleased, for he senses that his prey has begun to tire. He wonders what the fish intends and what he will do. He wishes that he might feed the fish, his brother, but knows that his own strength must be the greater if he is to prevail, and worries about the paralyzing cramp that stiffens his left hand.

Suddenly the line grows slack; the fish surfaces, leaping out of the water. It is the largest marlin Santiago has ever seen, longer even than his skiff. Santiago prays for victory, sure that he can "show him what a man can do and what a man endures." All afternoon and again into the night the fish tows the skiff, now to the east. To bolster himself, Santiago recalls a titanic hand wrestle he won years ago at a tavern. Hungry, he catches and eats a dolphin. During the night the marlin jumps again, cutting Santiago's hands once more. He dreams of Africa and the lions.

At sunrise on the third morning, the line almost tears through Santiago's hand as the fish begins a series of leaps. Now the old man begins to shorten the line even though each tug lacerates his hands anew. He washes his bleeding hands in the sea, then continues to draw in his line as the fast-tiring marlin circles the skiff in ever-narrowing arcs. Just before the fish is close enough to harpoon, the old man pleads with it not to kill them both. For a fleeting moment, in admiration— almost in love—he exclaims that he would not care if the noble creature, at once his brother and his enemy in nature, killed him. But the old man knows that he must overwhelm the marlin. He harpoons the mighty fish and lashes it to the side of his boat.

The return to Havana is a nightmare that begins an hour after the marlin has been tied to the skiff. A Mako shark attacks the corpse and mutilates it before the old man can kill it. As other sharks come, the old man fights them off tenaciously, defending not only his own victory but the dignity of the dead marlin. He wonders whether it was a sin to kill his fish, but he realizes that man must struggle against defeat by nature. Sorry that the fish is dead, its corpse ravished, he knows also that he had to do what he did. Although he continues to battle the sharks, his struggle is in vain. His knives break, and his torn hands will not even hold the club he tries to wield. All he can do is steer his boat toward harbor as the ravenous sharks strip the marlin to a skeleton. To himself, Santiago says that he went out too far. That was why he suffered defeat.

His boat beached, only the head and tail of his catch remaining, the old man shoulders his mast and climbs slowly up the hill to his shack. Once he stumbles and falls, but he rises and struggles on. He sleeps sprawled face down on his bed, his arms outstretched, his palms turned up. Manolin comes to the old man in the morning and tends to him. Despite Santiago's insistence that his luck has turned bad, Manolin says that it will turn good again and that he wants to sail again with the old man. As the novel ends, the old man sleeps, dreaming about his lions. Manolin sits beside him.

Critical Opinion

Read literally as an adventure yarn, *The Old Man and the Sea* grips young and old. The prose is simple, the approximations of Spanish dialogue poetically affecting and appropriate, the narrative pattern lucid and economical. Santiago's stubborn courage, rugged strength, and marvelous skill sustain suspense till the tragic end. As almost every critic has noted, however, the reader who casts for subtler meanings may net a more rewarding haul. Hemingway said of the story that the old man, the boy, the sea, the fish, and the sharks were all real. "But if I made them good and true enough," he went on, "they would mean many things."

For some readers the novel has deep, religious implications. Santiago's scarred palms, the crosslike mast he carries up the hill—these symbols suggest the Christian overtones that sound throughout the tale. Although Santiago loves the fish, his pride compels him to destroy it—a human failure for which both man and nature suffer.

Others see the struggle between man and nature as the ancient bond between hunter and hunted. Respecting his prey, the hunter must nevertheless assert at any price the power of man. Ironically, the price is often death or defeat for the hunter as well. Santiago becomes an embodiment of all of Hemingway's "code" heroes—the first of them, however, as Philip Young observes, to have grown old.

The Old Man and the Sea is also significant as a study of initiation, for in it the boy Manolin learns what it means to be a man. He has been consummately tutored in the craft of big-game fishing. More important, however, he has, like all of Hemingway's initiates, absorbed knowledge about love, death, courage, and endurance.

The Author

In *Death in the Afternoon* (1932), a study of the art of bull-fighting, *Ernest Hemingway* wrote: "All stories, if continued far enough, end in death, and he is no true storyteller who would keep that from you." Violent death, often the subject matter of his fiction, shaped Hemingway's life. It also triggered his exit—with a blast from a shotgun he held in his mouth.

Hemingway's boyhood in Oak Park, Illinois, was quiet, his chief enthusiasms fishing and hunting trips in northern Michigan or making medical rounds with his father, a physician (who years later committed suicide). Shortly after his high-school graduation, Hemingway joined the Italian Army, first as an ambulance driver, then as an infantry officer. In 1918, at nineteen, he was almost killed by a shrapnel burst. For the rest of his life, Hemingway flirted with destructive forces, both human and natural. As a journalist after the war, he reported battles in the Near East. During the twenties and thirties, he divided his time between bullfights and wild-game safaris in Africa. He was in Spain during the Civil War and in Europe (often farther ahead of the lines than the Allied troops) during World War II. In 1954 he survived two plane crashes in the African jungle. Throughout, Hemingway's code was courage in a world of crisis. Almost compulsively he sought danger in order to prove himself man enough to face —perhaps to overwhelm—the threat of extinction.

In Paris after World War I, Hemingway joined the expatriate group of artists and writers described by Gertrude Stein as "the lost generation." From her as well as from Ezra Pound and others, he learned the discipline of his craft—the taut sentences, monosyllabic vocabulary, stark dialogue, and understated emotion that are the hallmarks of the Hemingway style. His earliest stories foreshadow his mature technique and his concern for values in a corrupt and indifferent world.

With the publication of *The Sun Also Rises* (1926) and *A Farewell to Arms* (1929), Hemingway's fame was secure for the rest of his life. But until *For Whom the Bell Tolls* (1940), his succeeding novels added little to his stature, though some of his short stories, notably "The Snows of Kilimanjaro" (1936) and "The Short Happy Life of Francis

Macomber" (1936), are distinguished and memorable. After *For Whom the Bell Tolls*, only *The Old Man and the Sea* (1952) approached the force of Hemingway's early genius. In 1953 *The Old Man* won him the Pulitzer Prize. A year later he was awarded the Nobel Prize

Some observers have commented that Hemingway's suicide resulted partly from his awareness that he was no longer, in his favorite term, "the champion." Although it is true that some of his late works seemed parodies of himself, in the pages of the posthumously published memoir of his early years in Paris, *A Moveable Feast* (1964), a reader may discover once more strong traces of Hemingway's deep sensibility, sinewy style, and resounding courage.

The Bridge of San Luis Rey

by

THORNTON WILDER (1897–)

Main Characters

Doña Mariá, Marquesa de Montemayor—An unprepossessing, eccentric woman who is also a superb letter writer, an intensely devoted mother who has compassion for no one but her daughter.

Doña Clara—Doña Mariá's daughter, beautiful, cold, intellectual.

Camila Perichole—An extraordinarily talented actress (called "the Perichole") whose social ambitions help to destroy her individuality and to mar the lives of other people.

Abbess Madre Mariá del Pilar—Directress of the Convent of Santa Rosa de las Rosas, an extraordinarily perceptive woman supremely dedicated to the church, to the poor and the outcasts.

Pepita—An orphan girl, the particular object of the Abbess's solicitude, who is being trained to carry on the Abbess's work.

Esteban—One of twin brothers, racked by excessive guilt for his brother's death.

Manuel—His twin, silently and unavailingly in love with the Perichole.

Uncle Pio—An adventurer endowed with the gift of love—
especially for beautiful women and beautiful language.
Jaime—The sickly young son of the Perichole.
The Viceroy—An aristocrat, now old and suffering from the
gout, but still charming and capable of ruling.

The Story

The bridge of San Luis Rey, a slat bridge with vine hand-
rails, was the most famous bridge in Peru. On Friday, July 20,
1714, at noon, it broke, and five travelers were hurtled into
the gorge it spanned. It was a deeply impressive event, and
Brother Juniper, who had long wanted theology to be an exact
science, felt that this was his opportunity to demonstrate
God's wisdom with laboratory precision. By gathering all
possible data about the five people who had fallen to their
deaths, he would be able to show the outline of His purpose,
the pattern of His providence.

Doña Mariá, Marquesa de Montemayor, is the most important personage of the five. She is remembered for the wit
and brilliance of her letters to her daughter. The Marquesa's
life is marked by almost unvarying suffering. An ugly child
without grace or charm, she grows into an equally unprepossessing young woman. Only her father's great wealth
procures her a husband. She gives birth to an exquisite
daughter, Doña Clara, who regards her adoring mother
with a cold indifference that develops into repulsion. Deliberately she accepts the offer of marriage that will require her
removal to Spain. The agonized mother—after one disastrous
visit—returns to Lima to write the letters that establish her
enduring fame.

Though ill and unhappy, she forces herself to go everywhere and to see everything that might be converted into
amusing material for her letters. She pours her love, her very
life, into these masterpieces. Her daughter answers seldom,
briefly, distantly. Increasingly the Marquesa finds relief and
oblivion in drinking wine.

Desiring a companion, she applies to the devout and saintly
Abbess Madre Mariá del Pilar, directress of the Convent of
Santa Maria Rosa de las Rosas. The latter chooses Pepita, a

twelve-year-old orphan whose devotion and intelligence have moved the Abbess to train her as a potential successor. Pepita's service in a great house, the Abbess believes, will further her education. But the Marquesa is willful, eccentric, and often unintentionally cruel to the young girl who suffers additionally from the contempt and practical jokes of the servants.

A curt letter arrives from Spain in which Doña Clara briefly announces her pregnancy. The Marquesa becomes frantic with worry over her daughter's well being. She deluges her with unwanted counsel, prays hysterically, even succumbs to pagan superstitions in the attempt to ensure a safe delivery. On a pilgrimage to a great shrine, the Marquesa and Pepita stop at an inn. Pepita, during a pause in her duties, begins a letter to the Abbess, a letter that cries out with her unhappiness at being with the Marquesa and away from the Abbess. The Marquesa reads it by accident. In it she finds revealed not only her wanton neglect of Pepita but also her oppressive love for her daughter—never brave and generous, always greedy. She prays to be allowed to begin again. Two days later the bridge falls as she and Pepita are crossing it.

Esteban is the third victim. He is one of twin boys, found-lings reared by the Abbess. He and his brother Manuel have been fused into a spiritual unity, a oneness for which the word love is too shallow. After leaving the Abbess, they earn their living as scribes, though sometimes they work at other jobs. Always they are together; all other men are strangers.

One day Manuel is asked to write a letter for Camila Perichole, the first actress of Peru. Idolized by her public, she is the mistress of the Viceroy but is having an affair with a matador. At her dictation, Manuel writes a very different letter to each lover. When he has finished his task, he is wholly infatuated with her. He broods over her continually, haunting the places where he is likely to see her. Esteban soon realizes his brother's condition and is saddened by the breach that follows. Sometime later, the actress visits them in their room. She wants Manuel to write an angry letter to the matador, who has failed to keep a rendezvous. He complies and she steals away. But Manuel has sensed the misery of his brother and by a powerful exercise of will he renounces her, telling Esteban that he will write no more letters for her.

Esteban realizes the nature of Manuel's sacrifice and refuses
to accept it. Manuel, however, insists.

Sometime later, Manuel cuts his leg which swells painfully.
Esteban nurses him faithfully through his delirium during
which he curses Esteban violently for coming between him
and the Perichole. In his lucid intervals Manuel grieves over
his outbursts. When Manuel dies in agony, Esteban is incon-
solable. He wanders desolately over Peru, seeking lonely and
difficult jobs, and once tries to commit suicide. At the instance
of his old guardian, the Abbess, a sea captain persuades
Esteban to join him in a voyage. It is on the way to the ship
that Esteban crosses the bridge of San Luis Rey at the fatal
moment.

Uncle Pio and Camila Perichole's young son, Jaime, are the
last victims. Uncle Pio ("Uncle" because of his willingness to
listen and advise—if also to profit) is a witty, acute, somewhat disreputable adventurer. Almost successful in a variety
of undertakings, he seems at the last juncture to will his own
downfall. The great passion of his life—a life devoted to
beautiful women and the theater—is for the actress Camila
Perichole. He finds her singing in cafés at the age of twelve
and undertakes her training. He teaches her to speak distinc-
tively, to convey the essential quality of a song, and to act
with fervor and understanding. She becomes the best actress
in Peru, perhaps in the Spanish-speaking world. As she
develops into a woman, she has intermittent love affairs
(never with Uncle Pio, though, for their attachment is deep
but passionless). Ultimately she attracts the Viceroy himself.
For a long time she admires him, even adores him, and learns
from him the habits and carriage of a great lady. She bears
him a son who is legitimized. Unhappily, however, she turns
from the stage to seek a place in society. Uncle Pio is heartbroken and attempts to convince her of her supreme talent,
but she spurns him. Shortly afterward she contracts smallpox
and her face becomes hideously marked. She goes into
seclusion, hiding herself from the world. By a stratagem
Uncle Pio manages to see her. He has only one request. For
one year he wants to take her young son, Jaime, who remains
secluded with her into the world to teach him fencing, Latin,
music—all that a gentleman should know. Reluctantly she
agrees, and together Uncle Pio and Jaime return to Lima.

They start across the bridge of San Luis Rey in the company of the Marquesa, Pepita, and Esteban.

The Perichole comes to the funeral service for her son and Uncle Pio. She visits the Abbess, tells of her profound despair, and is comforted. She enters the service of the Church as aide to the Abbess. Doña Clara, too, comes to see the Abbess. The daughter at last realizes the greatness of her mother, not merely as a writer but as a person. And the Abbess muses over the meaning of all that has befallen, concluding that love is the only meaning, the only answer to the tragedies of life.

The large book that Brother Juniper wrote was seized by the Inquisition—all but one copy, upon which the narrator draws. The others were burned, together with their author. His deductions were perhaps too scientific—or too inconclusive.

Critical Opinion

The Bridge of San Luis Rey is generally considered Thornton Wilder's best novel. It is certainly his best known. It seems a slight-enough work: three "case histories" and a somewhat ironic commentary. But the case histories are not only acute psychological studies. They also illuminate, though they hardly solve, an age-old philosophical problem: Is there a reason for man's suffering in this world, for his blighted hopes and shattered purposes?

The findings of Brother Juniper, Wilder's theological investigator, are deliberately withheld. Yet while Wilder "spares" us the generalizations, he tells us that Brother Juniper "thought he saw in the same accident, the wicked visited by destruction and the good called early to Heaven." Brother Juniper, however, has decided in advance; he is scarcely to be trusted.

Through the Abbess, who seems to speak for Wilder, we may infer the answer that the book projects to the problem of man's pain-fraught existence. It is that there is no answer —or else that the answer is shrouded in darkness. In the last sentence of the novel, the Abbess insists that "love is the only survival, the only meaning."

The Bridge of San Luis Rey is a remarkable achievement.

The incisive portraits, especially of the Marquesa (modeled after Mme. de Sevigné), the sensitive, slightly ironic style, which reaches a real eloquence, the deft evocation of the atmosphere of a different era and an exotic place—these continue to make the book a rich and absorbing experience.

The Author

Thornton Wilder has won the Pulitzer Prize three times: twice for plays—*Our Town* (1938), a glowing, sentimental, but not cloying piece of nostalgia, and *The Skin of Our Teeth* (1942), "a sort of Hellzapoppin with brains"—once for *The Bridge of San Luis Rey* (1927). In almost any year in which he has written either novel or play, he has been a contender for the prize.

The Cabala (1926), his first published novel, describes the fragmented lives of aristocrats in Rome as viewed by a young American. *The Woman of Andros* (1930), though based on a play by the Roman dramatist Terence, is a contemporary novel on the values of love. *The Ides of March* (1948) is a witty and serious fictional study of the life of Julius Caesar. Wilder's first novel of the contemporary American scene, *Heaven's My Destination* (1934), a comic story about a traveling salesman, deals with the problem of belief in an unbelieving age.

Wilder's plays, perhaps more derivative than his novels, are still admirable creations. *The Matchmaker* (1955) reworks an earlier Wilder play, *The Merchant of Yonkers* (1938), which was adapted from Johann Nestroy's farce. Currently Wilder is working on a cycle of fourteen plays, the first three of which have had a successful off-Broadway production under the title *Plays for Bleecker Street*.

Thornton Wilder, born in Wisconsin, grew to young manhood in China where his father was American Consul General. In America he attended Oberlin College (1915–17), interrupted his academic studies to serve as a corporal in the Coast Artillery during World War I, and completed the work for his bachelor's degree at Yale in 1920. He did post-graduate work at the American Academy in Rome, taught French at the Lawrenceville School, took his master's degree at Princeton (1925), and then became a member of the University of

Chicago faculty (1930–36). In World War II he served as an Air Force intelligence officer in Africa and Italy, and was discharged with the rank of lieutenant colonel. He has lived most of his life in a suburb of New Haven, reading at the university library and frequently lecturing abroad.

Wilder, it has been remarked, "is a curious anomaly in the American literary scene, a widely cultured man who writes as he pleases and yet has managed to captivate the masses in his best work." He has written broadly and in a half-dozen fields. Moreover, he has several absorbing literary hobbies, ranging from the analysis of Joyce's *Finnegans Wake* to the tracing of Lope de Vega's dramatic productions. His scholarly avocations and his vocation as writer, however, dovetail, for, he has commented, "My writing life is a series of infatuations for admired writers."

Giants in the Earth

by

OLE EDVART RÖLVAAG (1876–1931)

Main Characters

Per Hansa—A Norwegian pioneer farmer in the Dakota Territory, proud, independent, resourceful.
Beret—His wife, deeply in love with him but assailed by a profound melancholy.
Ole ("Olamand") and *Hans*—Their stalwart young sons, happy in the new life on the prairie.
Anna Marie ("And-Ongen")—Their small blonde daughter.
Hans Olsa—A loyal friend to the Hansas, a kindly, hardworking giant.
Sorine—Olsa's sweet-tempered, dutiful wife.
Syvert Tönseten—Another Norwegian settler, short, stout, excitable, self-important.
Kjersti—Tönseten's sharp-tongued but good-hearted wife.
The Solum brothers—Two Norwegian settlers, bachelors, who unlike the other pioneers can speak some English.
The Minister—An itinerant minister, ungainly, ill-dressed, spiritually gifted.

The Story

In 1873 Per Hansa, a Norwegian immigrant, moves west by ox wagon from Minnesota to the Dakota territory, with his family: his wife, Beret, a loving, deeply religious woman, who at times becomes deeply melancholy; his two sons, Ole (or *"Olamand"*) and Hans, the former about nine, the latter seven—both stalwart, eager boys; and his small blonde daughter, Anna Marie (pet-named *And-Ongen*, "The Duckling"). The family arrive at a fertile spot where they have been preceded by friends who now joyfully welcome them: the kindly giant, Hans Olsa; his devoted wife, Sorïne, and their ten-year-old daughter, Sofie; Syvert Tönseten, a short, stout man, perpetually excited and garrulous, and his good-natured but sharp-tongued wife, Kjersti; and two bachelors, the Solum brothers, the only settlers who can speak English at all.

Per Hansa falls in love with the stretch of land that has been set aside for him. With one of the Solum boys he travels to Sioux Falls, a fifty-two-mile journey, to file an application for his quarter section, his new "kingdom." On his return he sets to work in an indomitable mood, brooking no opposition from man or nature. He dreams of his land at night and awakens at daybreak to labor on it—fourteen, then sixteen hours a day. He begins building an enormous sod house and completes it in an astonishingly short time, making an arduous trip to another settlement to get timber for the house and young trees to plant around it. He enlists all his family, but especially Ole and Hans, for his eager labors.

Once Indians come when Per's comrades have made a trip to town. The settlers are terrified, but Per visits the Indians, cures a sick chief, and receives a pony as a gift.

Life in the settlement is a continual struggle. Even little events seem very important, for on them depend the life of the community. Per prospers and everyone regards him as a fortunate man. He plants potatoes, raises a good crop, sells it profitably. He catches a large quantity of fish and ducks. He is the first man to whitewash the interior of his sod house. Because of his extraordinary energy and resourcefulness, he is admired by his sons, looked up to by his neighbors.

But there is a deep sorrow in Per's life. His wife, Beret, has never been happy on the prairie. The great expanse of flat, lonely land, the frontier mores, the lack of religious dedication among the settlers all distress her. Per, who has found markers

left by earlier pioneers, destroys them, then repulses the settlers when they return. He is legally justified, since they have
not filed official claims, but Beret fears the vengeance that
must follow such a sinful act. She recalls, too, her passionate
love for Per, her child born out of wedlock, her desertion of
her parents to follow him. Pregnant now, she is sure that a
terrible punishment awaits her guilt, sure that she will "fall
into the hands of the living God." And in fact she almost dies,
as tended by Sorïne and Kjersti, she gives birth to the child
while Per waits in agony of spirit outside the house.

But Beret lives and the child is chistened Peder Victorious
—a heathen name, Beret thinks, and the ceremony, performed by Hans Olsa, is unhallowed. After the birth of the
child, Beret sinks into a more profound melancholia. Just after
the wheat that her husband had so proudly and joyfully
planted is destroyed by great swarms of locusts, Beret, quite
mad, prepares for death. She lies down in the huge chest that
they had brought from Norway, her baby in her arms and her
daughter And-Ongen at her knees. His heart bursting with
grief, Per rescues them.

An itinerant minister comes to the settlement. Ungainly and
ill-dressed, he nevertheless has a real spiritual gift. His understanding counsel, his intense sincerity, his powerful preaching,
and, not least, his approval of the name Peder Victorious
and his christening of the child, help to remove the pall that
has fallen over Beret's spirit. Though she recovers her sanity,
she remains always touched with sadness, and her religious
fervor increases.

The settlement suffers from a plague of locusts, from rain,
snow, and freezing cold. But it endures. Tragedy, never far
distant, falls upon Hans Olsa. Attempting to repair his cattle
shed, he is prevented from making his way home by a fierce
blizzard. He spends the night in the shed. When he returns
home it is clear that the exposure to the blizzard has made
him deathly ill. Beret decides that he must be saved and
earnestly begs him to repent. Hans asks for the doctor, but
Beret insists on a minister. And she prevails upon Per to go
after one, despite the weather. Tenderly bidding his children
goodbye but saying nothing to Beret, Per sets forth on skis

for the long journey to fetch the minister. But with evening, the snow begins to fall and the drifts become deeper.

One day, during the spring after Hans Olsa died, two boys find the body of a man with his back against a moldering haystack. Though it is May, there are two pairs of skis with him, one on the ground, the other on his back. His eyes are set toward the West.

Critical Opinion

Giants in the Earth, a "Saga of the Prairie," is dedicated "to those of my people who took part in the great settling, to them and their generations. . . ." Like all of Rölvaag's works, it was written in Norwegian and translated with astonishing skill by the author in collaboration with Lincoln Colcord—a collaboration, it has been said, as remarkable "in its way as that of Joseph Conrad with Ford Madox Ford."

Giants in the Earth is not so widely read now as it used to be, perhaps because the American pioneer experience has faded, perhaps because it has so frequently been recounted— by Hamlin Garland, Willa Cather, Ruth Suckow, and others. But the novel has not sunk into oblivion, nor does it deserve to. It has been called "the fullest, finest, and most powerful novel that has been written about pioneer life in America. . . . a great and beautiful book that suggests the wealth of human potentialities brought to America year after year by the peasant immigrants who pass through Ellis Island and scatter the length and breadth of the land."

Giants in the Earth is an American book, too, despite its high position in Norwegian literature. To know that, Lincoln Colcord suggests, one has merely to look at Johan Bojer's *The Emigrants*, which explores a similar theme and which Rölvaag's novel anticipated by only a month. As both Bojer and Rölvaag agreed, they had wholly different perspectives: "Bojer saw it from the viewpoint of Norway, not of America." To him, it was a story of emigration; to Rölvaag, one of settlement. It fulfilled Rölvaag's ambition from student days: to become the spokesman of one people to another, to tell them "the immigrant's part in the making of the great new nation."

The Author

Ole Edvart Rölvaag was born in Norway, on the island of Dönna, "just south of where the Arctic Circle cuts the coast of Norway." His parents, like all the people on the island, were fishermen. He went to school for seven years, nine weeks a year, walking seven miles each way to and from the schoolhouse. Ole, however, seemed to have no aptitude for learning, though he read widely and indiscriminately.

After five years as a fisherman, Rölvaag decided to go to America. An uncle in South Dakota sent him a ticket, and in 1896, aged twenty, he came to America. He farmed for three years, an occupation he thoroughly disliked. Then, without much confidence or inclination, he entered Augustana College, a preparatory school in South Dakota. There he performed brilliantly, and upon graduation entered St. Olaf College in Northfield, Minnesota (1901–05). Despite poverty and ill health, he was graduated with honors, and set off for graduate study in Norway with five hundred borrowed dollars. Upon his return to the United States, he was offered a post at St. Olaf teaching Norwegian literature. He remained at the college for the rest of his life, dying from a heart attack in 1931.

All Rölvaag's books were written in Norwegian and gained their first recognition in Norway, yet he belongs to American literature. As his translator comments, he deals with American life and characteristically American episodes; his "material is altogether American." His most important works bear this out: *Giants in the Earth* (1927), *Peder Victorious* (1929), and *Their Father's God* (1931), an epic trilogy depicting in harsh, realistic detail the struggle of the Norwegian pioneer to survive on the American prairie—and the terrible human cost of that struggle.

Look Homeward, Angel

by

THOMAS WOLFE (1900–1938)

Main Characters

Oliver Gant—A huge, exuberant, eloquent man, harried by his wife and children, often drunk.

Eliza Gant—Oliver's wife, a sharp-tongued, shrewd, avaricious woman.

Steve Gant—Their eldest son, a foul-mouthed, dishonest braggart.

Daisy Gant—Their eldest daughter, timid, conventional, dutiful.

Helen Gant—Their third child, temperamental, unstable, loving, the father's favorite.

Grover Gant—One of the twins, a sad, gentle boy who dies young.

Ben Gant—His twin, a tormented, proud, independent man, Eugene Gant's beloved brother.

Eugene Gant—The youngest of the family, a brooding dreamer, hungry for life, love, beauty.

John Leonard—Principal of the private school that Eugene attends, a good but not very intelligent man.

Margaret Leonard—Eugene's teacher, who recognizes his talent and encourages him to develop it.

Laura James—A guest at the Dixieland, with whom Eugene falls madly in love.

The Story

Oliver Gant is a huge, haunted man driven by undefined longings. After the death of his wife, he wanders into Altamont, a small mountain town in North Carolina. There he marries Eliza Pentland, a shrewd, calculating woman, amassing property with almost insane greed. Oliver works as a stonemason, often interrupting his labors to go on drinking sprees, returning to denounce his wife in madly inflated rhetoric. The Gants steadily produce children of whom the seventh is Eugene, born when Eliza is forty-two and Oliver fifty.

Through Eugene's childhood run three memories: his father's violent, drunken rages and his mother's terrified responses; his love of words and his joy on learning to write; and the affection, alternating with cuffs, showered on him by his elder brothers and sisters. They are an eccentric and unstable crew. Steve, the eldest, is the one unregenerate member, foul-mouthed, foul-minded, whining, crooked. Daisy, next born, is timid, dutiful, industrious. Helen, the third child, is passionate, dissatisfied, loving, fiercely devoted to her father who in his debauches will be quieted only by her. Grover and Ben are twins, the former sad and gentle, the latter tormented, proud, afflicted. Luke, the youngest except for Eugene, is clever and sharp. He shares, beyond the others, his mother's lust for possessions.

When Eugene is four, Eliza takes all her children, except Daisy, to St. Louis, the world's fair city, to open a boarding-house. Daisy stays behind to finish school and keep house for Oliver who opposes Eliza's venture. But Eliza soon returns to Altamont, for Grover contracts typhoid fever and dies.

There, at the age of six, Eugene begins school. He is tormented by his schoolmaster, who senses that he is different. Eugene is dark, brooding, given to fantasy. Nevertheless the books he now begins to devour make school tolerable. And after a while, too, he becomes part of a boy's gang and so is able to inflict pain on people even more helpless than he.

Eugene is soon forced to endure more serious suffering. From childhood Ben had delivered newspapers and Luke had been an energetic agent for the *Saturday Evening Post*. As a result of Eliza's insistence, Eugene also becomes a wage earner. First he assists Luke; later he gets a newspaper route of his own. Eugene hates his jobs which expose him to danger when he delivers his papers to the worst parts of town. Only Ben seems to sympathize with him, upbraiding their mother for her neglect.

Before Eugene is eight, Eliza buys Dixieland, a large boardinghouse in town. The purchase means her separation from Oliver. Helen, who is hostile toward her mother and adores her father, stays to keep house for him. Eliza takes Eugene with her, while Ben and Luke float from one house to the other. Steve has already begun his vagabondage, existing by odd jobs and small forgeries. Daisy marries a grocery clerk and moves to another town. Eliza regularly complains of her hard lot despite the fact that it is self-imposed. Working from early to late at the Dixieland, engrossed in land speculation, she can devote little attention to her family.

In his eleventh year, Eugene wins a school essay contest. The principal, John Leonard, about to start a school of his own—the Altamont Fitting School—prevails upon Eliza to enroll Eugene. There, for the next four years, he comes under the spell of a highly gifted teacher, Margaret Leonard, the principal's wife. She recognizes and directs his passion for knowledge and beauty, his confused gropings toward understanding and self-realization. Eugene reads hungrily, memorizes great quantities of poetry, learns Latin and some German. At the same time he continues to work his paper route. It is small wonder that at fifteen he has only 130 pounds of flesh on his six-foot-three frame.

Eugene is tortured by erotic desire, but is at the same time plagued by sexual fears. Once, when he stops to make a collection on his paper route, a Negro prostitute arouses him. But he runs away. On a trip to Charleston, he has an affair with a waitress, but again he does not consummate it.

Eugene is not quite sixteen when he enters the state university. He is happy to go. Eliza has become richer and more grasping and miserly than ever. His brother Ben, whom he loves more than any other member of his family, suffers from weak lungs. Oliver, the powerful, raging man, is debilitated by cancer. Steve, though he has married a sluttish older woman with a small fortune, keeps returning to the Dixieland—and with him he always carries the stench of rottenness. Helen has become a professional singer and, as one of the Dixie Melody Twins, is touring the South with indifferent success.

At college, Eugene at first seems out of things. He is the victim of practical jokes. His gullibility and ignorance of college traditions are exploited unfeelingly. But gradually he adjusts to college life. He joins the staff of the student literary magazine, does well in his studies, especially in English literature and in Greek, subjects in which he has imaginative teachers. He makes some disreputable friends and visits a brothel where his fear and revulsion make him impotent.

During his first summer holiday, Eugene falls in love with Laura James, a guest at the Dixieland. But he is fifteen, she twenty-one. They have a brief but intense love affair. Then she returns to her home in Richmond—for a week, she promises. But from Richmond she writes to tell him that she has been engaged for a year and is to be married the next day. He is sunk in despair which is intensified by the malicious teasing that he gets from his family.

Eugene's sophomore year is uneventful. He is accepted by his fellow students, joins clubs and societies, promises to become a "big man" on campus. He spends a desolate summer working at several jobs in Richmond where he has gone in the forlorn hope of somehow seeing Laura. Returning home, he is further depressed by his father's decline and his mother's callous pursuit of money.

In October of his third year at college, Eugene is summoned home. His brother Ben is dying of pneumonia; Eliza had neglected to call a doctor till too late. On his deathbed, Ben rejects Eliza's faltering attempts to approach him. After his death, he is given an expensive funeral. The Gant family spends more money on Ben dead than they ever did when he was alive.

At the university, Eugene becomes editor-in-chief of the newspaper, does brilliantly in his courses, and is graduated with honors. He returns home to his family which has grown more divided than ever, each suspecting the others of wanting more than a just share from the estate of their dying father. Eugene remains aloof. After Eliza promises to send him to Harvard for a year's graduate study, Luke asks Eugene to sign a paper acknowledging that the college fees and expenses he had received eliminate him from sharing in the estate. He signs the release willingly.

On his last night in Altamont, under a blazing moon, Eugene has a vision of his beloved brother, the dead Ben. Ben tells him that there is only one voyage, that there is no happy land, that the world is always within—that there is no more to be found in life than Eugene has found so far. But Eugene, filled with hope, looks forward to the great voyage of discovery he is about to take, the voyage that is life.

Critical Opinion

Thomas Wolfe's *Look Homeward, Angel,* a biographer points out, "fell on critically evil days and they have taken their toll of his reputation, if not of his steadily increasing number of readers." Published in 1929 in the month of the stock-market crash, it was regularly attacked by the critics of the thirties for its lack of social commitment. The attacks have never ceased. Only recently an influential English critic has said that Wolfe is not a novelist at all: "He is an obsessional neurotic with a gift for words who could write only about himself and who could not create other people."

The charges against Wolfe vary, but those most frequently leveled are that he is guilty of "sprawling profusion," that he is "monstrously rhetorical and oratorical," that he constructs formless, bulging pseudo-narratives that he then calls "novels." Not all the charges are baseless. Wolfe himself divided writers into two classifications—those who "take out" and those who "put in," and named as the great practitioner of the selective novel, Flaubert and of the inclusive novel, Tolstoi.

Wolfe further wrote, to Margaret Roberts (the model for Margaret Leonard), that *Look Homeward, Angel* was the story of a powerful creativity "trying to work its way toward an essential isolation; a creative solitude; a secret life—its fierce struggles to wall their part of life away from birth, first against the public and savage glare of an unbalanced, nervous, brawling family group, later against school, society, and all the barbarous invasions of the world." And this analysis may indicate the reason for the novel's continuing appeal. *Look Homeward, Angel* is intense autobiography, the record of the author's struggle for self, for individuality. People, especially but not exclusively young people, identify with that struggle, feel the novel with a force and directness that make negative criticism largely irrelevant. The novel still proves for them a vitalizing, even a liberating experience, and they still find their way to it in undiminished numbers.

Besides, the novel has three qualities that make it rise above its faults: its lyrical, soaring prose which forms an effective counterpart to its harsh and bitter realism; its moving, pungent dramatic dialogue; its vivid portraiture, which has etched for us a gallery of real, memorable people. Few American novelists can boast a greater accomplishment.

The Author

Thomas Wolfe was born in Asheville, North Carolina, and died in Baltimore, Maryland, of a brain infection. The thirty-nine years of his tumultuous life are chronicled in his four novels: *Look Homeward, Angel* (1929), *Of Time and the River* (1935), *The Web and the Rock* (1939), and *You Can't Go Home Again* (1940). Though the last two novels have a different hero (George Webber displaces the Eugene Gant of the earlier novels), all are essentially autobiographical.

Thomas Wolfe's father was a stonecutter, fond of reciting Shakespearean verses and impelled from time to time to go on roaring drunks. His mother ran a boardinghouse. In Asheville, Wolfe attended first a public school, then a private school where he came under the influence of a superb teacher, Margaret Roberts. He escaped a tempestuous family life by going to the University of North Carolina where he "joined everything" and wrote prodigiously. Two of his plays were produced at the university. Later he studied playwriting at Harvard under George Baker who conducted the famous "Workshop 47" course. The plays were not important in themselves, but they developed in Wolfe the dramatic sense that informs his novels.

The rest of his life Wolfe dedicated to writing, though he taught intermittently at New York University (1924–30) and went abroad several times. The stage designer Aline Bernstein, with whom he had a long love affair, showed the manu-

script of his first novel, *Look Homeward, Angel,* to Maxwell
Perkins, editor of Scribner's. It was a huge, sprawling, shapeless, unpublishable work, but Perkins saw in it the marks of
genius. Together with Wolfe, he edited the novel, eliminating,
condensing, sharpening. Their "creative partnership" was generously acknowledged by Wolfe in *The Story of a Novel*
(1936). The manuscript, one wit commented, was brought to
Perkins by truck and he returned it by taxi.

Despite the unfortunate timing of publication—the month
of the 1929 stock-market crash—*Look Homeward, Angel* was
successful. Wolfe worked for the next six years on the monu-
mental *Of Time and the River,* the second installment of his
vast fictional autobiography, publishing in the interval some
stories and one excellent short novel, *A Portrait of Bascom
Hawke.*

After his second novel, Wolfe changed publishers, perhaps
because it had not been as favorably received as his first,
perhaps because he resented the frequent remark (originating
in jealousy) that Perkins ought to be listed as co-author at
least. In any event, Edward C. Aswell of Harper and Brothers
proved a splendid editor, too. Wolfe's untimely death prevented the kind of intimate collaboration that he had had
with Perkins, but Aswell expertly sifted through the huge
stack of manuscript that Wolfe had left and from it shaped
three novels: *The Web and the Rock, You Can't Go Home
Again,* and *The Hills Beyond* (1941), the last a book of stories. Together with the Eugene Gant novels, they form a vivid,
astonishingly full account of one man's artistic growth and
fulfillment.

The Sound and the Fury

by

WILLIAM FAULKNER (1897–1962)

Main Characters

Jason Compson, Sr.—The alcoholic head of the Compson family. Weak and cynical, he loves his brood but lacks the initiative to do more than advise them of the futility of struggling against life.

Caroline Bascomb Compson—His wife, a selfish hypochondriac, more concerned about her status than the psychic welfare of her children. Her favorite child is Jason.

Quentin Compson III—The eldest son, born 1891, a Harvard undergraduate, obsessed with tradition, purity, and death, a suicide at nineteen.

Candace Compson—Nicknamed Caddy, beautiful, indiscriminately amorous, but capable of profound self-sacrifice.

Jason Compson—Brutal, devoid of human feeling, responsive only to money.

Benjy Compson—Youngest of the children, born 1895; a gelded idiot who loves three things: the Compson pasture, Caddy, and firelight.

Miss Quentin—Caddy's seventeen-year-old daughter, separated by family will from her mother, living with Mrs. Compson, Jason, and Benjy. She is headstrong and rebellious, beautiful and promiscuous.

Uncle Maury—Mrs. Compson's only brother, handsome, lecherous, and always unemployed.

Dalton Ames—Caddy's lover, probably young Quentin's father, as stereotypically Southern as his name—romantic, bold, and egotistic.

Herbert Head—Caddy's husband, an Indianan, a former Harvard undergraduate, remembered at college for cheating at cards and during examinations.

Gerald Bland, Spoade, and *Shreve*—Quentin's classmates. Bland and Spoade are Southerners, the former a shallow parvenu, the latter a lazy man but a sexual athlete. Shreve, a Canadian and Quentin's roommate, remains an outsider.

Dilsey—The Compsons' Negro housekeeper. Strong of will and faith, she scolds and submits as circumstance demands and struggles to keep the declining Compsons together.

Roskus—Dilsey's husband.

Luster—Dilsey's grandson. Aged fourteen, he is assigned the man's task of caring for Benjy.

Frony—Dilsey's daughter and Luster's mother.

T.P., Versh—Dilsey's sons.

Deacon—A Negro factotum at Harvard who earns his living by providing for Southern students the Uncle Tom image they seem to need.

The Story

The Sound and the Fury is divided into four books, each narrated from a different point of view, each told on a different day. Thus the opening section takes place in the mind of the idiot Benjy on Holy Saturday, April 7, 1928. The second section is a record of Quentin's stream of consciousness on June 2, 1910, the day Quentin commits suicide. Jason narrates the third section on Good Friday, April 6, 1928. The final section, dealing with the events of Easter, April 8, 1928, is told from an external point of view.

The first two sections present difficulties for the reader. The latter two are readily comprehensible. Benjy's tale—since he is an idiot—shifts time and events rapidly and apparently incoherently. Moreover, Benjy's responses to stimuli are sensory, never rational. Quentin, despite his highly sophisticated intelligence, is obsessed by memory, compelled by suicidal drives. As a result he, too, fuses time and freely associates

words, things, and episodes so complexly that his narrative
may confuse the reader even more than Benjy's. To enable
the reader to follow the sequence of events in these first two
sections, the following summary chronologically orders the
events. Such an arrangement, of course, is a convenience, not
a substitute for Faulkner's brilliantly realized evocation of
dislocation and decay.

Benjy, April 7, 1928

a. The Present.

On his thirty-third birthday, Benjy, attended by Luster,
watches the golfers across the fence from the Compson yard
and moans as they call for their caddies. (The word reminds
him of his sister.) Luster has lost a quarter he needs for the
visiting carnival that evening and, while searching for it, keeps
Benjy quiet by giving him a jimson weed to chew on. They
reach the creek and Luster takes off Benjy's shoes so he can
wade. Thinking that he may have lost his quarter elsewhere,
Luster leaves Benjy alone and goes off to search further.
Benjy wanders off to a grove where Miss Quentin and a carnival pitchman are embracing. When Luster—still without his
quarter—arrives, Quentin berates him for letting Benjy intrude
on her.

Luster tries without success to sell the pitchman a golf
ball for twenty-five cents. A few minutes later, a golfer takes
the ball from him without paying anything. Frustrated and
angry, Luster relieves his boyish irritation by tormenting
Benjy. He overturns the bottle in which Benjy keeps his weeds
and whispers "Caddy" in his ear.

Benjy's howls reach the house and Dilsey calls the two
back, then placates Benjy by sitting him before the oven fire
and lighting the candles on his birthday cake. When Dilsey
leaves the kitchen, Luster mischievously closes the oven door
and blows out the candles. Benjy howls and Dilsey returns to
open the door and warn Luster. Again, however, with Dilsey's
back turned, Luster shuts the door, and this time Benjy reaches
out for the fire and burns his hand on the oven. Dilsey slaps
Luster, salves Benjy's burn, and gives him Caddy's old slipper
to appease him. Moaning softly, clenching the slipper, Benjy
sits before the library fire.

At dinnertime Jason refuses Luster's request for a quarter

and warns Quentin to stay away from her carnival boyfriend. Quentin defies Jason and when he ridicules her, throws a glass of water at him and runs from the room.

At bedtime Benjy looks at his gelded body and cries. Luster, putting Benjy's nightclothes on him, hears a noise and, together with Benjy, watches Quentin climb down a tree from her window and walk out across the lawn.

b. The Past.

In 1898, while all the children are playing in the creek, Caddy, squatting, wets her dress and takes it off despite Quentin's protest. Quentin slaps her and she falls, muddying her drawers. Angrily, she splashes water on Quentin. Jason says he will tell his parents what they have done and as soon as the children return home, he tells his father. Sent to bed after supper, the children, led by Caddy, sneak out to the Negroes' cabin to play. Later, Caddy climbs a tree to see what the adults are about. The children below look up at Caddy's muddy drawers—all except Quentin, who remains aloof and sullen. What Caddy thinks is a party is in fact a funeral gathering for her dead grandmother, "Damuddy."

The years of Benjy's adolescence are dominated by memories of Caddy's smelling like rain, her gentle embraces, and her sleeping beside him. Other memories also intrude: delivering Uncle Maury's love notes to a neighboring lady and seeing Maury's eye blackened by her husband; watching his beloved paper dolls being cut up by Jason; crying when Caddy, at fourteen, first uses perfume, and again, after discovering her in a swing with a boy who tries to kiss her, and still again, when at the age of thirteen, he is forbidden to stay in Caddy's bed.

At fourteen Benjy howls when Caddy returns home after losing her virginity. He tries to pull her into the bathroom to wash, as before when he cried at her using perfume and her being kissed. The next year, at Caddy's wedding party, T.P. gets Benjy drunk on champagne in the cellar. Standing atop a box to look inside, Benjy sees Caddy in her wedding dress and cries. Then he slips, hits his head, and begins to bellow. Quentin discovers Benjy and T.P., beats the Negro boy sober, and watches as Benjy vomits and passes out.

With Caddy gone, Benjy stands sobbing at the Compson

fence. When Quentin's body is sent home from Harvard a month later, Benjy is kept from the house. Just a few weeks thereafter, Benjy chases some girls passing along the fence and touches one of them. Yielding to town pressure, the family sends Benjy away to be castrated. Two years later Benjy smells death once more, this time the death of his father. Holding a flower in his hand, Benjy rides to the cemetery in a horse carriage with his mother and T.P. On the way they drive through the town square of Jefferson to pick up Jason at his store, but he refuses to attend the funeral. The carriage drives on.

Quentin, June 2, 1910

a. The Present.

It is the last day of Quentin's life. He awakens early, hears his watch ticking, and turns it face down. His roommate, Shreve, urges him to hurry lest he be late for Harvard chapel. But Quentin lingers, watching Spoade dawdle across the campus. Then he breaks his watch crystal and twists off the hands, cutting his fingers in the process. He packs his trunk, addresses some letters indicating to whom his clothes are to be given, and lays out a fresh change of clothing. After bathing and shaving, he rides the tram to Boston, breakfasts, and brings his watch to a jeweler, noting with interest that none of the clocks in the jeweler's window has the correct time.

At a hardware store he purchases two six-pound flatirons (to weight his body) and reboards a trolley for Cambridge. At the Charles River, the drawbridge opens and Quentin gets off the trolley to watch Gerald Bland row by. Within the next hour, he mounts and leaves several trolleys, each headed in a different direction. At last, just after noon, he rides to a stop in the country near a stone bridge that seems right for his purpose. Under one edge of the bridge he hides his flatirons.

He stands at the bridge with three boys watching a trout swim by and then begins to walk toward the adjacent town, guided by the church steeple whose clock face he tries not to see. At a bakery where he stops to buy a bun for lunch, he meets a little girl, buys her a bun, too, and then some ice cream as well. The child follows him silently despite his efforts to get her to leave. Two men suggest that he take her to the section of town across the tracks. He does, but the child refuses to tell him where she lives or to leave him. Quentin climbs a wall to elude her but finds her waiting for him on the other side. Together they approach the river, and there the sheriff and the child's brother accuse Quentin of having assaulted the girl.

Quentin laughs wildly at the charge, but he is nevertheless arraigned before a justice of the peace. Spoade and Shreve arrive to pay the six-dollar fine. As the three leave, they find Gerald Bland, his mother, and two girls waiting to take them all to a picnic. Angered by Gerald's cynical remarks about women's purity, Quentin punches him, but is himself battered, his nose bloodied, his eye blackened. Quentin returns to Cambridge alone at dusk, hiding his bruised eye from the passengers on the trolley but watching his own reflection merge with a woman's hat feather in the car window.

Back in his dormitory, Quentin changes into the clothes he had laid out early in the morning, and pauses to clean his vest with gasoline. As the campus clock tolls, he puts a letter to Shreve on the table and his watch in Shreve's drawer. He brushes his teeth, rubs up the nap on his hat, dons it, and leaves—to commit suicide.

b. The Past.

Like Benjy, Quentin recalls first the episode of Caddy's dirtying her drawers on the day of Damuddy's death. All his subsequent recollections spiral outward from that primal stain upon his sister's purity. When Caddy at fifteen kisses a boy and twits Quentin, saying she made the boy kiss her, Quentin rubs her face in the grass. She taunts him further by reminding him that he kissed a girl named Natalie not long before. In that episode Quentin and Natalie kissed and childishly imitated the gestures of intercourse, unaware that Caddy was watching. After the incident Quentin, humiliated and ashamed, threw himself into the hogwallow. Then, seeing Caddy, he tried to make her understand what happened. When she turned away from him, he grabbed her, knocked her down, and smeared her with the mud from his body. Caddy scratched his face, apologized, and together they washed themselves in the creek.

Quentin's central memory is of Caddy's loss of virginity to Dalton Ames. When Benjy howls at Caddy's new smell, Quentin, who understands Benjy's strangely perceptive sensory insight, determines to ask Caddy whether she yielded or was forced. Finding Caddy squatting in the creek, he asks her, swears to kill Ames if he has harmed her, and offers to run away with her. When she asks him whether he has ever experienced sex, he weeps, and recalls for her the day she muddied her drawers. He presses a knife to her throat, offering a death compact, but she rightly doubts his willingness to go ahead with his offer.

Failing to dissuade Caddy from meeting Ames, he goes along with her and watches as they embrace. He runs off distraught, and Caddy follows him to the creek and offers herself to him. Torn between desire and horror, he shakes her and bids her be still. A few days later Quentin confronts Ames alone and threatens him. Ames gently dismisses Quentin's warnings, reminding him that all women are bitches. Enraged, Quentin tries to hit Ames but is easily held off. Ames takes a pistol and shoots a bit of wood in the river, then offers the pistol to Quentin. Quentin takes it, but trying again to hit Ames, he faints. Caddy, hearing the shot, runs to the scene, thinking Ames has hurt Quentin. She sends Ames away forever, she says, but when Quentin asks her later whether she still loves Ames, she admits that she does.

Mrs. Compson (who wore black the day she first knew Caddy had kissed a boy) now takes Caddy away hoping to find her a husband other than the unacceptable Ames. While they are gone, Quentin tries to convince his father that he, not Ames, has made love to Caddy. Aware that his son is a virgin, Mr. Compson tries to help Quentin gain perspective on Caddy's loss of virginity as a normal process, one hardly conducive to thoughts of suicide. All of this is temporary, Mr. Compson argues, persuasively but unavailingly.

Just before the wedding, back from Harvard where he enshrined the wedding invitation on his desk as an altar for the dead, Quentin meets Herbert Head, Caddy's fiancé, and despises him for his flattery and ostentation (he has bought Caddy a car for a wedding present and promised Mrs. Compson to give Jason a job in his bank) and for his attempt to bribe Quentin not to tell about his reputation at Harvard. When he is alone with Caddy, he begs her not to marry Head, but Caddy insists he let her have her chance for marriage. The night before the wedding, she asks him to care for their father and for Benjy. Again he pleads with her not to marry Head but rather to go away with him. As he tries to embrace her, Caddy pushes him away, telling him that she is pregnant and must marry, and that she has had other lovers, too. Quentin's responsibility, she insists, is to finish college and help the family.

Jason, April 6, 1928

With Quentin and his father dead and Caddy exiled, Jason is the head of what is left of the Compson family. "You are the only one of them that isn't a reproach to me," his whining mother tells him. Jason's thoughts ("Once a bitch always a bitch, what I say . . . ." is the opening phrase in this section) and actions do little to support his mother's misplaced faith. Deprived of his promised banking post when Herbert Head abandons Caddy, Jason has compensated by stealing for fifteen years the monthly $200 checks Caddy has sent Mrs. Compson to care for her daughter Quentin. Though Mrs. Compson knows about the money, Jason has kept the authentic checks aside, giving his mother worthless forged copies which she innocently burns, proud of her refusal to accept money from her sinful child.

Once partner in a general store, Jason has sold the interest his mother had purchased for him to buy a car. He remains as a clerk just to keep his mother ignorant of what he has done with her investment. Ironically, the car yields Jason more grief than pleasure, for he is allergic to gasoline fumes and cannot venture any distance without carrying along as antidote a camphor-soaked handkerchief. His attempts to make money on the cotton market meet with little more success, for he is so busy spying on Quentin that he misses opportunities to buy and sell at a profit. Thus, on Friday, April 8, while the market fluctuates wildly and demands his constant attention, Jason pursues Quentin up and down back alleys, trying to trap her with her boy friend from the carnival. Not only does he fail to catch her, but he misses an important message about a stock transaction. When he does at last try to telegraph his instructions, the stock market has closed. His revenge is to taunt

Quentin at dinner with thinly veiled obscene allusions to her activities.

Jason's bitterness extends beyond his family: he hates Jews and Negroes, because he fancies that the former control the stock market and the latter his life. He resents Dilsey's place in the family pattern and regards all Negroes as stupid or stubborn or both. When Luster, still hoping to attend the carnival even though he has lost his quarter, asks Jason for one of the two passes he has, Jason retorts that he needs cash and will sell one pass for a nickel. Despite Dilsey's anger, Jason baits the boy, rejects his fervent promises of repayment, and at last drops both passes into the fire.

Easter Sunday, April 8, 1928

Three episodes are interwoven in this brief final section. Ironically contrasted with the chaos of the Compson family is Dilsey's orderly preparation of breakfast and her trip with her family to Easter services conducted by a wizened, inspired Negro preacher from St. Louis, Rev. Shegog. After the service, her face tear-streaked, her head held high, Dilsey walks toward home and says, prophetically, "I seed de beginnin', en now I sees de endin'."

Meanwhile, Jason discovers that Quentin has run off with the nearly $7,000 Jason had hidden beneath a plank in his room. When the sheriff refuses to join in a chase on evidence he regards as too circumstantial, Jason drives off alone—without his camphor-soaked handkerchief. His headache rages even when he tries to think about his weekends with his blowzy mistress Lorraine. At the carnival, where he hopes to find Quentin and her pitchman lover, Jason irrationally demands of an elderly cook that he produce the couple. The cook has no notion of what Jason is talking about, but when Jason strikes him, the cook goes berserk and chases him with a rusty hatchet. Others prevent the cook from killing Jason after Jason falls and strikes his head. Exhausted, unable to carry on his search or to drive his car back to Jefferson, Jason offers various Negroes a dollar to drive him home. All refuse until one stops by and demands four dollars. Jason counters with an offer of two, but the Negro insists upon and gets what he asked for.

In the final scene, Dilsey allows Luster to drive Benjy to town. Holding a narcissus in his hand, Benjy sits quietly as the carriage moves toward the town square in Jefferson. Suddenly determined to show off, Luster decides to turn the carriage to the left, counter to traffic. Unaccustomed to seeing objects in reverse order, Benjy bellows. Just back from his unhappy trip, Jason hears the noise, leaps across the square, turns the horse about, pounds Luster on the head, and directs him to return to the house. As the pattern returns to normal, Benjy sinks into a serenely quiet blankness, the broken narcissus stem clenched in his fist.

Critical Opinion

Life, says Macbeth, is "a tale told by an idiot, full of sound and fury, signifying nothing." In Faulkner's complex paraphrase of Shakespeare's grim utterance, man's prospects grow no brighter. True, Dilsey endures and seems a symbol of man's endurance. But Dilsey is a Negro housekeeper, courageous yet subjugated and oppressed by the white society she lives in. Her strength is internal. Its impact on the world outside is small.

One cannot turn away, however, from a work of literature because its author's vision of life is neither idyllically happy nor glowingly hopeful. Critics have argued lengthily about theme and technique in *The Sound and the Fury*, but only a few have denied its overpowering force. Unquestionably a difficult book, it rewards the painstaking reader with deep insight into the private and public life of a degenerating Southern family. A haunting sense of the glories of their ante-bellum past torments the Compsons, and their failure to adjust to a modern world hastens their decay. False views of caste, chivalry, morality, and love distort Quentin's approach to experience as thoroughly as Jason's total absence of any but material values distorts his. Caddy, like her daughter Quentin, is essentially a decent human being trapped by the inflexibility of outworn or inhumane conventions. Poor Benjy, though he understands nothing, feels and smells the effects of the disorder that surrounds him. His tale, a tale told by an idiot, nevertheless signifies much.

To tell his powerful story, Faulkner uses his novelistic techniques with consummate skill. Structurally, he moves from
the disordered, irrational world of Benjy's uncomprehending
consciousness to the lucid, objective, external narrative of the
final section. Some critics have argued that the novel would
read better were the order reversed. Others have justly shown
that the small gain in clarity would be offset by great loss of
perspective, mood, and insight.

Other devices also add density to Faulkner's searching revelation of the fate of modern man. The novel is rich in symbols
that render concrete many of the abstract problems Faulkner
treats. Thus, Quentin's obsessive interest in time is imaged in
his broken watch—a sharp contrast, incidentally, to Dilsey's
faulty alarm clock which never disturbs her assurance about
time. The theme of incest is presented against the sensually
aromatic background of honeysuckle. Jason's materialism
evokes the noxious odor of gasoline. And there is, of course,
the central myth of Easter to underscore the agony of man
and to hold forth in Dilsey's experience at the service the possibility of resurrection.

The Sound and the Fury, then, affords the reader a rich and
complex philosophical and psychological perception of life. Its
art orders a chaotic universe, and though it provides no final
answers to man's problems, it dramatizes them with power,
insight, and understanding.

Light in August

by

WILLIAM FAULKNER

Main Characters

Joe Christmas—The protagonist, an agonized spirit, violent,
rebellious, destructive, unable to discover his identity, and
doomed to wreak vengeance on himself as well as on others.

Joanna Burden—Joe's mistress, a forty-one-year-old New Englander whose moral inheritance commits her to helping the
Negro even though she believes him inferior.

Gail Hightower—Once a Presbyterian minister, now a recluse willfully isolated from the world of reality and from all possibility of either pleasure or pain.

Lena Grove—Pregnant with an illegitimate child, yet the symbol of natural innocence, never questioning the essential goodness of life and man.

Lucas Burch—Alias Joe Brown, the father of Lena's child. Shiftless and irresponsible, he wants from life only the pleasures of sex and drink.

Byron Bunch—Until he meets Lena Grove, he is lonely, austere, dutiful, bound by moral strictures and social taboos.

Doc Hines—Joe Christmas' grandfather, a sin- and race-obsessed fanatic who hovers over Joe like an avenging angel.

McEachern—Joe's foster father, a bloodlessly religious and ruthless tyrant.

Mrs. McEachern—Gentle, maternal, but wholly submissive to her husband's will.

Bobbie Allen—Joe's first woman, a waitress and prostitute, capable of both affection and cruelty.

Percy Grimm—A young National Guardsman, a chauvinist and a racist.

The Story

Although the stories of Joe Christmas, Gail Hightower, and Lena Grove are entirely separate, during the eleven eventful August days in Jefferson, Mississippi, their lives intersect dramatically and bring to the novel a powerful unity. At the beginning Lena Grove has been walking from Alabama toward Jefferson for nearly a month to find Lucas Burch, the father of her unborn child, rumored to be working at a lumber planing mill in Jefferson. Ignoring her swollen, uncomfortable body, Lena plods along the road, gratefully accepting a wagon ride or a night's hospitality. Lacking these, she trudges on serenely, confidently, resting and sleeping in the open fields. One Friday morning she arrives in Jefferson where she sees columns of smoke rising from a burning house in the distance.

Three years earlier—also on a Friday morning—a silent young stranger named Joe Christmas was hired at the mill. Just six months before Lena's arrival, another young man, brash and talkative, calling himself Joe Brown (he is, in fact, Lucas Burch), also began work there. For some months before the novel begins, neither Burch nor Christmas has worked at the mill, being partners in a lucrative bootlegging operation. A third millworker is Byron Bunch who has labored there for nine years. The men at the mill respect Christmas for his diligence but dislike him for his rude aloofness. They ridicule Lucas' laziness and despise his loudness, and they wonder about Byron who is friendly and hard-working but reticent about his personal life.

Only one townsman, the Rev. Gail Hightower, knows about Byron's private life: on weekends Byron drives to the country to sing with a church choir, and several nights a week he spends hours in conversation with Hightower. Thus on the evening of Lena Grove's arrival in town, Bunch tells Hightower about certain significant events of the day: Lena's visit to the mill, the murder of Joanna Burden, and the burning of her house. At the mill, Lena has spoken with Bunch about Lucas. Byron, knowing of Lucas' involvement in the Burden case, regrets now that he did not deny to her that Lucas and Joe Brown are the same man. Byron tells Hightower only that he wants to shield Lena from knowing the grim sequence of events coincident with her arrival. But Hightower senses what Byron himself does not yet realize—that he has already fallen in love with the tranquil but determined girl. About Joanna Burden's death, Byron tells what he has learned from the townspeople. Having heard of a reward for the capture of Joanna's murderer, Lucas has told the police that Joe Christmas is the culprit and lived with Joanna for three years even though he apparently merely shared with Lucas a cabin on her property. Finally, he has told the police that Joe has admitted he is a Negro, despite his coloration.

During Byron's recital, Hightower sits silent, rigidly erect, his expression one of "denial and flight." Years have passed since he came with his young wife to preach in Jefferson, since he abandoned his ministry, and since he has accepted reality. From the outset, parishioners found his sermons too frenzied, as if he sought to find religion rather than to dispense it. And Hightower's wife, too, seemed objectionably strange, rarely attending service, disappearing on weekends, and once interrupting services by screaming hysterically. Briefly confined as a mental patient, she was soon thereafter discovered in a Memphis hotel room with a strange man and leaped from a window to her death. Despite pressure from his flock, Hightower refused to resign his post. But at last, accused of relations with his Negro cook, beaten by Klansmen, he yielded. In time the townfolk came to ignore him and to accept his self-imposed isolation.

Now, listening to Byron's narrative of love and violence, Hightower is afraid these events may disrupt his determination to turn away from experience. Ironically, he also fears that Byron's involvement—especially with Lena—will deprive him of his single remaining human companion.

The novel now shifts to Joe Christmas, tracing in multiple flashbacks his recollection of the past and the events leading to his murder of Joanna Burden. He recalls first a key episode during his fifth year when he lived in a white orphanage. Hidden behind a curtain in the room of Miss Atkins, the dietitian, Joe sits eating toothpaste and, when Miss Atkins and a young doctor unexpectedly enter, uncomprehendingly hears the sounds of their lovemaking. When the toothpaste sickens him, Joe vomits and thus is discovered by the woman. Angered, distraught, she calls him a spy and, in an outburst of rage, "nigger." Joe understands only that he is being punished for eating toothpaste, but the trauma of sex and racial identity stirred by this episode haunts him forever.

Afraid that Joe will tell and cause her to lose her post, Miss Atkins seeks help from Doc Hines, the janitor, who began work at the orphanage just after Joe's arrival. Since then, as Miss Atkins says, Hines has stayed on just "to watch and hate" the child. Though he regards Miss Atkins as a harlot and her discovery by Joe as a triumph for God, he nevertheless tries to steal the child and place him in a Negro orphanage. Meanwhile Miss Atkins, hoping to have Joe sent away, tells the matron of the orphanage that he is a Negro. Hines's kidnaping venture is unearthed, the child brought back, and the matron, believing that a shift in Joe's racial identity will hurt him, places him with a white family, the McEacherns.

Joe's years in the McEachern home harden the mold of his sexual and racial bitterness. As a child of eight he is mercilessly beaten by his rabidly moralistic foster father for failing to learn his catechism. At fourteen, confronted with the possibility of his first sexual experience, he kicks and beats the Negro girl his white friends have been making love to. At seventeen, after arduous daytime work on McEachern's farm, Joe begins to slip away at night to meet Bobbie Allen, a woman in her thirties, with whom he has his first sexual experience. During one of their amorous moments, he tells her of his belief that he is part Negro. Shocked but not entirely convinced, she continues with their affair. When Joe learns that Bobbie is really a prostitute, he beats her brutally, yet remains her lover, but he pays her each time, using money he has stolen from his kindly foster mother.

One night McEachern follows Joe and finds him at a dance with Bobbie. McEachern denounces the girl as a whore and attacks Joe who fells him with a chair. With Bobbie's imprecations roaring in his ears, Joe returns home, steals his foster mother's money as she looks on (he has loathed her kindness even more than her husband's brutality), then steals and beats the horse he rides to Bobbie's house. He spills the stolen money on her bed, then punches her viciously. She calls out for help, denounces Joe to her friends as a Negro, and watches as he is beaten up.

For the next ten years Joe drifts through the country, working at several jobs, sleeping with innumerable women, afterward telling them he is a Negro and suffering the curses or beatings that follow. One woman shows indifference to his race and he nearly beats her to death, sickened at the possibility of her lack of prejudice. For two years after this experience, he lives as a Negro in the North, his mistress an ebony-hued girl. But he fails here again to prove his racial identity to himself.

At last—at the age of thirty-three—he arrives in Jefferson. Attracted by the large house just beyond the town, he walks there. Once inside the gate, Joe smells food and steals into the kitchen. He is eating when the lady of the house, Joanna Burden, discovers him. She allows him to stay on and live in a cabin across the field from her house. Although they rarely meet, Joe is always infuriated by her aloofness. His rage increases and one night he rapes her, startled by her "hard, untearful and unself-pitying and almost manlike yielding." Joe expects that Joanna will seek revenge for what he has done to her. He is shocked when nothing happens. He continues to work at the mill and to live at the cabin, wondering what his strange benefactor and victim will do next. Some time later, Joanna comes to his cabin and in great detail recounts her history: her abolitionist forebears, the murder of some of them who moved to Jefferson to help Negroes, and her ancestrally imposed task—to expiate the guilt of her race at whatever cost to herself.

Her confession over, Joanna initiates the "second phase" of her relationship with Joe. The days remain as before, but at night—in her bed and sometimes even in the fields—she forces him beyond sin, demanding of him total corruption in word and deed. Always during their lovemaking, she whispers, "Negro, Negro, Negro." Her passion and fury terrify Joe. Yet knowing he should escape, he stays on, not understanding why.

Two years later, the third and final phase begins—Joanna's quest for salvation. Pregnant, desperate to be forgiven her carnal sins yet unwilling to forego them, she turns to prayer. Trying to force Joe to share her expiation, she urges him to attend a Negro college or, since he refuses, at least to pray for his soul. Again Joe refuses. The struggle grows in intensity until one night Joanna points a Confederate revolver at him, and Joe cuts her throat. The next morning, after Joe has fled, the drunken Lucas Burch discovers the body and accidentally sets fire to the house.

Catastrophe follows Joe swiftly in his flight. Bloodhounds and posse pursue him while Lucas clamors for the reward money. Along his way, Joe bursts into a Negro revival meeting, knocks the preacher from the pulpit, and looses a tirade against God. When the preacher's son tries to slash Joe with a razor, Joe fractures his skull with a bench leg. The flight and pursuit continue, the dogs thrown off the scent when Joe dons a Negro's shoes. Running, no longer aware of time or place, Joe enters Mottstown, twenty miles from Jefferson, on Friday morning, just seven days after his flight began. In Mottstown, Joe has his hair cut by a white barber, buys new clothes, and then walks the main street until he is recognized and arrested.

Among the would-be lynchers in the mob that quickly gathers, none is more eager for Joe's blood or more difficult to restrain than Doc Hines. The erstwhile janitor of Joe's orphanage has for the past thirty years been a preacher in Mottstown, his gospel—white supremacy as the price of salvation; his audience—Negroes. A lynching is averted and Joe is returned to the jail in Jefferson. Doc Hines and his wife follow the pris- oner, Doc to try once more to stir the crowd to action, his wife to learn the truth she has never heard about the boy whose existence Hines has kept hidden from her since the child's birth. She reveals the tale to Hightower after Byron Bunch brings her to him.

The truth about Joe's origins emerge. The Hineses are Joe's grandparents. Their daughter Millie bore a son from her affair with a man she described as a Mexican. Doc Hines killed the man and, denying his daughter the post-natal care she needed, allowed her to die. Then he stole the newborn child and de- posited it on Christmas Eve on the doorstep of a brothel, later telling the madam its name was Joseph. Once Joe went off with the McEachern family, Doc thought his God-assigned task of revenge was complete. Soon, however, his haunted sense that Joe was "a pollution and an abomination" returned to torture him until the climax of Joe's final arrest.

As Joe is led from his cell across the square to the court- house for arraignment, he breaks and runs. Handcuffed but with a gun gripped between his hands, he clears a path through the stunned crowd. Alone among the pursuers, Percy Grimm keeps Joe in sight, chasing him from behind a Negro's cabin and finally into Hightower's house. Inside the house, Joe cracks his gun against Hightower's face and runs into the kitchen, overturning the table and taking refuge behind it. When Grimm enters the house, Hightower, who has sworn to Byron Bunch that he would not help Joe in any way, now cries to Grimm that Joe is innocent, that he was with Joe the night of the murder. Grimm, disgusted with the pretense, brushes Hightower aside and enters the kitchen firing. When the other deputies arrive, they discover Grimm bending over the dying but still conscious Joe and castrating him.

As Joe dies in Hightower's house, Lena Grove gives birth to her child in the cabin Byron Bunch had sheltered her in, the same cabin Joe and Lucas had shared on Joanna Burden's property. Mrs. Hines, sent by Bunch to attend Lena, helps de- liver the child. Then, crazed by her recent knowledge, she mistakes the child for Joe, Lena for Millie. Despite Byron's love for Lena, he has the sheriff bring Lucas (who thinks he is being taken to receive his reward) to Lena's cabin. Within a very few minutes, Lucas leaves, promising to return. Instead, he escapes, chased by Byron, who catches him near the railroad. But Byron is no match for the aroused Lucas. Beaten, Byron watches as Lucas leaps aboard a departing freight.

Thus Joe Christmas dies, Lena Grove bears her child, and the Rev. Hightower is thrust reluctantly, and at best temporarily, back into the agony of life. As the novel ends, a furniture dealer from the eastern part of Mississippi, lying in bed with his wife, tells of picking up in Jefferson and carrying along to Tennessee in his truck a young woman with a baby in her arms and, with her, a nervous young man. He recalls how, when the truck paused for the night, the young man (whose name, the dealer recalls, was Bunch) crawled in to lie beside the young woman and was promptly ousted. The next morning only the girl and the baby were aboard the truck as it drove off. But around the bend, the dealer found the young man waiting. When he jumped aboard, the young man said to the girl, "I done come too far now. I be dog if I'm going to quit now." The girl's reply was, "Ain't nobody never said for you to quit."

Critical Opinion

Acknowledged as one of Faulkner's finest and most readable novels, *Light in August* is nevertheless a difficult work. The sources of its difficulty are many: complex structure, diversity of points of view, intricate imagery and symbolism, and involved themes. A summary merely suggests the novel's dazzling technical complexity and its profound insight into human behavior.

Critics have taken pains to demonstrate how Faulkner's technique serves his theme in the novel. The separate plots about Joe, Lena, and Hightower, for example, testify powerfully to man's isolation. And even when people do meet, or, as with Joe and Joanna, collide, they never do really communicate with one another. Each is sealed off in his own traumatic world of self. The same fate befalls even the minor characters: Doc Hines, McEachern, and Percy Grimm. By keeping characters like Joe and Lena from ever meeting, Faulkner not only underscores the theme of alienation and frustration, but counterpoints Joe's agony against Lena's serenity.

Similarly, the varied points of view used to narrate the story suggest how impossible it is for any single mind to comprehend the range of experience. Shifting from Lena's intuitive mind to Joe's inwardness and then to Hightower's agonized detachment, the reader begins to appreciate the kind of omniscience required to understand the power and weakness of man.

Many critics have seen in the story of Joe Christmas an ironic parallel to the New Testament account of Jesus Christ. Among the more obvious analogies are these: Joe's initials, Lucas' Judas-like betrayal of Joe for money, Joe's wanderings in his early manhood, and his inevitable progress toward crucifixion during the last seven days of his life. But Joe is no savior. His death saves no soul, frees no spirit. Indeed, as Edmond Volpe points out, Joe alone finds release, not the society whose racist concept crucifies him: "The fear and guilt of his society . . . are reinforced . . . and the concept will be imposed, during childhood, for the heirs of the executioners and make these victims, in their turn, executioners." Joe cannot save the South from its puritanical mentality. He can serve only as a scapegoat, suffering torment for a tormented people, white and black alike.

Joe dies trying to discover some justification for living. Hightower, on the other hand, surrenders his quest. "I am not in life any more," he says, rejecting at last the forces of life and death symbolized by Lena and Joe. Only Byron Bunch and Lena Grove survive to face the future. Yet Faulkner holds forth no shining promise for them: Lena is too primitive, Byron more dogged than delighted about his commitment to experience. Lena's delivery of her child is only an affirmation of a natural process—she is "light in August," as a cow might be; she has delivered her bodily burden. But no other "light" shines through to beckon her or the others. The "shadow" of Joe Christmas still falls darkly across the land when the novel ends.

The Author

Since the Civil War, the Faulkner family has been distinguished in Mississippi history. None, however, has attained the eminence of *William Faulkner,* winner of both the Pulitzer and the Nobel prizes for his fiction. Although he never graduated from high school and failed the only English course he took at the University of Mississippi, Faulkner tirelessly labored at the craft of writing and won recognition as one of the finest American novelists of the first half of the twentieth century.

After World War I, during which he trained as a pilot for the Canadian Air Force, Faulkner determined to be a writer. He started out as a poet, but soon after he met Sherwood Anderson in New Orleans, he began work upon his first novel, *Soldier's Pay* (1926), later published with Anderson's help. Though it brought him no fame, it encouraged him to go on writing. Three years later, with the publication of *The Sound and the Fury,* his finest work, Faulkner had arrived as a major writer.

That same year Faulkner married and found himself compelled to undertake odd jobs to earn a living. In 1931 he published *Sanctuary,* a novel avowedly written to make money. The brutal portrait of the degenerate Popeye and of the charming young decadent Temple Drake produced a sensation and earned Faulkner the fortune he sought. Shortly afterward he began the first of several jaunts to Hollywood, where, as he later noted, "I made me some money and had me some fun."

Such instances of potboiling, however, are fleeting and minor in Faulkner's creative life. Most of the years after 1930 found him living quietly and working diligently in his old colonial house in Oxford, Mississippi, the town where he grew up and where he spent most of his adult life. Out of that town and its environs he fashioned the mythical world of *Yoknapatawpha,* its inhabitants a cross section of the rigidly stratified Southern society. The Sartoris and Compson families, for example, represent the genteel aristocracy, a shade above Faulkner's own upper-middle-class origins. The Snopes stand at the other extreme, a clan of grasping, virulent usurpers.

And always there are the Negroes, embodying the qualities of human endurance and, by their very existence, nagging the dormant guilt and fear of the white man.

A small but handsome, quiet man, Faulkner—until his very last years—avoided publicity. Only intense family pressure persuaded him to go to Sweden, don formal attire, and accept the Nobel Prize. When he did go, however, he delivered a memorable acceptance speech. In it he declined to accept the doom of man: "I believe that man will not merely endure, he will prevail."

The 42nd Parallel

by

JOHN DOS PASSOS (1896–)

Main Characters

Mac—Restless, socially conscious, and theoretically committed to the cause of the proletariat, but unable to act creatively.

Janey Williams—The epitome of the career girl who ineffectually apes her betters.

J. Ward Moorehouse—An opportunist, the symbol of the corruption destructive to both capital and labor.

Eleanor Stoddard—Dedicated to the pursuit of a sterile estheticism that can never turn her into a warm human being.

Charley Anderson—A talented young mechanic with a zest for ideas and experience who is still emotionally uncommitted.

The Story

The 42nd parallel is a latitudinal line along which American climate travels from west to east. In Dos Passos' novel, it is also the imaginary track along which most of his characters travel. To tell his story, Dos Passos uses four different simultaneous narrative techniques. Each of these appears within the first thirty pages of the novel.

The novel opens with a *Newsreel*, a composite of headlines,

217

songs, speeches suggesting the national mood at the opening of the twentieth century. Carefully selected, the items of the *Newsreel* record the political, social, and cultural chaos of American life until 1917, when the novel ends. *The Camera Eye* follows immediately, an autobiographical stream-of-consciousness treatment of the themes of idealism and frustration in Dos Passos' childhood, adolescence, and young manhood. With *Mac*, the third and most conventional of the narrative devices begins. Mac is one of five characters whose lives are presented in the course of the novel. Each characterization is complete in itself, yet all the lives are interrelated. Finally, there are the *Living Biographies*, free-verse sketches of businessmen, scientists, and politicians drawn from contemporary history: case studies of notable Americans who represent the possibilities and the dangers along the 42nd parallel. Included are Andrew Carnegie, Minor Keith, Edison, Steinmetz, Debs, Bill Haywood, LaFollette, and William Jennings Bryan.

No summary can effectively represent either the *Newsreel* or the *Living Biographies*. Because the interspersed sections of *The Camera Eye* would interrupt the fictional narrative, a brief, general summary of that material has been appended to the summary below which concerns itself with the fictional narrative.

Mac

Fainy McCreary, known as Mac, is the son of poor Connecticut parents. Daily, as a child, he fights the sons of his Polish and Bohemian neighbors, finding moments of peace only in his own back yard. When his mother dies and his father loses his job during a strike, Mac's uncle Tim O'Hara, a printer and a socialist, takes him and his sister to live in Chicago. There Mac grows up, learns the printing trade and the principles of socialism.

When his uncle is driven out of business by anti-labor forces, Mac ventures forth alone, guided by Tim's words: ". . . read Marx, study all you can, remember that you're a rebel by birth and by blood." Hired by an unctuous lecher, the Rev. E. R. Bingham, with whom he travels, Mac soon learns that most of the books he is supposed to peddle are pornographic. When an irate farmer discovers Bingham with his wife and chases him with a shotgun, Mac's career as a book salesman ends.

For several months thereafter, Mac rides the rails westward, working at lumber camps and on railroad jobs. By late fall, 1905, Mac reaches San Francisco and finds work again as a printer. He attends socialist meetings, hears Upton Sinclair lecture about Chicago's stockyards, and meets Fred Hoff, a member of Bill Haywood's newly organized I.W.W.— the Industrial Workers of the World. Hoff invites Mac to join him and others in Nevada in publishing a newspaper supporting a miner's strike. Though he wants go, Mac has become amorously involved with Maisie Spencer, a pretty salesgirl.

Having seduced Maisie, Mac promises to marry her, but first he leaves for Nevada. Several months after he learns that Maisie is pregnant, he returns and marries her. Settled now in a printing job in San Diego, Mac assumes a domestic role for at least another year, long enough for Maisie to have a second child. Increasingly, however, he frets about having sold out to the bourgeois world. When Maisie's brother makes it possible for them to move into a suburban cottage, Mac's rancor mounts. Everywhere about him he hears about the Mexican revolution, the fall of Diaz, the murder of Matero, the revolutionary leader. When Maisie berates him for drawing from their savings to pay for Uncle Tim's funeral, Mac uses the quarrel as an excuse to leave for Mexico.

Americans in Mexico assure Mac that Zapata is vicious, the revolution an affair for bandits. But Mac is resolutely determined to join the fighting forces of revolution. Somehow Mac never gets beyond talk. Instead he settles for a printing job with a newspaper in Mexico City, a mistress, and a comfortable apartment. A few months later he buys a bookstore: "It felt good to be his own boss for the first time in his life." Ironically, Mac's shop specializes in radical literature. Grudgingly Mac admits a kind of admiration for J. Ward Moorehouse who is trying to work out major investment deals in Mexico for American firms. Still committed to the revolution, however, Mac fails to help Moorehouse. When Zapata comes into Mexico City, Mac sells his bookstore and flees with Concha and her mother. Once in Vera Cruz, he buys a single steerage passage for the United States, planning to abandon

Concha. But he has a change of heart and remains in Vera
Cruz. From that point on, settled with his Mexican girl,
Concha, in Vera Cruz, Mac and his friends serenely and
safely toast the coming of reform in the new Mexico.

Janey Williams

Janey Williams, a plain, sandy-haired girl from Georgetown,
Washington, D.C., adores her older brother Joe and despises
their father for beating him. In her adolescence Janey falls in
love with Joe's best friend, Alec, though Alec knows nothing
of her infatuation. When Alec is killed in a motorcycle accident, Janey feels emotionally dead. She never really recovers.

When Joe joins the Navy, Janey, now a stenographer, lives
vicariously the excitement in his postcards. For a brief period
she comes close to a life of her own when Jerry Burnham, a
genial, left-wing cynic, tries to win her. Almost in love with
him, she resists his lovemaking and frightens him away. Janey
decides to become a career woman instead of a woman. She
bleaches her hair, smokes, and flirts mildly and safely.

When the war in Europe starts, Janey leaves her job because her employer is pro-German. After a brief period of
unemployment and a single day's work for G. H. Barrow (an
unscrupulous publicist and labor organizer, more gifted as a
lecher than as a leader), Janey comes to work for J. Ward
Moorehouse. When Moorehouse's secretary is injured, Janey
becomes his private secretary and goes off with him on his
trip to Mexico.

When she returns to New York, infatuated with Moorehouse, who barely acknowledges her existence, Janey aspires
to a better set of friends. When Joe comes home (he has
deserted from the Navy, joined the merchant marine, and
been torpedoed twice), Janey is too embarrassed to invite him
to her apartment lest her friends see her sailor brother. But
the next evening she goes with Joe to a restaurant and listens
disapprovingly to his vitriolic attack upon the war as fraudulent and crooked. Janey shares Moorehouse's patriotism.

G. H. Barrow, who has been dating Janey during this time,
proposes marriage to her. Janey considers him briefly—
especially after finding him listed in *Who's Who*—but decides
she cannot love him and refuses. The wisdom of her decision

is confirmed when Moorehouse (strictly for business reasons) makes her a member of his new corporation. Her affection for him doubles because of this action and because she knows that his wife has started divorce proceedings over an alleged affair with Eleanor Stoddard.

J. Ward Moorehouse

Ward Moorehouse was the eldest and brightest of six children. As school marble champion he rented marbles to his peers. Winner of a college scholarship, Ward leaves college after a year when his father, drunk, suffers an injury that prevents his working. Determined to rise in the world, Ward gets a job with a real estate firm and impresses his employers with his energy and insight. In Maryland, where he has been sent to report on some company holdings, he meets and falls in love with wealthy Annabelle Strang. Not long after their honeymoon abroad, Ward discovers Annabelle with another man and leaves her.

In Pittsburgh, Ward works briefly as a reporter, then gets a job as a publicist for a steel company. He rises swiftly in the esteem of his employers, and again a lucky match—at least financially—helps him on his way up. This time he marries Gertrude Staple, a millionaire's daughter. Now thirty-two and wealthy, he returns from Europe and his second honeymoon, ready to move to New York to set up his own firm. With G. H. Barrow, he devises a plan for labor-capital rapport during the war, a plan that has nothing to do with principle but much with profits.

Eleanor Stoddard

From childhood on, Eleanor Stoddard has hated the smell and sight of blood. Nightly her father brought home with him the stench of the Chicago stockyards. What Eleanor loved was the exquisite purity of pre-Raphaelite art and the idealism of the poets her high-school English teacher introduced her to. Mobs and sex also frightened and sickened Eleanor. After her mother died, Eleanor found peace working in a lace shop, and beauty in her courses at the Art Institute.

A friendship with cultured Eveline Hutchins leads to their establishing an interior-decorating shop in New York where they barely cover expenses. When a Shubert play for which they designed the costumes fails, Eveline returns to Chicago, but Eleanor rents an apartment in Greenwich Village. Her opportunity comes when Ward Moorehouse commissions her to decorate his summer home on Long Island.

Eleanor and Ward become close friends, though she is shocked to learn that his wife suspects an affair. One afternoon Eleanor decides to confront Mrs. Moorehouse and tell her how purely platonic the friendship is. But before she can, she learns that the United States has entered the war. Ward tells her that he has offered his services free to the Government. Eleanor, after confronting Mrs. Moorehouse, says that she will join the Red Cross to serve in France.

Charley Anderson

When Charley Anderson is growing up in Fargo, North Dakota, his mother, owner of a railroad boarding house, takes note of him only on Sundays when she marches him diligently to church. But Charley's interests are mechanical, not theological. From his earliest years he tinkers with machinery. At fourteen he works in a garage, and at seventeen he is busy in an amusement park repairing the roller coaster.

For a passing moment a girl almost snarls Charley's career. Having teased Charley, she sleeps with his friend, becomes pregnant, and traps Charley into a promise of marriage. At the last possible moment, Charley escapes.

On the road toward New York, Charley absorbs much socialist indoctrination and almost as much sexual experience. Just before he leaves the Mardi Gras in New Orleans, he meets Doc Rogers, a Floridian on his way to enlist in a volunteer ambulance corps. Doc has no patriotic motives but wouldn't dream of missing a big war. Charley has no feeling about the war, but after a few days in New York, where he listens dispassionately to violent pro- and anti-war arguments in bars and on street corners, he decides to join Doc. As the novel closes, Charley stands at the bow of a liner bound for France.

The Camera Eye

In Holland during the Boer War, the "narrator," aged four, walks carefully to avoid hurting the tender grass blades. All about him an angry Dutch mob stones a mother and child suspected of being English. Thus the conflict between poetic sensibility and harsh reality enters Dos Passos' consciousness in childhood, never to end, never to be resolved. He hears among his countrymen clichés about racial equality but sees actions that rob the clichés of meaning. Negroes, Mexicans, Poles, Bohemians—all are treated as inferior; only the English and the Americans are thought to be truly civilized.

School, church, and home fashion him according to the dictates of the upper class. But his private dreams deny his caste, and his personal experiences disprove the stereotypes. The brutality of a streetcar strike, the poverty of a Southern farm during a drought, contrast sharply with the portrait of America others have drawn for him. At Harvard he spends "four years under the ether cone," encouraged to be a good student but not too good, and to avoid being seen with Jews and socialists.

Just before the war, he attends a pro-Russian rally at Madison Square Garden and also hears Emma Goldman. At the end, like Charley Anderson, he stands aboard a troopship heading for France.

Critical Opinion

To comprehend the full impact of Dos Passos' study of despair, defeat, and disillusion, one must read all three volumes of the trilogy *USA*, of which *The 42nd Parallel* is the first volume. *1919* and *The Big Money* (published in 1932 and 1936) round out the portraits begun in the earliest novel and add several others. But even in the initial work, the sustaining purpose is clear, the pervasive technique manifest. All four narrative techniques merge to shape a nightmare vision of human exploitation.

Dos Passos' method, as critics have noted, enables him— except in *The Camera Eye*—to stand apart and record events dispassionately. The testimony of history thus indicts the capitalistic system without reducing the novelist to the role of propagandist. Unhappily, the results do not entirely fulfill the promise of Dos Passos' purpose. Too often his carefully selected characters lack flesh to body forth their symbolic intent; they seem clinical specimens rather than full-blooded human beings. Similarly, in choosing subjects for his *Living Biographies*, Dos Passos has ignored many who have survived or prevailed in our society without selling out or being sold out.

Before the trilogy ends, the reader becomes aware that Dos Passos has not intended to indict only capitalism. Acts of betrayal and distortion indict Communism as well. What Dos Passos seems to argue for most passionately is the dignity of man and his right to freedom from the encroachments of any ideology that diminishes him. Precisely how to achieve his goal Dos Passos fails to make clear, but his nobility of motive and dramatic force move the reader.

The Author

Of Portuguese ancestry and fairly wealthy parentage, *John Roderigo Dos Passos* studied abroad and at Harvard. In 1916 he went to Spain to continue his studies in architecture, but a year later, like many other American writers—Hemingway and e. e. cummings, for example—he volunteered in World War I as an ambulance corpsman. Out of his war experiences grew his first novels, *One Man's Initiation—1917* (1920) and *Three Soldiers* (1921).

In New York after the war, Dos Passos published several volumes of poetry, produced some plays, and was one of the founders of the Marxist periodical *New Masses*. His novel *Manhattan Transfer* (1925), written during this period, was his first attempt to master the technical form he perfected in *The 42nd Parallel*. Later in the twenties, Dos Passos worked actively in behalf of Sacco and Vanzetti—writing, picketing, and even going to jail.

Throughout the 1930s, his most creative years, Dos Passos dedicated himself to such causes as miners' strikes, the defense of political prisoners, and support of the Spanish Loyalists. In the 1940s, Dos Passos increasingly wrote historical tracts as well as novels, again arguing the case for the rebel, the outsider. Today the onetime radical of the left has swung so far to the other side (a supporter of Taft and later of Goldwater) that many of his former admirers find his position intolerable. Whatever Dos Passos' political views, they continue in one way or another to reflect his original dedication to protest against whatever threatens to silence the affirmation of the individual voice.

The Good Earth

by

PEARL BUCK (1892–)

Main Characters

Wang Lung—A poor Chinese farmer, devoted to his land above all else.

O-lan—His wife, a faithful, self-sacrificing, and seldom-appreciated helpmate.

The Sons—Nameless in the novel, they are nevertheless sharply distinguished. The *eldest* is an unfulfilled scholar whose overriding ambition is to establish a great house. The *second* is a shrewd merchant whose main concern is profit. The *third* is a passionate young man whom his father intends to be his successor to the land but who wants to be a soldier.

Lotus Blossom—Wang Lung's concubine, pretty and ineffectual, with whom he is for a time infatuated.

Wang Lung's Father—An old man who once toiled unremittingly on the land and now sleeps peacefully in the sun.

Wang Lung's Uncle—A lazy good-for-nothing member of a robber band, whom Wang Lung supports partly out of respect but mostly out of fear.

Wang Lung's Cousin—The son of his uncle, an insolent and immoral young man who plagues Wang Lung and his eldest son.

Pear Blossom—The lovely, timid young slave who is Wang Lung's last love.

Cuckoo—Once the concubine of the master of the House of Hwang, finally the paid companion of Lotus Blossom.

The Story

Wang Lung, a poor Chinese farmer living in a house made of earthen bricks, has for the past six years since his mother died cared for his old father, rising early in the morning to light the fire and boil hot water for him to drink and, after laboring in the fields all day, preparing his simple evening meal. Now Wang Lung's domestic labors, at least, will be eased, for he has persuaded his father to choose a wife for him. She is to be a slave from the House of Hwang, not too young and not too pretty (for a pretty one would be no virgin, since the Hwang men had their will with female slaves).

After washing his whole body, Wang Lung sets out to fetch his bride. He is overwhelmed by the great family—even by the gatekeeper. The old mistress of the house, smoking her opium pipe, receives the awed farmer and allows him to take her slave, but orders him to return when their first child is born. Wang Lung and his bride stop at the temple to light sticks to the god of the fields and his lady. It is their only marriage ceremony.

The woman, O-lan, is not beautiful. She has square cheeks, a strong, graceless body, and large feet (they have not been bound)—but she is hard-working and good-tempered. Not only does she perform all her domestic tasks expertly and serve Wang Lung and his father devotedly, but she helps him in the fields each day. Before long a son is born to O-lan. She will accept no aid during the birth. The next day she waits upon the men, and soon after she works in the fields again. On the second day of the New Year, the three, dressed in new clothes, go to the House of Hwang to pay their respects.

Wang Lung, who has had a good harvest, learns during their visit that the great house feels pinched and is willing to sell land. Eagerly he buys. The buying is a symbol of his lust for land. The next year O-lan bears a second child. Again the harvests are good, but this time Wang Lung does not buy

more land because his rascally uncle borrows money from
him, ostensibly for a dowry for his daughter, actually as a
gambling stake.

Wang Lung's fortunes decline. A third child arrives, a girl
this time and a simple-minded one, as the years prove. The
earth is parched, the crops scanty. Wang Lung nevertheless
buys another, larger field from the House of Hwang. Famine
comes to the province. The family eats its ox and then nearly
starves. Another baby girl is born, but O-lan chokes the meager
life from it. Desperate as he is, Wang Lung will not sell any
of his land to the shrewd, grasping men who offer only a
fraction of its value. But he does sell them his few furnishings
for two pieces of silver.

Finally Wang Lung and his family decide to go south
where they hope somehow to find food. They join a multitude
of others on the same quest. In a large city in the south they
build themselves a fragile house of reed mats and go to the
public kitchen for rice. O-lan and the children beg each day,
and Wang Lung pulls a rickshaw. Still, they have scarcely
enough for rice, and Wang Lung is in danger of being seized
for the Army, for there is a war going on. Finally, as the
enemy approaches, people flee from the city. There is no work
to be found nor anyone to beg from. Wang Lung wants to return to his good land, but O-lan asks him to wait a little longer.

When the enemy enters the city, the poor of the slums break
the gates of rich men's houses. Carried along by O-lan's directions and by the surging mob, Wang Lung enters one such
house and encounters a terror-stricken fat man who has
lingered and who offers him money to spare his life. Thinking
of his land, Wang Lung grabs the money, gathers his family,
and hurriedly goes back to his land.

Wang Lung finds his old house looted, but with the silver he
has acquired, he purchases everything he needs. He discovers,
too, that O-lan has been even more successful than he at the
rich man's house. She has found a collection of precious
jewels. Wang Lung allows O-lan to keep two pearls, and with
the rest of the treasure he makes his way to the House of
Hwang, deserted now save for the old master and his shrewd
concubine, Cuckoo. Without difficulty Wang Lung buys the
land belonging to the great house. After that he prospers.
He hires men to work in his fields, employs the honest farmer

Ching to be his overseer, and builds additions to his earthen dwelling. His two sons he sends to school so that they will not be unlettered like himself.

Seven years later the river bursts its bounds and floods Wang Lung's lands. Though he does not worry, he grows restless, finds fault with his sons, and sees all at once that O-lan is no longer beautiful. He begins to frequent the new tea house and looks longingly at the pictures of beautiful women hanging on the walls. Cuckoo, who works for the tea house now that her old lord is gone, tells him they are portraits of women in the rooms who may be had for silver. He buys the favors of the beautiful Lotus Blossom. Soon he finds that he cannot live without her.

Meanwhile, his uncle, aunt, and their son have moved into his house, much to his disgust. But now he finds a use for his aunt. She bargains with Cuckoo. For a large sum Lotus Blossom, attended by Cuckoo, comes to live with Wang Lung. He sets her up in a special court, for O-lan, from whom he has heartlessly taken the two pearls to give to Lotus Blossom, will not recognize her presence or her companion's.

Now that Lotus Blossom is easily accessible, Wang Lung's infatuation cools. Peace, however, does not settle on his house. His eldest son demands a woman, and Wang Lung arranges a marriage for him with a grain dealer's daughter. The marriage is to take place in three years. The young man is restless and sullen. One day Wang Lung catches him in Lotus Blossom's court, talking and laughing. Furious, Wang Lung whips both, then sends his son off to the South. To prevent difficulties with the second son, he apprentices him to the grain merchant.

For a long time O-lan has been ailing. Her health worsens. Wang Lung goes for the doctor who pronounces her condition hopeless. Though he has no love for her any more, Wang Lung is deeply unhappy at O-lan's illness and feels guilty about the way he has treated her. He buys two coffins, one for her and one for his now ancient father. But O-lan refuses to die until her eldest son is married. The latter is recalled, an elegant marriage takes place, and that night O-lan dies. Wang Lung's father dies soon after.

Wang Lung's uncle and his uncle's son behave grossly, but Wang Lung dares not oust them, for he has learned that his uncle is second in command of a robber band that has been terrorizing the village but so far has never harmed Wang Lung's house. At the suggestion of his eldest son who is angry with his cousin because the latter has been ogling his wife, Wang Lung buys opium for them. Before long they are addicts, too engrossed in dreams to threaten his peace again. Next, at his eldest son's urging, he once more rents the inner courts of the House of Hwang and furnishes them expensively. His second son marries a good and careful village maid, as he had desired. A sumptuous wedding is held in the new residence. His eldest son's wife and then his second son's wife bear him grandchildren. Wang Lung seems ready to pass into a contented old age, especially when his uncle's son joins the Army.

But the sons and the sons' wives bicker continuously. His youngest son, who, Wang Lung has hoped, will take his place and care for the family's lands, resents his fate bitterly. When Wang Lung, his desires returning for a season, takes Pear Blossom, a lovely young slave, as his concubine, the youngest son, who had longed for her, runs off to join the Army. Finally the vicious cousin returns with a troop of soldiers and arrogantly quarters himself in Wang Lung's courts for a month and a half. Only the old man's simpleton daughter and Pear Blossom offer him comfort. His sons have deeply disappointed him.

One day Wang Lung walks over his land accompanied by his sons. He overhears them speaking softly of the fields they will sell after he is gone. Trembling, he protests that the land is their source of unity and stability. They comfort their father, assuring him they will not sell the land—but over his head they smile at each other.

Critical Opinion

The Good Earth is the first of a trilogy, *House of Earth*. The second novel, *Sons* (1932), traces the destinies of Wang Lung's three sons, an idle man of wealth, a merchant, and a war lord. The third, *A House Divided* (1935), carries the story forward to the decline of the family in revolutionary China. The trilogy, a historian of the American novel observes, "is more epic than dramatic in its development." Nevertheless, there are dramatic episodes—war, famine, pestilence—all intensely projected through the experience of the characters. They live, they suffer, they love, they sometimes are briefly visited by happiness, they die; and then the cycle is continued through their descendants.

Clearly *The Good Earth* is the best novel of the three—so good, in fact, that it has been suggested that the others seem unfulfilled beside it. Some scholars have challenged the accuracy of Pearl Buck's description of Chinese life and customs. She has vigorously rebutted these objections. For the American reader the argument does not seem especially significant. As Oscar Cargill points out: "The great merit of *The Good Earth* . . . is the conviction it carries of verisimilitude to all the vicissitudes of Chinese life—nothing changes or passes which does not seem probable."

The Biblical simplicity of Pearl Buck's language, her gift for making the strange and distant appear familiar, her feeling for the fundamental truths of life—these have established *The Good Earth* as a contemporary classic. Though she has sunk in critical esteem—the two largest histories of American literature give her no more than a few sentences of consideration—Pearl Buck is still an enormously popular author, both in America and abroad. "*The Good Earth* was almost the first book to unlock for the West the interior of China. . . ." It remains one of the very best.

The Author

Pearl Buck, born in Hillsboro, West Virginia, was brought up in China. (She would have been born there if her missionary parents had not come home on furlough.) Both father and mother—about whom she has written two "passionate but critical biographies," *The Exile* (1936) and *Fighting Angel* (1936)—belonged to liberal, distinguished families. "From my ancestors," she writes, "I have the tradition of racial equality."

Living in the far interior of China, Pearl Buck learned Chinese before she learned English. She delighted in the marvelous Buddhist and Taoist stories she heard as a child from her Chinese nurse. Indeed, she came to think of herself as Chinese.

When she was seventeen, she was taken to England and then America where she entered Randolph-Macon College. Earlier, save during her stay at a boarding school in Shanghai, her mother was her chief teacher. Apparently she was an excellent one, too, for Pearl Buck gives her mother high praise, particularly for teaching her "the beauty that lies in words and in what words will say." Pearl Buck did extraordinarily well at college, becoming president of her class and in her senior year winning two literary prizes.

Returning to China after graduation, she married Dr. John Lossing Buck, whom she describes as a "soil missionary." For five years they lived in a town in North China, then came to Nanking. There, from 1921–31, she taught English at the University of Nanking, at Southeastern University, and at Chung Yang University; and there she gave birth to two daughters. In 1934 she came back to New York alone and joined the editorial staff of John Day, the publishing company. The next year, after obtaining a divorce, she married Richard J. Walsh, president of the publishing company.

Pearl Buck began to write as a girl in China. She published articles and stories, and her first book, *East Wind, West Wind* (1930), achieved critical recognition. Not till 1932, however, when *The Good Earth* appeared and won for her the Pulitzer Prize, did she become a significant figure in American letters. Since then she has written many novels (the best of them with Chinese settings), plays, essays, and biographies, and translated the Chinese classic *All Men Are Brothers* (1933). She was awarded the William Dean Howells medal by the American Academy of Arts and Letters in 1935, and in 1938 she became the first American woman and the third American to win the Nobel Prize for literature. Over 70 now, she still writes with distinction on such varied subjects as racial unity, retarded children, and of course, China.

Mutiny on the Bounty

by

JAMES NORMAN HALL (1887–1951)

and

CHARLES NORDHOFF (1887–1947)

Main Characters

Roger Byam—A young man of seventeen when he first sails from England, he already shows the integrity, courage, and firmness that mark his whole career. As an old man, retired from the British Navy, he narrates the *Bounty* story.

Mrs. Byam—Roger's mother.

William Bligh—A superb mariner, resolute and forceful, but as captain of the *Bounty*, petty, harsh, and tyrannical.

Fletcher Christian—Master's mate, brave and generous, whose fatal flaw is excessive pride coupled with a capacity for fierce resentment.

John Fryer—Master, an honest, fair, capable officer.

Robert Tinkler—Midshipman, carefree, good-humored, and good-hearted.

Thomas Hayward—Midshipman, vengeful and untrustworthy, a bully and a coward.

John Hallet—Midshipman, like Hayward, less than brave and less than truthful.

Thomas Huggan—Surgeon. Whiskey is his sovereign cure for all troubles, his own as well as other people's.

David Nelson—Botanist, a quiet, dedicated scientist.

James Morrison—Boatswain's mate, a sound-hearted, wholly
   honest, steadfast man, Byam's good friend.
Sir Joseph Banks—President of the Royal Society, a good man,
   a devoted worker for science and a staunch friend to Byam.
Tehani—Byam's wife (through a Polynesian ceremony), a
   lovely, sweet-tempered, charming, faithful young woman.
Hitihiti—The noble Tahitian chief who becomes Byam's loyal
   friend.

The Story

In 1787 Lieutenant Bligh visits Mrs. Byam and her seventeen-year-old son, Roger. Bligh has come at the suggestion
of Sir Joseph Banks, President of the Royal Society, friend of
the late Mr. Byam, an astronomer who has done important
navigational research. Bligh has just been given command of
the *Bounty* and is scheduled to sail to Tahiti to procure breadfruit trees which West Indian planters hope will prove a cheap
and wholesome food for their Negro slaves. Bligh invites
young Byam to join his crew. Since the boy has a gift for
languages—a gift that Sir Joseph thinks will enable Byam to
compile a dictionary and grammar of the Tahitian language—
he gladly accepts.

The *Bounty* sails. It will be four and one-half turbulent years
before she returns to England. The voyage out is fairly
uneventful, marked chiefly by Bligh's at-times insane ferocity.
For the slightest infractions or insubordinations, he orders men
flogged. He is insufferably rude to his officers, insulting and
upbraiding them before the crew. Petty, avaricious, unaffected
by the needs of others, he doles out short rations to the crew
and pockets his small gains.

Gradually Byam learns his duties and gets to know the
crew. The master's mate, Fletcher Christian, a stalwart young
man of twenty-four, is bold, fair, resolute but excessively
proud, fiercely resenting the wrongs inflicted by the captain.
The master, John Fryer, is a bluff, steady, capable officer. The
surgeon, Thomas Huggan (nicknamed "Old Bacchus"),
prescribes brandy for everyone and especially for himself. Of
Byam's fellow midshipmen, two prove ultimately to be enemies
—Thomas Hayward and John Hallet, a cowardly pair. The

others turn out to be his firm friends, particularly the carefree and brash Robert Tinkler and the solid and generous George Stewart. Three others are on his side: James Morrison, boatswain's mate, a steady and cool but deep-feeling Scotsman; William Muspratt, a loyal and conscientious able seaman; and Thomas Ellison, a foolish, brash, light-hearted boy.

When Tahiti is sighted, Byam is struck by the loveliness of the island and its inhabitants. He goes ashore to begin learning and recording their language, a task for which he will have several months, since it will take that long for the botanist to collect young breadfruit plants. Almost immediately he finds his island *taio*, or intimate friend, an important chief, Hitihiti, a middle-aged man of superb bearing. With him and his large family, Byam spends an idyllic season and learns to love the land and its people, while working steadily and productively at his language lessons. Unlike Christian and some others, he does not choose a sweetheart.

The voyage homeward begins unhappily and grows tragic. Bligh has regularly annexed the gifts that the Tahitians have offered to the crew—pearls as well as pigs, cloth, fruit. Christian has bitterly resented this highhanded action. A day out from the island, Bligh falsely accuses Christian of stealing some coconuts, cursing him in front of crew members.

That night at watch, Christian asks Byam to notify his people in Cumberland if anything happens to him. As Byam says, "You can count on me" and shakes hands, Bligh appears on deck. He exchanges some words with the two officers, then retreats. Midshipman Tinkler, lying in the shadow of the guns, has witnessed the brief, apparently innocuous episode.

Before daybreak Byam is awakened by two of the crew—one bearing a pistol, the other a musket with fixed bayonet. The explanation soon becomes terribly clear: a mutiny has broken out, led by Christian. Four officers and twelve seamen have seized all weapons, tied Bligh up, and disarmed the twenty-eight loyal members of the crew (of a ship's company numbering forty-four). Bligh cajoles, snarls, promises. To no avail. Christian is adamant. "I have been in hell for weeks past," he declares.

At first a rotten cutter is allotted to Bligh, but at Byam's intercession, a small launch is substituted. Bligh and eighteen of his loyal men board it. There is less than eight inches of

freeboard amidships. Byam, Stewart, Morrison, and seven
others who have been delayed want to enter the launch, but it
will hold no more. Cursing bitterly, Bligh and his men sail
away.*

The mutineers with the nine loyal men who remain aboard
turn back. Christian regrets his action, but is determined to do
what he can for his co-conspirators. After voyaging among the
islands, he attempts a settlement on one, but the Indians are
hostile. He sails to Tahiti again, and several weeks later allows
Byam, Stewart, Morrison, and more than a dozen others to stay
on Tahiti—though he realizes that he endangers himself and
his followers by the act, since the Navy search for the *Bounty*
will surely begin at Tahiti. Eight Englishmen remain aboard
ship with him, plus eighteen Polynesians, twelve men, and six
women (among the latter his sweetheart). Together they will
seek an uninhabited island in the South Seas.† Before he
leaves, he again asks Byam to tell his people the story as
Byam knows it. Christian assures him that the mutiny was not
planned, that ten minutes before Bligh was seized, Christian's
only intention was to cast himself on a raft he was having built,
hoping it would take him to a nearby island.

On Tahiti, Byam and his companions soon adapt themselves to the tranquil ways of the islanders. Byam falls in love
with Tehani, niece of an important chief, and fathers a girl.
He continues working devotedly on his Tahitian dictionary,
but the days slip by imperceptibly in a land where it is always
summer. In March, 1791 a British frigate, the *Pandora*, anchors
off Tahiti. As duty commands, Byam paddles out to her,
identifies himself, and is promptly clapped into chains by the
captain, Edward Edwards. So, too, are thirteen others of the
crew—some of them, ironically, seized while attempting to return to England on a craft they had painstakingly constructed.

During the return trip they suffer a variety of hardships, not
least among them the severities of the captain and the sadism
of one of the officers. Only the ship's surgeon is Byam's friend,
informing him of the charges against him. Bligh, on the night
of the mutiny, heard his innocent words to Christian—"You

---

* After fantastic hardships, they manage to reach England. The details of
the amazing journey are recorded in the authors' *Men Against the Sea*, the
second narrative of *The Bounty Trilogy*.
  † *Pitcairn's Island*, the concluding narrative of the trilogy, tells the fascinating history of their quest and settlement.

can count on me"—and afterward wrongly deduced Byam's complicity. Since everyone who can give decisive testimony to his innocence is with Christian, Byam is in an exceedingly dangerous position.

Fifteen months after they are placed in irons—four and one-half years after their initial departure—Byam and his crewmates return to England. Though Byam has devoted and influential friends—Sir Joseph Banks, especially—the court, composed of eleven sea captains and presided over by a vice-admiral, is clearly unsympathetic. The malicious testimony of Hallet and Hayward, midshipmen on the *Bounty*, seems final, since none of the crew who sailed from the *Bounty* with Bligh can prove Byam's innocence, though most are morally certain of it. Midshipman Tinkler, who overheard Byam's conversation with Christian, is the desperately needed witness, but he has been reported lost at sea.

The court finds not only the mutineers guilty but also Muspratt, Morrison, and Byam. All are sentenced to be hanged. The first two, after enduring agonies of suspense, are granted unconditional pardons at the recommendation of the court, apparently activated by more than a suspicion of doubt concerning their guilt. Byam's case, though, appears hopeless, and he resigns himself to his fate. But his fortunes take a spectacular turn. Tinkler has been rescued at sea, has landed in England, and has been seized by Sir Joseph who immediately carries him to the admiral. Examined by the Admiralty Commission, he easily persuades them of Byam's innocence. They reverse the decision of the court-martial. Byam is free.

Byam intends to return to Tahiti, but is induced to continue his naval career so that he may remove any trace of dishonor clinging to his name. He serves gallantly during England's wars with the allied nations of Europe, attaining captain's rank. Not till sixteen years later, in 1809, does he have the opportunity to sail to Tahiti. En route he touches Port Jackson in New South Wales, there briefly glimpsing Bligh again. Bligh's notable tactlessness has again bred insurrection. Appointed governor of New South Wales, he has alienated the settlers who have revolted and imprisoned him. He has been relieved of his post and is sailing for home, once more to figure in a dramatic trial.

In Tahiti, Byam discovers that his wife and nearly all his friends are long since dead, his daughter married. He sees her and her child without identifying himself. Sadly he returns to England, and as an old man writes his recollections of the mutiny.

Critical Opinion

Mutiny on the Bounty is a splendid novel of adventure on the high seas and on the islands of Polynesia. The narrative is compounded of shadow and light, of gallantry and romance, steadfast courage and cowering fear, nobility and villainy. It has impressed an image of the lovely islands of the South Seas on the American imagination, an image that seems likely to last for a long time to come. In the snarling Captain Bligh, the resolute mate Christian, the enchanting Tehani, the noble Hitihiti, the harsh Captain Edwards, the cheerful "Bacchus," Nordhoff and Hall have projected a gallery of memorable, vividly realized characters.

Mutiny on the Bounty is not only an exciting sea story. It is also a completely documented account of a real voyage. To discover the facts of the mutiny, the authors ransacked libraries, photostatted every page of the court-martial report, even prevailed upon the British Admiralty first to make copies of the deck and rigging plans of the *Bounty* and later to make a detailed model of the ship. Books, charts, maps, photographs were collected and painstakingly studied. Though *Mutiny on the Bounty* is fiction, it is fiction with the authority of comprehensive and precise scholarship behind it. While the authors invented episodes, conversations, and characters, they nevertheless produced a history that is truer than a flat, unadorned recital of facts could possibly be.

The Authors

James Norman Hall and *Charles Nordhoff* have become in the public mind a fused novelist whose specialty was romantic adventure. Hall, born in Colfax, Iowa, in 1887, attended public school in his home town and later Grinnell College.

After graduating, he became a social worker in Boston. In 1914, he joined Lord Kitchener's volunteer army, enlisting as a private and serving as a machine gunner in France until 1916. On his release, he joined the Escadrille Lafayette, France's crack air unit. When it combined with the American Air Service, he was commissioned a captain. In May, 1918, he was shot down behind German lines and remained a prisoner in Germany for the last six months of the war.

Charles Nordhoff, born in London (1887) of American parents, came to the United States at the age of three and lived at different times in Philadelphia, California, and Mexico. He attended Stanford University for one year and Harvard for three, receiving his bachelor's degree in 1909. In 1916, after serving as an ambulance driver in France, he became a member of the Escadrille Lafayette, and by the end of the war had been commissioned first lieutenant.

It was in the Escadrille Lafayette that Nordhoff and Hall became friends. After the war they decided to combine forces. Besides distinguished war records, they had several things in common: both were contributors to *The Atlantic Monthly,* both had a taste for high adventure, both felt that the "stridency and vulgarity of post-war civilization was beyond endurance." Financed by an advance royalty from a book publisher, they set sail in 1920 for the most glamorous island in the world, Tahiti. They remained there, with the families they subsequently acquired, for the rest of their lives.

Nordhoff and Hall each published books separately. Their chief fame, however, rests on the works they have written in collaboration—notably on *The Bounty Trilogy: Mutiny on the Bounty* (1932), *Men Against the Sea* (1933), and *Pitcairn's Island* (1934).

Young Lonigan: A Boyhood in Chicago Streets

by

JAMES T. FARRELL (1904—)

Main Characters

Studs Lonigan—The fifteen-year-old hero whose real name is William. Outwardly tough and determined to prove his manliness to all, he remains nonetheless inwardly sensitive and lonely, yearning romantically after pure love and chivalric honor.

Patrick Lonigan—Studs' father, a boss painter of solid means. He prides himself on being "a good Catholic, a good American, a good father, and a good husband," but he has no real understanding of his son's desperate problems.

Mary Lonigan—His wife, an earnest, unimaginative woman whose fondest hope is that her son will become a priest.

Frances Lonigan—Studs' thirteen-year-old sister, bright, eager, and determined not to fall prey to the deteriorating forces of her environment.

Loretta and *Martin Lonigan*—The youngest children of the family.

Weary Reilley—Studs' classmate and gang associate, though never his friend, a vicious and sadistic bully, son of a hard-working father and a plodding mother who hopes to see her Frank become a lawyer.

Danny O'Neill—Twelve years old, bespectacled, and an authority on baseball. Curious about the activities of the gang, he remains aloof from their excesses and is often the butt of their games.

Davey Cohen—A Jewish member of the gang, tolerated in most activities, but ostracized from others.

Paulie Haggerty, Kenny Killarney, Red Kelly, Tommy Doyle —Members of the Prairie Avenue gang.

T.B. McCarthy, Three-Star-Hennessey, Johnny O'Brien, Jim Clayburn—Members of the Indiana Avenue gang, the latter two more or less outsiders because they go on to high school.

Lucy Scanlan—Studs' girl friend, a sweet, proud girl.

Helen Shires—The local tomboy and confidante of Studs.

Iris—A fourteen-year-old nymphomaniac.

The Story

The events of the novel take place within a six-month period beginning June, 1916, the day that Studs Lonigan graduates from St. Patrick's Grammar School in Chicago and Woodrow Wilson is nominated for a second-term as President. As the novel opens, Studs is in the bathroom secretly smoking, assuming various expressions of leering toughness as he studies himself in the mirror, and delighting in the prospect of being free of the intellectual, moral, and physical discipline imposed by the nuns and priests of St. Patrick's. Outside the bathroom door, his sister Frances loudly complains about Studs' keeping the bathroom to himself. While the argument goes on, Studs tries to clear the room of smoke.

Meanwhile Patrick Lonigan sits contentedly on the back porch smoking his cigar, glancing at the pages of the Chicago *Evening Journal* and sentimentally recalling his own childhood and his achievements since then. He alone of his family has had any real success. One of his brothers ran off to sea, another was killed in the Spanish-American War, a third married unhappily, and a fourth struggled along as a motorman. His sister became a prostitute. Mr. Lonigan and his wife feel proud of their accomplishments, confident that they have done right by their children.

During Father Gilhooley's delivery of the St. Patrick's

Grammar School commencement address, the bored graduates tickle one another, whisper obscenities, and indulge in all sorts of horseplay. Studs feels a certain sentimental appeal in the proceedings, but sternly represses the emotion as unworthy. After the ceremonies several of the children come to the Lonigans' for a party. While the older Lonigans and Reilleys sit in the living room discussing the marvels of parochial education, the youngsters experiment with a variety of kissing games, Studs and Lucy delicately and timidly, Weary Reilley and Helen Borax passionately, almost brutally. After the party Studs' parents discuss his prospects with him, Mr. Lonigan wanting him to go on to high school and then enter the painting trade, Mrs. Lonigan beseeching him to think seriously about the priesthood. Studs listens to both with feigned interest. His real aim is to become as tough as Weary Reilley. In his bedroom later Studs and Frances, roused by the light sexual play at the party, find occasion to study one another surreptitiously, even to knock against each other accidentally. Horrified and self-reproaching, Studs leaves and kneels beside his bed praying that his soul may be washed of sin.

A month later, having abandoned his lackadaisical efforts to secure a job, Studs lies in bed late each morning shadow-boxing and scowling for a while before the mirror, then wanders along the streets kicking cans and batting stones. He wonders about the "goofy" middle-aged music teacher, Leon, who strokes his arm and urges him to visit and begin to learn about the more beautiful things in life. Disgusted by Leon, Studs feels comfortable with tomboy Helen Shires. Helen tells him about Weary's attempts to make sexual advances to her and how she has put him off. While Helen and Studs dribble a basketball (at which she is far better than he), Weary comes along to join them. Even less skilled with the basketball than Studs, Weary irritatedly smashes his shoulder into Helen's breast. Hurt and angry, she hits Weary in the mouth with the ball and he rushes toward her furiously. When Studs interferes, Weary curses them both and a fight ensues between Studs and Weary. Helen—as well as Danny O'Neill and Lucy Scanlan, who happen by—cheers Studs on during the long and brutal fracas. A host of spectators, young and old, gathers to watch the smaller Studs give

Weary a thorough beating. When the fight is at last stopped by Diamond-Tooth, a detective, Studs emerges as the "champ fighter of the block." His reward at Helen Shires' party is a shower of kisses from Lucy Scanlan.

As the pride of Indiana Avenue, Studs occupies a niche he has aspired to, and he enjoys its minor rewards of respect and admiration. He still finds little that holds his interest for any length of time. He presses the less combative into wrestling and boxing matches with each other and, when he cannot match their skills in another sport, makes them box with him so that he can prove his superiority. Thus when Danny O'Neill repeatedly beats him at stoop ball, he decides to teach Danny how to box. Although he batters and humiliates the younger boy, he cannot reduce him to tears and concludes merely that Danny. like so many others, is "goofy." At home Studs resents his father's increasing insistence that he find a job, come home earlier, and occupy himself more usefully. When his father gives him a baseball novel to "improve his mind," Studs dutifully reads for ten minutes, then leaves to rejoin his friends at the playground.

A day in early July brings complete happiness to Studs. On that day he and Lucy Scanlan walk hand in hand through the park, climb a tree together, and sit there sharing an idyllic dream of love. Though they kiss, Studs represses the passion that surges through him. He thinks of how he would like most to win her as his pure love, yet he cannot bring himself to speak about his feelings. When at last they return home, Studs is in a joyous daze, but tells himself that he is a "Goddamn goof." The lyric episode is short-lived, for the next day Studs finds chalk signs everywhere announcing that Studs and Lucy love each other. When Danny O'Neill laughs at Studs' discomfiture, Studs beats him. At home he lashes back at the family's teasing, and when Helen Borax, Lucy's girl friend, twits him, he insults her obscenely. When Lucy learns how he has treated Helen, she snubs him in the street.

By the end of July, the promise of a happy summer has faded. Studs is conscious only that he wants something, but he cannot articulate what it is. Though he now knows that he loves Lucy, he has not seen her; and as a hard-boiled youth, he refuses to seek her out. Drifting from his haunts on

Indiana Avenue, he seeks adventure on Prairie Avenue. By fighting and beating Red Kelly, the champion of that block, he gains acceptance. But with his new friends, Davey Cohen and Paulie Haggerty, the games are essentially the same, though they promise a deeper plunge into degradation. After Studs twists the arm of a youngster who will not obey him, Studs feels a certain renewal of assurance. As he gains mastery of the skill of spitting tobacco juice from either side of his mouth, he senses that passers-by will recognize that he is a young man to be reckoned with. Unfortunately, Lucy Scanlan happens by and rebukes him for being a show-off.

In addition to their usual escapades of hitching rides and stealing candy and fruit, Studs' new friends prove even more effective than his former cronies in baiting Jews and Negroes, shaking them down for money, and beating them. In such activities, the young men have the tacit approval of their parents who daily complain about how the neighborhood has run down since these minority groups have moved in. At Bathcellar's Billiard Parlor and Barber Shop, Studs hears from the older men lewd talk about sexual exploits and yearns for his sexual initiation. When he sees Weary Reilley (who has left his parents' home and now carries a rusty, empty .22-caliber pistol) go off with Iris, Studs grows jealous and even more eager.

A few days later, Studs' desires are satisfied when Iris entertains all of the boys at a "gang shag," all, that is, except Davey Cohen, whom she rejects because he is a Jew. Bitter and frustrated, Davey avenges himself on a hostile world by beating up both an Irish and a Jewish boy, each considerably younger than himself. After the session with Iris, the boys stand at the corner and rehearse their deeds. But as Lucy Scanlan passes by, Studs experiences a deep sense of guilt and contemplates with terror the possibilities of death and hell.

The last section of the novel opens in November as Weary, Studs, and Paulie—all playing hookey from high school—wander along the streets seeking some kind of interesting activity. Paulie has contracted a venereal disease, Davey Cohen has left Chicago hoping to find a world that will accept him, and Iris has been sent off to boarding school after Weary Reilley's mother has caught the two of them in sexual activity. At home Studs listens with ill-disguised resentment to his father's nagging insistence about a job, his mother's importuning him about the priesthood. Mr. Lonigan, however, confides to his wife that the children are coming along wonderfully well and that, as successful parents, they can indulge themselves more frequently in vacations. Alone at the window, Studs stares out upon the cold streets and "felt like he was a sad song."

Critical Opinion

Studs Lonigan is not, as James Farrell has pointed out, a tough or a gangster. Nor is he the product of the slums. In the first novel of the trilogy, at least, Studs displays many of the qualities of an average American boy—dreams of grandeur, a rebellious spirit, an essential decency. And his family, with its faith in church and home, work and duty, represents a characteristically American approach to life. Moreover, the Lonigans have the economic means and security to translate that approach into reality. What, then, goes wrong?

According to Farrell, Studs' downfall is caused by "spiritual poverty," the failure of church, family, school, and community to provide a significant direction for the boy and for his friends. Platitudes have taken the place of purpose, allowing social and moral decay to seep into and rot the vital substance of youth. Studs is not a villain, then, but a victim of the world he inhabits, and his story, Farrell has asserted, is "the story of an American destiny in our time."

Young Lonigan, like the other books in the trilogy, is compelling and affecting. It records disillusion, degeneration, and despair with an almost photographic accuracy and with meticulous attention to fine detail. Farrell has sought to emulate the compass of Balzac and the scientific detachment of Zola, the thundering power of Dreiser and the stylistic elegance of Joyce. Unfortunately, he achieves less than he aspires to. Farrell's prose style is almost featureless, his accumulation of details often repetitious to the point of ennui, and his sense of life's ceaseless boredom nearly suffocating. The naturalistic novel—of which Farrell has been the outstanding writer since Dreiser—often falls prey to these faults, and Farrell's novel sometimes reads more like a case history than a novel. Nevertheless, *Young Lonigan* and the two novels that follow it belong to the great tradition of American naturalistic writing, a tradition that sharply contrasts romantic dream and hideous reality.

The Author

Like Studs Lonigan, *James T. Farrell* was born, attended parochial school, and grew up on Chicago's South Side. But Farrell's career more closely resembles that of Danny O'Neill, about whom he has written several novels: *A World I Never Made* (1936), *No Star Is Lost* (1938), *Father and Son* (1940), *My Days of Anger* (1943), and *The Face of Time* (1953). After a successful career as an all-round boy athlete, Farrell attended the University of Chicago for three years without taking a degree. There, he studied writing and in one course wrote a short story called "Studs," published in *This Quarter*. Encouraged by two of his professors to expand the story, Farrell worked at it for the next three years while holding a variety of jobs that provided material for his expanding manuscript. "I worked on with this project," Farrell has written, "setting up as an ideal the strictest possible objectivity." What began as a short story in 1929 became at last a thousand-page trilogy completed in 1935, the three novels—*Young Lonigan* (1932), *The Young Manhood of Studs Lonigan* (1934), and *Judgment Day* (1935)—providing a panoramic study of Chicago life and a close analysis of the forces that destroy Studs by the time he is twenty-nine.

The trilogy won Farrell a considerable reputation. But despite the success of some of the Danny O'Neill novels, little of Farrell's prolific output since that time has added to his stature as a novelist. He has now written eighteen novels and several volumes of short stories and literary criticism. He has frequently expounded Marxist political as well as esthetic points of view.

God's Little Acre

by

ERSKINE CALDWELL (1903–)

Main Characters

Ty Ty Walden—A shrewd, shiftless, amoral Georgia hillbilly. For fifteen years he has been digging holes in quest of gold.

Buck—His son, sullen and brutish, violently jealous of his beautiful wife.

Shaw—Another son, frequently seduced from digging holes by the local female population.

Jim Leslie—The third of Ty Ty's sons, who has somehow escaped the family pattern. He has become a wealthy cotton broker and married a society girl. Not unreasonably, he avoids his father and brothers.

Darling Jill—Ty Ty's pretty, provocative, and promiscuous daughter—"careless," he calls her.

Rosamond—Ty Ty's other daughter, married now and relatively placid, but nevertheless with explosive potential.

Griselda—Buck's wife, "the finest-looking girl in the country," with creamy skin, golden hair, and an untapped passionate nature.

Pluto Swint—Monstrously fat, timid, ineffectual, he is Darling Jill's suitor and an unlikely candidate for sheriff.

Will Thompson—Rosamond's husband, a weaver from Carolina whose mill is shut down.

247

The Story

Ty Ty Walden, head of a Georgia mountain family, suffers from gold fever. For fifteen years he has been digging pot-holes, his obsession no whit diminished by the fact that he has found not a trace of gold. Though shiftless, he works long, hot hours at his digging, and he has infected two of his sons, Buck and Shaw, with the fever. While completely amoral, he nevertheless is religious, after a fashion. He has set one acre aside, God's little acre, for the church. If he strikes the lode on that acre, he will turn over the proceeds to the church. To keep this from happening, however, he regularly shifts the location of the acre so that it is never the one on which he is digging.

While Ty Ty and his sons are at work, they receive a visit from Pluto Swint, an obscenely fat man with eyes like water-melon pits, a candidate for Darling Jill and sheriff. It seems unlikely that he will win either. Pluto, who is allergic to work, declines to take hold of a shovel. He suggests, however, that an albino would help Ty Ty's cause for albinos have a special gift for divination, and Pluto has seen one not far away who ought to be able to locate the lode easily. Ty Ty takes fire, for though he doesn't believe in conjure men and such superstitions, the albino has scientifically proved powers. The male Waldens set out with ropes to capture him and enlist Pluto and Darling Jill to fetch daughter Rosamond and her husband, Will Thompson, a Carolina weaver whose plant has shut down and who may want to help. Pluto is happy to drive Darling Jill because though she scorns and torments him, he is infatuated with her.

Late at night they arrive in Scottsville where the Thomp-sons live. Will has been drinking more than ever since he has been unemployed and occasionally beating Rosamond. She complains, of course, but accepts her beatings as stand-ard marital procedure. She loves Will, has a deep intuitive understanding of him. What sets her crying, however, is his uncensored expression of desire for Griselda, the wife Buck so jealously cherishes, "the prettiest girl in the country," golden-haired and creamy-skinned. Will can't quite under-stand Rosamond's tears: "It's all in the family, ain't it?" Before going to sleep he also tells Pluto of his plans for taking over the mills and turning the power on if the company doesn't start up soon.

Next morning, while Rosamond is downtown and Pluto sits on the porch, Will eagerly accepts Darling Jill's open invitation and takes her. They are still embracing when Rosamond returns. She furiously whacks him and then Darling Jill. Will tries to explain that Darling Jill can't go anyplace without someone taking her: "She was made that way from the start." The explanation infuriates Rosamond, who pulls out a little pearl-handled .32 from a convenient drawer and shoots at Will. She misses and Will dives through the window to run naked down the street. Immediately after, with Pluto's flushed assistance, Rosamond applies lard ointment to Darling Jill's buttocks.

The party departs, after a late breakfast of ice cream, for God's little acre. There, the albino has been captured and is being guarded by Ty Ty and his sons. With Darling Jill about and vividly demonstrating her affection for the captive, however, the guard is no longer needed, there or elsewhere. For Will cordially despises the hillbilly brothers, Scott and Buck, and they are even less enthusiastic about the visiting linthead. Buck especially hates Will, since he accurately suspects that the latter has designs on the beautiful Griselda. The brothers and their brother-in-law fight viciously. Ty Ty intervenes because among other reasons, it interferes with his obsession to dig for gold.

His crops neglected and his small funds exhausted, Ty Ty determines to try once more to extract money from his successful son, Jim Leslie, a wealthy cotton broker in town, married to a society girl. Jim has escaped his family and refuses to have anything to do with them. But Ty Ty, accompanied by Darling Jill and Griselda, manages to sneak into the house and confront him. Astonishingly they wheedle $300 from Jim. His capitulation seems much more the result of his lust for Griselda than his sympathy for his father whom he regards as a fool. Though his wife is in the house ill, Jim makes a fevered pass at Griselda as she sits in Ty Ty's decrepit automobile. Only Ty Ty's quick getaway prevents Jim Leslie from grabbing her.

Will feels he must get back to Scottsville, his mill town,

to rejoin his comrades, perhaps to start the mill running. Pluto is persuaded again to drive the Thompsons and Darling Jill. After some negative grunts, Buck allows Griselda to accompany the party. At Scottsville, Will attends a meeting of the unemployed mill workers who have decided to turn on the power in the shut-down mill. The decision generates a flow of passion, long dammed, between Will and Griselda. Rosamond can do nothing to stop it. Serenely she rocks while her husband tears the clothes from her willing sister-in-law and fulfills his promise to make startling love to her.

The morning following Will leads a party of millhands to the mill and turns on the power. But the company guards, murderously armed, have filtered into the mill. They shoot Will. With his death the hopes of the men collapse. That night Pluto for the first time possesses Jill. Excitement working with pity has brought her to his arms.

After Will's funeral everyone returns to Ty Ty's home. Buck guesses what has happened to Griselda, but Will's death leaves him without possibility of revenge. At this juncture, Jim Leslie appears. His lust for Griselda has possessed him completely. Buck grapples with him, and Ty Ty tries vainly to dissuade him, but he breaks through them and into the house in pursuit of Griselda. Buck grabs a shotgun, levels it at his now mindless brother, and pulls the trigger. While Ty Ty stoops over Jim's lifeless body, Buck, carrying the reloaded gun, walks off to kill himself. Ty Ty does not stop him—merely relocating God's little acre so that it will bound Buck's body when he falls. Then he begins digging again.

Critical Opinion

God's Little Acre has now endured for a third of a century, and it is still widely read. Yet few twentieth-century novels have been accused of so many literary sins. The most common charge—that it is a deliberately obscene work, devoted to the delineation of degenerates—may easily be disposed of. Dismissing an action brought against the novel, the court affirmed that *God's Little Acre* was an honest work that attempted to tell "the truth about a certain group in American life." And the *Atlanta Journal* added that Caldwell's are passionately sincere novels whose "appeal is to humanity, to fairness and decency."

Other charges are not so easily countered. Critics agree that the characters of *God's Little Acre* are for the most part too broadly presented, often turning into comic grotesques. The situations are occasionally preposterous (for example, Jim Leslie's terminal visit to Ty Ty's household for the unconcealed purpose of ravishing Griselda). The climax of the novel (Will's heroic return to the mill and his murder by the mercenaries who have preceded him there), while melodramatically effective, is hardly convincing.

Obviously, *God's Little Acre* is an imperfect work. But so are a number of other significant American novels—*Uncle Tom's Cabin, The Grapes of Wrath, The 42nd Parallel,* to name only three. And like them, *God's Little Acre* describes in a new way, authentically and compassionately, a submerged part of America and the people who inhabit it. At first these people may arouse our laughter. But as one Southern critic observes, it is laughter that dissolves into pity even if the pity is mixed with revulsion.

Caldwell's dialogue is masterly—vivid, real, and racy. His plot, though marred by sensationalism and slapstick in particular episodes, is expertly and suspensefully contrived. And at least one character, Pluto Swint, promises to become a permanent part of the gallery of great fictional grotesques.

The Author

Few writers have had greater variety of experience than *Erskine Preston Caldwell*. Though born in Georgia, he claims the "entire South, from Virginia to Florida, from the Atlantic to the Mississippi," as his home. It was the duty of his father, a Presbyterian minister, secretary to his denomination, to live in each parish for a few months. Consequently Caldwell, until he was twenty, "rarely lived longer than six months in the same place." He attended primary school in Virginia, grammar school in Tennessee, and secondary school in Georgia—each for one year. The three years constituted his total early schooling, his mother supplying all his other formal education. In spite of his sporadic school attendance, Caldwell was admitted to Erskine College in South Carolina, the University of Virginia, and the University of Pennsylvania, but stayed in none for very long.

Caldwell has been by turns a poolroom attendant, a gun runner, a hack driver, a stagehand, a sodajerk, a cook, a waiter, a bodyguard, a lecture-tour manager, a variety-store clerk, a professional football player, a newspaperman, a script writer, an editor, and a war correspondent. He has frequently traveled across the United States, and has visited every country in South America and Europe at least once. He has been married four times.

Punctuating Caldwell's multitudinous activities are about forty published books, which have sold more than 25 million copies. He began to write seriously in 1928, when he abandoned newspaper work and settled in Maine. After five years the story, "Country Full of Swedes," which had made the rounds of the magazines, won the *Yale Review*'s $1,000 Award for Fiction. From then on, Caldwell's graphic studies of the disinherited in America, the poor whites and Negroes of the South, especially, have made him one of America's best-selling authors. *Tobacco Road* (1932) was an enormously successful novel, and its dramatization established a new Broadway record for number of continuous performances. *God's Little Acre* (1933) sold even more widely. *Trouble in July* (1940), *Georgia Boy* (1943), and *Tragic Ground* (1944) have also enjoyed great popularity.

Appointment in Samarra

by

JOHN O'HARA (1905–)

Main Characters

Julian English—President of a Cadillac agency, aged thirty, handsome, charming, sensual, and compulsively driven to destroy everything he cherishes.

Caroline English—Julian's wife, a year older than he, pretty, sensitive, and deeply in love with her husband—less with the present reality than with the memory of their past and the improbable hope for their future.

Lute Fliegler—A salesman at Julian's agency, lower middle class in taste and manner, but endowed with candor, courage, and compassion.

Irma Fliegler—Lute's wife, mother of three, simple, unsophisticated, and not overly intelligent.

Ed Charney—Bootlegger and owner of the Stage Coach Inn. A devoted family man during holiday seasons, he prefers his mistress during the rest of the year.

Al Grecco—A young hoodlum and ex-boxer, jailbird, and errand boy for Ed Charney. Born Anthony Murascho, he gained his nickname from a lady sportswriter who decided that his physical beauty recalled the canvases of El Greco.

Harry Reilly—A former suitor of Caroline, part owner of Julian's agency, a loud low-brow, shrewd and dangerous.

Helene Holman—Ed Charney's mistress, nightclub singer, alcoholic, and nymphomaniac.

Dr. William English—Julian's father, a prosperous though incompetent surgeon. Proud, cold, and vindictive, he has tried to live down the shame of his father's suicide.

Mrs. Waldo Walker—Caroline's mother, a widow, an efficient committeewoman, but emotionally sterile and intellectually vapid.

The Story

The events leading to Julian English's "appointment in Samarra"—that is, his death—fill three days that begin just after midnight on December 25, 1930. During that time, Julian plods a liquor-sodden course across the caste lines that stratify Gibbsville's social system. A wealthy anthracite mining town of 25,000 in southern Pennsylvania, Gibbsville has suffered from the impact of union strikes and the advent of the oil burner. But even the stock market crash of 1929 has not seriously perturbed its wealthy citizens or shattered its lower middle class. The marginal group—the bootlegger and his hirelings—is thriving. Julian English still manages to sell Cadillacs, Lute Fliegler, his salesman, earns enough to stay out of the coal mines and the ranks of the proletariat. Ed Charney, the bootlegger, rides the crest of Prohibition.

The upper and middle classes of Gibbsville have much in common. They have faith in Herbert Hoover's conviction that the nation's economy has undergone a "strong technical reaction." They attend parties, get drunk, and make tentative passes at other men's wives. They belong to a variety of clubs, social and charitable. While they tolerate certain Catholics (especially those who can afford Cadillacs), they despise all Jews (whether or not they can afford Cadillacs). Within this tidy framework, the population of Gibbsville enjoys the advantages of democracy, and when the novel opens, rejoices after its fashion in the heightened pleasures of the Christmas season.

Julian English, who grew up on fashionable Lantenengo Street with his rich childhood friends, played with the sons of parents less affluent. The boys enjoyed a variety of conventional and some less conventional games. While playing Five-Finger Grab, Julian was arrested for stealing merchandise. From then on, Julian's father has regarded him as nothing more than a common thief.

Julian avoided World War I by staying at Lafayette College until he was graduated. He refused to study medicine, as his father wished him to, or to join his father's fraternity. After graduation he entered the garage and auto business. Before his marriage to Caroline he had only one serious love affair, with á beautiful, lower-class Polish girl named Mary.

When the novel opens, Julian has been married five years, has no children, and has fallen considerably into debt, especially to Harry Reilly. His charm and grace, however, help him maintain his status as one of the most popular members of the exclusive Lantenengo Country Club.

Caroline English's past is more colorful than her husband's. A well-bred Bryn Mawr graduate, she taught briefly among the underprivileged, but soon concentrated on her essential interest—men. Though she had known Julian from childhood, he was the last man she thought about seriously as a lover. There was a wounded but dashing British officer, her cousin, who first roused but refused to take advantage of her youthful passion. Then there was Joe Montgomery, gentle, wealthy, daring. (He took Caroline swimming at night, nearly nude.) Caroline loved Joe but refused to give herself to him until she returned from a European trip with her mother. While Caroline lingered abroad, Joe wrote her, ending their relationship.

In 1926, at the age of twenty-seven, Caroline had at her disposal several men, including Harry Reilly and Julian. She thought Harry "too lavish and considerate," Julian too much a "habit." Her most likely prospect, Harvard-bred Ross Campbell, proved to be a stingy stuffed shirt. Caroline was beginning to believe that no man would ever meet her demands, when she realized that she had loved Julian since childhood. Swiftly, their love burst into passion, sustained itself, and led them to marriage.

As the novel begins, the Englishes are attending a Christmas Eve party at the Lantenengo Country Club. Julian has been listening disgustedly to Harry Reilly tell another of his dirty stories in an Irish brogue and has been contemplating

the pleasure of throwing a drink (complete with ice cube)
into Harry's "fat, cheap, gross Irish face." Julian savors the
impulse, then acts on it. By Christmas morning, news of
Julian's act has spread through Gibbsville, leaving a wake of
speculation about the form of Harry's revenge. Furious with
her husband, Caroline insists that he apologize to Reilly. She
reminds him that he owes Reilly money and that Reilly, a
prominent Catholic, can dissuade many other Catholics from
buying Cadillacs. Julian consents but hints nastily that Caroline is as interested in Reilly as in himself. To prove otherwise, Caroline promises to be in their bed waiting to make
love when Julian returns that afternoon from meeting Reilly.

Reilly refuses even to see Julian, and Mrs. Gorman,
Reilly's sister, tells him that her brother, humiliated and
enraged (the ice cube blackened his eye), has determined
to "fix" Julian. Julian's concern about the threat diminishes
a few minutes later when he returns to Caroline's arms. That
evening, on their way to a dinner party, Caroline begs Julian
to stay sober and promises him as a reward his favorite
recreation—a lovemaking bout in their Cadillac. At the
party, however, twitted by friends about the Reilly fracas,
Julian grows sullen and drinks too much. When Reilly's
priest, Father Creedon, confides to Julian in the men's room
that he, too, dislikes Reilly, Julian's spirits revive and he goes
to Caroline and asks her to join him now in their car. Aware
that he is drunk, she refuses him. Antagonized, Julian begins
to drink in earnest.

Later in the evening, Julian takes Caroline and several
other friends to the Stage Coach Inn, Ed Charney's nightclub. Already there is Al Grecco, assigned by Ed to keep
close watch on his mistress, Helene Holman, the club singer.
At home for Christmas with his wife and children, Ed knows
that Helene's alcoholic and amorous inclinations may lead
her astray. Also present are Lute and Irma Fliegler, with a
group of earthy friends who nag and bait one another while
reaching under the table for their friends' wives.

Julian drifts to the Flieglers' table, then to the table where
Al Grecco has been trying with difficulty to keep Helene in
line. Al warns Julian, whom Ed likes and admires, about Ed's
relationship with Helene, but Julian, stung by his wife's
rebuff earlier in the evening, takes Helene to his car—where

he promptly falls asleep. Al, Caroline, and others have seen what he has done and react with varying degrees of irritation.

The next morning, gossip about Julian's behavior is again rampant. Irma Fliegler teases him when they meet on the street, but Lute adopts a sterner tone in the office, pointing out that Julian has humiliated his wife and alienated Ed Charney, one of their most powerful business connections. Caroline, no longer able to tolerate Julian's behavior, turns to her mother but finds only platitudes of small comfort.

Alone in his office, having failed once more to win Harry Reilly's forgiveness and having discovered how deeply he is in debt, Julian briefly contemplates the possibility of suicide. Instead, he lunches at the country club and argues about his recent behavior with Froggy Ogden, a one-armed veteran whom Julian has long thought of as his best friend. To Julian's astonishment and chagrin, Froggy not only berates him (especially for his treatment of Caroline) but adds that he has always hated him. Froggy rises and offers to fight Julian. Though Julian refuses, other club members rush to their table thinking that Julian intends to hit a cripple. Suddenly Julian goes berserk, smashing the face of one intruder (a Polish lawyer and thus another potential Catholic customer), punching Froggy, and throwing bottles in all directions. Then Julian drives away, feeling strangely sleepy but not wanting to be awakened.

Julian meets Caroline in the street as she leaves her mother's house. Again they argue, agreeing only to cancel the party scheduled at their house for that evening. Julian returns to their home alone. Only one guest shows up—Miss Cartwright, a reporter checking the names of the invited guests. Julian makes an unsuccessful play for her. After she leaves, Julian gets very drunk and listens to jazz records. Half-aware of what he is doing, he goes to the garage outside his house, locks himself in his Cadillac, smashes the clock, and starts the engine.

The doctor who verifies Julian's death is his father. Because of the history of suicide in their family, Dr. English is eager to avoid a coroner's verdict. He knows, however, that the Jewish coroner—whom Dr. English deliberately did not invite to a local medical dinner—will allow no irregularities.

When Dr. English tells Caroline that he will try in every way
to alter the verdict, she screams at him that Julian's death
was as much his fault as anyone's and that the manner of
death was Julian's choice and should be so recorded.

The novel ends with three brief, ironically juxtaposed
scenes: Harry Reilly expresses astonishment that "a real gentleman" like Julian would kill himself; Julian's Polish friend,
Mary, and Caroline's stuffy suitor, Ross Campbell, arrange a
weekend rendezvous; and Lute and Irma Fliegler wonder
what effect Julian's death will have upon their economic
future.

Critical Opinion

The loosely structured plot of *Appointment in Samarra* centers, of course, on the catastrophe that befalls Julian English.
But the novel's true force lies elsewhere. O'Hara never satisfies us about the reasons for Julian's compulsive self-destruction. His father's psychic cruelty and his own sensitivity are
inadequate explanations for his own explosive and often
sadistic behavior. Nor do we really understand what—other
than sex—binds Julian and Caroline. Analysis in depth of
human motives lies beyond O'Hara's skill.

O'Hara's power—and it is considerable—derives from
other sources. Above all else, O'Hara is, as Edmund Wilson
has written, "a social commentator; and in this field of social
habit and manners . . . he has done work that is original and
interesting." With his unerring ear for dialogue, keen eye for
detail, and rich store of information about the minutiae of
daily life, O'Hara captures the mood and movement of the
American middle class in the Gibbsvilles throughout America.
If he fails to discover the psychological motivation of his
characters, he compensates in part by precisely locating their
social drives.

For each of the classes he describes, O'Hara documents
domestic and communal life: furniture, cars, songs, stories,
and sprees, insulated egos, and deeply graven prejudices.
With reportorial detachment and irony, O'Hara communicates his vision of a part of the American way. Because he
cannot penetrate the deepest recesses of his character's hearts,
he falls short of greatness. But in his delineation of surfaces,

he has no master among observers of the twentieth-century American scene.

The Author

Son of an Irish physician, *John O'Hara* was born in Pottsville, Pennsylvania, and attended private schools in preparation for admission to Yale. But his father's death compelled him to give up the hope of college and undertake a variety of odd jobs, among them working as secretary to Heywood Broun, the well-known journalist. After newspaper and movie-script writing, O'Hara began to devote himself to fiction.

His first and best novel, *Appointment in Samarra,* which appeared in 1934, immediately won him a large and appreciative audience. Although he has published nine novels and as many volumes of short stories since then, his skill as a narrator and his insight as a keen critic of American middle-class mores remain substantially the same as in the first book. Nevertheless, several of his subsequent works deserve attention. *Butterfield 8* (1935) captures the sterile gaiety of the Jazz Age. *Pal Joey* (1940), originally a collection of stories from *The New Yorker,* later a musical comedy and a film, epitomizes the opportunism and cynicism of diverse Broadway types. O'Hara's most ambitious novels since *Appointment in Samarra* have been *A Rage to Live* (1949) and *Ten North Frederick* (1955). The first of these is a vigorous study of upper-class amours in a typically O'Hara-like Pennsylvania town; the second, another study of Gibbsville, ranges from the Civil War to the present as it analyzes the career of Joseph B. Chapin, an aspirant to the presidency of the United States. *Ten North Frederick* won for O'Hara the National Book Award.

The Late George Apley

by

JOHN P. MARQUAND (1893–1960)

Main Characters

George Apley—An upper-class Bostonian whose initial impulse to revolt has faded. He has lost touch with his son and daughter and feels that his world is careening toward destruction.

Horatio Willing—His very conservative Bostonian biographer, a good man but a little obtuse.

Thomas Apley—George's father, a pillar of Boston society, moral, dominating, very sure of what is right for George.

Elizabeth—George's mother, a tender, loving, but exceedingly possessive woman.

Mary Monahan—The "unsuitable" Irish girl with whom George falls in love.

Catharine Bosworth—George's wife, a Boston lady who is of George's own class and who exerts firm control over him.

John Apley—George's non-conformist son whom he loves but does not understand.

Eleanor Apley—George's daughter whose bohemian preferences puzzle and grieve him.

The Story

The story of George Apley, Bostonian, unfolds in the papers he has left behind—letters, memoranda, occasional essays. These are presented by an official biographer, the very conservative and slightly obtuse Horatio Willing who has been instructed by George Apley's son, John, to tell the truth, to make the proper Bostonian seem real.

George Apley was born into an old Bostonian family. Its fortunes were founded by Moses Apley, his grandfather, a ship's captain who got his wealth by shrewd trading during war and maintained it by relentless dealing. George's father, Thomas, though educated for the law at Harvard, went into the textile business and, with an acuteness equal to his father's, branched out in partnership with his brother William.

George's childhood was a happy one. He spent his summers at Hillcrest, the Apley home in Milton, where only the boredom of Sundays at the Unitarian church marred the idyllic weeks. The winters in Boston were less perfect, but at Mr. Hobson's school he formed the friendships that would endure for a lifetime. His mother, Elizabeth, a tender woman with literary leanings, taught him the manners that always distinguished him. His father, Thomas, a much more severe parent, planted the attitudes—toward money, toward class, and especially toward family—that controlled him all his life.

Harvard, of course, was the goal of all the Apleys. George distinguished himself there not by scholarship (he was always in the middle of his class) but by his talent for good fellowship and by his prowess as a boxer. The former brought him all sorts of honors, among them appointment to the board of the *Lampoon*, selection as one of the first ten of the D.K.E. Society, and ultimately, the chief accolade, election to the Club. His boxing skill enabled him to become the university titleholder for his weight.

For the Apleys, Boston was the hub of the universe, their class the peak of social evolution, their family the epitome of culture. Despite his youthful fondness for pranks, George never challenged the opinion of the Apleys and frequently won their guarded approbation. In his senior year, however, he fell headlong in love with a lovely Irish girl, Mary Monahan, and she loved him, too. When the senior Apley discovered the relationship, George, protesting, was shipped off to Europe as soon as final examinations were over. The tour through France and England, with stops at all the conventional places, was a dull ache to George, especially since he was accompanied by his Aunt Martha, Uncle Horatio, and Cousin Henrietta and regularly advised and cautioned in letters from home. Indeed, George felt hardly out of Boston at all. His companions carried Boston with them.

Returning home, George entered Harvard Law School, where he did well if not brilliantly, joined his father's Boston clubs and the boards of his father's several charities. One summer he worked for his Uncle William at the family mills in Apley Falls, proving (at least to his uncle's satisfaction) that he was not cut out to be a real businessman and that he ought instead to become an estate lawyer.

George gradually adjusted to Boston, not happily, perhaps, but tranquilly. His mother and father were particularly pleased when he asked Catharine Bosworth, a young lady of considerable will power, to marry him. Catharine belonged to his own class, came from the same background, and held the same prejudices. The families, of course, were intimately involved in the marriage. James Bosworth gave them a summer home at Mulberry Beach, and Thomas Apley a house on Gloucester Street in Boston. Catharine's parents clung to her and George's to him, but Catharine's more active cooperation with the Bosworths gave them the advantage.

The marriage was not an unhappy one, though George often thought longingly of Mary Monahan. He escaped regularly to his clubs, writing a paper that brought him a good deal of local fame—a history of a Boston Street, "Cow Corner," and the people connected with it. He found hunting and fishing trips more congenial than he had as a single man. Before long, a son was born to Catharine and George. Both the Bosworths and the Apleys insisted that the child bear the first name traditional to each family. Finally the child was christened "John," which was fortunately both a Bosworth and an Apley name. The daughter who shortly followed was called "Eleanor"—a Bosworth triumph.

George's sister, Amelia, another firm Boston lady, married well—that is, to a young man who had the right background and a large fortune. Soon after the marriage, Thomas Apley died quite suddenly, leaving a large fortune in trust for George as well as about two and a half million dollars to charities. One estate expenditure came as a surprise. A woman living in New York alleged that she had been the mistress of Thomas Apley and that he was the father of her twelve-year-old son. George Apley refused to credit the allegation, but to avoid scandal he settled the claim by payment of a lump sum.

For some years George's life passed uneventfully. He devoted himself to his philanthropic enterprises, to civic movements (especially the Save Boston Association which was dedicated to honest government and good morals), and to his camp at Pequod Island. He had purchased Pequod Island as a retreat for himself and his male companions. But soon the Apley women invaded it, and Amelia organized it ruthlessly. George formed a kind of sub-organization of male campers, but Pequod was never quite the same. He developed an interest in bird watching, and went on Sunday jaunts with an old friend, Clara Goodrich. The jaunts were beyond criticism, but they nevertheless were criticized by an old family friend. George, however, persisted and the bird watching ultimately became a serene part of his life.

During World War I, George waxed fiercely patriotic, resenting any lukewarm attitude toward the Allies and suspecting German espionage everywhere. His son, John, who had attended Groton unwillingly and then Harvard without passionate commitment to Boston ideals, seemed far less willing than George had been to conform to Apley ways. At first he pretended neutrality toward the war, but when trouble broke out on the Mexican border, he enlisted. When war was declared he was sent to France, fought at the front, and was wounded. Long after his recovery, he stayed on in France, despite George's impatience to see him again and apprentice him to his Boston duties.

When John did return to Boston and to Harvard Law School, he resisted the round of activities that engrossed his father. Upon graduation, John accepted a position in a New York law firm. George, who loved his son deeply, felt aggrieved. Other troubles came, too. His daughter, Eleanor, would not behave in the approved way of the women of her class. She did not direct her total energies toward marrying well. She occasionally took two cocktails before dinner and discussed Freud at the dinner table. She even turned down a thoroughly eligible suitor. George's worry grew. His world had changed and he could not adjust to it. More and more, he complained about politicians, literature, manners. Often he sounded like an echo of his father. Nevertheless, to George's satisfaction, John married a woman of excellent background though she was a divorcée. George was thoroughly displeased, however, by Eleanor's choice: a penniless journalist, whom he suspected of marrying her for her money and position.

An almost disastrous adventure interrupted George's smooth professional progress in the early twenties. In pursuit of his reforming activities, he tried to bring charges against an astute Irish politician named O'Reilly. The latter got George to a hotel room, lured by the prospect of getting additional information for his case. When the door to the room shut, there was no informant. Instead, a nearly nude woman faced him. And the police were not long in arriving to arrest him. George was determined to fight the frame-up until he received a letter from his boyhood sweetheart, Mary Monahan, a relative of O'Reilly's. When George and Mary met again, she found it easy to persuade George to abandon the case. He was happy to do her the favor. Charges were dropped, and his reputation suffered scarcely a mark.

Not much else happened to George. The crash of 1929 affected his fortune not at all. He had seen it coming. Gallantly he came to the aid of friends who had been caught. He campaigned for Hoover. He made a trip to Rome, during which he discovered that he had a heart condition. Upon returning home, though still quarreling with the doctor's diagnosis, he set his affairs in meticulous order—even sending John a diagram of seating arrangements for his funeral service. In December, 1933, he died in his Boston Street House.

Critical Opinion

The Late George Apley is a delightful and dexterously written novel. The memoirist, Horatio Willing, who belongs to the same class and shares the same ideals as his subject, exposes himself thoroughly in the process of exploring George Apley's life and times. Both excessively proper Bostonians are conformists, a trifle pompous and more than a trifle smug. Yet George Apley earns our affection. He is lost in a world in which all the old markers have been destroyed. He has had engraved on his consciousness the watchwords "City, Class, and Family," and he learns sorrowfully that his own beloved children reject them. He has been rigidly molded, and can find no way out of the mold. Indeed, he finally sees it as a product of the highest art.

Then why do we come to like and appreciate George Apley? Because he tries always to do the right thing—as he conceives of right. What he does is often mistaken and misdirected, but he is motivated by an admirable code of decency and service.

Marquand's pervasive irony sometimes flattens Horatio Willing, makes him too obviously a type. Though, however, we see George Apley's similarities to other men of his place, time, and class, he never becomes a caricature. We always recognize him as an individual creation. And we mourn that someone so intelligent, so compassionate, so loving, should find no worthier outlet for his talents than protesting electric signs along Beacon Street or crusading against suggestive books and plays.

The novel, constructed largely as a series of flashbacks—through letters, reminiscences, diary entries and the like—is generally acknowledged to be Marquand's masterpiece: "the most experimental in form among Mr. Marquand's books," one critic says, "and quite the most brilliant." Some years after it won the Pulitzer Prize, *The Late George Apley* was converted into a successful play by Marquand in collaboration with George S. Kaufman, and later into an equally successful movie. But neither play nor movie manages to convey the tenderness and satire implicit in the novel, or the discreet biographer's reluctant disclosure of his hero's humanity, or the gallantry and misbegotten idealism that make men co-operate in their own defeat. *The Late George Apley* firmly established Marquand's reputation and is today still the most widely read of his novels.

The Author

John Phillips Marquand was born in Wilmington, Delaware. His family had their roots in Newburyport, Massachusetts, to which they returned when he was fourteen, and to which, despite excursions to New York and Tokyo, Marquand always returned, in his life and in his novels.

After Harvard, he became a reporter for the Boston *Transcript*. During World War I, he served as a lieutenant, first on the Mexican border and later in France. Home from the war, he returned to reporting, on the New York *Tribune* this time, but shifted to advertising. He soon abandoned that occupation to devote himself to writing. After a good deal of miscellaneous romantic fiction published in *The Ladies' Home Journal* and *The Saturday Evening Post,* some detective stories featuring an amiable Japanese secret-service agent, Mr. Moto, and one delightful biography of a New England eccentric, *Lord Timothy Dexter* (1925), Marquand wrote his first important work of fiction, *The Late George Apley* (1937), a story firmly grounded in his own background and experience. In it Marquand sounded his distinctive satirical note and established his fundamental themes: the decline of a family and the human waste entailed in the refusal to adjust to changing conditions. *Wickford Point* (1939) and *H. M. Pulham, Esquire* (1941) satirically yet compassionately portray the rigidities of the Boston Brahmin, and *So Little Time* (1943), *Repent in Haste* (1945), *B. F.'s Daughter* (1946), and *Point of No Return* are poignant studies in human terms of frustration and failure.

All of Marquand's later novels have been enormously successful, critically and financially. After *The Late George Apley* won the Pulitzer Prize, book clubs, magazines, and motion-picture companies competed for the right to purchase Marquand's novels, reviewers praised them, and the reading public bought them eagerly.

Though Marquand will probably not survive as an important name in the literature of the twentieth century, he is nevertheless a masterly writer. As Granville Hicks has observed, "He is a social novelist of great talent, and neither his slick past nor his successful present should blind us to that fact."

The Grapes of Wrath

by

JOHN STEINBECK (1902–)

Main Characters

Ma Joad—Matriarch of the Joad clan, a large woman, as ample in spirit as in body. She shoulders the responsibility of welding the family together in its time of despair.

Pa Joad—A hard-working, dogged man, earnestly trying to help, but spiritually tired.

Tom Joad—Loyal to family and friends, quiet, but capable of violence in the face of injustice.

Jim Casy—Tom's friend, an erstwhile itinerant preacher who has lost his "calling" but none of his fervor. For God he has substituted Man and set himself the task of preaching the gospel of human brotherhood.

Grampa Joad—A salty, cantankerous old man filled with zest for life as he remembers it—fighting Indians and tilling the soil.

Granma Joad—Testy and lecherous and, until she sinks into senility, almost as vibrant as her husband.

Rose of Sharon Joad—The pregnant young daughter (also called Rosasharn), yearning simply for a sensual, comfort-filled life.

Connie Rivers—Her husband who hates farming and wants to open a radio-repair shop.

Al Joad—Aged sixteen and lusty. A gifted auto mechanic who would prefer to be off on his own, he stays with the family because he admires Tom.

Ruthie and *Winfield Joad*—The youngest children, mischievous but deprived of the experience of normal childhood pleasures.

Noah Joad—Deformed and disfigured by a birth injury, he finds peace in solitude and in nature.

The Story

The spring rain was light in Oklahoma, enough to raise the corn but not enough to settle the dust that had already begun to sweep across the fields. By June the crops were dry, the land crusted, the air fogged with dust—and the sharecropping farmers had grown frightened. Thus, in the opening chapter, Steinbeck describes the setting against which his novel develops. In succeeding chapters, he alternates narrative and exposition. The events in the lives of the Joads hold the narrative center. Their drama is played out against a series of interchapters concerned with the socio-economic, political, and philosophical issues that have bred disaster. In the following summary, the story of the Joads occupies the foreground. The related material is interwoven wherever appropriate.

Just paroled from prison after serving four years of a seven-year sentence for homicide, Tom Joad hitches a ride home with an inquisitive truck driver. As Tom walks across the fields later, he picks up a turtle that has just been spun off the road by the wheels of a truck. The up-ended turtle, seeds of oat and barley embedded in its shell, has righted itself, dropping some of the seed onto the ground. Pocketed by Tom, the turtle carries within its shell other seeds to be planted elsewhere. This symbol of struggle and regeneration links Tom's arrival with his meeting Jim Casy, who remembers having baptized Tom years earlier. Jim confesses his loss of faith but vows to find a new way to help his fellow man.

Together the men discover the Joad farm, desolate and deserted. Like other sharecroppers, the Joads have been ousted, unable to meet payments on their land because it has dried up and failed to produce a paying crop. Forced by the economic squeeze to produce cotton, unable to rotate crops, the farmers have knowingly though unwillingly ruined the soil. Now the landowners—themselves pressured by Eastern money interests—refuse to share the crops. By displacing their tenants and using a single tractor, they need pay only a single wage and can take the entire crop. Thus, the farmers' homes must go, the land must be drained of its last resources and then sold to satisfy the bankers' demands. The frustrated and embittered farmers struggle hopelessly against an enemy they cannot even see.

Tom and Jim find the Joad family staying with an uncle near by and learn that they are scrimping to raise money to head toward California, where (they have learned from widely distributed handbills) work seems plentiful. The family decides to invite Casy along, making a total of thirteen jammed aboard a wheezing Hudson truck. To buy the truck, the Joads have sold nearly all their personal belongings as well as their farming implements. Almost half the paltry $200 they get for their worldly goods goes for the truck. At the last moment Grampa decides not to leave, arguing, "This country ain't no good, but it's my country." The family drugs the old man, loads him aboard, and the Joads head West.

Along Route 66, the truck groans toward the state line. Once Tom crosses it, he is violating his parole, but he knows that his family needs him and he chooses to be with them. Before they reach the line, however, Grampa suffers a stroke and dies. Lacking the money to hire an undertaker, the family digs a wayside grave. Casy performs the burial rite. A kindly couple, the Wilsons, driving a battered sedan, join the Joad caravan. On the road, gas-station and hamburger-stand owners incredulously gape at the bizarre, overladen truck. Occasionally a compassionate waitress underprices a loaf of bread or some candy for them. But as they move farther west, they are received with increasing suspicion and hostility.

In Texas, where the Wilsons' car breaks down, Pa and Tom urge Ma to drive on ahead in order not to lose time. Already worried about the possible break-up of the family (Rosasharn and Connie intend to settle in the city when they reach the Coast), Ma Joad adamantly refuses to budge: "All we got is the family unbroke," she argues, bolstering her reasoning by brandishing a jack handle. She compromises by agreeing to stop at a campsite just ahead until the car is repaired. From this point forward, her indomitable will sustains the family's courage and determination, even when increasingly ominous signs undermine her resolve. Thus, before they leave Texas, a returning migrant tells them how the work handbills deceive the farmers. Owners advertise for 800 workers. As many as 5,000 appear. Then the owners, confident that the 800 hungriest workers will labor for little, lower the hourly rate to the barest minimum.

The Joads press on—across New Mexico and Arizona, to the edge of the California desert. There, for the first time, they hear the word Okie, an epithet for an Oklahoman migrant that "means you're scum." At a river's edge, just before they enter the desert, Noah abandons the family. When they stop for a night, sheriffs threaten them with arrest, treat them like vermin. Ma refuses to be browbeaten and challenges one deputy with a skillet. Tom teases her, then tells her of Noah's departure. Saddened by this, by Granma's weakness and senility, and by Mrs. Wilson's illness, which prevents the Wilsons from continuing the journey, Ma still goads her brood on.

As they reach the end of the desert, the fertile valley extends before them. They gaze at it, awed and exultant. Ironically, at this moment Ma tells them that Granma died during the night's journey across the desert. Fearing they might be delayed if she spoke, Ma lay silently beside the dead woman all night. On the other side of the truck, Connie and Rosasharn made love. Despite everything, they are in California, land of plenty and poverty, of patriotism and terrorism, a land where Okies—the enemy invaders—breed fear and hate in the hearts of native Californians.

At a Hooverville camp, the Joads set up a tent and Ma tries to organize a household. But there is no work. Uncle John gets drunk, and Connie deserts his pregnant wife. When a deputy intrudes, threatens them all, and shoots a woman, Tom disarms him and Casy kicks the felled man unconscious. To save Tom from arrest and jail as a parole violator, Casy takes full blame and goes off with the police. The camp breaks up when it learns that American Legionnaires plan to burn it. As the Joads leave, Tom refuses to obey the deputies' order to head south. Defiantly, he drives north. Ma soothes him, assuring him that he will not lose his integrity: "They ain't gonna wipe us out. Why, we're the people—we go on."

At a Government-run camp, Weedpatch, things go more promisingly. Treated like human beings, protected from invading sheriffs, the migrant farmers govern themselves cooperatively, and even the children learn once more how to play. A humane but beleaguered employer hires Tom and warns him to beware of an invasion of the camp's Saturday-night dance by troublemakers. Quietly the campers plan their strategy. During the dance, as the toughs arrive, armed deputies wait outside the camp for sound of a riot—the only legal justification they have to enter. The riot call never sounds, for Tom and others spirit away each rowdy as he tries to stir up trouble and efficiently dump him over the camp fence. The dancers continue unmolested.

A month later the Joads have had a total of only five days of work, all of it Tom's. Ma insists that they move on lest Pa lose all his spirit and determination. Above all, she counts on Tom, her favorite, to maintain the level of decency she wishes for all her family. They move north to a peach farm and are hired to pick fruit at a nickel for each three-gallon bucket of unbruised fruit. By sundown, with the entire family working, the Joads have earned a dollar. To cap their disillusion, the prices set by the ranch store are so high that their dollar will not even buy them a decent meal.

That night Tom steals out of the camp past armed guards who tell him they are protecting the pickers against Communist agitators. At a tent in the fields, Tom finds Jim Casy, now a labor leader and strike organizer, trying to stop the wage-cutting methods used by ranch owners. As Tom and Jim talk, they hear voices near by and then stare into a flash light. Two men leap at Casy, one swinging a pickhandle that crushes Casy's skull. Tom wrests the club from the man and bashes in his head. Grazed by a blow, Tom escapes and manages to crawl back to the Joads' camp house. He tells his family what has happened and insists that he must leave. Ma begs him to stay for the sake of the family, especially as Rosasharn will soon have her child. Tom agrees to remain.

Next day the wage for peach picking drops to two and a

half cents, young Winfield collapses from hunger, and a
posse searches for Tom. Nearly distraught, the Joads leave,
hiding Tom between two mattresses. Continuing north, they
come to a cotton camp and are assigned housing in a boxcar.
Tom, his face still bruised, must hide in a culvert. During a
childish fracas, Ruthie boasts to another youngster that her
brother has killed a deputy. Ma realizes that she must now
tell Tom to flee. When she goes to him, Tom tells her that he
intends to carry on Jim Casy's mission, for he has become
convinced of Casy's rightness: "a fella ain't got a soul of his
own, but on'y a piece of a big one. . . ." Ma gives the reluctant Tom money, and they part stoically after Tom's assurance that he will return when things have settled.

At the camp, Pa Joad feels that command of his family has
slipped from his grasp. Worse, he has ceased to care, despite
Ma's assurance that what has happened simply proves that
women are more flexible than men. For a brief time the
cotton picking continues, but all work ceases when the tor-
rential seasonal rains pour down on the land. Disease sets in
among the workers. Stealing and begging replace dignity and
pride. And the native Californians, now more hostile than
ever, swear in new deputies to cow and beat the Okies. Only
their wrath—the grapes that have matured during their terrible experience—keeps the downtrodden together.

In the final chapter of the novel, a counterpoint of life and
death echoes the imagery of turtle and seed. As the men dig
banks against the rising flood waters, Rosasharn delivers her
child in the boxcar. It is born dead, "a blue shriveled little
mummy." As the flood waters rise toward the floor of the car,
Ma and Pa Joad remove Rosasharn to a dry barn. There they
discover an elderly worker dying of starvation. Lying beside
the ailing man, Rosasharn nurses him, "and her lips came
together and smiled mysteriously."

Critical Opinion

In recent years critics have grown increasingly impatient with
John Steinbeck. He has been called a "naïve mystic" and,
worse, a "hausfrau sentimentalist." Yet a quarter of a century

ago, when *The Grapes of Wrath* appeared, Steinbeck's work stirred intense reactions. Supporters called his novel "The *Uncle Tom's Cabin* of the Depression." Antagonists joined Lyle Boren, an Oklahoma Congressman, in attacking the novel as "a lie, a black, infernal creation of a twisted, distorted mind."

Today distance enables us to adopt a more judicious attitude. Few view the novel as a mere piece of left-wing propaganda despite the warning sounded by its title, a title Steinbeck chose "because it is in our own revolutionary tradition and because in reference to this book it has a large meaning." The novel does, however, urge the development of a communal spirit and affirms a sense of the mystical spirit of the group. Jim Casy possesses this instinctive sense of the surging force of mankind, and Ma Joad expresses it in her insistence upon the unity of the family. Tom Joad moves gradually toward awareness of this higher sanctity and, at the end of the novel, assumes the responsibility for pressing forward its ineffaceable truth.

Because of Steinbeck's interest in marine life, some critics have argued that he has reduced life to a series of animalistic patterns like those he had observed in the sea: survival of the fittest, rejection of alien elements by the established group. Certainly the migrant farmers of *The Grapes of Wrath* represent intruders who upset the balance. And in this, as in other Steinbeck novels, property, ownership, indeed the land itself —all upset the natural balance disastrously. But Steinbeck is a man of compassion, not a clinical precisionist. Like Jim Casy, he seems to say, "All things are holy," and to urge all men and women to love one another, to march forward together. His confidence in man triumphs over despair.

The style and structure of *The Grapes of Wrath* seem at times overwrought, the symbols transparent, and the episodes —especially the much-debated closing scene of Rosasharn nursing the starving man—often melodramatic. Nevertheless, at its best—which it often is—the novel nears the level of epic in its lyric sweep and agonized power. And in Ma Joad, Jim Casy, and Grampa, among others, Steinbeck has created a gallery of American portraits that body forth our American heritage of courage, compassion, and humor.

The Author

Born and raised in Salinas, California, son of a local politician and a schoolteacher, *John Steinbeck* worked on farms and in laboratories as a high-school student. At Stanford he registered only for courses that interested him, and remained there intermittently for six years without taking a degree. Determined to write, he set out for New York in 1925 and arrived there by way of the Panama Canal. The side trip provided him with material for his first published novel, *Cup of Gold* (1929), a tale about Henry Morgan, the pirate. During his two years in New York, he worked variously as reporter, chemist, and hod carrier.

Back in California, his first novel published, he married and began to work in earnest. His succeeding novels got favorable reviews but little money—even the best of them, *Tortilla Flat* and *In Dubious Battle*. With *Of Mice and Men* (1937), Steinbeck became a best-selling novelist. Two years later he published *The Grapes of Wrath,* his finest book, the outgrowth of a newspaper series about migrant workers he had published three years earlier in the San Francisco *News.*

During the war years, Steinbeck served overseas as a correspondent. Since *The Grapes of Wrath,* he has been enormously productive but has failed to maintain his earlier force. *Cannery Row* (1945) and *Sweet Thursday* (1954), for example, are gentle, sentimental tales based upon his recollections of Ed Ricketts, a marine ecologist. But they lack the point and purpose of *The Sea of Cortez,* a semi-scientific work he had written earlier with Ricketts. In 1962 Steinbeck won the Nobel Prize for Literature, largely for *The Grapes of Wrath.* Despite his fame, Steinbeck has remained shy, avoiding publicity, preferring to travel the length and breadth of the nation with his poodle (*Travels with Charley,* 1962), observing, reflecting, and recording.

The Ox-Bow Incident

by

WALTER VAN TILBURG CLARK (1909–)

Main Characters

Gil Carter—A good-natured cowhand, tough, ready to fight on little or no provocation.

Art Croft—His friend, the narrator of the episode, a more sensitive and perceptive man.

Jeff Farnley—A trigger-tempered, proud, vengeful cowboy.

Drew—A rancher whose cattle have reportedly been rustled.

Canby—A saloonkeeper, efficient, shrewd, and a little cynical.

Greene—The young excitable cowboy who reports Kinkaid's death.

Risley—The capable, level-headed sheriff.

Mapes—The deputy sheriff, brutal, stupid, touchy.

Smith—The town drunk, a vicious blowhard.

Bartlett—A rancher whose cattle have been stolen in the past and who is all-out to hang rustlers.

Moore—Drew's foreman, a firm, fair-minded man.

Winder—The perpetually angry stage-coach driver.

Gabe Hart—Winder's powerful, moronic, but gentle hostler.

Ma Grier—A huge, loud, easy-going woman, owner of the town's boardinghouse.

Major Tetley—The leader of the posse, cruel, poised, power-mad.

Gerald Tetley—His frightened, oversensitive son.

Amigo—Tetley's amiable Mexican cowhand.

275

Osgood—The town minister, pompous, timorous, ineffectual.

Tyler—The town judge, florid, eloquent, but as ineffectual as Osgood.

Sparks—A Negro handyman, simple, religious, good.

Davies—A storekeeper, idealistic, intense, but wholly powerless to stop the posse from acting.

Rose Mapen—Formerly Gil's girl friend, driven from the town by jealous women.

Swanson—Her poised, dangerous new husband.

Donald Martin—A courageous and honest rancher who, along with his Mexican cowhand and a feeble, half-insane old man, is accused of rustling Drew's cattle.

Kinkaid—Farnley's friend, the man supposedly shot by the rustlers.

The Story

After spring round-up in the year 1885, two cowhands, Gil Carter and Art Croft, come to the small Nevada town of Bridger's Wells. Gil is a powerfully built, proud, pugnacious but essentially good-hearted man. Art, the narrator, is slighter, more equable, and much more sensitive. Occasionally Gil feels the need for a fight, and now, after a poker game with Jeff Farnley, a trigger-tempered cowboy, he gets it. He knocks Farnley out and is similarly treated by the saloonkeeper, Canby, who breaks a bottle over his head. More violence seems to be in the offing, but the men in the saloon are distracted by a young fellow who furiously breaks in to report that cattle have been rustled from Drew, a local ranch owner, and that one of his hands, Kinkaid, has been killed.

The report is circumstantial but suspect. Greene, who retails it, has observed nothing firsthand: he was asked to ride for the sheriff and was told only that Kinkaid had been shot. Cattle rustlers have been active in the region, and the men are quickly inflamed. They decide not to wait for the sheriff, Risley, though nobody denies his effectiveness because they want immediate justice, not the slow and doubtful process of law.

The posse formed by the vigilantes and illegally sworn by Mapes, the brutal deputy sheriff, has some odd members:

Farnley, Kinkaid's buddy, bristling for revenge; Smith, a drunkard and blowhard; Bartlett, a rancher, who has had some of his cattle stolen and who is nearly as eager as Farnley to get the rustlers; Moore, Drew's foreman, a firm and fair-minded man; Winder, the stage-coach driver, perpetually angry and avid for action first, explanations later; Gabe Hart, his gentle, moronic, apelike hostler; Ma Grier, a huge, loud, easygoing woman, owner of a boardinghouse; Major Tetley, a former Confederate officer, cruel, perfectly poised, driven by an abnormal craving for power; Gerald, his son, sensitive, weak-willed, terrorized; and Amigo, his Mexican cowhand. Major Tetley at once emerges as the leader of the posse through his force of will and singleness of purpose.

Opposed to the vigilantes are an impotent few: Osgood, the minister, pompous, timorous, wholly out of touch with the hard-living cowboys and ranchers; Tyler, the judge, florid, eloquent, full of law but as empty of understanding as Osgood; Sparks, a Negro handyman, simple, religious, and good; and Davies, a storekeeper, deeply troubled, idealistic, passionately dedicated to the law which he regards as the conscience of society. He pits himself against the posse. But despite his eloquence and good sense, he fails to sway them from their purpose: to pursue the rustlers and to hang them.

The most likely stopping-place for the rustlers is the Ox-Bow, a little valley named for a creek in the middle that winds back on itself. The men riding in the bitter cold are diversely motivated: Farnley utterly set on killing the rustlers, Sparks hoping somehow to help them if they are caught, Tetley triumphant at having achieved command. Most, perhaps, stay with the posse simply because they are hemmed in by a few resolute men and because they are ashamed to desert. Art is troubled by the moral issue and Gerald Tetley despairs at his inability to oppose his father.

At the summit of a hill, where the wind bites most fiercely, the posse pauses in a clearing. Art makes Sparks borrow his coat—he is wearing only jeans and a thin shirt. The tension of the posse grows. Art lights a cigarette and is threatened by Winder, but the danger passes when Sparks notes that half a dozen men have lighted up. Suddenly they are startled into immobility. They hear horses and see the stagecoach crashing toward them. The driver, thinking the group he sees are bandits, whips the horses madly onward. The men pursue, trying to halt the stagecoach. Art, in the lead, is hit by the guard's bullet. Finally, Ma Grier raises her big voice and the driver pulls the stagecoach to a precarious halt. The passengers, two women and a man, descend. They are Rose Mapen, with whom Gil had an affair from which he has not recovered and who was driven from the town by jealous women; her new husband, Swanson, an elegant but clearly dangerous young man; and the latter's sister. Gil and Swanson exchange guarded words—Swanson with fluency and pointed politeness. Art's wound is bound up, and though he faints, he is determined to continue in pursuit of the rustlers.

After the stagecoach departs, the men go ahead with their mission despite the now relentlessly falling snow. At Ox-Bow they come upon their quarry, three men sleeping round a campfire: a swart Mexican, shrewd and alert; an old gray man, obviously feeble-minded; and their leader, a tall, thin, dark young fellow. When they are awakened, only the Mexican retains his alertness and bravado. The old man mumbles, seized with a vague dread. The young man, brave despite his chattering, asks what the charge is. Hearing that it is rustling and murder, he protests their innocence. Farnley is in an agony of impatience, but Tetley sternly quiets him in order to question the presumed criminal. The story he tells is hardly convincing. His name is Donald Martin; he is from Ohio and has recently purchased a ranch near Pike's Hole; he has bought fifty head of cattle from Harley Drew and is now driving them. But the ranch he says that he has bought is part of a larger ranch owned by someone else; and he has no bill of sale for the cattle, Drew allegedly having promised to mail it. Martin's protests do not impress the vigilantes. Davies tries vainly again to persuade the men to check on Martin's story. The Mexican tries to escape, but is shot in the leg. The old man blabs the charge that the Mexican committed the murder, but is put down by Martin. Davies promises to find someone to look out for Martin's wife and children and to see that Martin's final letter gets to her. Then, in the gray light of dawn, Major Tetley supervising, the three criminals are hanged. But young Tetley bungles the job his father assigns him; he fails to prod Martin's horse, and Martin, who has at the end exhibited his proud courage, is left dangling and has to be shot. The major strikes his son with the butt of a pistol and drops him where he stands.

The posse leaves the scene to return to town. On the way back they meet the sheriff, Tyler, Drew, Davies' clerk—and Kinkaid, the man reported dead. Judge Tyler denounces them as murderers, promises to try every man for murder. But Sheriff Risley refuses to recognize any of them, asking for volunteers for a legal posse. They all volunteer, but Risley passes up Mapes and Tetley and eight others.

In town, Art's wound is expertly treated by Canby. Art falls into a deep sleep. When he awakes, Davies is there. He is tortured by guilt, desperately wants someone to confess to, and Art seems to have the necessary sympathy and sensitivity. Davies accuses himself of the sin of omission—for not, apparently, exercising leadership equal to Tetley's. In agony of spirit, he insists that he lacked real courage. His self-castigation, though unquestionably sincere, is nevertheless tinged by a sort of pleasure, as Art acutely notes. Davies tells Art that young Tetley has hanged himself from a rafter upon returning home. The major seems unmoved. But Gil comes in and adds to the story: the major has killed himself.

Gil and Art come down to eat, contribute to the collection for Martin's family, and casually discuss Rose Mapen and her new husband. Gil wants to fight Swanson because his self-assured possession of Rose irritates him, but Gil knows that a fight with him would come to shooting. "I'll be glad to get out of here," he says. Art agrees.

Critical Opinion

The Ox-Bow Incident, Walter Van Tilburg Clark's first novel, may be read (and often has been) simply as a western. And on that level it is a remarkably satisfying story: the episodes are exciting, the action mounts steadily toward the climax, the characters are real, the style is hard and lean, the backgrounds are graphically drawn. However, Clifton Fadiman comments, "It bears about the same relation to an ordinary western that *The Maltese Falcon* does to a hack detective story."

The core of *The Ox-Bow Incident* is the lynching of three

alleged cattle rustlers in Nevada in 1885. But Mr. Clark gives
the vigilantes and their victims faces, converts the "incident"
into a significant study of mob cruelty and irrationality, dissects the separate motives of the members of the posse and
shows how their motives reinforce one another. He does more,
too, for as Frederic I. Carpenter points out, "The novel is the
story of the tragic failure of an idea in action—the idea of
law and justice. It can also be taken, if you will, as a parable
on the tragedy of Western civilization."

There are faults in the novel, certainly. The reader would
like to know a good deal more about several of the characters:
massive, easygoing, loud "Ma" Jenny Grier, for example, or
humane yet steel-purposed Sparks. But detailed analysis of
all the characters might have impaired the force and drive of
the story. As it stands, *The Ox-Bow Incident* is one of the two
or three important westerns in contemporary American literature.

The Author

Born in Maine in 1909, *Walter Van Tilburg Clark* spent part
of his childhood in Nyack, New York, and in 1917 moved
with his family to Reno, Nevada. His life there supplied the
background for his sensitive novel of adolescence, *The City of
Trembling Leaves* (1945). He attended the University of
Nevada, of which his father was president, getting his
bachelor's degree in 1931 and his master's in 1932. After two
more years of graduate study at the University of Vermont,
he taught for ten years in the public schools of Cazenovia, a
small town in upstate New York. Married in 1933, Clark is
the father of two children. He has taught with distinction in
several colleges, but his main efforts are now devoted to
writing.

Though he has published both poetry and essays, Clark's
special bent is for fiction. He has been represented with unusual frequency in the O. Henry Memorial Collections of short
stories, and in 1945 he won the O. Henry Short Story Award
for "The Wind and the Snow of Winter." *The Ox-Bow Incident* (1940) and *The Track of the Cat* (1949), the latter a

stirring, symbol-laden tale of the pursuit of a mountain lion, have been made into superb movies.

Mr. Clark's novels and some of his stories are westerns—but with a difference. His uniqueness, one critic says, is in "the total 're-interpretation' of the traditional western stock-type characters and the subdued but penetrating insight into their motives, their human and universal passions." Moreover, the realistic settings, natural dialogue, and the taut, spare language put the stamp of authenticity on everything he writes.

The Heart Is a Lonely Hunter

by

CARSON MCCULLERS (1917–)

Main Characters

John Singer—A deaf-mute, thirty-two years old, with a deep
wisdom that makes people confide in him.
Antonapoulos—Singer's beloved deaf-mute companion, a
gross, unbalanced Greek.
Mick Kelly—A fourteen-year-old tomboy who idolizes Singer
and is bewitched by music.
Dr. Copeland—A Negro physician whose mission is to raise
the Negro people to freedom and a sense of purpose, and
who is bitterly disappointed at his children's failure to share
his vision.
Portia—Dr. Copeland's daughter, servant of the Kellys, a
good, loving, but unintellectual woman.
Jake Blount—A driven man, short, ugly, hammer-fisted, who
is maddened because people will not understand that a
better life is possible for them.
Biff Brannon—Proprietor of a restaurant, a lonely, impotent
man whose tenderness and love are never realized.

The Story

Singer, a deaf-mute about thirty-two years old, has been
living in a Southern town for ten years working as an en-

graver. Living with him is another deaf-mute, a Greek named Antonapoulos. The latter is gross, greedy, cretinous, but Singer adores him, attributing to him intelligence and sympathy that he does not possess.

When Antonapoulos's odd behavior becomes intolerable and he is sent to the state insane asylum 200 miles away, Singer is distraught. He moves into a furnished room in a house run by the Kellys, a large, impoverished family. He begins taking his meals at the New York Café, a restaurant owned by Biff Brannon, a lonely man filled with a tenderness that finds no outlet. Biff's wife, Alice, treats him with contempt, especially since he has become impotent.

Singer soon becomes, without his willing it or understanding it, a magnet for four unfulfilled, spiritually restless people. First there is Jake Blount, a five-foot, huge-fisted, raging wanderer who goes on periodic drunks. Jake is maddened by the hopelessness of people, their refusal to learn what they can do to improve their miserable lot. He goes from place to place in the South, always unheeded or misunderstood. Singer seems to him to comprehend and even to share the emotions that drive him. On Sundays, when he is free from his job as a carnival mechanic, Jake comes to Singer's room to talk tumultuously of his experiences, his hopes, his ideals.

Mick Kelly, a gangling fourteen-year-old girl, is another who finds in Singer a sensitive understanding of things she cannot fully articulate. A bit rough, she is nevertheless a girl who loves her little brothers until it hurts, and who has a passion for music that leads her to sacrifice her lunches in order to take lessons from a more fortunate girl who can play the piano. Music is with her always—little tunes that go through her head and that she tries, without technical knowledge, to put down on paper. She comes to identify music and Singer, and she worships the deaf-mute for his apparent compassion and, she supposes, empathy.

Dr. Benedict Copeland, a tubercular Negro physician, also feels that Singer shares his ideals. The doctor is filled with suppressed fury at the brutality of white men and at the ignominy of his race. He has always striven to invest his people with a sense of mission—freedom to serve humanity as equals and receive their due. He names his children Karl Marx, Hamilton, William, and Portia, but they reject his ambitions for them and remain content with their trivial round of pleasures. Only Singer, different from all other white men he has known, will respond to his impassioned statement of purpose which has alienated his wife whom he loved but who rejected him and drove his children from him.

Finally Biff Brannon, inquiring and skeptical, a searcher but not a devotee, comes often to see Singer. Restless, unceasingly interested in penetrating beneath the surface, feminine in spite of his hirsute masculine appearance, Biff is misinterpreted by Jake who cannot understand that Biff feels an affinity for him though not for his beliefs, and by Mick who distrusts him intuitively and feels that he harbors animosity toward her. Biff, in fact, likes freaks and children. He likes freaks, his wife once sharply informed him, because he is a bit of a freak himself. He has a secret fondness for perfume, which he dabs under his ears, and he keeps a complete file of newspapers dating back twenty years to World War I. He likes children, too, in an ambiguous fashion, varying from a tender parental longing for children of his own to a diffuse sexual longing for Mick.

Other people are drawn to Singer, imagining that he possesses a great silent wisdom. They ascribe superhuman qualities to him and construct a number of myths about him—always in their own image. He is variously said to be a Jew, a Turk, a union organizer, a wealthy man, a poor man. And Singer is supported by a myth of his own. He builds for himself the illusion that Antonapoulos—the poor, deranged Greek —is a godlike man. He writes letters to the illiterate Antonapoulos, then destroys them. Whenever he can, he visits Antonapoulos, bringing him expensive gifts and talking to him eagerly despite the Greek's unresponsiveness.

The four cling to Singer, wanting to love, wanting to be loved, and being continually disappointed. Jake is ravaged by his desire to communicate his message. He is scorned and repelled by everyone except Singer who appears to agree. Jake thinks he has discovered another comrade, a man who scrawls warnings to the rich and mighty of the earth. But he proves to be a half-crazed evangelist.

Dr. Copeland tries to draw nearer to his children, to enlist them for his true purpose. They, however, fear and resent him. Only Portia visits him, but neither can achieve any kind of spiritual union. With none of his race, in fact, does he experience it. At a family party he sits stiff and alien, refusing to eat or drink and leaving as early as he can. As judge of an essay contest for Negro high-school students on the subject of advancing the Negro race in society, he awards the prize by default to a wild composition full of racial hatred. The other students have really nothing to say. During the Christmas party following the award, Dr. Copeland speaks of his hopes for his people and preaches his version of Marx's gospel. But his belief that his meaning has been perceived and appreciated is momentary. His son Willie gets involved in a knifing, is sent to jail, and because he attempts to escape, is punished by being put in a freezing room for three days until his feet swell, develop gangrene, and have to be amputated. When Dr. Copeland attempts to approach the local judge, he is beaten as an uppity Negro and thrown into jail. After his release, Singer and Jake call on him. With Jake he gets into a fierce argument about what must be done to improve conditions for Negroes, becomes enraged, and is seized with a severe attack of tubercular coughing.

Mick, gangling and awkward, suffers more than than most adolescents. She tries to "belong," to be one of her high-school crowd. She throws a "prom" party that becomes a disaster when some neighborhood rowdies break it up. She struggles unsuccessfully to put down on paper the tunes that haunt her. She finds no suitable response to her emotional needs in her family. Her seven-year-old brother, torn by an ecstasy of love for a little girl, Biff's niece, and unable to express it otherwise, shoots her. Mick's impoverished family goes deeper in debt as they toil to pay the medical bills. Only one brief fulfillment comes to her—and that is marred. Harry, a Jewish boy, hires bicycles and they go on a swimming outing. They have a glorious time; but afterward the fourteen-year-old girl and the sixteen-year-old boy come together in a sexual encounter. Guilt-ridden, Harry flies home to take a job as mechanic in another city while Mick remains behind and endures. Finally she is subtly persuaded by her family to take a job in a five-and-ten-cent store.

Biff Brannon goes from disillusionment to disillusionment. He remains friendless. His aunt and her spoiled daughter exploit him. Jake rejects him. After a while he does not even have the satisfaction of illusion: he realizes that Singer has none of the qualities that the hopes and needs of people endow him with.

As for Singer himself, on one of his periodic visits to Antonapoulos, he is informed that his friend has died from nephritis. The world is henceforth blighted, hopeless. Singer shoots himself.

Singer's death arouses despair in his disciples. Dr. Copeland, perhaps fatally ill, goes off to the country farm of his father-in-law, convinced that his life has been a failure and is now at an end. Jake gets into a murderous fight at a carnival and leaves town, determined to continue spreading his futile doctrine of rebellion through the South. Mick, chained to her onerous job, no longer hears the music that once filled her being and looks forward to nothing at all. Biff fleetingly undergoes a kind of illumination, catching a glimpse of the human struggle, of men and women laboring and seeking love. But then he glimpses darkness and terror, too—the realization of aloneness. And he is suspended between the two, the radiance and the blackness.

Critical Opinion

The action of *The Heart Is a Lonely Hunter*, which Carson McCullers wrote when she was twenty-three, is contained within the winter of one year and the summer of the next. It is a tightly constructed and intensely concentrated novel. Yet remarkably, it presents a panorama of the "strangled South." As Ihab Hassen notes, "The novel finds a way of acknowledging the social realities of its time."

Its central theme is the inevitable isolation of each man. Each reaches out, lonely and longing, for communion with another human being. And each finds it is only an illusion— an illusion that must be ultimately shattered. Nevertheless, the illusion is what makes life livable.

The characters in the novel are realistically, sometimes ironically drawn—but always the quality of mercy mitigates the irony. Mick Kelly, who loves music and strives dimly for a kind of beauty, perhaps touches readers most poignantly. But the unexpressed tenderness of Biff Brannon, the futile rage of Jake Blount, the unfulfilled purpose of Dr. Copeland—these, too, evoke compassion. Richard Wright, an important Negro novelist, especially praises Mrs. McCullers for "the astonishing humanity that enables a white writer, the first time in Southern fiction, to handle Negro characters with as much ease and justice as those of her own race."

Singer, a deaf-mute, is the centripetal force of the novel. Toward him all of the characters gravitate to speak their deepest wants and to hear the saving words—and he can neither hear nor speak. Though *The Heart Is a Lonely Hunter* is set in the deep South during the early thirties, it is more than reportage, even spiritual reportage, dealing with a particular place and time. It is a parable on the human condition, men's fragile visions, their frustrated aims, their shut-in agonies, their necessary self-deceptions and, not least, their valorous endurance.

The Author

Carson McCullers was born in 1917 in Columbus, Georgia. Though her first ambition was to be a concert pianist, she began writing at fifteen and published her remarkable first novel, *The Heart Is a Lonely Hunter,* at twenty-three. When she was seventeen, she came to New York to study at the Juilliard School of Music. On her second day in the city, she lost her tuition money in the subway. She worked at a series of part-time jobs, going to school at night and writing in her scant spare time. In 1940, three years after her marriage to Reeves McCullers, she sold two of her stories to *Story* magazine and embarked on a full-time writing career. She has won several literary awards and two Guggenheim fellowships which have allowed her to live and work abroad where she has read widely, particularly the French novelists and poets. She lives in Nyack, New York.

Carson McCullers' novels explore the world of the lonely, the isolated, the misfits. Her dominant theme is the futile search for love and identity. Her most characteristic and important novels are *Reflections in a Golden Eye* (1941), a brilliant, grotesque study of the failure of love; *The Member of the Wedding* (1946), a foray into the adolescent world of its twelve-year-old heroine, which Miss McCullers turned into a first-rate play; *The Ballad of the Sad Café* (1951), dramatized in 1963 by Edward Albee, a mirror of the distortions of personality created by love bitterly mixed with pain.

Miss McCullers, it is true, works within a small compass and perhaps develops her central theme too often. "But within the small, lonely, lost world which she has created in her fiction," Stanley Kunitz observes, "she moves with sure and steady artistry. She is one of the most admired and imitated authors of her generation."

The Human Comedy

by

WILLIAM SAROYAN (1908–)

Main Characters

Katey Macauley—A widow of limited economic means, abundant faith in mankind, and endless resources of love. Her creed: "Nothing good ever ends. . . . And the world is full of people and full of wonderful life."

Homer—Her fourteen-year-old son, a schoolboy and a telegraph messenger.

Ulysses—Her youngest son, four years old. Like his namesake, he is an adventurer to whom the whole world represents an exciting voyage of discovery.

Marcus—Her eldest son, a soldier in World War II.

Bess—Her daughter, aged seventeen, sweet, understanding, gentle.

Mary Arena—Marcus' girl friend, the girl next door, seventeen, innocent and lovable.

Thomas Spangler—The genial, fatherly manager of the local telegraph office, onetime high-school low-hurdle champion whom Homer idolizes.

Mr. Grogan—An elderly, kindly drunkard and philosopher, once the world's fastest telegrapher, now perhaps the last of his kind and fearful of being replaced by machines.

Tobey George—Marcus' buddy in the Army, a homeless orphan.

Lionel Cabot—Ulysses' seven-year-old friend, a bungling but eager fellow traveler in the wonderful world of Ithaca, California.

Miss Hicks—Teacher of ancient history at Ithaca High, antiquated but wise, compassionate, and just.

The Story

As the novel opens, Ulysses Macauley watches in wonder as a gopher emerges from a hole and squints at him. A moment later he joyously gazes at a bird settling in a walnut tree. Even more exciting than the worlds of bird, beast, and tree, however, is the world of man and machines that comes into view as a freight train passes through Ithaca, California. All of the men aboard ignore Ulysses' happy waves except for a Negro who waves and cries out to him, "Going home, boy —going back where I belong!" Without comprehending just what the Negro means, Ulysses senses that the world is a funny, lonely, but wholly exciting place. What he fears most is having the people he knows best go away, for they seem not to come back. His father has never returned, and now he is worried that Marcus may not, either. When Homer tells of his plans for travel, Ulysses pleads with him not to leave and Homer assures him that he will not go for a long, long while.

At fourteen, Homer has taken on a job as messenger boy to help support his mother. Mr. Spangler and Mr. Grogan are astonished at his eagerness to prove that he is the best messenger boy they have ever had. He delivers messages and returns to the office with amazing speed. He and Mr. Grogan enjoy long discussions about the ways of the world, and Homer feels a deep urge to help Mr. Grogan keep the job he has always performed so commendably. Unfortunately Mr. Grogan often falls into drunken stupors and ignores the signals of the telegraph ticker. Mr. Grogan receives and Homer delivers to a Mexican woman a War Department message notifying her of the death of her son in combat. When Homer reads the note to the illiterate mother, she refuses at first to accept the truth, and then insists that Homer sit with her, eat candy, and even become her boy to take the place of Juan. When Homer returns home that night, he tells his mother of the events of the day and confesses to her that they have made him feel lonely, though why or for what he cannot say. She explains to him that he has reached the end of childhood, and that loneliness is a worldwide affliction. War, she tells her son, does not make loneliness; rather, it is man's loneliness that makes war.

Homer's immediate goal is to win the 220-yard low-hurdle race at Ithaca High. Rising early each morning, he exercises while the fascinated Ulysses watches, then practices leaping fences on his way to school. But Homer's ambitions encounter more opposition than he anticipates. For one thing, Coach Byfield, the bigoted, tyrannical athletic coach, has been training Hubert Ackley III, son of a wealthy townsman, to win the event. On the day of the race, a more formidable obstacle looms before Homer. Miss Micks, who teaches ancient history, keeps Homer and Hubert in after school because they have exchanged insults during the class hour. Homer's dislike of Hubert is based not only on that young man's snobbishness but also on his friendship with Helen Eliot, the prettiest girl in the class and also a snob but, in Homer's eyes, nonetheless adorable. Coach Byfield tries to get the principal to release Hubert, and when the principal refuses, lies to Miss Hicks that the principal has authorized Ackley to run. Annoyed at what she recognizes at once as a lie, Miss Hicks releases both boys and goes to the track meet to root for the best man.

Homer, arriving at the meet too late to change into track clothes, runs as he is—to the chagrin of both Hubert and Coach Byfield. For most of the race, Hubert and Homer run almost side by side, Homer a bit ahead despite Ackley's insistence that he slow down. Meanwhile Coach Byfield, furious at the way things have turned out, steps onto the track and makes Homer stumble. Ackley has the decency to wait until Homer is back on his feet, and then the race continues to a close finish with Ackley the winner by the narrowest of margins. Miss Hicks prevents Coach Byfield from punishing Homer for almost winning the race and even makes him apologize for a slurring remark he makes to Homer's Italian friend. Then she sends all the youngsters home, urging them to be cheerful about the future.

On his way home, Homer is called to rescue Ulysses from

an unexpected and unusual situation. During an afternoon of wandering about town, Ulysses has drifted into a sporting-goods store where the proprietor is demonstrating to a prospective customer a new and improved bear trap. It suspends the bear in mid-air, keeps turning him around, but does him no other physical harm. By some mischance, when the trap is sprung, Ulysses gets caught. Though somewhat puzzled, Ulysses seems more interested in the consternation of the onlookers than in his own plight. No one seems to know how to release the trap though several persons, including the local policeman, try. When Homer arrives, he takes charge of matters and sees to it that the trap is destroyed and the still curious but undisturbed Ulysses set free. A few minutes later Ulysses is amusing himself at Mr. Spangler's telegraph office where Homer has gone to catch up with the messages that have accumulated in his absence.

Homer has worked for three days at the telegraph office, and, as Mr. Spangler points out, has already matured considerably. That night Homer has a dream that marks just how far he has come toward manhood. Riding his bicycle down a street, Homer dreams that Coach Byfield tries to stop him. Homer manages to make the bicycle fly over Byfield's head and on upwards into the clouds. As he sails along he sees another cyclist, and they race along side by side until Homer suddenly realizes that the other cyclist is Death. The phantom rider moves swiftly toward Ithaca, and Homer tries desperately but unsuccessfully to stop him. Homer's sobs waken Ulysses who watches his brother's anguish, then goes to fetch their mother. She comes and gently reassures the boy. She takes the alarm clock from his room so that he may enjoy a long night's rest.

The next morning Homer tells his mother that delivering telegrams to people whose sons have been killed in the war caused his sad dreams and made him cry even though he knows that grown boys ought not to. Mrs. Macauley tells him that pity has led him to tears, and that pity for one's fellow man is essential to a humane spirit. ". . . out of pity comes balm which heals." She tells Homer, too, that his sobbing as he slept was but the echo of the world's grief. When Homer leaves, Mrs. Macauley sees—as she has innumerable times before—a vision of her dead husband,

Matthew, standing before her. He tells her that Marcus must join him in death, and quietly, as she turns to her daily chores, Mrs. Macauley says, "I know, Matthew."

Ulysses and his friend Lionel continue their excursions into the outside world, watching a funeral, visiting the library and examining carefully the pictures in books they marvel at despite their inability to read. Only once does terror invade Ulysses' happy world of innocence, and it reduces him to terrified sobs. As he watches a waxen-faced man made up as a robot to advertise a quack medicine in a store window, Ulysses senses death without consciously knowing the word, and he flees into the darkness, lost until a newsboy discovers him and brings him to Homer who comforts him.

Across the sea, en route to battle, Marcus Macauley and his friend, Tobey George, talk about the Macauley family, a source of pleasure and hope for the orphaned Tobey who laments the fact that he does not even have a clear national identity. Marcus assures him that he is an American and that that is all he need know about himself. After a brief silence, the two young men pray, Marcus for a home for all the homeless of the world, Tobey for the survival of Ithaca and all the people there whom he has learned to love through Marcus.

Letters arrive from Marcus for each member of the Macauley family. Homer brings his with him to the telegraph office where Mr. Grogan urges him to read it aloud. The letter tells Homer that he is "the best of the Macauleys" and must go on being so. Marcus bequeathes all his possessions to Homer and urges him to welcome Tobey when he arrives with Marcus after the war. Moved to tears by his brother's letter, Homer tells Mr. Grogan that if his brother dies in the war, he will spit at the world and hate it.

Six months later—after soldiers have begun to return to Ithaca and Ulysses has watched with his usual enthusiasm a host of new marvels—the inevitable tragedy befalls the Macauley family, As Homer and Ulysses walk through town, Homer sees a penny and tells Ulysses to pick it up for good luck. Across the street Homer sees Mr. Grogan alone in the telegraph office and stops by to see whether he needs any help. Mr. Grogan seems again to have fallen into a drunken stupor, and since the machine is clicking, Homer resorts to his usual water splashing to revive the old man, then goes out for coffee. When he returns, the old man has slumped across the machine, the incoming message only partly typed. Homer moves the old man, sees that he is dead, and then notices that the incomplete telegram is from the War Department, announcing the death of Marcus.

Mr. Spangler takes Homer away from the office and listens as the boy tells him that the hate he wishes to feel cannot emerge, but that he cannot find any direction for the love he wishes to feel. "Who's the enemy?" the boy asks the man, hoping to find a target for his pent-up anger. Mr. Spangler tells him that one cannot hate, but must carry on through the love he feels for those closest to him. A good man never dies, Mr. Spangler argues, and at the heart of a good man is love.

That same night Tobey George, limping from a war wound, arrives in Ithaca. He wanders about the town and comes upon Mr. Spangler and Homer pitching horseshoes. Homer feels he knows the youth but cannot be certain. Tobey walks on and comes to the Macauley house where Bess is astonished when he greets her by name and tells her he knows all of them. She senses that he has come to tell of Marcus' death, but instead he tells her that Marcus is not dead. Homer arrives and, now realizing who Tobey is, tells him that the telegram about Marcus' death arrived that afternoon. Tobey tells him to destroy the message because it is not true. Together they enter the house where Mrs. Macauley greets her son's friend who is now also her son.

Critical Opinion

From the outset, William Saroyan has rebelled against the formalities of literary craftsmanship. He boasts of writing swiftly and easily, and of paying little heed to such matters as plot construction, grammar, punctuation, and diction. His writing proves his assertion, and provides hostile critics with an easy target. But despite Saroyan's technical naïveté, his best writing has an undeniable appeal. However slap-dash the structure of *The Human Comedy*, however indifferent it is to the niceties of language and imagery, the novel manages to win the hearts of readers open to a simple, unabashedly sentimental approach to experience.

The Macauley family is perhaps too beautiful to be true, but in its gentle commitment to an unmaterialistic way of life and in its passionate dedication to the worth and dignity of all men, it argues for an approach to living that few readers can resist. Homer's approach to maturity is accomplished with poignancy and humor, and Ulysses' wide-eyed embrace of all experience enchants as it delights. He represents, if not the reality of childhood, at least our dream of what it might be if the world would only allow it to be so. Saroyan, then, tries to substitute a different kind of American dream, one of protracted innocence in which evil does not exist except to be absorbed and transmuted back into innocence. His is a primitive version of the possibilities available to modern man that will not withstand the critical scrutiny of historical evidence. But at his best Saroyan communicates his sense of a fantasy world of goodness with abundant good humor, tenderness, and an astringent insight into the limitations of the world most of us accept as real.

The Author

Son of an Armenian minister and vineyard worker who died very young, *William Saroyan* was born in Fresno, California, and attended public schools there until he was fifteen. During those years he worked as a newsboy and as a telegraph messenger, much like Homer in *The Human Comedy*. At sixteen, to help his family, he worked in his uncle's vineyards for a time, and then drifted into a series of jobs that were to contribute much to his later fiction. Though he read widely, he found much that was considered great literature was of little consequence to him. "In order to write the way the world wanted me to write," he said later, "I would have to work twice and three times as hard as I would writing the way I wished to write, so I decided to write the way I wished to write."

In 1934 the first of his short stories began to appear (he has since written more than 350 stories), and with the appearance of the first collection, *The Daring Young Man on the Flying Trapeze,* in that same year, his fame was immediately established. His output from that time on has been extraordinarily prolific. Among the most popular and most admired of his works are *The Human Comedy,* two plays— *My Heart's in the Highlands* (1939), a warmly affecting plea for rent-free housing for poets, and *The Time of Your Life* (1939), his best play, awarded the Pulitzer Prize (which Saroyan rejected)—and *My Name Is Aram* (1940), a collection of stories about an Armenian family in the San Joaquin Valley, supposedly narrated by one of the sons, Aram Garoghlanian.

All the King's Men

by

ROBERT PENN WARREN (1905–)

Main Characters

Jack Burden—The narrator, aged thirty-five, onetime journalist, then aide to Willie Stark. An apprentice to life, he
passes through phases of cynicism, defeatism, and escapism
en route to maturity.

Willie Stark—The "Boss," Governor of a Southern state, a
pragmatic despot who tries to shape men, affairs, and even
nature to his will.

Anne Stanton—Jack's friend who becomes Willie's mistress;
intelligent, sensitive, and idealistic.

Adam Stanton—Anne's brother, Jack's friend, and Willie's
assassin; director of the State Hospital and an absolute
idealist who refuses to believe that good can come from
evil.

Judge Irwin—The "upright judge," a man of integrity, decency, compassion, and fallibility.

Sadie Burke—Willie's mistress (before Anne). Pock-marked,
hot-tempered, and vile-mouthed, she is fiercely and jealously
devoted to the "Boss," and ruthless when he crosses her.

Tiny Duffy—A fat, unprincipled wardheeler whom Willie
makes Lieutenant-Governor.

Sugar-Boy—Willie's chauffeur and bodyguard, a dim-witted,
stuttering Irishman, fanatically loyal to Stark.

Mrs. Burden—Jack's mother. Vain and shallow, she manages at least once in her life to love selflessly, wholly.

Ellis Burden—The "scholarly attorney," long since separated from his wife and now a religious fanatic.

Lucy Stark—Willie's wife, patient, loyal, and utterly alone.

Tom Stark—Willie's arrogant, irresponsible son.

The Story

Ostensibly, Jack Burden is narrating the story of Willie Stark and his career as Governor of a Southern state from 1936 until his assassination in 1939. But *All the King's Men* is also the story of Jack Burden, and he intersects the present with flashbacks that fill in his own boyhood, adolescence, and young manhood. Thus in the second chapter Jack recalls meeting Willie for the first time in 1922 when Stark, running for the post of county treasurer in Mason City, unsuccessfully tried to block local politicians from handing out a crooked school-building contract. As a young reporter assigned to cover Stark's campaign, Jack found Willie a teetotaling idealist inspired by his schoolteacher wife, Lucy, and hoping to keep local politics clean. Badly beaten in the election, Willie supported his family by peddling during the day, but at night he diligently studied law. When the jerry-built school collapsed, Willie became a local hero. But later he chose to ignore politics and pass his bar examination.

Soon after Willie sets up as a lawyer, a group of incumbent Democratic state politicians decide to use Willie's local popularity in order to split the primary support for the rival candidate for the governorship. Tiny Duffy is delegated to offer Willie the candidacy. Unaware that none of his supporters expects or wants him to win, Willie accepts. Again Jack is assigned to cover Stark's campaign. This time Willie irritates no one; he simply bores them. Speaking quietly and keeping to the facts, Willie loses audiences with painful ease. He has, Jack says, "galloping political anemia," an opinion voiced more boldly though less quotably by Sadie Burke who has been assigned to guide his candidacy to failure.

Just before the election, Sadie tells Willie the facts about his candidacy. Shocked and angry, he gets drunk and passes out. At a political rally next day, still half-drunk, he ignores his prepared speech and tells the astonished audience how he has been duped by Duffy and the machine. Willie withdraws from the campaign, throws his support to the opposition, and helps them win. Then Willie vanishes from the political scene. In 1930, when he does return, as Jack observes, "there wasn't any Democratic Party. There was just Willie . . . he had a meat axe in his hand and was screaming for blood." No longer the pure-hearted idealist but a shrewd opportunist, Willie lashes the electorate to a political frenzy and wins by a landslide. To remind himself forever that hacks are useful and despicable, he creates a post for Tiny Duffy—but Tiny is too grateful to recognize the irony.

During the campaign, when Jack's newspaper insists that he support Willie's opponent, he resigns and sinks into what he calls "The Great Sleep," a period of disengagement during which Jack refuses to acknowledge reality except as a succession of sensory impressions. Unlike his earlier experiences with The Great Sleep, this one is short-lived, for soon after Willie Stark becomes Governor, he hires Jack as his all-round aide, friend, consultant, and research specialist in digging political dirt.

When the novel opens in 1936, Governor Stark (who has already survived impeachment proceedings and won re-election) assigns Jack the most painful—and painstaking—dirt-digging job of his career: to search the past for something that will destroy the reputation of Judge Montague Irwin, the man who has, since Jack's childhood, been his idol. Irwin has, in fact, been a surrogate for Ellis Burden, Jack's legal father. But because Irwin refuses to support Stark's candidate for the Senate, Jack must find Irwin's Achilles' heel. And Jack finds it—though the search is long, intricate, and agonizing.

As he begins his research into what he calls "The Case of the Upright Judge," Jack remembers his last scholarly venture into the past, his unfinished doctoral dissertation in American history. For several years Jack sifted the journal and letters of Cass Mastern, the uncle of the "scholarly attorney," hoping to reconstruct a social portrait of the pre-Civil War era. The facts were relatively simple. Cass seduced Annabelle Trice, his best friend's wife. Her husband, aware of her infidelity, placed his wedding ring under her pillow, then committed suicide. Phebe, Annabelle's young Negro slave, discovered the ring and silently returned it to her. To silence Phebe, Annabelle took her downriver and sold her. Horrified when he learned this, Cass purchased Phebe himself and then gave her her freedom. Haunted by the episode, Cass sought atonement in death on the battlefield. In the past Jack could not understand the truth inherent in the tale. Not until he completes his research on Judge Stark does he realize the significance of the Cass Mastern episode: that all experience is interrelated, that good and evil are inextricably linked. In those early days, however, Jack walked out of his study, leaving his notes and his doctoral thesis behind, and entered into The Great Sleep.

Jack's research in the Irwin case is more intricate but more successful. His quest begins with a single word, "foulness," spoken by the "scholarly attorney" when Jack asks him about Irwin. From Adam Stanton he learns that long ago the judge was poor; from Anne Stanton, that his second marriage in 1914 brought wealth. Court records reveal that in 1907 Irwin borrowed more than $40,000 on his home mortgage, in 1910 repaid a small sum, but nothing more until 1914. When foreclosure proceedings were initiated, he suddenly paid his account in full. Irwin's wife, having squandered her wealth, could not have helped him.

Where, then, had the money come from? No, not from Irwin's piddling salary as attorney general under the distinguished and honorable Governor Stanton (father of Anne and Adam). But in 1915, the records show, Irwin resigned this post to become an executive in an electric power company at $20,000 a year. Jack's suspicions aroused, he searches stock-market records and learns that Irwin also owned 500 shares of stock. Next he scans the newspapers for a further lead, and strikes a lode in a story about the suicide of Mortimer Littlepaugh, Irwin's predecessor as counsel to the power company. Tracking down a possible survivor, Jack locates in Memphis the sister of the dead lawyer, a penny-pinching medium and fortuneteller whom he pays to give him the truth: Littlepaugh, discovering that his company had bribed Attorney General Irwin not to prosecute a conspiracy case, carried the evidence all the way to Governor Stanton who refused to listen to him. The company fired Littlepaugh and hired Irwin. In despair, Littlepaugh took his own life. But he left with his sister a letter giving the details of the swindle. Jack buys the letter from her. His seven-month search has disclosed the meaning of the word "foulness."

While Jack plays out his role as ferret, Willie makes plans for a state hospital and medical center to be the finest in the nation. He fends off Duffy and others who want to make a financial plum of the $6,000,000 building contract, insisting upon absolute assurance that all will be orderly, legitimate, perfect. To head the medical organization, Stark wants the capable and unqualifiedly honest Adam Stanton, and he sets Jack the task of enlisting his boyhood friend for the job. Again, it is a difficult assignment because Adam despises everything Willie represents. When Jack offers him the post, Adam categorically rejects it.

A few days later Anne sees Jack and demands that he make Adam accept the job. Jack suggests that one way may be to teach Adam a "history lesson" about good and evil, that is, to show him evidence of his own father's corruption in protecting Judge Irwin. Anne shows photostats of Littlepaugh's letter to Adam. Adam, damning his father and without further comment, accepts the hospital job. One question still puzzles Jack: How did Anne know that Stark wanted Adam for the job? Neither he nor Adam had told her. He learns the answer to this, too. Just a few days later Sadie Burke tells him in a jealous rage that Anne has become Willie Stark's mistress.

Shattered by this knowledge about the woman he has loved since childhood, Jack takes flight to the West, hoping to find refuge in sheer movement. But as he lies on a hotel bed in California, he relives their burgeoning love, its aspirations and frustrations, its failure ever to reach consummation because of Jack's confused sense of purity and morality (as wrong a sense, he realizes, as Cass Mastern's sense of sin). He recalls, too, his absurd and short-lived marriage to Lois Seager whose mechanized sexuality and crude banality drove him to his first experience with The Great Sleep. Jack thinks that the events of his life have no central relevance, that will and aspiration mean nothing—"for nothing was your fault or anybody's fault,

for things are always as they are." A man with an uncontrol-
lable tic and a lobotomized patient, now symbolize for Jack
the absurdity of man's will before the force of what he calls
The Great Twitch, the thoughtless, mechanical power that
determines human behavior.

Once Jack returns East, the innumerable strands of his and
Willie's life swiftly and tragically spin out their fates. To beat
off his opponents, Willie reluctantly gives the hospital-building
contract to Duffy's friend, Gummy Larson. But when his son,
Tom, has his spine crushed in a football game, Willie's conscience compels him to withdraw the contract. The next day
someone telephones Adam to tell about Anne's affair with
Stark. Sickened by the belief that his sister's body has earned
him his job, Adam approaches Willie on the steps of the
Capitol and shoots him. Willie dies a few days later, protesting to Jack that things might have been different. Adam is
shot to death by Sugar-Boy. Some weeks later Jack learns that
it was Sadie Burke, infuriated by Willie's determination to return to his wife after their son's injury, who told Tiny Duffy
and Gummy Larson about Anne and Willie, and it was
Duffy's voice that Adam heard on the telephone.

Jack presents to Judge Irwin the damning evidence against
him. Broken by the revelation of an event so remote he has
nearly forgotten it, Judge Irwin tells Jack he still may block
disclosure of the evidence by one further revelation. The next
morning, "a bright, beautiful, silvery soprano scream" awakens
Jack: It is his mother, who has just been told that Irwin has
committed suicide. She tells Jack that he has killed his father.
For the first time in his life, Jack realizes that his vapid, silly
mother has been capable of love, ironically, for a man Jack,
too, has loved and, in effect, killed.

That terrible scream wakens Jack from The Great Sleep and
compels him to abandon the easy despair of The Great Twitch.
That his mother could love, that Adam and Anne, Lucy and
Willie could live despite their pre-ordained doom—all of this
convinces Jack that man must act against his fate. As the
novel ends, Jack and Anne, married, live in the house Irwin
has willed him. Jack works to complete his study of Cass
Mastern, after which he and Anne "shall go out of the house
and go into the convulsion of the world. . . ."

Critical Opinion

When *All the King's Men* appeared in 1946, the obvious parallel between Willie Stark and the late Huey Long, Governor of Louisiana, aroused greater attention than the more significant merits of the novel. To those who insist that the novel is an apology for Long's life, Warren's own answer serves best: "There is really nothing to reply to this kind of innocent boneheadedness or gospel-bit hysteria."

Most critics since those first days of stormy dissension have recognized the novel for its more relevant qualities. They have seen that Willie Stark and Jack Burden are alike in their quest for self-knowledge and for the identity that enable a man to shape his destiny in a chaotic world. Willie's moral neutrality leads him at last to destruction, but so too does Adam's moral absolutism. Jack Burden alone comes to a maturity that permits survival. He experiences the extremes of idealism and despair but settles at last for a kind of pragmatic realism that opens the way to meaningful life.

The novel has tremendous narrative impact, even though its episodes occasionally border on the melodramatic. The prose style has energy and sweep, except when the contrast between Jack Burden's rhetorical asides to the reader and his hard-boiled, laconic dialogue tax the reader's credulity. Warren draws upon a rich fund of imagery and certain basic mythic patterns—the motifs of journey and return, birth and death, sin and repentance—to deepen the implications of his narrative. The abiding strength of *All the King's Men* remains in its characterizations, not only the masterly handling of Willie Stark, but also the shrewdly and vividly portrayed minor figures who cluster about him.

The Author

Novelist, poet, dramatist, biographer, critic, and teacher, *Robert Penn Warren* was born in Guthrie, Kentucky, attended Vanderbilt University as an undergraduate and Oxford as a Rhodes Scholar. A member of the *"Fugitive* group" of young Southern agrarian poets and critics dedicated to creating a

Southern literature more vital than sentimental, Warren wrote
for their magazine, *The Fugitive,* and later helped found and
edit the important journal *Southern Review.*

Winner of the Pulitzer Prize for *All the King's Men,* Warren
has for the past twenty-five years taught English at several
universities—Louisiana State (where he gathered material for
his novel), Minnesota, and Yale. He collaborated with Cleanth
Brooks on the important college text *Understanding Poetry*
which has introduced students and teachers to the "new
criticism."

From the outset, Warren's fiction has dealt with regional
problems that touch universal themes. In *Night Riders*
(1939), his first novel, an account of a historical struggle
between Kentucky farmers and tobacco companies, Warren
stresses Percy Munn's conflict as he tries to reconcile principle
with reality. In *World Enough and Time* (1950), *The Cave*
(1959), and *The Flood* (1964), Warren also draws on historical events, past and present, to highlight the complexities of
man's fate.

The Naked and the Dead

by

NORMAN MAILER (1923–)

Main Characters

General Edward Cummings—Division commander, a Mid-
westerner and a graduate of West Point, a fascist-minded
despot, loather of men, a pseudo-intellectual, and a subtle
homosexual.

Lt. Robert Hearn—The General's aide, Chicago-born and
Harvard-educated, a sensitive but ineffectual dilettante who
has played with love and radicalism without ever embracing
either. To escape the emptiness of his mother-dominated
life, he enlists just before Pearl Harbor.

Sgt. Sam Croft—A platoon leader, son of illiterate Texas
parents, a hunter from his boyhood and as cold and ruthless
toward men as he is toward animals. ("I hate everything
which is not in myself.")

Red Valsen—Son of a Montana coal miner killed in a shaft
explosion. At fourteen he is a miner; at nineteen, a vagabond drifting eastward through America's hobo jungles; at
twenty-nine, a complete nihilist who, to keep moving and
to avoid any lasting involvement with women or jobs, joins
the Army.

Joey Goldstein—Son of poor Brooklyn candy-store keepers,
a welder before his induction, settled in a gray but tolerable
marriage, deeply sensitive to the anti-Semitism of his Army
comrades.

Roy Gallagher—An ugly, acne-ravaged Boston Irishman, viciously anti-Semitic, and a minor bully-boy hoodlum in right-wing groups before being drafted.

Julio Martinez—A lithe young Mexican from Texas, shy, mannerly, and though frightened, a fine soldier. Nicknamed "Japbait."

Woodrow Wilson—Aged thirty, married and devoted to his wife and children, but nevertheless the most virile, free-booting lover in his Southern hillbilly environs. He amuses himself and his fellow soldiers with recollections of his amorous prowess.

William Brown—Formerly a salesman in Tulsa, Oklahoma, popular, middle-class in fortune and taste, blandly interested in his wife but more willing to repent the morning after than to forego whoring and drinking.

Polack Czienwicz—Product of a Chicago slum and a stern parochial education, a butcher, numbers runner and, when he is drafted, about to become a white slaver.

Roth—An intelligent, hypersensitive youth, wholly alien to his comrades in interests and sensibilities.

Steve Minetta—An Italian soldier from New York, terrified of the rigors of combat and willing to use any device to avoid battle.

Major Dalleson—Operations officer of the division, a dull-witted but persistent opportunist.

The Story

Aboard the troop convoy, the men variously occupy the hours before the assault craft will be lowered to land them on the Pacific island of Anopopei. Wilson, Gallagher, and Croft play poker, Red Valsen sneaks on deck at night and watches the shore line, Brown discusses the faithlessness of wives, and Martinez lies in his bunk tensely anticipating the violence of the morrow. Next morning, as the assault craft moves toward the shore, Croft senses that young Hennessey, who seems overly cautious and tense, will be the first to die. When his prediction is swiftly borne out, Croft experiences a surge of self-confidence. For Martinez, the boy's death merely frees him of the terror he suffers before battle begins.

The progress of General Cummings' task force inland from the beaches is slow and costly, but gradually the men infiltrate the Japanese positions. General Cummings expects that the campaign will consume time and men but satisfies himself that he has both in abundance and sets about establishing for himself quarters as luxurious as the jungle permits. At the officers' mess that afternoon, Cummings demands that a loud argument between Hearn and his fellow officers cease at once. Hearn had listened impatiently while several of his superiors discoursed ignorantly but vituperatively about labor unions. Finally Hearn interposes questions and comments that challenge the intelligence of his fellow officers. Just when the others seem ready to discipline him, Cummings intervenes, saving Hearn.

Later, in the general's tent, Hearn tries to answer Cummings' query about his behavior. Hearn's replies move Cummings to ridicule his aide as a foolish liberal hopelessly out of line in a century that belongs to the power-lusting reactionary. To prove his point, Cummings compels Hearn to snap to attention and salute him. Angry, humiliated, Hearn nevertheless grudgingly admires his commanding officer, partly because he shares the general's snobbery, partly because he takes pride in Cummings, singling him out as a fit intellectual companion. But above all, Hearn is fascinated by the riddle Cummings poses for him, the "shoddy motive" that he is certain he will ultimately discover, the hidden core that has always aroused Hearn's curiosity.

After a month of confused battle plans, the division has advanced almost twenty-five miles, seriously overextending supply and communication lines. For some time, Croft's platoon has served only in reconnaissance duty and has experienced no combat. Rain soaks the men's spirits as well as their bodies, typhoons rip up their tents, interrupting their card games and windy conversations. For Cummings, the storms represent a form of natural chaos he cannot tolerate in the orderly, disciplined world he hopes to control. Nevertheless, despite the disorganization of his forces by the storms, Cummings orders that no general retreat take place. He determines to risk an assault by the Japanese.

Anticipating an enemy attack that night, Cummings orders Croft's reconnaissance squad to the front in support of the forward lines. Croft anticipates the battle with eagerness, Valsen with absolute indifference, most of the others with varying degrees of fear and anticipation. A mile from the front, Croft receives orders to drag two anti-tank guns through the jungle mud to the front lines. The trail along which the men slog is only a few feet wide, their progress tortuously slow. At a bank, the gun dragged by Goldstein and two other soldiers slips from their grasp and tumbles down the embankment into a creek. Croft, calling Goldstein "Izzy," places the blame on him and accuses him of goldbricking. Goldstein was not solely responsible for the accident, but no one comes to his defense.

The next evening, lying at the edge of a river, the men hear the enemy calling across softly that they are coming to kill. Croft roars at them to come on, fires his machine gun, and attracts a volley of enemy fire. When the Japanese begin to charge, Croft enthusiastically mows them down like wheat stalks before a thresher. The sound of a wounded Jap near by irritates him, and he tosses a grenade to silence the dying man. But the slaughter leaves Croft still unsated. "One of these days I'm gonna really get me a Jap," he says as he watches the dead bodies drift downstream.

While the battle continues at the front, Cummings' electric refrigerator arrives at the bivouac with a supply of fresh meat to stock it. The general puts Hearn in charge of establishing an officers' recreation tent, and Hearn quickly discovers, while working with several incompetent enlisted men, that he shares some of the general's contempt for them and their transparent efforts to balk him in his assigned task. That night the general calls Hearn to his tent to play chess. Though Hearn is a competent player, he finds Cummings more than his match. Cummings uses the chess game to draw an analogy with human experience, "a concentration of life," he calls it. As in the game, Hearn feels that during the ensuing conversation about the worthlessness of all but supremely powerful men, he has been outmaneuvered and kept off balance by Cummings. Whenever he attempts a crude retort, Cummings responds by treating him as a subordinate. Something in the general's voice and manner, nevertheless, makes Hearn realize Cummings' intentions are sexual. He has, he now knows, found the "shoddy motive," and nothing Cummings tries will any longer disturb him.

At the front, Croft, Red, and Gallagher come upon four Japs and hurl a grenade at them. Valsen, sent by Croft to mop up the wounded, is attacked by a survivor when his gun jams. Croft disarms the Jap and sends Valsen on ahead. Croft makes Gallagher give the prisoner candy, allows him to smoke a cigarette and show pictures of his wife and family. As the prisoner relaxes against a tree at Croft's invitation and closes his eyes with a smile of pleasure on his face, Croft fires a bullet through his head. Gallagher looks on, horrified. A few hours later, the platoon is ordered to the rear where the men sit about listening to Croft recount the death of the prisoner. By the time they are all drunk, however, Croft's brief pleasure has disappeared and his hunger for blood surges within him again. Restless, the men set out to plunder a ravaged Japanese camp. Martinez recovers the gold teeth of one corpse. The others rampage among bodies and parts of bodies, sickened by the stench but driven by their desire to bring home some tangible evidence of their expedition. But a snake appears and they flee even after Red blasts its head off.

One day the chaplain brings Gallagher word that his wife has died in childbirth. Stunned, Gallagher can think only that a Jew must have been the doctor. Her letters bring Gallagher close to breakdown. Ironically, it is Roth, a Jew, who feels most deeply for Gallagher but cannot even talk to him or attempt to console him.

Little progress in the campaign rewards Cummings' ingenious plans. Stalled and unable to effect any significant advance, Cummings rages inwardly, conscious that he may lose his command, powerless to alter the course he thought he could control. The butt of his frustration becomes Hearn upon whom he imposes all sorts of petty and humiliating tasks that make his aide a laughingstock among the officers. In revenge, Hearn executes the maneuver he knows may cause his own destruction. After having the general's quarters spruced and the floor scrubbed absolutely clean, Hearn drops a match near the general's footlocker and grinds a cigarette butt into the middle of the floor.

Later, when the general calls him to his quarters, Hearn deliberately avoids the kind of tact he knows the general insists upon. To Cummings' query about the reason for the war, Hearn answers too pointedly, "It's a bad thing when millions of people are killed because one joker has to get some things out of his system." Cummings' theory is that the war is an expression of "power morality," that all men are moved toward omnipotence and those who cannot adjust to such a course must be crushed. To prove his point he demands that Hearn pick up a cigarette he throws at his feet. The men exchange stares, but Hearn picks up the butt and puts it into an ashtray. Hearn then asks for a transfer, but Cummings assigns him to Major Dalleson's section for further humiliation until he can conceive a more fitting resolution to the problem Hearn poses for him. Hearn, Cummings knows, represents the kind of rebellion his theories cannot survive.

Cummings' proposed solution seems demoniacally clever since it purports to rid him of Hearn and simultaneously to set in motion a plan to further the campaign. He places Hearn in charge of Croft's reconnaissance platoon and assigns the men to travel by assault boat to the farthest end of the island, there to land, march through the jungle to the rear of the Japanese lines and, by reconnaissance, determine the feasibility of a large-scale amphibious attack.

Hearn assumes command of the patrol, aware of Croft's competence and sure that the sergeant resents the presence of an officer. He is right on both counts but has no real measure of Croft's bitterness toward him. Most of the other men accept Hearn as a decent person, though Red Valsen resents him as he does any figure of authority. The men march wearily through the jungle, cutting a trail along the river until they come to a flat valley at the foot of tall, rugged Mount Anaka. Thus far, apart from physical exhaustion and Wilson's desperate case of diarrhea, the patrol has experienced neither incident nor accident. All of them know, however, that on the morrow, when they attempt to work their way through a narrow pass leading to the rear of the Japanese lines, they face the threat of a Japanese ambush.

Croft's instinct tells him to have the men climb Mount Anaka, but he keeps his counsel to himself for the moment, reluctantly ordering the men to enter the pass as Hearn has directed. Shortly after the patrol enters the pass, they are ambushed, but with the exception of Wilson, who is shot in the stomach, all scurry to safety. That night Croft, along with Red Valsen, Gallagher, Goldstein, and a Southerner named Ridges, worms his way through the tall grass and brings the wounded Wilson back to the encampment. The men improvise a litter and Hearn and Croft assign four men (including Brown, Goldstein, and Ridges) to try to carry Wilson back to the beachhead where they originally landed.

While the men are cutting the stretcher poles, Roth picks up a small crippled bird and gently cups it in his hand. The other men crowd about him, concerned and sympathetic. Annoyed by the interruption, Croft breaks into the circle and demands to see what Roth is holding. Taking the bird from Roth's hand, Croft is momentarily torn between compassion and his lust to kill. Possessed by the urge to destroy, he squeezes the bird to death, then hurls it into the valley. Instantly the men recoil in horror, then, led by Red, denounce Croft. Only Hearn's intrusion prevents a violent flare-up. But Hearn's insistence that Croft apologize to Roth deepens Croft's hostility toward his superior officer.

While the litter bearers begin their agonizing journey to the rear—Wilson's cries of pain tormenting them more than the burden of his heavy body—Croft sends Martinez out on a mission intended to lead to Hearn's destruction. Martinez' assignment, Croft tells him, is to determine whether a second Japanese bivouac lies beyond the one in the pass. If so, Croft wants Martinez to report only to him. Croft's hope is that if the enemy is present, Hearn, leading the patrol, will be the first killed. Martinez ventures forth, discovers a Jap sentry, kills him, then reports that the pass is cleared. Within a half-hour after the patrol enters the pass the next morning, Hearn is killed by a machine-gun bullet. Croft assumes command at once, telling the men that they will climb Mount Anaka and, after they descend on the other side, scout the Japanese rear.

Under Croft's orders, Martinez tells the men that Hearn, despite knowing that the pass was Jap-infested, insisted upon making the entry. But even the knowledge that the lieutenant was a fool fails to diminish the growing irritation the men feel toward Croft as he drives them brutally and relentlessly toward the crest of Mount Anaka. To Croft, climbing the mountain has become an obsession, almost a "human thing" he must conquer. When they reach a point less than a thousand feet from the top, the ledge along which they have been alternately walking and crawling narrows to less than a foot. Below, the mountain sheers off into a walled abyss. The only way to proceed, Croft recognizes, is to leap across the crevice to surer footing on the other side. The leap is only four feet, but because of the awkward terrain, the men, laden with full packs, must leap sideways and gain an immediate foothold. The alternative is death. All of the men except Roth make the leap successfully. Exhausted, frightened, bullied a few minutes earlier by Gallagher, Roth simply lacks the force to propel himself to safety. Bellowing in horror and disbelief, he hurtles to his death.

By the next morning, the already limp morale of Croft's platoon has crumbled. While Croft sleeps, the men determine that they will not go on, and ask Martinez, whom Croft most respects, to tell the platoon leader about their intention. By challenging Martinez' good sense, loyalty, and courage, Croft regains his support. A few minutes later, however, Valsen forces Martinez to reveal the truth about Hearn's death by frightening the superstitious young Mexican into believing that his knifing of the Japanese sentry has brought him nearer to his own death. As Martinez again wavers about defying Croft, Red announces that he has no intention of moving on. Croft threatens to shoot him, but Red suggests that Croft will have to shoot everyone. Unfortunately the other men are too awed by Croft to stand beside Red. With Croft's rifle pointed at his stomach, Red at last yields.

The climb continues for a few more hours, the last ounce of energy dwindling even in Croft. Just beyond the dense foliage through which he is leading the men, Croft sees sunlight and knows he is nearing the summit. At that instant, however, he stumbles and falls upon a hornets' nest. The insects swarm over the men, driving them frantically and aimlessly down the sides of the mountain they had so laboriously climbed. Silently and uneventfully, they retrace their steps through the jungle trail to the beachhead. The stretcher bearers are waiting, but Wilson has already died. On the assault boat returning them to their base, Croft looks at the unconquered mountain and experiences again the old hunger and with it the knowledge that he has failed and will never have another chance to learn just how far he might have gone.

When the men return, they learn that their expedition was wholly unnecessary. Cummings' clever schemes have amounted to nothing, for the enemy resistance has simply collapsed because their supplies are exhausted. To add to the absurdity, the Japanese defeat was achieved in a single day while General Cummings was away at headquarters. The conquering hero is the bumbling Major Dalleson, who (wholly unaware of what he was about) mounted a full-scale attack on the crumbling Japanese supply depot. All that remains is to mop up stray Japanese soldiers. The American patrols take few prisoners, shooting most of the wounded, and rifle-butting others to death. As the novel ends, Major Dalleson, contemplating his promotion, thinks of a brave new idea to further his career: a field map with an overlay of a pin-up girl so that trainees will attend more carefully to instruction.

Critical Opinion

In the early short story "A Calculus at Heaven," which provided the basis for *The Naked and the Dead*, Mailer wrote: "In America, men live, work, and die without the rudest conceptions of dignity." The blighted lives of the men involved in the campaign on Anopopei extend to a bitter conclusion the deep pessimism implicit in the short story. At first glance the reader may be misled into assuming that war alone has fashioned the dead end toward which all the events seem to lead. But by means of the technical device he calls the "time machine" (a technique for which he is indebted to John Dos Passos' *U.S.A.*), Mailer flashes back to the pre-war lives of his characters and reveals that their doom had already been spelled out before they entered the Army.

Racial and religious discrimination has foreshortened possibilities for Martinez, Goldstein, and Roth, and distorted truth for the bigoted Gallagher. Yet Gallagher, too, has been victimized by an economic environment which precluded open-mindedness. Beyond economic and social handicaps, nearly all of the characters have also suffered the tensions resulting from America's ambivalent sexual attitudes. Towering over and beyond these forces is the climactic struggle between the representatives of absolute power (Cummings and Croft)

and those of liberalism (Hearn) or compassionate nihilism
(Valsen). What is most terrifying about Mailer's resolution
is that it is not a resolution at all. Good and evil cancel each
other out. Hearn is killed, Valsen is faced down by Croft.
Cummings' victory is hollow since it comes by accident rather
than by plan. Croft suffers humiliation (ironically, a stinging
defeat by hornets) at the hands of the natural forces he wants
most to control. Mount Anaka thus becomes, as Mailer himself has indicated, "a consciously ambiguous symbol" suggesting the hopelessness of aspiration as well as the defeat of
evil intention.

Not all readers agree that the novel ends in despair. Some
prefer Mailer's interpretation of his own work, in which he
argues that although he acknowledges the corruption and
confusion of man, he tries in *The Naked and the Dead* to
prove that "there are limits beyond which [man] cannot be
pushed," and that despite the corruption, "there are yearnings
for a better world."

Mailer's novel, whatever we may think about its philosophical orientation, is thoroughly absorbing throughout. Although
the characters are more prototypical than real, the episodes
in which they appear more often than not obscure the psychological limitations of type casting. The language is commonly harsh, the vulgate familiar to men at war, but because
of its accuracy only the prudish will object to it. In all, *The
Naked and the Dead*—the first novel of a young man of
twenty-five—still remains the best war novel to emerge from
World War II.

The Author

Brooklyn-bred, *Norman Mailer* set out to become an aeronautical engineer, but shifted to writing during his freshman year
at Harvard. A year after graduation, Mailer entered the
Army, served for two years in the Philippines and in Japan
as clerk, cook, surveyor, and rifleman. Before he was out of
the Army, he had won story-writing contests. One of his
stories, "A Calculus at Heaven," contains the germ of *The
Naked and the Dead*.

Mailer's success with his first novel, *The Naked and the*

Dead, was immediate and widespread. His reputation has not diminished since, though several of his experiences in public and private life have added notoriety rather than dignity to his stature. His second novel, *Barbary Shore* (1951), blasted by most critics, tells about a young man settled in a Brooklyn boardinghouse writing a novel about the war. Politics (chiefly left-wing) and neuroticism invade Mikey Lovett's privacy and distort his artistic purpose. Mailer's third novel, *The Deer Park* (1955), received mixed but essentially admiring notices for its satirical analysis of the debauchery and sterility of Hollywood life.

Since his first three novels, Mailer has completed no full-length novel, though he has published a novella, *The American Dream* (1964), and *Advertisements for Myself* (1959), a collection of stories and essays. Mailer's anti-Stalinist Marxism and his profound interest in existentialism find voice in the essays published in *Advertisements* and in the more recent *The Presidential Papers of Norman Mailer* (1964), a collection of articles he wrote about the late President Kennedy and about the problems Mailer regarded as central to a successful Administration. He has also published a volume of poems, *Deaths for the Ladies* (1962).

The Catcher in the Rye

by

J. D. SALINGER (1919–)

Main Characters

Holden Caulfield—A seventeen-year-old boy who believes that the world is dominated by "phonies," and is in frantic search of some refuge.

Ackley—A classmate at Pencey Prep, whom Holden finds repulsive.

Stradlater—Another classmate, a clean-looking young man whom Holden regards as a lecher.

Mr. Spencer—One of Holden's teachers, kind but ineffectual.

Phoebe Caulfield—Holden's younger sister, a sweet, innocent, very precocious girl, one of the few people Holden loves and admires.

Mr. Antolini—A former teacher of Holden's, a bright, sophisticated man whom Holden suspects of homosexual intentions toward him.

The Story

Holden Caulfield, a seventeen-year-old student at Pencey Prep, writes this autobiographical account of his misadventures in a world of "phonies." He sees them everywhere: the headmaster who snoots people with the wrong accent while kowtowing to those with the right moneyed-manner; the jazz pianist who plays showy and false to please the crowd; and almost all professional actors, especially movie actors. Partly because of his hypersensitivity and his low threshold for boredom, he has just flunked out of Pencey—the third prep school he has attended. Among Holden's companions there is Ackley who constantly squeezes the pimples on his face, dislikes everybody he thinks at all superior to him, and doggedly pesters his classmates. But Ackley is perhaps preferable to Holden's roommate, Stradlater, a clean-looking, athletic young man whose goals seem to be conforming, avoiding work, and seducing young ladies.

Holden has a brief fight with Stradlater about a girl, Jane Gallagher, whom he likes and whom he suspects Stradlater of attempting to seduce. After the fight, Holden bids an uncomfortable farewell to an old teacher, Mr. Spencer, and leaves Pencey for New York.

Holden knows that his mother will be heartbroken and his father furious at his latest failures, but they won't have the news from Pencey for three days. Since he has plenty of money, he decides to check into a hotel and have as good a time as he can before confronting them. Though he is six feet two and a half and has grey hair, he does not look older than sixteen. When he descends to the Lavender Room of the rather sleazy hotel he has chosen, the waiter refuses to bring him whiskey. Disgruntled, he settles for a coke. Then he attempts to pick up a girl who is sitting with two friends— "witches," Holden calls them. He dances with each of them, buys them drinks, but is once again snubbed as a child.

Restless, he takes a cab to Ernie's, a Greenwich Village nightclub where anyone over six can get a drink. On the way he asks the driver one of the questions that has been plaguing him: Where do the ducks that swim in the Central Park lagoon go in winter? The driver isn't helpful. At Ernie's, while sipping Scotches, he is repelled by all the prep-school and college phonies who talk vacuously and applaud the music because they think it sophisticated. He meets an old flame of his big brother, D.B.—now in Hollywood writing scripts (selling himself, Holden believes) after producing a first-rate book of stories. She exerts her charm, but to no avail. She's a phony, too, hoping to work on D.B. at long distance through Holden.

Returning to the hotel, Holden is asked by the elevator man if he wants a girl to visit him in his room. Because he is depressed, he answers Yes without thinking. When the girl arrives, he is unable to carry the affair off. He pays her the five dollars agreed upon, but she insists he must give her ten. He refuses. A little later the prostitute returns, accompanied by the elevator man who punches Holden in the stomach, knocking him on the floor, while the prostitute extracts five more dollars from his wallet.

The next day Holden leaves the hotel, phones a girl friend named Sally (whom he likes only intermittently), and arranges a theater date for the afternoon. He checks his bags, has breakfast, and offers ten dollars that he can now ill afford to two nuns whom he meets, then wanders around Broadway. He really wants to phone Jane Gallagher or his sister Phoebe. Phoebe is a wonderful ten-year-old—wonderful as almost all children are in Holden's eyes (in contrast to adults). The theater date proves disastrous, first, because the Lunts are good but don't behave like people, and second, because Sally meets an Andover student who activates every phony fiber in her. They go skating afterward, and when she rejects Holden's suggestion that they go away to some cabin camp in the woods and escape the tedium and falsity of New York, he insults her. He is immediately sorry, but she won't accept his apologies.

Holden phones an older acquaintance—somebody who was at a prep school with him—and they meet at a swanky bar. Holden teases him, drinking heavily the while, until his former schoolmate goes off to an engagement. Drunk, Holden goes to the park to check on the ducks. It begins to rain. He has very little money left. He decides to sneak into his parents' home and see his sister Phoebe for whom he has been longing. Luckily for him, his parents aren't in, and he negotiates the passageway without awaking the maid. Phoebe is ecstatic at seeing him until she deduces that he's been kicked out of Pencey. She upbraids him, and his attempts to explain to her his exasperation about school are only partly successful. In spite of this, their meeting is filled with affection.

Their parents suddenly arrive. Before Holden hides, Phoebe attempts to convince him of the importance of school. He says he's going West. Phoebe quickly puts out the light just before her mother enters the room. She questions Phoebe, who conceals the fact that Holden is with her, even confessing to puffing a cigarette to explain the smell of cigarette smoke in the room. (Holden is a chain smoker.)

Holden sneaks out and goes to the home of a former English teacher, Mr. Antolini, whom he has phoned. Though it is now very early in the morning, he is greeted warmly, and he listens to Mr. Antolini's witty lecture as attentively as his sleepy mind will allow. Mr. Antolini tells Holden that education would be valuable for him because it would teach him the size mind he had and what it would fit. Holden agrees, yawning. Finally he is allowed to go to sleep on the sofa. He awakens suddenly to feel Mr. Antolini's hand stroking his head. He jumps up and despite Mr. Antolini's protests, scurries out of the apartment. He is convinced of Mr. Antolini's perverse intentions.

Holden spends the rest of the night in the Grand Central waiting room, snatching what sleep he can. Next morning he leaves a note at Phoebe's school asking her to meet him at the Metropolitan Museum of Art. At the school he is perturbed by the obscene scrawls on the walls. Phoebe arrives at the museum lugging a suitcase. She has determined to go with Holden on his projected journey West. Holden is moved, but he firmly declines her offer. She becomes angry, refusing to talk to him—though when he walks into Central Park past the zoo to the carousel, she follows him. He persuades her to ride the carousel. After some protests, she does. As she rides, it begins to rain. But Holden has made his decision. He will not run away. He will face whatever he must.

At the end Holden implies that he is writing the book from a sanitarium. His psychoanalyst keeps asking him if he is going to apply himself when he goes back to school in September. Holden thinks so, but he doesn't know. How can one know what one's going to do until one does it?

Critical Opinion

The Catcher in the Rye is Salinger's only published novel. (It may be that the stories about the Glass family will take the shape of a novel of sorts eventually.) Its hero, Holden Caulfield, is a modern version of Huck Finn, like him a moralist in

spite of himself, racked by the frauds and shams and cruelties
he sees everywhere about him. Huck, of course, comes through
sound, and Holden may, too; but at our last glimpse of him
he is still under treatment by a psychoanalyst.

The dominant objection to Salinger is that he is sentimental,
that he holds a number of unrealistic attitudes about life and
society, especially his notion that children are basically innocent and good and that they degenerate as they grow older.
Salinger has confessed his fondness for children: "Some of my
best friends are children. In fact, all my best friends are children. It's almost unbearable for me to realize that my book
will be kept on a shelf out of their reach." (In Windsor, at the
library nearest Salinger's home, it is.)

However, not Salinger's attitudes but Holden's are relevant
to *The Catcher in the Rye*. And it is completely believable that
Holden—an adolescent with nerve endings where he ought to
have skin—might love the innocence he sees (or thinks he
sees) in children but not in adults. The psychoanalyst Ernest
Jones, though less than enthusiastic about the novel, says it
reflects "what every sensitive sixteen-year-old since Rousseau
has felt, and of course what each one of us is certain he has
felt."

Even antagonistic critics agree that *The Catcher in the Rye*
is a fascinating, witty story. Indeed, one may extract from their
comments a small anthology in praise of Salinger. For example,
George Steiner, a hostile critic who objects that the reputation
of the book is inflated, admits that "Salinger has caught with
uncanny precision the speech and thought—rhythms of the
young." And Harvey Breit, discounting *The Catcher in the
Rye* as a serious novel, nonetheless declares it "a brilliant
tour de force, one that has sufficient power and cleverness to
make the reader chuckle and—rare indeed—even laugh
aloud."

The Author

Jerome David Salinger, for a decade now one of the favorite
authors of American college undergraduates, was born in New
York City. After attending public schools in Manhattan, a military academy in Pennsylvania, and three colleges (none of

which conferred a degree upon him), he spent a year abroad. During the war he served with the Fourth Infantry Division as a staff sergeant, took part in five campaigns from D-Day to V-Day. He began writing at fifteen, published his first story at twenty-one, and since then has appeared in a number of magazines (as he says, "mostly—and most happily—in *The New Yorker*"). He lives with his second wife and their two children in Cornish, New Hampshire, in virtual seclusion.

Besides three volumes of short stories—*Nine Stories* (1953), *Franny and Zooey* (1961), and *Raise High The Roof Beam, Carpenters* (1963)—Salinger has published only one other work in book form, *The Catcher in the Rye*. His best stories concern the trials, aspirations, frustrations, and occasional successes of the nine members of the Glass family: an Irish mother and a Jewish father (former vaudeville performers), and their seven eccentric, charming, perceptive, and neurotic children.

Salinger's are delightful pieces, sometimes funny, sometimes touching, sometimes painful—but always gracefully constructed and admirably phrased. He has an extraordinary ear for dialogue. Readers are virtually unanimous in praise of the uncanny accuracy of his crisp, colloquial lines.

A few critics have called Salinger a "slick middle-brow writer," "a delayed adolescent," "a garrulous pseudo-mystic." A far greater number, however, have compared him to Mark Twain, have found his stories "original, first-rate, serious, and beautiful," and have termed him "a twentieth-century classic." The truth probably lies somewhere between. While Salinger is no Mark Twain, he is an interesting, intelligent, often perceptive writer, and a consummate craftsman.

Lie Down in Darkness

by

WILLIAM STYRON (1925–)

Main Characters

Milton Loftis—The head of the decaying Loftis family of Port Warwick, Virginia, who at forty-three has betrayed his aspirations and degenerated into a weak, guilt-ridden sensualist.

Helen Loftis—Milton's wife, possessive, bigoted, her heart "a nest of little hatreds," she yearns to rid herself of but cannot.

Peyton Loftis—Their intelligent, seductive daughter. She is a suicide at twenty-two, victim of her relationship to her family and to her Southern world.

Maudie Loftis—The youngest daughter (already dead when the novel opens), retarded and crippled, the center of her mother's life.

Dolly Bonner—Milton's mistress, flighty, sensuous, silly, but deeply in love with Milton.

Pookie Bonner—Dolly's husband, hearty, uncouth, well-intentioned.

Carey Carr—A failure as a poet, he turns minister without "having been able to attain a complete vision of God."

Adrienne Carr—Carey's sophisticated, skeptical, and rather cynical wife.

Dick Cartwright—Peyton's first lover, a carefree, unimaginative college boy.

322

Harry Miller—Peyton's husband, a New York artist, who tries
ardently but unsuccessfully to save his wife.
La Ruth, Ella, Stonewall—The Negro family employed by the
Loftises.
Daddy Faith—A Negro evangelist whose preaching about love
unifies and inspires the local Negro community.

The Story

One morning in August, 1945, a small group gathers at the
railway depot in Port Warwick, Virginia, a shipbuilding city
near Richmond. An undertaker and his chauffeur work furiously to repair the broken radiator pipe of an empty hearse.
Near by in a limousine sits the weeping Dolly Bonner who
has joined her lover, Milton Loftis, to await the arrival of
the body of his daughter, Peyton, from New York. Helen
Loftis has coldly refused to accompany her husband, promising only to attend the funeral services with the Rev. Carey
Carr.

In the present, the seven sections of the novel trace with
brief notations the slow progress of the cortege from the depot
to the cemetery. The past, however, holds the true center of
dramatic interest. Thus in each chapter one or more of the
major characters recalls those crucial events of the past years
leading to the tragic climax.

By refusing to attend the funeral with her husband, Helen
hopes to make him experience a lonely despair that will at
last reveal to him what intense suffering can really be. She
recalls how the death of her youngest child, Maudie, emptied
her spirit but hardly affected Milton's. Now, with the death
of Peyton, whom he loved with a passion beyond fatherliness,
Helen prays that Milton, too, will suffer comparable agony.
As he waits at the depot, Milton more .than fulfills Helen's
desire. Two memories invade his tormented consciousness:
first, his father's urging him in adolescence never to let passion
be his guide, advice he has abysmally failed to follow since
his college days, and second, Peyton's last, despairing letter
from New York with its hauntingly prophetic images of birds
and falling. As these recollections of the past torture him,

Milton is obsessed by a desire to be reunited with his estranged
wife.

Peyton's body arrives and is placed in the hearse, and the
ride to the cemetery begins. Unwillingly seated beside the
adoring Dolly, Milton recalls the beginning of their affair. A
dozen years earlier, Dolly and her fat, balding husband,
Pookie, along with their young son, Melvin, visit the Loftises'
home one Sunday. Dolly boldly flirts with Milton and he freely
studies her shapely legs. Alone for a brief moment, they admit
their mutual affection but are interrupted by a shrill cry.
La Ruth, the maid, has discovered the crippled Maudie tied
and gagged by Peyton and Melvin. Helen grasps the sobbing
child to her, slaps Peyton, and takes Maudie into the house.
After the Bonners leave, Milton quiets Peyton and gently persuades her to apologize to Helen. Later, Peyton curls up beside
him and he is filled with a strangely profound love for the
child. Though he resents Helen for hitting Peyton, he hopes to
make her understand his special love for his daughter and
even his sensual need of Dolly.

As the cortege moves past the town dump, Dolly sadly
realizes that Milton no longer loves her and that she will soon
be utterly alone since Pookie has long since divorced her.
She recalls the night in 1939 when Milton first made love to
her at the country club. At this moment Milton and Helen
also think back to that evening, the night of Peyton's sixteenth
birthday party. Helen is jealous of Dolly, at once loving and
despising Milton, resenting Peyton's youth, beauty, and, most
of all, her love for her father and cool disdain for her mother.
When Helen discovers that Peyton has been drinking party
punch spiked with liquor, she demands that the girl return
home. Milton intercedes in Peyton's behalf, and Helen, after
denouncing him as a sinner and an atheist who has destroyed
love, stalks off alone. Milton consoles himself by getting drunk
and then, finding Dolly alone, leads her to the darkened golf
museum room and distractedly makes love to her. On the lawn
Peyton, saddened by the evening's cruelties, lies weeping in
the embrace of a teen-age boy.

As Milton and Dolly sit in the cemetery-bound limousine
waiting for the last of a long procession of Negroes to pass on
their way to Daddy Faith's revival meeting, the Rev. Carey
Carr drives to the Loftis home to pick up Helen and bring her

to the funeral. As he drives, he remembers when Helen first came to him for spiritual advice just after Peyton's unhappy birthday party. Helen tells him of her adoration for her father, a strict, severe military man known as "Blood and Jesus Peyton." From him, she insists, "I learned what's right and what's wrong." And she recalls her happy years with Milton— before he begins drinking and lusting. Carr remembers, too, how Helen recounted with horror Peyton's easy display of her physical charms, a sure sign, Helen believes, that she will sin and be damned. Helen admits to Carr that she wants to stop hating and he tries, with little success, to convince her that God is love. Finally, he remembers hearing from several people about Helen's confronting Dolly in a local restaurant two weeks after Peyton's party and loudly accusing her of having carried on a six-year affair with Milton. Coolly, but as audibly as Helen, Dolly replies that their love had first been consummated at Peyton's party but that the affair would continue as long as Milton wanted her.

When Carr arrives at Helen's house, she is upstairs dressing. La Ruth weeps and prays as she helps her. In a gesture of love and compassion, La Ruth grasps Helen's hand and begs her to take Milton back to fill her loneliness. Helen recoils at the woman's touch and sharply rejects her advice. Helen descends the steps and, as she leaves with Carr, says, "The end is upon us."

In fact, Milton and Helen do not separate after Peyton's party. For the sake of the children, they maintain a working relationship, Milton tactfully keeping Dolly and his drinking under cover. A brief crisis interrupts the peace when Peyton returns from college for her Christmas holiday in 1941. She and Helen clash bitterly, but Milton embraces Peyton and begs her not to leave. During the next year, Peyton does not return for her vacations and Milton's dreams are tormented with her image.

In the fall of 1942, Helen takes Maudie to the university hospital in Charlottesville for a check-up. One night while they are away and Milton has returned from his rounds as an air-raid warden (he has daydreamed of being a colonel in Libya) determined to finish writing a letter to Peyton, he discovers Dolly on the living room couch. Milton tries to talk to Dolly about Peyton but she manifests only mild interest. They get drunk together, and in a moment of bitter vengefulness, Milton leads Dolly to Helen's bed and makes love to her there. Ironically, after his passion, Milton dreams of Peyton. Milton and Dolly are interrupted by a call summoning Milton to the hospital where Maudie is dying.

At the hospital Helen pleads with Milton to stay with her and he agrees. Alone in the waiting room, Milton watches a blue kite flying like a bluebird in the distance, and he recalls his adolescent search for love, a romantic quest he has never abandoned. An old college classmate chances by to interrupt his reverie and insist that Milton join him for one drink at their old fraternity house. Remembering that Peyton's boy friend, Dick Cartwright, will probably be there with her, Milton goes along. Caught up in the wild pre-football-game party, Milton fails to see Peyton who, however, is there. He drifts into a restaurant and meets Pookie Bonner with his girl friend. Jealous of Pookie's wealth and insensibility which, Milton thinks, free him from responsibility and guilt, he patronizes and then insults Pookie. Drunkenly seeking Peyton, he wanders into the football stadium, sits beside a drunken woman for a while, then stumbles out of the arena into the street, careens along the roadway, and at last falls face down in a muddy culvert. There he is found by a Negro, and later, by Peyton and Dick. When he tells Peyton about Maudie, she reproves him. "I love you," she says, adding, "I just think you're a jerk." Milton's image of their perfect union has been shattered, but he recovers enough to go with her to the hospital.

There Helen tongue-lashes them, Milton as a sot, Peyton as a whore, both as utterly incapable of love. She tells how years earlier, Maudie, despite her illness, came closer to genuine love in a fleeting, momentary embrace with an ugly little man named Bennie who would stop in the fields to amuse her by juggling and making faces. Then Helen walks off. Peyton goes off with Dick, gets drunk, and sleeps with him, their relationship pathetically loveless. In the background the radio blares out news of the war.

At a filling station along the road to the cemetery, the limousines of Carey Carr and Milton meet. Milton tells Carr that he wants Helen back, that there must be something left for them. He reminds Carr that the year after Maudie's death was a reasonably happy one for him and Helen. He stopped

drinking and seeing Dolly and even controlled his guilty longing for his daughter. All went well until the day of Peyton's
wedding to Harry Miller.

Peyton's determination to get married in her home represents not sentiment, as she tells Milton the morning of the
wedding, but an effort to come to terms with her past, to
achieve a normalcy despite all the trauma: "Oh, I feel so sorry
for us all. If just she'd had a soul and you'd had some guts."
Milton tries to control his emotions during Carr's reading of
the wedding ceremony, but his hunger for Peyton obsesses
him. Meanwhile Helen behaves well, graciously, and amiably.
During the party, Milton begins to drink, kisses Peyton too
often and too strongly—all in full sight of Harry and Helen.
Peyton begs her father as they dance not to smother her.
Minutes later, Helen and Peyton argue violently in the bedroom. Peyton claws her mother's face and rushes out of the
house with Harry. Milton follows her to the lawn, clings to
her, then lets her leave. Then he telephones Dolly to tell her
that he and Helen are finished.

The final section of the novel—except for a brief prologue
and epilogue—rehearses Peyton's stream-of-consciousness as,
nude, she prepares to leap to her death from a window in
Harlem. In the prologue, Harry and a friend reclaim her body
from potter's field. Harry remembers their meeting at a Greenwich Village party in 1943, his fascination with her beauty,
intelligence, and psychic anguish. Though his friends warn him
that she will bring grief to both of them, he is certain that
together they will triumph. Peyton's stream-of-consciousness
proves how false his expectations are.

The failure of Peyton's marriage lies in the fact that she
needs Harry more than she loves him. Because Harry is fully
aware of this, Peyton irrationally punishes him for his insight
by taking lovers—Tony, the milkman, and Earl Sanders, one
of their artistic friends. Finally disgusted, Harry leaves,
pursued by the hysterical Peyton who begs him to give her
another chance—not, as she says, to let her drown. She brings
him a clock, explaining that they can lose themselves within
its fine mechanism, safe at last from the terror of time: "Not
out of vengeance have I accomplished all my sins," she tells
him, ". . . only in order to lie down in darkness and find, somewhere in the net of dreams, a new father, a new home." But

Harry rejects her. Peyton rides the subway to Harlem, enters a loft building, and climbs the stairs. In the ladies' room, she undresses, envisions flights of birds soaring free, and leaps from the window.

In the epilogue, Milton rushes to Helen in the anteroom of the funeral parlor, demanding that she return to him. When she refuses, he begins to choke her. Then suddenly, he stops and walks alone into the rain. Helen presses her head against the wall, murmuring "Nothing! Nothing! Nothing! Nothing!" Down the road, La Ruth, Ella, and Stonewall share with other Negroes the joyous frenzy of Daddy Faith's river baptism.

Critical Opinion

The title of Styron's novel derives from a passage in Sir Thomas Browne's seventeenth-century study of ancient urn burials. Like the people of old, Browne reminds us, it cannot be long before we lie down in darkness and have our light in ashes. Styron's novel is an analysis of the contemporary forces that cause a whole family to lie down in darkness or, more explicitly, to rot.

Thus no single character can be isolated as chief protagonist or victim. In a sense, it is a whole society wasting away. The raging hatreds that corrode the Loftis family bond are mirrored in the racial tensions and religious bigotry smoldering just below the surface. Moreover, both the society and the characters are ridden with guilt and strive to find forgiveness through love. The tragedy lies in the failure of love to bring them together. Only the Negroes, in a primitive way, discover a path to spiritual redemption.

Styron's narrative fragmentation underscores the fractured psyches of his characters. "The business of the progression of time seems to me one of the most difficult problems a novelist has to cope with," Styron has observed. In *Lie Down in Darkness* he achieves a masterly solution by recording varied points of view as they hover about, then plunge into the crucial episodes of the past. Moreover, his use of dreams, stream-of-consciousness, and, on occasion, omniscient narration, lend variety as well as density to his writing.

Some critics, though admiring Styron's skill, have protested against the novel's solemnity and despair, assigning it to "the dread-despair-and-decay camp of U.S. letters." Styron scorns this attitude, insisting that "new writers haven't cornered any market on faithlessness and despair, any more than Dostoevski or Marlowe or Sophocles did." Several critics share Styron's view. While admitting that Peyton's suicide on the day the atom bomb dropped on Hiroshima seems rather overdrawn, they argue that the novel truthfully and graphically analyzes certain tensions afflicting contemporary man and his society. *Lie Down in Darkness* is not a cheerful novel, but it is an honest one, its characters deeply and closely studied, its techniques imaginatively developed.

The Author

Born in Newport News, Virginia (the actual setting of *Lie Down in Darkness*), *William Styron* attended Duke University until World War. II. After three years of service with the Marines, he returned to Duke to complete his education, especially to study writing with William Blackburn. Later he came to New York, writing at the New School under the tutelage of Hiram Haydn. Haydn advised and encouraged Styron during the writing of *Lie Down in Darkness,* his first novel. Published when Styron was twenty-five, it won wide acclaim and was awarded the Prix de Rome of the American Academy of Arts and Letters. While in Rome, Styron married. Today he lives with his wife and three children in Roxbury, Connecticut.

Recalled to Marine duty during the Korean War, Styron gathered material for his short novel, *The Long March,* published in 1952 as a magazine story and in 1956 as a book. Styron has written one other novel, *Set This House on Fire* (1960), a long, disappointing, rather static analysis of the conflict of wills between two men—Mason Flagg, a gifted but cruel American playboy, and Cass Kinsolving, an artist who panders to Flagg's whims in order to keep himself supplied with liquor.

Invisible Man

by

RALPH ELLISON (1914–)

Main Characters

The Narrator—A young Negro, unnamed and "invisible." His
invisibility, however, is spiritual rather than physical, the
result of his inability to discover the identity he desperately
seeks. He is a man of fine intelligence, great sensibility, and
courage.

Brother Jack—A one-eyed Brotherhood district leader, cold,
ruthless, willing to sacrifice anyone to his cause.

Tod Clifton—A young Negro worker for the Brotherhood
cause. Like the narrator, he is seeking his reason for being.

Ras, the Exhorter—A fanatical black-race-supremacy leader
in Harlem.

Sybil—A white woman obsessed with fantasies of being raped
by a Negro.

Lucius Brockway—A Negro boilerman at the Liberty Paint
Company, violently anti-union and terrified of losing his job.

Mary Rambo—A gentle and sympathetic Negro landlady.

Dr. Bledsoe—President of the narrator's college in the South,
a hard-headed opportunist who kowtows to important white
men to win financial support for his institution.

The Rev. Homer A. Barbee—A blind preacher from Chicago,
guest speaker at the college, who believes in the Negro's
courage and endurance.

Mr. Norton—A white benefactor of the college, driven by a
sense of personal as well as social guilt.

Jim Trueblood—A Negro farmer guilty of incest, but happily surprised by the social approbation the episode wins him among the white community.

The Story

"I am an invisible man," says the narrator in the opening sentence of the Prologue. Hiding in the abandoned basement of a white man's apartment building, the narrator has tapped electric wires to provide himself with more than a thousand lights—free—to illuminate his home and to make himself visible. The light really represents his quest for the truth about himself—his psychic identity. The novel tells how and why the narrator became "invisible," sought an underground refuge, and chose to remain there until, as he hopes, he can emerge into real rather than artificial light.

The narrator's earliest recollection is of a white stag "smoker" in the South in which, after the usual striptease, a group of Negro boys—including himself—entertain by boxing while blindfolded and by picking up coins from an electrified rug. At the close of the festivities, the narrator is made to deliver his recent commencement address. His reward is a scholarship to the state college for Negroes.

During his junior year at college, the narrator is assigned one day by Dr. Bledsoe to drive the visiting white benefactor, Mr. Norton, about the countryside. The sightseeing tour proves disastrous. First, the narrator unwisely allows Norton to meet an elderly Negro farmer, Jim Trueblood, who tells the horrified white man how, while abed with his wife and daughter, he mistakenly made love to his daughter. Ironically, though the local Negroes ostracize Trueblood, the white population is understanding and generous. Before Norton leaves—his agonized memories of his incestuous love for his own daughter stirred by the narrative—he gives Trueblood a hundred dollars. When the distraught Norton demands a drink, the narrator stops at the Golden Day, an inn and brothel where Negro inmates of a mental institution (most of them educated professional people whose advanced ideas qualify them for commitment) are brought for recreation under the supervision of a menacing attendant named Supercargo. One of the patients insists that Norton is his grandfather, and a prostitute genially strokes his forehead. Faint with terror and aghast when one patient, a former doctor, diagnoses him as an hysteric, Norton shrieks to be released. A brawl ensues and Norton's head is cut before the narrator gets him into the car.

For the trouble he has caused, the narrator is expelled. First, however, he listens to Dr. Bledsoe lecture him about the need to please white men and to acknowledge his own insignificance. "I had to be strong and purposeful to get where I am," Bledsoe says. "Yes, I had to act the nigger!" With that advice and a sealed letter of reference from Bledsoe, the narrator ventures North to search for identity beyond the black world that he had thought his.

Wherever the narrator displays his letter of reference, he is turned away. At last a homosexual whose father has turned the narrator away, tells him that the letter warns employers against hiring him. The homosexual offers the narrator employment as a valet or companion, is refused, and finally recommends that the narrator seek employment at the Liberty Paint Company. He is hired there to add the ingredients needed to make a special Government-contract paint known as Optic White and used specially on national monuments. To mix the paint, the narrator must add a specific number of drops of black until the black is dissolved and makes the white even more brilliant. Unfortunately, the narrator adds the wrong substance and allows the black to show.

He is given another chance to keep his job, but in a different department, as assistant to Lucius Brockway, an elderly Negro long employed in the boiler room, deep in the bowels of the factory. Brockway created the slogan "If It's Optic White, It's the Right White" and believes himself essential to the success of the company. In fact, his terror of being a Negro in a white company has made him a complete Uncle Tom, blindly loyal to the management, frantically suspicious of his fellow employees. When Brockway suspects the narrator of belonging to the union, he starts a violent fight and tricks the inexperienced narrator into overpressuring a boiler which explodes, nearly killing him. In the company hospital, the narrator is treated by electric shock that deprives him of memory and identity.

Released from the hospital, the narrator travels to Harlem

and, after a brief time in a "Y," rents a room from Mary Rambo who tries gently to orient the young man to his environment. Walking the streets of Harlem, he tries unsuccessfully to reassert his Negro identity by eating his favorite Negro food, baked yams. Later he tries to destroy the image of himself as Negro by smashing a cast-iron figurine of a Negro (used as a doorstop in his room) and tossing it away. But someone, thinking he has dropped the figure accidentally, follows him and returns it.

While his inward struggle continues, he is suddenly thrust into the violence of the outside world. Watching the eviction of an elderly Negro couple, he first holds off the bystanders who threaten the marshal, arguing that Negroes are "a law-abiding and a slow-to-anger people." Then, when the white marshal refuses to let the old people re-enter their apartment to pray, the narrator rouses the mob to action. They beat the marshal off and are carrying furniture back into the apartment when the police arrive. A handful of whites who have encouraged the Negroes during the fracas help the narrator escape from the police. One of them, Brother Jack, later invites the narrator to join his organization as a speaker for the underprivileged.

At the insistence of his new white friends, who have admired his skill in haranguing the mob, the narrator attends a party and enlists in the party of Brotherhood. Hired at a good salary, the narrator delivers his first address to a large group of Negroes assembled in a meeting hall. His subject—as in his eviction speech—is the dispossessed; his theme, "We'll be dispossessed no more." Despite the enthusiasm of the audience, Brother Jack and Hambro, the Brotherhood theoretician, condemn the narrator for his speech. They object to its emotional content, its evasion of principles. For the next four months, the narrator leaves the rostrum to study with Hambro the doctrines of scientific materialism. His lessons have a single purpose: to teach him to submerge his own deeply felt passion. "You will have freedom of action," he is told, "and you will be under strict discipline to the committee." Once more the narrator has stumbled into a blind alley from which he can emerge only as an invisible man.

In the arena of love, as in that of politics, the narrator discovers that he lacks identity. Sex-starved white women lust after him as a stereotype of potency. One seduces him, and another, Sybil, drunkenly demands that he rape her. When she passes out, the narrator—who has not touched her—writes in lipstick on her flesh, "Sybil, you were raped by Santa Claus. Surprise."

One aim of the Brotherhood is to oppose the aggressive, terroristic methods of Ras the Exhorter. Tod Clifton, youth leader of the Brotherhood, takes the narrator along to help disrupt a street meeting led by Ras. After a violent battle in which they subdue Ras, Tod and the narrator listen to his impassioned argument that the only possible cause they share is the unity of blacks. Cooperation with white men is both futile and treasonous. Tod retorts that this is emotion, not reason, and that what Ras asks is that the Negro plunge outside the current of history.

Ironically, only a few weeks later, Tod (whose name in German means "death") himself takes that plunge, fatally. Disillusioned by party discipline, incapable of following Ras, Tod symbolically destroys himself by peddling dancing Sambo dolls in the street. When Tod punches a policeman who shoves him, the policeman shoots him dead. Rejecting the party's judgment of Tod as a traitor to their cause, the narrator delivers an eloquent funeral oration before a Harlem audience. Ras, however, accuses the narrator of merely bandying words, not avenging Tod's murder. No longer Ras the Exhorter but Ras the Destroyer, the extremist leader incites the angry mob to violence.

While the riot rages, the narrator has a series of strange encounters. A girl approaches him and addresses him as Rinehart, mistakenly thinking him her lover; a policeman calls him by the same name, assuming him to be a local payoff runner. Always using the name Rinehart, others mistake him for a gambler, a bookie, and a minister. Stunned, the narrator suddenly realizes that this total loss of identity—he is at once all men and no man—has granted him absolute freedom from responsibility to white or to black, to North or to South, to the Brotherhood or to Ras. Denied existence and identity by the external world, he can turn his gaze wholly inward and discover for himself who he believes himself to be.

When Ras, mounted on a horse and carrying a spear, tries to have the mob apprehend and hang the narrator, the narrator knows that he wants desperately to live. Hanging, he realizes, will not make him visible any more than assenting to the white man's will or rising in anger against the white man. He flees from the scene of danger and plunges into an open manhole. In the underground world—where he opens his narrative —he continues to contemplate his place in the universe. Shorn of illusion, he is neither barren of hope nor empty of love. "There's a possibility," he says as the novel ends, "that even an invisible man has a socially responsible role to play."

Critical Opinion

The years since World War II have produced several outstanding novels by Negro writers, Richard Wright's *Native Son* and James Baldwin's *Go Tell It on the Mountain* among the very best. But Ellison's *Invisible Man,* many critics insist, cannot be classed simply as a novel by a Negro about Negroes. It is rather a novel about mankind written by a man of enormous skill and profound sensibility.

Ellison's vision has its sources in Dostoievski's insight into the "underground man," the alienated, isolated, neurotic child of disorder and chaos. But Ellison's expression of the theme is wholly American. Folk materials, evangelical fervor, and the language of jazz, especially the blues, endow the narrative with nervous, rhythmic energy. About the blues, for example, Ellison has written that it "is an impulse to keep the painful details and episodes of a brutal experience alive in one's aching consciousness . . . and to transcend it, not by consolation of philosophy, but by squeezing from it a neartragic, near-comic lyricism." All of these techniques combine in *Invisible Man* to render what Ellison has called "the bright magic of the fairy tale."

The fairy tale he tells is grim and gothic, a nightmarish story of violence and guilt narrated by a haunted hero. Nevertheless, the very irrationality of the narrator's situation— whether in the illuminated basement or in the raging world above—breeds a sense of the comic as well as of the tragic. Deeply involved as he is in the drama of seeking his identity, the narrator maintains a certain ironic detachment. By refusing to recognize him as a man, both white and black races have cloaked him in invisibility. Thus garbed, he is utterly alone, but he can also see those about him and judge them for their failures. More important, he can begin to recognize himself and perhaps discover the selfhood he has never really known.

The novel is an existential work because the hero sloughs off all abstract notions about reality and attains a total freedom that demands choice and a course of action. In his underground habitat, the narrator must reevaluate everything afresh. Only then can he possibly venture forth confident of his own existence. Although the narrator is a Negro, experiencing the agony of blackness in a white society, he emerges symbolically as Everyman. His problem of self-discovery is a universal one affecting men of all races.

The Author

Ralph Ellison was born and educated in Oklahoma City, and later won a scholarship to Tuskegee Institute where he majored in music. In 1936 he came to New York City to study musical composition and sculpture. A friendship with Richard Wright, already famous as the author of *Native Son*, encouraged him to write. During the seven years he was writing *Invisible Man*, Ellison worked as photographer, jazz trumpeter, and waiter.

Invisible Man remains Ellison's only published novel, though one chapter of a second novel has appeared in *Partisan Review*. Meanwhile, since winning the National Book Award in 1952 for his first novel, he has published several short stories, critical and sociological essays, and reviews in *Horizon* and *The Saturday Review*, among other publications. In addition, he has lectured widely and taught courses in literature and creative writing at Bard College and, currently, at Rutgers University.

The Adventures of
Augie March

by

SAUL BELLOW (1915–)

Main Characters

Augie March—The picaresque hero, fiercely dedicated to a
free-style pursuit of his fate. Sympathetically open-minded
and insatiably curious, he refuses to commit himself to any
of the creeds that shape human destiny.

Simon March—Augie's elder brother, intelligent but ruthless
in his quest for wealth and power.

Georgie March—The youngest March, a gentle idiot, as happy
in an institution as he was at home.

Mrs. March—Their mother, deserted by her husband, a kindly,
well-meaning woman but passive and ineffectual.

Grandma Lausch—An aged Russian-Jewish boarder at the
March home. Proud, Machiavellian, she influences the lives
of the young March brothers.

William Einhorn—A total paralytic, but a man of enormous
energy and gusto—economic, intellectual, and sexual; a
major influence in Augie's youth.

Tillie Einhorn—His patient, devoted, and self-effacing wife.

Arthur Einhorn—The Einhorns' self-centered, self-indulgent,
and wholly unproductive Harvard-educated son.

Mrs. Renling—A wealthy, motherly woman who vainly undertakes to adopt Augie and make him "successful."

Thea Fenchel—A rich, passionate, and lovely young woman who pursues men, eagles, and iguanas with equal determination.

Stella Chesney—A beautiful actress, a mildly compulsive liar, and the woman with whom Augie more or less settles down at last.

Mimi Villars—An intellectual waitress, tough and experienced, who is willing to suffer for the only cause she holds dear —love.

Hooker Frazer—Mimi's lover (succeeded by Arthur Einhorn), a brilliant political theorist and a Trotskyite.

Charlotte Magnus Einhorn—Simon March's wife, a shrewd complement to her husband.

Renee—Simon's attractive, predatory mistress.

Robey—An eccentric millionaire engaged in writing a history of happiness from the point of view of the rich.

Harold Mintouchian—A wealthy Armenian lawyer and businessman, worldly, cynical.

Hyman Basteshaw—A ship's carpenter, but also a gifted, if mad, scientist who insists he has discovered a method to create protoplasm.

Tom Gorman, Jimmy Klein, Sylvester—Boyhood friends of Augie's.

Padilla, Kayo Obermark, Clem Tambow—Friends of Augie's at the university.

Hilda Novinson, Sophie Geratis, Esther Fenchel—Onetime loves in Augie's life.

Wiley Moulton, Iggy, Oliver—Expatriate friends of Thea's in Mexico.

The Story

Narrator of his own inexhaustible experience, Augie March begins with his boyhood in Chicago. Poor and Jewish, Augie starts life economically and socially alienated, yet he is neither bitter nor vengeful, only eager to absorb the knowledge and experience he hopes will help him discover a "good enough fate" to live by.

"A man's character," Augie quotes from Heraclitus, "is his fate," and Augie learns at the outset that he must shape as well as be shaped by his encounters with life. Grandma Lausch, his first "teacher," sets for him and his brother Simon a single goal—to rise above the laboring class. But though she teaches Augie at the age of eight how to deceive municipal officials into issuing free eyeglasses for his mother, she cannot force Augie into the mold she envisions for him. Simon, determined to succeed, labors shrewdly and effectively, but Augie shows little inclination to accept the conventional notions of successful living. At school and at work, Simon easily outshines his younger brother. Moreover, when Simon cheats, he escapes unscathed; Augie is usually caught or outwitted. As a twelve-year-old elf, for example, working with Santa Claus, Augie and his fellow elf expropriate every tenth quarter the children pay to receive a surprise package. A store inventory quickly reveals the elfin duplicity, and Augie suffers humiliations and ostracism at home.

By the time Augie enters high school, his ties to his family have weakened. His beloved idiot brother, Georgie, has been institutionalized, and Grandma Lausch, her ambitions for her chosen family far short of fulfillment, has suffered a decline and accepted with her usual dignity a place in an old folks' home. In her stead, Augie finds as his new mentor William Einhorn, "the first superior man I knew." Hired as the paralyzed Einhorn's general factotum, Augie carries him about on his back, dresses him, runs his errands, and listens attentively to his searching comments about life. Einhorn, Augie realizes, refuses to be intimidated by his physical limitations. All life beckons him, and Einhorn reaches out in all directions to absorb and, if possible, to dominate. Augie admires his courage and genius but not his cheapness and occasional cruelty.

When the stock market crash of 1929 ruins Einhorn, Augie yields to the pleas of a local tough, Joe Gorman, to participate in a robbery. Although he eludes capture, Augie has been deeply shaken and sickened by the experience. When Einhorn, now managing one of his few remaining properties, a poolroom, hears of Augie's escapade, he berates him as a fool. He perceives, however, a reason for Augie's adventure outside the law. "You've got *opposition* in you," he observes. "You don't slide through everything."

Gratified by this astute insight into his character, Augie rewards Einhorn by rejecting his efforts to shape his life, even as he had fended off Grandma Lausch and Joe Gorman. Einhorn does not, however, disappear from Augie's expanding world. As a graduation present for Augie, Einhorn takes him to a brothel.

That fall Augie joins his brother Simon at the college, but again finds himself disinclined to accept the rigorous discipline of the academic community. Nor does he apply himself enthusiastically to the demands of his sales job in the basement of a department store. Fortunately, he is hired to sell luxury items in a suburban sporting-goods store. Leaving school to work for the Renlings, owners of the store, Augie is thrust into a millionaire's world. Moreover, Mrs. Renling, a middle-aged woman as forceful and energetic as Grandma Lausch, determines to make the attractive youth her protégé, paying his tuition for courses in advertising, enrolling him in a riding school, and taking him along as her companion at a health resort.

At the wealthy vacation spot, Augie sees the beautiful and fabulously wealthy Fenchel sisters, Esther and Thea, and after a brief inward struggle, decides that he has fallen in love with Esther. For days Augie follows her about at a distance, fantasying their love for one another, aspiring yet not daring to try to win her. When at last he musters courage to ask Esther for a date, she flatly refuses him. Augie promptly faints. Later, Thea tells him that she and Esther thought he was Mrs. Renling's gigolo. Disabused of that false notion, Thea goes on to tell Augie of her own love for him. She offers herself to the confused and embarrassed young man, who manages to flee.

Mrs. Renling, although annoyed at Augie's indifference, decides to adopt him. She tempts him with wealth and status, hinting that through these he may gain access to the enviable world of the Fenchel sisters. Uncertain, Augie seeks Einhorn's advice, but discovers that his erstwhile mentor is too involved with a new mistress to concern himself about Augie's problem. When Augie realizes that yielding to Mrs. Renling would necessitate surrendering his fate to another's will, he refuses the offer and departs.

After trying a variety of odd jobs, Augie encounters his

old tempter, Joe Gorman, now engaged in smuggling immigrants across the Canadian border. Halfheartedly Augie joins Joe, but takes flight when police trap them in the stolen car they have been using. Hours later, taking refuge in a crowd, Augie sees Joe in the custody of the police. For the next few weeks, Augie rides the rails and, after spending a night in jail as a suspect, hitchhikes back to Chicago.

During Augie's absence, Simon, desperately in love with Cissie Flexner, has tried in many ways to earn enough money to marry. He has sold the furniture from their apartment and moved their mother in with neighbors. He has borrowed money from Einhorn (on the pretext of sending it to Augie) and lost it in a crooked baseball pool. When, after all his effort, Cissie breaks their engagement and marries an older cousin of the Marches', Simon goes berserk and lands in jail—the same night that Augie, on the road, is imprisoned. When the brothers are reunited, Simon swears to Augie that henceforth he will fix upon success, not love. Within weeks after his statement of purpose, Simon wins Charlotte Magnus, chosen because her father owns a successful chain of coal-yards. Simon's rise is swift, but Augie senses in it a "consent to death." As Simon grows more opulent and more powerful, he also becomes more vicious and, as Augie constantly fears, suicidal—qualities hitherto alien to his personality, now apparent as a kind of self-imposed punishment for having sold his birthright of independence.

While Simon surges toward a success he is secretly ashamed of, Augie continues his quest for his personal destiny. As always, his approach veers from the conventional. From a young Mexican student, Padilla, Augie learns the art of shoplifting scholarly texts which are much in demand by college students. Though Augie proves adept, he irritates his accomplice by insisting upon reading the pilfered texts before he sells them. Although his income suffers, Augie's intellectual resources grow enormously.

At the rooming house where he lives and carries on his business, Augie befriends the mistress of Hooker Frazer, a political-science student who is one of his best, though non-paying, customers. Mimi Villars, Frazer's girl, is like Augie in her opposition to accepted norms. But whereas Augie is still seeking his fate, Mimi has already—to her endless pain

—found hers in love. Ironically, when Mimi becomes pregnant, Frazer (who already has a wife) disappears and it is Augie who sees her through an abortion.

Helping Mimi extricate herself from her predicament plunges Augie into one of his own. For several months Simon has been trying to force Augie to share the delights of marriage and wealth. He has involved Augie in a mildly amorous arrangement with Lucy Magnus, Charlotte's sister. Almost ready to drift into Simon's prearranged order for his life, Augie stops short. What halts his final step toward marriage is the report to Lucy and her family—communicated by a cousin—that Augie and a young woman were seen together leaving an abortionist's office. Lucy and Simon banish Augie. Augie comments, "I didn't mount the step of power. I could have done so from love, but not to get to the objective."

Once more Augie ventures forth in search of his fate, and soon embarks on the wildest of his many adventures. For a brief time he works as a labor organizer for the C.I.O. and takes his recreation with a Greek girl named Sophie Geratis. One evening his recreation is disturbed by a knock at his door. Thea Fenchel, his ardent pursuer of an earlier time, stands at the door. Conscious that Augie is not alone, Thea decently asks only that Augie call her at her hotel. The next day, after he has been beaten by a goon squad from an opposing union and decides that his fate does not include political or labor leadership, Augie hastens to Thea. They embrace passionately when they meet in the elevator, and in Thea's apartment their ardor continues unabated for the next three days.

En route to Mexico to obtain a divorce and to hunt iguana with a man-trained eagle, Thea urges Augie to join her. Deeply conscious of Thea's obsessive need to have her way, Augie knows, too, that he has never been so fully absorbed with or by another human being. In love, he accepts, and for a considerable time, as he says, "I followed her sense wherever it went." Once Thea has arranged the details of their trip (insisting that Augie take whatever cash he needs from the refrigerator where the bills lie mingled with salad leaves), the two set forth on their first enterprise to purchase and train an eagle.

With Thea as his tutor, Augie undertakes the physical task

of training the eagle, not, however, without wondering why training an eagle should seem to Thea an adventure even greater than their love.

They settle in Acatla at Thea's Mexican home, Casa Descuitada (Carefree House), and continue to train the eagle, now christened Caligula. Augie flinches as Caligula learns to kill and eat small lizards. Thea twits Augie for his sentimental objections, arguing that natural law cannot be altered for beasts or for men. Augie refuses to accept her creed and takes considerable pleasure in Caligula's fright when one of the lizards bites the eagle before dying. On the day of the supreme test, the hunting of the iguana, Caligula disproves Thea's assumption and demonstrates that even eagles can be "in opposition," and can seek an independent fate. Thus, though Caligula soars gracefully above the iguana and swoops murderously down for the kill, the violent resistance the iguana offers convinces Caligula that discretion is better than valor. As Thea shrieks in fury, Caligula flies back to Carefree House and safety. Augie's compassion and affection for the bird increase immeasurably.

Some days later Augie persuades Thea to give Caligula another chance. This time, with Caligula perched on his gauntlet and himself mounted on Old Bizcocho, Augie climbs high into the hills while Thea waits just below to stir iguana from their rocky hiding places. At the critical moment Augie spurs the horse downhill and releases Caligula. But the slope is too steep, the horse balks, throws Augie, then kicks him in the head. Caligula performs as before, sighting the iguana and soaring back to its perch in Carefree House. Disgusted with the bird's cowardice and Augie's horsemanship, Thea ships the bird to a zoo and confines Augie to the house. During Augie's confinement (which he welcomes as a refuge from hunting), Thea goes off daily to hunt rare snakes.

Conscious that they are drifting apart, Augie offers Thea marriage on the day her divorce becomes official. But she refuses, fearful of jeopardizing her inheritance. To restore their happiness, Thea argues, Augie must begin again to hunt with her and cease his bouts of drinking and gambling with the American expatriates of their community. Thea despises the "faulty humanity" Augie tolerates. They try to reconcile their differences, but a party given by Oliver, one of the

American colony, forces the issue. Leaving Thea to dance with a man she loathes, Augie walks into a garden with Stella Chesney, Oliver's mistress. Stella begs for Augie's help, telling him that her lover is about to be arrested by American agents and that she wants to escape. Stella offers herself to Augie if he will take her to Mexico City. Augie, however, volunteers only to take her to a nearby town where she can find transportation. As Augie tries to crank his ancient station wagon to begin the journey, Thea discovers the two of them and stalks off angrily. Augie and Stella drive off into the hills, where the car stalls on the edge of a precipice, compelling them to stay there for the night. Almost instinctively they make love. The next morning, with the aid of natives, Augie drives Stella to Cuernavaca, lends her money to make good her escape, and returns to Carefree House.

His reception by Thea is predictably hostile. She makes clear that their relationship is at an end. Her emotions, she insists, are stirred less by jealousy than by disappointment. Augie's quick humanitarian responses, she protests, leave him open to all people and thus prevent the absolute commitment to idealism she had hoped they might share. Augie's retort that his indulgence of her eccentricity about hunting deserves at least some reciprocal tolerance infuriates Thea and she leaves. Frustrated and miserable, Augie kicks open all of Thea's snake boxes and wrecks the house furnishings. When he calms down, he ponders the failure of his affair. He realizes that once more he has discovered that he cannot be shaped absolutely by another person, even one with whom he is deeply in love. Nevertheless, he believes that Thea's determination to triumph over nature represents a quality he must further explore if he is to achieve roundness and fullness as a personality. He determines to pursue her and beg her to renew their love. As he sets out, however, one of Thea's friends tells him that Thea already has another lover, one she entertained before Augie and during the time he was recuperating from his injury. Shattered but persistent, Augie goes to Thea, but she tells him she no longer feels anything toward him but indifference.

Despondent, Augie journeys back toward Chicago. En route he is briefly involved in a plot to save Trotsky from assassination. In Chicago he visits his brother Georgie and his mother, contemplating sadly what he regards as their imprisonment in mental and old-age institutions. Whatever else he may lack, Augie remains deeply proud of his freedom. When his mother asks him whether he is making a living, he replies, "I *am* living." Renewing his long-broken union with Simon, Augie feels deep pity for his brother, now a millionaire, a bully, and a lecherous brute. Augie denies to Simon that he feels superior because he has no money, but to himself Augie admits that money, though good to have, must follow the discovery of a fate significant enough to tolerate prosperity. And Augie has not yet discovered that fate.

As he visits his old friends—Mimi, Einhorn, Padilla, and others—he listens as each argues a cause for Augie's failure to have made his mark in the world. He has placed too much faith in the good, ignored the basic evil that dominates the universe, failed to adjust to reality, thought too abstractly. Acknowledging to himself the partial validity of each claim, Augie nevertheless refuses "to lead a disappointed life." It has not been at all bad, he observes, to have been "a runner after good things, servant of love, embarker on schemes, recruit of sublime ideas, and Good Time Charlie."

Augie, nevertheless, decides to find a career and returns to the university, taking courses to prepare for teaching. He envisages a school in some idyllic pastoral setting where children can learn and experience the joy of living. To support himself, he accepts a job assisting an eccentric millionaire, Robey, who has embarked on a history of happiness as the rich have experienced it. Plunged into histories of materialism, Augie discovers that he has no desire, as Robey has, to turn his complex knowledge to any single, directed purpose. "I don't want to prove a single thing," he tells himself, and adds that he has no compelling need "to beat life at its greatest complication and *meshuggah* power, so I want to start in lower down and simpler."

The outbreak of World War II disrupts Augie's determination to simplify his life. After an operation for a hernia suffered when he was unhorsed, he joins the merchant marine. While he is in training, Stella Chesney suddenly re-enters his life. They fall in love and plan to marry as soon as possible. In the happy weeks preceding their marriage, Augie meets and holds long discussions with Harold Mintouchian, the wealthy lover of one of Stella's friends. Mintouchian lectures Augie about love and reality, insisting that love, for example, is a form of adultery, an expression of the need for change, and that a variety of loves affirms the principle of reality that moves the universe. Although he recognizes once more the partial truth of Mintouchian's thesis, Augie (especially because he is in love) refuses to accept it. He observes, too, with ironic detachment, that Mintouchian, who is married, knows that his mistress is cheating him.

Two days after their wedding, Augie ships out and Stella leaves for Alaska to join a USO troupe. Off the Canary Islands, Augie's ship is torpedoed and he finds himself adrift in a lifeboat with Hyman Basteshaw, the ship's carpenter, a mad genius who has been fired from six universities for claiming to have discovered a technique for making protoplasm. A self-designated superman, Basteshaw rejects Augie's pleas that they use every means possible to locate a rescue ship. Basteshaw intends that they reach the Canary Islands, have themselves interned, and continue with experiments on protoplasm. Basteshaw fells Augie and binds him, but during the night Augie frees himself and secures the now-feverish madman. The next day they are rescued, briefly hospitalized, and soon afterward, Augie returns home.

After the war, Augie and Stella live abroad, chiefly in Paris, where she makes movies. Though he loves her, Augie learns that his wife has a compulsion to lie and that she has hidden from him her involvement with a previous lover, one more powerful and influential than her American refugee in Mexico. But Augie accepts these weaknesses in his determination to simplify his life and have a family. As the novel ends, Augie is on a business trip as an agent for Mintouchian. Traveling with him on her way to visit relatives is the Marches' maid Jacqueline, an ugly woman but consummately proud of her sex appeal. Observing her stubborn refusal to accept disappointment in life, Augie feels renewed in his faith in his own quest for a suitable fate. He thinks of himself as a "laughing creature, forever rising up," refusing to be cowed by nature or man, a kind of Columbus eternally exploring the unknown. "I may well be a flop at this line of endeavor," he thinks, but adds, "Columbus too thought he

was a flop, probably, when they sent him back in chains.
Which didn't prove there was no America."

Critical Opinion

In an interview shortly after publication of *The Adventures of
Augie March,* Saul Bellow pointed out that, a Chicagoan, like
his hero, he nevertheless composed not a single word of his
novel in that city. Most of it was written in Paris, but sections
were set down in Austria, Italy, Long Island, and New Jersey,
as well as in the Pennsylvania Station in New York and in
his publisher's office. What Bellow found significant in this
he has summed up thus: "I do not see what else we can do
than refuse to be condemned with a time or a place. We are
not born to be condemned but to live."

In theme and in style, *The Adventures of Augie March*
bears out the validity of Bellow's observation. Breaking from
the modern novel's concern with form and structure, Bellow's
has the shapeless, episodic structure of the picaresque novel,
a twentieth-century version of Henry Fielding's *Tom Jones.*
Out of the apparent chaos, however, emerges an order imposed by sheer exuberance for living, a vibrant affirmation of
the joy contained in infinite variety and ceaseless experimentation.

But although Augie is above all else determined to remain
a free man, he is by no means indifferent to the claims of
the world about him. What he does, however, is to sift ideas
and experiences through his consciousness, impatiently rejecting whatever he believes to be temporary or irrelevant.
Lured by the temptations of body and mind, he refuses to be
trapped by either. Conscious of the alienation of man—
especially the Jew—he assumes the role of the opposition
but he rejects flight. If the family has been dissolved as a
cohesive unit in modern life, then man must search for other
means to come to terms with the world. In other words, no
matter how hostile the world or society, Bellow insists that
man remains. Those men who, like Simon, surrender to the
conventions accepted by the Establishment, face psychic
annihilation. Augie discovers the comic possibilities in man's
tragic condition and, at the end, sees himself as *homo ridens,*

man laughing. Experience suffered, enjoyed, but always felt to the utmost—this becomes the measure of affirmation in Bellow's version of modern society.

Apart from its complex philosophic implications, *The Adventures of Augie March* enthralls readers with its marvelous control of language, its seemingly endless range of narrative invention, and its brilliant array of unforgettable characters. Like Augie—who accepts all of these people regardless of their faults—the characters possess an animation and vivacity that quicken interest and never let it flag. In an age when the fashionable literary attitude seems to be one of despair, Saul Bellow has placed himself in opposition. Without sinking to the banal or the sentimental, he has expressed a resoundingly vigorous affirmation of life.

The Author

Youngest of four sons of Russian immigrants, *Saul Bellow* was born in Canada and moved to Chicago nine years later. Schooled in Chicago, which he regards as his cultural home, Bellow left the University of Chicago after two years and completed his course at Northwestern where he was graduated with honors in anthropology and sociology. A brief venture into graduate study proved abortive, and Bellow, just married, turned at once to the writing that has since preoccupied him. He has taught at several colleges, most recently the University of Chicago.

Bellow's first novel, *Dangling Man* (1944), deals with the anxiety of a young man awaiting his call to the Army. Critics found promise rather than fulfillment in this novel, but felt more hopeful about his second novel, *The Victim* (1947). At first glance an analysis of anti-Semitism, *The Victim* penetrates to far deeper levels, searching beyond the relationships between Jew and Gentile for ways in which man can translate alienation to reconciliation. With the appearance of *The Adventures of Augie March* in 1953, Bellow's reputation reached its height, and he won the National Book Award for distinguished fiction. In *Seize the Day* (1956), a short novel, Bellow again deals—less melodramatically but perhaps more poignantly than in *Augie March*—with man's need to recognize the absurdity of his world, yet to live in it as well as he can. *Henderson, the Rain King* (1959) pursues a similar theme but locates the action in Africa. Bellow's most recent novel, *Herzog* (1964), acclaimed by many critics as his finest novel thus far, deals with the spiritual crisis confronting Moses Herzog, a Canadian-born college professor whose second marriage has just collapsed. In 1964 Bellow's first play, *The Last Analysis,* was produced on Broadway.

The Assistant

by

BERNARD MALAMUD (1914–)

Main Characters

Morris Bober—A kindly, gentle, long-suffering Jewish grocery owner.

Ida Bober—His constantly complaining but wholly devoted wife.

Helen Bober—Their daughter who longs without fulfillment for love, education, and a better life.

Karp—The smug owner of a liquor store adjoining Morris' grocery.

Frank Alpine—The young man with an affinity for suffering who is Morris' assistant and (for a while) Helen's lover.

Ward Minogue—The hoodlum son of an honest policeman.

Nat Pearl—A law student, bright and ambitious, with whom Helen has had a brief affair but whom she rejects because she thinks his interest in her is merely sexual.

The Story

Morris Bober, sixty, a kind and gentle Jew to whom hard luck clings, owns a grocery store in a run-down section of Brooklyn. His wife, Ida, complains incessantly about their lot but devotedly helps him tend the store. Their daughter,

Helen, longs for college, for a larger and better life. But she works as a secretary, turning over most of her salary to her father to help him survive.

One night Karp, the owner of the flourishing liquor store next door, asks Morris to phone the police. Two men have been driving around the block and Karp suspects that they intend to break into his store. Karp closes the store and hurriedly drives off. The holdup men enter Morris' grocery instead. There is fifteen dollars in the register, but one of the men insists that Morris is hiding the rest. Though his companion tries to dissuade him, he hits Morris with his gun.

Morris, seriously injured, lies in bed for a week. During this time a tall, seedy, melancholy young man haunts the neighborhood. He is Frank Alpine, one of the two holdup men. Bad luck pursues Frank, too. He had been unwilling to take part in the robbery, but had been talked into it by Ward Minogue, the hoodlum son of an honest cop. He tried to dissuade Ward from striking Morris, and he gave the grocer a drink of water when Ward slapped him. Now, torn with guilt and obscurely attracted to his victim, he wants to atone for his part in the crime. When Morris recovers, Frank helps him carry cases of milk in the morning and cleans his store windows. He asks Morris for a job without wages—so that he can learn the business, he says. Morris, supported by Ida, refuses.

Then one night Morris finds Frank in his cellar which he has entered through a door that the grocer generally forgets to lock. Frank has been keeping alive by stealing milk and rolls from Morris. Over Ida's objections, Morris allows Frank to sleep on a couch for the night. Next morning, dragging in some milk boxes, Morris reopens the wound on his head and collapses. Frank takes over the store and manages it much more successfully than Morris. Ida, still suspicious, becomes almost reconciled to his remaining, even pressing five dollars of the meager profits on him despite his reluctance to take the money.

Troubled by conscience, Frank puts the seven and a half dollars that the robbery yielded him back into the store's register. He visits Ward, too, trying to recover the gun used in the robbery, but leaves without it. Ward accuses him of being after the "Jew girl." And in a way that Frank is yet

unaware of, Ward is right. For Helen profoundly attracts
Frank. He undresses her in fantasy, and once he secretly
watches her as she undresses.

After Morris returns, Frank stays on. During the winter the
two men exchange intimate conversations and come to like
each other. Finally Frank gets to know Helen, too. He goes
frequently to the library hoping to meet her there. One night
they walk home together, confiding their ambitions to each
other. She wants to go to college. He tells her he does, too.

Despite Helen's resistance, their relationship grows. She
chooses books for Frank to read, listens to him sympathetically.
At Christmas he gives her two expensive gifts. When she
returns them, he throws them out. Quite by accident she
sees them and rescues them from the rubbish. She finally accepts one of the gifts, and he promises to return the other to
the store. Helen begins to respond seriously to Frank, even
spurning dates with Nat Pearl, a law student with whom she
had an affair but whom she has rejected. At last, acceding
to Frank's urgings, she goes to his room where they kiss and
neck. She refuses to sleep with him.

Ida has become increasingly suspicious of Helen's activities. She follows Helen one night and sees her kiss Frank.
She pleads with her to stop seeing Frank, but Helen will not
agree. Morris, though perturbed when Ida informs him that
Helen has kissed Frank, refuses to fire Frank. Ida extracts a
promise from Helen to go on a date with Nat. While she is
with him, Morris catches Frank stealing—ringing up less
money than he has taken in. While he has regularly pilfered
in this fashion, he frequently has restored sums and he intends to repay the whole. Morris, despite his pain at discovering Frank's thefts, fires him. Disconsolate, Frank goes to meet
Helen who has arranged to see him after her unsuccessful
date with Nat.

At their meeting place Helen is accosted by Ward who
attempts to rape her. Frank arrives in time to rout him, and
Helen melts into his arms. But Frank, his desires long pent
and heightened by the whiskey he has drunk, pulls her to
the ground. She pleads, "Please not now, darling," but Frank
takes her.

From this point on, Helen, disgusted with herself and with

men, will have nothing to do with Frank. One night Morris, by either design or accident, neglects to light the gas radiator and is saved by Frank from dying in the fumes. When Morris is taken to the hospital, Ida very reluctantly allows Frank to continue working at the store. A new grocery has opened around the corner and Morris' profits have shrunk disastrously. Frank gets a job as a counterman from 10 P.M. to 6 A.M. to supplement the store's earnings, snatching what sleep he can during the day. Helen, unaware of Frank's sacrifice, continues to snub him. And as soon as Morris is home from the hospital and able to tend the store again, he discharges Frank. Before that, however, Frank confesses that he was one of the holdup men, a fact that Morris has already deduced.

The grocery slides downhill rapidly. One day Morris is visited by an arsonist who offers, for a fee, to set fire to his store so that the grocer can collect the insurance. Morris declines, but that night he experiments, using a piece of celluloid in accordance with the directions he received. After setting the fire, though, he becomes terrified and smothers it —nearly burning himself in the process. Frank appears, having apparently been near the store, and saves Morris. But the grocer still will not take him back.

Another fire almost changes Morris' luck. Ward breaks into Karp's prosperous liquor store next door, gets drunk, and burns the store down—himself with it. Karp, Morris' longtime antagonist, offers to buy Morris' grocery and convert it into a liquor store. Morris and his family are delighted, but the change in luck proves illusory. On the last day of March, Morris, not wearing warm clothes, shovels snow away from the sidewalk fronting his store, catches pneumonia and dies. At his funeral, the rabbi lauds him for his endurance, his kindness, his probity—for his "Jewish heart."

Karp suffers a heart attack and backs out of his offer to buy the store. Once again Frank takes over, renting the store for more than it can possibly be worth. He works with Morris' dedication and slowly business picks up. Frank determines to send Helen to college. He approaches her, and while she is no longer furious with him, she abruptly turns down his offer. He insists that he owes her father a debt, confessing that he was one of the robbers. Helen screams, denounces him, and runs off.

Frank persists, nevertheless. He slaves in the store, denying himself necessities to give Ida—and through her, Helen— the money that will enable her to survive. He has become, in fact, the poor, deprived, nearly hopeless man Morris was. He has become, in effect, the man wedded to suffering—the Jew. His affinity for pain convinces him. One day in April he goes to the hospital to have himself circumcised. And after Passover he becomes, literally, a Jew.

Critical Opinion

On its surface Bernard Malamud's *The Assistant* seems a drab story, "a grocery-store idyl" bounded by pain on every side. It is, nevertheless, "a lyrical marvel," has run through dozens of printings, and is increasingly the subject of critical comment.

One explanation for *The Assistant's* vogue lies in its language. Malamud's ear for speech rhythms and nuances, especially of the poor Jews who figure most largely in his story, is nearly perfect. There is scarcely a line of dialogue that does not ring true. It has, Ihab Hassan comments, "a Hemingway clearness. . . , a kind of humility and courage, but also a softness Hemingway never strove to communicate."

And the characters, too, convince through their authenticity. Morris Bober, the gentle Jew, filled with suffering but retaining pity and love; Helen, hemmed in by squalor and frustration, but still cleaving to her ideals; Frank Alpine, the man with Bober's "talent for suffering," but enduring and even hoping. These are people whom the reader is drawn to because of their essential humanity, which is, finally, more important than their condition.

The characters determine the novel's structure. It is taut and pointed, every incident leading to Morris' death and Frank's conversion. The dramatic effect, as Ben Siegel notes, is enhanced by "implication, compression, and suggestion." *The Assistant* is a short work, but powerful and major in its effect and implications.

The Author

Bernard Malamud was born in Brooklyn, attended public schools there, then went to the City College of New York and later Columbia University where he received his master's degree. He has taught in several universities, mainly in the Pacific Northwest, and now lives in Vermont. He won the National Book Award for *The Magic Barrel* (1959) and was a Ford Foundation Fellow in 1959–61.

Malamud has written only three novels and two books of stories, yet he is generally ranked among the half-dozen best novelists in America. *The Natural* (1952) is a fantastic saga of a baseball player, "wild and nutty" but with mythic overtones. *The Assistant* (1957) is the moving record of Morris Bober, a Jew born to suffering, and his relations with his Italian assistant, Frank Alpine. *A New Life* (1961) tells, with mingled satire, indignation, and compassion, the story of S. Levin, "formerly a drunkard," who journeys from New York to teach in a college in the Pacific Northwest. The stories in his two collections, *The Magic Barrel* (1959) and *Idiots First* (1964), are alternately grotesque, poignant, bizarre, realistic—haunting fragments of experience.

Malamud's subjects are characteristically poor Jews, but the understanding penetration with which they are treated makes them representative of all mankind. Malamud's affirmation of the human spirit that transcends suffering and loneliness has been called "the humanism of the unfortunate."

Appendix

50 American Novels, arranged by date of publication

The Last of the Mohicans   1826
The Scarlet Letter   1850
Moby Dick   1851
The House of the Seven Gables   1851
Uncle Tom's Cabin   1851
The Adventures of Tom Sawyer   1876
The Adventures of Huckleberry Finn   1885
The Rise of Silas Lapham   1885
The Portrait of a Lady   1888
Looking Backward   1888
The Red Badge of Courage   1895
The Turn of the Screw   1898
Sister Carrie   1900
The Octopus   1901
The Call of the Wild   1903
Ethan Frome   1911
My Ántonia   1918
Winesburg, Ohio   1919
Jurgen   1919
Billy Budd—Foretopman   1924 (written between 1880
    and 1890)
Babbitt   1925
An American Tragedy   1925
Arrowsmith   1925
The Great Gatsby   1925
The Sun Also Rises   1926
The Bridge of San Luis Rey   1927
Giants in the Earth   1927
A Farewell to Arms   1929
The Sound and the Fury   1929
Look Homeward, Angel   1929
The 42nd Parallel   1930
The Good Earth   1931
Light in August   1932

Mutiny on the Bounty   1932
Young Lonigan   1932
God's Little Acre   1933
Appointment in Samarra   1934
The Late George Apley   1937
The Grapes of Wrath   1939
The Heart Is a Lonely Hunter   1940
The Ox-Bow Incident   1940
The Human Comedy   1943
All the King's Men   1946
The Naked and the Dead   1948
The Catcher in the Rye   1951
Lie Down in Darkness   1951
The Old Man and the Sea   1952
Invisible Man   1952
The Adventures of Augie March   1953
The Assistant   1957

Bibliography

Books about the Novel

1. Aldridge, John W. (ed.). *Critiques and Essays on Modern Fiction, 1920–1951.* New York: The Ronald Press Company, 1952.

2. Bowen, Elizabeth. *Collected Impressions.* New York: Alfred A. Knopf, Inc., 1950.

3. Chase, Richard. *The American Novel and its Tradition.* New York: Anchor Books, Doubleday & Co., 1957.

4. Cowie, Alexander. *The Rise of the American Novel.* New York: American Book Co., 1951.

5. Fiedler, Leslie. *Love and Death in the American Novel.* New York: Meridian Books, Inc., The World Publishing Co., 1960.

6. Forster, E. M. *Aspects of the Novel.* New York: Harvest Books, Harcourt, Brace & World, 1956.

7. Goodman, Theodore. *The Technique of Fiction.* New York: Liveright Publishing Corp. 1955.

8. James, Henry. *The Future of the Novel: Essays in the Art of Fiction,* ed. Leon Edel. New York: Vintage Books, Random House, 1956.

9. Kazin, Alfred. *On Native Grounds: An Interpretation of Modern American Prose.* New York: Anchor Books (abridged edition), Doubleday & Co., 1956.

10. Lubbock, Percy. *The Craft of Fiction.* New York: Compass Books, The Viking Press, 1957.

11. Quinn, Arthur Hobson. *American Fiction: An Historical and Critical Survey.* New York: Appleton-Century-Crofts, 1936.

12. Trilling, Lionel. *The Liberal Imagination.* New York: Anchor Books, Doubleday & Co., 1953.

13. Van Doren, Carl. *The American Novel: 1780–1939.* New York: The Macmillan Company, 1940.

14. Wagenknecht, Edward. *Cavalcade of the American Novel.* New York: Holt, Rinehart and Winston, 1954.

Index

British Novels

British Novels

Contents

Contents

The Seventeenth Century

The Pilgrim's Progress

by

JOHN BUNYAN (1628–1688)

Main Characters

Christian—A simple, earnest man making a pilgrimage from
the City of Destruction to the Celestial City.
Evangelist—Christian's faithful guide through his travail.
Faithful—A fellow pilgrim who receives his heavenly reward
when he is martyred in Vanity Fair.
Hopeful—Christian's companion during the latter part of his
journey, who keeps up his courage even in Doubting Castle
and the River of Death.
Mr. Worldly Wiseman—A man of the world who tries to lead
Christian astray with tales of town life.
Apollyon—A giant fiend who nearly kills Christian.
Giant Despair—The bloodthirsty master of Doubting Castle
who keeps Christian and Hopeful prisoner.

The Story

Wandering through the wilderness of this world, John Bunyan falls asleep in a cave and has a dream. In it he sees Christian who is dressed in rags and carries a Bible in his hand and a great burden on his back. Christian cries out that he has left his city because he has read in the Good Book that the wrath of God is about to descend on it. His family has refused to escape with him from the City of Destruction, and he doesn't know which road to take in order to reach the Celestial City.

When Evangelist, the Preacher of Christianity, shows him a vision of the destruction to come, Christian tries to warn his family and neighbors, but they all think him mad. Evangelist tells him to knock at a wicket gate where he will find Eternal Life, but Christian does not know the way to the gate.

He is joined in his search by two neighbors, Pliable and Obstinate, who ask him where he is going. When he tells them, Obstinate turns home in disgust but Pliable promises to go with Christian. Not noticing the road they are taking, Christian and Pliable fall into a treacherous mire, the Slough of Despond. Weighed down by the great burden of sins on his back, Christian is in danger of sinking into the mud over his head, but Help soon comes and rescues him. When Pliable, by a great effort, emerges from the Slough, he leaves Christian in dismay at the difficulty of the journey, and makes his way home.

Resuming his pilgrimage, Christian next encounters Mr. Worldly Wiseman, a suave, sophisticated man who tries to convince the pilgrim that his journey is folly. He tells Christian that Christian would be happy if only he allowed Mr. Legality and Mr. Civility, dwellers in the village of Morality, to remove his burden from him. Christian nearly falls into Mr. Worldly Wiseman's persuasive trap (it would be so much more pleasant to live in the easy-going town than to continue the hard journey in search of salvation) but Evangelist intervenes. He warns Christian that Mr. Legality is a fraud and Mr. Civility a hypocrite, and sets Christian on the right path again.

Christian finally arrives at the wicket gate, on which is written, "Knock, and it shall be opened unto you," and is met by Good-Will. An Interpreter invites him into the gatekeeper's house and explains the Christian mysteries to him. Shown a vision of the Day of Judgment, Christian is filled with fear of Hell and hope of Heaven.

Continuing on his journey, he comes to the Holy Cross and the Sepulchre of Christ, where miraculously his burden of sins falls from his back. He is beside himself with joy. Passing Sloth, Presumption, Simple, Formalism, and Hypocrisy, and escaping two terrifying lions who block his path, Christian makes his way to the House Beautiful where he is given hospitality and a good sword by four fair maidens, Charity, Discretion, Prudence, and Piety.

Armed with the sword and shield of Christian faith, the pilgrim next finds himself in the Valley of Humiliation, where the foul fiend Apollyon, who takes pride in his shiny scales, blocks Christian's way and warns him, "Prepare to die." Christian joins battle with Apollyon and finally, after a desperate struggle in which he is wounded by flaming darts, drives the beast away. Christian heals his wounds with leaves from the nearby Tree of Life and is able to resume his journey.

Even more terrifying than the Valley of Humiliation is the next place Christian comes upon: the Valley of the Shadow of Death. There, on one side of a narrow path, he sees a deep ditch into which the blind have led the blind to eternal death. On the other side is a bottomless quagmire. Christian must travel the straight and narrow path between these two dangers, past one of the mouths of Hell from which devils taunt him. Christian drives them off by declaring, "I will walk in the strength of the Lord God!" When day breaks, Christian resumes his journey past the caves of the giants Pope and Pagan, and is joined by Faithful, a neighbor from the City of Destruction.

Warned by Evangelist of its dangerous lures, Christian and Faithful come to the town of Vanity, which holds a year-long Fair created by Beelzebub and the fiends of Hell where all the people are consumed with the vanity that entices men away from the true road to salvation. The cruel townspeople taunt Christian and Faithful, arrest them on false charges of disturbing the peace, and beat them. (The pilgrims' "crime" is their refusal to buy the town's goods.) Christian is thrown into prison and Faithful is burned alive. As Faithful gives up the ghost at the stake, a great chariot descends from Heaven and carries him off to the Celestial City. Christian is rescued from jail by a young man named Hopeful who has been impressed by Faithful's heavenly reward.

Christian and Hopeful come upon a lovely plain named Ease which has in it a silver mine called Lucre. The mine is open to all, but those who dig in it are smothered. Christian and Hopeful leave the plain and come upon Lot's wife, who was turned into a pillar of salt when she disobeyed God's command and looked back upon Sodom and Gomorrah. They come to the River of Life where they refresh themselves.

The road now becomes stony and hard. It leads to Doubting Castle, which Christian and Hopeful reach in dark, stormy weather. There Giant Despair captures them and throws them into a dreadful dungeon, where he flogs them. Because they survive the floggings, the giant tries to persuade them to commit suicide, but Christian and Hopeful pray fervently and retain their faith. Christian remembers that he has a key called Promise with him, and they use this to escape from the prison. Giant Despair pursues them but is blinded by radiant sunlight.

Continuing on the stony path around Doubting Castle, Christian and Hopeful meet four shepherds named Knowledge, Experience, Watchful, and Sincere, who lead them to the peak of the Delectable Mountains, from which they can see, in the distance, the Celestial City. But the shepherds warn them that they can still mistake the road and take the path to Hell. On the narrow path down the mountain, they meet Flatterer, a dark man in shining costume, who says he will guide them. Instead, however, he entangles them in a net from which they finally extricate themselves with great difficulty.

Eventually the pilgrims pass through the Enchanted Land into the lovely land of Beulah, where the air is so clear that they can see the Celestial City before them, glistening with pearls and precious stones and paved with gold. Although their strength is now failing, Christian and Hopeful are determined to go on. Before the gates of the city, however, is the River of Death, deep and treacherous, with no bridge spanning it. The pilgrims plunge into the river. As the billows swirl around him, Christian fears the river is bottomless, but Hopeful shouts to him to be of good cheer. Christian touches bottom. A great darkness comes over him, but he recovers and finds he has made it to the opposite shore where Hopeful gives him a hand. Having left their mortal garments behind, the two pilgrims ascend the steep hill to the Celestial City where the gate is opened wide for them. They are greeted joyously by a company of the Heavenly Host, are given shining raiments and harps, and join the angelic choir in praise of God. With this glorious vision John Bunyan awakens from his dream.

Critical Opinion

In the years since its first publication, *The Pilgrim's Progress* has taken an honored place next to the Bible and Milton's *Paradise Lost* in the hearts of devout Englishmen. That its appeal is not restricted to England, however, is demonstrated by the fact that it has been translated into 108 different languages and dialects.

In form *The Pilgrim's Progress* is an allegory, a narrative in which such abstractions as virtue, sin, love, and evil are personified by individual characters through whom the moral of the story is made dramatically effective. Thus Christian is not only a Bedfordshire peasant of the seventeenth century but also a symbol of every man in search of salvation. We become simultaneously involved with his physical and his spiritual travail; and because of the simple but compelling suspense of the individual episodes in the story, we are inexorably caught up in Bunyan's moral vision.

Although allegory was a traditional device of the lay preachers of Bunyan's day, it is an extremely difficult form to handle successfully. No one has handled it more vividly or interestingly than Bunyan.

The Pilgrim's Progress is not a ponderous religious tract. It is rich in clever satire of the eternal human foibles. Bunyan is very hard on the glib, the hypocritical, and the superficial; his Vanity Fair is a brilliantly terse commentary on the materialistic life. The nonreligious Thackeray found it a useful title for his great satiric novel about society.

Although allegory is rare in English fiction, *The Pilgrim's Progress*, for all the crudeness of its fictional technique, exercised a great influence on the English novel, particularly in the eighteenth century. Its vivid handling of scenes from common English life—the roads, the scenery, the simple peasant homes that Christian comes upon—was not lost upon the more sophisticated novelists such as Fielding, Smollett, and, later, Dickens.

Because an unauthorized sequel to *The Pilgrim's Progress* by one Thomas Sherman appeared in 1684, Bunyan decided to write a sequel himself, narrating the path to salvation taken by Christian's wife, Christiana, and her children. As so often happens with sequels, the second part of *The Pilgrim's Progress* is not as successful as the first, largely because Bunyan did not think the road to conversion was fraught with as many dangers for women and children as for men. Thus the second part, though full of charming, homely detail, lacks the high suspense of the first part.

The Author

The man who gave to the English language the concepts of "Vanity Fair" and "Slough of Despond" came, as he said, "of a low and inconsiderable generation." *John Bunyan*, the son of a tinker, was born in Bedfordshire in 1628. He learned to read and write at the village school, but was soon apprenticed to his father's trade.

When he was sixteen, Bunyan served in the Parliamentary Army for two years. During his youth, he had a reputation as a roisterer who indulged "in all manner of vice and ungodliness." The "vices" of which he later accused himself were cursing, swearing, dancing, and unwarranted ringing of the church bell. In 1648 or 1649 he married a poor, devout woman who brought with her a few religious books which deeply influenced Bunyan.

When his wife died in 1656, leaving him to care for four children, Bunyan immersed himself in the study of the Bible. He had done some itinerant preaching, and had, in 1653, joined a Nonconformist church in Bedford. But after his wife's death he "was never out of the Bible either by reading or meditation."

Bunyan remarried in 1659, and the following year was arrested for preaching without a license. The next twelve years Bunyan spent in prison, where he wrote many of his early religious tracts and books. The most important of these is *Grace Abounding* (1666), the autobiographical account of his conversion and early career as a preacher. Released in 1672 by Charles II's Declaration of Indulgence, Bunyan was appointed pastor of the Bedford church, but was again imprisoned for preaching in 1675. During this six-month sentence he composed *The Pilgrim's Progress from this World to that which is to come,* published in 1678.

At two-year intervals thereafter, Bunyan published his two other major works, *The Life and Death of Mr. Badman,* a demonstration "that wickedness like a flood is like to drown our English world," and *The Holy War,* a complex political and spiritual allegory based in part on Bunyan's early military experiences.

Bunyan's last years were spent preaching in many places, including London, but he never ran into trouble with the law again. He died in 1688 and was buried in Bunhill Fields, London.

The Eighteenth Century

Robinson Crusoe

by

DANIEL DEFOE (1660–1731)

Main Characters

Robinson Crusoe—An ingenious and self-reliant sailor who carves out an existence for himself while a castaway on a desert island.

Friday—The cannibal who, civilized by Crusoe, becomes his loyal servant and friend.

The Story

Although his father wants him to become a lawyer, young Robinson Crusoe is determined to go to sea. On September 1, 1651, in the seaport town of Hull, the nineteen-year-old boy decides to ship aboard a vessel bound for London. Just out of port, they strike a great storm, and young Crusoe vows that if he ever reaches shore alive he will obey his parents and never go to sea again. But when the sea becomes calm, he forgets his resolution. Impressed by the courage and good fellowship of his shipmates, he takes up a life of adventure.

Aboard an African trading vessel, when it is boarded by Turkish buccaneers, Crusoe is sold into slavery. He manages a desperate escape in a boat no larger than a dory and is picked up by a Portuguese freighter bound for Brazil. There he sets up as a successful sugar planter; but, finding that he needs slaves for his plantation, he is persuaded by another English planter to sail to the slave coast of Africa. The ship is wrecked off an unknown island near the northeast coast of South America. Crusoe is the only survivor.

He is washed ashore on a deserted island with only his knife, a pipe, and some tobacco. Fortunately the ship has not actually sunk, but has foundered on some rocks. The next day, in clear weather, Crusoe is able to swim out to the wrecked ship which he finds loaded with useful supplies in good condition. Back on the island he constructs a crude raft which he plies back and forth between ship and shore for two weeks, bringing back with him firearms, powder, saws, an ax, and a hammer. He also finds £ 36 aboard the ship. He takes the money with him although he realizes that all the gold in the world is of no use to a castaway. Crusoe thanks Providence that his life has been spared and that he now has a chance for survival on the island. He begins to keep a daily diary of his activities and reflections.

After he recovers from a fever, Crusoe slowly starts building a permanent dwelling. For food and clothing he hunts wild goats and tans their hides. He plants some barley and corn— half of his precious stock from the ship—but finds to his horror that he has planted them at the wrong season and they are wasted. His every effort, from making pottery in which to store fresh water to felling and planting trees for his shelter, is enormously difficult and often meets with failure. Most frustrating of all is his attempt to build a canoe that will carry him away from the island. For five months he works on a great cedar tree, hewing and shaping it until it is seaworthy, only to find that it is so heavy he cannot get it from the construction site to the shore.

Eventually Crusoe learns to plant crops, domesticate goats

for milk, and even train a parrot for a pet. Although he has never seen another living soul on the island, he makes himself a safe hiding place. It is well that he has done so, for after twelve years of utter isolation on the island, Crusoe one day makes a startling discovery: On the beach far from his shelter he finds a human footprint in the sand. Determined to find out who the intruder is, Crusoe constructs a hiding place in a cave near the footprint and spends years searching that part of the island.

When he has been on the island about twenty-two years, Crusoe makes another shocking discovery. On the beach where he first saw the footprint are human bones and mutilated flesh. Apparently cannibals from the mainland have paddled over with their prisoners of war whom they murdered and ate.

Crusoe's first reaction is one of terror, but soon he becomes so indignant that he determines to ambush the savages the next time they arrive and kill as many as he can. He sets up a small fortress in a cave. One day, from his lookout post, he sees about thirty savages dancing obscenely before a fire. They have already cooked one prisoner and are getting ready to murder two more when Crusoe attacks them with his two loaded muskets and a sword. He shoots several of the cannibals. The others run off in panic, leaving one of their prisoners behind. After twenty-four years of solitude, Crusoe at last has a companion.

The man he rescues is also a cannibal, but Crusoe soon teaches him to loathe his former habits. He names him Friday, for the day of his rescue. Crusoe brings Friday back to his shelter and gradually teaches him enough English so they can communicate with one another. The grateful Friday, who is basically intelligent and comes from a superior tribe, becomes Crusoe's loyal and trustworthy servant and friend.

Friday informs Crusoe that on his native island seventeen white men are unharmed but being held captive. Crusoe decides to get to them and perhaps with their help return to civilization. Aided by Friday, Crusoe builds another seaworthy boat—this time right at the shore.

They are just about to set sail when three canoes full of savages land on the island with three prisoners—one a white captive. Crusoe and Friday attack with all the firepower at their command, kill all but four of the twenty-one savages, and save two of the captives. One of them turns out to be Friday's father. Father and son greet each other joyfully.

The white man they save is an old Spaniard who had been aboard a ship that Crusoe had seen wrecked some years before. Crusoe sends the Spaniard back with Friday's father to the island in his newly made boat to rescue the other white prisoners. Meanwhile, he sights an English ship anchored off shore. The captain and two loyal crew members are sent ashore by a rebellious crew. Crusoe and Friday help them recapture the ship, and they depart with the captain for England. The crew say they would rather remain on the well-stocked island than face trial and inevitable hanging in England. They are left behind.

Learning later that the Spaniard and Friday's father have succeeded in rescuing the captive seamen on Friday's island, Crusoe determines to visit them someday.

But first he returns to England with Friday, after an absence of thirty-two years. Crusoe is now a rich man. Besides the money from the sunken Spanish ship, he has an estate in Brazil, kept intact all the time he was away by an honest Portuguese captain, and £ 10,000 waiting for him in Portugal. He learns that both his parents are dead. After a visit to Portugal to settle his estate, Crusoe returns to England, marries, and has children. When his wife dies, Crusoe sets sail once again to see what has happened on his island.

In Defoe's sequel, *The Farther Adventures of Robinson Crusoe,* the shipwrecked Spaniards and the mutinous English sailors have joined forces, married native women from another island, and established a thriving colony.

After several more adventures, in one of which the faithful Friday is killed, Robinson Crusoe returns for the last time to England, where he lives out the rest of his years in peace and contentment.

Critical Opinion

In 1711 Alexander Selkirk caused a sensation in England. Having run away to sea, he returned after spending five years as a solitary castaway on Juan Fernandez Island off the coast of Chile. Selkirk, after a quarrel with his captain, had been put ashore the island at his own request, and was ultimately rescued by one Captain Woodes Rogers.

The ways in which the castaway had survived on his island fascinated people, and several accounts of his story were published on his return. Never one to let a literary opportunity pass, Defoe wrote his most famous book, *Robinson Crusoe*, a fictional elaboration of Selkirk's adventures, couched in so plain and unadorned a narrative style that it appeared to be true.

Robinson Crusoe has influenced many authors, including Swift *(Gulliver's Travels)*, Stevenson *(Treasure Island)* and, of course, Wyss *(The Swiss Family Robinson)*.

Despite its plain, crude style, *Robinson Crusoe* has epic qualities often reminiscent of the *Odyssey*. Frightfully lonely, sometimes sick, and often afraid, Crusoe manages not only to stay sane during his long years of isolation, but to build a little civilization of his own on his island. Defoe seems to be saying that no matter how morally weak the average man may be, he has unknown and untapped sources of courage, stamina, and ingenuity.

While a modern writer would have been much more concerned with Crusoe's psychology, Defoe concentrates on his physical activities. Crusoe suffers, to be sure, from moments of terrible loneliness and pangs of religious guilt for having disobeyed his parents. But early in his stay on the island, he makes his peace with God, who, he feels, has mercifully spared his life and provided him with the wherewithal for existence. From that point on, he spends his time in making a little England of his island. The resourcefulness and single-mindedness with which he goes about this task is the most appealing aspect of the book.

When Friday appears on the scene, Crusoe, a slaveholder in Brazil, naturally makes him a servant and forms a two-man colonial system. But Friday is also a valued friend who shows his loyalty and gratitude to his master in countless ways.

The people of Defoe's time had limitless faith in man's ability to carve a life for himself out of the wilderness. This faith, which made possible the exploration and taming of the American continent, is implicit in almost every page of *Robinson Crusoe*.

The Author

Daniel Defoe was born in London, probably in 1660, the son of a butcher. Not much is known of his early life except that he married Mary Tuffley when he was about twenty-three years old, became a hosiery merchant, traveled extensively in Europe, and joined William III's army in 1688.

In 1702 Defoe published an ill-fated pamphlet called "The Shortest Way with Dissenters," in which he ironically advised brutal suppression of the religious sect to which he belonged. Intending it as a satire against intolerance, Defoe was completely misunderstood and fined, pilloried, convicted of slander, and thrown into jail.

His jail sentence seems to have affected his character, for Defoe became suspicious and very careful with money. He wrote extensively, publishing in his lifetime more than 250 separate works, many of them political tracts.

The five years after the publication of *Robinson Crusoe* in 1719 were the years of Defoe's great fiction. They saw the appearance of *Moll Flanders* and *Roxana,* two classic studies of women of easy virtue, and the *Journal of the Plague Year.* In the *Journal,* Defoe's powers as a realistic writer were employed to their utmost. He recounted the Great Plague that swept London in 1665 as if he had been an eyewitness to it, when in actual fact he was only five years old at the time. His novels were immensely important in establishing fiction as a genre in English literature. Their realism and their concern with everyday life rather than with idealized fantasy inspired the most enduring strain in English fiction.

Defoe was also a prolific and facile journalist. He wrote nine volumes of a newspaper called *The Review,* and contributed regularly to other papers.

By contemporary accounts Defoe appears to have been a rather shifty, shrewd man, and a political opportunist. His contemporary, the great essayist Joseph Addison, once described him as "a false, shuffling, prevaricating rascal . . . unqualified to give his testimony in a Court of Justice."

As a religious dissenter and a political hack writer of extraordinarily persuasive force, Defoe was always in danger of imprisonment or worse, but he generally managed to keep a few steps ahead of his enemies. He died on April 26, 1731, in his London lodgings.

By the Same Author

Moll Flanders: Even more than *Robinson Crusoe, Moll Flanders,* written three years later, is of paramount importance in the early history of the English novel. Based on the theme that "poverty is the worst of all snares," it tells about the exciting life of Moll Flanders. Born in Newgate Prison, desired and won by many men, often married, and the mother of twelve children, Moll Flanders is sent to Newgate for pickpocketing. She successfully convinces her captors that she is remorseful; and, instead of being hanged, she is allowed to go to Virginia with her new consort, a highwayman she met in Newgate. In Virginia she ends her days as a respectable matriarch and plantation owner. In the course of her adventures, a vast panorama of life in early eighteenth-century England unfolds. Moll leads a lusty and dangerous life, but with an unconquerable spirit akin to Robinson Crusoe's, she always manages to survive for still another adventure. Although she is often no more than a prostitute, Moll has Defoe's own middle-class outlook, which patiently survives all disgrace and sordidness, determined to make its way in the world. She is one of the timeless heroines of English fiction.

Gulliver's Travels

by

JONATHAN SWIFT (1667–1745)

Main Characters

Lemuel Gulliver—A simple, naïve, English surgeon and seaman whose love of adventure sends him journeying to
distant and exotic lands.

The Emperor of Lilliput—A monarch a little over six inches
high, referred to by his loyal subjects as the "delight and
terror of the universe."

Flimnap—The wily, jealous Treasurer of Lilliput, he becomes
Gulliver's mortal enemy at court.

Reldresal—The Lilliputian Secretary for Private Affairs, Gulliver's friend.

Glumdalclitch—A Brobdingnagian farmer's daughter who befriends Gulliver and treats him as gently as a little doll.

The King of Brobdingnag—A peace-loving giant who nevertheless maintains a standing army.

Lord Munodi—An efficient Laputian out of favor at court
because his house stays up and his fields yield crops.

The Struldbrugs—A race of unhappy immortals whose only
wish is that they may be allowed to die.

The Yahoos—A filthy race of ape-like creatures who claim
Gulliver for one of their own.

The Houyhnhnms (pronounced Whinnims)—A race of rational, gentle horses who rule over the Yahoos.

Pedro de Mendez—The kindly Portuguese sea captain who
tries to convert Gulliver from his hatred of mankind.

The Story

When Lemuel Gulliver's medical practice in London fails because he is too ethical, he books passage as a ship's doctor aboard the *Antelope*. The ship leaves Bristol for the South Seas on May 4, 1699. Northwest of Van Diemen's Land it is wrecked in a sudden storm, but Gulliver manages to swim ashore where he falls asleep on the beach. When he awakes, he finds himself tied to the ground by thousands of delicate threads. He is the prisoner of the natives of Lilliput, a hitherto unexplored island inhabited by people six inches high who swarm all over him and threaten him with poisoned arrows.

Gulliver is a source of wonder to the Lilliputians, who have never seen anyone his size. He is brought to the capital city of Mildendo where he is instructed in the language and inspected by the Emperor. His comb, pistol, and watch cause great wonder among the Lilliputians who refer to him as Quinbus Flestrin, or Great Man-Mountain.

For a time Gulliver charms the Lilliputians by his simple, friendly manner and his desire to learn their language and customs, which are very curious. Lilliput is at war with Blefuscu, another country exactly like it, and is torn by internal conflict as well. There are two political parties, the High-Heels and the Low-Heels, and two opposing religious sects, the Big Endians and the Little Endians, who fight bitterly about which end of an egg it is better to break. Political favor at court is won by doing a complicated and degrading rope dance.

The Lilliputians, Gulliver learns, seem physically beautiful to him because they are so small that he cannot see their blemishes. Their tiny size makes them ingenious at mechanical work but petty and small minded as well.

Gradually, Gulliver becomes involved in court intrigues. He is given the honorary title of Nardac, and becomes an archenemy of Flimnap, the Treasurer. (Flimnap wants him killed because he costs too much to feed [1,728 Lilliputian portions of everything], and because he suspects Gulliver of carrying on an affair with his wife.) Gulliver's new friend, Reldresal, warns him of the indictments being prepared against him at court. When Gulliver tries to ingratiate himself by putting

out a fire in the Queen's Palace, he is only further condemned
for the unorthodox way in which he does it.

Gulliver is informed that there is one great service he
can do for the Lilliputians. The enemy island of Blefuscu
is preparing an invasion. With his superior size he can easily
destroy their fleet. Gulliver obligingly wades the 800 yards
between the islands, and, under the fire of Blefuscudian arrows, succeeds in hauling the Blefuscu fleet back to Lilliput.

This action momentarily regains for Gulliver the favor of
the court; but a new dispute arises when Gulliver refuses to
crush the Blefuscudians completely and make them the slaves
of Lilliput. Championing Blefuscudian freedom makes Gulliver a marked man in Lilliput. When he learns that he is to be
killed, Gulliver seeks shelter in Blefuscu where he is well
treated.

One day a large boat is washed ashore and Gulliver, homesick for England, outfits it for the voyage. At sea he is picked
up by a passing ship and returns home, bringing with him
samples of the minute Lilliputian cattle to prove his story.

Back in England with his wife and children, Gulliver becomes restless again and sets sail for India aboard the *Adventure*. The ship veers from its course. The sailors make for an
unknown land to look for supplies. Gulliver loses the rest of
the landing party and finds himself in a field of grain forty
feet high where giant farmers are threshing the grain. One of
them discovers Gulliver and brings him home in his pocket
to entertain his nine-year-old daughter, Glumdalclitch. Gulliver learns that he is in Brobdingnag, a land 6,000 miles long
and 5,000 miles wide. The people there are giants as gross
and coarse-featured as the Lilliputians were delicate.

In Brobdingnag, Glumdalclitch treats Gulliver like a pet.
Her father, hoping to make a fortune, goes about the country
displaying Gulliver in a box as a freak. When Gulliver gets
sick as a result of this rough handling, the farmer increases
the number of shows in order to make as much money as
possible before Gulliver dies. Fortunately for Gulliver, the
farmer eventually sells him to the Queen who adopts him as
a pet.

At the court the philosophers and wise men laugh at Gulliver. How can there be a whole race of men so tiny? The
King asks him many searching questions about life in England,
and Gulliver, filled with pride and homesickness, tells him of

the great glories of English military might. Gulliver is startled, however, to find the King appalled at the effrontery of such small creatures carrying on war.

Life in Brobdingnag is a daily source of terror to Gulliver. His size makes him vulnerable to all sorts of disasters. He must fight off immense, ferocious rats and is menaced by hailstones as large as tennis balls. Even in the palace he is in constant danger. One day the thirty-foot court dwarf becomes jealous of him and tosses him into the cream pitcher. He barely escapes drowning. When Gulliver looks into a mirror, he seems, even to himself, puny and insignificant. The court ladies behave coarsely before him, unable to take his manhood seriously.

After two years of constant peril, Gulliver escapes one day when a giant bird lifts the box in which he lives and carries it in its beak over the water. The bird drops the box into the sea. Gulliver is spotted by a vessel heading for England and is hauled aboard.

When he has recovered from his adventures in Brobdingnag, Gulliver is once again attacked by wanderlust and sets out to sea a third time. On this voyage, his ship is attacked by pirates, and he is set adrift in a small boat. He lands on the island of Balnibarbi, just east of Japan. Balnibarbi is a colony ruled from above by a floating island called Laputa. The Laputians are normal in size, but they have only two interests in life: music and mathematics. They are keen theoreticians, always rapt in abstract thought from which they must be roused by servants rattling bladders in their faces. For all their intellectual prowess, however, the Laputians are totally unable to do anything practical. Their clothes do not fit, and their houses are lopsided shambles. Only one of them, Lord Munodi, has been able to build a real house and farm his land profitably. For these accomplishments he is scorned by the other Laputians.

The King of Laputa keeps the colony of Balnibarbi under control by dropping huge rocks on it from above to prevent the natives from revolting.

The pride of Laputa, Gulliver discovers, is the Academy of Projectors in the capital city of Lagado. Here Laputian scientists labor for years on such foolish projects as extracting sunbeams from cucumbers and reducing human excrement to its original food. In the Academy the blind select colors by touch. Houses are built from the top down.

From Lagado Gulliver travels to Glubbdubdrib, an island of sorcerers. There the Governor summons for Gulliver such famous figures of history as Alexander the Great, Hannibal, Caesar, and Pompey. One after another they appear and answer Gulliver's questions about their great deeds. Each has a disillusioning story to tell, showing that the official accounts of history are a pack of lies.

A further disillusionment awaits Gulliver on the island of Luggnagg, where he meets the Struldbrugs, a race of immortals. Gulliver assumes that these must be the happiest and wisest of men because they have had so much time to learn the secrets of the universe. He finds, however, they are merely senile and embittered. Although they do not die, they keep growing progressively older and weaker, losing all zest for life and yearning for the blessed release of death.

Gulliver then returns to England by way of Japan. Once again, in August 1710, after staying with his family for a short time, he sets sail for foreign parts, this time as captain of the ship. In the South Seas, Gulliver's crew seizes the ship and confines Gulliver to his quarters. Eventually they set him adrift in a longboat. He lands on a strange shore where he encounters a filthy, disgusting race of ape-like men known as Yahoos. After befouling Gulliver, the Yahoos flee in terror at the approach of some horses called Houyhnhnms (after the whinnying sound they make). They are the masters of the island.

The Houyhnhnms assume that Gulliver is a Yahoo—albeit a more delicate and rational one—because he looks more like a Yahoo than like a horse. Just as the Yahoos are savage and irrational, the horses are gentle, civilized, and highly reasonable creatures. They marry according to genetic laws, and they accept death calmly. Gulliver is housed in the stable of a family of Houyhnhnms where he even learns to enjoy their diet of milk, herbs, and oatcakes. Ever resourceful, he makes his own clothes when necessary, but the Houyhnhnms are amazed that he does not go naked. They attribute this eccentricity to his inferior physique.

Gulliver describes life in England to the Houyhnhnms who (like the King of Brobdingnag) are appalled that such a cantankerous, evil race as men should think themselves lords of creation when in fact they are only slightly more refined Yahoos. The horses cannot understand the concept of lying, for they consider words to be meant for communication, not for concealment. They are insulted that horses should be used as beasts of burden in England. When Gulliver describes the horrors of war, he is more cautious and less patriotic than he was during his stay in Brobdingnag. He agrees with the Houyhnhnms that man is vile, and finds himself living happily with the horses in a totally rational society.

His happiness and peace, however, are short lived. The Houyhnhnm Grand Assembly, a sort of parliament, decides that Gulliver must really be a Yahoo although he may seem more civilized than the vile local breed of apes. He is even sexually attractive to the female Yahoos. As an intelligent Yahoo, the horses reason, he poses a threat to their ideal civilization. So, much against his will, Gulliver is ordered to leave. He builds a canoe and sails away, being picked up eventually by a Portuguese ship under the command of a kindly, understanding captain, Pedro de Mendez.

Gulliver has now become a complete misanthrope. He sulks in his cabin on the return trip to Europe. But Mendez tries to bring him back to his own kind by showing, in his own actions, that not all men are as detestable as Yahoos. Nevertheless, when Gulliver finally returns home from his last voyage, he is unable to endure his family, and for a long time is able to bear only the company of horses.

Critical Opinion

A satirical fantasy in the form of a travel book, *Gulliver's Travels* is known both as a delightful children's book (in expurgated editions) and as the most bitter attack on human depravity in the English language. Some of the objects of Swift's scathing satire are politics, court intrigue, bigotry, and human selfishness and cruelty in all their forms. In his four travels to distant parts of the earth, Gulliver discovers that for all their physical and cultural differences, men everywhere are basically the same. Starting out as an easy-going optimist, Gulliver eventually comes to the conclusion that, in the words of the King of Brobdingnag, human beings are "the most pernicious race of little odious vermin that nature ever suffered to crawl upon the surface of the earth." Only a few decent individuals escape Swift's withering condemnation of the human race.

Gulliver's Travels is representative of Swift's satiric genius at its best. His obsession with language finds an outlet in the invention of languages for all the strange lands Gulliver visits. His involvement with politics is reflected in the satire on English government intrigues in the court of Lilliput. His distrust of theoretical science emerges from the satire on the Grand Academy of Lagado, a parody of the English Royal Society.

Each country Gulliver visits thinks itself the greatest on earth, inhabited by the lords of creation. But everyone, large or small, apes or horses, suffers from gross human defects. Gulliver, as his name suggests, is gullible, naïve, and innocent. But in the course of his travels he is exposed to the petty, scheming Lilliputians, the gross, selfish Brobdingnagians, the abstracted, inhuman Laputians, and the foul, subhuman Yahoos. Even the Houyhnhnms, the most sympathetic creatures in the book, are too rational, as their expulsion of Gulliver demonstrates. By the end of his travels, Gulliver has become a sadder, wiser man.

Swift believed that man's inhumanity to man is made even more detestable because he is capable of reason but either misuses it or doesn't use it at all, and because he takes inordinate pride in himself—a pride hardly justified by his love for war, cruelty, and bloodshed.

The Author

Jonathan Swift, the greatest English satirist, was born in Dublin of English parents in 1667. A cousin of the poet John Dryden, he was educated at Trinity College, Dublin, where he got into trouble for offenses against discipline. He became secretary to Sir William Temple, in whose service he wrote his first major satires, *The Battle of the Books* and *A Tale of a Tub,* published together in 1704. At this time, too, he fell in love with Esther (Stella) Johnson whom he may later have secretly married.

When Temple died in 1699, Swift became a clergyman and was given a living in Ireland. On his frequent trips to

England, he became deeply involved in politics and literature. Although he started out as a Whig, he went over to the Tories in 1710 and became Dean of St. Patrick's three years later.

Although Swift is known for his caustic view of human nature, he seems to have been an amiable man capable of great friendships with the leading literary lights of his day, Pope, Arbuthnot, and Gay, with whom he formed the Scriblerus Club. He also became a hero to the Irish whom he defended against English rule in a series of savage satires of which "A Modest Proposal" (1729) is the most famous.

In Swift's last years he suffered from a progressive mental disease. Nothing sums up Swift's character as well as the epitaph he wrote for himself: "Here lies one . . . whose heart was lacerated with savage indignation."

Tom Jones

by

HENRY FIELDING (1707–1754)

Main Characters

Squire Allworthy—Rich, generous, and good-natured, the model of an English country squire.
Bridget—Squire Allworthy's plain, kindly sister.
Blifil—Bridget's scheming son.
Tom Jones—Open-hearted and outgoing, a foundling whose indiscretions always get him into trouble.
Mr. Partridge—A poor, naïve schoolmaster.
Squire Western—Red-faced and hot-tempered, chiefly addicted to eating, drinking, and hunting.
Sophia—Squire Western's beautiful, headstrong daughter.
Thwackum and Square—Two hypocritical pedagogues.
Black George—Squire Allworthy's drunken, good-for-nothing gamekeeper.
Mrs. Fitzpatrick—Sophia's cousin, running away from her insanely jealous husband.
Lady Bellaston—A sophisticated London friend of Mrs. Fitzpatrick's.

The Story

Of all the landed gentry in Somersetshire, Squire Allworthy is the most highly regarded for his benevolence, good nature, and wealth. He lives in peaceful retirement with his maiden sister, Bridget. Returning one night from a several months' stay in London, he is shocked to find a baby boy lying in his bed. He takes to the foundling and insists on bringing it up himself rather than leave it on the churchwarden's doorstep.

The foundling's parentage is a great mystery. The Squire and his sister act on the assumption that the mother must be Jenny Jones, a servant of the local schoolmaster, Partridge; Jenny Jones had spent some time nursing Bridget during an illness. Fearing local gossip, Squire Allworthy sends Jenny away. The schoolmaster leaves the county, too. The foundling is named Tom Jones.

Soon after, Bridget marries the fortune-hunting half-pay officer, Captain Blifil, by whom she has a son. The two boys are brought up together. Captain Blifil, who had hoped to inherit Squire Allworthy's money, dies of an apoplectic fit while his son is still a boy.

Tom and young Blifil don't get along together, for Tom is good-natured, easy-going, and highly mischievous, while Blifil is a spiritless prig, always concerned with the impression he is making on his elders. Allworthy hires Thwackum and Square to educate Tom. This they try to do with frequent beatings. But when Tom catches the pompous Square in bed with the local slut, Molly Seagrim, his education ends. Tom's one friend is Allworthy's lazy, shiftless gamekeeper, Black George, and together they go poaching about the countryside and getting into scrapes which sadden the affectionate Squire.

On an estate nearby lives Squire Western with his lovely daughter, Sophia. The Squire is a hard-drinking, hard-riding, choleric man. Tom spends a good deal of time with the Westerns because the Squire admires his rough and ready manners and his horsemanship while Sophia is impressed with his goodness of heart. One day while out hunting, Tom breaks his arm catching Sophia's runaway horse. He stays with the Westerns while recovering. He and Sophia fall in love.

When Tom learns that Squire Allworthy is ill and not likely to recover, he rushes to his benefactor's bedside, where he finds Blifil in obsequious attendance. But Allworthy makes a miraculous recovery, and Tom is so delighted that he gets roaring drunk. Blifil, whose mother has recently died, takes offense at Tom's behavior. Tom offers to apologize, but Blifil insultingly refers to his illegitimate birth and the two lads fight.

Meanwhile, Sophia becomes interested in Blifil, a favorite with the ladies, in order to conceal her real love for the penniless, imprudent Tom. When her aunt arrives from London, she assumes that Sophia and Blifil will marry, and tells Squire Western to prepare for the wedding. When Sophia's aunt learns the truth, both she and Western are outraged. Much as the fox-hunting squire likes Tom, he refuses to consider a foundling as a son-in-law.

Now that Squire Allworthy is fully recovered, Blifil tells him about Tom's drunken behavior the night he was so sick, implying that Tom didn't care what happened to him and couldn't wait for the reading of the will. Enraged and disillusioned with Tom, whom he liked more than his legitimate nephew, Allworthy reproaches Tom—who is too dismayed to defend himself—and banishes him from the house. He gives Tom £500 to help him make his way in the world. Tom carelessly loses the money.

Sophia, too, is in disgrace. Refusing to marry Blifil under any circumstances, she is locked up in her room by her father. But with the connivance of her maid Honour, she manages to slip out at night and heads for her aunt's house in London.

On the road, Tom falls in with a band of rowdy soldiers and gets into a fight with them at an inn. His wounds are treated by the local barber, who turns out to be the banished Partridge. Partridge becomes Tom's companion on his adventures. They meet a beautiful, middle-aged woman named Mrs. Waters, who is fighting off the advances of a soldier in a forest. Tom rescues her and takes her to the inn at Upton, where she lures him into her bed.

Also arriving at the Upton inn on their way to London are Sophia and her maid. Before long the inn is in an uproar when an enraged husband looking for his runaway wife shows up and is led to Tom's room, where he discovers Tom with Mrs. Waters, who starts to scream. The man is a Mr. Fitzpatrick, not Mrs. Waters' husband at all; but by the time everything is straightened out, Partridge has inadvertently revealed to Sophia her lover's infidelity. Sophia departs in a fury, leaving her muff behind for Tom to discover in the morning.

Soon after she leaves the inn, Sophia meets Mrs. Fitzpatrick, her cousin, who fled the inn when her jealous husband caused the row with Tom. Together they travel to London. Here Sophia is introduced to the sophisticated Mrs. Bellaston, who promises to show the unspoiled country girl the pleasures of the town.

Tom and Partridge follow Sophia to London, where they find congenial lodgings at the home of Mrs. Miller. Soon Tom is admitted to the social circle and to the beds of Lady Bellaston and Mrs. Fitzpatrick. One night, seeing Sophia at a play, he assures her of his eternal devotion and promises to reform. The quarrel is patched up. Partridge finds love, too, in London with Nancy Nightingale, whose father objects to him as a suitor. However, Tom good-naturedly persuades Nightingale to allow the match, to the delight not only of Partridge but of Nancy's friend Mrs. Miller, as well.

When he learns of Sophia's escape from his house, Squire Western abandons fox-hunting long enough to pursue his daughter to London. He finds her at Lady Bellaston's lodgings and removes her to his own. Tom is broken-hearted because he knows the squire will never approve of his marriage to Sophia. To add to his misery, Partridge brings the news that Squire Allworthy has also arrived in London with Blifil who is now going to marry Sophia. Tom goes to Mrs. Fitzpatrick for advice, but with typical bad luck he is discovered there by her jealous husband, who challenges him to a duel. Tom wounds him and is immediately hustled off to jail.

In his cell Tom is visited by the Mrs. Waters with whom he spent the night at Upton. Partridge later identifies her as the former Jenny Jones, reputedly Tom's mother. The lad is so shocked by this coincidental incest that he determines to reform his casual, promiscuous ways. Mrs. Miller defends Tom, telling Squire Allworthy that Tom was not at fault in the duel with Mr. Fitzpatrick, a fact that Mr. Fitzpatrick, on recovering from his wound, graciously acknowledges.

Indeed, Squire Allworthy is about to forgive Tom when he learns of Tom's behavior with Mrs. Waters. Once again the good man is furious with Tom, but Mrs. Waters assures him that she is not, indeed, Tom's mother. The real mother, she tells the Squire, was his own sister, Bridget. On her deathbed, Bridget left a message with Blifil concerning Tom's true parentage. Blifil had treacherously destroyed the message.

Blifil had also tried to bribe witnesses to get Tom hanged
for the duel with Mr. Fitzpatrick, even though that gentleman
had not died of his wounds.

Now that Tom is exonerated, he is released from prison and
his fortune improves. Squire Allworthy's affection for him
returns. He apologizes to Sophia for trying to force Blifil on
her and tells Squire Western that Tom is his heir, for the
young man is indeed his nephew. This convinces Squire
Western that Tom, after all, is worthy to marry Sophia, and
the match takes place. Everyone rejoices except the odious
Blifil who is sent away with a yearly stipend. Tom and Sophia
live happily on Squire Allworthy's estate.

Critical Opinion

As in *Joseph Andrews*, Fielding was concerned in *Tom Jones*
with writing what he called the comic epic in prose—a work
in which "the plain and simple workings of honest nature"
would be explored on a large scale, but without fanciful
diction, absurd events, or lofty moralizing. Drawing on his
long experience as a dramatist, Fielding plotted *Tom Jones*
with consummate skill. Writing while the English novel was
in its infancy, he set for it standards of structure, characterization, and tone that have endured to this day.

Tom Jones is neatly and evenly divided into three parts:
the first in the country, at the Allworthy and Western estates;
the second on the road, culminating in the farcical scene at
the inn at Upton; and the third in London. Thus Fielding
managed, without distorting his plot, to delineate the whole
of English life of his day. His section on the highways and
country inns of eighteenth-century England particularly influenced Dickens. The panoramic sweep of *Tom Jones* has
inspired many English novelists since.

Each book of *Tom Jones* is prefaced by a delightfully witty
essay analyzing the action up to that point and making shrewd
observations about the characters and about human nature.
These asides to the reader also had their influence—not always
beneficial—on Dickens, Thackeray, and Trollope. In these
asides Fielding's tone is invariably that of the wise and humane man of the world addressing his peers.

The theme of *Tom Jones* lies deeply rooted in eighteenth-century enlightened optimism. In pitting Tom against Blifil, Fielding is saying that, in general, human nature is careless, imprudent, and pleasure loving, but essentially good, and is best left alone to develop a moral sense in its own time. While Tom blunders thoughtlessly into one scrape after another, he finally emerges a genuinely righteous man.

Blifil, on the other hand, observes all the proprieties, is exceedingly polite and, on the surface, thoughtful. But he is a complete hypocrite and villain, resorting to every possible treachery to obtain Squire Allworthy's fortune. Ultimately his scheming brings about his downfall. Fielding's world is moral, but not puritanical.

The Author

Although *Henry Fielding* was a gentleman, the great-grandson of the Earl of Desmond, he had to struggle for a living most of his life. Born on April 12, 1707, at Sharpham Park, near Glastonbury in Somersetshire, he attended Eton and studied law at the University of Leyden. When he returned to England, he supported himself by writing farces and musicals for the popular stage. Between 1728 and 1737, he produced a number of potboilers, the most notable being a burlesque of serious stage conventions, *Tom Thumb* (1730).

In 1734 Fielding married Charlotte Cradock, supposedly the model for Sophia in *Tom Jones* and for Fielding's last heroine, Amelia. Fielding returned to the law and was admitted to the bar in 1740. To eke out a living, however, he managed a small London theater and practiced journalism, editing the *Champion* between 1739 and 1741. His wife died in 1744, and three years later Fielding married her maid, Mary Daniel.

Fielding first tried his hand at fiction with *Joseph Andrews* (1742) and the savagely ironical *Jonathan Wild* (1743); but it was the experience with all segments of society that he had gained during his appointment as justice of the peace for Middlesex and Westminster in 1748 that provided the broad scope of his last two novels, *Tom Jones* (1749) and *Amelia* (1751).

In 1740 Samuel Richardson published what is generally considered the first true English novel, the heavily moralizing

Pamela. Offended at what he considered the false, hypocritical morality of this immensely popular book, Fielding
first wrote a brief parody of it called "Shamela," and then
set to work on a more detailed ironic treatment in *Joseph
Andrews.* But what started as mere burlesque became a
typically robust, good-humored Fielding novel, rich in character and incident.

Fielding was an intensely vital and humane man whose
experiences as a Grub Street hack and as a man of the law
made him deeply aware of social injustice. Much less sheltered
than Richardson, Fielding developed a common-sense view
of life which pervades his great novel, *Tom Jones.* Nothing
human was alien to him except injustice, against which he
argued both from the bench and in a multitude of pamphlets
and essays in *The Covent Garden Journal,* which he founded
in 1752.

In 1754 his health broke down and he traveled to Portugal,
leaving a very moving account of his journey in search of
health in the posthumously published *Journal of a Voyage to
Lisbon.* He died in that city on October 8, 1754.

By the Same Author

Joseph Andrews: Amused by the sentimental puritanism of
Richardson's *Pamela,* Fielding set out in *Joseph Andrews* to
chronicle the adventures of Pamela's brother, footman to
the lascivious Lady Booby, who tries to seduce this hyper-
virtuous young man. Failing, she dismisses both Joseph and
his true love, Fanny Goodwill, from her service. Fanny is
saved from the wicked world, however, not by Joseph but by
Parson Adams, a man of great simplicity and charm, who
dominates the book and who probably served as a model for
Dr. Primrose, the Vicar of Wakefield. Writing, as he admitted,
"in imitation of Cervantes," Fielding created in *Joseph Andrews* a novel that starts out as burlesque and ends up as a
vision of English life in the eighteenth century.

Amelia: Written at the end of Fielding's life, *Amelia* lacks
the high spirits of his earlier novels. It is, in fact, a completely
serious treatment of the injustice of eighteenth-century law
courts and jails. A weak-willed, innocent man, William Booth,
confined to debtors' prison, tells a fellow prisoner of his love

and courtship of the long-suffering Amelia. The listener, a
murderess named Miss Matthews, seduces William. Meanwhile Amelia is having difficulties outside the jail. Eventually,
through a last-minute inheritance, William and Amelia are
able to achieve peace as husband and wife outside the confines of the debtors' prison.

The Vicar of Wakefield

by

OLIVER GOLDSMITH (1728–1774)

Main Characters

Charles Primrose—The kindly, unworldly vicar of Wakefield, whose innocence and simplicity often lead him into trouble, but who bears good fortune with humility and ill fortune with fortitude.

Deborah Primrose—The vicar's wife, a good woman, although sometimes inclined to be a social climber, who must be brought back to reality by her husband.

George—The Primroses' eldest son, who joins the army after trying his hand unsuccessfully at many careers.

Moses—The Primroses' younger son, educated at home and intended for business, who is even more naïve than his father.

Olivia—The Primroses' older daughter, gay, vivacious, and flirtatious, the family beauty who becomes the family heartache.

Sophia—Olivia's younger sister, soft, modest, and gentle, a more serious, less coquettish girl than Olivia.

Squire Thornhill—Mr. Primrose's landlord, a handsome, unscrupulous ladies' man.

Mr. Burchell—Actually Squire Thornhill's uncle, Sir William Thornhill, in disguise, whose honesty antagonizes the Primroses until they discover his merits.

Arabella Wilmot—George Primrose's fiancée.

Ephraim Jenkinson—A rogue in many disguises, whose surface knowledge of philosophy and ancient languages impresses his victims.

The Story

Mr. Charles Primrose, the vicar of Wakefield, is one of the most contented men in England. Married to a good wife and father of six healthy, beautiful children, he takes pleasure in the simple things of life. As the novel opens, his oldest son, George, just down from Oxford, has fallen in love with Arabella Wilmot, a neighbor's daughter, and both families are joyfully preparing for the wedding.

One day, however, Mr. Primrose quarrels with Arabella's father about whether a man should remarry after his wife's death. (Mr. Primrose is a strict monogamist. Mr. Wilmot is about to wed for the fourth time.) Suddenly Mr. Primrose learns that his comfortable fortune has been lost by a broker and that he is now dependent solely on his meager living as a vicar. Because of this sudden change in fortune and the quarrel with Mr. Wilmot, the engagement between George and Arabella is broken off.

George is sent off to London to make his way, and the Primrose family move to another, even less lucrative living. On the way to their new home, they meet Mr. Burchell, a handsome man who endears himself to them by his impulsive act of charity to another traveler. Riding with the Primroses a way, Mr. Burchell tells them about their new landlord, Squire Thornhill. He is the wealthy, woman-chasing nephew of Sir William Thornhill, a great and magnanimous man. Mr. Burchell further endears himself to the Primroses when he rescues Sophia who is thrown from her horse. He is assured of a warm welcome any time he cares to visit the Primroses in their new home.

One autumn afternoon shortly after the Primroses are established in the vicarage, they meet their landlord, Squire Thornhill, while he is out riding. Olivia falls in love with the gallant squire, but her father is troubled by Thornhill's reputation for seducing all the pretty girls in the neighborhood. Mrs. Primrose, however, impressed by his wealth and social position, encourages his attentions to her older daughter, certain that he will marry her. She finds him more eligible than the far less wealthy Mr. Burchell, now a frequent visitor. Mr. Burchell is interested in serious, quiet Sophia, and makes a point of bringing gingerbread cookies for the Primroses' youngest boys, Dick and Bill. Mr. Primrose is worried because Mr. Burchell does not seem particularly prudent with the little money he has.

The women of the household are all agog one evening when Squire Thornhill brings two finely dressed ladies to visit. Lady Blarney and Miss Carolina Wilelmina Amelia Skeggs make a grand entrance, taking the Primroses by surprise while they are playing homely fireside games with their rough, honest, farmer neighbor, Mr. Flamborough. Sophia and Olivia are impressed with the sophisticated conversation of the ladies, and are overwhelmed with pleasure when the ladies suggest that they join them in London as companions. Mrs. Primrose welcomes the suggestion, feeling that some time spent in London will polish her daughters' manners and make them more suitable for fine social matches. But Mr. Primrose and Mr. Burchell object to London as a place not fit for innocent, well-bred young ladies.

Mrs. Primrose begins to get grand ideas, and insists that the family sell its clumsy horse and buy a finer one to take them stylishly to church on Sundays. So Moses, the Primroses' second son, who is supposedly training for a business career, is sent to town to make the trade. He manages to sell the horse for a fair price but then is cheated by a smooth-talking confidence man into buying a gross of green spectacles. He proudly brings his purchase home, only to discover that it is worthless; the "silver" rims are only copper.

Despite Mr. Burchell's strong objections to the project, all is set for the girls to go to London. But the trip is abruptly canceled because Mrs. Primrose learns that the London ladies have received slanderous reports about the character of her two daughters. When the Primroses learn that the slanderer is Mr. Burchell, the vicar tells him to leave the house. Unrepentant, Mr. Burchell leaves.

Squire Thornhill now calls even more frequently at the vicarage, but Mrs. Primrose begins to suspect that marriage is not uppermost in his mind. She and Olivia decide to spur Squire Thornhill's interest in marriage by concocting a plot to convince him that Olivia is shortly to marry Mr. Williams, a local farmer. Mr. Primrose disapproves of the plot, although he thinks Olivia actually ought to consider marrying the good but somewhat plodding Mr. Williams if Squire Thornhill still fails to ask for her hand. All thought of this marriage disappears, however, when, four days before the wedding is supposed to take place, Dick Primrose sees Olivia going off with two men in a carriage.

At first the Primroses assume the abductor is Squire Thornhill, but he protests his innocence. The finger of blame points to Mr. Burchell. Mr. Primrose sadly determines to go in search of his errant daughter. During the search he falls ill and is bedridden at an inn for three weeks. On recovering, he sets out on his journey once again and meets Arabella Wilmot who asks him about George. Mr. Primrose replies that he has not heard from his son since George went to London to seek his fortune. Arabella is now being courted by Squire Thornhill who rubs salt into the vicar's wounds by asking Olivia's whereabouts.

The missing George turns up with a troupe of actors at a country house where Mr. Primrose meets them. George has been wandering through Europe, tutoring and playing music, but he has less money now than when he first left for London. Squire Thornhill, wanting George out of the way, buys him a commission in the army.

The vicar finds Olivia, abandoned and wretched, at a country inn, where she confesses the story of her abduction. It was Squire Thornhill after all, and not Mr. Burchell, who had run off with her. After a fake wedding ceremony performed by a bogus priest, the squire had seduced her. Soon tiring of her, he abandoned her in London, leaving her to make her way home alone. The two fine London ladies whom he had introduced to the vicarage were in fact prostitutes. The vicar forgives his penitent daughter, and together they set out for the homeward journey.

Just as they arrive home that night, the vicar sees his house going up in flames and his wife Deborah crying that the two little boys, Dick and Bill, are lost in the fire. Mr. Primrose rushes into the burning house and rescues his sons, but he is badly burned. Now the Primroses must settle in an outbuilding on the estate, for all their possessions have been destroyed. Kind neighbors help them move into the wretched little shack.

Olivia's misery is increased by the news that Squire Thornhill, whom she still loves, is about to marry Arabella Wilmot. This news infuriates Mr. Primrose, who treats the squire to a stern lecture when the squire has the effrontery to ask the vicar's blessing on the impending marriage and to suggest that Olivia be married off to a local man in order to be always at the squire's disposal. The squire reacts to being thrown out of the Primrose shack by demanding his quarterly rent which the vicar cannot pay. On the following day despite the angry protests of his parishioners, the vicar is led to debtors' prison. His family finds wretched accommodations in town to be near him, and the two youngest boys stay with their father in his prison cell.

While in jail, Mr. Primrose meets Ephraim Jenkinson, the confidence man who had fobbed off the worthless green spectacles on Moses, and had even cheated the vicar. Sick of his life of crime, he is trying to reform. Mr. Primrose preaches to him and to the other wretched convicts, taking his mind off his own misfortunes and giving them the strength to endure theirs. These misfortunes turn into tragedy when Jenkinson tells the vicar that Olivia, who has been pining away with remorse ever since her abduction, is dead. Deborah Primrose adds to the gloom of the occasion with the awful news that Sophia has been carried off by a gang of kidnappers.

Mr. Primrose is cast further into the depths of despair when his son George, battered and bruised, is led into the jail. When informed of Squire Thornhill's ill-treatment of Olivia, George had sped to Thornhill Castle to seek vengeance on the squire. There he was attacked by some servants, one of whom he injured in the scuffle. George is now to be hanged. Wretched and ill, Mr. Primrose writes to Sir William Thornhill, detailing his nephew's treachery and cruelty.

At this lowest ebb in the fortunes of the Primroses, things begin to look up. First Mr. Burchell arrives with Sophia, whom he has rescued from the ruffians who had abducted her. Overwhelmed with joy, the vicar promises Mr. Burchell Sophia's hand in marriage. It is then revealed that Mr. Burchell is actually the wealthy and magnanimous Sir William Thornhill, the squire's uncle, in disguise. (He had not revealed his identity to make sure that Sophia loved him for his own merits and not for his money.) The slanderous letter to the ladies in London had been written because he knew they would corrupt the Primrose girls if the girls ever fell into their clutches. Sophia's abductors were in the pay of Squire Thornhill, who, seeing that he could not have the one daughter, was determined to get the other. Sir William has pieced the story together with the aid of Mr. Primrose, and is thoroughly disillusioned with his nephew.

Then Ephraim Jenkinson informs everyone that Olivia and Squire Thornhill had been legitimately married all along. Jenkinson had been ordered by the squire to procure a fake priest for the wedding; but thinking he would be able to blackmail his master later if the squire were really wed, Jenkinson had obtained an ordained priest to perform the marriage.

Best of all, Mr. Primrose learns that Olivia is still alive. Jenkinson had spread the false tale of her death to persuade Mr. Primrose to give his blessing to the wedding of Squire Thornhill and Arabella Wilmot, thinking this would be the only way to stop the squire's persecution of Jenkinson's new friend. Since the marriage between the squire and Olivia is a real one, the squire cannot, of course, marry Arabella Wilmot. To cap the climax, the broker who absconded with Mr. Primrose's fortune is caught at Antwerp; the money is refunded to its rightful owner. There is nothing more for the sorely tried vicar to wish for in this life but that his "gratitude in good fortune should exceed [his] submission in adversity."

Critical Opinion

The Vicar of Wakefield has always been one of the best-loved novels of the eighteenth century. The reasons for its enduring appeal are clear. First, the various reversals in the fortunes of the Primrose family are sufficiently dramatic (the prison scenes particularly remind us that Goldsmith was a skilled playwright) to intrigue most readers, although the most sophisticated are likely to be put off by Goldsmith's sentimentality and his heavy reliance on coincidence. Second, we all like to read about a good man whose fortunes keep getting worse and worse until at the end all goes well for him again. Mr. Primrose is one of the most successful in a long line of innocent English country clergymen, starting with Fielding's Parson Adams in *Joseph Andrews*. Finally, Goldsmith possessed one of the finest styles of his time: easy and fluent, mildly satiric, elegant without being pretentious. The prose of *The Vicar of Wakefield* is classic in its simplicity.

For the more mature reader, Goldsmith's novel is a matchless description of humble country life in eighteenth-century
England. As in his poem, "The Deserted Village," Goldsmith is
expert at genre painting. He shows us vividly the inns,
roads, and prisons, the country estates, and best of all, the
vicar's family gathered around the fireside to enjoy the pleasures of a less complex, less harrowing age than our own.

In a sense, *The Vicar of Wakefield* is a Christian version of
the Greek tale of Prometheus or the Hebrew story of Job. Unlike Prometheus and Job, however, Mr. Primrose never curses
or even questions the God who seems to have turned against
him. Instead, he bears up with cheerful fortitude, convinced
that all will turn out for the best in the end, as indeed it does.

For all its unpretentious charm, *The Vicar of Wakefield*
is essentially a serious treatment of the theme of stoic fortitude. And for all its naïve plotting and reliance on coincidence,
it has had an immense influence on the English novel. Dickens
loved it and learned much from it. In fact, his early pen name,
"Boz," comes from the way he pronounced, as a child, the
name of Mr. Primrose's second son, Moses. Goldsmith's
charming pictures of rural life influenced Jane Austen and
George Eliot. Although the cynical may ridicule it, *The Vicar
of Wakefield* has a unique place in the history of English
fiction.

The Author

The vagabond life of George Primrose in search of a living,
as narrated in Chapter XX of *The Vicar of Wakefield,* is essentially autobiographical. For *Oliver Goldsmith,* born November 10, 1728, the son of an Irish clergyman, enjoyed far more
wit and talent than money during his lifetime. He was educated at Trinity College, Dublin, and, after running away from
school at least once, finally received his BA in 1749. He tried
to take holy orders, but was rejected. He then studied medicine at Edinburgh and Leyden, probably receiving his
medical degree on the continent during his year of wandering
about France, Switzerland, and Italy.

Arriving in London in 1756, he tried desperately to make
a living in medicine and teaching, but failure in these fields
drove him to doing hack work for various periodicals. In 1761

he made one of the most important friendships of his life, with Samuel Johnson, the great dictator of the English literary scene. Goldsmith became a member of the informal but famous "Club" which included such luminaries as James Boswell, Johnson's biographer; David Garrick, the great actor; and Sir Joshua Reynolds, whose portrait of Goldsmith is the best we have.

One day Johnson received a panicky summons from Goldsmith to keep Goldsmith out of debtors' prison. Seeing the manuscript of *The Vicar of Wakefield* in Goldsmith's poverty-stricken room, Johnson took it to a publisher, from whom he got £60, enough to pay Goldsmith's debt.

Johnson had a high opinion of Goldsmith's literary abilities although most other members of the "Club" saw him as a poor, fumbling buffoon, inarticulate in the presence of the great. (Garrick made affectionate fun of Goldsmith's stutter in the epitaph: "He wrote like an angel, and talked like poor Poll.")

Goldsmith was proficient in all genres, from poetry and plays to political journalism and history. His works are filled with gaiety, charm, and common sense. Besides *The Vicar of Wakefield*, Goldsmith's best-known writings are: "The Deserted Village," (1770); two delightful plays, *The Good-natur'd Man* (1768) and *She Stoops to Conquer* (1773); and the fine series of satiric "letters," *The Citizen of the World*, (1762).

Despite the popularity of some of the poems and plays during his lifetime, Goldsmith was never free of worry and debt. He died, ironically enough, of his own medical treatment, on April 4, 1774. Johnson's "Club" erected a monument to Goldsmith in Westminster Abbey.

Tristram Shandy

by

LAURENCE STERNE (1713–1768)

Main Characters

Tristram Shandy—The narrator and "hero" is an ill-starred
nonentity who is not even born until halfway through the
novel.
Walter Shandy—Tristram's father, fond of far-ranging philo-
sophical speculations on the subtlest points, but somewhat
divorced from reality.
Toby Shandy—Tristram's Uncle Toby, an old soldier and a
kindly gentleman who delights in recalling his past cam-
paigns.
Corporal Trim—Uncle Toby's loyal and innocent servant.
Mr. Yorick—An absurdly fanciful clergyman.
Dr. Slop—An ill-humored, inept quack doctor.
Widow Wadman—An amorous widow who lives near Shandy
Hall and hopes to entice Uncle Toby into marriage.

The Story

Tristram Shandy can always attribute the peculiarity of
his nature and the strange events of his life to the fact that,
when he was on the point of being conceived, his mother
asked his father, the eccentric, henpecked Walter Shandy,
whether he had not forgotten to wind the clock.

Immediately after Tristram's conception, which occurred sometime between the first Sunday and the first Monday of March, 1718, Tristram's father journeyed from Shandy Hall, the ancestral estate, to London, a trip his sciatica had hitherto prevented him from making. Both noteworthy occurrences can be verified in Mr. Shandy's meticulously kept diary.

The reason that Tristram was born in Shandy Hall, instead of in London, and delivered by a mere midwife, instead of a real doctor, is ascribed to the peculiar marriage settlement between the elder Shandys. According to its terms, Mrs. Shandy would be allowed to bear her child in London, but if she ever falsely persuaded her husband to take her to the capital, she surrendered this right and would have to settle for a home delivery. Since she has done this once, Mr. Shandy feels justified in sparing himself the expense of taking his wife on a second trip to London, although he enjoys going there by himself.

On the night Tristram is born, his father and his Uncle Toby are comfortably debating some complicated and endless issue before a cheerful fire. When Susannah, the maid, informs them of the impending birth, they send for a midwife and for Dr. Slop, a local quack practitioner who had once written a cheap pamphlet on the history of childbirth. Dr. Slop's chief function at local births is to allow the midwife to do the delivering while he charges a handsome fee for drinking the father's best wine.

Before either doctor or midwife can arrive, Walter Shandy and his brother have some fine conversations about their past life. Uncle Toby was an honorable soldier in his day, but during the Siege of Namur in 1695 he received a wound in an embarrassing place and left the army to retire to the country. His loyal servant, Corporal Trim, joined him and suggested an ideal occupation for the retired military man. Near Shandy Hall is a patch of lawn where Trim constructed a miniature battlefield. There Uncle Toby reconstructs his campaigns by means of toy fortifications, trenches, and soldiers.

His delight in this pastime is not, however, shared by his more philosophical brother, who constantly interrupts his long-winded tales of vanished military glory with equally long-winded philosophical speculations. Walter Shandy has theories about everything, and they are often highly ingenious, but they are never even remotely applicable to the problem at hand, and usually get bogged down in oceans of arcane facts and meaningless, if charming, lore. One such philosophical divertissement, begun while the brothers await the arrival of the midwife and Dr. Slop, concerns itself with the reasons for Mrs. Shandy's preference for a female rather than a male attendant at her delivery. Uncle Toby suggests it might just be female modesty, but this idea is too simple to suit Walter Shandy who goes into a long and incomprehensible philosophical harangue about the complex nature of women.

The talk is interrupted by the arrival of Dr. Slop. While Corporal Trim diverts the Shandy brothers with the reading of a long sermon, Dr. Slop goes about his work with typical ineptitude. Mistaking the infant's hip for his head, the doctor flattens Tristram's nose with his forceps. Another portion of Tristram's anatomy will receive an insult on a later occasion when, as a boy, Tristram relieves himself out of a window only to have the window come crashing down on him. These episodes, Tristram feels, with some justice, have blighted his life.

Finally, the lad is born, while Mr. Shandy reads the company his translation from a Latin treatise on noses by a German scholar named Hafen Slawkenbergius. (Both author and work are Sterne's inventions.) When Mr. Shandy hears of the nearly disastrous episode with the forceps, he fears for his child's safety. Learning that the baby is unusually sickly, he sends immediately for the local parson, Mr. Yorick, to baptize the infant before any further mishaps occur.

Hastening to dress for the event, Mr. Shandy sends Susannah on ahead to tell Yorick that he wants his son baptized "Trismegistus" in honor of his favorite philosopher. But Susannah finds the odd name difficult to remember, and by the time she conveys the request to Mr. Yorick, she has transformed the name into Tristram, which also happens to be the clergyman's first name. This coincidence thrills Mr. Yorick. The child is baptized accordingly, and by the time Mr. Shandy arrives, fully clothed at last, he is too late to change matters, although he thinks Tristram is the worst name in the world and can only bring bad luck. The only hope for this disaster-hounded child now is a proper education.

Tristram's boyhood is marred by one sad event—the death at Westminster School of his older brother, Bobby. Different members of the family react differently to the untimely tragedy: Mr. Shandy philosophizes about the nature of death; in her grief, Susannah finds joy in the thought that she will inherit all her mistress' dresses when Mrs. Shandy goes into mourning; and Corporal Trim symbolically drops his hat as if he himself had died and delivers a magnificent funeral oration on the spot.

The Shandy family's next problems concern the sort of tutor, if any, to get for Tristram and the age at which the boy will be ready to wear long trousers. But these practical considerations take second place to the tale of Uncle Toby's pursuit by the Widow Wadman, a buxom lady who lives near Shandy Hall. The gentle Uncle Toby bears up well under the widow's efforts to win his heart.

One day, however, the Widow Wadman, more anxious than ever to be married, asks Uncle Toby an embarrassing question: precisely where was he wounded? He assures her he will allow her to touch the actual place where he received his famous wound; he then produces a map of Namur and puts her trembling finger on the appropriate portion of the battle-field.

Corporal Trim, less naïve if just as good-hearted as Uncle Toby, has to point out to him that it is the spot on his person, not on the battlefield, that the Widow Wadman has in mind. When he is finally made to realize the awful truth, Uncle Toby beats a hasty retreat from any idea of marriage.

At the end of the novel, Tristram's mother asks, reasonably enough, "Lord, what is all this story about?"

"A Cock and a Bull," replies Yorick, "and one of the best of its kind I ever heard."

Critical Opinion

It is one of the glories of the English novel that at its very inception in the mid-eighteenth century a work should have appeared which mocked all its newborn conventions; which told its minuscule story backwards and at great length with absurd digressions; and which was, in fact, that very modern phenomenon, an anti-novel with an anti-hero, with impotence as one of its major themes.

It is no accident, then, that *Tristram Shandy* should have

exerted a profound influence on the fiction of James Joyce, for both Sterne and Joyce are irrepressible jokers who delight in exploding the possibilities of prose fiction into something very different from the ordinary novel—perhaps best called the comic epic in prose. By means of caricature, digressions, absurdly inflated language to describe the most mundane things, puns, and a panoply of wildly eccentric characters, Sterne makes glorious fun in *Tristram Shandy* of such a sober predecessor as Samuel Richardson, and even of the more worldly Fielding.

Beneath the practical jokes played on his fellow novelists and on his readers, however, Sterne has laid a very solid substratum which gives *Tristram Shandy*, for all its seeming chaos, a strength of form and theme that has made it endure long after most practical jokes are forgotten. This substratum consists of the very human story, told in loving, even sentimental detail, of the two immortal Shandy brothers—Walter and Toby—and their occasionally philosophical, occasionally ridiculous responses to the world around them. Both men are henpecked; Walter Shandy by his wife, Uncle Toby by the voracious Widow Wadman. Both men see the world conspiring against their pleasure and ease. And both refuse to submit to the pressures of the world.

Uncle Toby's "hobbyhorse," by means of which he escapes from a drab world, is his military past, which he and Corporal Trim never tire of discussing. It is one of the infinite number of paradoxes in the book that so gentle and considerate a man as Uncle Toby should have been a menace on the battlefield.

Totally unsympathetic to the military, and riding a "hobbyhorse" of his own, is Walter Shandy who escapes from the burdens of existence through a super-subtle and highly abstract philosophy that nobody else can understand. Occasionally, like lunatics in an asylum, the two brothers cooperate in each other's manias, and the resulting fun is both hilarious and heart-warming.

Underlying the extraordinary technical virtuosity of the novel are a complex and very modern philosophy of time (it takes the hero four books in which to be born) and a sentimentality about the sacredness of life and individuality that give emotional coherence to an otherwise seemingly slapdash effort of the imagination.

The Author

Laurence Sterne's early years were spent in the military environment that he was later to describe with such affectionate amusement in the career of Uncle Toby in *Tristram Shandy*. He was born in 1713, son of an ensign in an infantry regiment, at Clonmel in Ireland. Until his father's death, when Sterne was eighteen, the family moved constantly from garrison to garrison, taking time out, when the boy was ten, for him to go to grammar school at Halifax.

When his father died, Sterne was left penniless. Through the good offices of a cousin he was enabled to go to Cambridge where he made friends with one John Hall (later Hall-Stevenson), who often played host to Sterne in his bizarre home known as Crazy Castle.

In 1736 Sterne took his BA and was ordained a clergyman. Two years later he became vicar of Sutton-in-the-Forest, where he met and married Miss Elizabeth Lumley in 1741. Sterne's philandering with other women became notorious, however. In 1758 his wife became insane. In addition to his amorous escapades in the years preceding the writing of *Tristram Shandy*, Sterne was also involved in the rather weird goings-on at Crazy Castle. Sterne and others formed a group calling themselves the Demoniacks, which indulged in practical jokes and experiments in mock diabolism, all considered terribly shocking for a clergyman.

It is therefore not surprising that in 1759 Sterne left his vicarage and began the writing of *Tristram Shandy*. The first two volumes, published in 1760, made an immediate sensation in London literary society. Never had a book so eccentric and idiosyncratic as this been presented in the form of a novel, although there were obvious precursors in Burton's *Anatomy of Melancholy* and Rabelais' *Gargantua and Pantagruel*.

Sterne went to London to capitalize on this success, and by 1761 four more volumes of *Tristram Shandy* had appeared. Its success was somewhat dampened by the denunciations from several pulpits of its alleged "immorality." Dr. Johnson and Goldsmith, among others, found the novel repugnant on both moral and literary grounds.

In 1760 Sterne became curate at Coxwold. Two years

later he voyaged to France because of ill health. His amorous experiences there led to the writing of *A Sentimental Journey Through France and Italy* (1768). In 1767 Sterne parted permanently from his wife. It was the year of the appearance of the ninth and final volume of *Tristram Shandy* and of the third and fourth volumes of Sterne's *Sermons.* In 1768, heartbroken at having to part also from his daughter, Sterne died of pleurisy in his London lodgings, insolvent and disillusioned.

By the Same Author

A Sentimental Journey Through France and Italy: Written in 1768 as Sterne was facing death, this charming travel story is a sort of epilogue to the unfinished *Tristram Shandy.* The narrator this time is the Reverend Mr. Yorick who is a barely disguised portrait of Sterne himself. Written partly as an answer to Smollett's highly unsentimental *Travels in France and Italy* (1766), Sterne's slim book recounts various adventures, usually with complaisant chambermaids and other damsels, in a series of self-contained episodes. Less eccentric and more elegant in style than *Tristram Shandy, A Sentimental Journey* was designed, in Sterne's words, "to teach us to love the world and our fellow creatures better than we do."

Humphry Clinker

by

TOBIAS SMOLLETT (1721–1771)

Main Characters

Matthew Bramble—A middle-aged hypochondriac, basically amiable except when his delicate sensibilities are offended.

Tabitha Bramble—His man-hunting sister, a unique combination of stupidity, primitive shrewdness, and religious hypocrisy.

Lydia Melford—Bramble's niece, a romantic girl just out of boarding school.

Jerry Melford—Bramble's nephew and ward, a recent Oxford graduate.

Winifred Jenkins—Tabitha's muddle-minded handmaid whose misspellings and malapropisms are often hilarious.

Humphry Clinker—A simple-minded but loyal servant.

Lieutenant Obadiah Lismahago—An ungainly middle-aged Scotch lieutenant who had once been scalped by Indians.

Mr. Dennison—A country gentleman and college friend of Bramble's.

George Dennison—His son who, disguised as an actor named George Wilson, is in loving pursuit of Lydia Melford.

The Story

Squire Matthew Bramble is a basically kind, if disillusioned, man, whose temper is sorely tried by persistent attacks of gout. Although he has little faith in the honesty or intelligence of doctors, he decides to take their advice and visit Bath, where the waters are reputed to have healing qualities. Accordingly, he sets forth for that elegant city accompanied by his starchy maiden sister, Miss Tabitha Bramble (who hopes to catch a fine husband at the resort), and by Winifred Jenkins, Tabitha's maid-servant.

Also accompanying the Brambles on their expedition are Mr. Bramble's niece and nephew, Lydia and Jerry Melford, pleasant young people and wards of the old gentleman. Mr. Bramble hopes that the journey will make Lydia forget the strolling actor whom she fell in love with at boarding school. Jerry Melford hopes someday to find and fight a duel with the actor who has wronged him. But so far the opportunity has not presented itself.

On the way to Bath, the actor, who goes under the name of George Wilson, presents himself, in the disguise of a Jewish eyeglass peddler, to Mr. Bramble. He manages to disclose his true identity briefly to the love-smitten Lydia, but they are interrupted and Lydia asks Winifred Jenkins to follow her swain and find out his true identity. Winifred does so, but she is so muddle-headed that she forgets his real name before she has a chance to divulge it to Lydia. All she remembers is that the actor told her that he was a true gentleman who hoped someday to court Lydia in a more appropriate style.

When the group finally arrives at Bath, Tabitha sets out to find a husband, while her brother Matthew samples the supposedly miraculous waters and finds them merely filthy and ill-smelling.

Bramble's disillusionment with the waters and Lydia's patent unhappiness over her lost actor cause the party to leave Bath for London. En route to London, however, their coach is upset, and there is a fracas between Tabitha Bramble and the squire's servant over Tabitha's lapdog, which has bitten the servant's hand. At his sister's imperious command,

Bramble must dismiss not only his servant but the coachman as well who, Tabitha feels, was responsible for upsetting the carriage.

To replace the clumsy postillion, Matthew Bramble hires a homely, ragged, shirtless youth named Humphry Clinker. Since Clinker's condition shocks Miss Bramble, Squire Bramble gives him a guinea to buy some respectable clothes before he can assume his new duties.

In London, Squire Bramble discovers that Clinker is preaching Methodist sermons. This he regards as unseemly behavior in a servant. Tabitha and her maid, however, are entranced by the lad's religiosity, and they beg Matthew Bramble to permit him to continue his sermonizing.

When Clinker is arrested and jailed on a false charge of being a brigand (the charge is made by a professional informer, himself a former convict), his preaching impresses even the jailer, and he makes converts of some of his fellow prisoners. Squire Bramble manages to find the man who had been robbed and whose evidence clears Clinker of any guilt. Clinker is released and continues his highly successful preaching.

After visiting the famous Vauxhall Gardens, the family leaves London to journey north to Scotland. At Scarborough, Bramble hires a bathing machine—a small cart rolled down the beach to the water in which he can change his clothes in privacy. The squire plunges nude into the surf which turns out to be so cold that he cries out in shock. Hearing his master's cries, Humphry assumes he is drowning and plunges into the ocean to rescue him. He drags the nude squire to the shore where Bramble is profoundly embarrassed by the crowd of spectators that has gathered.

In Durham, the party meets a gaunt, middle-aged Scots lieutenant named Obadiah Lismahago. A sad-faced, lantern-jawed man, he entertains the Brambles with tales of his exploits among the North American Indians. The ex-army officer captivates Tabitha Bramble, and even her normally misanthropic brother enjoys the company of the tough, proud Lieutenant Lismahago. Meanwhile, Tabitha's simple-minded maid, Winifred Jenkins, finds herself falling in love with the loyal, mild-mannered Humphry Clinker.

Eventually the party reaches Edinburgh, where they are

royally entertained everywhere. But the squire realizes that his niece has still not forgotten her actor suitor, George Wilson, when she faints in the street at the sight of someone who looks like the missing man. Setting back toward England again, the party is rejoined by Lieutenant Lismahago, who once more becomes the object of Tabitha's amorous attentions. He helps Jerry Melford rescue the women when the coach is upset in a river, but the squire is trapped in the coach and is in danger of drowning until Humphry, by heroic effort, manages to free him and bring him to safety.

While resting at the local inn until the coach can be repaired, Bramble meets an old college acquaintance named Dennison, now a prosperous local gentleman farmer. Dennison addresses Bramble as Lloyd, a name that the squire once adopted for legal reasons for a short time. When Humphry Clinker hears the name, he becomes very excited and shows the squire certain papers he has always carried with him proving that he is Bramble's illegitimate offspring. Bramble welcomes him as his son and clarifies the matter before the whole group. Poor Winifred is afraid that Humphry will put on airs and refuse to have anything to do with her, now that he has been established as the squire's son. But Humphry remains simple and unspoiled.

Squire Bramble is again surprised when he learns that the mysterious actor who has been pursuing his niece, Lydia, is in reality his old friend Dennison's son. The young man had run away from home to become a strolling player only because his father wanted to force him into a marriage he detested. Because he knew Squire Bramble only as Lloyd, Dennison had not realized that the Lydia his son had spoken of so glowingly was the niece of his old friend.

Now, with all complications cleared up, Lydia and George are at last united. A triple wedding follows, for Tabitha manages to get Lieutenant Lismahago to propose to her, and Humphry Clinker proposes to Winifred Jenkins.

With all his friends and relatives married off, there is nothing further for Squire Bramble to do but to return to the comfort of his own home, Brambleton Hall, to argue with his doctor and reflect on his past adventures.

Critical Opinion

Humphry Clinker, Smollett's last and greatest novel, combines two fictional traditions with grace and mastery. The first is that of the epistolary novel—a novel told in the form of letters to and from the various characters involved. This was the form of what some critics consider the first English novel, Samuel Richardson's *Pamela* (1741), and the form also of Richardson's masterpiece, *Clarissa* (1748).

The use of letters as a narrative device occasionally proves awkward, but it can, nevertheless, be invaluable as a means of characterization. We learn, for instance, much about the character of the relatively minor figure Winifred Jenkins from the hilarious malapropisms strewn throughout her letters written during the Brambles' journeys. Even more important, however, is the ease with which different and sometimes opposite points of view can be explored through letters. Thus Matthew Bramble's clear-sighted, level-headed view of the snobbery and affectation of Bath society is cleverly juxtaposed against his sister Tabitha's all-accepting, unthinking attitude toward the same society. The middle-aged responses of Matthew Bramble stand in sharp contrast to the fresh, naïve responses of his niece Lydia. Thus the theme of youth versus middle age is subtly explored.

The other tradition employed in *Humphry Clinker*, dating back to Cervantes' *Don Quixote* and to Le Sage's *Gil Blas*, is that of the picaresque novel. This genre, which Smollett employed in *Roderick Random* and *Peregrine Pickle* as well, consists of a loosely strung-together series of adventures, usually taking place on the road and in local inns. The hero may be a *picaro*, or rogue, as in *Roderick Random*, but not necessarily so. During the course of his travels the central character meets a variety of characters representing all levels of society, some of whom enrich the story with their own life histories. The meeting with the Quixote-like Lieutenant Lismahago, who tells the group of his adventures fighting Indians in North America, is a typical picaresque episode.

Humphry Clinker presents a refinement of the picaresque adventure tale, for although the group travel all over England and Scotland, their adventures are credible and are not as

loosely strung together as usual. Thus Lieutenant Lismahago does not appear only to disappear and be forgotten. He
becomes an intrinsic part of the plot and marries Tabitha. The
adventures are woven into a more coherent and tightly knit
plot than in Smollett's earlier novels, and offer us a splendid
view of life in eighteenth-century England.

The Author

Although with typical hard-headed irony *Tobias Smollett*
referred to himself as "a lousy Scot," he was born into a very
good family in Dumbartonshire, in 1721. He attended Glas-
gow University, where he studied medicine, and soon drifted
to London in search of fame and fortune. Like his hero,
Roderick Random, Smollett soon found himself working as a
ship's surgeon aboard the *Chichester*, a vessel that took part
in the 1741 attack on Cartagena in the West Indies, a campaign challenging Spain's dominance in South America.

Smollett's stay in the navy provided him with invaluable
material for the novels he was later to write. The rough and
ready life on board ship supplied much of the material for
satirical treatment both in *Roderick Random* (1748) and
Peregrine Pickle (1751).

For a while Smollett settled in Jamaica, where he married.
In 1744 he returned to London with his wife to settle down
as a surgeon. In Chelsea he engaged in a great deal of hack
journalism and translating, writing an English version of *Don
Quixote* in 1755 and editing the *Critical Review* the next year.
An article in the *Critical Review* brought a libel suit against
Smollett for which he was briefly imprisoned in 1759.

Smollett's fresh attempt at periodical journalism, *The
Briton*, met with little success. Broken in health, he traveled
abroad to France and Italy in 1763, spending most of his
time at Nice. An inveterate traveler, he returned to England
two years later; and in 1766 he incorporated his continental
experiences into a typically humorous but ill-tempered travel
book, *Travels in France and Italy*, a work that so enraged
Laurence Sterne that he called its author "Smelfungus" and
tried to set the record straight with his own *A Sentimental
Journey Through France and Italy*.

Back in England, Smollett lived generally at the fashionable resort of Bath, scene of some of the finest escapades in what was to prove his last and greatest novel, *Humphry Clinker.* He left England on his last trip in 1768, living in Leghorn in northern Italy. Here he wrote *Humphry Clinker* which was published three months before his death in 1771.

Like Matthew Bramble, who is generally recognized as a somewhat idealized self-portrait, Smollett had few illusions about life. He was often quick-tempered but basically kind and of a philosophical cast of mind. His medical training made him hypersensitive to the wretched sanitary conditions of the England of his time. Much of his corrosive satire is directed at the physical rottenness and decay underlying the elegant pretensions of eighteenth-century society. Nevertheless, such is the vigor of Smollett's satire and the vividness with which he portrays the world around him that his books still hold and interest readers.

By the Same Author

Roderick Random: Smollett's first novel is a semi-autobiographical account of a young rogue determined to make his way in the world by fair means or foul. A vivid evocation of low life in the eighteenth century, *Roderick Random* traces its hero's course from a childhood marked by cruel treatment at school, through his apprenticeship to an apothecary, his nightmarish adventures as a sailor and later as a surgeon's mate, and his love affair with the beautiful Narcissa. Accompanied on many adventures by his faithful friend, Hugh Strap, he is finally able, after a stroke of good fortune, to marry Narcissa and settle on his ancestral estate in Scotland. Loosely strung together, the individual episodes of *Roderick Random* have a dash and vigor that were to become typical of Smollett. The work is most noteworthy for its scenes aboard various men-of-war, the first serious naval scenes in English fiction.

Peregrine Pickle: For his second novel Smollett chose an English rather than a Scottish hero, but in all essentials the formula is much as before. Pickle could be a blood-brother of Roderick Random. Secondary characters, however, are more richly realized than in the earlier book, the most memorable being a grand old eccentric, Commodore Hawser Trunnion, a man so in love with the sea that he has outfitted his country house to look like a battleship. Commodore Trunnion's riding gallantly off to his wedding to Pickle's Aunt Grizzle is one of the most richly comic scenes in eighteenth-century fiction.

Pride and Prejudice

by

JANE AUSTEN (1775–1817)

Main Characters

Mr. Bennet—The drily humorous father of five daughters, a gentleman with a modest estate in Hertfordshire.

Mrs. Bennet—His silly wife, a confirmed gossip and matchmaker.

Elizabeth Bennet—The Bennets' second daughter, witty and vivacious, and a keen observer of society.

Jane Bennet—Elizabeth's beautiful older sister, docile and gentle.

Charles Bingley—An amiable, wealthy young gentleman who rents Netherfield, an estate near the Bennets'.

Fitzwilliam Darcy—Bingley's immensely wealthy, proud friend.

George Wickham—A dashing, dissolute young officer.

Caroline Bingley—Bingley's younger sister, who wants to marry Darcy.

The Reverend William Collins—A remarkable combination of conceit and fatuity, whose patroness is the Lady Catherine de Bourgh.

Charlotte Lucas—A plain young woman, Elizabeth's friend.

Lady Catherine de Bourgh—Darcy's arrogant aunt, who exacts complete, unswerving subservience from everyone.

The Story

When Mr. Bingley, a rich young bachelor, rents Netherfield Park, one of the neighboring estates, excitement stirs in the Bennet family, which includes five marriageable daughters. The flighty Mrs. Bennet immediately begins plotting which daughter to marry off to the unsuspecting Bingley, but her long-suffering husband suggests that Mr. Bingley might want some choice in the matter. Before long Mr. Bennet is persuaded by his wife to pay a formal call at Netherfield Park.

The Bennet daughters meet Mr. Bingley at the Meryton Ball. Also in attendance is Mr. Bingley's aristocratic friend, Fitzwilliam Darcy, who turns up his nose at the vulgarity of Mrs. Bennet and snubs her daughters. Elizabeth Bennet, the liveliest and most intelligent of the Bennet girls, overhears the newcomer making condescending remarks about the local provincial society. When he refuses to be introduced to her, Elizabeth Bennet becomes instantly prejudiced against him, despite his good looks and great wealth.

More successful at the ball are the amiable Mr. Bingley and Elizabeth's lovely, good-natured older sister, Jane, to whom Elizabeth is closely attached. Soon after, Bingley and his sisters become friends with Jane Bennet, and the romance between Bingley and Jane seems to flourish. Eventually Darcy unbends a bit toward Elizabeth, and the two engage in ironic banter.

One day while visiting the Bingleys in the rain, Jane comes down with a bad cold and is compelled to stay at Netherfield Park. Elizabeth walks three miles through the mud to visit and nurse her sister. Her disheveled appearance when she arrives is meat for Caroline's gossip, but Mrs. Bennet sees the episode as a great opportunity to cement relations between Jane and Bingley. While Elizabeth is nursing her sister, Darcy pays her more attention, and Caroline's jealousy rages.

Bingley's sister Caroline is interested in Darcy herself. She tries unsuccessfully to poison his mind against Elizabeth. A more serious obstacle to the romance is Darcy's distaste for Elizabeth's vulgar, scheming mother and for the younger Bennet girls: flighty, officer-crazy Lydia and Kitty, and dull, plain Mary.

Meanwhile the Reverend William Collins, a cousin of the Bennets, who is in line to inherit Mr. Bennet's estate, comes to visit. The supremely conceited Mr. Collins talks constantly about his patroness, the rich and arrogant Lady Catherine de Bourgh, an aunt of Darcy's. Since she has urged him to marry (and her word is his command), he proposes to Elizabeth in a ludicrously pompous manner. She rejects him immediately, displeasing her mother but immensely satisfying her father who is fonder of her than of his other daughters.

Unabashed by his rejection, Mr. Collins proposes again, but finally concedes defeat. Immediately after, he becomes engaged to a friend of Elizabeth's, the placid, unimaginative Charlotte Lucas.

One of Darcy's acquaintances is a dashing young officer, George Wickham, who poisons Elizabeth's mind against Darcy by telling her that Darcy is a wicked, cold-hearted man who has refused to carry out the wishes of his father's will, cheating Wickham out of a legacy. Fearing to meet Darcy face to face, Wickham stays away from a ball which he knows Darcy will attend. Misinterpreting Wickham's motives, Elizabeth becomes increasingly suspicious of Darcy.

Shortly after the ball, Bingley and his sisters suddenly leave Netherfield for London. Elizabeth is convinced that Bingley's sisters are trying to keep him from marrying Jane whom they consider beneath him. Jane accepts the break with outward composure, but soon visits her aunt, Mrs. Gardiner, in London, hoping to see Bingley there by chance. When Elizabeth joins Jane in London, she learns that Bingley has never called on Jane. Elizabeth believes that Darcy has deliberately kept Jane's presence in the city from Bingley.

In March, Elizabeth visits her friend Charlotte Lucas, now married to Mr. Collins, in Kent. She realizes with a sudden wave of sympathy that Charlotte, a rather homely girl of advancing years, married Mr. Collins out of necessity, fearing a lonely and poverty-stricken life as an old maid.

While in Kent, Elizabeth again meets Darcy who is visiting his aunt, Lady Catherine de Bourgh. Again, Darcy is attracted to Elizabeth. He proposes to her in so haughty a manner that she rejects him and upbraids him for what she considers his mistreatment of her sister and of the unfortunate Wickham. Darcy listens to her accusations in silence. The next day he writes her a letter admitting that he has tried to keep

Bingley from Jane because he considers the Bennet family
beneath his friend's attentions. He strongly denies having
wronged Wickham, however, and demolishes the officer's
claim that he has been cheated out of an inheritance. Furthermore, he informs Elizabeth, Wickham had been carrying on
an intrigue with Darcy's sister Georgiana.

Despite its condescension toward the Bennet family, the
letter begins to allay Elizabeth's prejudice against Darcy.
Under no illusions about her mother and younger sisters,
Elizabeth begins to see Darcy's inherently honest character.
Her new impression of him is strengthened by the evidence
of an old Darcy family retainer who has nothing but good to
say of Darcy. Elizabeth again meets Darcy while she is
traveling with her intelligent and fashionable uncle and aunt.

Earlier Lydia has insisted, over Elizabeth's objections, on
going to Brighton, where Wickham's regiment is now stationed.
Before long, Elizabeth is shocked by a letter from Jane informing her that Lydia has run off with Wickham. Elizabeth
tells Darcy what has happened and returns home, full of
anxiety for her irresponsible younger sister.

To add to Elizabeth's woes, she now feels that Darcy, whom
she has begun to love, will have nothing to do with her, for
Lydia's behavior confirms all he has ever said about the com-
monness of the Bennet family. To Elizabeth's surprise, however, Darcy, who is now deeply in love with her, has gone off
secretly to London, where he finds Lydia and Wickham, pays
Wickham's many debts, and gives him £1,000 with which
to marry Lydia.

Mr. Bennet had also gone in search of the couple but has
returned from London without success. When Lydia returns
home, she tells Elizabeth that Darcy had attended her
wedding. Elizabeth's suspicions of Darcy's part in the affair
are confirmed by a letter from her aunt, Mrs. Gardiner, whom
Darcy had sworn to secrecy.

After Lydia and Wickham leave, Mr. Bingley returns to
Netherfield Park, accompanied by Darcy. Bingley soon becomes engaged to Jane, much to the Bennets' satisfaction.

The arrogant Lady Catherine de Bourgh descends on Long-
bourn, furious because of a rumor that Elizabeth and Darcy
have become engaged. (Lady Catherine wished Darcy to
marry her own daughter, a pathetically listless and un-

attractive girl.) Haughtily she demands that Elizabeth give up Darcy. Elizabeth, however, is more than adequate to the challenge. Without losing her temper, she coolly tells Lady Catherine to mind her own business. When Lady Catherine tells Darcy that Elizabeth refuses to give him up, Darcy begins to hope that Elizabeth returns his love.

Thus encouraged, Darcy again proposes to Elizabeth, this time with proper humility, and is happily accepted. Mrs. Bennet, having married off three of her daughters, is filled with joy. Mr. Bennet philosophically awaits any further suitors who may come along.

Critical Opinion

"I write about Love and Money; what else is there to write about?" Jane Austen once remarked. *Pride and Prejudice* is a perfect example of a social comedy based on the interaction of love and money: the class differences between Darcy, the Bingleys, and the Bennets shaping the love affairs between Bingley and Jane, Darcy and Elizabeth. Influencing these differences is the emergence of the middle class as a social force in England; hitherto a match between a man like Darcy and the bourgeois Elizabeth would have been a rarity. Even at the time in which the story takes place, many barriers must be hurdled before the couple are happily matched.

The conflict that gives the novel its title centers around Darcy's coldly aristocratic pride and Elizabeth's instinctive feminine prejudice against a man who has snubbed her at a dance. Before it is resolved, this conflict is the basis for the exquisite play of wit between hero and heroine, reminiscent of the ironic banter between Beatrice and Benedick in Shakespeare's *Much Ado About Nothing*.

Despite its surface wit and lightness, *Pride and Prejudice* is not without its underlying pathos. It stems largely from Jane's acceptance of Bingley's supposed indifference, and from the plight of Elizabeth's friend, Charlotte Lucas, a symbol of any girl on the brink of spinsterhood who makes the best of a bad bargain in choosing a spouse. Although Elizabeth deftly escapes from the attentions of Mr. Collins, we are haunted, after putting down the book, by the thought of the life to which the less fortunate Charlotte has consigned

herself. The pathos of her condition is all the more moving for
the tact with which Jane Austen treats it.

The uniqueness of Jane Austen's art lies in the way she
plumbs such emotional depths within the extremely circumscribed life she knows. Her world consists of visits to
country houses, teas, dances, and other minor social functions.
She never describes any aspect of life she has not personally
witnessed, and for that reason there is never a scene in any
of her novels in which two men are together without a woman.
Within these limitations, however, Jane Austen is matchless in
her analysis of the pressures of society, especially on young
people in love. Sympathizing equally with the needs of the
individual and the often conflicting demands of social
decorum, she finds comedy in the resulting stresses.

The Author

Jane Austen was born on December 16, 1775, in the small
rural rectory of Steventon, in Hampshire, where her father
was a clergyman. The family was large, consisting of six boys
and another girl, Jane's beloved sister Cassandra. Although
the Austens were an educated family, they were never particularly well off. Like most girls of her time, Jane was educated at home. Her matchless ear for dialogue first revealed
itself when, at fourteen, she began writing little plays for
home theatricals. As a girl, she also wrote satirical burlesques
and nonsense stories intended solely to give her family pleasure. These were filled with references to friends and neighbors
which only the Austens could understand.

The family seems to have been a happy one; and, more
important for the future novelist, the Austens were, in Jane's
words, "great novel-readers and not ashamed of being so."

When her father retired in 1801, the Austens moved to the
then fashionable seaside resort of Bath where Jane's social
perspective broadened. Five years before the move, however,
Jane had written the first draft of *Pride and Prejudice,* then
entitled *First Impressions.* Undiscouraged by her failure to get
it published, she continued with her writing, producing in
1797 first drafts of what were later to be *Sense and Sensibility*
and *Northanger Abbey.*

The years spent in Bath were more productive of observations of society to be used in later books than of novels themselves. When Mr. Austen died, the family moved to Southampton where they stayed from 1806 to 1809, but Jane seems to have found the town uncongenial. It was only when the Austens moved to Chawton, a town as small as Steventon, that Jane felt ready to continue with her writing. She began *Mansfield Park,* her most ambitious novel, in 1811; *Emma* in 1814, and what was to prove her last novel, the unusually romantic *Persuasion,* in 1815.

Thus, Jane Austen's six major novels fall into two groups separated by about a decade of silence. Discouraged by the neglect of publishers and public, Jane Austen gave her last novels a graver and more serious tone than the first three. Indeed, *Mansfield Park* and *Persuasion* have little of the ebullience and high spirits of her earlier books.

Jane Austen's outward life was singularly free of conflict. Even the Napoleonic Wars, which raged through Europe during her lifetime, seem to have had little effect on her although two of her brothers were in the Royal Navy. She died on July 18, 1817, generally unrecognized for the perceptive novelist she was.

By the Same Author

Sense and Sensibility: This early novel announces most of the major themes with which Jane Austen was to be concerned during her writing life. It describes in loving detail two sisters of opposite character: Elinor, the paragon of good common sense, and Marianne, a girl filled with romantic "sensibility," or hypersensitivity. Both experience unhappy love affairs: Elinor with Edward Ferrars, who is in the clutches of Lucy Zouche, ask for directions to Rotherwood, the home of Cedric a dashing scoundrel, John Willoughby. Ferrars ultimately comes back to Elinor, while Marianne, like Lydia in *Pride and Prejudice,* nearly ruins her reputation by following her caddish lover to London. She ultimately abandons her romantic notions and marries an upright, if less dashing, middle-aged man.

Emma: Emma is a richly comic exploration of class distinctions and courtship customs in a small English village. Emma Woodhouse, a vigorous, restless girl, takes under her

wing the rather commonplace Harriet Smith, hoping to educate her in the ways of the world and enable her to attract
the local rector as a mate. Emma's well-intentioned interfer-
ence in her friends' affairs, however, nearly goes awry. But
when Harriet mistakenly imagines that John Knightly is in
love with her, Emma, who had always regarded Mr. Knightly
as a friend, realizes that she is in love with him herself. The
comedy of errors comes to a close when Knightly proposes
to Emma and Harriet marries a farmer. *Emma* is a richer and
more complex novel than *Pride and Prejudice*, but has less
of the earlier novel's vivacity.

The Nineteenth Century

Ivanhoe

by

SIR WALTER SCOTT (1771–1832)

Main Characters

Cedric the Saxon—Lord of Rotherwood Grange, bitterly opposed to the Normans.
Rowena—Cedric's lovely niece and ward.
Athelstane of Coningsburgh—Rowena's nobly born Saxon fiancé.
Wilfred of Ivanhoe—Cedric's son, disinherited for following the Norman King, Richard the Lion Hearted, on the Crusades.
Sir Brian de Bois-Guilbert—The haughty commander of the Norman Order of Knights Templar.
Reginald Front de Boeuf—A tyrannical Norman knight.
Lucas de Beaumanoir—Grand master of the Knights Templar.
Isaac of York—A persecuted Jewish moneylender.

Rebecca—Isaac's beautiful, strong-willed daughter.

King Richard I—Called Richard the Lion Hearted for his valor during the Crusades, absent from England for many years.

Prince John—Richard's evil, ambitious brother, Regent of England in Richard's absence.

Gurth—An honest Saxon swineherd.

Wamba—Gurth's companion, a court jester.

The Story

Gurth, the swineherd, and Wamba, the court jester, are talking late one evening in the forest when Prior Aymer of Jorvaux and the arrogant Sir Brian de Bois-Guilbert, commander of the Order of Knights Templar, who are on their way with their retinue to the royal tournament at Ashby de la Zouche, ask for directions to Rotherwood, the home of Cedric the Saxon, where they hope to get shelter for the night. The Saxon serfs deliberately mislead the hated Normans, but a pilgrim returning from the Crusades, also headed for Rotherwood, guides them there. Cedric and his retainers are already seated at the great wooden table when the Normans arrive.

Although Cedric has not yet reconciled himself to the Norman conquest of England, he obeys the laws of hospitality and offers food and shelter to the visitors. When Cedric's lovely niece and ward, the lady Rowena, enters, Brian de Bois-Guilbert stares lustfully at her. Rowena, descended from the Saxon royal family and engaged to be married to Athelstane of Coningsburgh, a descendant of King Alfred, veils her face.

A dispute arises at the table over who served the Crusade most worthily—Norman or Saxon. When Bois-Guilbert boasts of his exploits, he is challenged by the pilgrim, who is actually Ivanhoe, son of Cedric, disinherited for following the Norman King Richard. Even his father is unaware that Ivanhoe has secretly returned to England and is sitting at his table. Bois-Guilbert admits that Ivanhoe is a valorous fighter but boasts that he would not fear meeting him again in hand-to-hand combat.

Also seeking shelter that night at Rotherwood is Isaac of York, an old Jewish moneylender. Isaac is warned by Ivanhoe, who has overheard a whispered conversation between Bois-Guilbert and his retainers, that the Knight Templar is after his moneybag. Early the next morning, Ivanhoe helps the Jew slip out of the house. In gratitude, Isaac equips Ivanhoe with horse and armor for the coming tournament at Ashby de la Zouche.

The tournament is attended by Prince John, Richard the Lion Hearted's evil brother, who is trying to usurp the throne while Richard is away at the Crusades. Prince John announces to the colorful throng that the winner of the joust will be allowed to name the Queen of Love and Beauty, and the passage of arms begins.

First, five Normans led by Bois-Guilbert take on all challengers, and are successful. Then a new champion enters, whose armor displays the motto, "Desdichado," or disinherited. It is, of course, Ivanhoe in still another disguise, and he challenges and defeats Bois-Guilbert and the other Norman knights. This wins him the privilege of naming the Queen of Love and Beauty who will preside over the next day's tourneys. He names Rowena, and then rides off before he can be properly acclaimed by the crowd.

The next day's combat is a free-for-all between two groups of fifty knights each, one led by Ivanhoe, the disinherited knight, and the other by Bois-Guilbert. Ivanhoe, set upon by three combatants, is hard pressed until a knight in black armor, called the Black Sluggard by the crowd because he had previously refrained from combat, comes to Ivanhoe's aid. Together they rout their opponents, even Bois-Guilbert, whose horse has been wounded.

When Ivanhoe removes his helmet to receive the prize from Rowena, she cries out in recognition. As he kisses Rowena's hand, he faints from the wounds he has received in combat. Rebecca, Isaac of York's beautiful black-haired daughter, suggests that they bring Ivanhoe home to nurse him back to health. The Black Knight rides away secretly, but Isaac, Rebecca, and Ivanhoe are joined by Athelstane and Cedric the Saxon, still unaware of his son's identity.

The party is soon waylaid, however, by Bois-Guilbert and his fellow knights, Maurice de Bracy and Reginald Front de Boeuf, and are carried off to Front de Boeuf's castle, Torquilstone. De Bracy covets Rowena because, even though she is a Saxon, she is of royal blood. Bois-Guilbert wants the lovely Rebecca, and Front de Boeuf hopes to ransom the party to get money from Isaac and his moneylender friends. Separating father from daughter, Bois-Guilbert tries to persuade Rebecca to become a Christian so they can marry. She scornfully rejects him.

Unknown to the Norman captors, Gurth, the swineherd, has rallied a group of Saxon yeomen and outlaws, including Robin Hood and his band. Led by the Black Knight, who is really Richard the Lion Hearted in disguise, the Saxons storm Torquilstone and set it on fire. The Black Knight succeeds in rescuing Ivanhoe and Rowena, but Bois-Guilbert abducts Rebecca, and Isaac prepares to ransom his daughter. In fighting, Athelstane tries to kill Bois-Guilbert with a mace, but is himself felled by a sword blow and appears to be dead. De Bracy, who escapes the flames, hastens to tell Prince John that the Black Knight is his brother, Richard Plantagenet, who knows of John's usurpation of the throne and has returned secretly to England to wrest it back from him. John determines to put Richard in prison.

Isaac goes to Lucas de Beaumanoir, the grand master of the Knights Templar, to beg that Rebecca be returned to him. Bois-Guilbert, to save his pride, claims that Rebecca is a witch who put a spell on him which he could not resist. Lucas condemns the girl to be burned at the stake, but when Rebecca demands a champion to defend her, as is the custom, de Beaumanoir agrees.

Tied to the stake, Rebecca awaits her champion. After the heralds summon him three times, Ivanhoe rides in, announcing himself as Rebecca's defender. Bois-Guilbert, champion for the Knights of Templar, at first declines to fight with the wounded Ivanhoe, but Ivanhoe insists, and the two lock in mortal combat. Following a desperate struggle, during which Ivanhoe is unhorsed, Bois-Guilbert falls dead of a stroke. Rebecca is released. She and her father will journey to Spain, hoping there to find refuge from persecution.

Meanwhile, grateful for his rescue from the burning Torquilstone, Cedric has invited the Black Knight to Rotherwood. Richard replies that he will accept but "will ask such a boon as will put even thy generosity to the test." Then, at a funeral banquet for the fallen Athelstane, the Black Knight reveals himself to Cedric as King Richard and asks his boon: that Cedric forgive Ivanhoe. Ivanhoe kneels to his father, and the old man relents. He knows that Ivanhoe hopes to marry Rowena but decrees that a two-year period of mourning for her fiancé, Athelstane, must elapse before he can claim her hand.

Just then, to everyone's surprise, Athelstane himself enters, pale and ghostly. He tells them that he was only stunned by the flat of Bois-Guilbert's sword, and recovered his senses when he was lying in an open coffin in a chapel. Admitting that Rowena loves Ivanhoe more than him, he offers her to the knight.

The Black Knight comes to the Knights Templar and accuses them of plotting against the lawful sovereign of England. He proclaims himself king again, and the royal flag flies once more over the Temple. Robin Hood and his outlaws affirm their loyalty to Richard who attends the wedding of Ivanhoe and Rowena.

Both Norman and Saxon nobles attend the ceremony. Now that Richard has been restored to his throne and his friend Ivanhoe to his rightful heritage, there is hope that peace will once again reign in divided England.

Critical Opinion

Ivanhoe was written during a brief respite from the ill health that plagued Scott in 1819. He decided to change the background if not the formula of his fiction and venture for the first time away from purely Scottish material. The result, although the most popular of Scott's novels, is not among his best.

For his departure from Scotland as a locale, Scott picked two favorites of English history and legend: King Richard the Lion Hearted and Robin Hood, weaving them into a complicated tale of chivalric honor and rivalry. Even bitter enemies like Ivanhoe and Brian de Bois-Guilbert address one another in high-flown chivalric rhetoric and fight strictly according to the laws of feudal combat. Athelstane the Saxon nobly gives Rowena over to his rival, Ivanhoe, when he sees she is really in love with him. Cedric the Saxon, for all his hatred of Normans, extends a courteous welcome to Bois-Guilbert in his home. All actions in *Ivanhoe* spring from a feudal code of honor which was to Scott the most important thing in life and which he punctiliously obeyed centuries after the death of feudalism.

The faults of *Ivanhoe* are legion. The plot is overcomplicated, depending too heavily on coincidence to please sophisticated modern tastes. The characters are without exception one dimensional, and they speak in a stilted, lofty, unnatural rhetoric that often makes for tedious reading. Too, Scott cannot resist frequent pedantic asides on twelfth-century English customs.

How then has the book retained its popularity? The answer is that Scott is a master of the conventions of adventure fiction and employs all its devices to great effect in *Ivanhoe*. Suspense is sustained by not one but *two* heroes in disguise (Ivanhoe and Richard I). The many scenes of high action and adventure (the prolonged tournament at Ashby, the storming of Torquilstone, and the rescuing of Rebecca from the stake) go far to redeem the novel from its pretentious style.

Above all, Scott had sufficient humanity to make even characters outside the aristocracy—Isaac and Rebecca, Gurth and Wamba—vivid and alive.

The Author

Sir Walter Scott was born in Edinburgh on August 15, 1771. He attended Edinburgh High School and University, and was called to the bar in 1792. His first great love, however, was folklore and ballads. In 1802–1803 he published a three-volume collection of *Minstrely of the Scottish Border*. Scott made his debut with romantic poetry strongly colored by legend and folk strains. The first of these poems, *The Lay of the Last Minstrel* (1805), was an immediate success, which Scott followed with *Marmion* (1808) and *The Lady of the Lake* (1810).

After the appearance of Byron's *Childe Harold* in 1812, which was a serious new rival in romantic narrative verse, Scott turned his attention to the novel, beginning his prolific career with *Waverley* in 1814. Because the fiction of the time was held in such low esteem, Scott allowed his novels to appear anonymously. He did not acknowledge their authorship until 1827, seven years after he was made a baronet.

Scott's passion for Scottish folklore formed the basis for his first novels, all of which deal with historic events from the Scottish past about which Scott made himself an authority. *Waverley* was followed by *Guy Mannering* (1815), *Old Mortality* (1816), and *The Heart of Midlothian* (1818), considered by most critics the finest of the Waverley novels.

It was not until *Ivanhoe*, in 1819, that Scott turned to other than Scottish material for his fiction; but despite the popular success of that novel, and of *Quentin Durward* (1823), which has a French historical background, it is the Waverley or Scottish novels that are considered his finest artistic accomplishments.

In 1812, Scott's love of the antique and his aristocratic pride inspired him to buy some farmland on the Tweed River and build Abbotsford, a great gothic castle. An ill-advised publishing venture and the general economic depression in England plunged Scott into financial disaster. In 1826, he found himself £130,000 in debt.

A less honorable man might have evaded his creditors, but Scott met with them and worked out a plan for repayment that ultimately hastened his death. He had always been a facile writer, but writing now at a superhuman pace (in two years he was able to pay back £40,000), Scott exhausted himself. The pace told not only on his constitution but on the quality of his work, for the later novels are slapdash and lack the credibility and high romantic spirit of the earlier ones. Nevertheless they remained popular with readers, and Scott managed to pay all his creditors. Traveling to Italy to regain his health, Scott was soon brought back to Abbotsford where he died September 21, 1832.

By the Same Author

Quentin Durward: Like *Ivanhoe*, *Quentin Durward* is not one of the Waverley novels, although its hero is a young Scot come to France in the era of Louis XI to make his fortune. He gets embroiled in treacherous court politics and succeeds in rescuing the beautiful Countess Isabelle de Croye from an attempted kidnapping by the villainous William de la Marck. After a series of harrowing adventures involving plots and counterplots, Quentin and Isabelle finally marry.

The Heart of Midlothian: Generally considered the finest of the Waverley novels, *The Heart of Midlothian,* based on a real event, is set in the city jail of Edinburgh where Effie Deans is imprisoned on charges of murdering her illegitimate infant. Although her half sister, Jeanie, is too honorable to tell the white lie that will rescue Effie, she goes to no end of trouble to win an acquittal for her. Free from the over-plotting and confusing number of characters that slow down most of Scott's novels, *The Heart of Midlothian* is unique in its psychological study of Jeanie Deans. A woman torn between love for her sister and a rigid sense of honor, she is probably the finest single character in Scott's fiction.

The Last Days of Pompeii

by

EDWARD BULWER-LYTTON (1805–1873)

Main Characters

Glaucus—A rich young Athenian living in Pompeii.

Clodius—Foppish and selfish. A Roman friend of Glaucus, he lives for pleasure and gambling.

Arbaces—A mysterious, evil Egyptian of great wealth, famous in Pompeii for his occult powers.

Ione—Arbaces' beautiful Neapolitan ward.

Apaecides—Ione's troubled brother, brought up in the Egyptian priesthood, but a skeptic about the cult of Isis.

Olinthus—A zealous convert to the new religion of Christianity.

Nydia—A blind young slave girl who sings and sells flowers for a living.

Diomed—One of the vulgar rich of Pompeii, who gives lavish banquets to achieve status with the aristocrats.

Julia—Diomed's pretty, scheming daughter.

The Story

In A.D. 79 the walled city of Pompeii on the Bay of Naples is a luxurious resort for the aristocrats of the Roman Empire. Two of these spoiled young men are Glaucus, an Athenian by birth, and his friend Clodius, a Roman dandy and gambler.

71

Strolling one day toward the fashionable baths, Glaucus tells Clodius of a hauntingly beautiful Greek girl he saw some months before in the Temple of Minerva in Naples, but whom he has since been unable to find.

As they chat lightly about love, the pair pass Nydia, a blind but appealing flower seller. She comes from Thessaly, a region of Greece noted for its witchcraft. Glaucus takes a friendly interest in her.

The young men also meet Arbaces, the powerful priest of Isis, whose vast wealth and magic powers are known and feared by all Pompeii. Unknown to Glaucus, Arbaces is the guardian of Ione, the girl Glaucus saw in the temple, and of her brother, Apaecides, whom Arbaces is training for the Egyptian priesthood with the help of the mercenary priest Calenus.

Glaucus soon meets Ione again at a fashionable party and declares his love, unaware that Arbaces desires the girl for himself. At the same time, Nydia, the slave of the gross and unfeeling innkeeper Burbo, finds herself falling in love with Glaucus who is far above her station in life.

One day Glaucus and Clodius stop at Burbo's wine shop in order to look over the gladiators drinking there. Clodius, an inveterate gambler, wishes to check on the prowess and stamina of the men he will bet on in the gladiatorial combats. One of the few gladiators not yet completely bestialized is Lydon, a youth who hopes to earn enough in combat to buy the freedom of his slave father, Medon. Clodius, however, decides to bet against him because he is young and inexperienced.

While the young men are in the tavern, they hear the cries of Nydia, who is being mercilessly beaten by Burbo's wife. Glaucus buys the slave girl on the spot as a gift for his beloved Ione, but his act of mercy only intensifies Nydia's love for him. Unaware of her love, Glaucus sends the girl to Ione with a letter declaring his passion for Ione and pleading with her not to listen to Arbaces' slanders against him.

Ione returns his love, but is enticed by Arbaces into his palace where with a show of magic the priest tries to force her to marry him. Warned by Nydia, Glaucus and Apaecides rush into the palace just in time to save Ione from rape. Glaucus engages Arbaces in combat. The priest is about to kill Glaucus when an earthquake shakes the palace to its foundations and topples a statue of Isis on Arbaces' head. Assuming that Arbaces is dead, the two young men escape with Ione.

After the earthquake, the people of Pompeii resume their normal lives, heedless of the great volcano, Mount Vesuvius, looming over them. Apaecides is now disillusioned with his guardian and loathes the rites of Isis in which he is being instructed by Calenus. He falls under the influence of the teaching of Olinthus, the humble, eloquent Nazarene who is trying to convert Pompeii to the new religion of Christianity before all its people are engulfed by their sins. Gradually Apaecides becomes converted, while the love of Glaucus and Ione matures.

But Arbaces, who was not killed in the earthquake, but merely stunned, vows revenge on his lovely ward and the Athenian who has stolen her from him. His opportunity comes at a party being given for eighteen select guests by a wealthy parvenu, Diomed. Diomed's daughter Julia, who is in love with Glaucus, comes to the Egyptian's palace a few days before the banquet for a love philter that will win Glaucus away from Ione.

Arbaces takes her to a witch's hovel at the foot of Vesuvius, where he procures a magic draught to drive Glaucus insâne. Julia plans to give it to him at her father's dinner, but Nydia hears of the potion and, hoping it will make Glaucus love her, steals it from Julia and gives it to Glaucus when he returns home from the party.

The potion drives Glaucus mad, and he rushes from his house to a cemetery where by chance Arbaces and Apaecides are quarreling over the youth's conversion from Isis to Christianity. Arbaces kills Apaecides and puts the blame on Glaucus who, in his madness, cannot defend himself.

Arbaces then stirs up the mob against the Athenian, claiming he killed Apaecides when the young priest tried to intervene in his affairs with Ione. Glaucus is arrested with Olinthus, the Christian zealot who has tried to defend him. A lion and a tiger have just been brought to Pompeii, and the crowd looks forward avidly to seeing the two prisoners fed to the beasts.

After Apaecides' funeral, Ione tries to save her lover, convinced he is innocent. But Arbaces imprisons her in his

palace, along with Calenus, who was an eyewitness to the
actual killing. When Calenus tries to blackmail the Egyptian,
Arbaces flings him into a dungeon to starve to death.

Nydia, who knows the guilty secrets of his dungeons, is imprisoned, but she bribes her guard to take a letter to Sallust, a
powerful friend of Glaucus, informing him of the truth. Sallust
is in a drunken stupor when the letter arrives and cannot read
it till the morning when the prisoners are to be put to death in
the arena.

On the last day of Pompeii a throng has gathered to watch
the gladiatorial combats. The bloodthirsty mob is indifferent
to the preliminaries, for the main event of the day is to be the
slaughter of Glaucus by the lion and Olinthus by the tiger.
Young Lydon, outmatched, dies horribly, and Clodius wins his
bet while the Christian father mourns for his son.

After this preliminary bloodshed, the lion, who has been
starved for days, is let loose in the arena. Glaucus is given
only a knife to defend himself. Miraculously, the lion refuses
to attack him, slinking back to its cage.

At this moment news comes from Sallust, who has finally
read Nydia's letter, that Glaucus is innocent and the murderer
of Apaecides is Arbaces. The mob, furious at being cheated
out of a spectacle, demands that the Egyptian take Glaucus'
place in the arena. Just as this is about to happen, however,
all Pompeii is overwhelmed by the great eruption of Vesuvius.

As smoke and ashes billow down upon them, thousands
flee the arena, desperately seeking safety in the streets which
are rapidly filling with molten lava. The weak are crushed
in the panic. Calenus, set free by Nydia in order to be a
witness against Arbaces, is killed by the sulfurous smoke as
he tries to loot Arbaces' palace. Julia, Diomed, and a group
of his friends take shelter in his capacious wine cellar, but to
no avail.

Because she is accustomed to finding her way in the dark,
the blind Nydia is able to lead Glaucus and Ione through
the pitch-black streets of Pompeii toward the waterfront.
Eventually they reach a small boat and escape to safety while
Arbaces, in hot pursuit, is killed by a second, even greater
earthquake.

By nightfall the eruption begins to subside. Asleep in their
boat, Glaucus and Ione do not notice that Nydia, despairing

of ever winning the handsome Athenian, has jumped overboard into the sea.

Ten years after the mighty eruption that destroyed the
sinful, pleasure-loving city, Glaucus and Ione, now married
and living in Athens, have become converts to Christianity
which they feel offers them a better life than the one they
knew in Pompeii.

Critical Opinion

While passing through Milan on his trip to Italy, Bulwer-
Lytton saw a painting of the destruction of Pompeii that
inspired him, he said, to reconstruct that fabled city at the
height of its glory as a pleasure resort for decadent Romans.
The basic drama of his book was to be the contrast between
the gay, heedless lives of the Pompeians and their hideous
deaths in the eruption of Vesuvius. Another drama would
emerge from the pagan sensuality of the public baths and the
pagan cruelty of the arena contrasted with the simple, lofty
devoutness of the persecuted early Christians.

Unfortunately, the grand moral drama of Good versus
Evil in Bulwer-Lytton's mind never comes fully to life in the
novel. One reason for this is that his research into the customs
of the period was voluminous, and he had no intention of
letting any stray fact go unnoticed. The result is that the
action often bogs down in a series of pedantic, undramatic
descriptions of daily life in Pompeii. As Disraeli noted, while
Bulwer-Lytton had literary flair, he was no thinker. The
essential meaning of the destruction of a great hedonistic city
eludes him.

Nevertheless, as an entertaining, if turgidly written, historical romance perfectly suited for the movies, *The Last Days of
Pompeii* has its virtues. When it is not clogged with extra-
neous research, its plot moves with great rapidity and high
suspense. Bulwer-Lytton is a master of plotting, and for
chapters at a time, notably when the "good guys" are menaced
in the palace of Arbaces, he keeps his reader's eyes glued
to the page; no small accomplishment in view of the clumsiness
of the prose style, the lofty unreality of the dialogue, and the
thinness of the characters. Of these, perhaps only Nydia, an
oversentimentalized study in the pathos of hopeless love, and

Arbaces himself, a stock villain with a certain grandeur,
endure in the reader's mind. Minor characters, too, such as
the vulgar Diomed, the foppish Clodius, and the brutal
innkeeper, Burbo, emerge with some liveliness. But as so
often happens in historical romances—even those of Scott—
the hero and heroine are singularly lacking in individuality
or human interest.

The Last Days of Pompeii is not to be compared with such
serious historical novels as *The Heart of Midlothian,* George
Eliot's *Romola,* or Pater's *Marius the Epicurean.* Rather, it
manages to hold its place with such popular romances as
Quo Vadis? and *Ben Hur.* Alone among Bulwer-Lytton's many
novels, it is still read today.

The Author

Parliamentarian and cabinet minister, prolific author and one
of the most notable dandies and poseurs of his day, *Edward
Bulwer-Lytton* was born in London on May 25, 1805. He was
the son of a famous general, Earle Bulwer, and heir, on his
mother's side, of one of the great English aristocratic families.
Considered a child prodigy, he was educated at Trinity
College, Cambridge, where he won the chancellor's medal
for a prize poem. He then went into Parliament as Member
for St. Ives and later for Lincoln.

Fond of romantic attitudinizing, young Bulwer-Lytton enjoyed reading, boating, and carrying on hopeless love affairs,
including one with Lady Caroline Lamb, Byron's former
mistress. He wrote prodigiously as a youth, mostly in imitation
of Byron and Scott, but few of his early poems or plays have
survived. When he married against his mother's wishes,
however, his allowance was cut off and he was forced to
write popular novels to support his and his wife's extravagant
tastes.

His early novels, *Falkland* (1827) and *Pelham* (1828),
are memorable largely for the light they shed on the life
and habits of an aristocratic dandy in the early nineteenth
century. Following in the footsteps of the famous Beau
Brummell, Bulwer-Lytton made a high art of dress—impress-
ing even the young Dickens with the variety and splendor
of his waistcoats.

He followed his early successes with two lurid tales of crime, *Paul Clifford* (1830) and *Eugene Aram* (1832). During a trip to Italy, inspired, no doubt, by the great success of Scott, he turned his hand to writing historical romances, of which *The Last Days of Pompeii* (1834) and *Rienzi* (1835) are the best known.

In 1838 he was made a baronet and, on inheriting the ancestral estate of Knebworth from his mother, took on the name of Lytton in 1843. In 1858 Bulwer-Lytton served as secretary for the colonies; in 1866 he was elevated to the peerage as Baron Lytton of Knebworth.

His familiarity with the highest political and social circles in England enabled him to feed his vast audience the details of high life they craved. A rival of the great Disraeli, who was also a novelist and a dandy, he drew from the prime minister the opinion that "his mind is full of literature but no great power of thought"—a verdict that seems even more just today than when it was made.

Bulwer-Lytton was a man of many talents, none very profound, and an extremely hard worker whose fingers were always on the popular pulse. He died on January 18, 1873, and was buried in Westminster Abbey.

The Pickwick Papers

by

CHARLES DICKENS (1812–1870)

Main Characters

Samuel Pickwick, Esquire—A genial, innocent, middle-aged man with an inquiring mind and a love of adventure.

Nathaniel Winkle—The most timid member of the Pickwick Club.

Tracy Tupman—The fat, amorous member of the Pickwick Club.

Augustus Snodgrass—The poetic member of the Pickwick Club.

Alfred Jingle—A strolling actor and confidence man who talks nonstop in short, telegraphic sentences.

Mr. Wardle—The stout and jovial owner of the Manor Farm near Rochester.

Rachael Wardle—Mr. Wardle's elderly spinster sister.

Emily Wardle—Mr. Wardle's daughter.

Arabella Allen—The love of Mr. Winkle's life though intended by her brother to marry a doctor.

Mrs. Bardell—Mr. Pickwick's London landlady who fancies he is in love with her.

Sam Weller—The resourceful and inimitable cockney, Mr. Pickwick's devoted servant.

Mr. Serjeant Buzfuz—Mrs. Bardell's unscrupulous attorney in her breach of promise suit.

Mr. Bob Sawyer—The lively young medical student rejected by Arabella Allen.

The Story

Mr. Samuel Pickwick, the genial, bespectacled founder and permanent chairman of the Pickwick Club, sets forth on May 13, 1827, for a stagecoach tour of the countryside accompanied by the three members of his Club, Mr. Nathaniel Winkle, Mr. Augustus Snodgrass, and Mr. Tracy Tupman. The members of the club propose to travel to remote parts of England and report on the local customs. While achieving this quasi-scientific purpose, they intend to have a good time together.

No sooner have they set out on their adventures than they are rescued from a gang of bullies by the suave, ingenious Mr. Alfred Jingle who regales them on the road to Rochester with a variety of colorful stories about his many careers. When they arrive at Rochester, after consuming barrels of oysters en route, they discover that a formal ball is planned at the inn for that evening. Mr. Jingle complains that he has no evening clothes because his luggage has been lost, and he intimates to Mr. Tupman that it would be a pity if he missed the ball because he could introduce the fat, shy Tupman to all the pretty girls there.

Mr. Tupman accordingly "borrows" Mr. Winkle's formal suit for Alfred Jingle, who proceeds to offend Dr. Slammer at the party by flirting with the middle-aged lady the choleric doctor has been courting.

The next morning Dr. Slammer's servant calls on Mr. Winkle to challenge him to a duel. Poor Mr. Winkle was too drunk the night before to remember giving offense. Not realizing that the culprit was Mr. Jingle wearing his clothes, the timorous Pickwickian arrives, shaking with fear, at the field of honor. His second is Mr. Snodgrass, the poet of the Pickwick Club. When Dr. Slammer arrives, he immediately sees that Mr. Winkle is the wrong man, and the affair is settled amicably. No one knows where Mr. Jingle is.

That afternoon the Pickwickians are invited to visit Manor Farm where the stout, jovial Mr. Wardle lives with his two daughters and his plump spinster sister, Rachael. The next afternoon, after a rather harrowing ride, the disheveled

Pickwickians arrive at the farm, some ten miles from their inn.

Mr. Tupman falls in love with the elder Miss Wardle and Mr. Winkle falls in love with the beautiful Arabella Allen. To prove his valor Mr. Winkle goes hunting although he is totally inexperienced with guns, and manages only to shoot Mr. Tupman accidentally in the arm.

During a cricket match, Mr. Pickwick meets Jingle again. Mr. Wardle invites the actor and mountebank to Manor Farm. Ever the opportunist, Jingle decides that Miss Wardle must be a rich heiress, poisons her mind against Mr. Tupman, and elopes with her. Mr. Wardle and Mr. Pickwick set off in hot pursuit and apprehend the pair in London, thanks to the intelligence of Sam Weller, a cockney servant in the White Hart Inn. Jingle is bought off for a tidy sum, and poor Miss Wardle is brought back in tears to Manor Farm.

Impressed by the wit of Sam Weller, the son of a London coachman, Mr. Pickwick hires him for his manservant, and they return to his lodgings in Gosling Street, where the widowed landlady, Mrs. Bardell, conceives the strange notion that Mr. Pickwick is in love with her and is proposing marriage. She manages to faint compromisingly in the innocent old gentleman's arms just as his three friends come in the door.

Deciding that London is no place for him with Mrs. Bardell in her present mood, Mr. Pickwick and his friends next journey to Eatanswill, where a hotly contested election between the Blues and the Buffs is in progress. The Honorable Samuel Slumkey of Slumkey Hall, a Blue, is triumphant, after a good deal of dirty politics, over his Buff rival, Mr. Horatio Fizkin of Fizkin Lodge. During the election excitement, Mr. Pickwick meets Jingle again and is led to think he has foiled Jingle's plan to elope with a rich young girl in boarding school.

When he returns to London, Mr. Pickwick is startled to be served by the firm of Dodson and Fogg with a legal writ informing him he will be sued by Mrs. Bardell for breach of promise. But before the trial opens, Mr. Pickwick spends a happy Christmas holiday with the Wardle family, and Mr. Winkle's romance with Arabella Allen prospers under the mistletoe.

Back in London for the trial, Mr. Pickwick must defend himself against the machinations of Mr. Serjeant Buzfuz, the attorney for Dodson and Fogg. The unscrupulous lawyer convinces the judge that a note Mr. Pickwick had written to his landlady requesting chops and tomato sauce for his dinner was really a love letter. Mr. Pickwick's case is not helped by the well-meaning but hopelessly inept Mr. Winkle who manages to antagonize the judge. Sam Weller rises to the defense of his master, but his shrewd wit is only interpreted as cockney impudence. While the judge dines handsomely on chops and sherry, the jury returns a verdict of guilty. Outraged at this patent miscarriage of justice, Mr. Pickwick refuses to pay even a penny of the £750 damages, insisting on going to prison instead.

Before being sent to the Fleet Street jail for debtors, Mr. Pickwick is allowed to spend a month quietly enjoying the waters at Bath. Here Mr. Pickwick tries to advance his friend Winkle's suit with Arabella Allen. When he learns that the lovely Miss Allen has rejected the medical student, Mr. Bob Sawyer, proposed as her mate by her brother, Mr. Pickwick arranges for her to have a lovers' meeting in a garden with Mr. Winkle.

Still refusing to pay damages (against the advice of his lawyer and Sam Weller), Mr. Pickwick is trundled off to prison. He makes his cell as comfortable as possible with the aid of Sam, who manages to get himself locked up in order to continue serving his master. In prison, Mr. Pickwick once again meets the irrepressible Jingle, now in a sorry financial state. He benevolently forgives the rascally actor his past sins and gives him money for food and clothing.

Mr. Pickwick is startled one day to find that Mrs. Bardell and her son have also been thrown into the Fleet Street jail. Dodson and Fogg, who took her case without a fee, expected to collect from Mr. Pickwick's damages. When she refused to pay, they sent their client to prison. Ever warmhearted, Mr. Pickwick gives the Bardells money, too, and promises to help them on his release from jail.

Meanwhile, against her brother's wishes, Arabella has married Mr. Winkle. The pair visit Mr. Pickwick in his cell and beg him to pay his damages so that he may be released in order to bring about a reconciliation between Arabella and her brother. Mr. Pickwick cannot refuse this appeal. After three months in jail, he pays Mrs. Bardell her damages and is released. He manages to bring Arabella's brother around, but finds that now Mr. Winkle's father objects to the marriage and threatens to cut his son out of his will. Furthermore, Mr. Wardle comes to Mr. Pickwick with his daughter, Emily, claiming that the girl is hopelessly in love with a poor poet, Mr. Snodgrass.

Mr. Pickwick soon resolves all these difficulties. The elder Mr. Winkle becomes reconciled to his daughter-in-law when he sees what a charming girl she is. Mr. Snodgrass marries Emily Wardle, and even Sam Weller gets married—to a housemaid who joins him in Mr. Pickwick's service.

Dissolving his club after his exhausting adventures, Mr. Pickwick retires to the country with the Wellers and serves as benevolent godfather to all the children of the Winkles and Snodgrasses.

Critical Opinion

One day in 1836 an artist named Robert Seymour approached the twenty-four-year-old Dickens to write captions for a series of hunting prints he was designing. The prints would jocularly show the misadventures of a group of amateur sportsmen, somewhat in the manner of the popular novels of Surtees. With the cockiness of youthful genius, Dickens agreed to the more experienced Seymour's suggestion, but with the proviso that the drawings should take second place as mere illustrations to the text he would write. Without really knowing where the book was heading, he began work immediately on *The Pickwick Papers* which was to appear, as was then the custom, in monthly installments.

The Pickwick Papers got off to a slow start, and not until the introduction of Sam Weller did the book catch fire with the reading public. The suicide of Seymour left Dickens in mid-novel without an illustrator. One of the men he interviewed for the job was the young Thackeray, then trying to make a career for himself as an artist. The job went, however, to Hablot K. Browne, who as "Phiz" became the illustrator for many of Dickens' early books, his place being taken later on by the brilliant George Cruikshank.

Meanwhile, as Dickens' genius took over, the original, rather trivial plan for *The Pickwick Papers* was forgotten. No longer bound to recount the misadventures of cockney "sportsmen," Dickens turned instead to his favorite childhood reading, the picaresque novels of Cervantes, Fielding, and Smollett, and shaped a great panoramic novel of English life in the early nineteenth century.

The most loosely constructed of his books, *Pickwick* nevertheless became one of the most famous. At the time he wrote it, Dickens had little experience or awareness of novel form. Writing in monthly installments, he pretty much made up the plot as he went along. Only later in his career did he learn how to impose formal order on a serialized novel.

The haphazard plotting, the interpolated stories that bog down the action, the superabundant wealth of characters all fail to detract from Dickens' vast imaginative powers. *Pickwick* remains a great delight. The glories of the inns and coaches of preindustrial England, the delight in eating and drinking, the sentimental pleasures of a family Christmas are balanced by the indignation at the absurdity and injustice of the law and the horrors of debtors' prison. Most of Dickens' themes make their first appearance in the sprawling, humane pages of *The Pickwick Papers*.

David Copperfield

by

CHARLES DICKENS

Main Characters

David Copperfield—The youthful narrator, who experiences many vicissitudes before he becomes a successful novelist.

Betsey Trotwood—David's eccentric but kind-hearted great-aunt.

Mr. Murdstone—David's cruel and saturnine stepfather.

Jane Murdstone—Mr. Murdstone's grim sister.
Peggotty—David's fat, jolly nurse.
Barkis—A quiet, reserved carrier.
Daniel Peggotty—Peggotty's staunch, simple brother.
Little Emily—Peggotty's innocent orphan niece.
Ham—Peggotty's sturdy and good-natured orphan nephew.
Mr. Creakle—The brutal headmaster of Salem House school.
James Steerforth—David's passionately romantic but deeply selfish boyhood friend.
Tommy Traddles—Another school friend, good-natured and open-hearted.
Wilkins Micawber—Eternally optimistic, certain "something will turn up" to pay his huge debts.
Mr. Wickfield—Betsey Trotwood's Canterbury solicitor.
Agnes—His daughter, a beautiful, sensible girl.
Mr. Spenlow—Senior partner of the law firm of Spenlow and Jorkins, who takes David on as an apprentice.
Dora—Mr. Spenlow's pretty, loving, and silly daughter.
Uriah Heep—Mr. Wickfield's unctuous clerk.

The Story

Shortly before David Copperfield is born at Blunderstone, in Suffolk, his father dies, leaving his young widow Clara with an annual income of £105 and a devoted servant, Peggotty. The night David is born, his great-aunt, the eccentric Betsey Trotwood, is present, but she leaves in a huff because she had hoped for a girl to be named after her.

David's early years are happy ones. His pretty, young mother dotes on him. Once Peggotty takes him on a wonderful excursion to the port of Yarmouth where her brother, Daniel, a simple fisherman, lives in a cozy boat beached on the shore. Daniel has an orphan nephew, Ham, and an orphan niece, Emily, who become David's friends.

On his return from Yarmouth David discovers that his mother has married Edward Murdstone, a darkly handsome, tight-fisted tyrant. Mr. Murdstone brings his pious, gloomy sister Jane to live with them, and together the Murdstones try to break the spirits of David and his mother. When David can stand the bullying no longer, he bites Mr. Murdstone on the hand and is instantly dispatched to the Salem House school, where he is put under the care of Mr. Creakle, the inept and sadistic headmaster.

David's one comfort at Mr. Creakle's ill-run school is the friends he makes there: handsome, aristocratic James Steerforth and the always cheerful Tommy Traddles. But his schooldays end abruptly with his mother's death in childbirth. Even the devoted Peggotty leaves to marry a taciturn carrier named Barkis. David is left alone, neglected by his stepfather.

When he is ten years old, David is sent to London to earn his living in the counting house of Murdstone and Grinby where he is almost starved to death. His job is to wash and label wine bottles in a rat-infested warehouse. His colleagues are the raffish Mick Walker and Mealy Potatoes. David lodges in London with Mr. Wilkins Micawber, an improvident husband and father, who tries to keep his brood of four children alive in spite of the creditors who constantly hound him. Mr. Micawber, an incurable optimist, keeps reassuring David that "something will turn up." But eventually Mr. Micawber is thrown into debtors' prison and David finds himself without a home.

Sick of his soul-destroying job and refusing to seek other lodgings because he has come to love the happy-go-lucky Micawbers, David leaves London for Dover, where his great-aunt Betsey Trotwood lives. Beaten and robbed on the way, David arrives dirty and penniless. Miss Betsey, who has always disapproved of him for not being a girl, nevertheless washes and feeds him. On the advice of her gently mad boarder, Mr. Dick, she decides to give David a permanent home, a decision which is enforced when the odious Murdstones arrive and highhandedly try to take David away.

This time, David is sent to a much better school than Mr. Creakle's, the good Mr. Strong's school in Canterbury. He lodges with his great-aunt's lawyer, Mr. Wickfield, and meets Mr. Wickfield's unctuous clerk, Uriah Heep, to whom David takes an instant dislike. David becomes very fond of Mr. Wickfield's pretty daughter, Agnes, who treats him as if she were his sister.

When David graduates with honors from Mr. Strong's school, he decides to become a lawyer, but first he goes to Yarmouth to visit the Peggotty family. On his way he meets his old school comrade, Steerforth, now an elegant, charming young man. David takes Steerforth with him, and in the two weeks they spend at Yarmouth, Steerforth and little Emily fall in love. Emily, however, is engaged to Ham.

David then returns to become apprenticed to the law firm of Spenlow and Jorkins. He falls in love with Mr. Spenlow's charming, silly daughter, Dora. Soon he receives the bad news that his aunt has lost all her money, and that Uriah Heep has wheedled his way into a partnership with Mr. Wickfield. On another visit to Yarmouth—for word has come that Barkis is dying—David is shocked to learn that Emily, despite her engagement, has run off with Steerforth. Broken-hearted, old Daniel Peggotty has gone in search of his niece.

David begins studying shorthand reporting in order to help out his aunt, who is no longer able to pay for his apprentice-ship to Mr. Spenlow. Despite his change in fortune, David continues to see Dora. When Mr. Spenlow learns they wish to marry, he strongly disapproves. Before very long Mr. Spenlow dies, penniless. David and Dora marry on his meager income from reporting. David tries to get his adoring but inefficient young wife to manage the household care-fully, but Dora is incapable of any economy, and the couple find themselves hard-pressed. They are still able, though, to prepare cheerful meals for their jolly bachelor friend, Tommy Traddles.

On a trip back to Canterbury, David finds his old friend Mr. Micawber now working for Uriah Heep who has gained complete control over him by giving him advances on his salary. Worse yet, Mr. Wickfield, too, seems strangely under his former clerk's greasy thumb. David is further appalled to learn that the odious Mr. Heep plans to marry Mr. Wick-field's lovely daughter, Agnes.

Eventually Mr. Micawber's basic honesty compels him to tell David that Uriah Heep has been embezzling money from Mr. Wickfield. His thefts have been responsible for the de-cline in Betsey Trotwood's fortunes. With the clerk exposed, some restitution is made, and Miss Trotwood finances Mr. Micawber's emigration to Australia where, he is sure, some-thing good is bound to turn up. Traveling with him on the ship are Emily and her uncle. Emily, who had returned in disgrace when Steerforth callously abandoned her, is forgiven by the magnanimous Daniel Peggotty, and together they hope to find a new life in the colonies.

Gradually Dora's health—always precarious—begins to

fail. David sorrowfully watches his child wife declining. During these sad days, Agnes is a constant solace to him. When Dora dies, Agnes suggests that David seek consolation abroad. He first visits Yarmouth, however, where a great storm is in progress. A ship is foundering offshore. Ham Peggotty swims out to save a man caught in the wreckage. He drowns trying to save Steerforth, who has gone under in the storm.

For three years David wanders about Europe. On his return to England, he learns from Miss Trotwood that Agnes is about to be married. Although he has always considered Agnes a sister, he is pained by the news. Under his aunt's matchmaking instigation, he goes to pay Agnes a visit. When they are together Agnes confesses she has never loved anyone but him. They marry, to Miss Trotwood's great delight, and have a large family. David becomes a highly successful author.

Critical Opinion

Among the best-loved novels of Dickens, *David Copperfield* is a huge, sprawling autobiographical work filled with characteristic Dickensian touches. Out of his unhappy career in a London blacking factory, Dickens shaped David's nightmare apprenticeship to the firm of Murdstone and Grinby. Mr. Micawber is a half-critical, half-affectionate portrait of Dickens' own improvident father. Superimposed on the autobiographical elements is a portrait gallery of a vast range of eccentrics, from the cryptic Barkis to the oily villian, Uriah Heep. These could have come only from Dickens' incredibly fertile imagination.

But the real strength of the book is the passionate honesty and indignation with which Dickens comes to grips with his early childhood. His six months in the blacking factory had been such a ghastly nightmare to him that in later life he completely suppressed the memory, never even telling his immediate family about it. Only through the medium of art was he able to cope with that nightmare. In *David Copperfield*, he shows us his early childhood—idyllic and innocent; his expulsion from this Eden by the cruel Mr. Murdstone; and his plunge, at an early age, into the grime of lower-class London.

Another early memory which haunts the pages of *David*

Copperfield is that of Dickens' love for Maria Beadnell, whom he knew before his marriage. She is the Dora of the novel. Dickens vividly imagines what marriage would have been like with a weak, silly but affectionate girl rather than with the stolid woman he actually married. The section describing David's young married career is immensely touching; but as he gradually becomes successful, the emotional impetus behind the first half of the novel begins to subside. Dickens' concern with tying the numerous plot threads together now becomes stronger than his interest in confession and self-analysis.

The plot becomes incredibly involved as Dickens introduces a wealth of characters, combining them in all sorts of fortuitous ways. As David, having passed through his childhood crises, becomes less interesting, the novel is largely given over to the galaxy of minor characters. When they are imaginatively conceived, like Micawber or Uriah Heep, the novel is lively. When they are romantic stereotypes of Byronic passion, like Steerforth, or Victorian stereotypes of saintly, betrayed womanhood, like Emily, the novel flags.

David Copperfield is typical of middle-period Dickens. The high humor and fierce indignation, the almost uncontrolled complexity of plot, the sheer number of characters, and the concentration on eccentrics are all Dickensian hallmarks, never combined to better effect than in this interpretation of the novelist's own youth.

A Tale of Two Cities

by

CHARLES DICKENS

Main Characters

Dr. Alexandre Manette—A once-strong, brilliant physician, almost destroyed by eighteen years in the Bastille.

Lucie Manette—Dr. Manette's tender, golden-haired daughter.

Jarvis Lorry—The "man of business" of Tellson's Bank, deceptively gruff.

Charles Darnay—The Marquis St. Evrémonde's handsome
nephew who has turned his back on the tyranny of the
aristocrats.
Sydney Carton—A self-destructive but brilliant lawyer who
looks like Charles Darnay.
Madame Defarge—A woman obsessed with vengeance against
the aristocrats.
Ernest Defarge—Mme. Defarge's "dark, angry, dangerous"
husband, owner of the wine shop in Paris where the revolu-
tionists frequently meet.
Miss Pross—Lucie's brusque servant and companion.
Jerry Cruncher—A bristly haired man-of-all-jobs, employed by
Tellson's bank and on the side a "Resurrection Man," or
supplier of corpses to medical students.

The Story

On a freezing November night in 1775, Mr. Jarvis Lorry,
agent for the old, respected banking firm of Tellson and Company, is riding on the mail coach to Dover where he is to meet
pretty, blonde Lucie Manette, a French refugee recently summoned from London. Together they set off for Paris where
Lucie's father, Dr. Manette, is being kept in hiding in a tiny
garret above the wine shop run by the Defarges. Dr. Manette
has spent eighteen years in solitary confinement in the Bastille.
Now, his mind failing, he is to be taken to sanctuary in England. Lorry and Lucie Manette are accompanied on their trip
to Paris by Jerry Cruncher, a loyal, odd-looking employee of
Tellson's bank.

The Defarges' wine shop is a center for revolutionary activities in Paris. Sworn enemies of the old regime, the Defarges
have sheltered Dr. Manette in their attic, where he has sat
long hours before a carpenter's bench, trying to recall his
past. Mme. Defarge, meanwhile, knits away at a strange scarf
inscribed with the names of all the aristocrats she hopes to
see executed when the revolution comes.

Five years after Lucie and Jarvis Lorry bring old Dr.
Manette back to London, where they are looked after by the
faithful Jerry Cruncher, they attend the trial of Charles
Darnay, a handsome young French language teacher accused
by a man called John Barsad of spying against England. The

Manettes testify that they met Darnay on the boat returning from France five years before. Darnay is saved by the brilliant lawyer Sydney Carton who so closely resembles the accused man that the attorney, Mr. Stryver, is able to shake the testimony of witnesses who "recognize" him.

After the trial, Darnay and Carton become frequent visitors at the humble Manette home. Darnay, it turns out, is the heir of the St. Evrémondes—a family of coldly selfish French aristocrats. Refusing to have anything to do with them, he has preferred to eke out a living in London as a French tutor.

Carton, brilliant but unstable, prepares Mr. Stryver's cases for him but is often too drunk to appear in court himself. Both young men court Lucie. When she chooses Darnay, Carton nobly assures her that he will always be ready to lay down his life for her or for one she loves.

Darnay and Lucie marry. Their little girl is six when the revolution breaks out in France with the storming of the hated Bastille and the release of its pathetic prisoners. One of the last provocations to the long-suffering French peasantry was the killing of a child run down by the coach of the callous Marquis St. Evrémonde, Charles Darnay's uncle. The child's father, having protested in vain, had murdered the Marquis in his bed and was subsequently hanged.

One day a letter arrives in England for the new Marquis St. Evrémonde. From it Darnay learns that an old family servant has been imprisoned by the revolutionaries. He begs the Marquis to intervene on his behalf, for he had been following Charles' orders to make restitution to the people when he was arrested. Darnay honorably determines to return to France to see what he can do.

Accordingly, he leaves for Paris with Jarvis Lorry, who has business to transact in the French branch of Tellson and Company. Darnay is arrested soon after his arrival and accused of being a returned aristocrat. When news of his imprisonment reaches England, Lucie and Dr. Manette go to France to help. Dr. Manette feels that his long imprisonment in the Bastille should count for something in his defense of his son-in-law.

The Manettes find Paris in the grip of the Reign of Terror. Although the old doctor is respected by the bloodthirsty revolutionaries, so implacable is the hatred of the Defarges for any member of the St. Evrémonde family that Charles Darnay is allowed to languish in prison for nearly a year and a half before he is tried. All this time Lucie is prevented from seeing her husband.

Finally Darnay is brought to trial. Mme. Defarge sits in the front row of the courtroom knitting her sinister scarf and demanding the death penalty. Charles insists that he had nothing to do with the St. Evrémondes, and, in fact, had ordered that all their wealth be returned to the people they had injured for so long. When the popular Dr. Manette testifies in his son-in-law's behalf, a cheer goes up in the courtroom. Darnay is freed.

Although the tribunal has freed him, Darnay is forbidden to leave France for England. No sooner have the Manettes held a victory celebration, than Darnay is arrested again, accused by the Defarges and a mystery witness of unspecified crimes against the people. While Darnay, wondering who his new accuser could be, is disconsolately awaiting his new trial, Miss Pross, Lucie's devoted old servant, meets her long-lost brother in the streets of Paris. He is John Barsad, the slippery, treacherous witness against Darnay during his Old Bailey trial years before.

Sydney Carton, now in Paris, interviews Barsad who has become a revolutionary spy. Carton manages to make a secret deal with him by threatening to expose him to the revolutionaries as a former English spy.

At Darnay's new trial, M. Defarge produces a paper accusing the St. Evrémondes of vile crimes. He names Dr. Manette as the other witness against Darnay, because the important, damning document was written by the old doctor during his years of imprisonment in the Bastille. When the notorious prison fell to the revolutionaries, Defarge had found the manuscript in Dr. Manette's old cell.

The paper tells how Dr. Manette was arrested because he had learned of a terrible crime committed by the Marquis St. Evrémonde against an innocent family. By the right of *"le droit du seigneur,"* the Marquis had raped a poor peasant girl—the sister of Mme. Defarge. Called in when the girl was dying, Dr. Manette became a witness to St. Evrémonde's guilt, and hence was thrown into the Bastille. In his document he calls for a curse on the whole house of St. Evrémonde.

The long-forgotten document has its effect on the tribunal. Despite his disclaimers and pleas for mercy, Dr. Manette is ignored. Darnay must pay for the sins of his ancestors. He is condemned to be guillotined within twenty-four hours.

But now Sydney Carton, long steeped in apathy and dissipation, prepares to act in behalf of the husband of the woman he loves. Aided by Barsad, whom he has blackmailed, Carton manages to gain admittance into Darnay's cell. On the pretense of having a farewell drink with him, Carton drugs Darnay, exchanges clothes with him, and gets Barsad to lead his friend out of the cell. Because he closely resembles the prisoner, Carton will be able to take Darnay's place at the guillotine. The mob outside is fooled by the deception, and Darnay is reunited with his family.

Meanwhile Mme. Defarge has made her way to the Manette lodgings in order to denounce the whole family, including Lucie's little daughter. Mme. Defarge meets her match in the stalwart Miss Pross, who keeps the French-woman at bay while the Darnays make good their escape from France.

Furious at being balked in her revenge and dismayed at missing even for a minute the terrible scene at the guillotine, Mme. Defarge struggles with Miss Pross and is shot to death when her own pistol goes off. The explosion deafens Miss Pross for the rest of her life.

As the tumbrels bring their prisoners to the place of execution, the absence of Mme. Defarge is noted and commented upon. In one of the tumbrels, Sydney Carton, noble to the last, is comforting a poor, innocent seamstress, also doomed by the vengeful tribunal.

"It is a far, far better thing that I do, than I have ever done," Carton declares before the guillotine descends; "it is a far, far better rest that I go to, than I have ever known."

Critical Opinion

Although its intricate, exciting plot has always made *A Tale of Two Cities* one of Dickens' most popular novels, he was never particularly comfortable writing historical fiction. His only other major-attempt in the genre, *Barnaby Rudge* (1841), is perhaps his least successful novel. As in the later book, *Barnaby Rudge* deals with retribution for a crime committed years before, and takes place against a turbulent background of mob violence—the Gordon Riots, a lurid anti-Catholic episode in English history.

Deeply impressed, however, by a reading of Thomas Carlyle's *French Revolution,* Dickens determined to try his hand once again at historical romance. Carlyle sent the novelist two cartloads of books for research in the period, but Dickens probably ignored most of them. He did not wish to rewrite the history of the revolution which he thought Carlyle had recounted as well as it could be done. Instead, he tried to capture the atmosphere of the time in a tale that would point the moral that Carlyle had found in those events: that blood begets blood; revenge is self-perpetuating; and only the kindness and selflessness of the individual human heart can terminate a series of bloodlettings as ferocious as those unleashed in revolutionary France.

The result is essentially a melodrama, curiously lacking in the high humor of Dickens' fiction. At the time he was writing *A Tale of Two Cities,* Dickens was involved, too, in some amateur stage productions and was fascinated by the dense plotting and heroic characterizations of Victorian melodrama. Thus *A Tale of Two Cities* is not as diffuse and leisurely as such earlier novels as *Pickwick Papers* or *David Copperfield.* Dickens' main concern here was to devise a fast-moving plot.

The theme of the novel is essentially the theme of Carlyle's *French Revolution.* Selfish and tyrannical, the aristocracy has brought upon itself the horror of revolution. But then the revolutionaries, carried away by revenge and cruelty, created the Reign of Terror—a match for the oppression before the revolution. At the end of the novel, Sydney Carton goes to his execution with a poor seamstress who has never harmed anybody but who is the pathetic victim of mob rule and blood-lust.

Only in the heroic self-abnegation of the redeemed Carton and in what Dickens saw as the essential goodness of the long-suffering French people does the novel hold out any hope for the future of humanity.

Great Expectations

by

CHARLES DICKENS

Main Characters

Pip—A lonely and imaginative orphan boy who receives an unexpected and unexplained education.

Joe Gargery—The decent, honorable village blacksmith who looks after Pip.

Mrs. Joe Gargery—Pip's shrewish older sister.

Miss Havisham—The eccentric mistress of Satis House, who was deserted years ago on her wedding day.

Estella—Miss Havisham's ward, beautiful and cold-hearted.

Herbert Pocket—Pip's warm-hearted and loyal friend in London.

Bentley Drummle—A clumsy, ill-tempered snob.

Abel Magwitch—An escaped convict with the assumed name of Provis who is obsessed with the idea of giving Pip a better chance in life than he (Magwitch) had ever had.

Arthur Compeyson—Magwitch's bitter enemy, sworn to his destruction.

Mr. Jaggers—The solicitor who informs Pip of his great expectations in life.

Biddy—Joe Gargery's gentle second wife.

The Story

Young Pip is an orphan boy being brought up by his older sister and her good-natured husband, Joe Gargery, the village blacksmith. In his loneliness, Pip often wanders about the forbidding moors and marshes of the neighborhood, sometimes stopping to mourn over the gravestones of his dead mother and father. One day, while out on the bleak moors, Pip

is startled by a hulking, menacing man who threatens him
if he does not bring him some food immediately. The stranger
is apparently an escaped convict, for he also demands that
Pip bring him a file with which to cut the chains binding his
legs.

Too terrified to refuse, Pip steals a pork pie from his sister's
kitchen and a file from a tool box, and returns to the spot
where the prisoner had accosted him. Here he sees another
strange man, engaged in a fierce fight with the first man. The
second man eventually disappears into the fog. Soon after, the
escaped convict, whose name is Abel Magwitch, is recaptured,
but before being returned to jail he promises to reward Pip
for helping him.

Pip soon forgets the incident. Before long, the eccentric Miss
Havisham requests Pip's sister to send the lad to gloomy Satis
House. Long ago, Miss Havisham had been jilted on her
wedding day. Ever since, she has had all the clocks stopped in
the great house where she lives in seclusion with her ward,
the beautiful, haughty Estella. The wedding breakfast, complete with decorated cake, has for years been lying on a table,
moldering. When Pip visits Miss Havisham, he is startled by
her extreme eccentricity.

The lonely Miss Havisham insists that Pip come often to
play with her ward. Estella torments him, however, and is
encouraged by Miss Havisham to tease him. In spite of himself, Pip is awed by Estella, the most beautiful girl he has
ever seen.

A studious lad, Pip hopes eventually to leave the limited
life he knows in the blacksmith shop. His opportunity comes
soon. One day Mr. Jaggers, a pompous London lawyer, arrives with the news that money has been secretly provided for
Pip to go to the city and become a gentleman. Pip, elated at
this prospect, assumes that the money is coming from Miss
Havisham with the hope that it will make him into a desirable
husband for Estella.

In London Pip is befriended by Herbert Pocket, a distant
relative of Miss Havisham and a dashing young man about
town, who shares the small but cozy rooms that have been
rented for Pip. Jaggers refuses to answer Pip's questions about
the identity of his benefactor, assuring the lad that in due
time he will know who has provided the money for him.

Before long Pip takes to the idle life of a London dandy. He becomes friends with an overbearing aristocrat named Bentley Drummle and learns the sophisticated ways of London society so well that he is embarrassed and irritated by the occasional visits of the simple, loyal Joe Gargery.

After Joe leaves, however, Pip feels remorse at the high-handed way in which he has treated him. Once, at Miss Havisham's request, Pip goes back home with Joe. The elderly recluse and her ward are impressed by the way in which Pip has outgrown his humble beginnings. Miss Havisham even goes so far as to tell Pip that she expects him to fall in love with Estella. Pip is more than willing.

Estella comes to London herself. Soon her dark good looks and aristocratic manner bring her a circle of suitors including Bentley Drummle. Although she still sees Pip occasionally, she obviously is not in love with him.

On Pip's twenty-first birthday, he receives a surprise visit from Magwitch, the convict he helped years before on the moor. A coarse, unprepossessing man, Magwitch at first repels the fastidious Pip, but when he reveals that he is Pip's secret benefactor, Pip is horrified. Magwitch tells him that he has made a great deal of money in the colonies where he had been transported, and has now secretly returned to London to see how Pip, whom he regards as a kind of son, has turned out. All he wants is for Pip to become a gentleman, something circumstances never allowed Magwitch to do. He is in England under the assumed name of Provis. If the police ever find out he has escaped from the convict colony, he will be condemned to death.

Pip reels at his dilemma. While he knows he should feel grateful to Magwitch, he is too snobbish to feel much sympathy for this brutalized man. He is also bitterly disillusioned that his benefactor is not Miss Havisham. Nevertheless, Pip vows to help Magwitch who tells him that the man who struggled with him on the moor was a sworn enemy named Arthur Compeyson. Pip learns from Herbert Pocket that Compeyson is the very man who jilted Miss Havisham on her wedding day.

Angry at his own folly in assuming Miss Havisham to be his benefactor, Pip goes to the gloomy mansion once more to upbraid the old woman for leading him on. With deliberate cruelty she informs him that Estella is soon to marry Bentley Drummle. Pip's anguish is precisely what Miss Havisham has counted on. Since her jilting, she has vowed vengeance on all men. In playing with Pip's affection for Estella, she satisfies her vow.

After Estella's marriage, Pip visits the Havisham mansion again. A fire starts in the mansion. Pip tries to rescue Miss Havisham. He is too late. The house is so filled with the dust and rubble of the past that it goes up like a tinderbox. Miss Havisham dies in the flames.

Back in London Pip learns that Magwitch is in fact Estella's father; her mother is apparently Jaggers' strange housekeeper. Even more startling is the news that Compeyson is in London, hunting down Magwitch to kill him. With Herbert Pocket's aid, Pip attempts to smuggle his benefactor out of England to safety in France, where Pip will join him. But just as they go aboard the boat that will take the convict across the Channel, Compeyson catches up with them. The two enemies lock in fierce hand-to-hand combat. Magwitch kills Compeyson. For this murder the old convict is once again returned to jail where he dies while awaiting trial.

Under the stress of recent events, Pip falls ill and is nursed by the faithful Joe Gargery. Pip's sister has died and Joe has married Biddy who really loves him and doesn't henpeck him. Pip finally realizes how wrong he has been to despise the humble, loyal Joe. He returns with him to his blacksmith shop and, while recovering from his illness, makes amends to Joe for having treated him so shabbily and snobbishly.

Still brooding over the loss of Estella, Pip joins Herbert Pocket in a business venture in London. Many years later he pays his final visit to the place where Miss Havisham's mansion once stood. He meets Estella there. Together they walk about the grounds where they had once been children together. Estella is now widowed. The surly Bentley Drummle, whom she had married for his aristocratic background, was kicked to death one day by a horse that he had been mistreating with his customary brutality. Her experiences with Drummle and her solitary widowhood have considerably softened the once cold and aloof Estella. As she walks hand in hand with Pip, the two understand that they will never part from each other again.

Critical Opinion

In many ways, *Great Expectations* is Dickens' finest novel.
Although it lacks the high spirits and wild inventiveness
of his earlier fiction, it is less diffuse and better organized.
Above all, it has a real theme—the corrosive effect of snobbery—treated in a serious and profound way.

Pip is early subjected to the snobbery of others. Although
he smarts under the contempt that Estella (ironically, the
illegitimate daughter of a convict and a housemaid) takes
no pains to disguise, when he is given the means to live in
London, he, too, falls easily into the ways of the snob. Once
a good, promising lad, Pip is so ruined by money that he
now callously condescends to his real friend, Joe Gargery,
while making his way in the superficial world of Bentley
Drummle.

Because he has become a snob, Pip is appalled to learn
that the source of his wealth is not the respectable Miss
Havisham, but the crude, ill-mannered convict, Magwitch.
Painfully, his early training under Joe Gargery breaks through
the superficial manners Pip has acquired in London, and he
vows loyalty to the hunted Magwitch.

Great Expectations, then, is an ironical title. The expectations of wealth that Jaggers presents to Pip seem great indeed,
but turn out to be ashes in the mouth as Pip scorns his old
friend Joe, loses Estella to Drummle (an even more consummate snob than he is), loses Magwitch, and is unable
even to rescue Miss Havisham.

It is only after these blows that Pip begins to realize his
duty to the dead Magwitch—to live up to the convict's expectations of him as the true gentleman he might become
given the necessary wealth and leisure. Pip must live the
good life that the haunted Magwitch was never able to attain
for himself.

Great Expectations is also a brilliant commentary on the
deadening influence that the past can exert on the present if
one allows an ancient injury to poison one's life. Because she
was jilted by Compeyson on her wedding day, Miss Havisham
has vowed vengeance on all men. For a time she seems
successful—her soured love nearly wrecks Pip's life. But
ultimately Miss Havisham's perverted will is thwarted. Sym-

bolically, her mansion—a museum of the dead past—is consumed in purifying flames which destroy her, too. It is Estella, not Pip, who suffers most from the marriage made for snobbish reasons.

The psychological insight into these thwarted lives shows Dickens at the zenith of his powers. The plot of this novel is more spare and austere than most of his others. Gone are the digressions and superfluous characters with which Dickens tended to pad his earlier novels. All is subordinated in *Great Expectations* to the theme: a devastating commentary on the moral perversions that wealth and the expectation of it can create in the human heart.

The Author

Charles Dickens, the best loved and most widely read of English novelists, was born into a lower-middle-class family at Portsea on February 7, 1812. His father, who later appears as Mr. Micawber in *David Copperfield*, was an ineffectual naval clerk whose fortunes continually fluctuated. When Charles was nine years old, the family fortunes took a catastrophic turn for the worse. Dickens' father was imprisoned in the Marshalsea debtors' prison, and the boy suffered the humiliation of working in a London blacking factory pasting labels on bottles in full view of passers-by.

These early experiences left an indelible mark on the sensitive, ambitious boy and shaped much of the fiction he was later to write. An improvement in the Dickens' fortunes enabled the boy to continue his interrupted schooling.

In 1835 he became a parliamentary reporter for a newspaper and began to contribute sketches of London life which were published in 1836 as *Sketches by Boz* (Dickens' early pen name). It was not until later that year, when the *Pickwick Papers* began appearing in monthly installments, that the name Dickens became a household word. The success of *Pickwick* enabled Dickens to marry Catherine Hogarth, the sister of the girl he really loved. Catherine, who bore him numerous children, was apparently a rather dull, unimaginative woman. The unhappy marriage ended in a separation in 1856.

Pickwick was followed by *Oliver Twist* (1838) and

Nicholas Nickleby (1839), both of which solidified Dickens'
reputation to such an extent that when he visited the United
States in 1842 in order to plead for a universal copyright
law, he was greeted as a conquering hero. Loathing slavery,
irritated by American piracies of his novels and by crude
American manners, Dickens pilloried the United States in
the middle section of *Martin Chuzzlewit* (1844) and in his
American Notes (1842).

In 1856 Dickens' public readings from his works enhanced
his reputation even further. A born actor, he put so much of
himself into these dramatic readings that they totally exhausted him and contributed to his death.

The novels of Dickens' middle period, *David Copperfield* (1850), *Bleak House* (1852), *Hard Times* (1854) and
A Tale of Two Cities (1859), show the exuberance and high
spirits of the early works giving way to a more serious concern with social injustice and the evils of industrialism. A
more somber, deeply symbolic style and a tighter and more
effective structure are evident in the last novels Dickens
wrote, the highly complex and haunting *Great Expectations*
(1860), *Our Mutual Friend* (1865), and the unfinished
mystery tale, *Edwin Drood.*

Dickens' later life was complicated by overwork and by
an unhappy affair with a young actress, Ellen Ternan. In
1867 he paid a second visit to the United States which he
liked better this time and which heaped even greater adulation on him than it had done before. The following year he
returned to England totally exhausted. On June 9, 1870, a
world famous but bitter man, he died in the mansion he had
built for himself, Gadshill Place, in Kent.

By the Same Author

Oliver Twist: Dickens' second novel is as somber as his first
is high spirited. Born in a workhouse of unknown parentage,
Oliver Twist is apprenticed to an undertaker by Mr. Bumble,
a monument of cruelty and hypocrisy. The lad then makes
his way to London where he falls in with a group of pick-
pockets including the Artful Dodger. Such notorious figures
of the London underworld as the greasy Fagin and the violent
Bill Sikes exploit Oliver and kidnap him when he is tem-

porarily rescued by the kindly Mr. Brownlow. Eventually, after Oliver finds a haven and Sikes brutally murders his wife, Nancy, the criminals are caught and punished. Oliver is adopted by Mr. Brownlow.

A Christmas Carol: This short tale of 1843 is one of Dickens' most sentimental and popular works. It tells of the old miser, Scrooge who in a series of dreams learns about the true Christmas spirit. Scrooge has always mistreated his impoverished but cheerful clerk, Bob Cratchit. When the Ghost of Christmas Present takes him to the Cratchit house, Scrooge sees himself through the Cratchits' eyes and realizes that his miserly, unloved life has been a waste. A changed man after his terrifying dreams, Scrooge contributes generously to the Cratchits' Christmas dinner and is blessed by the clerk's crippled son, Tiny Tim.

Jane Eyre

by

CHARLOTTE BRONTË (1816–1855)

Main Characters

Jane Eyre—An orphan who grows up to be a resourceful, self-reliant schoolmistress.

Mrs. Reed—Jane's cold-hearted aunt, mistress of Gateshead Hall.

Edward Fairfax Rochester—The brooding master of Thornfield Manor.

Adele Varens—Rochester's beautiful, precocious, half-French ward.

Mrs. Fairfax—A relative of Rochester, chief housekeeper of Thornfield Manor.

Grace Poole—A servant under Mrs. Fairfax.

Blanche Ingram—Beautiful, snobbish, and self-assured, she fancies herself in love with Rochester.

Mr. Mason—A mysterious visitor to Thornfield from the West Indies.

St. John Rivers—Clergyman of the parish of Morton who befriends Jane Eyre.

The Story

Orphaned as a baby, Jane Eyre is placed in the care of a cold-hearted aunt, Mrs. Reed of Gateshead Hall. Mrs. Reed's husband, a brother of Jane's mother, instructs his wife on his deathbed to care as tenderly for Jane as for her own three children. But Mrs. Reed, a somber and severe woman, ignores this request for the ten miserable years that Jane spends under her roof. She pampers her own spoiled children and brings Jane up as little better than a servant. One day, as punishment for a bit of childish willfulness, she puts Jane into the room in which Mr. Reed died. The highly imaginative child falls into a faint and becomes very ill.

After being nursed back to health by Bessie Leaven, a sympathetic nurse at Gateshead, Jane is sent to the Lowood School, fifty miles away. Although life in this school is very austere, it is generally a relief after Gateshead Hall. Jane is befriended by a Miss Temple and learns her lessons rapidly. Tragedy strikes when an epidemic kills some of the girls at Lowood. This leads to an investigation into conditions at the school and some subsequent improvements.

Jane becomes a teacher at the school, but leaves at eighteen to become governess to the precocious Adele Varens who lives in isolated Thornfield Manor near Millcote.

Jane does not at first meet Edward Rochester, the girl's guardian. She is engaged by the kindly, capable Mrs. Fairfax, chief housekeeper and relative of the lord of the manor. Jane finds contentment in the quiet, rustic life at the manor and in her imaginative young charge, but she is puzzled when Mrs. Fairfax warns her that she is never to enter a mysterious, locked room on the third floor. One day, Jane hears a shrill, blood-curdling laugh coming from the room, but Mrs. Fairfax pretends that the maniacal noise was made by Grace Poole, a rather dumpy, unprepossessing servant.

One January afternoon, while out walking, Jane meets her employer, Mr. Rochester. Rochester has been thrown by his horse, and his dog comes to Jane seeking help. But the gruff, surly Rochester insists on getting home unaided although he is in great pain. He questions Jane and learns she is the new governess. Rochester's manner to her becomes more gracious when she is obviously not cowed by his overbearing manner. In confidence, he tells her that little Adele is his daughter by a French ballerina who deserted both father and child long ago.

One night Jane is awakened by the same shrill scream she had heard before. Opening her door, she sees smoke billowing from Rochester's room. His bed on fire, Rochester is awakened just in time by Jane. He refuses to allow her to awaken the household, telling her the fire may have been set by Grace Poole, who has periodic fits of insanity. The rest of the servants are told the fire was accidentally caused by a candle falling.

Jane, sensing that her employer is suffering from the consequences of some mysterious sin of the past, gives him all her sympathy and gradually finds herself falling in love with him. But her hopes are thwarted when Rochester begins going to parties in the neighborhood where he is courting the beautiful, frivolous Blanche Ingram. At a party Rochester gives in Thornfield Manor, the aristocratic Blanche and her friends treat Jane with haughty condescension. Jane feels she can never compete with these snobbish, elegant people.

While the house guests are staying at Thornfield, Rochester receives a mysterious caller—a Mr. Mason from the West Indies. That night Jane hears a scuffle and a cry for help in the room just above hers. Rochester quiets the household's alarm but asks Jane privately to help nurse Mr. Mason who is bleeding and unconscious. Before dawn the wounded man is spirited away from the house.

One day soon after, Jane is enjoying the lovely midsummer evening in an orchard when Rochester comes upon her and informs her he is shortly to be married. Jane, miserable, assumes he intends to marry Blanche Ingram. She asks him tearfully how he can expect her to remain on at Thornfield under the circumstances. Rochester kisses her and tells her it is she whom he wishes to marry.

Jane's happy excitement before the wedding is interrupted one night when she awakens in horror to see a strange, ugly woman trying on her bridal veil and then tearing it to pieces. Rochester assures her it is only a bad dream, but in the morning Jane finds the ripped fragments of the veil.

On the wedding day the service is interrupted by Mr. Mason who has slipped into the church to announce that the marriage is illegal because Rochester still has a living wife. Forced to reveal the truth at last, Rochester takes Jane to the forbidden chamber on the third floor where Jane sees a hideous creature, crawling on all fours in her madness. It was she who had attacked Mason and torn Jane's wedding veil. Rochester explains that the creature is Mason's sister Bertha whom he had been tricked into marrying fifteen years before in Jamaica and who comes from a family of lunatics and degenerates. His married life has been an unmitigated hell, with the insane Mrs. Rochester kept under lock and key in the care of Grace Poole.

Jane is filled with sympathy for the misanthropic Rochester. Nevertheless, she realizes she must now depart. Taking just a little money with her, she wanders about the Midland moors, vainly seeking employment. Close to starvation, she is finally befriended and nursed back to health by a clergyman named St. John Rivers and his two sisters, Mary and Diana. Under the new name of Jane Elliott, she finds a job as village schoolmistress and tries to forget her seemingly hopeless love for Rochester.

One day Rivers learns that an uncle of Jane's, John Eyre, has recently died in Madeira and has left Jane £20,000. Jane insists on sharing this legacy with Rivers and his sisters who, a lawyer discovers, are really her cousins. St. John Rivers asks Jane to be his wife and to go with him to India where he plans to become a missionary. Although he is not in love with her, he feels she would make an admirable assistant in his mission.

While Jane is considering the offer, she has a dream that Rochester is calling for her. Failing to find him in the neighborhood the next morning, she journeys back to Thornfield where she is shocked to find the great manor house gutted by fire and completely in ruins. Making inquiries at the local inn, she discovers that Mrs. Rochester one night succeeded in setting the house on fire. Rochester managed to lead the servants to safety and then went back into the burning mansion to rescue his wife. She eluded him, was able to climb to the roof, and was then killed in a plunge to the ground.

Rochester barely managed to get out of the burning house alive himself. A flaming staircase had fallen, blinding him and crushing one arm so badly it had to be amputated. Rochester is now living in morose solitude at the lonely nearby manor of Ferndean. Jane hurries to see him.

Overjoyed that she has come to him, Rochester asks her to become his wife. She happily accepts and they are married. They soon have a child. Two years later, Rochester regains the sight of one eye.

Critical Opinion

Unlike her great predecessor, Jane Austen, Charlotte Brontë never possessed the ironic aloofness from the world that distinguishes such works as *Pride and Prejudice* or *Emma*. Instead, *Jane Eyre* is infused with passionate involvement and poetic imagination, sometimes bordering on the melodramatic. While Charlotte Brontë's hopeless love for M. Héger is undoubtedly the basis for Jane's love for Rochester, the figure of Rochester is larger than life; his sorrows and furies are titanic.

Rochester is a typical romantic hero, sharing some significant traits with the doomed heroes of Byron and with Heathcliff in Emily Brontë's *Wuthering Heights*. A man of great sorrow and great passion, a man too noble to be seduced by the superficialities of society, he is at the same time tormented and tormenting, tender and ruthless, and very much the figment of a lonely, romantic girl's imagination.

Although much of *Jane Eyre* is autobiographical, especially the scenes in the Lowood School, much is taken from the tradition of gothic romance popularized in the late eighteenth century by such shockers as Walpole's *Castle of Otranto* and Ann Radcliffe's *Mysteries of Udolpho*. Such elements in *Jane Eyre* as the lord of the manor haunted by a mystery from the past, the isolated, ghost-ridden mansion hiding its guilty secret, and the innocent but self-reliant girl trying to unfathom the mystery, are stock devices of the gothic novel.

Jane Eyre triumphs by giving these melodramatic devices a new lease on life and by investing them with unique personal passion and energy. They are no longer fictional clichés, but living facts in Charlotte Brontë's treatment. Because the Brontës' actual lives in lonely, haunted Haworth Parsonage really contained much of the "gothic," *Jane Eyre* is more convincing than most of its predecessors.

Rochester may divert attention from the book's modest, unassuming heroine; but the novel really centers on Jane's moral growth from the impudent, unhappy girl rebelling against her aunt's oppressive religiosity to the woman of delicate sensibility and strong character who eventually marries the crippled Rochester. Such experiences as those in the Lowood School (very Dickensian in tone), the teaching of the spoiled but adorable Adele, and the interrupted first marriage to Rochester give Jane strength to endure the blows of fate that eventually bring her to serene womanhood. *Jane Eyre* is in some respects a Cinderella-like fantasy of wish fulfillment, but one infused with an original and powerful romantic genius.

The Author

Charlotte Brontë was born on April 21, 1816, shortly before her family moved to bleak Haworth Parsonage in Yorkshire. Her father, Patrick Brontë, was a highly eccentric Irish clergyman. Her mother died when Charlotte was five, after bearing six children in all—three of whom, Charlotte and her sisters Emily and Anne, were to become famous novelists. The only son in the family, Patrick Branwell, showed considerable artistic gifts which he dissipated in drink.

In 1824 all the girls except Anne were sent to a school rather like the Lowood School in *Jane Eyre*. Here the two older daughters died, probably of tuberculosis. Charlotte and Emily then returned to Haworth where they were left on their own to roam the wild moors and make up stories for their own entertainment. Out of these tales and poems about a mythical northern kingdom called Angria came the *Gondal Chronicle*, an immature but fascinating saga in prose and verse on which the girls collaborated.

In 1831 Charlotte was sent to a boarding school where she was trained, like Jane Eyre, to become a governess. She hoped to open a school with Emily. In order to perfect their French, the two sisters traveled to Brussels, where they studied at the Pensionnat Héger. They were called back to England in 1842 by the death of their aunt. Shortly thereafter Charlotte returned to Brussels alone, spending a year as a teacher there and falling hopelessly in love with Constantin Héger, the married master of the establishment.

Discovering that her sisters Emily and Anne had been writing poems, Charlotte added some of her own. These poems were published in 1846 as *Poems by Currer, Ellis, and Acton Bell,* the pseudonyms the three girls used. The volume attracted no attention, but soon the three were writing novels. Although Charlotte's first effort, *The Professor,* was rejected, she was encouraged by a sympathetic publisher's reader. Her second work, *Jane Eyre,* became a great success on its publication in 1847.

Shaken by the deaths of Emily and Branwell and forced to care for her now blind father, Charlotte nevertheless managed to write two other novels, *Shirley* (1849) and *Villette* (1853). *Shirley* solidified her success. It was with the publication of that novel that she revealed the true identity of "Currer Bell." In London she met such literary lights of the day as Thackeray, Matthew Arnold, and Mrs. Gaskell, who was later to be her friend and biographer.

In 1854 she married her father's curate, the Reverend Arthur Bell Nichols. The marriage was tragically brief. Charlotte died on March 31 of the following year.

By the Same Author

Shirley: Shirley is a generally successful attempt to treat something Charlotte Brontë had only read about—the strife between workers and mill owners in Yorkshire in 1807–1812. Shirley Keeldar, its heroine, is concerned with the social changes brought about by the Industrial Revolution. She is a lively heiress whose character is partly modeled on Emily Brontë's. Shirley marries a man with a spirit like her own, Louis Moore, brother of a mill owner whose newly installed machinery provokes the laborers to riot. The novel is filled with keenly observed and sharply satirized clergymen whose moral rigidity in the face of changing times draws Charlotte Brontë's scornful fire.

Villette: This is a semi-autobiographical account of Charlotte Brontë's lovesick years as a teacher in the Pensionnat Héger in Brussels. The loneliness and despair she felt in her love for the married Constantin Héger is transmuted into the yearning of Lucy Snowe for Paul Emmanuel. Written after her brother and sisters had died, and while she herself was in ill health, the prevailing mood of *Villette* is the darkest of Charlotte Brontë's novels.

Wuthering Heights

by

EMILY BRONTË (1818–1848)

Main Characters

Mr. Earnshaw—the kindly owner of Wuthering Heights, a
storm-beaten house on the moors.
Catherine—His intense and passionate daughter.
Hindley—His weak-willed, snobbish son.
Heathcliff—An orphan boy adopted by Mr. Earnshaw.
Mr. Linton—The owner of neighboring Thrushcross Grange.
Edgar—His highly civilized son who deeply loves Catherine
Earnshaw.
Isabella—Edgar's sister who becomes infatuated with Heath-
cliff.
Frances Earnshaw—Hindley's sickly, childish wife.
Hareton Earnshaw—The son of Hindley and Frances, brought
up by Heathcliff to be crude, ignorant, and dirty, who is
nevertheless affectionate and loyal.
Cathy—Daughter of Edgar Linton and Catherine Earnshaw,
who has her mother's willfulness and pride.
Ellen Dean—The devoted housekeeper at Thrushcross Grange,
who narrates much of the story to Mr. Lockwood.
Mr. Lockwood—A tenant at Thrushcross Grange, who hears
most of the tale of the Earnshaws and the Lintons while
laid up with a cold.
Joseph—A sour, bigoted servant at Wuthering Heights.

109

The Story

One winter day in 1801 Mr. Lockwood, a tenant at Thrushcross Grange, decides to pay a visit to his landlord, Mr. Heathcliff, whom he has never met and who lives in the storm-battered old farmhouse nearby known as Wuthering Heights. He gets a surly reception from Heathcliff's dogs and from the landlord himself, a powerfully built, darkly handsome man, extremely sullen and abrupt in manner. Fascinated, Mr. Lockwood returns for a second visit to Wuthering Heights and meets Heathcliff's widowed daughter-in-law, a pretty but silent and haughty young woman, and a clumsy and unkempt young man named Hareton Earnshaw.

While Mr. Lockwood is at Wuthering Heights, it begins to snow heavily and it becomes obvious that he will have to stay the night. Heathcliff inhospitably tells him he will have to share a bed with Joseph, a dour and ill-tempered servant. Unwilling to do this, Mr. Lockwood is about to set forth in the snow when Zillah, a kindly cook, finds him an unused room in the house.

That night Mr. Lockwood has a nightmare in which he thinks he hears the branch of a tree knocking against his window. He tries to open the window to remove the branch. In the attempt, he breaks the window. He reaches for the branch but, instead, finds himself holding the icy hand of a woman. Crying that her name is Catherine Linton, she tries to get in through the window. Mr. Lockwood's screams bring Heathcliff rushing into the room, and in a fury the landlord orders him out of the haunted chamber. Heathcliff then throws himself on the bed and implores the spectral woman to come back to him.

His curiosity aroused by these strange events, Mr. Lockwood returns to Thrushcross Grange and asks the wise old housekeeper, Nelly Dean, to tell him about his landlord, for she has known Wuthering Heights from earliest childhood.

Mrs. Dean tells him that years before Mr. and Mrs. Earnshaw lived at Wuthering Heights with their daughter, Catherine, and their son, Hindley. Returning from a trip to Liverpool one day, Mr. Earnshaw brings back with him a filthy, ragged, dark-complexioned orphan boy whom he found in the slums. He christens the boy Heathcliff and tells his children they are to treat him like a brother. Soon Mr. Earn-shaw and Catherine grow to love young Heathcliff, for he is brave, sturdy, and self-sufficient. Hindley grows jealous of Heathcliff for stealing his father's affections. The atmosphere at Wuthering Heights becomes so tense that Hindley must be sent away to school because he is constantly baiting Heath-cliff and making him perform menial chores.

Soon after, Mr. Earnshaw dies, and Hindley returns to Wuthering Heights with a sickly, vapid bride named Frances. As master of Wuthering Heights, he now behaves even more cruelly to Heathcliff who vows that he will one day make Hindley pay for his brutality. Heathcliff's one joy in life is roaming about the wild moors with Catherine who finds in him the ideal companion for her own wild, restless spirit.

One night, when Heathcliff and Catherine are mischievously spying on a grand ball being given at Thrushcross Grange, they are set upon by a watchdog, and Catherine is bitten in the leg. She is taken into the house where she stays for five weeks until her leg is healed. There she meets the kindly, civilized Lintons, their charming son, Edgar, and lovely daughter, Isabella. When Catherine returns home, she is full of stories about the Lintons' life of ease and gaiety. Her tales make Heathcliff wildly jealous.

Tragedy soon strikes Wuthering Heights. Hindley's delicate wife, Frances, dies giving birth to a son, Hareton. Hindley drowns his sorrows in drink and continues to torment Heath-cliff. Meanwhile, Catherine confides in Nelly Dean that al-though she really loves Heathcliff, she thinks she will marry Edgar Linton, for she is tired of being a tomboy and it would degrade her to marry a servile orphan who is content to take orders from her brother. Heathcliff, overhearing the last part of the conversation, leaves Wuthering Heights that night in a fury, determined to make his way in the world before he returns to claim Catherine for his wife. Realizing what has happened, Catherine searches for him on the moors in a rainstorm but cannot find him.

While Heathcliff is away, Catherine eventually succumbs to Edgar Linton's charm and good manners. Not hearing from Heathcliff for three years, she marries Edgar and goes to live in the peace and tranquillity of Thrushcross Grange with Nelly Dean as housekeeper. There life proceeds placidly until one day Heathcliff returns and startles the Lintons with his

elegant clothes and fine manners. Heathcliff does not reveal
what he has been doing over the years, but he has obviously
prospered, and now wants to become a tenant at Wuthering
Heights. Edgar suspects his motives, but Catherine, overjoyed to have Heathcliff back, urges her husband to consent.
Hindley, overwhelmed by gambling and drinking debts, is
happy to have anyone pay him some rent for Wuthering
Heights, which has now fallen into a state of disrepair.

Accordingly, Heathcliff moves in and begins taking his
revenge on Hindley by inveigling him into more and more
gambling and drinking. Ultimately Heathcliff becomes the
real master of Wuthering Heights. He avenges himself on
Edgar Linton for marrying Catherine by getting Edgar's sister,
Isabella, to fall in love with him. Edgar, appalled at this turn
of events, assaults Heathcliff and orders him thrown out of
Thrushcross Grange. Heathcliff later persuades the flighty
Isabella to elope with him to Wuthering Heights.

Now Thrushcross Grange is barred to Heathcliff. But one
day he hears that Catherine, who is about to give birth, is
suffering from a fever. He forces his way to her bedside. She
confesses to Heathcliff that she was wrong in marrying Edgar
when she really loved him. There is a tender reconciliation
between the lovers a few hours before Catherine dies giving
birth to her daughter, Cathy Linton. Heathcliff, consumed
with guilt and frustrated love, calls upon Catherine's ghost
to haunt him forever.

Meanwhile Isabella Linton, completely disillusioned with
Heathcliff and aware of his true motives in marrying her,
leaves for London where she bears his son, Linton. Eventually Hindley dies of drink, having mortgaged all of Wuthering
Heights to the unrelenting Heathcliff.

Now, as complete master of Wuthering Heights, Heathcliff
is prepared to carry his revenge into the second generation
as he brings up Hindley's son, Hareton, in the most squalid
and brutal fashion. Poor Hareton, as rightful heir to the
Heights, is denied everything but meager subsistence and is
never allowed to forget that as the son of Heathcliff's mortal
enemy, he lives at the Heights only by Heathcliff's charity.

Twelve years after her son Linton's birth, Isabella dies
brokenhearted in London. Edgar Linton adopts the frail lad.
Heathcliff, however, demands that his son live with him at
Wuthering Heights. Heathcliff's plan, pathetically opposed

by the ineffectual Edgar Linton, is for young Linton and young Cathy eventually to marry. Linton's health is precarious, and Cathy comes to the Heights to visit him. Heathcliff imprisons her for five days until she consents to marry the invalid.

These events hasten Edgar's decline. He dies before he can disinherit Cathy and thwart Heathcliff's plans. Cathy inherits Thrushcross Grange. Soon after, the sickly Linton Heathcliff dies, and Cathy becomes dependent on Heathcliff who now controls both Wuthering Heights and Thrushcross Grange.

After a business trip to London, Mr. Lockwood returns one autumn to Wuthering Heights where he learns that Heathcliff has died three months before after deliberately starving himself for four days, sick of his vengeance and yearning to be united in death with his lost Catherine. Now Cathy and Hareton are alone at the Heights, and the girl takes upon herself the task of bringing out the long-submerged, finer elements in Hareton's character, giving him the education that Heathcliff had denied him.

When Mr. Lockwood visits the local cemetery, he finds Catherine's grave between her husband's and Heathcliff's. Local legend has it that on stormy nights the erstwhile lovers, Catherine and Heathcliff, are seen to roam the bleak moors they loved so much when they were young.

Critical Opinion

Wuthering Heights is one of the supreme masterpieces of English romanticism. In it, Emily Brontë explores two worlds: the world of the passionate emotions of love and revenge as symbolized by Wuthering Heights ("wuthering" is a Yorkshire dialect word for stormy weather), and the rational, civilized world symbolized by Thrushcross Grange. If the world of Wuthering Heights is often cruel and barbaric, as in Heathcliff's monstrous revenge against Hindley and the Lintons, it is also capable of a passionate love that transcends even death. If the world of Thrushcross Grange is cozy, comfortable, and civilized, it is also somewhat bloodless and ineffectual. The pitting of these two worlds of passion and reason against each other over the course of three generations is the essence of the book.

The novel really centers on Heathcliff, perhaps the most fascinating hero-villain in English fiction. A true figure of the Romantic Age, Heathcliff is consumed with a demonic passion which destroys all less vigorous life around him until he himself is destroyed by it.

Realizing that the demonic passions of the novel could easily turn into melodramatic rhetoric, Emily Brontë controls events through an enormously complex structure involving time shifts, shifts in point of view, and a highly sophisticated method of narration, all of which point to the style of such modern novelists as James, Conrad, and Joyce. Most of the events in *Wuthering Heights* are given a credibility they would not otherwise possess by being filtered through the common sense of Nelly Dean and Mr. Lockwood.

Thus, while the emotions of the book hark back to the romanticism of Byron and the gothic novel, the form looks forward to the control and sophistication of the modern novel. Somehow Emily Brontë manages to avoid completely the conventions of Victorian fiction. If the typical scene of the Victorian novel is a rectory garden or a middle-class drawing room (and this is true even of *Jane Eyre*), the typical scene of *Wuthering Heights* is a storm-swept, infinitely lonely moor. In this sense the novel is imaginatively closer to the world of *King Lear* than to the comfortable and commonplace world of Victorian fiction.

The Author

Although the tragically brief life of *Emily Jane Brontë* was highly circumscribed, her inner life must have been extremely rich. She was born on July 30, 1818, at Thornton, in Yorkshire, before the Brontë family moved to the famous Haworth Parsonage. Although she had very little formal schooling, Emily Brontë went to Halifax for a brief period as a governess in 1836, but returned home discouraged with teaching and homesick for the barren moors she loved. Like Catherine Earnshaw and Heathcliff, Emily Brontë felt an almost mystic passion for this bleak area of England. Except for brief excursions with her sisters, which always resulted in home-sickness, she never left the moorland.

Emily seems to have been rather different from the placid Anne and the passionate but practical Charlotte. Perhaps she was closest to her doomed brother, Branwell, who may have been a model for Hindley Earnshaw in *Wuthering Heights*. From what one can gather in brief family glimpses of her and in the character of Shirley, Charlotte's portrait of her, Emily was fiercely independent, stoically accepting loneliness, disease, and privation, and always infused with a transcendental mysticism which gave special significance to the world around her.

Of the three sisters, Emily was the most talented novelist and poet. Her strange, metaphysical poetry somewhat re-sembles that of the American mystical recluse Emily Dickin-son. The prose of *Wuthering Heights* is the most poetic to be found in the English novel before Virginia Woolf.

Wuthering Heights was published in 1847 under the pseudonym of Ellis Bell. Each of the Brontë sisters chose pseudonyms of ambiguous gender in the hope of avoiding what they felt was a prejudice against female authors. Its original critics misunderstood the book and were shocked by its intensity of feeling. Gradually, however, the novel came to be accepted for the masterpiece it is.

Fame, however, came too slowly for Emily Brontë to en-joy. Like her two sisters, she died of tuberculosis on December 19, 1848, in the parsonage at Haworth.

Vanity Fair

by

WILLIAM MAKEPEACE THACKERAY (1811–1863)

Main Characters

Becky Sharp—A clever, attractive, ruthlessly self-seeking orphan.

Amelia Sedley—Becky's kind and gentle friend.

Joseph Sedley—"Jos," Amelia's lazy brother.

Sir Pitt Crawley—The penny-pinching, slovenly baronet of Queen's Crawley, Hampshire.

Rawdon Crawley—Sir Pitt's second son, an army captain and "man about town."

George Osborne—Amelia's fiancé, but selfish and forgetful of his duty to her.

William Dobbin—Osborne's steadfast friend and Amelia's long-time admirer.

Lord Steyne—A rich, lecherous old aristocrat.

The Story

In the early days of the nineteenth century, two close friends are graduating from Miss Pinkerton's genteel academy for girls. They are Amelia Sedley, the gentle, well-brought-up daughter of a rich London businessman, and Becky Sharp, the poor orphaned daughter of an artist and a French opera girl, who is kept at the snobbish finishing school only because she can teach the other girls French. Amelia is kind-hearted and innocent. Becky is totally selfish and determined to make good in the world by fair means or foul.

As the girls leave the school, Becky, who hates the mean, penny-pinching life she has been subjected to, defiantly tosses a copy of Johnson's *Dictionary* at the headmistress' sister. Then the coach takes the girls to the Sedley home, where Becky is introduced to Amelia's fat, shy older brother, Jos, home on leave from the army in India. Becky decides that although Jos is lazy and an absurd fop, she will marry him for his wealth and position.

Her plan is balked, however, at a party she arranges with Amelia's matchmaking help at the famous Vauxhall Gardens. There Jos drinks too much punch, makes a fool of himself, and is persuaded by Amelia's old friend, George Osborne, to return to India as soon as possible. With Osborne at the party is his faithful friend and admirer, Captain William Dobbin, also stationed in India. Dobbin has long loved Amelia in secret but is willing to stand aside for his more dashing friend, George.

After the disaster of the Vauxhall party, Becky tearfully leaves her friend Amelia to serve as governess to the two small girls at Queen's Crawley in Hampshire. The miserly, thoroughly nasty Sir Pitt Crawley, baronet, tyrannizes over his family. Becky instantly decides to have little to do with the mousy wife or the girls she is supposed to care for. The object of her attention and flattery will be Sir Pitt and Miss Crawley, the rich spinster aunt of the family.

Miss Crawley's favorite is the young rakehell, Rawdon Crawley, Sir Pitt's son by his marriage to the late Lady Grizzel Crawley. Rawdon is a dashing army captain whose many gambling debts his aunt gladly settles. Becky captures Rawdon's heart and manages to ingratiate herself with the entire Crawley family. When old Miss Crawley falls ill, she will allow nobody to care for her but Becky. When the second Lady Crawley dies, Becky receives a startling marriage proposal from the smitten Sir Pitt.

Tearfully, Becky informs the old man that she cannot accept his proposal, flattering though it is, since she is already married. The announcement that she is married to Rawdon throws the haughty Crawleys into consternation. While Becky and Rawdon go off to Brighton on their honeymoon, Sir Pitt rages impotently and old Miss Crawley cuts her favorite nephew out of her will in favor of his older brother, Pitt.

Meanwhile, knowing that Amelia is pining for George Osborne, Dobbin tells the regiment of his friend's intention to marry Amelia. George is furious. He wants to marry the girl, but he wants his freedom, too. Now he feels honor-bound to marry and senses that he has been trapped into it by the loyal Dobbin.

The steady decline in Amelia's father's fortunes raises further difficulties. When Mr. Sedley finally goes bankrupt, George Osborne's father forbids his son to have anything to do with the now penniless Amelia. Egged on by Dobbin, however, George defies his father's will and marries Amelia, and the couple honeymoon in Brighton. There they meet Rawdon and Becky, who are deeply in debt as a result of living handsomely on "nothing a year."

Dobbin undertakes to reconcile George's father to the marriage but is peremptorily dismissed by the bitter old man. He arrives in Brighton with this sad report and with the exciting news that Napoleon has escaped from Elba and his forces are sweeping into Belgium. George, Rawdon, and Dobbin must proceed at once to Brussels. Meanwhile, George, after only six weeks of marriage to the docile but unexciting Amelia, has made overtures to Becky Sharp. The Battle of Waterloo interrupts his adulterous plans, however, and at the battle's end, George Osborne lies dead with a bullet through his heart.

Rawdon fares better in the battle. Promoted to a colonelcy for courage in action, he takes Becky to Paris for the gay and extravagant winter season following Napoleon's final banishment. Rawdon is highly successful for a time at cards and gambling, and Becky, as usual, attracts a host of admirers. She even finds time to bear Rawdon a son, to whom he immediately becomes passionately attached.

Amelia, too, has a son, but her life is hardly as glamorous as her friend's. Despite his son's death on the field of Waterloo, old Osborne still refuses to see Amelia or his grandson. Amelia, living in penury with her bankrupt parents, has only her baby to console her.

After two years of living beyond their means in Paris, Becky manages to buy off Rawdon's many creditors and both return to London to amass some new debts. Unlike her husband, Becky cares nothing for their little boy. She is preoccupied with adorning herself and flirting with rich men. Unable to live on what Rawdon wins at gambling, Becky begins circulating among the London aristocracy and catches the experienced eye of the rich, unscrupulous Lord Steyne. Steyne manages to have Becky presented at Court where she meets her husband's older brother, Pitt Crawley, now the wealthy member of the family, who falls in love with her.

While Becky is teetering on the verge of adultery, poor virtuous Amelia has finally been forced to consent to let her unrelenting father-in-law rear her baby in order to take the financial burden from her impoverished family. Old Osborne refuses to let the heartbroken mother see much of her son after he becomes the guardian.

Although Rawdon has been getting progressively deeper into debt, Becky sports fine new jewels and trinkets. When Rawdon asks her for money, she refuses him. Finally, Rawdon is hauled off one day to a "sponging house," a kind of debtors' prison for gentlemen. He appeals to his brother, who has him released. On unexpectedly returning home that night, Rawdon finds Becky alone with Lord Steyne. It is his final disillusionment. He leaves, never to see Becky again.

Ten years after Jos Sedley and Dobbin leave for India, they return home to find Mrs. Sedley dead and little George Osborne tyrannizing over his doting grandfather. Dobbin once again proclaims his love for Amelia, but she is still faithful to her dead husband. Jos helps out his family, and old Mr. Osborne's eventual death provides for little George. Together Joseph, Dobbin, and Amelia tour the continent, meeting Becky Sharp in a tenth-rate German spa. Amelia, softhearted as ever, wants to give her old friend a home, despite Dobbin's warnings about her character. Becky's life, after Rawdon's departure, has been hard. She allows Sir Pitt Crawley to adopt her child. Excluded from the London aristocracy, which fears a scandal, she journeys from one watering place to another, picking up men and living off them for a while, then going somewhere else where she is not known.

When she meets Jos, she once again manages to entrance him and becomes his mistress. She persuades the naïve, blundering Jos to take out a large insurance policy in her name. When Jos dies a few months later under mysterious circumstances, Becky is at last a rich woman—wealthy enough now to play the part of a widowed Lady Bountiful, a role she greatly enjoys. Despite her conniving, there is some good in Becky after all. When she learns that Amelia has been steadily refusing the suit of the steadfast Dobbin because she insists on remaining faithful to the memory of her dead husband, Becky shows Amelia a letter that George Osborne had written her on the eve of Waterloo, begging her to elope with him. This evidence finally opens Amelia's eyes, and she accepts Dobbin's proposal. They marry and live happily in the country.

Critical Opinion

Vanity Fair is perhaps the greatest English comic novel of manners, embracing in its many pages a vast spectrum of English life during the Napoleonic period. Thackeray, whose burlesques of historical fiction showed his awareness of the dangers inherent in that genre, nevertheless chose to write of the past—albeit the immediate past—rather than the present. Nevertheless, in the tradition of Fielding and Jane Austen, he managed to portray a society filled with hypocrisy and greed that is recognizable even today.

Thackeray's manner in *Vanity Fair* is that of an urbane, sophisticated, slightly cynical man of the world talking at ease to his fellows. Where Fielding interposed his comments on the characters and actions of *Tom Jones* in prefatory essays before each book, Thackeray injects his comments to the reader throughout *Vanity Fair*. These comments tell the reader essentially what to think about the characters, but never in a condescending or peremptory manner.

One of Thackeray's faults is his tendency to veer from the cynical to the sentimental, never quite hitting reality en route. Thus his experience as a caricaturist, both with pen and pencil, makes him portray the Crawleys as monsters of snobbery and selfishness. On the other hand, Amelia, whose name derives from the heroine of Fielding's last novel, is too saccharine for modern tastes. Perhaps only in Becky Sharp was Thackeray entirely successful in portraying a real human being. It is Becky's indomitable scheming for which the novel is best remembered.

The novel's brilliant structure follows the rise and fall in the fortunes of Becky Sharp and Amelia Sedley. At the beginning, Amelia is the daughter of a wealthy merchant; Becky a poor charity girl. Then as Mr. Sedley's fortunes decline and Becky's schemes mature, the positions are reversed. Mr. Sedley goes bankrupt and Becky marries Rawdon Crawley.

When Becky overplays her hand, however, and, in seeking a grander position in society, compromises herself with Lord Steyne, her fortunes begin to plummet, while Amelia's slowly rise again. It is through this dramatic graphing of social success and failure that Thackeray provides his memorable fleshing-out of Ecclesiastes and of the marketplace in Bunyan's *Pilgrim's Progress*.

The Author

William Makepeace Thackeray was born on July 18, 1811, in Calcutta, the son of a British civil servant. When his father died, young Thackeray was sent to England, where he was a miserable schoolboy at Charterhouse and later an indifferent scholar at Trinity College, Cambridge. He left there in 1830 without a degree.

After his undistinguished school career, Thackeray traveled on the continent for a year and returned to England to study law. He also began drawing caricatures and writing little comic magazine sketches, some of which are hilarious burlesques of the prevailing modes of popular fiction. In 1836 he made a tragic marriage with Isabella Shawe whose subsequent fits of insanity darkened Thackeray's later life.

After several years of struggling as a comic journalist, contributing to *Fraser's Magazine* and *Punch*, Thackeray settled down in 1847 to writing his masterpiece, *Vanity Fair*, which was published serially. He followed this triumph of Victorian fiction with the autobiographical *Pendennis* (1849) and with a historical novel of the eighteenth century, *Henry Esmond* (1852).

The research that went into *Henry Esmond* began during a series of lectures Thackeray delivered in 1851 on the English humorists of the eighteenth century. He repeated these lectures on a money-making tour of the United States in 1852, and gave a series of popular talks on the four Georges during a

second tour in 1855. Thackeray enjoyed his tours of the United
States more than Dickens enjoyed his, being in general a more
tolerant and urbane man than his great contemporary.

America inspired a sequel to *Henry Esmond, The Virginians*
(1859). After standing unsuccessfully for Parliament in 1857,
Thackeray took over the editorship of the *Cornhill Magazine*
in 1860, a job he found irksome. He died on December 24,
1863, in London.

Never quite as popular as Dickens, Thackeray appealed to
fewer but more sophisticated readers. Unlike Dickens, he had
firsthand acquaintance with the English aristocracy, about
whom he wrote more convincingly and less melodramatically.
Although the care of his insane wife and his two daughters
prevented Thackeray from ever attaining financial security,
his urbanity, wit, and easy good manners made him far more
comfortable in society than the tormented Dickens ever was.

By the Same Author

Henry Esmond: More controlled but less vivacious than
Vanity Fair, Henry Esmond is an account of the brilliant
society of England in the time of Queen Anne. Such actual
historical figures as Marlborough, Addison, and Swift appear
in its pages. The style is a triumphant imitation of Augustan
prose. Esmond himself, the allegedly illegitimate dependent
of the house of Castlewood, persistently woos Beatrix, the
flirtatious daughter of Lady Castlewood. Like Dobbin in
Vanity Fair, he is patient and stalwart in his wooing, but
unlike Dobbin, he finally decides he has had enough of
Beatrix's haughty rejections. When she helps thwart the
Jacobite Restoration plot in which he is involved, he marries
her mother, Lady Castlewood, instead and emigrates with
her to Virginia.

Pendennis: This autobiographical novel traces the growth to
maturity of Arthur Pendennis, nephew of the suave Major
Pendennis. Arthur Pendennis falls in love with two women,
Emily Costigan, an Irish actress older than himself, and Fanny
Bolton, a naïve servant girl. Both women are outside his social
caste. The novel chronicles the ways in which Arthur is ex-
tricated from what would be a misalliance and becomes the

mature husband of Laura, his adoring adopted sister. Thackeray's experiences at college, his gambling debts, his flirtations and jiltings are all amusingly recounted in this vast, sprawling novel.

Barchester Towers

by

ANTHONY TROLLOPE (1815–1882)

Main Characters

Bishop Proudie—The pompous new Bishop of Barchester.
Mrs. Proudie—The Bishop's strong-minded wife.
The Reverend Obadiah Slope—Bishop Proudie's self-centered
and power-hungry chaplain.
The Reverend Septimus Harding—Former warden of Hiram's
Hospital, a kindly, morally scrupulous old man.
Mrs. Eleanor Bold—Mr. Harding's newly widowed younger
daughter.
Dr. Grantly—Mr. Harding's son-in-law, competent, ambitious,
and opposed to the Proudie faction in Barchester.
The Reverend Vesey Stanhope—A clergyman who has just
returned after several years in Italy.
Charlotte Stanhope—His scheming spinster daughter who
professes great friendship for Eleanor Bold.
La Signora Madeline Vesey Neroni—Charlotte's vain, affected
sister, a semi-invalid and a flirt.
Bertie Stanhope—The Stanhope brother, a weak-willed dab-
bler in the arts.
The Reverend Quiverful—Poor father of a very large family,
who becomes a candidate for warden of Hiram's Hospital.
The Reverend Francis Arabin—A cultivated, well-mannered
Oxford divine and friend of Dr. Grantly's.
Squire Thorne of Ullathorne—Most notable member of the
Barchester local gentry.

The Story

One summer in the 1850's the placid old cathedral town of Barchester is in a turmoil about who will succeed the dying Bishop Grantly as Bishop of Barchester. As he watches over his father's deathbed, Dr. Grantly, the local "high-church" archdeacon, yearns to fill the post. But just as the old man peacefully expires, the government in which Dr. Grantly has powerful friends also falls, and the new government selects Dr. Proudie, a stranger to Barchester, for the coveted post.

Dr. Proudie arrives with his strong-minded wife, a woman with low-church sympathies, and a conniving, self-seeking chaplain, Obadiah Slope, who preaches the first sermon of the new bishop's regime. The sermon shocks the conservative elders of the church with its puritanical objections to ritual, to the chanting and intoning of services, and to church music.

Soon the lines of battle are drawn. Dr. Grantly quickly realizes that the new bishop is completely dominated by his wife—an intolerable state of affairs—and that she has insisted on giving power in cathedral affairs to the odious Mr. Slope who proposes to make radical changes in the way things have always been done at Barchester.

Aside from doctrinal differences, another point of dispute between the old and new factions at Barchester is the wardenship of Hiram's Hospital, a charitable institution for destitute old men, which is controlled by the diocese. Everyone assumes that the Reverend Septimus Harding, Dr. Grantly's father-in-law, who resigned from this post when a government scandal connected with it persuaded him he could no longer serve in good conscience, will now resume the wardenship. Mr. Slope, however, has different ideas. Seeing another opportunity to impose his clerical ideas on Barchester, Mr. Slope, unknown to Dr. Proudie, attaches such demeaning conditions to Mr. Harding's resumption of his post that the old gentleman feels he must refuse. Dr. Grantly is furious, but momentarily powerless to do anything about it.

Another "reform" of the new bishop's party is to force absentee clergymen to return to the diocese. This decree affects Dr. Vesey Stanhope, an elegant dilettante who has been living in Italy all these years, leaving his parish in the hands of his curates. Dr. Stanhope is head of a remarkable family: a sick wife; a sour spinster daughter, Charlotte; an affected, semi-invalid daughter who, after an unfortunate Italian marriage, calls herself La Signora Madeline Vesey Stanhope Neroni; and a hopelessly lazy and irresponsible son, Bertie, who has taken up a series of professions—never for very long—and has even gone to Palestine to convert the Jews. (He was himself converted for a time.)

One day the entire Stanhope family descends on Barchester for Bishop Proudie's first formal reception, and causes quite a stir. La Signora Neroni, borne by four men to the bishop's sofa, holds court there. With her exotic beauty and fine continental manners, she enthralls poor Mr. Slope who has never seen so glamorous a woman before. His attentions to her infuriate the jealous Mrs. Proudie who determines from then on to keep her husband's chaplain as well as her husband more carefully under her thumb. At the party, too, Bertie Stanhope irritates Bishop Proudie with his asinine opinions on religion.

Soon Dr. Grantly has a chance to strike back at the odious Proudies. The living of St. Ewold's becomes vacant, and Dr. Grantly travels to Oxford to ensure that his high-church friend, the Reverend Francis Arabin, will accept the appointment. Mr. Arabin, a suave, well-bred bachelor of about forty, can be counted on, Dr. Grantly feels, to awe the presumptuous Proudie faction.

Meanwhile, however, Eleanor Bold, Mr. Harding's younger daughter, a widow with an infant son, becomes the object of Mr. Slope's designs. The young clergyman sees a chance to defeat the high-church party, while gaining Mrs. Bold's inheritance for himself, by wooing the lovely young widow. Mr. Slope mistakes Eleanor's native politeness for encouragement and continues to press his attentions on her. Hoping to impress her, he decides to back Mr. Harding for the post of warden.

Unfortunately for his plan, Mr. Slope discovers that his patroness, Mrs. Proudie, has her own plans for the wardenship. She wants to give it to Mr. Quiverful who could certainly use the extra income. Desperately trying to rear a family of fourteen children on £400 a year, the naïve Mr. Quiverful proves no match for the intrigues of Mr. Slope, who easily persuades him to refuse the post by promising him something even more lucrative in the near future.

When she hears of this latest maneuver by her overly

ambitious protégé, Mrs. Proudie is furious, for she has already promised the wardenship to Mrs. Quiverful and has graciously received that humble lady's blessing. Mrs. Proudie stalks into her husband's study, expecting to lay down the law to him, but finds him in conference with Mr. Slope, who refuses to leave. Temporarily frustrated but by no means defeated, Mrs. Proudie breaks the sad news to Mrs. Quiverful.

Mr. Slope's attentions to Eleanor increase, much to the chagrin of Dr. Grantly. But the chaplain soon has a rival in Bertie Stanhope, encouraged by his sisters to woo the well-to-do widow in the hope that her inheritance will pay his debts. In order to help her inept brother in his suit, La Signora Neroni starts exercising her charms on Mr. Slope, not realizing that Eleanor had never even considered him as a possible mate.

Dr. Grantly, under the same misapprehension, hopes to take Eleanor's mind off Mr. Slope by inviting her and her father to visit with him at Plumstead Episcopi. There she meets Mr. Arabin who falls in love with her but, through lack of experience with women, does not know how to press his suit. When Eleanor receives a note from Mr. Slope at Dr. Grantly's home, her brother-in-law furiously assumes she is about to marry his arch-enemy. Mr. Harding shares this feeling, and wistfully prepares to accept Mr. Slope as a son-in-law. But when even Mr. Arabin believes she intends to marry Mr. Slope, Eleanor angrily leaves the house and returns to Barchester.

Affairs come to a head at a splendid lawn party given by the rich and old-fashioned Thornes of Ullathorne, the local country squire and his eccentric spinster sister. Eleanor, driven to the party in a carriage with the Stanhopes, finds herself seated next to Mr. Slope who decides to propose to her. When he does so later in the day, Eleanor slaps him in irritation.

Then Bertie, egged on by his sisters, tries half-heartedly to propose, but he naïvely tells Eleanor that his sister Charlotte has convinced him he should marry the widow to repair his broken fortunes. Eleanor is now furious with the entire Stanhope family, especially when she sees Mr. Arabin being played up to by the Signora Neroni. When Dr. Stanhope learns that Bertie has failed once again, he orders him out of the house. A few days later Bertie sets out for Italy, hoping to make his fortune as a sculptor.

Now Dr. Trefoil, the old Dean of Barchester, has a stroke and is on his deathbed. This means a new ecclesiastical position to fill—and the final test of strength between the warring factions. Mr. Slope, who would like the deanship for himself, plunges into action, writing letters to powerful friends in journalism and the government. He gets his newspaper friends' support and assumes he has Bishop Proudie's blessings. He does not, however, count on the unrelenting fury of Mrs. Proudie who has not forgotten how he danced attendance on the Signora Neroni and thwarted his patroness in the Quiverful affair.

Mrs. Proudie has made her husband's life so miserable that he has completely surrendered to her. He offers the deanship to Mr. Harding to preserve domestic peace. Mr. Slope's defeat is complete. Not only does he not get the deanship, but Mrs. Proudie also sees to it that he is no longer her husband's chaplain, and he must leave Barchester to try his luck elsewhere. He is also subjected to a scornful dressing-down by the Signora Neroni.

Now that Mr. Slope has left, the relieved Stanhopes feel they can safely return to Italy, but before leaving, Signora Neroni summons Eleanor to her home to tell her that Mr. Arabin is deeply in love with her but lacks the courage to make his feelings clear.

Mr. Harding decides he is too old for the deanship. Mr. Arabin is appointed instead, a great victory for the high-church faction, comparable only to the ousting of Mr. Slope from Barchester. Mr. Quiverful finally gets the wardenship of Hiram's Hospital, and Dr. Grantly is content.

With his new power, Mr. Arabin is emboldened to speak to Eleanor, and a meeting is arranged at Ullathorne, where Miss Thorne, a great matchmaker, sees to it that Mr. Arabin proposes. Eleanor accepts him, and peace once again returns to Barchester.

Critical Opinion

Henry James once said of Trollope that "his great, his inestimable merit was a complete appreciation of the usual." Unlike Dickens, his great contemporary, Trollope generally avoided writing about the grotesque, the bizarre, or the desperately poor people of this world. His novels describe in detail the average middle-class lives of mid-Victorian English-men going about their business in a normal way. A keen observer of the niceties of social behavior, Trollope is comparable to the Dutch genre painters who rendered middle-class life in faithful detail, uncharged with passionate emotion.

Thus *Barchester Towers,* although it is about the clergy, can hardly be said to seethe with religious emotion. Trollope's clergymen are average men with average ambitions and desires. The doctrinal disputes between high and low church factions are treated not as genuine theological issues but rather as counters in a political chess game. A religious zealot would be ludicrously out of place in Barsetshire.

Trollope's satire in *Barchester Towers* is milder than the indignant humor of Dickens or the sophisticated wit of Thackeray. It is best exemplified in his portraits of Mrs. Proudie and her henpecked husband, and in such scenes as the bishop's reception and the Ullathorne fete.

Trollope tries to be fair-minded in his judgment of people. None are wholly virtuous or wholly wicked. Mr. Slope, odious as he is, is described neither as a fool nor a coward. Trollope's satire, in short, unlike Dickens' or Meredith's, has nothing in it of the "corrective." He is not a campaigner for any radical change in society. He tends to accept life as it is. This is not to say that Trollope does not moralize. Like Thackeray, George Eliot, and other Victorian novelists, he addresses the reader directly, giving his opinions of the characters at crucial moments in the action.

Trollope's attitude toward his characters is almost remorse-lessly sane and reasonable. He never attains any grandeur, but neither does he ever become ridiculous or absurd. Although some of his later political novels probe deeper beneath the surface of Victorian society, it is the six-novel Barsetshire series that stands as Trollope's finest achievement. Like Balzac in his *Comédie Humaine,* Hardy in his Wessex novels, and Faulkner in his Yoknapatawpha novels, Trollope, by means of characters who reappear from novel to novel and by means of geographical and thematic unity, brings alive a whole area of human experience. Because the society he depicts is seen in such detail, many of his readers today still find his novels, especially the Barchester group, remarkably real and engrossing.

The Author

Anthony Trollope, born in London on April 24, 1815, attended Harrow and Winchester sporadically until the family, plagued by his father's mismanagement of the family fortunes, moved to Belgium to escape their creditors.

In 1834 Trollope entered the General Post Office as a clerk, but rapidly rose through the ranks. In his travels as postal inspector he began to write his extensive series of novels, beginning with two novels of Irish life in 1847 and 1848, and proceeding to the first of the famous Barsetshire series, *The Warden*, in 1855.

Aside from this series, of which the most famous novels are *Barchester Towers* (1857) and *The Last Chronicle of Barset* a decade later, Trollope's major novels are *The Eustace Diamonds* (1873) and *The Way We Live Now* (1875), an inveighing against the ills of Victorian England. Most of Trollope's novels deal either with clerical or political life.

Trollope was able to write a great number of novels (most of them quite long), indulge in his favorite sport of fox hunting, and travel extensively while performing his duties in the postal service because he worked so systematically at his writing. He planned and wrote his novels in trains while going from one postal inspection job to another, keeping himself to a rigid schedule of literary production. He even set a fixed number of words to write every quarter hour and kept a watch constantly in view. In his fascinating *Autobiography*, published posthumously in 1883, Trollope confessed that up to 1879 he had earned the staggering sum of £70,000 from his writing.

Enormously popular during Trollope's lifetime, his books began to decline in popularity almost immediately after his death, perhaps because the unromantic, businesslike revelations of his *Autobiography* shattered his readers' notions about how his novels were written. Interest in Trollope revived, however, shortly before World War II, when readers under wartime pressures found satisfaction in his leisurely, mildly humorous accounts of everyday life in a more stable world. One modern novelist, the late Angela Thirkell, was so entranced by the world of Barsetshire that she also wrote a series of novels about it.

By the Same Author

The Warden: The first of the Barsetshire series, coming just before *Barchester Towers,* this brief work introduces us to Dr. Grantly and Mr. Harding, who has been happily performing the functions of warden of Hiram's Hospital. When his daughter, Eleanor, falls in love with John Bold, an idealistic, rather priggish young physician, trouble begins. Bold has found out that according to the original stipulations of John Hiram's will, Mr. Harding has been getting a stipend much larger than he should. The kindly, cello-playing old choirmaster of Barchester is willing to resign his post, but Dr. Grantly will not hear of it. He finds it disgraceful that an outsider should meddle in church business, and he opposes Mr. Harding's resignation as a matter of principle. Mr. Harding becomes a pawn in a battle between Dr. Grantly and Mr. Bold, a conflict that raises a furor in the London newspapers. All ends well, however, when Mr. Harding is finally allowed to resign.

The Last Chronicle of Barset: This huge conclusion to the Barsetshire series was considered by Trollope to be his best novel. It deals with the events that follow when the Reverend Josiah Crawley is unjustly accused of stealing £20. Mr. Crawley finds himself in conflict with Mrs. Proudie over the affair (she tries to replace him in his own church). Before he is cleared, Mrs. Proudie, the most fascinating and, in her peculiar way, one of the most lovable characters in the series, dies of an apoplètic fit. Old Mr. Harding dies, too.

Adam Bede

by

GEORGE ELIOT (1819–1880)

Main Characters

Adam Bede—A strong and upright young carpenter.
Seth Bede—Adam's brother, in love with Dinah Morris.
Dinah Morris—A serious-minded Methodist preacher.
Martin Poyser—A neighborhood landowner who runs prosperous Hall Farm.
Mrs. Poyser—His voluble wife, Dinah's aunt, filled with folk wisdom and a sense of her own importance.
Hetty Sorrel—Another niece of Mrs. Poyser's, a vivacious, curly-haired girl of seventeen.
Arthur Donnithorne—The selfish, aristocratic grandson of the local squire.
Jonathan Burge—The master builder and carpenter who employs Adam Bede.

The Story

Adam Bede is a powerfully built young carpenter working for the builder Jonathan Burge in the small village of Hayslope in the year 1799. Adam is universally admired, and counts among his friends young Captain Arthur Donnithorne, grandson of the local squire.

One evening as Adam leaves his spacious workshop, his

brother Seth goes courting the earnest Dinah Morris, a gentle Methodist who is preaching on the village green. Escorting Dinah home after her sermon, Seth asks her to become his wife, but she replies that although she likes him she cannot marry because she is called to preach the word of God. When Seth returns home, disconsolate, he finds Adam working on a coffin that their father was commissioned to make but neglected to finish. Old Matthias Bede has of late become a frequenter of the local inn, and his wife, Lisbeth, complains bitterly about his irresponsibility while Adam hammers vigorously at the coffin.

On his way home from the tavern that night, the drunken Matthias Bede falls into the Willow Brook and drowns, leaving Lisbeth more than ever dependent on her two sons who will have to wait before they can think of getting married.

Mr. Burge is so pleased with Adam's work that he wishes he would marry his daughter, Mary. But Adam is in love with Hetty Sorrel, a pert, flirtatious girl of seventeen who lives with her aunt, Mrs. Poyser, at Hall Farm. However, the dashing Arthur Donnithorne visits the Poyser dairy one day, and since then Hetty thinks of no one but him. Her uncle, Martin Poyser, would like Hetty to marry the stable, honest Adam, but she dreams of the luxuries that the heir to Squire Donnithorne can offer her.

During the summer, Donnithorne leaves with his regiment and Adam hopes that Hetty will now turn her attention to him. But when Donnithorne returns to celebrate his twenty-first birthday, the whole village is astir with excitement over the feast that is to be held on the Donnithorne estate. Adam is honored with a place at Donnithorne's table. This act of friendship worries Adam's mother. She fears that it may give him notions above his station in life. The feast is a great success and Donnithorne becomes more than ever a glamorous figure in Hetty's romantic eyes.

Three weeks after the birthday celebration, Adam is returning home when he sees two figures in intimate embrace. His dog frightens them and the girl runs off, but Adam has seen that they are Arthur Donnithorne and Hetty Sorrel.

Knowing that the young aristocrat has no intention of marrying Hetty, Adam calls him "a coward and scoundrel," and soon the two former friends are exchanging blows. Adam easily defeats Donnithorne and makes him promise that he will write a letter to Hetty calling off the affair which Arthur insists was only a harmless flirtation. He gives the letter to Adam to deliver the next day, hoping that this action will prejudice Hetty even further against the carpenter.

When Adam gives the letter to Hetty, she is plunged into despair. After Adam is offered a share of Mr. Burge's business, he proposes marriage to the flighty Hetty. Again the Poysers urge her to accept, and this time, to their joy, she gives in. The wedding is put off for a while so that the Bede house can be enlarged to receive the newlyweds.

In February, Hetty, pretending that she is going to visit Dinah Morris in the mill town where she is currently preaching, impulsively leaves in search of Donnithorne. She learns to her dismay that his regiment has gone off to Ireland. She gives birth to his baby and abandons it in a wood. Then, filled with remorse, she returns to the spot where she left the infant and finds it dead.

When Donnithorne's grandfather dies, the young squire returns to Hayslope. He learns that Hetty is in prison awaiting execution for the murder of her child. He tries desperately to win her release, apparently to no avail. Dinah returns to Hayslope and visits the condemned girl, trying to ease her misery and get her to make a full confession. Hetty breaks down and says she did not intend the baby to die, and in fact was overcome with guilt when she learned what had happened. For a while she even considered killing herself.

Just as Hetty is about to die on the scaffold, Donnithorne, remorseful at his role in the tragedy, wins a reprieve for the girl. Instead of imposing the death sentence, the court orders that she be exiled to the colonies. Donnithorne leaves for a new life in Spain. He later learns that Hetty has died after serving her sentence.

Meanwhile, Adam Bede tries to find solace at his workbench. The following autumn Dinah Morris returns to the Poyser farm but leaves soon after to preach in the town. One day she accompanies Adam to his house, where his mother is ailing. On the way there, Adam shyly confides that he wishes Dinah were his sister so they could be together always. Dinah blushes at this but keeps her silence. Then her mother hints outright that Adam ought to propose to the good, earnest Methodist girl.

Adam first consults with his brother Seth who, he feels,

has a prior claim to Dinah's hand. Seth assures him, however, that all is over between them and that Adam can lose nothing by proposing to her.

Adam finally asks Dinah to marry him. She tells him that, although she is strongly attracted to him, she must await divine guidance. Accordingly, she goes back to the town to live. After a while Adam comes to see her and he learns that Dinah will marry him after all.

Critical Opinion

Although *Adam Bede* is the first of George Eliot's novels, it was written when she was forty years old and is consequently more mature than the first work of most novelists. From its initial publication in 1859—the year also saw the appearance of *A Tale of Two Cities, The Ordeal of Richard Feverel,* and *The Origin of Species*—it became a favorite with readers, including Dickens, Charles Kingsley, and Alexandre Dumas.

All of George Eliot's characteristic concerns and skills appear in *Adam Bede.* Her brooding compassion for weak humanity caught in moral traps of its own devising is movingly set forth in the tragedy of Hetty Sorrel, a sensuous girl of great sensitivity to life whose sin and expiation form the moral backbone of the novel. As one who had herself "sinned," or at least flouted the conventions of society, George Eliot was keenly aware of the temptations of love and at the same time sharply perceptive of its morally destructive qualities.

Another achievement of George Eliot's in *Adam Bede* is her ability to portray with gentle, uncondescending humor the uncomplicated lives of the rural lower middle class. Mrs. Poyser, Hetty's bumbling, officious aunt, is a triumph of comic art. Her sayings, folk wisdom mingled with self-important sententiousness, remain a delight. In her portrayal of rural types, George Eliot is matched in English literature only by Shakespeare and by her follower, Thomas Hardy, whose *Tess of the D'Urbervilles* in many ways resembles *Adam Bede.*

Central to George Eliot's moral doctrine is the influence of one soul on another. It was here that George Eliot touched upon themes that made her so unpopular for years after her death. The purity of Dinah and of Adam himself tends to be less acceptable to the modern reader than to George Eliot's contemporaries. In the story of Hetty she refurbished the stock Victorian cliché of the sinning girl, seduced and abandoned by an aristocratic weakling.

George Eliot transcends the limitations of her period, however, by the keenness of her analysis of a man who is amoral and basically selfish but who nevertheless has considerable charm and who redeems himself. She is most expert at outlining the conflict between the weakness of the flesh and one's moral duties to oneself and to others, a theme richly explored by her for the first time in *Adam Bede*.

The Author

George Eliot was the pen name of Mary Ann Evans, who was born in Warwickshire on November 22, 1819. Her father was an estate agent of somewhat conventional religious and social views which Mary Ann rebelled against. At an early age she had come under the influence of a Coventry manufacturer named Charles Bray.

Characteristically, the first work of this gentle, intensely serious and intellectual girl was a translation of the controversially rationalistic *Life of Jesus* by the German scholar, D. F. Strauss. Her father died in 1849, unreconciled to his daughter's views of religion.

Between 1851 and 1853, she was assistant editor of the *Westminster Review* and did further translations of significant German works. As an editor of this important liberal publication, she met the leading intellectual and artistic lights of her day, including the philosopher Herbert Spencer and the author of a standard biography of Goethe, George Henry Lewes. She fell in love with Lewes who was separated from his wife but could not obtain a divorce.

From 1854 until Lewes' death in 1878, George Eliot lived unconventionally with him. They never married. Although this step was initially shocking to Victorian morality, the rectitude and high moral tone of the match soon silenced most scandal, but the ambiguous social position George Eliot occupied shaped her later thinking about morality in the novels she began to write, of which *Adam Bede* was the first.

She followed this success with *The Mill on the Floss* (1860) and *Silas Marner* (1861). During the composition of these works, George Eliot visited Florence, where she did research in Renaissance life for her historical novel, the vast, somewhat inchoate *Romola* (1863). She returned to England for the subject matter of *Felix Holt* (1866) and her masterpiece, *Middlemarch* (1871–1872), the most complex and artistically successful of her novels.

After *Middlemarch*, George Eliot's talents seemed exhausted. Her final novel, *Daniel Deronda* (1876), is more noteworthy for its moral philosophy and for its prophetic treatment of Zionism (the hero, unique in Victorian fiction, is a Jew) than for any unusual qualities as fiction.

In May 1880, George Eliot married John Walter Cross. She died on December 22 of the same year. At the time of her death she was widely recognized as one of the outstanding novelists of the day, but her reputation underwent an eclipse from which it only recently has begun to emerge.

By the Same Author

Silas Marner: *Silas Marner* is a brief tale, told in classically simple style, of the redemption of an embittered miser through love. Falsely accused of theft in a small religious community, Silas Marner, a linen weaver, settles in Raveloe, where he lives for a while only to accumulate wealth. After fifteen years of loneliness, Marner is accused of a new theft, but his troubles begin to disappear when he discovers and adopts a pretty stray child named Eppie. As Eppie grows up, her selfless, unquestioning love for the old man purges his soul of the crabbed suspicion of his fellow beings which had formerly consumed it. The real culprit is discovered eventually, and Silas is allowed to live out the rest of his days with Eppie in peace and contentment.

Middlemarch: This, the most complex and richest of George Eliot's novels, was once cited by Virginia Woolf as one of the few English novels written for adults. Several stories are intertwined in it, the central "hero" really being the outwardly placid small English town of Middlemarch. In it Dorothea Brooke, an idealistic young woman, makes a bad marriage with the dry pedant Casaubon and later falls in love with his charming, irresponsible cousin, Will Ladislaw. At the same time, an idealistic young doctor, Lydgate, marries the shallow, spendthrift beauty, Rosamond Vincy, whose unceasing demands for a more luxurious life destroy him as a pure scientist. Out of these unhappy marriages, George Eliot weaves an immense tapestry in which the material life is seen in constant battle with the life of the spirit, and in which the social fabric of a town is scrupulously but compassionately analyzed.

The Ordeal of Richard Feverel

by

GEORGE MEREDITH (1828–1909)

Main Characters

Sir Austin Feverel—The embittered, possessive Lord of Raynham Abbey, suspicious of women and determined to protect his son from the world by a strict but eccentric system of education.

Richard Feverel—Sir Austin's only son, the "Hope of Raynham," a headstrong, idealistic, and thoroughly· aristocratic youth who chafes at his father's "System."

Adrian Harley—Sir Austin's nephew, the "Wise Youth," a parasitical and cynical young man who reports to Sir Austin on Richard's doings and enjoys trading epigrams with the Lord of Raynham.

Austin Wentworth—Richard's sensible, humane uncle who thinks the "System" is all nonsense.

Ripton Thompson—Richard's middle-class playmate and friend who joins him in his youthful escapades.

Tom Bakewell—A local farmhand who becomes Richard's loyal servant.

Blaize—The neighboring farmer, blunt, straightforward, and totally unimpressed by the grandeur of the Feverels.

Lucy Desborough—Blaize's Catholic niece, who loves Richard despite Sir Austin's disapproval and Richard's infidelity.

Lord Mountfalcon—A debauched aristocrat who flirts with Lucy after her marriage to Richard.

Bella Mount—A "fallen woman" who seduces Richard when he tries to have her accepted by society.

Clare—Richard's cousin, secretly and hopelessly in love with him.

Lady Emmeline Blandish—A wise, sophisticated woman whose admiration for Sir Austin Feverel does not prevent her from trying to intervene on Richard's behalf.

Heavy Benson—Sir Austin's serpentine butler.

The Story

When Sir Austin Feverel's wife ran off with a minor poet, the Lord of Raynham Abbey vowed that he would bring up his only son, Richard, according to a system that would spare him such disagreeable experiences. A confirmed woman hater and author of the cynical book of anti-feminist epigrams, *The Pilgrim's Scrip*, Sir Austin is determined that Richard should have no serious contact with women until he is twenty-five.

Placing Richard's education in the hands of his worldly-wise nephew, Adrian Harley, Sir Austin takes great pains to ensure Richard's innocence of the world and tries to instill in him a fine moral sense. He brings Richard up to be everything a young aristocrat should be: honorable, chivalrous, and high-spirited. But as he approaches adolescence, Richard becomes impatient with the kind of life he is leading. Sir Austin decides he must have a safe companion for his son, one he can trust not to lead Richard astray. He selects Ripton Thompson, the rather plodding son of his lawyer, who proves a willing follower in all of Richard's youthful pranks.

One of these escapades gets Richard into the first serious trouble of his life. Out hunting one day with Ripton, he unintentionally trespasses on the neighboring estate of Farmer Blaize, a political enemy of his father, and illegally shoots a pheasant. Blaize accuses the boys of poaching and orders them off his land. When Richard, insulted that a mere farmer should address him in this way, refuses to leave, Blaize horsewhips him.

On Richard's return, his father sends him to his room after dinner. Unrepentant, Richard meets Ripton and they plot a suitable revenge on Farmer Blaize. The boys set fire to Blaize's hayricks, with the aid of Tom Bakewell, a local farm laborer. Sir Austin suspects the truth, but does not accuse his son because he wants to see whether the boy will behave honorably without any prompting, as the system has taught him to do. Ripton, however, is immediately sent back to his father.

Tom Bakewell is arrested for arson, but he protects Richard by not mentioning the bribe Richard gave him to set the ricks on fire. When he hears of Tom's courage, Richard immediately goes to Farmer Blaize to confess. He does not know that his father has already quietly paid for the damage. Humiliated by Blaize's refusal to take his confession seriously, Richard stalks out of the house, failing to notice the farmer's pretty, young orphan niece, Lucy Desborough. Tom is acquitted at the trial and becomes Richard's lifelong loyal servant.

When Richard turns eighteen, his father decides to go to London to find a suitable wife for him. When Richard reaches the age of twenty-five, Sir Austin plans to let him marry a girl worthy of his fine upbringing.

But while Sir Austin is away, Richard meets the lovely Lucy Desborough, and they have an idyllic, innocent love affair. Richard had been earlier attracted to his cousin Clare, who passionately but secretly loves him. Now, however, he can think only of Lucy. The pair meet frequently in the meadows and woods surrounding the abbey to swear their love to each other. Lucy unfortunately has, in the eyes of the Feverels, one major defect. She is a Catholic.

In their innocence Lucy and Richard are unaware that they are being spied upon by Heavy Benson, Sir Austin's woman-hating butler. When Richard learns of this, he beats Benson nearly to death, but it is too late. Sir Austin has been informed of the affair and summons Richard to London to meet the girl he has chosen for him, Carola Grandison.

When Richard, unwilling to part from Lucy, puts off going to London, Adrian tells him his father is ill with apoplexy, and the dutiful son then hurries to London. Here, he finds his father quite healthy, but angry with him for carrying on with Lucy behind his back. Sir Austin lectures his son about the dangers of women, pointing out that every Feverel is doomed to an ordeal brought about by a woman. He insists on Richard's meeting Carola Grandison, who is nice enough but hardly the girl to drive Lucy from Richard's mind. Soon, however, Lucy stops writing him, and Richard, distracted, insists on returning to Raynham. There he discovers that Farmer Blaize, who also disapproves of the affair, has sent the unwilling Lucy off to a distant school.

Now Richard determines to take matters in his own hands. He persuades his old friend, Ripton Thompson, to procure lodgings in London for Lucy, and then, accompanied by his dyspeptic and inefficient Uncle Hippias, sets off for London himself. Giving his uncle the slip, Richard secretly establishes Lucy in a lodging house run by Mrs. Berry, his childhood nurse. He persuades the seventeen-year-old Lucy to marry him; but just as he is hurrying to the church, he accidentally meets Adrian Harley, Cousin Clare, and her mother. In his embarrassment, he drops his wedding ring which Clare picks up. Aware now of what Richard is about to do, Clare loyally keeps his secret, even though it is an agony for her to know that Richard is marrying another girl.

Delegating Ripton to break the news to Sir Austin, Richard marries Lucy and the pair go to the Isle of Wight for their honeymoon. Sir Austin's reaction to the news is cold and philosophical. He recognizes that the elopement means the defeat of his system. His old friend and admirer, Lady Blandish, tries to persuade him to meet Lucy, for she knows that the lovely girl will surely captivate him. But Sir Austin refuses even to answer Richard's conciliatory letters.

Efforts made by Lady Blandish and by Adrian, who has visited the honeymooning couple, to reconcile father and son fail. Sir Austin is deeply hurt by Richard's deception. Journeying from the Isle of Wight to London in the hope of meeting his father there, Richard innocently leaves Lucy in the care of the wicked Lord Mountfalcon. Mountfalcon arranges with a friend of his, the notorious Mrs. Bella Mount, to seduce Richard in London and to keep him there while Mountfalcon has his way with Lucy. Disregarding the warnings of friends, Richard falls into the trap by determining to rescue the reputation of Mrs. Mount while he is in London. After three months of waiting for his father to show up, Richard finally succumbs to Mrs. Mount's charms, unaware that his own Lucy, now staying with Mrs. Berry in London, is about to bear his son.

Meanwhile Richard's cousin Clare, having realized the

hopelessness of her love for him, has consented to marry an old man chosen by her mother. She dies soon after, leaving a diary telling of her love for Richard which fills him with remorse for his callousness. He feels further guilt about his relations with Mrs. Mount and goes wandering vaguely about Europe, unsure of himself and unable to face Lucy.

While Richard is wallowing in self-pity and guilt, his reasonable uncle, Austin Wentworth, returns to England after five years abroad. Wentworth, who never approved of the system, learns of the unhappiness it has produced and brings Lucy to Raynham to meet Sir Austin. In his loneliness Sir Austin has relented somewhat. He is charmed by his daughter-in-law and the handsome grandson she has borne him. Richard, informed that he is a father, returns to England. But before he can get to Raynham, he receives a letter from Mrs. Mount divulging Lord Mountfalcon's plot to seduce Lucy. He challenges Lord Mountfalcon to a duel, not realizing that whatever his original intentions may have been, the old roué never succeeded in undermining Lucy's virtue.

Then Richard returns to Raynham. He embraces the ecstatic Lucy and sees his son for the first time. Overcome with remorse, he confesses his infidelity and receives Lucy's forgiveness. Leaving a distraught Lucy behind, Richard rushes off to France for his duel. He is only slightly wounded by Lord Mountfalcon. But Lucy, in her anxiety for his safety, contracts brain fever and dies. When Richard hears of her death, his spirit is completely crushed. Lady Blandish wonders if Sir Austin, in his grief at the double tragedy, realizes that he has destroyed his boy with the rigors of his system.

Critical Opinion

The Ordeal of Richard Feverel is a strange and not altogether successful novel, a fact Meredith tacitly admitted when he revised it twenty years after its first publication. The plot is often incoherent and cluttered with minor characters, many of whom disappeared in the revised version. Its outstanding quality is its mingling of sophisticated comedy with passionate lyricism and somber tragedy. Many readers have felt, for instance, that the death of Lucy and the ruin of Richard's future are insufficiently motivated by that unimportant last-minute duel. The novel oscillates between high comedy (the court of admiring females hoping to marry Sir Austin, the determined but attractive woman-hater) and lyricism (Richard's love for Lucy, couched in a style that reminds us that Meredith thought of himself primarily as a poet).

Much of *Richard Feverel* is autobiographical. The desertion of Sir Austin by his wife before the book begins is a reflection of Meredith's own loss of his first wife. The tragi-comic efforts of Sir Austin to educate his only son represent Meredith's own nagging fears of the kind of father he might prove to be.

The greatness of the book lies in its ironic sense of the difference between reality and romance, and in its perception of the folly of trying to force a young, independent spirit into the rigorous, life-denying mold of an egoistic system of education. Warm-hearted and idealistic, Richard genuinely wants to help the "fallen woman," Bella Mount, but only succumbs to her charms and neglects the wife who really needs him. Similarly, Sir Austin's adoration of his son ironically leads to the most tragic consequences. For all Sir Austin's witty aphorisms and Adrian Harley's cynical appraisal of life, *The Ordeal of Richard Feverel* is a profoundly pessimistic book, underscoring the tragic consequences that flow from any effort to mold another human being after one's own sterile image.

The Author

George Meredith was born on February 12, 1828, the son and grandson of prosperous naval outfitters in Portsmouth. A consummate snob, he kept his ancestry secret throughout his life. His mother died when he was a child, and Meredith was sent to a German school where he received a thorough education. In 1849 he married the widowed daughter of Thomas Love Peacock, the distinguished satiric novelist.

It was an unhappy marriage, but it had one bright aspect: the friendship between Meredith and Peacock. The older novelist's sparkling wit and cosmopolitan view of the world strongly impressed Meredith and was later to influence his own fiction.

In 1858 his wife ran off with a lover, leaving Meredith, like Sir Austin Feverel, to bring up their son alone. The next year he published *The Ordeal of Richard Feverel,* his first real novel. Although the book did not sell well, it caught the attention of Swinburne, Rossetti, and others of the Pre-Raphaelite group of artists and writers. From that point on Meredith became the darling of the English intelligentsia although his novels never won the vast audiences that Dickens and Thackeray reached.

In 1861 Meredith's estranged wife died. Brooding over the failure of his marriage, Meredith wrote the great, tragic *Modern Love,* one of the finest long poems of the nineteenth century. At the same time he became a reader and editor for Chapman and Hall, a job he kept until 1894. He made some strange mistakes as a reader, rejecting, for instance, Samuel Butler's *Erewhon* and the early works of George Bernard Shaw, but he was also responsible for the encouragement of his great contemporary, Thomas Hardy.

In 1864 Meredith married again, this time more successfully. With his new wife, Marie Vulliamy, the novelist settled down at Box Hill in Surrey, where he lived the rest of his life. There he wrote some of his most famous novels, *The Adventures of Harry Richmond* (1871), *Beauchamp's Career* (1876), *The Egoist* (1879), and *Diana of the Crossways* (1885).

Meredith's second wife died in 1885, but Meredith lived on for another quarter century. Lonely and ailing, his productive powers waning, Meredith became the recipient of many honors, including the highly coveted Order of Merit. His brand of intellectual comedy had not won him a vast audience. Only a small, fiercely loyal group mourned his death, on May 18, 1909.

By the Same Author

The Egoist: Like Sir Austin Feverel, Sir Willoughby Patterne of Patterne Hall, the hero-villain of *The Egoist,* is a man consumed with a sense of his own importance. Again, like Sir Austin, Sir Willoughby is hounded by women who are at once attracted and repelled by his arrogance. After he is jilted by one of them, Constantia Durham, he falls in love with the beautiful and intelligent Clara Middleton, who stays with her father at Patterne Hall during a six-month engagement.

Sir Willoughby meanwhile maintains an interest in another

intelligent young lady, Laetitia Dale. His great fear is that he will be jilted a second time, something his ego could never bear. This inevitably happens when, in his blind conceit, he fails to see that Clara has fallen in love with Vernon Whitford, Willoughby's scholarly cousin and secretary. After a series of brilliant maneuvers and intrigues, Clara and Vernon marry, and poor Laetitia ends as the wife of the man she knows to be a "vindictive and incorrigible egotist." *The Egoist* is probably Meredith's richest and most complex novel. It is consistently comic, although tinged with pathos.

Diana of the Crossways: Meredith's last important novel, and during his lifetime one of his most popular, *Diana* is based on an actual scandal that shook early nineteenth-century England. The scandal concerned Mrs. Caroline Norton, the granddaughter of the famous playwright and parliamentarian, Richard Brinsley Sheridan. Mrs. Norton was unjustly accused of selling to a newspaper an important political secret she had obtained from her lover. In the novel, Mrs. Norton becomes the beautiful, witty, and misunderstood Diana Merion. Diana, trying to escape a loveless marriage with Augustus Warwick, becomes involved in a trial over her innocent but suspect relation with the powerful Lord Dannisburgh. Her beauty and wit make her a popular hostess, but she arouses the jealousy of most society women whose rumor-mongering nearly brings her to ruin.

Alice in Wonderland

by

LEWIS CARROLL (1832–1898)

Main Characters

Alice—A well-mannered little Victorian girl, full of curiosity.
The White Rabbit—Nervous, elegant, and very anxious about missing an appointment with the Duchess.
The Duchess—An extremely ugly creature, in mortal fear of the Queen.
The Queen of Hearts—Her favorite expression is "Off with his head!"
The Cheshire Cat—With its broad grin, it can appear and disappear at will.
The Mad Hatter—The host at the Mad Tea Party.

The Story

One drowsy summer afternoon, Alice is sleepily reading over her sister's shoulder when all at once she sees a White Rabbit, dressed for a party, consulting his pocketwatch and fretting about being late. Curiously she follows the Rabbit across a field and suddenly tumbles down the hole into which he has scuttled, falling and falling until she comes to a stop on a pile of leaves. There she sees the Rabbit again, but before she can question him he scurries away, leaving her in a long hall bounded by many locked doors.

Spotting a golden key on a glass table, Alice manages to unlock the smallest of the doors. Although she sees an inviting garden with a cool fountain through the door, she is too tall to get in. On a table she spots a bottle labeled "Drink me." When she drinks, Alice finds she has shrunk to ten inches— but she still cannot get into the garden because she has foolishly left the key on the table, and it is now far above her reach.

On a dish beneath the table, however, Alice finds a cookie labeled "Eat me." Alice does and immediately becomes nine feet tall.

Now Alice sees the White Rabbit again, but when she tries to talk to him, he scampers off, dropping his gloves and fan. Alice picks them up and begins to fan herself, only to discover that it is the fan that is reducing her height again. The White Rabbit reappears, frantically searching for his gloves. Under the impression that she is his maidservant, he curtly orders Alice to fetch new ones. Alice dutifully obeys and runs through a wood until she comes to a small white house with a doorplate reading "W. Rabbit."

In the Rabbit's house she finds the new gloves and fan, and also a very tempting-looking bottle. Unable to resist, Alice drinks from it and immediately begins growing again. This time she grows to such a size that she barely saves herself from being crushed by the house by putting one leg up the chimney and her elbow out the window, with her head drawn up to her chin.

Suddenly, Alice hears someone throwing pebbles against the window of the house. These become little cakes, which she eats, and soon she is small enough to emerge from the Rabbit's house. Running through the wood, Alice comes to rest beside a giant mushroom. Perched lazily on it is a caterpillar smoking a hookah. After rudely insulting her intelligence, the caterpillar tells Alice that she will grow if she eats from one side of the mushroom; she will shrink if she eats from the other. At first Alice shrinks so much that her chin hits her foot. In a panic, she quickly eats from the other side, and her neck becomes so long it reaches up to the treetops where an indignant pigeon scolds her for being an egg-stealing serpent.

Finally Alice is the right size. Proceeding through the wood, she comes upon the Duchess' cottage where a fishlike servant is handing to a froglike servant an invitation to the Duchess to play croquet with the Queen of Hearts. Without knocking, for she cannot be heard above the din, Alice enters the cottage and finds the Duchess rocking her infant in her lap while a cook is sprinkling pepper into some soup. The noise is deafening. The baby is squalling, and the Duchess is sneezing violently from the pepper. At the hearth is the Cheshire Cat grinning enigmatically from ear to ear.

The Duchess gives Alice her baby to hold for a while and disappears. As Alice tries to quiet the infant, its cries gradually become grunts, and she suddenly finds herself holding a little pig in her arms. It slips out of her arms and runs into the forest. Alice looks up and sees the Cheshire Cat grinning at her from the treetops. He tells Alice to go to a tea party being given by the Mad Hatter and then disappears in sections, his grin remaining to the last.

At the tea party, Alice meets the Mad Hatter, the March Hare (who is also mad), and a drowsy dormouse who keeps falling into the teapot and has to be rescued. Everyone is very rude to Alice, asking her unsolvable riddles and making personal comments. Finally, the Dormouse is persuaded to tell a long, involved story that puts even him to sleep.

Alice escapes from the party and comes to a garden where gardeners are painting talking flowers to please the Queen. The Queen catches the gardeners painting some white roses red and immediately orders them away to be executed, but Alice saves them by hiding them in a flowerpot. Now a royal procession begins, with soldiers and courtiers made out of playing cards followed by the Duchess, the White Rabbit, and the Queen of Hearts herself.

The royal croquet game gets under way. Live flamingoes are used as mallets and hedgehogs as balls. The wickets are formed by the card soldiers bending over. The Queen hands Alice a flamingo and peremptorily orders her to start playing. The game is impossible. Everyone plays at once. The hedgehogs crawl away just as the players are about to strike them. The flamingo keeps turning its head up to stare at Alice. Since the Queen shouts "Off with his head!" every time someone's playing displeases her, the soldier-wickets keep leaving their positions.

The Cheshire Cat materializes on the scene and asks Alice how she likes the game. Alice says she does not, and the Cat then looks at the King of Hearts and grins his famous grin. The King complains to the Queen who orders the Cat beheaded; but since, by now, only the Cat's head is in view, nobody knows how to go about executing him, and he is ignored.

When Alice is ready to give up the game in despair, the Duchess corners her and takes her to the seaside. Here Alice meets the Mock Turtle and the Gryphon, two lugubrious characters. The Mock Turtle describes his education, which has consisted of Reeling, Writhing, and all the parts of Arithmetic: Ambition, Distraction, Uglification, and Derision. These creatures invite Alice to join them in the Lobster Quadrille, a very complicated dance performed on the sands.

While they are dancing, they hear news that a trial is in progress. The Knave of Hearts has stolen the Queen's tarts and is being tried for his life. The Queen is all for delivering the verdict before the jury can deliberate. Several witnesses, however, give their testimony, none of which has anything to do with the case. (The jurymen are the dormouse, a ferret, a frog, a hedgehog, and other animals.)

Alice is finally called upon to give her testimony, but she denounces the trial as unfair, and the Queen orders, "Off with her head!" By now Alice has grown to such size that she inadvertently upsets the jury box, and all the creatures in it spill helter-skelter on the floor. After returning them to the box, Alice tells the Queen her procedure of "sentence first— verdict afterwards" is stuff and nonsense.

Screaming for Alice's head, the Queen becomes wild with fury, but Alice, now her full size, retorts, "Who cares for you? You're nothing but a pack of cards!" The cards all rise in the air and start flying at her. With a little scream, Alice awakens and finds that the cards are really dead leaves that have fallen on her face. Her sister shakes her and tells her she has been asleep all the time. Alice has been to Wonderland in a dream.

Critical Opinion

The Alice books (*Alice in Wonderland* and *Through the Looking-Glass*) appeal to adults and to children alike. A century after they were written, they remain as popular as ever. Children are delighted by the magic changes in size, the strange creatures Alice meets, and the perfectly sustained fairy-tale atmosphere. Adults find in the books witty social satire and profound commentaries on illusion and reality and on the relations between children and the adult world.

Most of the creatures Alice meets are abominably condescending. The White Rabbit, the Caterpillar, the Mad Hatter, and the Queen all believe devoutly in the topsy-turvy logic which they hold superior to Alice's simple, pragmatic values, and which they are usually too busy or too full of their own superiority to explain. To a child the rigid rules and seemingly meaningless regulations of the adult world must be what they seem to Alice—arbitrary, unreasonable, and foolish.

The world in both Alice books is essentially a looking-glass world (although the image is explored more consistently in the second work). Holding a glass up to the foibles and conventions of society, the very conventional Carroll shows how absurd they must appear to the clear, unspoiled intelligence of a child.

In a sense, then, *Alice in Wonderland* is as much a book about the problems of growing up as is *David Copperfield, The Way of All Flesh,* or *Sons and Lovers.* Alice must learn in the course of her dream what to take seriously about the adult world and its standards and what to ignore. Significantly, she achieves her full physical height in the trial scene, when she is no longer upset by the ludicrous behavior of the adults around her. When she tells the Queen and all the court that they are nothing but a pack of cards, she has made the difficult journey from childhood, which is abashed by adult standards, to maturity, which is able to judge them.

Two particularly delightful contributions to the Alice books are the now classic illustrations by Sir John Tenniel and the poems that Carroll scatters through the stories. Carroll delights in wickedly distorting into sheer nonsense scraps of the sickly sweet verse that good Victorian children were taught to spout to their approving elders. Even the great Wordsworth is parodied in the White Knight's song in *Through the Looking-Glass,* the book that contains the verbal fireworks of "Jabberwocky."

The Author

Lewis Carroll was the pen name of the Oxford mathematician
Charles Lutwidge Dodgson who was born on January 27,
1832, in Darebury, Cheshire. He was educated at Rugby and
Christ Church, Oxford, where he took a first in mathematics
in 1854, and was appointed lecturer the following year—a
position he held until 1881.

A shy, retiring bachelor, Dodgson wrote many books on
mathematics, the most important of which is *Euclid and his
Modern Rivals* (1879). Indeed, when Queen Victoria, delighted with *Alice in Wonderland,* asked the professor for
more of his books, she received a crateful of recondite tomes
on mathematics.

One trait, however, colored Dodgson's otherwise conventional life. He found small girls charming and would
entertain them by the hour with tales, puzzles, and magic
tricks, and loved to photograph them. (Carroll was a highly
gifted amateur when photography was in its infancy.) One
of the girls of whom he was especially fond was Alice Liddell,
daughter of the Dean of Christ Church.

On July 4, 1862, Dodgson and a clergyman friend took
Alice—who was ten at the time—and her two sisters on a
rowing trip up the Thames near Oxford. To repeated demands
for a story to beguile the afternoon, Dodgson told what was
in essence the tale of *Alice in Wonderland* which, at Alice's
insistence, he later wrote down and illustrated as a little
book entitled *Alice's Adventures Underground.* Three years
later, expanded and altered somewhat, it was published. It was
an immediate success and its popularity has grown over the
years.

Dodgson's personality presents a fascinating paradox. The
author of the most delightful and durable children's book in
English was in private life a dry, convention-ridden man.
He was handsome, although his face was rather asymmetrical,
but he suffered from partial deafness and a pronounced stammer that prevented his delivering many sermons (although he
was ordained a deacon) and made his lectures excruciating
to hear. In addition, he was an orthodox member of the
Church of England, a devout Tory, and a considerable snob.

The other Dodgson—the Lewis Carroll whom he kept

rigidly separate from the Oxford don—delighted in tricks, magic, and games, and published the great sequel to *Alice, Through the Looking-Glass* (1872), and one of the finest comic poems in the language, "The Hunting of the Snark" (1876).

Dodgson died at Guilford on January 14, 1898. In our Freud-ridden age, his personality may inspire some psychiatric interest, but children play around the statue of Alice in the Children's Zoo at Central Park, and no shadow falls on the Carroll Wonderland.

By the Same Author

Through the Looking-Glass: Disproving the unwritten law that all sequels must be inferior to their originals, Carroll wrote in *Through the Looking-Glass* a child's fantasy that is, if possible, even better and richer than *Alice in Wonderland.* Where the first book consists of an adventure in an underground world peopled partly by characters from card games, the second deals with a looking-glass house where everything is turned backward, and the characters are chessmen. Alice is a pawn. She meets the Red and White Queens, and the country through which she travels is a giant chessboard. Some of the most memorable things in the book are the meeting with Tweedledee and Tweedledum who sing the profound song "The Walrus and the Carpenter," and the brilliantly punning parody of songs of knight-errantry, "Jabberwocky." Ultimately, Alice reaches the eighth square of the chessboard and is made a queen herself. When she shakes the Red Queen, it turns into her kitten, Dinah, and Alice once more awakens to reality.

Erewhon

by

SAMUEL BUTLER (1835–1902)

Main Characters

George Higgs—A priggish, conventionally religious young
sheep rancher who adventures over the range into Erewhon.
Chowbok—A native guide baptized but not converted by
Higgs.
Yram—Daughter of Higgs' jailer in Erewhon.
Senoj Nosnibor—An Erewhonian gentleman of great fortune
found guilty of defrauding a widow.
Zulora—Mr. Nosnibor's unappealing elder daughter.
Arowhena—The Nosnibors' beautiful younger daughter.
Thims—A cashier in the Musical Banks who takes Higgs to
visit the Colleges of Unreason.

The Story

In 1868, when George Higgs is twenty-two years old, he emigrates to New Zealand to seek his fortune as a sheep rancher.
He soon finds a position in sparsely settled country.

One day, while tending his sheep, Higgs sees a series of
mountain peaks in the distance and wonders what lies beyond
them. He questions a drunken old native, Chowbok, about
the land beyond the range. Chowbok merely says it is forbidden territory into which no man dare venture. Higgs, never-

theless, prevails upon him to act as his guide. The mountains seem impassable, and Chowbok keeps trying to dissuade Higgs from completing his expedition. One day Higgs finds a pass that he thinks will lead him through the tall peaks. When he returns to camp for Chowbok, the old native runs away, and Higgs is left to explore the terrain alone.

The pass is rugged. A swollen, treacherous river bars his way, but Higgs fashions a crude raft and makes the crossing. On the other side he is startled to hear strange music of what sounds like a giant Aeolian harp. The source of the music, he finds, is a number of grotesque statues equipped with organ pipes on which the wind plays. These gave rise to Chowbok's superstitious fears.

Next morning Higgs is discovered by some girls who are tending goats. The girls, more beautiful than any he has ever seen, lead him to the local town where Higgs is closely inspected by the men and his clothing confiscated. The men, too, seem a handsome, superior race, but they are shocked when they discover Higgs' watch. They immediately take it from him and show him a museum where all sorts of dilapidated machinery is kept in glass cases. The men of Erewhon (for this is the name of the country) seem impressed by Higgs' blond hair and fair complexion, for they themselves are all swarthy. After a close physical examination, Higgs is put in jail.

He is well treated by the jailor and his pretty daughter, Yram, who teaches Higgs the language of the country. Hoping to win Yram's sympathy, Higgs one day complains of a cold. Instead of being sympathetic, Yram berates him severely for his illness. Higgs learns that in Erewhon illness and disease are considered serious crimes, one reason for the health and vigor of the people. Conversely, people who in England would be considered criminals are hospitalized and treated carefully by so-called "straighteners" until their moral defects disappear.

A conventional Christian, who even baptized the crude Chowbok, Higgs decides that the Erewhonians are really the ten lost tribes of Israel, whom it is his duty and privilege to convert to Christianity.

Higgs learns from his jailor that he is to be summoned to the King and Queen who are curious about him. He is to travel blindfolded a great distance across Erewhon to the

capital city where he will live in the house of Senoj Nosnibor
who has cheated an impoverished widow of her inheritance.
According to Erewhonian justice, Nosnibor is still considered
a respectable member of society although he is under the care
of the straighteners. The widow, however, was tried and convicted for being unfortunate enough to be victimized. The
Erewhonians, Higgs learns, worship success and have little
patience with gullible people.

At Mr. Nosnibor's house, Higgs meets his devout wife and
his two daughters, the overbearing, ill-mannered Zulora and
the fair young Arowhena. Higgs learns that he is well thought
of in Erewhon because he is so fair-skinned and healthy although he is the object of some suspicion because he was
found with a watch.

Higgs is introduced to society by the Nosnibors, who also
take him to the Musical Banks—the Erewhonian churches.
At the Musical Banks one pays the cashiers or priests with a
strange, valueless sort of money and receives equally valueless
change. Although all respectable Erewhonians profess great
devotion to the Musical Banks, Higgs notices that only a few
women attend them, and the cashiers are a disconsolate lot.
He makes friends with a cashier named Thims who takes
him on an expedition to visit the Colleges of Unreason where
young Erewhonians are instructed at great cost in Hypothetics
—dead languages and obsolete science. This education assures
the youths of a place in society but makes them unfit for any
useful work.

The religion the Erewhonians really follow is Ydgrunism, a
conforming creed governed by a fear of what the neighbors will think. Higgs learns that the Erewhonians have experienced epidemics of puritanism ever since an Erewhonian
prophet 2500 years before wrote a book on "The Rights of
Animals," in which he condemned the eating of meat unless
the animal had already died of natural causes or had committed suicide. The Erewhonians usually ignored these laws
unless there was some plague or national disaster. Then they
enforced them. A professor of botany at the College of Unreason decreed that since there was no real distinction between
the animal and vegetable worlds, the killing and eating of plant
life should also be forbidden. The Erewhonians, starving for
their beliefs, eventually overthrew both laws and became a

healthy, happy race again when instinct triumphed over reason.

Higgs also reads "The Book of the Machines," in which an ancient Erewhonian claimed that machines evolved as animals and plants did, and with great ingenuity demonstrated that the day would come when men would be slaves to their machines as dogs are to men. This so appalled the Erewhonians that they destroyed all their machines, saving only a few for the museum. (This was followed by an unsuccessful counter-revolution of the lazy who did not want to live in a machineless society.) Now the Erewhonians live a simple life without tools or appliances invented more recently than 271 years before the laws were originally adopted.

Although Higgs dislikes the Nosnibors, especially Zulora, he falls in love with Arowhena. Unfortunately, according to Erewhonian law a younger sister cannot be married before the older sister, and so Higgs must either wait until someone else marries the disagreeable Zulora (an unlikely prospect), or try to elope with Arowhena. He resolves to elope, when rumors reach him that he is no longer in favor at court. The King is still suspicious of Higgs because he was found with a watch in his pocket; his health is showing signs of strain, and Mr. Nosnibor suspects he is having an affair with Arowhena. Higgs carefully plans his escape.

Erewhon has not had rain for some time. Higgs persuades the Queen that if she will have a balloon built for him he will ascend and speak to the air god about the drought. The Queen and King both agree to this plan. (The King hopes Higgs will fall and be killed.)

When the balloon is ready to be launched, Higgs bribes Arowhena's maid and the chief mechanic and spirits Arowhena into the cabin. Arowhena is missed at breakfast by her family, however, and Higgs sees Mr. Nosnibor running toward the balloon. Without waiting for the King and Queen to appear, he cuts the ropes and they ascend. For days and nights they are propelled through the air by the trade winds. One day they find themselves descending over the ocean. Desperately Higgs drops their ballast overboard and wins some more time. Eventually he must even throw overboard "The Book of the Machines" which he hoped to bring back to England with him.

At the last moment, when the balloon is in the sea, the

pair are rescued by an Italian liner which transfers them to a ship bound for England. Higgs and Arowhena are married on board.

Back in England, Higgs determines to organize an expedition to return to Erewhon and enslave the people for work in Queensland, converting them to Christianity at the same time.

Critical Opinion

Erewhon is a complex and often ambiguous satirical utopia in which Butler both approves and disapproves of Erewhonian beliefs which are sometimes the same as those of Victorian England and sometimes radically different. Just as the word "utopia" is Greek for "nowhere," so "erewhon" is "nowhere" spelled backward. (Similarly, Yram is Mary, Senoj Nosnibor is Jones Robinson, Thims is Smith, and the goddess Ydgrun is Grundy, symbol of English middle-class morality.)

Never at ease in writing fiction, Butler barely clothes his ideas with plot and characterization. After the prosaic account of Higgs' trek over the range, the novel becomes an intellectual fantasy, its characters essentially mouthpieces for ideas. Many parts of the book, such as the chapters on "The Book of the Machines," were written earlier as essays. In essence Arowhena is a stock Victorian heroine, vapid and colorless, whose only function in the book is to listen to what the hero has to say.

In the character of Higgs, however (we first learn his name in the sequel, *Erewhon Revisited*), Butler creates a masterpiece of self-satisfied Victorian piety. Unable to accept the validity of another way of life, Higgs is primarily interested in converting the obviously happy and healthy Erewhonians to the life-denying perversion of Christianity in which he has grown up. It does not even strike him as odd to propose an expedition that will simultaneously enslave and convert the Erewhonians who ask only to be left alone. The Erewhonians are happy because they have found an ideal social system. Since pain and sickness are punishable by imprisonment, few hypochondriacs exist. Immorality is treated as a disease, not as a crime.

Butler is most prophetic in his vision of the "straighteners" who talk to criminals and try to "cure" them of their crimes. The shadowy borderland between the sick and the immoral, blurred even further in today's psychiatry, is explored with vivacity and wit in *Erewhon.*

Originating as a satire on Darwinism, "The Book of the Machines" is also oddly prophetic. Butler ironically foresees in it the subjugation of men by machines. The Erewhonian solution to the problem—destruction of all machinery—has, in more desperate moments, been entertained by the victims of automation in our time.

The Way of All Flesh

by

SAMUEL BUTLER

Main Characters

Mr. Overton—The narrator, a friend of the Pontifex family, who tries to make young Ernest's life endurable.

Ernest Pontifex—Brought up in a strict religious household, Ernest struggles against all the forces of Victorian hypocrisy and narrow-mindedness in order to find his own identity.

John Pontifex—The founder of the Pontifex family, a humble carpenter and music lover.

George Pontifex—Ernest's grandfather, publisher of religious books, and the first of the money-minded, joyless Pontifexes.

Theobald Pontifex—Ernest's father, a priggish clergyman who represses all his natural instincts and nearly ruins his son.

Christina Pontifex—Theobald's hypocritical wife.

Alethea Pontifex—Ernest's sensible, good-natured aunt.

Ellen—The Pontifexes' drunken maidservant.

The Story

The founder of the Pontifex family is old John Pontifex, a carpenter and music lover, who leaves his son George moderately well off. George, however, inherits none of his father's love of music nor any of his simple, humane spirit. Apprenticed to a printer uncle, George amasses a fortune printing religious books for the great religious revival of the Victorian age now in full swing. George has five children whom he thrashes and bullies, determined to rid them of their "self-will."

One of George's children, Theobald, is so shy and ill at ease that George decides he can make a living only in the clergy. Accordingly, Theobald is sent to Cambridge, against his will, to prepare for ordination. He bows to his father's repeated threats of disinheritance and takes holy orders. He becomes curate to Mr. Allaby, rector of Crampford, near Cambridge, and Mr. Allaby's daughter Christina, who is four years older than Theobald, decides she will marry the young clergyman. She "wins" him in a game of cards with her other unmarried sisters.

The naïve and unsuspecting Theobald easily succumbs to Christina's wooing. His father disapproves of the match. But Theobald feels he is too deeply committed to Christina to terminate their relationship. After a five-year courtship, they are married, and Theobald gets a fairly remunerative post at Battersby. George settles £10,000 on his son and daughter-in-law.

Immediately after the wedding, Theobald asserts his position as master and by the time their first son, Ernest, is born on September 6, 1835, five years later, Christina is entirely subject to Theobald's every whim.

The birth of Ernest so pleases old George Pontifex that he settles some money on the infant. Theobald, who feels he has satisfied his father's expectations of him for the first time in his life by producing a male heir, is piqued that the boy should receive this bequest and never forgives him for the independence it implies. Soon another boy, Joseph, and a girl, Charlotte, are born into the Pontifex family. Both take after their parents far more than Ernest does.

The upbringing of the children is harsh, rigorous, and typical of the Victorian middle class. At the age of three Ernest begins his studies and is learning Greek and Latin by the time he is five. Lessons are driven home with frequent beatings. Sunday is the worst day of all, when the children are forbidden to play but must spend a dismal day in religious observance.

An old friend of the Pontifex family, Mr. Overton, remembers his boyhood affection for old John Pontifex. Now he is appalled at the harsh, dreary life John's grandson Theobald is imposing on his children. One day he sees Ernest beaten within an inch of his life—for his own "good," of course—when he mispronounces a word. Mr. Overton tries to improve the boy's condition, but he is essentially powerless against the Pontifex philosophy of breaking a child's spirit.

At twelve, Ernest is sent to school at Roughborough and placed under the discipline of Dr. Skinner, an incompetent teacher and a bully like Theobald Pontifex. At Roughborough Ernest is as miserable as he was at home. Puny, gloomy, and indecisive, Ernest has one great consolation, music, a love inherited from his great-grandfather.

The only human warmth the boy knows at school is the affection of his Aunt Alethea who moves from London to be with him. She is a kind, generous woman who sees great potentialities for happiness in her nephew and refuses to allow him to succumb to his father's discipline. She helps the boy to build an organ, thus giving him exercise, skill in carpentry, and encouraging the love for music that his father considers degenerate and sinful. When Alethea dies a year later, she leaves £15,000 to Mr. Overton with the understanding that he keep it secretly in trust for Ernest until he is twenty-eight.

Ernest's last scrap of respect for his parents disappears one school holiday when he sees them summarily dismissing Ellen, a pregnant maidservant. In a moment of pity for her, he gives her his watch and pocket money. For this he is severely punished. Indeed, his mother suspects that he is responsible for Ellen's condition.

Ernest is in such disgrace at home that Theobald journeys to Roughborough to find out all he can about his son's behavior. He learns that Ernest is guilty of occasionally smoking, drinking, and running up insignificant debts for lack of pocket money. He informs Dr. Skinner, and Ernest, ignominiously punished, becomes a martyr to his schoolfellows.

After Roughborough, Ernest is sent to Cambridge to prepare for the ministry. Although the boy has no interest in religion, he finds the freedom and intellectual liveliness of the

great university refreshing after the stultifying atmosphere of
Dr. Skinner's school. For the first time he makes friends and
participates in sports. He writes an original article attacking
the Greek dramatists and wins some notoriety and a small
scholarship.

After leaving Cambridge, Ernest dutifully continues to prepare for a church career although his heart is not in it. As
a social worker in the London slums, he has many misadventures. He entrusts the legacy he received from his grandfather
to a Mr. Pryer who promises to increase it in the stock market.
Instead, Mr. Pryer cheats him out of all the money.

Totally innocent about the world and unprepared by his
education to cope with people, Ernest idealistically moves
into a slum district to be close to the real poor. Attempting
to convert an articulate freethinker to belief in God, Ernest is
himself converted to atheism. His greatest blunder, however,
comes when he visits the room of a girl he believes to be a
prostitute. She is really respectable and Ernest is summarily
arrested, charged with assault, and sentenced to six months
in prison.

Ernest's fortunes are now at their lowest. Unable to emi-
grate to Australia for lack of funds and barred from the clergy,
Ernest decides to set up a modest tailoring shop in London
upon his release. At least he will not have to endure the
middle-class life he now loathes. But just as he emerges from
jail, he is met by his parents who are filled with pious forgiveness and high moral sentiments. Finally Ernest has the
courage to tell them he never wants to see them again. With
Mr. Overton's help, he is able to set up his tailoring establishment.

Soon after his release from prison, Ernest meets Ellen
(his parents' dismissed maid) in the streets of London. In
his loneliness, he falls in love with her, partly because he
sees in her another helpless victim of his parents' way of life.
Against Mr. Overton's advice, Ernest and Ellen marry and
have two children. But it is soon apparent that Ellen is a
hopeless drunkard. Her drinking puts a great drain on
Ernest's modest income, and she becomes more sluttish and
slatternly every day. Utterly miserable at the way his marriage
has turned out, Ernest despairs of ever making his way in life.

One day Ernest meets John, his family's old coachman,
who tells him that he is the father of Ellen's illegitimate

child; soon after she left the Pontifex family he had married her. Since Ernest's marriage is thus bigamous, Mr. Overton is able to make an arrangement with Ellen under which she receives a weekly stipend on condition that she never bother Ernest again. Fearing to become as bad a parent as his own, Ernest boards his two children with the simple, happy family of a bargeman utterly free of any middle-class pretensions. The children will be allowed to live their own lives.

On Ernest's twenty-eighth birthday, Mr. Overton tells him of his Aunt Alethea's bequest, which through wise investment now amounts to £70,000. The money enables Ernest to fulfill his real ambition—to be a writer—which has lain dormant in his troubled mind ever since the publication of his successful article at Cambridge. A few years traveling abroad provides him with experiences and background for a book.

When he learns that his mother is dying, Ernest tries to become reconciled to his family. But his father is resentful that Ernest has become independently wealthy despite his follies. No real reconciliation is possible. Ernest never marries again but spends his days writing iconoclastic books and living a decent, civilized life. Although he becomes a prolific author, he never gets around to writing his own story. This is done for him by Mr. Overton.

Critical Opinion

The Way of All Flesh is one of a number of autobiographical novels which were highly popular in late Victorian and Edwardian England. Written between 1873 and 1885, it was not published until after Butler's death because he was fearful lest it give offense to his still-living sisters. Indeed, it is one of the most brilliantly devastating attacks in all literature on religious hypocrisy and on the family as an institution.

Theobald and Christina Pontifex are cruelly and wittily portrayed by Butler as monuments of complacency, smugness, false religiosity, and unfeeling brutality to their children. In almost every particular, they match Butler's own parents. Butler sees himself partly as Ernest and partly as Mr. Overton, the wise, civilized, easy-going man of wide culture.

The book begins unpromisingly with a long, somewhat tedious account of the early Pontifexes—John and George. Ernest is not even born until Chapter 17. One of Butler's deepest interests in the story was the question of heredity. A disciple of the biologist, Lamarck, Butler had several notions of heredity (at variance with the prevailing Darwinian doctrine of his day) which he wished to explore in *The Way of All Flesh*. One of these ideas is that inherited characteristics can skip one or even two generations. Thus Ernest is interested in carpentry and music, like his great-grandfather John and unlike his grandfather and father. Because traits can skip generations, Butler felt that parents and their children may have little in common and thus rarely understand each other.

The book's appeal, however, hardly depends on its biological assumptions or on its autobiographical core. Generations of rebellious youths, feeling themselves trapped in an oppressive home environment, have drawn spiritual aid and comfort from Butler's furious assault on the hypocrisies of parents and the life-denying rigors of a puritanical household. The "way of all flesh" is to seek freedom and self-fulfillment, Butler feels, but too often in practice it is to tyrannize over the young.

The Way of All Flesh is Butler's only full-fledged novel, and the number of years required for its composition are testimony to the pain it cost him. This arose not merely from the psychological difficulty of contemplating his own wretched childhood and youth but from the esthetic problems posed by the novel as well. Because Butler was primarily a controversial essayist and not a novelist, *The Way of All Flesh* is a far from perfect novel. Whole chapters are merely extended diatribes on the follies of Victorian life with very little plot holding them together. The end, where Ernest's story diverges widely from Butler's, tends to disintegrate into a series of connected essays.

Nevertheless, if a fertile Dickensian imagination was not one of Butler's gifts, he shared with the earlier novelist a lively sense of humor, at once bitterly indignant and humane. The brilliantly rendered portrayal of Ernest's soul-destroying youth and education remains the classic picture in English of family life at its worst.

The Author

Like the hero of *The Way of All Flesh*, *Samuel Butler* came from a religious family. Born on December 4, 1835, Butler was the grandson of Dr. Samuel Butler, the famous headmaster of the Shrewsbury School and bishop of Lichfield. Butler's father was a domineering clergyman—cruelly portrayed as Theobald Pontifex in *The Way of All Flesh*—who made the boy's life a nightmare.

Educated at Shrewsbury and St. John's College, Cambridge, Butler was headed for the clergy but revolted against that fate and decided to become a painter. Butler's father could not accept this career for his son. So they reached a compromise. Butler went to New Zealand in 1859 to take up sheep breeding. In time he became quite wealthy. His first book, *A First Year in Canterbury Settlement* (1863), is really a series of letters to his father describing his life in New Zealand.

In 1864 Butler returned to England and settled for the rest of his life in Clifford's Inn, London. *Erewhon* was published in 1872 and brought Butler more fame and notoriety than any other book he wrote. His father was mystified and enraged by the irreligious irony of *Erewhon* and of its successor, *The Fair Haven* (1873), which ironically defends the evidence for the Resurrection. On one occasion, he told Butler that the books had killed his mother. Butler's father claimed he never read any of his son's works.

A lonely, eccentric bachelor, Butler lived with a lawyer named Pauli who defrauded him of nearly all his income. Butler also became friends with a Miss Savage, a crippled artist who was the model for Aunt Alethea in *The Way of All Flesh* and who probably nurtured an unrequited love for the author.

Butler's interests were many and varied. He continued with his painting, played Handel on the piano, and even collaborated with another friend, his eventual biographer, Henry Festing-Jones, on two mock-Handelian oratorios. He traveled a good deal, especially in Greece and Italy, in search of evidence to support his theory that the author of Homer's works was a woman—specifically Nausicäa in the *Odyssey*—and that Odysseus' trip could be precisely charted in the neighborhood of Sicily.

Science, too, was a major interest of Butler's. He wrote several books, of which *Unconscious Memory* (1880) and *Luck or Cunning?* (1887) are best known as challenges to Darwin's theory of heredity. A man ahead of his time, Butler remained a sort of Don Quixote tilting at the windmills of Victorian ideas. He died on June 18, 1902. The masterpiece on which he had been secretly working for several years, *The Way of All Flesh*, was published in 1903. It was not until World War I, when Bernard Shaw became a passionate proselyte for them, that Butler's works began to be widely known.

By the Same Author

Erewhon Revisited: In this sequel to *Erewhon*, written thirty years later and published the year of Butler's death, Higgs returns to Erewhon to find himself worshiped as a child of the Sun God for his miraculous ascent long ago in the balloon. A cathedral has been consecrated in his name, old Chowbok has become Bishop Kahabuka, and the dominant religion in Erewhon is no longer Ydgrunism, but Sunchildism, explained and preached by Professors Hanky and Panky. Higgs finds that he has a son by Yram, the jailor's daughter. Eventually he must escape from the country once again. Less inventive and vivid than *Erewhon*, the sequel is very much the book of an old, disappointed man. It, nevertheless, contains some entertaining blasts at the evidence for miracles and revealed religion.

The Return of the Native

by

THOMAS HARDY (1840–1928)

Main Characters

Diggory Venn—An itinerant seller of reddle, a dye used for marking sheep.

Damon Wildeve—A romantic ex-engineer who has become the restless proprietor of the Quiet Woman Inn.

Thomasin Yeobright—A fair, simple, birdlike girl engaged to Wildeve.

Mrs. Yeobright—Thomasin's aunt, a strong-willed, middle-aged woman.

Clym Yeobright—Her son who returns to Egdon Heath after becoming successful in the diamond business abroad.

Eustacia Vye—A dark, passionate girl who hates Egdon Heath and yearns for a glamorous life.

The Story

Across somber, barren Egdon Heath in the south of England only the cart of Diggory Venn, the reddleman, is visible as it slowly makes its way late one November night. The scene is illuminated, however, by a series of bonfires lit by the local peasants to celebrate Guy Fawkes Day, the fifth of November.

In the cart, worn out and sick, is young Thomasin Yeobright, who two years before had refused to marry Venn. She is now being taken home to Blooms-End. They meet a group of peasants who assume that Thomasin has just married Damon Wildeve, the proprietor of the Quiet Woman Inn. But the marriage has not taken place because at the last moment the license was found to be technically invalid. Thomasin has asked the faithful Diggory Venn to take her home.

Thomasin's aunt, Mrs. Yeobright, is disturbed because she knows of Wildeve's weak character and fears that the invalid license was merely an excuse for him to get out of marrying her simple, trusting niece. Indeed, Wildeve is secretly in love with the wild, mysterious Eustacia Vye, granddaughter of a retired sea captain. Eustacia has lit her own bonfire on Guy Fawkes Night to signal Wildeve to meet her, although all she has in common with him is a loathing for the brooding, impersonal heath on which they live. Eustacia has always hoped for a great love which would take her away from Egdon Heath; she now feels she must accept Wildeve as a poor substitute.

Meanwhile, Mrs. Yeobright goes to Wildeve and asks him not to stand in the way of Thomasin's marrying another man, for she knows that Diggory Venn is still in love with her niece. When Wildeve learns that Thomasin has another suitor, he is torn by indecision and proposes to Eustacia that they leave the heath together and go to America. But now it is Eustacia who is indecisive. She has heard that Clym Yeobright is returning to the heath after a brilliant career in the diamond business in Paris.

Unsuccessful in her attempts to meet Clym in a casual encounter, Eustacia bribes one of the boys taking part in a Christmas pageant at the Yeobrights' to let her substitute for him. Clym notices her and is piqued by her daring disguise as a boy. He asks her to remove her mask, but she coquettishly refuses. Feeling she has finally attracted Clym, Eustacia finally breaks off with Wildeve, who marries Thomasin to spite her.

Eustacia hopes that if she can persuade Clym to marry her he will take her to Paris, which she longs to see. But Clym has left his successful business there precisely because he is sick of the sophisticated life. He now wishes only to live on his native heath and open a school, teaching the ignorant yeomen to give up their superstitious beliefs. He is strengthened in this purpose when he hears that Eustacia has been attacked as a witch by a local woman.

Mrs. Yeobright also thinks Clym is wrong to stay on the heath, but for a different reason; she fears that her son will fall into Eustacia's clutches. The mother's concern comes too late, for Clym has fallen in love with this strange, unhappy girl. He asks Eustacia to join him in teaching, but she refuses because she wants to leave the heath entirely.

Against his mother's advice, Clym marries Eustacia and begins studying to be a schoolteacher. Through overwork he strains his eyes and, unable to read any more, becomes a furze cutter to keep from dipping into his savings. Eustacia becomes increasingly disillusioned with her moody husband as she sees her chances of going to Paris fading.

Reconciled somewhat to her son's marriage, Mrs. Yeobright entrusts some money to a local rustic, Christian Cantle, to be equally divided between Clym and Thomasin. Christian loses the money gambling with the unscrupulous Wildeve, but the money is won back by Diggory Venn who loyally gives it all to Thomasin. Thinking Wildeve has given the sum to Eustacia, Mrs. Yeobright accuses her daughter-in-law of receiving it from the innkeeper. Furious, Eustacia tells Mrs. Yeobright of her disillusionment with her son, and they part bitter enemies.

Bored with her existence as the wife of a humble wood-cutter, Eustacia one night goes to a gypsy camp where she meets Wildeve, and once more feels attracted to him. They are seen by Diggory Venn who tells Mrs. Yeobright that she must become reconciled to her son and daughter-in-law before disaster strikes their marriage.

Mrs. Yeobright agrees and trudges across the vast heath in the burning sun to visit them. When she knocks at the door, however, there is no answer, for while Clym is asleep in one room after his morning's hard labor, Eustacia is entertaining Wildeve in another. Fearing that the knocking will awaken her husband, Eustacia shows Wildeve out the back door. When she returns, Clym is still asleep, but Mrs. Yeobright has left. Making her way back across the heath, Mrs. Yeobright, parched, exhausted, and grief-stricken at what she imagines is a rebuff from her son, is bitten by an adder.

When Clym wakes up, he sets forth across the heath to visit his mother, and discovers her dying in agony. Eustacia tells Clym that she did not open the door to his mother because she did not know he was asleep and assumed he would open it. Eustacia conceals from her husband the real reason, her fear that Mrs. Yeobright would discover her and Wildeve together.

At first Clym is consumed with grief and guilt. But when he learns the truth, he turns on his wife and demands that she leave his house. Remorse-stricken, she agrees, feeling that the only salvation for both of them is for her to leave Egdon Heath.

Eustacia returns despondently to her grandfather's house and tries to commit suicide, but is prevented by Charley, Captain Vye's servant. She knows that Wildeve is still willing to run away with her. When the innkeeper unexpectedly comes into a considerable fortune, flight becomes a possibility. One night Eustacia leaves the house for a tryst with Wildeve without seeing on the mantelpiece a letter that Clym, at Thomasin's instigation, had written in the hope that it might bring them together again.

Searching in the dark for the spot where she is to meet Wildeve, Eustacia loses her way and drowns in Shadwater Weir. Nearby, Clym meets Wildeve who is searching for Eustacia. The two men who loved her see Eustacia's body in the lake. Wildeve jumps in to save Eustacia. He, too, drowns. In turn Clym tries to rescue him, and is saved from the treacherous waters only by the arrival of Diggory Venn.

Several months later, Diggory marries the widowed Thomasin, and Clym becomes a preacher wandering about the heath in the hope of bringing light to the dark lives of its people.

Critical Opinion

As in all Hardy's major fiction, man in *The Return of the Native* is seen as the plaything of the gods, buffeted about by fate and ultimately destroyed by an uncaring universe. The blind, heedless power of nature is symbolized in the novel by Egdon Heath, a forbidding, uninhabited stretch of land that quite literally consumes its victims; by heat and the serpent's bite in the case of Mrs. Yeobright, by darkness and drowning in the case of Eustacia and Wildeve. The insignificance of struggling man in the face of a cosmic order he does not understand is thus embodied in the heath.

But novels are primarily about people, not about scenery, and Hardy's real interest is in the struggles of his characters against their destiny which Hardy views with a unique combination of irony and compassion. Like her famous French prototype, Emma Bovary, Eustacia Vye is a passionate romantic at odds with the dull, commonplace world around her. In revolt against the slow, plodding natural world of the heath, she yearns for a life of excitement in Paris. A perverse fate links Eustacia with a man who longs only for peace and solitude, having been disillusioned with the worldly life she so admires.

Thus, the tragedy of Eustacia and Clym is only partially caused by fate and coincidence. Essentially it stems, as all great tragedy does, from character. The wild coincidences of which Hardy is so fond merely contribute a touch of the grotesque to something foreordained by the very nature of the characters involved.

In the subtle interplay between predestination and free will, then, Hardy finds the philosophic basis for his fiction much as the Greek dramatists had done centuries before. Man is foredoomed to tragedy, according to Hardy, but the seeds of doom lie in his character—constantly striving, never at peace with the universe or with other human beings.

The plot of *The Return of the Native* is carefully organized, each section of the novel having its individual climax, starting slowly and building inevitably to the final disasters. The reliance on coincidence, for which Hardy has been taken to task, has come into its own today in a period that relishes the drama of the absurd. For the point of Hardy's coincidences (all the mislaid letters in his novels, for instance) is that life is not rational; events do not happen as in a "well-made" novel, but blind chance constantly intervenes in man's fate.

The only comforting note in Hardy's fiction is provided by his peasant types, like Christian Cantle. Inured to the blows of fate by centuries of experience, they live more or less at one with nature, refusing, in their folk wisdom, to make the mistake the major characters make—of trying to impose their puny wills on an unseeing, indifferent universe.

The Mayor of Casterbridge

by

THOMAS HARDY

Main Characters

Michael Henchard—The passionate and self-destructive grain merchant who becomes mayor of Casterbridge.

Susan Henchard—Henchard's long-suffering wife whom he sells to a sailor.

Richard Newson—The sailor who buys Susan Henchard for five guineas and takes her to Canada.

Elizabeth-Jane—Henchard's beautiful, loyal stepdaughter, who falls in love with Henchard's rival in Casterbridge.

Donald Farfrae—A bright, easy-going Scotsman who makes his fortune in the grain business in Casterbridge.

Lucetta Le Sueur—A young lady from Jersey who compromises herself in a love affair with Henchard.

Joshua Jopp—Fiercely envious of Farfrae.

The Story

Three dusty, tired travelers arrive late one summer afternoon at the small farming village of Weydon Priors: Michael Henchard, a bitter young man looking for work, his wife, Susan, and their little girl, Elizabeth-Jane. Arriving in time for a country fair, the youthful parents seek refreshment in the tent of a woman selling furmity, a kind of rustic milk punch. Henchard persuades the woman to spike his furmity with rum, and before long he becomes drunk and abusive.

In his drunkenness, Henchard, who is resentful at having married too young to be able to make his way in the world, publicly offers to sell his wife and daughter to any buyer. Richard Newson, a sailor, out of pity buys the downcast

172

Susan Henchard from her drunken husband for five guineas and leaves the refreshment tent with his new "family."

When Henchard awakes the next morning, he is appalled at what he has done. Swearing never to drink liquor for the next twenty years, he sets off in search of his wife and daughter. He learns at a seaport town that they have just emigrated from England with Newson, and he gives up the search. Arriving ultimately at the ancient town of Casterbridge, Henchard decides to make his fortune there in the grain business.

When Newson takes Susan Henchard and her daughter to Canada, he convinces the docile, unquestioning young woman that she is no longer legally bound to the husband who has so mistreated her. Susan's daughter dies soon after, but Newson and Susan have a daughter of their own. Susan and Newson live together as man and wife, but eventually Susan learns that she is still legally married to Henchard. Before she can act on this knowledge, Newson is reported drowned in a shipwreck, and Susan sets out for England with her daughter, now eighteen, in search of Henchard.

A meeting with the old furmity woman leads Susan to Casterbridge. In the intervening years, Henchard, true to his vow, has not touched liquor. By sheer energy and force of will he has become the leading citizen of Casterbridge. When his wife and stepdaughter arrive, he is mayor of the town.

Another recent arrival in Casterbridge is an ambitious, personable young Scotsman, Donald Farfrae. Overhearing Henchard's complaint about some rotten grain he has inadvertently sold, Farfrae makes an ingenious suggestion about how to make the grain edible. Although Farfrae is bent on seeking his fortune overseas, Henchard is so enthusiastic about the corn expert that he persuades the young man to stay in Casterbridge and become his manager.

When Susan meets Henchard, she does not tell him that Elizabeth-Jane is not really his daughter. The two women are set up in lodgings nearby so that Henchard can "court" his wife and "marry" her before the whole town. But in his loneliness, Henchard has confided to Farfrae that he once had an affair with a beautiful girl named Lucetta Le Sueur who became an object of scandal in her native Jersey because of Henchard's attentions.

Eventually, Henchard marries Susan and brings his wife and Elizabeth-Jane to live with him. The beautiful Elizabeth-

Jane finds Farfrae intensely attractive. When Henchard wants the girl to take his legal name, he is surprised at Susan's refusal.

Relations between Henchard and Farfrae become strained as Henchard grows envious of the popularity of his employee. Farfrae has none of the harshness at the root of Henchard's character. When the two men set up rival festivities at a country dance, Henchard is infuriated to see the townspeople flock to Farfrae's entertainment.

Realizing that his association with Henchard is ending, Farfrae begins his own grain business, but is so ethical that he refuses to take any trade that might otherwise go to his former employer. Henchard refuses to allow Elizabeth-Jane to see Farfrae.

One day Henchard receives word from his former love, Lucetta, that she will visit Casterbridge to obtain the love letters she had written to him. He goes to meet her, but when Lucetta fails to appear, Henchard puts the incriminating letters into his safe. Meanwhile, Susan, who has fallen mortally ill, writes a letter to Henchard which he is not to open until the day of Elizabeth-Jane's marriage.

When Susan dies, Henchard, hoping to draw Elizabeth-Jane closer to him, tells the girl the story of how he had lost his wife and daughter twenty years ago. Searching among his documents for evidence to convince the girl, he finds Susan's deathbed letter and discovers that Elizabeth-Jane is the daughter of Newson. Shocked, Henchard immediately becomes cold and abrupt with the girl who cannot understand the reason for this sudden change in him.

In one of her lonely excursions to the village graveyard, Elizabeth-Jane meets a handsome, rich woman who comforts her and offers to employ her as a companion. Having just inherited property in Casterbridge, the woman intends to live in the ancient town. She gives her name as Lucetta Templeman, but in reality she is Henchard's former love, Lucetta Le Sueur. Having Elizabeth-Jane in her house is designed to provide a convenient pretext for Henchard to visit her.

One day when Farfrae comes to the house to see Elizabeth-Jane, he meets Lucetta who is immediately drawn to him. In her new love for Farfrae, Lucetta completely forgets about Henchard. As Elizabeth-Jane sees her former lover falling in love with Lucetta, Henchard becomes infuriated with Lucetta for refusing to see him any more.

Determined to ruin Farfrae for this latest affront, Henchard buys immense quantities of grain when a weather prophet forecasts a rainy harvest. The weather stays fine, however, and Henchard is forced to sell his grain at a loss while Farfrae buys it very cheaply. The rains eventually do come, and Farfrae becomes wealthy overnight selling his cheaply bought grain at high prices.

In despair at this financial setback, Henchard warns Lucetta that unless she marries him he will expose her past to Farfrae. She agrees. She leaves the town, however, when the old furmity seller arrives in Casterbridge and reveals that many years before Henchard had sold his wife and daughter. Lucetta learns the truth for the first time. While she is away from the town, Lucetta secretly marries Farfrae. Elizabeth-Jane, heartbroken, leaves her employ and Henchard repeats his threat to reveal Lucetta's past.

Henchard's ruin is completed when creditors, hearing the furmity woman's story, demand their money from him. Henchard becomes ill and is reunited with Elizabeth-Jane who nurses him through his illness. When he finally recovers, he is bankrupt and must become a common laborer in Farfrae's employ. Having kept his vow to stay away from drink for twenty years, Henchard once again takes to drink, even more violently than before. The crowning blow to his pride comes when Farfrae, richer and more popular than ever now, is elected the new mayor of Casterbridge.

Now Joshua Jopp, who used to work for Henchard and who knows Lucetta's past, begins to blackmail Lucetta into getting him a good job with her husband. Henchard, whose own misery has made him relent, decides to send the incriminating love letters back to Lucetta, but he makes the mistake of asking Jopp to deliver them. Jopp first regales his cronies at the inn with a reading of the spicier portions of the letters.

When the Duke of Windsor visits Casterbridge, Henchard makes a last attempt to become a power once again in the town. He drunkenly attempts to join the pillars of Casterbridge society who are entertaining the royal visitor, but is humiliated anew when Farfrae brusquely pushes him aside. When Henchard later gets Farfrae alone in the warehouse, he is tempted to kill his former friend and manager, but, shamed by Farfrae's contemptuous pity, he lets him go.

Jopp's malicious reading aloud of Lucetta's letters has its tragic consequence. The townspeople place models of Henchard and Lucetta on a donkey which they lead through the streets of Casterbridge. Farfrae is away at the time of this mummer's parade, but Lucetta, appalled when she sees it, dies later that night of a miscarriage.

Richard Newson, the sailor who was thought lost, arrives in Casterbridge looking for Susan and Elizabeth-Jane. Henchard, who cannot bear the thought of losing his stepdaughter, the last prop of his life, tells the sailor that both women are dead. With Elizabeth-Jane, Henchard opens a fairly successful seed shop, but soon the widowed Farfrae begins to court the girl again.

Newson, too, returns, now aware of the truth. Henchard sees a lonely old age confronting him, for Newson is Elizabeth-Jane's father. Now she is to be married to Farfrae. Bereft of the only person in the world he loves, Henchard goes into a decline and dies. In his will he stipulates that he is not to be buried in consecrated ground.

Critical Opinion

Of all Hardy's novels, *The Mayor of Casterbridge* most closely resembles a classic Greek tragedy, for it is concerned with the downfall of a great man resulting from a combination of flaws in his character and repeated, ironic blows of fate. Henchard's initial act, selling his wife and child, so typical of his headstrong, unthinking temperament, comes back years later to haunt him with classic inevitability, when he has reached the heights of prosperity and honor in his little world of Casterbridge. Relying more heavily than ever on coincidence, Hardy, bit by bit, tears away the props that have raised Henchard to power in Casterbridge, until he is a completely broken and disillusioned old man.

For all his savagery when drunk, Henchard is a man of many fine qualities. He is open-hearted and generous, incapable of sustained guile or malice, and a man of abundant energy. When he has the power to blackmail Lucetta with her love letters, he is unable to bring himself to use it even though she has betrayed him by marrying his rival, Farfrae. But with typical Hardyesque irony, Henchard's well-intentioned return of the letters backfires. In the malicious hands of Jopp they have their full evil effect.

Henchard, like Heathcliff in *Wuthering Heights*, is a typically romantic figure—a single-minded, almost demonic man possessed of vast energy. He is deeply passionate and capable of inadvertently doing much harm. He seems always doomed to kill whatever he loves.

In contrast Hardy draws the thoughtfully energetic young Farfrae whose star inevitably rises while Henchard's sinks. Farfrae is like Horatio in *Hamlet*: a good, whole man always in control of his passions, emotional but capable of coolly intelligent behavior. Virile and energetic as Farfrae is, he is not the stuff of tragedy because his character is almost flawless. The disaster of his life—the death of his wife in a miscarriage—is not the result of his own passion or folly but is imposed on him by the trickery of the gods. He can later marry Elizabeth-Jane with a clear conscience.

The Mayor of Casterbridge is one of Hardy's most tightly knit novels and also one of his most blatantly coincidental. As if managed by a puppeteer, characters appear and disappear, always in time to bring more disaster crashing down on Henchard's head. The book's magnificence stems in large part from the stoic grandeur with which Henchard accepts the consequences of his early folly.

Jude the Obscure

by

THOMAS HARDY

Main Characters

Jude Fawley—An intensely serious, self-educated stonemason who yearns for a higher intellectual life.
Drusilla Fawley—Jude's great-grandaunt.

Arabella Donn—A coarse peasant girl who initiates Jude
into the world of sex.
Richard Phillotson—The country schoolmaster, Jude's sole
contact with the world of education.
Sue Bridehead—Jude's neurotic, self-assertive cousin, one of
the restless "new women" of the late nineteenth century.
Little Father Time—The prematurely sad and wizened son
of Jude and Arabella.

The Story

Young Jude Fawley, an orphaned baker's boy, gets his first
taste of what his life will be like when he is hired by a local
Wessex farmer to frighten the rooks away from the farmer's
garden. When Jude takes pity on the birds and feeds them
instead of scaring them away, the farmer beats him unmercifully. Some light comes into the lad's life, however,
when the local schoolmaster, Richard Phillotson, introduces
him to the magic world of learning. Jude decides to emulate
his teacher; but when the boy is eleven years old, Phillotson
leaves Marygreen to go to the great university town of
Christminster in order to get an advanced degree.

Jude wishes to go, too, but must content himself with the
Latin textbooks that Phillotson sends him from Christminster,
for Jude's great-grandaunt, Drusilla Fawley, insists on his
helping her in her bakery. Jude eagerly studies the grammar
books that Phillotson sends him but realizes they are no
substitute for a formal education.

As he grows into young manhood, Jude, who secretly
yearns to study religion, is apprenticed to a stonemason whose
job is to restore local medieval churches. One evening, while
returning home from work, the nineteen-year-old Jude, who
is still innocent in the ways of love, passes three peasant girls
who are washing pigs' chitterlings. The boldest of them,
Arabella Donn, attracts Jude's attention by throwing a bit
of pig's flesh at him and provoking him into agreeing to meet
her later. In his inexperience, Jude fancies himself in love with
the lusty Arabella. Before long she traps him into marriage.

The marriage becomes a nightmare. Arabella, who is all
coarseness and vulgarity, derides Jude's yearning for higher

things. After a series of quarrels, Arabella leaves him and emigrates to Australia.

Free at last of the shackles of marriage, Jude determines to journey to Christminster and try somehow to enter the academic community. Denied admission, he takes a job there as a stonemason, for that is as far as the hidebound university authorities will permit him to enter the life of Christminster.

Jude knows that his cousin, Sue Bridehead, is living in Christminster, but at first he avoids her because his Aunt Drusilla had warned him against her, pointing out with some justice that "the Fawleys were not made for wedlock."

In his loneliness, however, Jude eventually seeks out Sue Bridehead who is working as an artist in a shop that sells religious articles. An agnostic, Sue seeks relief from her job by reading Gibbon and by keeping large plaster casts of Venus and Apollo in her room. Jude is immensely impressed by his cousin's nervous, restless intelligence and suggests that she leave her job to assist his old schoolmaster, Phillotson.

Before long Phillotson, too, is captivated by Sue and becomes intimate with her. In his unhappiness Jude takes to drink and loses his job. Discouraged, he returns home to Marygreen but is soon attracted to the town of Melchester where Sue is studying at a teachers' college. Jude abandons his own tentative studies for the ministry in order to be near her, and once again turns to stonemasonry for a living.

Their lives in Melchester end disastrously when Sue is expelled from her college for her innocent relationship with Jude. She then marries Phillotson, leaving Jude to return, again defeated, to Christminster. There Jude encounters his wife Arabella who has returned to England and is working in a local bar. Gradually tales come to Jude of Sue's intense unhappiness with Phillotson. At the funeral of Jude's Aunt Drusilla, he and Sue decide that she should come and live with him since she has already left the schoolmaster. Phillotson, who is too "civilized" to make much of a fuss, allows his wife to live with Jude in the city of Aldbrickham where nobody knows them. He willingly grants Sue a divorce. Jude, too, divorces Arabella. Sue, however, will hear nothing of a formal church wedding with Jude; her deep-rooted anticlericalism and her fear of binding herself permanently to any man make her prefer to live out of wedlock with Jude.

For a while the pair live in reasonable happiness which is

shattered when Arabella arrives and tells Jude that she has remarried and is unhappy. She sends to Jude a pathetically aged-looking young son she claims to have had by him after she arrived in Australia. The wizened boy is nicknamed Little Father Time. Soon word that Jude and Sue are not really married begins to circulate, and Jude loses one job after another. He is forced to travel about the countryside looking for work, living an unhappy gypsy life with Sue, Little Father Time, and two children of their own. Jude's health begins to fail. Since the arduous work of stonecutting is bad for his lungs, he is reduced to becoming a baker. Sue sells his cakes at local fairs.

In his discouragement Jude is more than ever unable to pry himself away from the old university town that has figured so largely in his dreams of a better life. Unfortunately, Christminster is so scandalized by his irregular relationship with Sue that they are forced to live in separate lodgings. One day, in her bitterness, Sue lectures Little Father Time about the sin of bringing children into an already over-populated world. The unnatural child takes her tirade to heart. When Sue returns to her rooming house after dining with Jude that evening, she finds that Little Father Time has hanged her two children and himself in a gesture of despair. The shock of finding their bodies sends Sue into a dead faint, and in a premature delivery she loses the baby she has been carrying.

Once an outspoken agnostic who did all she could to destroy Jude's simple, innate faith and who finally succeeded in making him an agnostic, too, Sue now becomes a religious fanatic. Filled with a sense of sin, she tells Jude she can have no more to do with him but must return to her first (and, as far as she is concerned, only legal) husband, Phillotson.

She remarries the schoolmaster, and once again, for the last time, Jude takes to drink. In a drunken daze he is again tricked into marrying Arabella whose husband has died. By now, Jude is near death. Years of masonry work have eaten into his lungs. Despite his precarious health, however, he goes out into the rain to see Sue once more, for Arabella has cruelly refused to summon her to Jude's bedside. The meeting is a failure. Sue will have nothing to do with Jude.

Returning home, Jude curses the day he was born. While Arabella is enjoying herself with a new lover at a sporting

meet, Jude dies tasting the final bitter irony as he hears
through the window the shouts and cheers from the nearby
theater where the Christminster faculty are conferring honorary degrees on a group of undeserving aristocratic dilettantes.

Critical Opinion

With *Jude the Obscure*, his last novel, Hardy reached the
pinnacle of his art and the depths of his pessimism. Unlike
his other novels, *Jude* is not illuminated by the faintest ray
of light or hope. Even the rough peasant humor that relieves
the tragedy of *The Return of the Native* is missing here.

The novel's publication led to such a hue and cry in the
press about its outspoken treatment of sex and the so-called
"new woman" that Hardy decided to return to his first love,
poetry, which he felt would give him a freer hand in ex-
pressing his tragic view of life. But although the critical
blast that greeted the publication of *Jude* was ostensibly
directed at its "immorality," it is difficult not to believe that
the critics were really disturbed at the novel's unalloyed
pessimism, for, from the first to the last, Jude's life and the
lives of those who come into contact with him are blighted.
The world view of the novel is symbolized by the grotesque
suicide of Little Father Time.

Much of the novel's disturbing effect stems, too, from the
savagery of its assault on the institutions of marriage and
the university as Hardy saw them operating in Victorian
England. His own first marriage, to a snobbish, empty-headed
woman who fancied herself his superior, was a desperately
unhappy one. Hardy brooded over the cruelty inherent in
the difficulty of obtaining an annulment when a couple is
patently mismated and over the cruelty society inflicted on
people living together illicitly. He offers no glib solution to
this problem, however, for Sue Bridehead, the believer in
free love who is opposed to binding contracts between men
and women, is scathingly portrayed as a frigid, deeply
neurotic woman who can hardly solve her own personal
problems, let alone those of society. As always in genuine
tragedy, a panacea is neither suggested nor does one seem
remotely possible.

The other major target of *Jude*, academic snobbery, was a subject of much concern in Hardy's day. Christminster is a combination of Oxford and Cambridge, toadying, in Hardy's view, to the inept sons of aristocrats instead of offering education to those genuinely desiring it and capable of appreciating it. *Jude the Obscure* is a powerful document for higher education based on merit rather than on social position. For if anyone deserves as good an education as his society can provide it is the serious-minded Jude, always striving to better himself and always excluded by a society that closes ranks at his approach.

By the time he wrote *Jude*, Hardy had become the complete master of his art. Although his reliance on coincidence is as strong as ever, he builds the book in blocks of chapters like a great gothic cathedral. The symmetry of plot and action that never obtrudes itself gives the book a seemingly inevitable structure and design. It is the ultimate triumph of the architect who became a novelist.

The Author

Thomas Hardy was born of old yeoman stock on June 2, 1840, in a small hamlet in Dorsetshire. His father was a builder and Hardy was trained to be an architect specializing in church restoration. As a youth, he was fascinated by the lore of old churches and by the centuries-old folk music and dances of the countryside, which he later immortalized as the "Wessex" of his novels.

After working five years as an architect in London, Hardy feared his eyes would not stand the strain of architectural drawing. Self-educated, he had read the great classics, especially the Greek tragedians, and he considered turning his hand to literature. He thought briefly, too, of entering the Church, but his readings in modern science and philosophy and his interest in architecture turned him in other directions.

His first novel, *The Poor Man and the Lady*, was rejected by George Meredith, then a publisher's reader, who encouraged Hardy to continue writing. A second novel, *Desperate Remedies*, was published in 1871. The novel that followed, *Under the Greenwood Tree* (1872), was the first in which Hardy's "Wessex" country appeared—a region of

England closely resembling his native Dorsetshire but stamped with the imprint of Hardy's own brooding, compassionate genius.

It was not until 1878, with *The Return of the Native*, that Hardy really hit his stride as a novelist. It is one of the four masterpieces that capped Hardy's career as a novelist, the others being *The Mayor of Casterbridge* (1886), *Tess of the D'Urbervilles* (1891) and *Jude the Obscure* (1896).

The bleak view of the human predicament expressed in these novels, combined with an honesty about sex unique at the time, brought a storm of criticism down on Hardy. The uproar over *Jude the Obscure* was responsible for Hardy's giving up the writing of fiction and spending the last three decades of his life writing poetry, his first love.

From 1898 until his death in 1928, Hardy wrote poetry exclusively, publishing seven distinguished volumes of sharply ironic lyrics, and rounding out his poetic achievement with a massive verse drama about the Napoleonic wars, *The Dynasts* (1904–1908).

As Victorian prudery subsided in the twentieth century, Hardy came to be appreciated as one of the master novelists of his day. In 1910 he received the Order of Merit as well as honorary degrees from the leading British universities. Reviled as a pornographer during his middle years, Hardy found himself revered as a grand old man in his old age. When he died on January 11, 1928, his ashes were buried in the Poets' Corner of Westminster Abbey, an irony Hardy would have been the first to appreciate.

By the Same Author

Tess of the D'Urbervilles: Tess is the story of the seduction, betrayal, and destruction of an innocent girl, Tess Durbeyfield, who is led by her foolish parents into thinking she comes from an ancient noble family, the D'Urbervilles. Encouraged to claim kinship with the family, Tess is seduced by the suave, plausible Alec D'Urberville, who abandons her when she bears his baby. The child dies, and Tess finds a new love with the egotistic, self-righteous Angel Clare. When he hears her story on their wedding night, he too abandons her. In despair, Tess murders Alec. She finds a few fleeting days of happiness with

Clare, who returns to her before she is captured and hanged. In the famous last lines of the novel, which could fit any other of Hardy's works almost as well, " 'Justice' was done, and the President of the Immortals . . . had ended his sport with Tess." *Tess* exemplifies Hardy's tragic irony which views through compassionate eyes the difference between the fate human beings deserve and the one that they suffer.

Treasure Island

by

ROBERT LOUIS STEVENSON (1850–1894)

Main Characters

Jim Hawkins—The brave young narrator of the story who becomes cabin boy aboard the *Hispaniola*.
Dr. Livesey—A physician friend of Jim's.
Squire Trelawney—A country squire with a love of adventure.
Captain Smollett—The highly capable, no-nonsense captain of the *Hispaniola*.
Billy Bones—A mysterious guest at the Admiral Benbow Inn.
Pew—A blind, bloodthirsty pirate.
Long John Silver—A plausible, shrewd, treacherous pirate who signs up as cook on the *Hispaniola*. He has a wooden leg and a pet parrot named Captain Flint.
Ben Gunn—A half-crazed pirate marooned for three years on Treasure Island.

The Story

Young Jim Hawkins has been helping his parents run the Admiral Benbow Inn, near Black Hill Cove, a secluded spot in the English west country. One day a mysterious seaman appears looking for room and board. The stranger's name is Billy Bones. Presumably a retired sea captain, he makes him-

185

self at home in the inn, drinking vast quantities of rum, nervously scanning the coast, and singing the strange chantey:

> "Fifteen men on the dead man's chest
> Yo-ho-ho, and a bottle of rum."

Bones offers Jim a fourpenny piece every month if he will keep his eyes peeled for strangers, particularly a one-legged sailor who might appear at any moment.

When Bones fails to pay his board, Jim's father tries to get rid of him, but the old salt is so rough and terrifying that Mr. Hawkins, a sick man, never evicts him.

Soon another old sailor, Black Dog, appears at the Admiral Benbow, and he and Billy Bones get into a terrible fight in the parlor. Bones chases Black Dog away from the inn. He then falls on the floor in a fit and is treated by Dr. Livesey who has been caring for Jim's sick father.

Jim's father dies; and on the day he is buried, still another mysterious stranger shows up, ominously tapping his cane. It is the blind beggar called Pew, and he forces Jim to lead him to Billy Bones. He gives Bones the Black Spot—a note informing him he is to be killed at ten that night—and leaves. Billy Bones is so frightened at receiving this traditional pirate's death notice that he has a second stroke and dies.

Jim and his mother take the key to Billy Bones's old sea chest, hoping to find money to pay the old sailor's back rent. They plan to take only as much as is due them, but are interrupted by the sound of Pew's stick tapping along the walk. Quickly taking the dead sailor's account book and a sealed packet that they find in his trunk, Jim and his mother leave the inn to search for help. Eventually they find some revenue officers who arrive at the inn in time to scatter a host of Pew's friends. One of the officers on horseback crushes Pew to death.

Jim shows the sealed packet to the local squire, Squire Trelawney, who, with the help of Dr. Livesey, discovers that it contains a map showing the location of buried treasure left on an island by Captain Flint, a notoriously bloodthirsty old pirate. Apparently Billy Bones was to be murdered for holding out on his former friends. Excited by the prospect of high adventure, Squire Trelawney decides to equip a ship and sail for the island with Dr. Livesey and Jim. Trelawney has a reputation as a gossip so Dr. Livesey warns him to keep silent about their mission.

In Bristol, Squire Trelawney buys and outfits the *Hispaniola,* a fine schooner, and engages Captain Smollett. He also hires Long John Silver, a Bristol innkeeper and an old sea dog, to be ship's cook. Silver eagerly helps in the selection of the rest of the crew.

When Jim arrives at Bristol and visits Silver's inn, *The Spyglass,* he is surprised to see Black Dog drinking there. Silver persuades Jim that he does not know his guest's identity, and Black Dog escapes.

Soon the *Hispaniola* is ready to sail. Captain Smollett tells Trelawney that he does not like the idea of the cruise. He complains that he is the only one aboard who does not know the ship's destination. All the hands seem to know exactly where they are bound in search of treasure. Trelawney quiets the captain's fears, and off they sail.

The cruise is uneventful. But one night, just before arriving at Treasure Island, Jim, who is looking for an apple in the apple barrel on deck, is surprised by the approach of Long John Silver. Jim hides in the barrel, where he overhears Long John Silver planning mutiny with Israel Hands, one of the crewmen. Jim learns that in reality the crew look to Silver as their real leader. Most of them have known him since they sailed together with Captain Flint. Their plan is to slay Trelawney and the loyal members of the crew as soon as the treasure is taken off the island.

Jim tells his friends the news as they reach the island. Captain Smollett, his worst suspicions confirmed, cleverly sends most of the crew ashore, and Jim sneaks along with them to find out what they are up to. He hears the screams of two of the loyal crewmen whom Silver has put to death for refusing to go along with his plans.

Exploring the island, Jim comes across Ben Gunn, a poor half-mad hermit who had been aboard Captain Flint's ship when the old buccaneer buried the treasure. On a later trip Gunn had tried to find it but failed, and was left on the island by his shipmates.

In Jim's absence Captain Smollett, Squire Trelawney, and Dr. Livesey decide to leave the *Hispaniola* with the few loyal crew members and occupy Captain Flint's old stockade on the island. They make several trips to take supplies ashore. On the last trip they are fired upon by the pirates remaining aboard the ship.

Despite attacks from the pirates on shore, the loyal party is able to hold the stockade. Jim, who has left Ben Gunn, takes his position in the old fort. The next morning the wily Long John Silver, carrying a truce flag, comes to parley. He offers the men safe conduct back to the ship if they will surrender the treasure map. Captain Smollett contemptuously sends Silver back empty-handed, and soon the pirates attack again. There are casualties on both sides.

After this attack is repulsed, Jim sneaks off again, this time in search of the coracle (a small, one-man boat) which he knows Gunn has built and hidden on the island. He finds it and sets off at night to cut the *Hispaniola's* anchor hawser. He succeeds in setting the ship adrift, but it bears down on him, smashing the little coracle. Jim is forced to go aboard the *Hispaniola* to escape drowning. Aboard he finds Israel Hands, wounded after killing the only other pirate left on the ship. Hands, in a drunken stupor, pretends to allow Jim to run the ship; but suddenly, just as Jim is bringing it into safe harbor, he goes after him with a dirk. He hurls the knife at him, pinning Jim to the mast, but the boy is just able to fire his pistols in time and kills the pirate.

With a wound in his shoulder, Jim manages to anchor the *Hispaniola* safely in a secret spot and make his way back to the stockade. There Silver and the other pirates have now taken over. Jim learns that his friends have abandoned the stockade and given the pirates the treasure map.

Jim is held captive by the pirates who want to kill him and depose Silver as their leader. But the old sea dog bullies the men and promises Jim safety on condition that when they get back to England Jim will stand up for him at his trial. Since most of the pirates now are wounded, drunk, or sick with swamp fever, Silver keeps the upper hand even after they give him the Black Spot.

Carrying the flag of truce, Dr. Livesey arrives to treat the men's wounds. He is curt with Jim who he thinks has deserted to the pirates. Jim cannot understand why Dr. Livesey gave the pirates the chart, but Dr. Livesey tells him he had a secret reason. When Jim recounts his adventure aboard the *Hispaniola*, Dr. Livesey is convinced of his loyalty and tries to get the boy to escape with him, but Jim has given Silver his word not to leave.

Now the pirates go in search of the treasure. The route is

arduous. When they reach the hiding place, they hear a mysterious voice singing "Yo-ho-ho, and a bottle of rum" and taunting them with the final curses of the terrible Captain Flint. Sick with superstitious fear, the men panic, but they finally realize that the mysterious voice is that of poor old Ben Gunn hiding in a tree.

When the men reach the place, they find that the treasure is gone. Furious, they want to kill Silver and Jim, but at that moment Jim's companions come to the rescue and rout the pirates. They bring Jim and Silver to Ben Gunn's cave where the treasure had been hidden by the lonely castaway long before the *Hispaniola* ever arrived. That was why Squire Trelawney was willing to abandon the stockade and give the pirates the now useless map.

With a few days' labor the treasure—thousands of pounds in the currency of almost every nation in the world—is safely stowed aboard the *Hispaniola,* and she leaves the blood-soaked island, abandoning the three remaining buccaneers as they had once abandoned Ben Gunn.

When the ship puts in at a West Indies port, Long John Silver escapes with his share of the treasure and is never heard of again. With a fresh crew hired at the port, the adventurers finally reach Bristol where they divide the remainder of the fortune. Jim decides he has had enough adventure to last him the rest of his days.

Critical Opinion

It would be absurd to read any solemn significance into *Treasure Island,* a book conceived to delight a boy. Stevenson himself, speaking of the treasure map he drew for his stepson, once said that the second voyage of the *Hispaniola,* when Israel Hands and Jim Hawkins are fighting for control of the ship, was written because he had drawn two ports on his map and wanted to make literary use of both of them. Freely admitting his debt to Washington Irving and Charles Kingsley, he pointed out that he got "a parrot from Defoe, a skeleton from Poe (indeed, "The Gold Bug" deeply influenced *Treasure Island*), a stockade from Marryat." The book was first serialized in a boys' magazine.

Treasure Island has nevertheless endured while much of the boys' fiction of its time has been relegated to the dust heap. Stevenson came at just the right moment in English literary history. With the death of Dickens, Thackeray, and Trollope, English fiction had more or less run out of steam. The novels of the 1880's tended to be either absurdly snobbish accounts of "high society" or dreary, naturalistic imitations of Zola, sordidly detailed accounts of the stifling common-places of lower-middle-class life. Stevenson, with his superb tale-spinner's imagination, gave English fiction a lift and a new dimension.

A romanticism rare in the novel after Scott makes *Treasure Island* memorable. The opening scenes in the Admiral Benbow Inn, nestled in its sea cove, have never been surpassed for imaginative re-creation of mood and local color. The sinister figures who invade the inn—Billy Bones, Black Dog, and Pew—lightly but unforgettably sketched, bring color and adventure as well as terror into the lives of Jim Hawkins and his stouthearted English friends.

Later on, in the re-creation of the island, Stevenson surpasses even Defoe in the use of imaginative detail that makes a highly romantic yarn altogether convincing. We know the geography and climate of *Treasure Island* more intimately than we know Crusoe's island.

Finally, *Treasure Island* lives because Stevenson, it is said, was incapable of writing a slipshod or ineffective sentence. Seldom has prose as supple and evocative been lavished on a mere "boy's book." Stevenson's keen ear for the rhythm of a sentence gives the style of *Treasure Island* a classic beauty that transcends the simple characterization, the "thriller" plot, and the modest intentions of the book.

The Author

Born on November 13, 1850, in Edinburgh—the home of that other great romancer, Sir Walter Scott—*Robert Louis Stevenson* was intended by his family to be either an engineer or a lawyer. Young Stevenson was educated at Edinburgh University and admitted to the bar in 1875, already determined to be a writer.

Falling in love with Fanny Osbourne, an American woman estranged from her husband and living in France, Stevenson followed her to California where he nearly starved to death waiting for her divorce to come through. In 1880, having broken with his puritanical family over his affair with Mrs. Osbourne, he was at last able to marry her. In order to support her, he began writing magazine essays, some of which were published the following year in the notable collection *Virginibus Puerisque.* Stevenson's first venture into fiction was a group of stories called *The New Arabian Nights* (1882).

One day, hoping to entertain his stepson, Lloyd Osbourne, Stevenson drew an imaginary treasure map which so intrigued him that he composed a novel to explain it—*Treasure Island.* Although it was unsuccessful in serial form, it made a great sensation when published as a book in 1883. Stevenson was even more successful three years later with the "shocker," *Dr. Jekyll and Mr. Hyde,* which appeared at about the same time as his great romance about the Jacobite uprising in Scotland, *Kidnapped.*

Afflicted with tuberculosis, Stevenson spent much of his life traveling for his health. He spent a winter at the tuberculosis sanatorium in Saranac. In 1888 he set out for the South Seas which had always intrigued him.

On the island of Samoa Stevenson, revered by the natives, recovered his health. In 1889 he published *The Master of Ballantrae,* his most ambitious work. Stevenson also enjoyed collaborating on stories with his stepson, and together they wrote *The Wrong Box* (1889), a fascinating puzzle, and *The Wrecker* (1892).

Although he was usually ill, Stevenson was always a great rebel and adventurer. In Edinburgh he had shocked staid society by his debauchery. In the South Seas he feasted with cannibal chiefs and was able to govern a tribe of savages. Forced to write "penny dreadfuls," or cheap shockers, for a living, Stevenson nevertheless brought a lively romantic imagination and a finely wrought prose style to everything he wrote. When he died in Samoa on December 3, 1894, he left behind an unfinished book, *Weir of Hermiston.* His flair for romance was deeply admired not only by his young readers but by such astute critics of the art of fiction as Henry James and Joseph Conrad.

By the Same Author

Kidnapped: Another exciting tale in the manner of *Treasure Island*, *Kidnapped* relates the efforts of young David Balfour to recover his rightful inheritance from his miserly Uncle Ebenezer. After the uncle's attempt to murder David fails, Ebenezer tries to sell him into slavery in America. David is kidnapped and taken aboard the brig *Covenant*, where he has the good fortune to meet the dashing Jacobite Alan Breck, who helps David defeat the crew and return to Scotland to wrest his inheritance from his uncle. *Kidnapped* ends abruptly because Stevenson fell ill while writing it. A sequel, *David Balfour*, was published in 1893. Both are rousing adventure stories, filled with vivid descriptions of the Highlands.

The Strange Case of Dr. Jekyll and Mr. Hyde: The idea for this psychological study of a split personality came to Stevenson in a nightmare. The highly respected Dr. Jekyll finds a drug that can reduce him to a hideous, evil, dwarf-like being whom he calls Mr. Hyde. The same drug will change him back to Dr. Jekyll, but the good doctor finds himself drawn beyond his control to the life of pure evil and power he knows as Mr. Hyde. One night, as Mr. Hyde, he commits a shocking murder and finds himself unable to return to his other self. The truth of his split personality is discovered, and with the police on his trail he kills himself. Written merely as an entertaining "penny dreadful," *Dr. Jekyll and Mr. Hyde* nevertheless reveals a psychological subtlety and insight Stevenson rarely achieved in his other books.

The Picture of Dorian Gray

by

OSCAR WILDE (1856–1900)

Main Characters

Dorian Gray—A young, rich, extraordinarily handsome, debauched dandy in the sin-ridden London of the 1890's.

Lord Henry Wotton—Dorian's witty, cynical mentor in sensuality.

Basil Hallward—A serious artist whose haunting portrait of Dorian is his masterpiece.

Sibyl Vane—A naïve young actress who catches Dorian's fancy.

James Vane—Sibyl's vengeful brother, a sailor.

Alan Campbell—A tormented young scientist being blackmailed by Dorian Gray.

The Story

Lord Henry Wotton, a cynical man about town, pays a visit to the luxurious studio of his painter friend, Basil Hallward, where he sees the full-length portrait of an exquisitely handsome young man whose features are marked by purity and innocence. Lord Henry asks Hallward who the model is. The artist replies that the young man's name is Dorian Gray, but that he does not want Lord Henry to meet the lad for fear he will corrupt him. He says that young Dorian has inspired him to do his finest work.

While they are talking, Dorian Gray arrives and Hallward is forced to introduce him to Lord Henry who engages the youth in charming, cynical banter while he poses. He begs Dorian to make the most of his youth and beauty while he has it, and deeply impresses the young man with his sophistication and epigrammatic wit.

Before long the portrait is finished and the three men admire it. Dorian is disturbed because the picture will remain eternally young and handsome while he himself will grow old and ugly. He says he would give his soul if only the portrait would age, and he remain perpetually young.

In the next few months, against the wishes of Basil Hallward, Lord Henry takes Dorian under his wing. The youth, who comes from a wealthy but unhappy family, is completely unspoiled. Lord Henry begins to change him. He takes him about London—to parties, plays, and operas—introducing him to society and to a life of pleasure and self-indulgence.

Lord Henry's influence is checked, however, when Dorian falls in love with the innocent seventeen-year-old actress, Sibyl Vane, whom he sees playing Juliet in a tenth-rate theater. At first Dorian is hesitant about letting Sibyl know his name, so she calls him "Prince Charming." Her mother, a faded, somewhat vulgar actress, entirely approves of the affair, but Sibyl's brother, James, becomes furious when he hears of it. James, a sailor, is soon to leave England, but first he warns Sibyl against her mysterious admirer, threatening to kill him if he ever betrays her innocence.

Lord Henry and Basil Hallward react coolly when Dorian tells them he is engaged to Sibyl. They see it as the unfortunate but necessary first affair of an inexperienced youth, and are sure that he will soon leave Sibyl for someone more worthy of his wealth and social position. Dorian insists that they come with him to the theater where she is acting Juliet to see what a paragon she is. That night Sibyl gives a stiff, unimaginative performance. Bored and embarrassed, Lord Henry and Basil Hallward leave the theater before the final curtain. When Dorian goes backstage to see Sibyl, she tells him that she acted badly because art means nothing to her now that her life has become fulfilled by his love. Suddenly Dorian realizes that his friends are right: Sibyl is "common."

He brutally tells her he no longer loves her, leaves her weeping in the dressing room, and storms out of the theater.

At home Dorian receives a terrible shock. Looking at the portrait of himself, he sees it has changed slightly. Although in the mirror his features are as fresh and innocent as ever, in the portrait a cruel grimace distorts his mouth. Dorian hastily writes a letter begging the girl's pardon and assuring her of his love. The next afternoon Lord Henry arrives with the news that Sibyl Vane had taken poison in her dressing room immediately after Dorian had jilted her. The girl is dead, but Lord Henry assures Dorian that he is well rid of her; she was unworthy of him anyway. Furthermore, he will be spared any scandal because nobody connects his name with hers.

Basil Hallward calls to offer his sympathy and asks to see the portrait which he is thinking of exhibiting. Dorian refuses to let him see the picture which he conceals behind a screen. Later he hides the portrait in an unused upstairs room. Fascinated by the idea that the picture will be a mirror of his soul, Dorian is terrified lest anyone else learn of its power.

During the next few years, Dorian falls deeply under the spell of Lord Henry Wotton. The older man gives him a "poisonous" French book to read (J. K. Huysmans' *A Rebours*) which details the infinite variety of sins and sensual pleasures in which a rich, selfish young man can indulge himself. Under its influence, Dorian collects rare gems and perfumes, flirts with Catholic ritual, and even frequents low haunts and opium dens. He takes pleasure in leading young men into a life of debauchery and soon finds himself barred from London society where evil rumors about him are circulating.

Dorian's greatest interest in life is to compare his still youthful, unravaged face in the mirror with the coarse, cruel face emerging in the portrait. Nobody else in London can understand how Dorian manages to remain physically unmarred by his vices.

Late one night, Dorian is visited by Basil Hallward. The artist tells him he is leaving for Paris where he will spend at least six months painting, trying to recover the inspiration that left him when Dorian and he became estranged. Before he leaves, however, he feels he must make one last attempt to talk Dorian out of his evil ways. He harangues him about his evil reputation and begs Dorian to assure him that the rumors are unfounded. Instead, Dorian angrily reveals the picture to the artist who painted it. Basil is appalled by the loathsome visage of evil staring insolently at him from the canvas. He pleads with Dorian to pray for his soul, but Dorian, in a sudden fury, grasps a knife and stabs Hallward to death.

Since Hallward was supposed to be going to Paris, Dorian is sure the murder will not be discovered if he can only dispose of the corpse. To do this, he enlists the aid of an old friend, Alan Campbell, a chemist whose life Dorian had ruined. Campbell has not been on speaking terms with him for years, but Dorian pleads with him to help destroy the body of Basil Hallward. When Campbell angrily refuses to do so, Dorian threatens to blackmail him for some secret sin of the past. Resigned to his fate, Campbell orders large quantities of nitric acid and in a few hours destroys every vestige of the artist's body. While this grisly work is going on, Dorian indulges in witty banter with Lord Henry at a fashionable dinner party.

One night in an opium den, Dorian comes close to death. James Vane, returned from his voyages and single-mindedly stalking his prey, has overheard a woman calling Dorian "Prince Charming," which he remembers as his sister's name for her lover. When Dorian emerges from the den into the fog, Vane is waiting for him with a pistol. Only Dorian's quick thinking saves him from the brother's vengeance. He reminds Vane that Sibyl had died eighteen years before, and then asks the sailor to look at his face under a street lamp. Since Dorian has not aged at all, he seems to be only twenty, and the would-be avenger slinks away. Later Vane realizes his mistake and stalks Dorian at a fashionable hunting party where Vane himself is accidentally killed.

Dorian now thinks himself completely safe. The minor flurry of interest about the disappearance of Basil Hallward has subsided. Sibyl's embittered brother is dead, and Alan Campbell has committed suicide. No one can possibly accuse Dorian of murder. Sick of the past and grateful for his new lease on life, Dorian tells Lord Henry that he is determined to lead a better, less selfish existence. When Lord Henry laughs, Dorian insists that he has begun by refraining from seducing a peasant girl he could easily have had. Filled with good intentions, Dorian wonders if his noble acts will also be recorded on the portrait. Perhaps it will not be so horrible now. He looks again at the picture, but to his horror the face is even worse. In addition to its grossness and cruelty, he can see a hypocritical smirk on the lips and blood dripping from the hand.

Seizing a knife, he slashes passionately at the picture which he feels has betrayed his good intentions and ruined his life. When the servants below hear an agonized cry, they break down the locked door and see on the wall the picture of Dorian Gray as it looked originally—godlike in its beauty and purity. But on the floor is the real Dorian Gray who, in stabbing the portrait, has actually killed himself. Old, debauched, and withered, he is unrecognizable to his own servants until they identify him by the rings on his gnarled, grasping fingers.

Critical Opinion

The Picture of Dorian Gray is Wilde's only full-length novel. It is a curious reworking of the Faust legend in which Dorian is Faust; Lord Henry Wotton, Mephistopheles; Sibyl Vane, Gretchen; and her brother, Valentine. The major difference is that while Faust wishes for eternal youth in order to experience all that life has to offer—including unselfish work. for good—Dorian wishes to remain young only to be admired and to experience all the lusts of the flesh. A very debased Faust, his end is appropriately sordid and essentially meaningless.

Like Dorian's portrait, the novel has aged badly. After its first notoriety as an exhibit used by the prosecution in Wilde's trial, it became a great favorite. Wilde, however, had very little talent for fiction: the plotting is heavy-handed, the characters one-dimensional. Whatever vigor the novel has today stems not from its allegorical treatment of the wages of sin but from its sparkling epigrams and its charm as a period piece of late-Victorian London.

Lord Henry's epigrams and paradoxes are still entertaining. "The only way to get rid of a temptation is to yield to it," he says to Dorian, and (later in the novel), "A man can be happy with any woman, as long as he does not love her."

Obviously, Lord Henry's wit is Wilde's own, and he may have seen himself in the novel as the cynical roué who debauched the "innocent" Lord Alfred Douglas. The pervasive sense of sin is largely unconvincing today, however, because Wilde is too conventionally Victorian to be specific about it. We are not told, for instance, just why Dorian can blackmail Alan Campbell, although we may assume that much of the sin talked about in the book is pederasty.

As a period piece, *The Picture of Dorian Gray*, like the Sherlock Holmes stories, paints the fog-muffled streets, the dandies, and the languors of London in the 1890's. The atmosphere of the book is still entrancing even if the basic plot has less impact today.

The Author

No other sensation in the literary and social world of the 1890's matched the meteoric rise and fall of *Oscar Fingal O'Flahertie Wills Wilde*. Born in Dublin on October 15, 1856, Wilde inherited his artistic tastes from his eccentric mother, a minor literary luminary of the time. He went to Oxford in 1874, where he came under the influence of the esthetic theories of John Ruskin and Walter Pater.

On leaving Oxford, Wilde made it his mission in life to bring a simplified version of the doctrine of art for art's sake to the philistine middle class, not only by means of brilliant essays, plays, and stories but by his own behavior. Dressed extravagantly, and usually clutching some such "esthetic" object as a lily in his hand, Wilde propagandized for an art free of any moral considerations. His lecture tour of the United States in 1882 was a great success largely because of Wilde's genius for self-advertisement. He was parodied as Bunthorne in the Gilbert and Sullivan comic opera *Patience*.

Wilde published a volume of poems that increased his notoriety, although they were little more than pastiches of Swinburne and the Pre-Raphaelite poets. In 1891, under the influence of the French decadent writer J. K. Huysmans, he published *The Picture of Dorian Gray*.

Wilde's real popularity came, however, from the series of comedies he wrote, starting with *Lady Windermere's Fan*, produced in 1892, and reaching a climax with perhaps the most brilliant farce in the English language, *The Importance of Being Earnest*, in 1895. Here all of Wilde's gifts for self-dramatization, for scintillating, sophisticated dialogue, and for gay absurdity reached fruition. He revitalized the English stage, which had lain dormant for over a century, and laid the groundwork for the plays of Bernard Shaw.

But disaster closed in on Wilde in the same year. Married and the father of two sons, Wilde had for some years been indulging in homosexual practices with a variety of young men ranging from the elegant, spoiled Lord Alfred Douglas, who resembled Dorian Gray, to male prostitutes in the lowest strata of the London underworld. When Lord Alfred's father, the Marquess of Queensbury, insulted Wilde at his club one day, Wilde sued him for slander. He lost the suit and in turn was prosecuted by the crown for his sexual crimes. The trials became the scandal of the age. Wilde answered flippantly to the prosecution's charges, rejected the advice of his friends to escape to France, and was condemned to two years at hard labor.

A broken man when he was released from Reading Gaol in 1898, Wilde went to France to live. His wife had left him, his plays had been immediately taken off the stage, his property had been sold at auction, and many of the powerful friends who had been delighted with his repartee at social gatherings now deserted him. Wilde's spirit was broken by the years in prison. Only two more works worth noting came from his pen: the long, self-explanatory letter *De Profundis*, written to Lord Alfred Douglas, and the poem "The Ballad of Reading Gaol."

In France, Wilde lived two years in squalor and poverty, and died on November 30, 1900, a broken man, victim both of his own weakness and folly and of a hypocritical, vengeful society.

The Twentieth Century

The Time Machine

by

H. G. WELLS (1866–1946)

Main Characters

The Time Traveler—An adventurous scientist who journeys
millions of years into the future by means of his time
machine.
Weena—A girl of the race of Eloi whom the Time Traveler
discovers inhabiting England in the year AD 802,701 and
who becomes his trusting and affectionate companion.

The Story

In the waning years of the nineteenth century, the Time
Traveler is entertaining some friends after dinner with a
discussion of time as the fourth dimension. All things, he says,

exist not only in length, breadth, and thickness, but in time as well. The only reason we cannot properly perceive the dimension of time is that we ourselves are moving in it.

To correct this condition and to test his theories, the Time Traveler has constructed a machine designed to help him move backwards or forwards through the centuries. He jolts his skeptical guests (a politician, a doctor, and a psychologist) when he shows them an actual model of the machine, which has taken him two years to construct. He persuades the psychologist to press a lever, and suddenly the model disappears. The Time Traveler tells his astonished guests that as soon as his machine is perfected he hopes to launch himself into the future.

The next week the same group gathers at the Time Traveler's house, joined by a newspaper editor. Their host is late for dinner, and his guests wonder what is keeping him. Can he actually have traveled into the future?

Suddenly the door bursts open and the Time Traveler appears, dirty, disheveled, and bedraggled, with a nasty cut on his chin. After he has cleaned up and dressed and they have all dined, he tells the guests his extraordinary story.

In the week after demonstrating his model, the Time Traveler perfected his machine. That very morning, strapping himself into the time machine, he took off like a rocket into the future. Travel was very uncomfortable, for the days and nights sped past in such rapid succession that his eyes hurt from the alternating light and dark. Eventually, in the misty, strange world of the future, he brought his machine to a jolting halt and found himself in the year AD 802,701.

Hoping to find a greatly advanced civilization, the Time Traveler sees in the misty, warm air only an ominous, giant white sphinx on a huge pedestal. Before long, some men approach. They are frail and delicate and only about four feet tall. One of them, childlike, asks the Time Traveler if he has come from the sun in a thunderstorm. Then these feeble creatures deck the Time Traveler with garlands of flowers and sing and dance around him. They are mildly curious about his time machine, and he allows them to touch it after taking the precaution of removing the operating levers. Together they dine on fruit and vegetables—animals have become extinct— and the Eloi, as they are called, teach the Time Traveler the rudiments of their language.

The Eloi, he decides, are an overcivilized race. Easily fatigued, like children they rapidly lose interest in things. They are extremely lazy, but beautiful, peaceable, and friendly. The Time Traveler realizes that this is the end of human evolution. In a world freed from the struggle for existence by better and more efficient machinery, the people have become unambitious and unassertive. Because the Eloi are no longer struggling with nature, which has long since been entirely subdued, they have become reasonable and cooperative. Having achieved the apparent goal of civilization, they seem to be leading a happy if uneventful life.

As night falls, the Time Traveler is dismayed when he discovers that his machine has disappeared. He tries to awaken the Eloi, but they are terrified of the dark and refuse to help him search for his machine. Uneasy, the Time Traveler finally falls asleep. The next morning he finds a path leading to the huge white sphinx, and realizes that his time machine is inside the statue. He tries vainly to open the door of the sphinx. The Eloi are uncooperative. The Time Traveler begins to despair of ever getting back to his own century.

At this point, however, the Time Traveler makes a special friend among the Eloi, Weena, an affectionate, childlike girl whom he saves from drowning. Like the other Eloi, Weena is easily fatigued and fearful of the dark, but she loyally joins the Time Traveler in his adventures.

On the fourth day of his sojourn, the Time Traveler understands why the Eloi are terrified after nightfall. In the dark ruins of an ancient building, he becomes aware of strange eyes staring at him. Following them, he discovers that they belong to a loathsome, ape-like creature that lopes along before him, eventually disappearing down a ladder into a shaft. The Time Traveler cannot believe that this creature is as human as the Eloi until he realizes that the Morlocks, as they are called, are also descended from the human beings of his time. The world has been divided between the fragile, helpless Eloi, who inhabit the surface of the earth, and the fierce, obscene Morlocks, who clamber about in the darkness of their underground tunnels, like human spiders, emerging only at night. The Eloi, obviously the masters, are descended from the nineteenth-century ruling class in England. The Morlocks, descended from the working class, do all the physical labor, but their brutality and savagery keep the Eloi in mortal terror of the day these servants will revolt.

Certain now that the Morlocks, and not the Eloi, are responsible for hiding his machine, the Time Traveler determines to follow them into their subterranean caverns, despite Weena's warnings. Clambering laboriously into one of the caves, the Time Traveler sees a group of the creatures gnawing at a chunk of meat. He is attacked by them, but by lighting matches before their eyes, he manages to escape above gound. Later the horrible realization comes to him that the Morlocks live on Eloi meat, carrying off their victims at night.

The only safeguard against these obscene creatures is light, which they fear as much as the Eloi fear darkness. As the Time Traveler is running out of matches, he goes exploring the next day with Weena to find some other sources of light. He discovers an ancient palace of green porcelain, apparently a science and natural history museum long forgotten by the Eloi. There he fortunately finds some matches and wax from which he can fashion a candle.

Weena is exhausted after the long trek to the museum, so the Time Traveler decides to camp out with her that night, building a fire to keep the beasts away. But when he sees some Morlocks crouching in the woods, he decides it would be safer to spend the night up on a hill where he builds a new campfire. During the night he awakens to discover that his new fire has gone out, his matches are missing, and Weena is no longer there. Fearing that she has been abducted by the Morlocks, he searches for her without success. He finds that his first fire has spread through the forest, killing thirty or forty Morlocks.

Sleeping by day and traveling by night, he makes his way back to the sphinx, which he is determined to open with a crowbar from the science museum. The door, however, is already open when he gets there, and, not suspecting a trap, the Time Traveler enters.

Inside he discovers his machine. But at that instant a group of Morlocks pounce upon him, and it is all he can do to fend them off while he starts the machine. Just as the Morlocks are about to carry him off to suffer Weena's fate, the machine hurtles him out of their grasp and far into the future.

Millions of years later, the earth has stopped rotating on its axis. The machine lands on a desolate beach where the Time Traveler discovers the only inhabitants are giant, evil-looking crabs. He sets the machine in motion again, and now, thirty million years after leaving the safety of his laboratory, he finds the world a cold, still hulk, faintly lit by a dying sun.

Horrified, the Time Traveler sets the machine back for the return journey, and eventually reaches home where he tells his story to his friends. Disillusioned though he is with the future, the Time Traveler has not lost his scientific curiosity. The next day he sets off again on a journey through time. Three years later he has still not returned, and his friends can only speculate about what misadventure has overtaken him in the depths of time.

Critical Opinion

The Time Machine is a scientific romance with philosophical and political overtones. More serious than Jules Verne, Wells in his first successful book set the tone for contemporary science fiction.

Wells has often been accused of having an over-optimistic faith in what science and intelligent planning could do for the human race. Recent critics have complained that his faith in science as a panacea failed to take into account the side of human nature which would pervert scientific learning into weapons of destruction like the nuclear bomb. In *The Time Machine*, however, Wells shows that he is far from being a facile optimist.

Essentially, this brief book is a speculation about the future of a race which rapidly, through science, finds itself less and less challenged by the physical universe. The soft, lazy, hypercivilized Eloi are as degenerate in their way as the bestial Morlocks who represent an aspect of human nature that can never be entirely suppressed. Wells merely extends into the future the existing society of his day, with its sharply divided ruling and serving classes. In AD 802,701 the rulers find themselves on the brink of being annihilated by their servants whom they depend on for physical sustenance but fear as their potential destroyers.

The only hope for human society, as Wells sees it in *The Time Machine*, is in a humane, intelligent blending of the

vigorous and the contemplative life, and in an amicable,
just relationship between the classes until such time as class
lines disappear.

Tono-Bungay

by

H. G. WELLS

Main Characters

George Ponderevo—The narrator of the story who is interested in aeronautical engineering but gets sidetracked
by his uncle into the patent medicine business.

Edward Ponderevo—George's enthusiastic, ambitious pharmacist uncle, who invents the patent medicine Tono-
Bungay.

Susan Ponderevo—George's sweet and unassuming aunt, who
humorously tries to keep Edward's ambitions in perspective.

Beatrice Normandy—The aristocratic love of George's life.

Marion Ramboat—The grasping, unimaginative girl George
marries.

Gordon-Nasmyth—A reckless soldier of fortune who interests
the Ponderevos in stealing a pile of radioactive material
from an East African island.

Cothorpe—An idealistic, self-educated engineer who helps
George in his flying experiments.

The Story

Young George Ponderevo spends his childhood learning at
first hand about the rigid class system that dominates late
Victorian England. As the son of the housekeeper of Bladesover—a large ancestral estate—he sees that everyone has
his predestined rank, from the regal Lady Drew down to the
lowliest tradesmen and servants. It is impossible to move

from one rank to another, and George quickly perceives that his is near the bottom.

When he is twelve, George falls in love with a high-spirited, aristocratic neighbor, Beatrice Normandy. Little Beatrice seems to return his puppy love; but when George gets into a fight with her overbearing half brother, Archie Garvell, Beatrice not only fails to help him, but betrays him to Lady Drew, pretending that he started the fight. It is George's first disillusioning experience with the clannishness of the English aristocracy, and he never forgets it.

Forced to leave Bladesover, George works for a while in a bakery run by his dull, pious maternal uncle, Nicodemus Frapp. But again the lad disgraces himself by uttering blasphemies before his hypocritically religious young cousins who inform against him to his uncle.

Finally, George finds a place with his paternal uncle, Edward Ponderevo, a pharmacist in the sleepy little town of Wimblehurst. His uncle is a sympathetic spirit. After his mother's death George is well brought up by his patient, humorous aunt, Susan Ponderevo. Uncle Edward, however, is constantly chafing at the dullness of life in the small village. He has great dreams of making a fortune with a single invention that would cater to the wants of the expanding middle class. He sees himself getting a monopoly on some commodity that industry desperately needs and thus becoming a captain of industry.

In his haste to make money, Edward Ponderevo invests his savings foolishly and loses the little he has as well as his small chemist's shop. He even dips into the money entrusted to him for George's upbringing. Unable to bear the sarcastic comments of their neighbors, the Ponderevos leave town to seek their fortune. George is reunited with his uncle and aunt in London when he gets a Bachelor of Science degree at the university.

Although he is angry with his uncle for appropriating his inheritance, George is still fascinated by his restlessness and eccentricity. One day Edward Ponderevo hints to George that he has come upon a great invention with the cryptic name "Tono-Bungay," but that is all he will divulge at the time.

While he is studying science, George meets Marion Ramboat, who helps him forget his childish love for Beatrice. George is naïvely smitten with Marion's wholly commonplace charms and wants to marry her, but she keeps reminding him that he is too poor to set up a household.

Just at this point, Edward Ponderevo summons George to a momentous meeting. Tono-Bungay has been perfected and is being advertised and sold all over England. Will George help him in the production of this unique product? As far as George can discover, Tono-Bungay will neither kill nor cure the people who swallow it. It is a secret formula, cheap and easy to make, but the demand for it has far exceeded Edward's ability to manufacture it. When his uncle offers him £300 a year to come in with him, George, seeing in this offer his chance to get married, agrees.

George's natural efficiency and scientific training enable him to expand the production of Tono-Bungay. He collaborates with his uncle on increasingly vulgar and ludicrous advertisements, and notes, to his amazement, that his uncle really believes in the product and is hurt to hear any criticism of it. The nostrum sweeps England, and the Ponderevos prosper. George's qualms about wasting his scientific skill on a perfectly useless and fraudulent product are assuaged by the fact that he can now finally afford to marry Marion. The marriage is a ghastly failure, however. Marion is interested only in material possessions and is intellectually and temperamentally unsuited to George. Before long George is seeking solace in a temporary affair with Effie Rink, his uncle's secretary.

Once Tono-Bungay is well launched, George can spare the time and money to cultivate his real interest—building and experimenting with gliders and balloons. While he is devoting himself to science, his uncle, ever on the alert to increase his fortune, has been giving to almost anyone who comes to him with a scheme for making money a favorable hearing and capital to go ahead with the project. One of these projects, which is eventually to bring disaster, is the stealing of some "quap," or radioactive slag, from the barren shore of an East African island. This scheme, broached by a soldier of fortune named Gordon-Nasmyth, hangs fire for a while because both Ponderevos are too busy to pursue it.

Meanwhile Edward Ponderevo moves from one elaborate home to another. Still restless, but by now immensely wealthy, he can find no home sufficiently grand to suit his Napoleonic concept of himself. His wife, Susan, tries vainly to keep a check on his pretensions by her quiet humor and by the example of her unaffected personality. Edward is determined to become one of the leading social figures of his time. As long as he has the money to spend, he seems able to break through the rigid class barriers. He tries to learn French and to be a wine connoisseur. The results are ludicrous. Ultimately he buys Crest Hill, as splendid a mansion as Bladesover, and employs a hundred workmen to "improve" it.

Meanwhile, with the money pouring in from Tono-Bungay, George continues his glider experiments with a talented assistant named Cothorpe. Once again he meets Beatrice Normandy, and their love is rekindled when she nurses him back to health after George is nearly killed in a flying experiment.

Edward Ponderevo's massive speculations backfire. Overextended financially, he finds himself dangerously close to bankruptcy. The public begins to lose confidence in him, his powerful friends refuse to help him, and he must call on George to take up Gordon-Nasmyth's scheme, to sail to Mordet Island in search of the mysterious quap. If he can bring back a substantial amount, the Ponderevos will have a monopoly of radioactive substances which are becoming vital in science and industry, and Edward may be able to recoup his losses in other enterprises.

Reluctantly but dutifully, George leaves Beatrice and his flying experiments to set sail aboard the leaky brig *Maude Mary*. George struggles to keep the mutinous crew in order. When they reach the barren island, the heat is nightmarish; stealing the heaps of quap is dangerous and backbreaking work. One day George spots a native staring at him. Afraid of being discovered in the illegal operation, he draws a gun and kills him. Loading the last of the quap aboard ship, he heads for home. In mid-ocean the boat springs a leak and sinks with the entire cargo of quap. George is rescued by a passing ship and returns to England only to learn that Edward Ponderevo has gone bankrupt.

Hounded by creditors and afraid of arrest, Edward decides to leave England. He and George take off in George's latest flying ship, a huge dirigible, and successfully cross the channel at night, landing near Bordeaux, where they pretend to be ordinary tourists. But the excitement and physical rigors of the trip prove too much for the broken-spirited Edward

Ponderevo. With all his grand financial schemes in ruins about
him, he falls ill and dies in a little inn near Bayonne with
only George at his side.

When George returns to England, he has a two weeks'
idyl with Beatrice Normandy. He sees no reason why they
cannot marry now, but Beatrice tells him she can never step
outside her class. She has become too accustomed to luxury
and easy living to share her life with a man who is starting
from scratch even though she admits that she loves him.

Disillusioned, George, now forty-five, becomes a designer
of warships and sets out to write his first and only book,
Tono-Bungay.

Critical Opinion

Although *Tono-Bungay* is often amusing, it is a deeply serious
analysis of the breakdown of values in pre-World War I
England. The character of George Ponderevo is much like
Wells's own, down to the details of being a housekeeper's
son and receiving a scientific, technical education rather than
the classical education of the upper class.

Three major symbols in the book illustrate Wells's theme.
The first is Bladesover, the great estate on which George is
raised and a symbol of the hidebound, snobbish England of
the late nineteenth century. Bladesover, and the whole system
of life implied by its existence, nevertheless had its good points,
George realizes. At least it was based on tradition and an
ordered way of life, not on exploitation and advertising. Lady
Drew belonged there, but after her death the estate was taken
over by members of the newly rich class—uneducated, vulgar
people who cared about its traditions only because they
enhanced their own status.

The second major symbol is the patent medicine, Tono-
Bungay. Utterly valueless, through saturation advertising it
makes a fortune for George and his uncle. Scientific experiment, which Wells felt should be subsidized by the government, is dependent on the financial success or failure of
such goods. As the first major satire on modern advertising
techniques, *Tono-Bungay* is still an effective novel.

Finally, the mysterious radioactive quap symbolizes the
folly of imperialism and industrialism, and the plunder of the

natural resources of the earth to satisfy men's greed. In order to get this substance, which is nauseating to smell and dangerous to hold, George, who is normally decent and honest, must lie, steal, and even kill. The quap is finally lost—returned to nature where it always belonged.

Although Wells never sermonizes in *Tono-Bungay,* it is clear that he is sharply criticizing the vulgar commercialism in the England of his day. Neither the self-destructive snobbery of Bladesover, symbolized by Beatrice's refusal to marry George, nor the aggressive unscrupulousness of the middle class, traditionless and socially unsure of itself, strikes Wells as good. The aristocracy dies because it is weak, insular, and self-indulgent. The middle class is rising to take the aristocracy's place, but its only system of values is a relentless materialism.

At first, science seems to be the only legitimate human concern in the book. But it is science that has taught the world the uses of quap, and we last see George putting his scientific training to use in designing destroyers. Fundamentally only the good-humored patience and bravery of George's Aunt Susan, like the spirit of Weena in *The Time Machine,* is worth anything. Underneath its ebullient humor and Dickensian high spirits, *Tono-Bungay* is a darkly prophetic book, richer in detail and human warmth than *The Time Machine* but every bit as pessimistic about the future.

The Author

Like his Time Traveler and like George Ponderevo, the narrator of *Tono-Bungay, Herbert George Wells* was fascinated all his life by the power of science to shape man's destiny. It was science that lifted Wells from the undistinguished, lower-middle-class world into which he was born on September 21, 1866. His father had tried his hand unsuccessfully at gardening and shopkeeping; his mother was a lady's maid and later housekeeper at Up Park in Hampshire, an establishment like the Bladesover of *Tono-Bungay.* Wells, who called himself "a typical Cockney," learned early what it meant to be a member of the lower social orders of Victorian England.

Determined to rise in the world, Wells rejected all attempts to make a shopkeeper or pharmacist of him. Instead, in 1881, he became a pupil-teacher at Midhurst Grammar School.

Wells's preoccupation with science won him a scholarship in 1884 to study biology under Thomas Henry Huxley at the Royal College of Science. Poor health and a foray into journalism cut short his career as a science teacher. By 1895, with the publication of *The Time Machine,* he had established himself as one of England's most popular and successful authors.

Wells was extraordinarily prolific—there are at least a hundred titles to his credit—in three genres. First are the scientific romances, precursors of modern science fiction, of which the most successful, besides *The Time Machine,* are *The Island of Dr. Moreau* (1896), *The Invisible Man* (1897), and *The War of the Worlds* (1898). Then come the novels about lower-middle-class eccentrics, filled with Dickensian humor and keen social observation. Among these the best known are *Kipps* (1905), *Tono-Bungay* (1909), and *The History of Mr. Polly* (1910). The third group is by far the largest, if the least enduring, of Wells's fiction and includes novels of ideas—ideas about love and sex, politics, war, religion, and education. They include *Ann Veronica* (1909), *Mr. Britling Sees It Through* (1916), and *The World of William Clissold* (1926).

With the publication in 1920 of his vastly successful *Outline of History,* Wells attained world-wide fame as a political and social pundit. Like his friend George Bernard Shaw, he had always been interested in Fabian socialism, which to Wells meant the only rational way of organizing the world in order to prevent waste, poverty, and war.

Never particularly interested in the esthetics of fiction, Wells, as he grew older, turned more frequently to the writing of popularized history, philosophy, and science, sometimes thinly disguised as fiction but more often straightforward expository or argumentative tracts. A lifelong hater of war, he found himself propagandizing for England in the two major wars of the century.

Before he died, on August 13, 1946, the Labour Party whose program he had done much to formulate had risen to power in England.

By the Same Author

The War of the Worlds: This grim tale of a savage, destructive invasion of earth by ruthless, super-intelligent Martians shocked a good many Victorian readers out of their complacency about man's inevitable progress. In it Wells describes the invasion, starting with the landing of a single, mysterious spaceship which is mistaken for a meteorite, and leading into a universal panic through wholesale destruction of the English countryside and of London itself. The Martians are all brain and no heart. They are the scientific superiors of men on earth, but finally, after literally sucking the blood of human beings for food, they succumb to the bacteria of earth for which their systems are unprepared. In the light of the immense accumulation of scientific knowledge about outer space since the book was written, it may seem rather primitive to sophisticated modern readers. Wells's vision of a universal holocaust destroying man's complacency, however, has in recent years become even more pertinent than at the time he wrote this short, terrifying book.

The History of Mr. Polly: This is a delightful novel about an especially charming lower-middle-class draper's apprentice's frustrations and glorious escape from a humdrum existence. After fifteen years of trying to run an unsuccessful shop and to cope with a shrewish wife, gentle, mild-mannered Mr. Polly decides to escape. He sets fire to his shop so his wife can collect insurance, pretends to commit suicide, and then takes off for high adventure as a tramp. Eventually he meets an unpretentious woman who runs a country inn and joins her in that more cheerful enterprise. *The History of Mr. Polly* reflects Wells's compassion for the average man who leads what Thoreau called a life of "quiet desperation" but who nevertheless refuses to close his eyes to the beauty and romance in life. Mr. Polly, however, is no stereotype for the "little man": he is one of the "originals" in our literature, and the novel is a gem, mined in the Dickensian vein.

Heart of Darkness

by

JOSEPH CONRAD (1857–1924)

Main Characters

Charles Marlow—An old, experienced seaman telling the story of a nightmarish youthful adventure.

Fresleven—A Danish captain, Marlow's predecessor in the Congo.

The Russian—An enthusiastic sailor Marlow meets deep in the Congo.

Mr. Kurtz—The mysterious European ivory trader whom Marlow is sent to search for.

Kurtz's "Intended"—His idealistic, loyal fiancée back in Brussels.

The Story

The experienced old sea dog, Marlow, is perched one evening like a Buddha on the deck of the cruising yawl *Nellie*, which is anchored in the Thames estuary. He is talking to a group of his boyhood friends. They are now grown to be important people—a director of companies, a lawyer, and an accountant —but between them there has always existed the "bond of the sea." Marlow, looking at the great city of London enveloped in the gloom of dusk, makes a cryptic remark to his friends. "And this also," he says, "has been one of the dark places of the earth."

Seeing London, now the apex of civilization but at one time a barbaric port where Roman legionaries came in fear and trembling, reminds Marlow of his experience many years before, sailing up the Congo River in search of the mysterious ivory trader, Mr. Kurtz.

As a boy, Marlow had always been fascinated by maps, especially those of unexplored continents. The map of Africa particularly intrigued him, with its gaps of uncharted land deep in the Congo. After growing up to be a sailor and spending some six years in the East, Marlow one day decides to take a job aboard a steamer headed for the Congo River. He visits an aunt in Brussels who has influence with one of the continental trading companies that are exploiting Africa and need brave men to sail their fresh-water steamers.

Marlow learns later that his predecessor in the company's employ was a Dane named Fresleven, who had been brutally murdered in an argument with some natives about a couple of chickens. Still full of the spirit of adventure, Marlow impresses his future employer. A strange, disquieting medical examination follows, performed by a doctor who measures Marlow's skull with calipers, all the time remarking ominously, "The changes take place inside, you know." The doctor also, significantly, asks Marlow if there is any history of insanity in his family.

Ultimately Marlow ships aboard a French steamer which follows the forbidding African coast past such bizarre places as Gran' Bassam and Little Popo. One day he sees a French man-of-war firing shells futilely into the continent; a nameless war is in progress, but the jungle has swallowed up the combatants.

Landing finally at the company's seaboard station, Marlow sees wretched Negroes engaged in slave labor. There is general apathy among the whites, and everything is going to ruin in the implacable grip of the jungle. One accountant, however, has managed to keep up European standards. To Marlow's delight and surprise, he wears a formal business suit, keeps up appearances, and even tries to do his job efficiently despite the general rot and decay surrounding him.

Marlow also begins to hear rumors of the great Mr. Kurtz who operates the company's inner station deep in the heart of the Congo. Mr. Kurtz is renowned, even on the coast, for the vast quantities of ivory he sends back. Nobody quite knows how he gets it, but they are all pleased that their agent is so efficient, even if his methods may be slightly unorthodox.

Trekking two hundred miles in two weeks through dense forest, Marlow reaches the company's central station on the shore of the river where he is to find his steamer. Here he learns that his boat has sunk, and it will take at least three months to dredge it up and make it seaworthy again. He is greeted with cold disdain by the inscrutable manager of the central station, who, like everyone else there, is obsessed with the profits to be made from ivory.

Again Marlow hears the name of Kurtz, as he waits for his boat to be repaired and meets the various people of the station, most of whom are intensely jealous of the great ivory trader. The rumor is that Mr. Kurtz is seriously ill. It will be Marlow's job to pilot the steamer up the river until he reaches Kurtz's station, and there to bring the sick man—and his accumulated ivory—back to the central station.

Eventually Marlow's boat is made seaworthy, and he begins the voyage, joined by a company manager, some pilgrims, and a few cannibals who have been paid by the company with useless little bits of wire to man the ship.

As Marlow penetrates deeper and deeper into the jungle, his boat is in constant danger of hitting snags, his cannibal steersman is enthusiastic but unreliable, and the trigger-happy pilgrims aboard are ready to fire at any natives they see ashore.

About fifty miles from the inner station, Marlow comes upon an abandoned hut where he finds a note urging him to hurry but to approach cautiously. He also finds an old English maritime manual with strange, cipherlike annotations in the margin. The sight of this book, a touch of sanity in the midst of the oppressive madness of the jungle, encourages him.

When the boat approaches Kurtz's station, however, the natives on the shore open fire on it with arrows. Marlow's cannibal steersman is killed. Marlow saves the situation by pulling on the boat's steam whistle. This sends the superstitious natives scurrying for shelter. At last the boat reaches the inner station.

There Marlow is greeted by a Russian sailor whose clothing is so patched that he looks like a tattered harlequin. The Russian had left the naval manual behind. (The strange notations were in Russian script.) He is a personable, enthusiastic young man who fills Marlow's disbelieving ears with hero-worshiping talk about Mr. Kurtz. The great ivory merchant is mortally ill, the Russian confides sadly. Marlow looks around and spots what seem to be highly polished wooden balls decorating the picket fence surrounding the compound. But when he looks more closely he realizes they are native heads impaled on poles and grinning hideously.

Gradually Marlow begins to learn the truth about the remarkable Mr. Kurtz. Entering the jungle as an idealist who thought that European commercial exploitation would bring culture and civilization to the natives, Kurtz had eventually succumbed to the savage lure of the jungle where he became all-powerful.

Although Kurtz has a fiancée back home in Brussels, whom he loftily refers to as "my intended," Marlow sees a savage native girl wailing on the shore. She is obviously Kurtz's mistress. As the jungle has taken its inexorable toll of Kurtz, he has allowed savage rites to be performed in his honor and has ruthlessly slain anyone who has stood in the way of his single-minded pursuit of ivory.

By the time Marlow actually meets the moribund Kurtz, he is filled with ambivalent feelings about him. On the one hand he detests him for being a hollow egomaniac who has lived for plunder while giving it the sweeter name of progress. But on the other hand Marlow realizes that at one time Kurtz had elements of genuine greatness in him. He was many cuts above the tawdry merchants of the central station. At least he started out his career in Africa with some ideals, even if they did ultimately disintegrate.

It is too late now, however, to bring Kurtz to any kind of justice. The dying man is placed on Marlow's steamer, and back they head down river, to the menacing hoots of the natives ashore. Soon after the return journey has begun, a native contemptuously comes to Marlow with the news, "Mistah Kurtz—he dead." The last words Marlow had heard him utter had been "The horror! The horror!" as the darkness of the jungle, of death, and of his knowledge of his own terrible sin had closed in on him.

Back in Brussels, Marlow resists the attempts of various interested parties to get at the papers Kurtz had entrusted to him. Physically and spiritually shaken by the experience and by the curious sense of identification he felt with Kurtz,

Marlow goes to see his bereaved fiancée. He discovers that she
has remained loyal to the idealistic Kurtz who first went to
Africa. Marlow decides that even though he hates nothing
more than a lie, he cannot tell the girl the truth about her
dead lover's last hideous moments. Instead, Marlow agrees
with Kurtz's "intended" that he was a great man, and tells
her his last word had been her whispered name.

Critical Opinion

On the surface, *Heart of Darkness* is a short novel about a
long voyage into the depths of the Congo. It is, however, an
allegory, like Bunyan's *Pilgrim's Progress* or Dante's *Divine
Comedy*. The narrator's actual, literal voyage is symbolic of the
more profound voyage of the soul on which it discovers that
the heart of man is dark and capable of monstrous evil.

Like Christian and Dante, Conrad's narrator, Marlow,
in the course of his nightmare journey, makes discoveries
about himself and his relation to good and evil.

As in *Lord Jim*, the narration proceeds by means of complicated time shifts. The prose style is lushly romantic and richly
suggestive, the words "dark" and "black" recurring with
haunting suggestiveness. Conrad says of Marlow that "to
him the meaning of an episode was not inside like a kernel
but outside, enveloping the tale which brought it out
only as a glow brings out a haze." This is the esthetic theory
that underlies the writing of *Heart of Darkness*, which is
mysteriously suggestive and allusive rather than explicit or
realistic.

The real "facts" of the story stem from a voyage like
Marlow's that Conrad made into the Congo in 1890 just after
he had begun to write *Almayer's Folly*. The voyage was
every bit as harrowing as Marlow's. The Mr. Kurtz who died
aboard Conrad's boat was in reality a Georges-Antoine Klein
whom Conrad had picked up at Stanley Falls. Eventually
Conrad fell ill, and the whole experience effectively ended
his career as a sailor.

What is significant about the story is not its foundation in
actual fact but the implications that Conrad draws from the
facts.

"All Europe contributed to the making of Kurtz," Marlow

tells us, and indeed he is a representative figure of the lust for plunder which ravaged Africa in the nineteenth century and which attempted to conceal its rapacity under the guise of idealism.

The true horror of the story lies not in Kurtz's degeneration and ultimate despair but in Marlow's growing realization that he, too, is capable of undergoing the moral regression that destroyed Kurtz. He is made painfully aware of the savagery pulsating behind the most civilized façade.

Lord Jim

by

JOSEPH CONRAD

Main Characters

Jim—The ruggedly built sailor son of an English country parson.

Charles Marlow—The main narrator of the tale, a sympathetic, experienced seaman who tries to help Jim.

Stein—A philosophical German trader and butterfly collector.

Cornelius—A corrupt white trader living on the island of Patusan.

Jewel—Cornelius' fanatically loyal, beautiful daughter.

Doramin—A stern old native chieftain on Patusan.

Dain Waris—His son, a loyal friend and comrade of Jim's.

"Gentleman" Brown—A bloodthirsty pirate fleeing the law.

The Story

Spotlessly clean and immaculately dressed, Jim at first glance is more prepossessing than any other water-clerk in the Eastern ports. But the job of water-clerk, which entails rowing out in a small boat to sell ship's supplies to vessels reaching port, does not seem to agree with him, for after doing satisfactory work for a while he will suddenly and mysteriously take off for a distant port.

Charles Marlow, an experienced old sailor, is intrigued by the tall, blond English lad with the haunted look. Although Jim, the son of a country parson, seemed to all the world "the right kind," a gentleman, he was involved in the disgraceful *Patna* affair, which Marlow learns about while attending the Court of Inquiry investigating the affair.

Twice in Jim's apprenticeship to the sea he had shown moments of indecisiveness that could easily have been interpreted as cowardice. Then he ships aboard the *Patna*, an old, unseaworthy vessel commanded by a drunken, cowardly old captain, and carrying eight hundred Malayan pilgrims. The crew, with the exception of Jim, is rough, disorderly, and mercenary. Jim is the only true gentleman aboard.

One supernaturally still night, while the pilgrims are sleeping in squalor on the deck of the overcrowded ship, the *Patna* runs into an unidentified, submerged object. One of the officers notices a bulging bulkhead and spreads the word among the crew that the ship is about to sink. With only seven lifeboats aboard, there is no hope of saving any of the eight hundred Malayans in the mad scramble that would follow a general alarm. So the crew, fearing the ship will go down at any moment, jump into the lifeboats, without even sounding an alarm lest the pilgrims awaken and panic.

Jim stays on deck for a moment, shocked at the crew's cowardice. After checking the rusty bulkheads, he is convinced that the ship will sink. The captain and crewmen call to him from the lifeboats and Jim impulsively jumps, not because he is afraid of dying but because he visualizes how helpless he would be when the horrified pilgrims awake.

The lifeboats reach shore, and tell the appalled British colonials what happened. The colonials had expected nothing better from the captain and crew but are embarrassed that one of them, Jim, should also have behaved so dishonorably. They even offer him money to flee before the Court of Inquiry meets, but Jim proudly insists on taking the consequences of his cowardly action.

It is this stubborn sense of his worth as a man responsible for his acts that attracts Marlow to the sailor. One day, for instance, after a particularly grueling session of the court, somebody refers to a dog ambling along as a "wretched cur."

Jim spins around, assuming the remark is meant for him, and Marlow realizes how deep the shame must have burned into the youth's soul.

Ironically enough, the *Patna* does not sink after all, but just drifts, crewless, until she is spotted by a French gunboat. The French captain orders the *Patna* secured by a rope to his own boat and, staying on the wretched ship all the time, sees her into port. The French captain, too, gives evidence. He tells the court that he was frightened to death himself while aboard the *Patna* but was merely doing his job. The board deprives all the officers of the *Patna* of their sailing certificates and closes its hearings.

Gradually, through his blunt, realistic sympathy, Marlow manages to make friends with Jim. He sees in the unfortunate young sailor a mirror of what might well have happened to him in the crises he has somehow managed to survive. He gets Jim a job with the owner of a rice mill. For a time Jim seems well-suited to his work. But one day a former officer of the *Patna* shows up, and at this reminder of his disgrace, Jim bolts without saying a word. He leaves one job after another, constantly heading east in the hope that somewhere far enough from civilization his disgrace will not be known. But by now everyone knows Jim's story. He is never able to stay on any one job for long, for, although people are too polite to mention the *Patna* affair to him, his own conscience keeps tormenting him.

Marlow, beginning to despair that Jim will ever find peace and salvation for his troubled soul, goes to visit an old German friend, Stein, the wealthy, widely respected head of Stein and Company, who is also an ardent butterfly collector and an amateur philosopher. Stein diagnoses Jim's trouble immediately: Jim is a romantic, unrealistic about human limitations in this world, with too noble a concept of himself. Thus he cannot forgive himself for his momentary, all-too-human lapse into cowardice.

Stein's solution for Jim's problem is to send him to the remote island of Patusan, where Stein and Company have a trading post. There, far from any white men who might know his story, perhaps Jim can forget the past and reclaim himself. Stein gives Jim a ring to present as identification to his old friend Doramin, an island chieftain, and Marlow bids Jim an emotional farewell.

At first Jim runs into trouble on Patusan. He is jailed by a tyrannical rajah who is fearful of the trade competition Jim may bring. But Stein's friend Doramin intervenes when Jim escapes from prison. 'Together with his stalwart son, Dain Waris, Doramin helps Jim defeat the rajah in a pitched battle.

Jim also meets his predecessor in Stein's employ, a corrupt old man named Cornelius, who first tries to persuade Jim to leave the island and then, when he is unsuccessful, watches with growing, impotent hatred as Jim falls in love with his beautiful daughter, Jewel. When Marlow pays him a visit two years after Jim has come to Patusan, all seems to be going well. Jim and Cornelius' daughter are deeply in love with each other, so much so that Jewel is cold to Marlow, whom she suspects of trying to lure Jim away from Patusan. She cannot believe that her strong, respected lover could never find acceptance in the outside world. Indeed, to the natives, Jim has become a hero for defeating the hated rajah and bringing prosperity to the island. They call him "Tuan" or "Lord" Jim. Marlow leaves the island satisfied that Jim's reclamation is proceeding well.

Trouble comes to the island in the ominous person of "Gentleman" Brown, a pirate fleeing from the law, who harbors his boat in Patusan, hoping to find provisions, money, and sanctuary. Jim is on a trip up-river when Brown and his crew attack the stockade, now temporarily commanded by Dain Waris. The natives manage to repel the attack, for Brown and his men are half-dead with exhaustion and hunger. Dain Waris drives Brown and his crew to take shelter on a hilltop. The stronghold they build there proves impregnable.

When Jim returns from his expedition, he goes himself, at considerable risk, to interview Brown. Brown cravenly begs Jim for a chance to escape—after all, did not Jim ever need a second chance in life? The words hit home. Jim sees himself as no better really than this cutthroat. He had been given a second chance; who was he to withhold one from "Gentleman" Brown? He returns down the hill and persuades the natives to lift the siege.

They do so reluctantly. The savage Brown repays Jim's benevolence by descending on the natives and slaughtering several of them, including Dain Waris. Heartsick at what he considers this second great betrayal, Jim presents himself before the slain warrior's father. Native justice demands that

Jim be punished for the slaying of Dain Waris, which was, after all, the result of his own misjudgment of character. Stoically, feeling this is the only way now to recapture his lost honor, Jim allows the heartbroken old native chieftain to shoot him through the chest. His tragic death, Marlow believes, was the only possible salvation for Jim.

Critical Opinion

Lord Jim has been called Conrad's *Hamlet,* for it is the complex tragedy of an indecisive man of great inherent nobility who nevertheless, with "the stamp of one defect," manages to bring death and destruction upon those he loves. In form, this novel of Conrad's greatest period is no less rich and complicated than *Hamlet.* Using constant changes of point of view, narrations within narrations, kaleidoscopic time shifts, and other highly sophisticated and masterly fictional techniques, Conrad weaves around the anecdote of Jim's desertion of the *Patna* a complex moral skein. A basically simple adventure yarn thus becomes a great parable of man's fate.

Originally, Conrad had intended to write a short story around the *Patna* incident. When he decided to develop it into a novel, he found great difficulty welding it together with the Patusan story into a single, coherent narrative. Realizing this was the "plague-spot" of his novel, Conrad once told a friend that the cleavage at the middle of the book made him feel "as if he were left with a lump of clay into which he had failed to breathe the right sort of life." He need have had no worry on that score, however, for *Lord Jim* ranks with his finest achievements.

A thoroughgoing romantic, Jim can never come to grips with reality, can never accept his limitations as a human being who is often indecisive, sometimes even cowardly. Only Stein and Marlow realize that in Jim's single-minded quest for redemption he is heroic as well as absurd and "wrong-headed"; his romanticism is his glory as well as his dilemma.

Jim is on the point of redeeming himself from the disgrace of the *Patna* affair by becoming a trusted and beloved native leader when the invasion of Brown and his crew of cutthroats leads him to make an unrealistic, foolishly chivalric error of judgment which destroys his friends. He would not have made this error had not Brown insidiously appealed to his sense of guilt. Thus, as in the greatest tragedies, Jim's character —haunted by the sin of his past and lost in his search for absolution—brings the ultimate catastrophe down upon him.

The Author

A great paradox of English fiction is that one of its supreme masters was born in the Ukraine, of Polish parents, and was totally ignorant of the English language until he was twenty years old. Born on December 3, 1857, the future novelist's full name was *Teodor Józef Nalecz Konrad Korzeniowski*. His father was a poet and revolutionary, a translator of Shakespeare who ended his life a political prisoner in Russia where Conrad's mother died, too, a brokenhearted exile.

The young Conrad was brought up by his conventional but understanding uncle, Tadeusz Bobrowski. Like Marlow in *Heart of Darkness*, Conrad as a youth was fascinated by maps and was filled with a desire to explore the world. Accordingly, he signed aboard a French vessel in 1874 and had some extraordinary adventures, including a duel while he was a gunrunner for the Carlist cause in Spain. Eventually he joined the English merchant marine in 1878, became a naturalized British subject, and gained his master's certificate in 1884.

For the next few years, Conrad sailed over much of the world, especially in the Far East. He taught himself English by reading the plays of Shakespeare and the novels of Trollope. Eventually he began trying his own hand at fiction. The result, *Almayer's Folly*, was shown to John Galsworthy, who encouraged the sailor to continue writing. In 1894, the year before *Almayer's Folly* was published, Conrad settled in England and became a struggling, full-time author.

Writing was always difficult for Conrad, who once said he wrote in English, thought in French, and dreamed in Polish. Nevertheless, with a wife and growing family, he struggled hard, publishing a sequel to *Almayer's Folly, An Outcast of the Islands,* in 1896; the masterful *Nigger of the 'Narcissus'* in 1897; and *Lord Jim* in 1900. Although he was immediately appreciated as a master by the novelists of his day—James, Galsworthy, and Wells in particular—the difficulty of his style, his psychological subtleties, his handling of time, and his somber, dry irony baffled the general public. At best, he was considered the author of unduly complicated boys' sea yarns.

Annoyed by this reputation, Conrad embarked on the writing of three political novels that had nothing to do with adventures afloat: *Nostromo* (1904), his longest work, about South American politics; *The Secret Agent* (1907), a completely ironic tale about anarchists in London; and *Under Western Eyes* (1911), a bitter look at Russian psychology.

Politically conservative, morally at one with the stern maritime traditions of loyalty and honor, Conrad was a unique voice in English fiction. A late starter as a novelist, he was more or less worn out by the time of World War I, although it was only with *Chance* (1913) and *Victory* (1915) that he really achieved a wide audience. Conrad died of a heart attack after a visit to the United States on August 3, 1924.

By the Same Author

Nostromo: Conrad's largest canvas and the work that was written with the greatest pains, *Nostromo* was inspired by Conrad's brief visit to South America during his days in the merchant marine. In the book, Conrad describes a typical Latin American country named Costaguana. The corrupt nation is beset by revolution, during which Nostromo, a virile young Italian working for the Gould silver mine, hides some silver treasure for safekeeping on a desert island. He spreads the rumor that the ship carrying the treasure has sunk and keeps the silver for himself. He is, however, found out and destroyed by the father of the girl he loves. Many subplots are woven around the central one to make *Nostromo* the richest and most complex of Conrad's novels. As an analysis of Latin American politics and character, it remains unmatched.

Victory: The last of Conrad's important novels, *Victory* is about a disillusioned, Hamletesque Swede named Axel Heyst who tries to escape involvement with other human beings and retreats to an island of his own. He becomes involved against his will with Lena, a girl being mistreated by the heavy-handed, coarse German hotel keeper, Schomberg. Heyst spirits Lena off to his island but is pursued by Jones, who, like "Gentleman" Brown in *Lord Jim,* is the incarnation of evil. In the ensuing battle, Heyst thinks Lena has betrayed him to Jones but learns, too late, of her moral victory in keeping unto death a faith and trust he had never been capable of returning.

Kim

by

RUDYARD KIPLING (1865–1936)

Main Characters

Kimball O'Hara—An impish and ingenious thirteen-year-old
  orphan educated in the teeming streets of Lahore.
Teshoo Lama—An ancient priest of Such-zen in Tibet, he
  is searching for a mystic, all-healing river.
Mahbub Ali—A crafty Indian horse trader working for the.
  British secret service.
Colonel Creighton—Ostensibly a member of the Ethnological
  Survey, actually the chief of secret service operations.
Hurree Chunder Mookerjee—A Bengali educated in English
  schools, a wily secret service agent.
Father Victor—A kindly Catholic chaplain attached to the
  Maverick regiment.
The Reverend Arthur Bennett—The Mavericks' blunt, un-
  imaginative Anglican chaplain.
Mr. Lurgan—A gem dealer and "healer of sick pearls" who
  trains Kim in the art of spying.

The Story

Kimball O'Hara, known as Kim in the crowded, colorful
streets of Lahore, is the orphan son of a dissolute sergeant in
the Mavericks, an Irish regiment in India, and an Irishwoman

who died when he was a baby. He has been carelessly brought
up by a half-caste woman who lets him roam the streets at
will. Deeply bronzed by the burning Indian sun, Kim looks
more Asiatic than European and is more proficient in Hin-
dustani than in English.

One day, idly perched on the great cannon of Zam-Zammah,
Kim sees a Tibetan lama obviously lost in the bustling city of
Lahore. The lama is searching for the River of the Arrow,
which reputedly washes away all sin. Kim, sensing a chance
for adventure, joins forces with the old man and promises to
take him to Benares, the holy city. He begs food for him and
protects him from the jeers of the other street boys.

But Kim now receives an assignment from Mahbub Ali, a
crafty horse peddler, to deliver a secret message to the British
command at Umballa. Although the message seems to be
about horses, Kim senses that it really is a code. His hunch is
confirmed that night when Mahbub Ali's house is unsuccessfully ransacked.

Kim and the lama arrive by rail at Umballa. After delivering
his message, Kim hides in the grass and overhears the conference among the officers. The coded note from Mahbub Ali
is the signal for eight thousand armed men to destroy some
far-flung native potentates who are planning a rebellion.

Then Kim and the old lama begin their travels along the
Grand Trunk Road, which stretches 1500 miles across India
and offers an unparalleled cross section of native life. The
holy man and his *chela*, or servant boy, are adopted by a rich
old Kulu woman traveling to visit her daughter. The old lady
is very talkative and nearly bores the lama to death with her
demands for religious talismans. But she feeds the two way-
farers handsomely during their search for the mystic river.

One evening the Irish regiment of the Mavericks encamps
near the road. Kim is attracted by their flag, displaying a red
bull on a green field. He recalls a prophecy that his fortunes
will rise when he finds a red bull on a green field. Stealing
closer to the camp, Kim is discovered by the Anglican chaplain, the Reverend Arthur Bennett, and his Catholic cohort,
Father Victor. The chaplains find an amulet hanging from
Kim's neck in which his birth certificate is kept. They are
astonished to learn that this Indian ragamuffin is the son of
the late Sergeant O'Hara.

For Kim the discovery spells disaster. He will be separated

from his beloved lama and sent to school, which he loathes. He assures the lama that he will escape from the soldiers in a few days. Meanwhile the old holy man is to follow the rich dowager lest he get into trouble without Kim to aid him.

But when the lama hears that the regiment will send Kim to school, he asks for Father Victor's name and address and promises to send some money for the boy's education. Kim astonishes the soldiers with a prophecy that soon eight thousand men will go into action. At first they laugh at his prediction, but soon it comes true, and they are ordered to march against the rebel potentates.

Meanwhile a letter comes from the lama enclosing three hundred rupees with a promise to send the same amount yearly for Kim's tuition at the fine St. Xavier's school. Father Victor is amazed that the lama, who looks like a woebegone beggar, should be able to command such a sum.

Kim is beaten by the drummer boy charged with seeing that he does not escape. He is desperately unhappy with the orderly, military routine of the regiment. He manages to get a scribe to send a letter to Mahbub Ali begging for help. One day the horse trader arrives and snatches Kim away with him. Kim thinks he is to be rescued from the military life, but Mahbub Ali turns him over to Colonel Creighton, a member of the Ethnological Survey, who extracts from Kim a promise that he will go to St. Xavier's. Kim recognizes the colonel as the man who gave the order for the eight thousand men to march.

Kim is unhappy at school, but he works hard and slips out from time to time to meet his lama. When vacation time comes, Kim dyes himself a dark brown, puts on a turban, and escapes to more adventure. He begs Mahbub Ali to let him travel with him, proving his worth to Mahbub by spying on some men who are planning to kill him and exposing the plot.

Mahbub Ali turns Kim over to a mysterious Mr. Lurgan at Simla. Mr. Lurgan, who calls himself the healer of sick pearls, has gems, totems, and even a phonograph in his shop. Mr. Lurgan is actually a member of the British secret service in India. He trains Kim to observe, to remember, and to be secretive, pitting Kim against his son in contests of observation and disguise. At Mr. Lurgan's house Kim meets fat Hurree Chunder Mookerjee, a babu or Indian who has been educated by the English. Mookerjee, also employed by the secret service, tells Kim that if he stays in school and learns well, he, too, may become a secret agent or join the "Great Game," as spying is called.

Accordingly, Kim returns to St. Xavier's where he studies for two more years to become a geographic surveyor, a useful occupation for spies. One day, when Mahbub Ali assures Colonel Creighton that the boy is ready, Kim leaves school and resumes his Indian color and costume. He joins the lama, who has kept his promise to pay Kim's tuition every year. Together they head for Delhi in search of the River of the Arrow.

On the train Kim meets E. 23, another Indian spy playing the Great Game, who is frantically trying to escape from some enemies waiting to kill him in Delhi. Kim disguises the spy so well that when they get off the train nobody knows who he is. Kim is praised for his skill and ingenuity and once again he and his lama ply the roads of India.

They meet the garrulous old Kulu woman again and Mookerjee, who tells Kim he is needed for more spy work. Two Czarist agents, one a Russian and the other a Frenchman, have penetrated the north country, bribing the treacherous kings there to let them do some secret surveys. Orders are to capture them. Kim and the lama head for the steep foothills of the Himalayas. Kim tells the simple old man he will find his river there. The lama is pleased to be in mountainous country once more, but the steep passes and heavy snow baffle Kim, who can barely keep up with his friend.

Meanwhile the babu encounters the Russian and the Frenchman and offers his aid as a guide. He finds their maps and some letters incriminating the local kings. He leads the two spies to Kim and the lama, and the foreigners begin to fight with the holy man, tearing the sacred drawing that he keeps with him at all times.

In a fury, Kim wrestles with one of them and wounds him. In the confusion sliding down the mountain, Kim makes off with the agents' basket, which he examines in the nearby village of Shamlegh. Keeping all the written evidence in an oilskin pouch next to his body, Kim tosses the spies' other belongings into a deep ravine.

Their mission a dismal failure, the spies are escorted out of the Himalayas by Mookerjee. But the adventures and the strange climate of the North have taken their toll of Kim.

The lama, too, is ill. They are both cared for by the old woman of the Grand Trunk Road, who adopts Kim as her son. When Kim awakens from a long, feverish sleep, he sees the babu at his bedside. He delivers the papers stolen from the Russian to Mookerjee, who compliments him on his fine work. Mahbub Ali also praises the lad.

The lama, who in his innocence has never realized that Kim is playing the Great Game, receives his reward, too. A stream on the old lady's property turns out to be the sacred river, and the holy man is washed of his sins.

Critical Opinion

Kim is a boys' book in much the same way as *Huckleberry Finn* is a boys' book—that is to say, it resonates far more deeply than the usual adventure tale. There is even some similarity in the character of the two protagonists. Both Kim and Huck are resourceful, mischievous, but open-hearted boys who hate the restrictions and confinements of "civilization" and seek adventure in the great world: Huck on his raft in the Mississippi, Kim on the Grand Trunk Road winding through India. Like *Huckleberry Finn, Kim* is a great, nostalgic evocation of its author's youth. The similarity in name between Kim and Kipling is not fortuitous.

The plot of *Kim* is rather halting and tenuous. It consists of separate episodes not really welded together either by the lama's search for the great river or by Kim's apprenticeship in the secret service. The episodes are so individually exciting, however, that the looseness with which they are strung together is barely noticeable. (Kipling's real forte was the short story, a form in which few Englishmen have excelled. Somerset Maugham—one of the few—has called Kipling the great English master of the art; and indeed he is, rivaled perhaps only by D. H. Lawrence.)

The sporadic plotting of *Kim,* which reveals Kipling's essential uneasiness in the novel form, is more than compensated for by the book's richness of local color and detail. Kipling loved India and understood it as few other Englishmen have. He reveled in its sights, sounds, and even smells. All of these he richly explored in *Kim.*

It is this love for India that the critics who assailed Kipling for his jingoism during the 1920's and 1930's failed to take into account. Although in *Kim* he is interested in observing the clash of temperaments and cultures between East and West, Kipling never asserts that the Western values are superior. The reverse would seem to be true, for such crafty Orientals as Mahbub Ali and Mookerjee can outwit practically any sahib in India. The natives, too, speak in a colorful, proverb-strewn language far more flexible and attractive than the stiff, correct English taught at St. Xavier's.

When the novel opens, Kim, at thirteen, is clever, self-sufficient, and warm-hearted. But he must learn discipline in order to become a man, and he does this by assimilating the best of both East and West.

The Author

Rudyard Kipling, born on December 30, 1865, in Bombay, was the son of a connoisseur of Indian art. As a boy, he spent most of his time, like Kim, learning the ways and languages of India. This idyllic period in his life came to an abrupt halt in 1871. The weak and nearsighted Kipling was sent to England in charge of a cruel and imperceptive guardian. He went to a Devon public school for Anglo-Indians, where he was a poor student and worse athlete. His adventures there he later recounted in *Stalky and Co.* (1899), a classic of English school life.

Deciding against going to a university, Kipling returned to India in 1883 and joined the Lahore *Civil and Military Gazette,* becoming a first-class journalist. Discontented with mere newspaper work, however, Kipling began writing tales for the paper about three wildly exuberant and eccentric soldiers in the British Army in India, the famous "soldiers three": Ortheris, Mulvaney, and Learoyd. These stories, collected in *Plain Tales from the Hills* (1888), were an instant success in England. They were followed the same year by *Soldiers Three* and *Under the Deodars,* and by an equally successful volume of verse, *Barrack-Room Ballads* (1892). Before long, Kipling's name became a household word in the English-speaking world.

He continued with journalism on the Allahabad *Pioneer,* returning in 1889 to England, where he settled down near

Fleet Street. In 1892 Kipling married Caroline Balestier and emigrated to his wife's home in Brattleboro, Vermont, where they lived four years until a quarrel with his brother-in-law sent Kipling back to England. In 1900 he covered the Boer War where his staunch imperialistic defense of British action in South Africa became widely known.

After two not entirely successful novels, *The Light That Failed* (1890) and *Captains Courageous* (1897), Kipling produced his fiction masterpiece, *Kim*, in 1901. With such poems as "If" and "Gunga Din," it remains his best-known work.

For all his wide success, Kipling was a truculent and combative man. He became increasingly shrill and embittered after World War I, in which his son was killed in action. An ardent propagandist for the war, Kipling afterward helped form the Imperial War Graves Commission.

Although the 1920's saw the rise of a generation that found Kipling's chauvinism and imperialism repugnant, honors continued to be heaped on him, including the Nobel prize (1907) and the Order of Merit, which he rejected. He died in London on January 18, 1936, on the eve of the destruction of the colonialism he had praised for so long.

By the Same Author

The Light That Failed: This sentimental, semi-autobiographical tale is about Dick Heldar, an artist, who wins fame during the fall of Khartoum, but who tragically begins to lose his vision as a result of a sword wound suffered at the same time.

Dick is brought up in England by Mrs. Jennett, a dour religious woman who starves the boy for love. He finds sympathy with a fellow orphan, Maisie, who encourages him in his study of art. As a correspondent at Khartoum, Dick sends back drawings of General Gordon's heroic action which (like Kipling's stories) take England by storm.

After the war, however, Dick's vision begins to fail. The model for what is to be his masterpiece ruins the painting in a fit of jealousy, and Maisie, too, deserts him now that he is going blind. Dick goes to Egypt, where fighting has broken out, and deliberately exposes himself to deadly enemy fire.

Captains Courageous: Like *Kim*, this is a story about a

youth growing up. However, its hero, Harvey Cheyne, is totally unlike Kim. A spoiled American boy, Harvey falls overboard from an ocean steamer and is rescued by some Gloucester fishermen. All his father's wealth cannot protect him from the rough life he must endure with the fishing fleet, but the experience with wind and waves—and heroism— makes a man of him. When he is reunited with his father, Harvey is no longer a spoiled brat but a youth ready to face the vicissitudes of the world.

Green Mansions

by

W. H. HUDSON (1841–1922)

Main Characters

Abel Guevez De Argensola—A twenty-three-year-old Venezuelan aristocrat who finds a tragic love and ultimate self-
knowledge in the dense jungles of South America.
Rima—Mysterious and elusive, half girl and half bird, friend
and protectress of all wildlife in the Green Mansions.
Nuflo—Rima's crafty old guardian.
Runi—The chief of an Indian tribe.
Kua-ko—An Indian youth who teaches Abel the ways of the
forest.

The Story

Abel Guevez De Argensola, known in Georgetown, British
Guiana, as "Mr. Abel," tells the story of his youthful passion
to an old friend. A member of a wealthy Venezuelan family,
Abel flees into the densely forested territory south of the
Orinoco River when a political coup in which he is involved
fails. Intending to cross the Rio Negro into Brazil, he is
diverted by tales of gold to be found in the Parahuari mountains in southern Venezuela.

Failing to find the gold, the young adventurer joins an
Indian settlement led by Runi, whose suspicions of the white

youth are allayed when Abel gives him a precious tinderbox. Abel is adopted by the Indians, particularly by Kua-ko, who promises to teach him how to hunt with blowpipe and bow and arrow. These primitive people fear only two things: Managa, the chief of a hostile tribe, and the enchanted forest, which Abel discovers some two miles west of the village. Although this lovely woodland is filled with wildlife, the Indians refuse to hunt there for they believe a malevolent spirit—the mysterious daughter of the Didi—lives there.

Abel laughs at their superstitions and explores the forest, which he calls his green mansions. He hears a seductive bird-like voice calling to him and vainly pursues it, until one day he sees a delicate girl, Rima, playing with a bird. Rima is a lovely, elfin sprite, shy and yet alluring, who constantly eludes Abel's attempts to capture her. Kua-ko tells Abel that some-day he may be proficient enough with the blowpipe to kill the girl, who has prevented them from hunting in the forest. Abel, who has already fallen in love with her, rejects the idea in horror.

One day Abel comes upon a poisonous snake in the forest and is about to crush it when Rima appears, dressed in a gossamer gown, with her lovely, iridescent hair reflecting the sun. She upbraids him for trying to kill the snake which slithers to safety at her feet. When Abel tries to embrace Rima, the snake bites him. He runs panic-stricken through the forest and falls down a precipice. When he regains consciousness, Abel finds himself in the hut of Nuflo, an old man dark as an Indian, who tells him that he is really Spanish. He calls for his seventeen-year-old granddaughter—Rima. In the hut, however, the girl is listless and spiritless—totally different from the wild wood sprite Abel had encountered in the forest. It was Rima who rescued Abel when he fell down the precipice. She nurses him back to health.

When Rima speaks to Abel in Spanish, he asks her about the lovely bird speech he had heard from her lips in the forest; but, resentful because he does not know the bird language, she runs away. Abel learns that Rima is so fond of the creatures of the woods that she will not allow Nuflo to kill any of them for food. So the strange pair exists on plants and berries. Nuflo, however, kills and eats animals on the sly.

Since Rima flies from Abel when he touches her hand, to teach her a lesson he leaves her grandfather's hut and returns for a few days' visit to the Indian village. There he finds that the Indians have given him up for dead and have gone to a neighboring settlement. Only the toothless old hag, Cra-Cra, is there to greet him. Abel, stricken with remorse for his treatment of Rima, returns to the forest.

There he and Rima spend an idyllic day on top of a mountain, where Abel tells the girl of the unimaginable vastness and diversity of the world. Lonely for people who can speak her language, Rima asks him if there are people like her anywhere on earth. Abel tells her she is unique. He mentions a faraway mountain called Riolama, which Rima suddenly recognizes as the place for which she was named, and where her mother had come from. She is furious with Nuflo for having kept Riolama a secret from her and descends the mountain to upbraid the old man. She insists that they make an expedition to Riolama immediately.

Although old Nuflo is unwilling to make the arduous trip, he fears that Rima, who is constantly communicating with her dead mother, is really a spirit who will damn him in the next world if he does not obey her. So he makes preparations for the long march.

Before they leave, however, Abel returns once again to the Indian village. The natives regard him with suspicion for having consorted with the daughter of the spirit Didi. In effect a prisoner, he is able to elude his captors after a week, and he returns to Rima and Nuflo.

As the three take the eighteen-day trek through the jungle to Riolama, Nuflo finally tells Abel the true story of Rima: Nuflo was a member of a group of outlaws. One day, he found a lovely woman hiding in a cave. She was weeping and was soon to give birth. Thinking her a saint and hoping for her intervention in heaven on his behalf, Nuflo went to her aid. She had slipped down a precipice. Nuflo rescued her, tended her broken ankle, and brought her back to health. The woman could speak neither Spanish nor Indian but only the bird language.

Nuflo took her to the nearby settlement of Voa, where she gave birth to Rima and taught her the bird language. When the girl was seven, her mother died. Since Rima, too, seemed sickly, Nuflo took her to the Parahuari mountains where she was restored to health. At first they lived near Runi's tribe, but Rima shared her mother's fear and loathing of the Indians.

She constantly balked their attempts to hunt in the forest, thus acquiring her reputation as an evil spirit.

When the trio reaches Riolama, Abel feels he must disillusion Rima. He tells her she will never find the tribe that bore her because if they were still in existence her mother would have told her about them. What must have happened, Abel sadly tells her, is that her people, a delicate, exotic breed, must long ago have fallen victims to an Indian assault. Rima, the last of the bird people, must accept her loneliness and seek comfort only in him, for he will be her protector. When she senses the truth of Abel's conjectures, Rima faints. Nuflo fears she is dead. When she recovers and moans that no one in the world can ever understand her, Abel once again swears his love and eternal constancy.

They set off on the long return trip, but Rima, impatient, gets far ahead of the two men. When Nuflo and Abel reach the old hut, they find it burned to the ground. Rima is nowhere to be found. Searching for her in the forest they both knew and loved so well, Abel meets an Indian hunting. He knows Rima cannot be around or else the Indian would never have dared invade her sanctuary.

Abel returns to Runi's tribe, hoping to get some news of what has happened to his beloved. He is greeted with even greater suspicion than before. A council of war is held to decide what to do with him. The Indians consent to accept him back into the tribe when Abel tells them he had merely been out searching for gold. With great patience he finally manages to elicit from the surly Kua-ko the story of what has happened to Rima.

When the Indians realized that Rima had left the forest, they began to hunt there again. A week before Abel returned, however, they caught Rima in a tree in the enchanted woods. Superstitiously fearing that arrows would be powerless against her, they had heaped wood around the tree and set it on fire. Her last despairing cry had been "Abel, Abel!" before she plummeted, like a great white bird, into the smoke and flame where she was burned to ashes.

Barely able to restrain himself from killing Kua-ko on the spot, Abel pretends to fall asleep and then leaps from the campfire and escapes through the woods with Kua-ko in hot pursuit. Half-crazed with grief and without his revolver, Abel kills the Indian in hand-to-hand combat. He then goes to the tribe of Managa, persuading the savage enemy of Runi to slaughter everyone in the village.

When Abel returns to the charred hut where he had once been so happy, he finds the bones of Nuflo, who had also been slaughtered by the Indians. A search through the forest reveals the tree where Rima met her death. Reverently Abel collects her remains and brings them in an urn to another part of the woods.

Here he tries to live as a hermit but finds he is unable to and fears he is going mad. So, Abel makes the great trek to Georgetown, carrying with him the ashes of his beloved Rima.

Critical Opinion

The modern attitude toward Hudson is perhaps best expressed by Ernest Hemingway in *The Sun Also Rises*. One of the characters in that novel yearns to go to South America after reading *The Purple Land*, which, Hemingway says, "is a very sinister book if read too late in life. It recounts splendid imaginary amorous adventures of a perfect English gentleman in an intensely romantic land, the scenery of which is very well described. For a man to take it at thirty-four as a guide-book to what life holds is about as safe as it would be for a man of the same age to enter Wall Street direct from a French convent, equipped with a complete set of the more practical Alger books."

In the romantic tradition, Hudson is obsessed with the oneness of all nature. Rima is part bird, part girl, speaking, or rather warbling, in birdlike tones incomprehensible to mortals. Completely at one with nature, she is unable to understand how man can plunder the Green Mansions which are her home. The tragedy of the book is that she herself dies horribly at the hands of savages who, although they too live intimately with nature, fail utterly to see any higher spiritual meaning in it.

Rima's impact on Abel is that of a powerful natural force. Coming to the jungle as a city-bred sophisticate, disgusted with the life of politics in which he has dabbled with unfortunate results, disillusioned with his early search for gold, Abel is ripe for a conversion to the gospel of nature. At first

he mistakenly thinks he has found the happy natural life with
Runi's Indians, but in the course of the book, beginning with
Kua-ko's suggestion that he kill Rima, Abel's attitude toward
these primitives begins to sour.

After the tragedy of Rima is complete, Abel, half-crazed,
wreaks bloody revenge on his former friends and finds
himself reverting to savagery as a hermit. He does not really
come to grips with nature and himself until he abandons his
primitive hut and returns to civilization.

What he emerges with is a kind of stoicism based on a
profound acceptance of man's relatively puny place in the
natural scheme of things. Abel's ultimate acceptance of the
hard facts of existence, coupled with Hudson's keen observation of nature rendered in classically simple prose, does much
to redeem a novel whose lush romanticism has proved generally alien to the modern spirit.

The Author

William Henry Hudson was a descendant of one of the
families that came to America on the *Mayflower*. His father,
however, after an injury sustained while working in a New
England brewery, became a sheep farmer near Buenos Aires,
where the future poet-naturalist and romancer was born on
August 4, 1841.

Hudson got his education on the wild pampas of Argentina,
which he loved as a boy and which sharpened his unique gift
for the observation of nature. At fifteen, however, he suffered
a debilitating attack of rheumatic fever after driving some
cattle through a blizzard. His health thereafter was always
frail.

In 1870 Hudson emigrated to England, where he entered
into an unhappy marriage with a dull, unimaginative older
woman, Emily Wingreave. For many years the couple
struggled for a livelihood, as Hudson's books went largely
unnoticed by the public. It was not, in fact, until *Green
Mansions* was reissued in 1916 with an enthusiastic preface
by John Galsworthy that Hudson won any measure of recognition outside his immediate circle of friends and other writers.

One of his most influential friends, Joseph Conrad, spon-
sored Hudson for British citizenship in 1900, and said of this

strange, irascible man, "Hudson writes as the grass grows. The good God makes it be there. And that is all there is to it."

While Hudson was struggling to make a living in London, his wife kept a boardinghouse. In 1901, however, a civil service pension was granted the author, and he moved to the isolated Cornish town of Penzance. He had begun his literary career as a writer of ornithological books, but his first important work was *The Purple Land* (1885), the narrative, in Hudson's words, "of one Richard Lamb's adventures in the Banda Oriental, in South America, as told by himself." This romantic work was followed in 1904 by *Green Mansions,* and in 1906 by *A Crystal Age,* Hudson's not entirely successful attempt at a utopian romance. He was never really a writer of fiction. Hudson's most readable book today is an autobiography he wrote late in life, *Far Away and Long Ago* (1918), describing his boyhood experiences on the pampas and setting forth his pantheistic religious beliefs.

Ill health and lack of recognition made Hudson a rather crusty man given to abrupt, savage laughter. Among his many antipathies, the killing of wildlife for sport ranked high. Despite his illnesses, Hudson managed to live past eighty, dying of a heart attack on August 18, 1922, a decade after his wife's death. He was buried in his beloved Sussex Downs. A fitting memorial to him is Sir Jacob Epstein's controversial statue of Rima standing in the Hyde Park bird sanctuary.

The Man of Property

by

JOHN GALSWORTHY (1867–1933)

Main Characters

James Forsyte—The stiff-necked, strait-laced founder of the firm of solicitors, "Forsyte, Bustard, and Forsyte."

Soames Forsyte—James' son, also a solicitor and man of property, who considers himself a connoisseur of art.

Irene—Soames' most beautiful possession, his unhappy wife.

Old Jolyon Forsyte—James' older brother who has become immensely wealthy as a tea merchant, the only Forsyte with a true appreciation of beauty.

Young Jolyon Forsyte—An artist disinherited by Old Jolyon for a scandalous love affair.

June Forsyte—Young Jolyon's impetuous, strong-willed daughter who has lived with her grandfather ever since Young Jolyon's elopement, a close friend of Irene.

Philip Bosinney—A talented, headstrong young architect, June's fiancé.

The Story

On a fine June afternoon in 1886, the formidable Forsyte family has gathered in Old Jolyon's home in London to toast the engagement of Old Jolyon's granddaughter, June, to a poor but talented young architect, Philip Bosinney. The elder

242

Forsytes, entrenched in wealth, are highly suspicious of the young man whom they call "the Buccaneer."

They justify their suspicions on the grounds that June is to be sole inheritor of her grandfather's vast wealth. (Old Jolyon had adopted her when his son, June's father, brought disgrace to the Forsyte name by running off with a governess whom he married after the death of June's mother. Perhaps even worse, Young Jolyon became an artist—an unheard-of calling in the Forsyte family—and an unsuccessful one at that.)

Now that June is to be married, Old Jolyon fears he will be left all alone in his vast, dark old house, now reverberating with the gossip and malicious small talk of the Forsyte clan. Fearing the loneliness of old age, Old Jolyon determines to pay a visit to his son's club. After the engagement party he sees Young Jolyon for the first time in years.

Old Jolyon is pleased that his son bears him no grudge for disinheriting him. Although he is leading a hand-to-mouth existence as an underwriter for Lloyd's and in his spare time is painting his unsuccessful water colors (which his father secretly collects), Young Jolyon is blessed with a happy family. The governess has proved a good wife and has borne him two lovely children, Holly and Jolly, who immediately capture Old Jolyon's fancy when he visits their cottage. Nevertheless, Old Jolyon feels guilty; the Forsytes would look upon this reconciliation as unseemly weakness.

Now that Philip Bosinney is engaged to June, he must call on all the Forsytes. They are a great family of upper-middle-class lawyers and businessmen who have amassed considerable fortunes and who live for their wealth and for the luxury the wealth has brought. The women of Old Jolyon's generation are crotchety old spinsters. They all look down upon the arts except possibly as profitable investments.

Bosinney, who lives for his architecture, finds little in common even with Soames, Old Jolyon's nephew, who fancies himself a connoisseur and collector. Irene, Soames' wife and the most beautiful "object" in his collection, immediately attracts Bosinney. At the many teas, dinners, and receptions given by the Forsytes, Bosinney sees more and more of Irene.

The Forsytes have long suspected that all was not well between Soames and Irene. Having bought her just as he bought his various art treasures, Soames regards her as a good investment reflecting credit on himself. When Irene agreed to marry Soames, she stipulated that she should have full freedom of action if the marriage proved unsuccessful. In his egoism Soames was unable to imagine such a possibility. In fact, however, Irene's aversion to the Man of Property has increased through the years. Rumor has it that Soames and Irene now occupy separate bedrooms.

Hoping to please his wife, whose "whims" he cannot understand, Soames decides to build her a great house worthy of her beauty. He buys some property at Robin Hill, outside London, and hires Philip Bosinney as architect. This, Soames feels, will be a fine opportunity for June's fiancé to make a name for himself. Soames wishes to please June because she is Irene's only close friend.

Immediately a contest of strong wills begins over the house. Bosinney refuses to listen to Soames' conventional ideas about what he wants. The architect is determined to build a masterpiece regardless of cost, but Soames, a typical Forsyte, wants showy magnificence at not too high a price. Soames realizes he has met his match in the young architect, whom he cannot bully, and gives him a more or less free hand in the planning and construction of the great country house.

One day Soames's Uncle Swithin takes Irene out to see the house under construction. Bosinney is there. While the old man dozes, Irene and Philip discover that they have fallen passionately in love with each other. For all their discretion in meeting later on, in out-of-the-way parts of London, June and the rest of the Forsytes soon learn of their affair. A fullfledged scandal is in the making. But Soames remains unaware of what is happening. Blinded by his self-esteem, he still cannot understand why his wife is so cold to him even though he lavishes expensive gifts on her.

As the house progresses, Soames and Philip begin to quarrel bitterly about the mounting costs. Philip agrees to decorate the house only if he is given a completely free hand, but Soames sets a limit to the amount of money he can spend. Philip finally agrees.

Meanwhile, Old Jolyon, troubled by the rumors of an affair between Philip and Irene, finds increasing comfort in the simple, unaffected lives of his son and grandchildren. He decides to take the trusteeship of his estate away from James and Soames Forsyte, who would ridicule his change of heart, and alter his will to leave Young Jolyon and his family in more comfortable circumstances. He asks Young Jolyon to speak to Bosinney about the rumors. Young Jolyon does so but realizes there is nothing he or anyone else can do to break up the architect's affair with Irene.

By the time the house is completed, Soames learns from the old gossips in the family that his wife has been seeing Bosinney. Furious, he decides to sue Bosinney for spending too much money on the house. If Bosinney loses the suit, he will have to pay Soames £350, which will bankrupt him. When she hears of Soames's intentions, Irene refuses to move to the house built for her. She locks her bedroom door against Soames. One night, consumed with jealousy and frustration, he manages to get in and forces himself on her.

Soames's suit comes to trial uncontested by Bosinney. June, who is in the courtroom, sees that her fiancé is not there, and, wondering what has become of him, she sets out for his apartment. He is not there either. But, while June is waiting for him, Irene enters, also worried about her lover. She tells June that she has left Soames; the two former friends argue bitterly and Irene leaves.

The next morning a policeman brings the horrible news that Bosinney has been run over and killed by a cab in the thick London fog. It was apparently suicide, for Bosinney had been seen earlier wandering distraught through the city. He had just learned from Irene of Soames's brutal act, and in the state of mind that this news produced he seemed not to care what happened to him.

In the wake of this final tragedy, Irene, numb with grief, returns to Soames, and June persuades Old Jolyon to buy the house at Robin Hill. She knows that Soames and Irene will never live in the mansion created by her dead fiancé.

A short epilogue, called "Indian Summer of a Forsyte," ties up the strands of the story. Some years after Bosinney's death, lonely Old Jolyon, now eighty-five, is living at Robin Hill. June, still unmarried, and Young Jolyon are away on vacation. One day Irene pays him a secret call. She has left Soames permanently now, supporting herself in a meager way by giving music lessons and occupying her time in charity. Gradually, through the hot summer, Irene wins the affection of Old Jolyon. He tacitly forgives her for stealing June's fiancé, and they are reconciled. He provides for her in his will and tries to persuade her to give music lessons to Holly and Jolly, but Irene cannot bear to see June again.

One day, sitting in the garden waiting for Irene's last visit, Old Jolyon, the only Forsyte ever to have known through suffering the values of love and beauty, dies in his sleep.

Critical Opinion

"This long tale," Galsworthy wrote of *The Forsyte Saga*, "is no scientific study of the period; it is rather an intimate incarnation of the disturbances that beauty effects in the lives of men. The figure of Irene, never present except through the sense of the other characters, is a concretion of disturbing beauty impinging on a possessive world."

Like Thomas Mann's *Buddenbrooks, The Forsyte Saga* is a magnificently detailed account of upper-middle-class morality, mentality, and tribal customs. One of its great appeals, despite its author's disclaimer, is unquestionably its almost scientific delineation of the world of business and professional men between 1886, when *The Man of Property* opens, and World War I. The later novels in the *The Forsyte Saga,* dealing with the postwar world, are not nearly as successful.

The conflict in *The Man of Property* results, as Galsworthy suggests, from the clash of two very different temperaments. The first is that of Soames Forsyte, self-assured man of the world, secure in his wealth, and a great "collector" of beauty. Yet his most beautiful possession, Irene, is drawn to the architect, Bosinney, because he is a creator of beauty rather than a mere collector and sees her as a living person rather than a museum exhibit. Soames's esthetic judgments depend mainly on the monetary value of a work of art. In a sense he cannot distinguish between his collection of "dead" beauty—his paintings and *objets*—and the live woman who is his wife. The climax of the book comes when Soames asserts his property rights to a wife who cannot abide him, thus destroying her lover and removing any affection or pity she might have had for her husband. Soames, however, becomes a more and more sympathetic figure, eventually dominating the story completely, as Galsworthy grows more and more disenchanted with the modern world and looks with increasing nostalgia at the good, stable, late-Victorian society so scandalized by

Irene's behavior. If it was a smug, self-satisfied world, if its values were essentially materialistic and philistine, it at least had some guiding principles, and principles of any kind, Galsworthy felt, were rapidly disappearing from the postwar world.

The Author

The seething passion that underlies the social satire in *The Man of Property* and makes it the finest of Galsworthy's many novels comes from the author's personal identification with the story. For just as Philip Bosinney, an honorable man, finds himself wooing another man's wife, so did *John Galsworthy* love his cousin Ada, whose relationship to her husband was essentially that of Irene to Soames Forsyte.

Although Galsworthy's love had a happier ending than Bosinney's—his marriage to Ada in 1905 proved a happy one —the difficulties and scandal leading up to the marriage transformed him from a rather superficial young dilettante into a novelist and playwright whose labors were crowned with the Nobel prize in 1932.

Galsworthy was born in Surrey on August 14, 1867, into a prosperous, upper-middle-class family that had risen from yeoman stock, much as the Forsytes had done. His father was a successful attorney. Galsworthy attended one of the finest English public schools, Harrow, and later went on to Oxford. He did not particularly distinguish himself. He was later a barrister without any observable talent or passion for the law.

A good deal of travel abroad opened horizons for him. On one voyage he sailed aboard a ship whose mate was Joseph Conrad, then wrestling with his first novel, *Almayer's Folly*. Galsworthy read the manuscript and persuaded Conrad, who later became a close friend, to become a professional writer.

Between the years 1897 and 1901, Galsworthy himself began writing stories and novels under the pen name of "John Sinjohn," but they are of very minor interest. It was not until 1906, the year after his marriage to Ada, that he produced his masterpiece, *The Man of Property*. Although he had no idea at the time of expanding this tale of the Forsytes into anything as massive as the three trilogies that eventually appeared, the theme of beauty trapped in a world of material complacency haunted him. Interspersed with other novels and plays, *The Forsyte Saga* and its sequels, *A Modern Comedy*, and *The End of the Chapter*, each comprising three novels, gradually emerged.

Galsworthy's fame spread as a result not only of his novels but also of his highly popular plays which dealt with social injustices of the day. Among these were *The Silver Box*, produced in 1906, *Strife* (1909), a play about labor unions, *Justice* (1910), and *Loyalties* (1922), concerned with English snobbery.

In many ways, Galsworthy was the ideal English gentleman. Tall and handsome, fond of animals and country life, gentle and honorable in his behavior to others, and an implacable foe of any manifestation of cruelty or injustice, he became one of the best-loved authors of his time. Since his death on January 31, 1933, however, his reputation has diminished considerably. Often, to the modern reader, his brooding over the vanished splendors of the Victorian past and his compassion for the weak and helpless seem mere sentimentality, and his refusal to take sides in viewing social conflict, mere lack of intellectual power.

By the Same Author

In Chancery: In Chancery begins in 1899 and ends two years later with a notable description of the funeral of Queen Victoria, the great monarch of Forsyteism. Soames Forsyte, hoping for a son to inherit his property, tries to effect a reconciliation with Irene but only manages to drive her into the arms of Young Jolyon whose children are now grown up. Irene and Young Jolyon eventually marry and live in the ill-starred house at Robin Hill. They have a son, Jon. Meanwhile Soames, after his divorce from Irene, marries a French girl, Annette. Instead of giving him the longed-for son, she has a daughter, Fleur. But Soames, ever the Man of Property, is able to reflect in pride at the baby's crib, "By God, this thing was . . . his!" *In Chancery* is less complicated emotionally and lighter in tone than *The Man of Property*.

To Let: Now we are in the postwar world of the 1920's. Jon, the son of Young Jolyon and Irene, meets and falls in love with Fleur, not aware of her parentage. Fleur, very much a Forsyte, strong-willed and grasping, determines that she wants Jon; she ignores the protests of the two sets of parents, who are aghast at the possibility of a marriage. Jon and Fleur, like Romeo and Juliet, must love each other against a background of bitter family feuding. Jon, deeply influenced by his mother, gives Fleur up, and she marries the son of a baronet instead. After writing a pathetic letter to Jon about why he had to renounce Fleur, Young Jolyon dies. The famous house at Robin Hill, tied up with so many thwarted lives from the day Soames first decided to build it, is finally "To Let."

The Old Wives' Tale

by

ARNOLD BENNETT (1867–1931)

Main Characters

Mr. and Mrs. Baines—Owners of a humble draper's shop in Bursley.

Constance Baines—Their pleasant, placid older daughter.

Sophia Baines—Constance's willful, headstrong sister.

Samuel Povey—The dull, unimaginative manager of the Baines' shop.

Daniel Povey—Samuel's cousin, unhappily married to a wife who drinks.

Cyril Povey—Constance's selfish, artistically inclined son.

Gerald Scales—A dashing and imprudent traveling salesman from Manchester who represents to Sophia the glamorous world outside Bursley.

Mr. Critchlow—A Bursley chemist and friend of Mr. Baines.

M. Chirac—A French newspaperman, friend of Gerald's.

Madame Foucault—Owner of a Paris rooming house of ill repute.

The Story

In Bursley, one of the Five Towns in the north of England dominated by the manufacture of pottery, Mr. and Mrs. Baines operate a humble draper's shop, aided by their two daughters: Constance, sixteen, and Sophia, fifteen. The two girls are very different in temperament and outlook. Constance, a good-natured, unimaginative girl, is perfectly willing to remain in the shop all her life. But Sophia, a proud beauty, is full of plans to see the great world. Her first step is to become a teacher, a plan that shocks her parents who see teaching as a profession for widows and spinsters.

Even Mr. Baines, a semi-invalid suffering from a paralytic stroke, tries to put pressure on Sophia to abandon her ideas, but the girl remains adamant and becomes apprenticed to the local schoolmistress. When she is not teaching, she takes turns watching over her sick father.

One day a dashing young commercial traveler from Manchester, Gerald Scales, enters the shop adjoining the Baines home, and Sophia leaves her father for a moment in order to meet him.

While she is talking to Gerald, her father slips off his bed and, unable to move, suffocates. Overcome with remorse at her negligence, Sophia promises to forget about teaching and help run the shop. But her real reason for staying in the draper's shop is that she hopes to see Gerald again on his occasional visits there.

Meanwhile, Constance has fallen in love with the unassuming, unglamorous Samuel Povey, manager of the shop. Mrs. Baines approves of this, but alarmed at Sophia's infatuation with Gerald Scales, she makes inquiries about the traveling salesman and becomes convinced he is not good for Sophia.

The two lovers nevertheless begin writing to each other. When as a last resort Mrs. Baines sends Sophia off on a visit to her Aunt Harriet, the willful girl elopes with Gerald who has inherited £ 12,000 and has quit his job. Together they go to London where Sophia forces him to marry her against his will. From London the couple move to Paris where Gerald begins spending his inheritance lavishly on fine clothes, elegant dinners, and gambling. Disillusioned with her husband, Sophia, a true Baines, manages to steal £ 200 from him and hide it against a rainy day.

After years of high living and a descent to increasingly cheaper rooms, Gerald's money is gone and he suggests that Sophia write home for more funds. When Sophia refuses to do this, Gerald abandons her in a wretched Paris hotel room. The shock of abandonment sends Sophia into a terrible fever, and for weeks she hovers between life and death. She is tended in her illness by a sympathetic journalist friend of Gerald's, M. Chirac, who brings her to the seedy rooming house of Madame Foucault. Madame Foucault and two kindly prostitutes who work for her nurse Sophia back to health.

When Sophia learns that Madame Foucault is badly in debt, she buys the house from her with the £200 she took from Gerald and makes the place a respectable rooming house. The Franco-Prussian War of 1870 is raging now, Paris is under siege, and food is extremely scarce. But with her determination and acumen Sophia, aided by Chirac, who keeps asking her to marry him, manages to make a go of it. Gradually the flighty girl becomes a successful, unsentimental businesswoman.

After the siege is lifted, Sophia buys the Pension Frensham, one of the favorite spots in Paris for visiting Englishmen. Here she is successful, too, and gradually amasses a considerable fortune. However, she still refuses to marry Chirac, of whom she has become very fond, because she does not know Gerald's whereabouts.

Back in Bursley, meanwhile, life has been placid and dull for Constance. After seven years of gradually increasing prosperity under Samuel Povey's plodding care, the couple have a son, Cyril, whom they dote on. Mrs. Baines dies while the boy is an infant, and young Cyril grows up selfish and unheeding of his dull parents. He has a talent for drawing, which he persists in cultivating despite the Poveys' wish that he enter the draper's shop.

Tragedy enters their life when Povey's cousin Daniel kills his drunken wife in a fit of desperation. Putting family loyalty above his own health, Samuel fights unsuccessfully in court for his cousin's acquittal. Soon after the trial Samuel succumbs to pneumonia.

Constance, now a widow, is increasingly lonely. Young Cyril gets a job as designer in the local pottery, which keeps him away all day. At night he attends art school. At nineteen the youth wins a national scholarship and goes off to London, leaving his proud but lonely mother to look after herself in Bursley. She has not heard from Sophia except for one Christmas card some years before.

One day a young Englishman comes to the Pension Frensham in Paris. Attracted by the stately, dignified Sophia, he reveals that he is a friend of Cyril Povey's. On returning to

England, he informs Cyril and Constance that he has found the missing Sophia. Constance immediately writes her sister a long, loving letter, asking her to return to Bursley for a visit.

At first Sophia is unwilling to leave her thriving business even for a short while. Soon, however, she suffers a mild stroke. When she is made a handsome offer for the Frensham by a hotel corporation, she accepts. After a quarter-century in the business, she sells her pension and visits England.

The two sisters are reunited once more. But soon the worldly, sophisticated Sophia begins to urge Constance to leave Bursley—which now seems utterly dingy and third-rate to Sophia—and move to Paris, or, at least, to London. But Constance resents what she considers Sophia's effort to dominate her, and remains stolidly in the decrepit old house where she was born. They live dully together for nine years, hearing infrequently from Cyril who is constantly traveling in pursuit of his art.

One day Sophia receives a telegram informing her that Gerald Scales is dying and wishes to see her. She rushes to his bedside only to find that he has died of exhaustion and malnutrition. Penniless and shabby, the once gay salesman has come to the end everyone predicted. Sophia is shocked not only at the sight of the wizened old man who had once been her dashing lover but at her incapacity to feel anything for him. "My life has been too terrible," she thinks at Gerald's deathbed. "I wish I was dead." Returning to Bursley after this deeply disturbing experience, Sophia suffers a second stroke and dies, leaving all her money to Cyril.

Now Constance is completely alone. At first she is relieved to be free of her sister's nagging domination. She suffers from sciatica and rheumatism. She almost never hears from her son. She is puzzled by the rush of events as Bursley is about to be officially incorporated into the Five Towns. When Constance dies a few years later, Cyril is off in Italy and cannot get home for the funeral. Only her poodle, last in a long succession of Baines's dogs, is there to mourn her.

Critical Opinion

In the autumn of 1903 Bennett used to dine frequently at a

small, undistinguished Paris restaurant. Once he saw the waiters and customers ridiculing a "fat, shapeless, ugly, and grotesque" old woman whose peculiar mannerisms soon "had the whole restaurant laughing at her." Reflecting that her case was a tragedy, Bennett realized that "this woman was once young, slim, perhaps beautiful." With the example of Guy de Maupassant's *Une Vie* in mind, Bennett decided to write a novel in which the hero and villain would be "time" as it remorselessly converts a lovely, spirited young girl into a pathetic old frump. Thus the idea for *The Old Wives' Tale* was born.

But where Maupassant had chronicled one woman's passage from innocent youth to disillusioned old age, Bennett decided to use two, in order to appraise and compare the effect of the forces of heredity and environment. Both Constance and Sophia are Baineses; that is to say, essentially granite-willed, indomitable North of England women. By separating them early in life, keeping Constance in the environment of her birth and sending Sophia to the totally different environment of besieged Paris, Bennett was able to show that, except for superficial differences, a person's character will remain essentially what it was at birth. Constance stoically endures her long, uneventful life in Bursley, while Sophia, as much a Baines as her sister, triumphs over a worthless husband, a totally foreign atmosphere, and even a great famine, to become a success in business. But like Constance, Sophia ends up a lonely old woman.

The triumph of *The Old Wives' Tale*, then, is in its subtle, meticulous study of time's erosions. Ever so gradually the girls become less frolicsome, less self-assured, but better able to take care of themselves and more inured to loneliness in their very different environments. Time works its havoc on them and in the end wins a hollow victory over these two indomitable women.

With quiet confidence in his power to keep two plots moving simultaneously, Bennett set out quite deliberately in *The Old Wives' Tale* to write what he knew would be his masterpiece. He even learned penmanship so that the manuscript itself would be a work of art, as indeed a published facsimile edition of it shows it to be. Following his usual rigid writing schedule, thinking out each episode a day in advance during long walks in the beautiful forest of Fontainebleu, Bennett attained his goal. *The Old Wives' Tale* combines the ruthlessly accurate detail of French realism with the gusto and humor that have always characterized English fiction.

The Author

Enoch Arnold Bennett was born on May 27, 1867, in Hanley, one of the Five Towns in North Staffordshire that he immortalized in his novels and stories. His father was a solicitor. After Bennett attended London University, he became a solicitor's clerk in his father's office. Following a family quarrel, he moved to London in 1893 and took up journalism, editing the magazine *Woman* for six years.

When Bennett began writing novels, with *A Man from the North* (1898), he was deeply influenced by the French realism of Zola and the Goncourt brothers. His second novel, *Anna of the Five Towns* (1901), was an attempt—on the whole successful—to transplant the French realist manner to the material he knew best: the hard, unyielding character of the potteries and their workers in the North of England. It was not, however, until *The Grand Babylon Hotel* (1902), a light detective romance, that Bennett achieved any popular success as a novelist. He maintained his popularity in the three following decades.

In 1900 Bennett moved to France, where he lived for eight years, marrying a French actress in 1907. Like Trollope, Bennett was an assiduous worker, turning out vast quantities of fiction and journalistic writing on a rigid schedule. With financial success he was able to indulge his tastes for high living, buying a succession of yachts and motor cars and staying in lavish hotels.

Aside from theater and book reviews, Bennett's work falls into three main categories. First are the serious novels, of which the most distinguished are *The Old Wives' Tale* (1908), *Clayhanger* (1910), and *Riceyman Steps* (1923). Then there are the lighter works, which Bennett called his "larks," of which the most popular are *Buried Alive* (1908) and *The Card* (1911). Least important, but most successful during his lifetime, are the numbers of self-help books such as *How to Live on Twenty-Four Hours a Day* (published in 1908, the same year as *The Old Wives' Tale* and *Buried Alive*) and *The*

Human Machine (1909). These shallow "pocket philosophies" essentially told readers how to organize their lives as efficiently as possible—as efficiently, in fact, as Arnold Bennett had organized his.

A genial, kindly man whose severe stammer was a lifelong embarrassment to him, Bennett loved what he conceived of as the glamorous life—hotels de luxe (his last major work, *Imperial Palace*, is a massive tribute to such a hotel), yachts, and French cuisine. Although he was popular chiefly with middle-brow readers, no educated taste in fiction could disregard such solid achievements as the *Clayhanger* trilogy. For many years Bennett was in essence the literary dictator of England. He died of typhoid fever in a grand hotel on March 27, 1931, years after a more esthetically oriented younger generation, led by Virginia Woolf, had ceased to take him seriously as a novelist.

By the Same Author

Clayhanger: Clayhanger is the first of three novels (the others are *Hilda Lessways* and *These Twain*) that tell of the rise to maturity of Edwin Clayhanger, a boy much like Bennett, living under a domineering father in the Five Towns. Edwin wants to become an architect, but his father insists on apprenticing him in his printing firm. Lonely and artistically inclined, Edwin defies his father's will and falls in love with the strange, free-spirited Hilda Lessways. The second novel tells of the courtship from Hilda's point of view, and *These Twain* details the difficulties of the marriage—difficulties that Edwin, with true Five Towns spirit, determines to overcome.

Riceyman Steps: Written in 1923, long after most critics had stopped considering Bennett a serious novelist, *Riceyman Steps* is the last real triumph of his art. It tells in brilliantly imagined detail—sometimes hilarious, sometimes poignant— the story of a miserly book dealer named Earlforward and his bizarre marriage to Mrs. Violet Arb. Earlforward is so cheap that he literally starves himself to death. The true heroine of the novel is Elsie, his maid and victim of his miserliness, who bears her lot in life with stoical good humor and remains loyal to her eccentric employer.

The Crock of Gold

by

JAMES STEPHENS (1882–1950)

Main Characters

The Philosopher—Kindly, wise, and eccentric, with ideas on every subject which he expounds at great length.
The Thin Woman of Inis Magrath—The philosopher's shrewish wife.
Seumas and Brigid Beg—The philosopher's children.
Meehawl MacMurrachu—A neighborhood farmer who gets into trouble with the leprechauns of Gort na Cloca Mora.
Caitilin—Meehawl's lovely daughter.
Angus Õg—A great Celtic god who lives in a cave far away.

The Story

At first there were two philosophers living in peace and contentment in the dark pine forest of Coilla Doraca near the leprechaun-haunted woods of Gort na Cloca Mora. But they both took shrewish wives who moved into the hut with them and constantly interrupted their philosophical discussions. One was the Grey Woman of Dun Gortin and the other was the Thin Woman of Inis Magrath. One couple had a boy named Seumas and the other had a girl named Brigid, but each wife decided she liked the other's child better than her own and so they switched children.

257

When Seumas and Brigid are ten years old, the first philosopher decides he knows everything he wants to know about life and is ready to die even though he is in perfect health. His friend tries vainly to dissuade him. For a quarter of an hour, the philosopher whirls around on the floor like a top and falls dead. Then his wife, the Grey Woman of Dun Gortin, follows suit, spinning about until she is dead. The Thin Woman of Inis Magrath buries the philosopher and his wife under the hearthstone and brings up both children, forgetting which is really her own.

The surviving philosopher is often sought out by the people of the wood to solve problems beyond their limited understanding. A small farmer named Meehawl MacMurrachu asks the philosopher one day what has happened to his wife's scrubbing board, which has mysteriously disappeared. After intensive Socratic questioning, the philosopher decides that the leprechauns must have made off with the scrubbing board and tells Meehawl to go to the woods where they live and steal it back.

Meehawl complies, but instead of the scrubbing board he finds, to his delight, the crock of gold which the leprechauns keep in order to ransom themselves when one of them is captured by a mortal. Since it is very hard work to accumulate a crock of gold by scraping the edges off coins they find in people's houses, the leprechauns are naturally furious when they discover the theft.

Knowing that Meehawl had sought the advice of the philosopher, the leprechauns decide to kidnap the philosopher's two children, Seumas and Brigid Beg. Pretending to teach them games, one of the leprechauns lures the children into their little house inside the root of a great tree. When Seumas and Brigid Beg do not come home for supper, the Thin Woman, who has occult powers, demands that the leprechauns return them, and the Little People, fearing her, obey.

Frustrated, the leprechauns then seek vengeance on Meehawl himself. They send for the Great God Pan, half goat, half man, who has not been seen in Ireland for many years. They persuade Pan to seduce Caitilin, the lovely daughter of Meehawl. With his magic pipes and his tales of the pleasures of the flesh, Pan succeeds in luring Caitilin away from her humble peasant life into his cave.

Once more Meehawl comes to the philosopher for advice.

The wise man sends his children to Pan's cave to beg him to release the girl, but the god refuses to have anything to do with them. Determined now to take matters into his own hands, the philosopher orders his wife to bake him some cakes for his long journey. First he goes to see Pan, but he is unable to persuade him to release Caitilin. Then he sets out to find the great old Irish god, Angus Og. After a long journey during which he meets all sorts of people—some helpful, others nasty and suspicious—the philosopher finds Angus Og and urges him to do something.

Angus Og visits the cave where Pan holds Caitilin a willing captive and wisely leaves it up to the girl to decide whom to follow. Pan represents all that is lusty in man, but only with Angus Og will Caitilin find love instead of lust, happiness and serenity instead of fear and hunger. The girl soon decides to follow the old god and leaves the cave of Pan.

On his way home from Angus Og's dwelling, the philosopher delivers several prophetic messages from him to the people he meets. When he eventually comes home, his wife is so happy to see him that she swears never to be ill-tempered with him again or serve his evening stirabout with lumps. All seems well for the present. The philosopher and his wife are blissfully unaware of the troubles to come.

Furious at being thwarted in their revenge and determined to get back their crock of gold, the leprechauns leave anonymous information at the police station about two dead bodies— murdered by the philosopher—lying buried under his hearthstone. The police break into the philosopher's house, find the bodies of the first philosopher and his wife, and accuse the philosopher of murder.

The philosopher, vainly protesting his innocence, is escorted to jail. It is a pitch-dark night, and the police have a hard time keeping watch on their prisoner, who talks them practically to death on such recondite philosophical matters as why only man, of all the social species on earth, needs policemen. Suddenly the police come upon a leprechaun, and in their amazement at this tiny, bearded being, lose sight of both philosopher and leprechaun, who escape.

Meanwhile, Seumas and Brigid, playing in the wood, have found the crock of gold where Meehawl buried it, and they return it to the leprechauns. The Little People are overjoyed, but it is too late to do anything about the information they

have given the police. The philosopher, now at home, decides
that since he is innocent of any crime, he will give himself up
to the police. In grateful surprise they put him in jail, and
here he listens to the pathetic stories of two other captives.

While her husband is in prison, the Thin Woman decides
to take matters into her own hands. She bakes some cakes
and sets off with Seumas and Brigid in search of Angus Ōg.
On her way she meets the Three Absolutes: the Most Beautiful Man, the Strongest Man, and the Ugliest Man. Terror-
stricken at these superhuman figures, the Thin Woman
nevertheless answers their questions and succeeds in saving her
children from them. Eventually she finds the dwelling of the
great Angus Ōg. He has been waiting for her to ask his help,
for the gods help only those who request their intervention.

Living now with the lovely Caitilin, Angus Ōg summons
a great conference of the gods of ancient Ireland, and together they dance and sing through the countryside. In the
town, moved by the life-affirming joy of the gods, the people
are transformed, and the police immediately release their
prisoners. The philosopher returns to his house in the pine
forest and once again offers his sage counsel to his neighbors.

Having done their good deed, the gods return to the
country of Angus Ōg and Caitilin to await the birth of their
child. Someday they will be able to leave their secret caves
for good and again dispense joy and wisdom (which are the
same thing) to the people of Ireland, for the gods are benef-
icent and wise; only people are sometimes misguided.

Critical Opinion

One of the characters in Stephens' *The Demigods* (1914)
remarks that "humor is the health of the mind." If this is so,
James Stephens must have been the healthiest of the many
figures who enriched Irish literature during the Celtic renaissance that began in the late 1880's and flourished until
World War I. For although most of the writers of that movement dealt, as Stephens did, with magic, myth, and legend,
none did so with as much vivacity and good humor as
Stephens, whose books combine the whimsical, fey, moonlit
quality of much Irish poetic prose with a gusty, almost
Rabelaisian appreciation of the joys of life.

Although the philosopher in *The Crock of Gold* is ludicrously henpecked, he never lets his wife get the better of him but simply ignores her when he is in full spate of eloquence. Similarly, in one of the most hilarious scenes of the book, he lectures his police captors when they come to arrest him, gives them the slip, and then surrenders in his own good time.

Such gods in *The Crock of Gold* as Angus Og represent to Stephens the good life, which is compounded of simplicity, respect for both the natural and supernatural worlds (which coexist in a miraculous alliance), benevolence, and good humor. The one rebel among the gods is Pan, a foreign deity who mistakes lust for love and is not spiritual enough for Stephens' people.

Essentially a fairy tale for adults, *The Crock of Gold* is a very difficult book to classify. In the words of Frank Swinnerton, "First it is a tale, and then it is a philosophy, and then it is nonsense; but all these qualities are so merged and, for the reader, confounded, that the effect is one of profound laughter."

Indeed, myth, folk tale, patches of poetic prose, domestic comedy, and even social commentary (in the prison scene) all give *The Crock of Gold* its unique flavor. The "philosophy" of the book is deceptively naïve. While Stephens gently mocks the long-winded platitudes of his philosopher, he never lets the reader forget that basically the philosopher is speaking the truth, which so often in our moon-struck world eludes both men and leprechauns.

The Author

James Stephens was born in Dublin on February 2, 1882, in the very hour in which his great compatriot James Joyce was born. This coincidence so impressed the superstitious Joyce that he once said only Stephens could complete his *Finnegans Wake* should he die prematurely.

Stephens' family was poor, and he received his only education in the Dublin slums. He taught himself to be a stenographer, however, and was discovered in an office by George Russell ("AE"), the Irish poet and statesman, who saw some of Stephens' early poems and sketches and encouraged him to become a writer. Recognition did not come to Stephens until 1912, when *The Crock of Gold* was published and won the Polignac Prize. It remained his most popular work, although Stephens began and ended his career essentially as a poet.

A student of Gaelic and an important figure in the Irish literary renaissance of the early twentieth century, Stephens was determined to give his country "a new mythology." He did so in such lyrical, mystic prose works as *Deirdre* (1923), which won the Tailteann Gold Medal, *In the Land of Youth* (1924), in the famous volume of short stories *Etched in Moonlight* (1928), and, of course, in *The Crock of Gold*.

Interested in all aspects of Irish culture, Stephens became an assistant curator of the Dublin National Gallery, a noted collector of Celtic folk songs, and a member of the Sinn Fein working to establish the De Valera government. During World War II, he protested against Irish neutrality, moved to London, and wrote to the *Times* that he was an Irishman who wanted "to elect himself an Englishman for the duration." Grateful for his services, the British government granted him a civil pension in 1942.

Stephens, who was married and the father of two children, traveled widely, living much of the time in Paris and visiting the United States in 1925 and in 1935, when he lectured at the University of California. Appropriately, the author of *The Crock of Gold*, according to his friends, resembled nothing so much as a leprechaun. Under five feet tall, bald, with the long, sad face of a stage Irishman, and speaking in a heavy brogue, Stephens seemed himself to have emerged from the forest of Gort na Cloca Mora rather than from a Dublin slum. He died in his home in London on December 26, 1950.

Sons and Lovers

by

D. H. LAWRENCE (1885–1930)

Main Characters

Walter Morel—A coal miner, crude and uneducated but full
of life and high spirits.
Gertrude Morel—Walter's unhappy wife who seeks a better
life for her children.
William Morel—The fun-loving, sociable, oldest Morel son.
Lily Western—William's snobbish and superficial fiancée.
Paul Morel—Sensitive and artistic, bullied by his father and
doted on by his mother.
Miriam Lievers—The intensely spiritual daughter of a neigh-
boring farm family.
Clara Dawes—A buxom and earthy suffragette who seduces
Paul.
Baxter Dawes—Clara's husband, a blacksmith.

The Story

When Gertrude Coppard, the refined, middle-class daughter
of an engineer, marries the coal miner Walter Morel, she is
twenty-three and he is a handsome, vigorous man in his prime.
But not long after the couple settles down in Bestwood, a
mining town in Nottinghamshire, Gertrude begins to realize
her marriage is a mistake. Her husband is a lazy drunkard,

crude, and ignorant of the things Gertrude considers important in life.

Over the years they have four children: William, Annie,
Paul, and Arthur. Mrs. Morel takes comfort in them, protecting them from their father's periodic drunken rages and
trying to bring them up to be refined and cultured, despite
the family's precarious finances. The oldest of her sons, William, a clerk in Nottingham, is socially ambitious and is always going to dances. When he is only twenty, he leaves the
unhappy family to make his way in London. The burden of
Mrs. Morel's frustrated love then falls on the next son, Paul, a
sensitive, artistically inclined lad who shrinks from his father's
crudities and hates him for his rough treatment of Mrs.
Morel.

As Paul is growing up, William becomes more and more
successful in a London lawyer's office, but his social engagements take up most of his money and time, and he has little
of either for his family. One day, however, he brings home
to Bestwood, Lily Western, the flighty brunette he has become
engaged to. Vain and superficial, Lily snobbishly condescends
to the Morels. Mrs. Morel strongly disapproves of her and
convinces William she is not the girl for him.

Shortly afterward, Mrs. Morel is summoned to London
where William is dying of pneumonia. After his death, Mrs.
Morel falls into a deep depression. It is not until Paul, too,
becomes ill that she realizes she still has him to live for. Paul
is more sensitive than the two younger children, and Mrs.
Morel feels he needs her protection against his loutish father
more than they do. She begins to smother him in mother love,
hoping that he will someday fulfill her frustrated ambitions.
Paul easily becomes her favorite, never realizing that his father,
too, has good qualities, including a vigorous, realistic acceptance of life that Mrs. Morel lacks.

Paul's first step toward independence is to get a menial
job in Nottingham working for Mr. Jordan, a manufacturer
of surgical appliances. He travels a considerable distance
from home and earns only eight shillings a week; but he
continues to draw in his spare time and finds the gossipy,
superficial lives of his fellow workers a relief from the dour,
passionate life at home.

One day Paul bicycles to neighboring Willey Farm, a
lovely pastoral spot far removed from the grimy coal town

in which he lives. Paul has become friends with the sons of the farm's owners, the Lievers, but soon he begins to notice their quiet, dark-haired, fifteen-year-old sister, Miriam. The Lievers, who are very religious, have brought up their daughter to be intensely spiritual. Shy and sensitive, Miriam comes to rely heavily on Paul's visits for solace when the crude life of the farm becomes too much for her.

While Paul is recuperating from an illness, he goes more and more frequently to the Lievers' farm, and while he tutors Miriam in French and mathematics, they fall deeply in love. Love to Miriam, however, is chaste and spiritual. She shrinks from any physical expression of love. Paul becomes increasingly frustrated. Mrs. Morel, too, who wants her son all for herself, disapproves of the generally unpopular Miriam and tries to persuade Paul to stop seeing her. Mrs. Morel knows that she is herself slowly dying of cancer. When Paul tells her one day that he is not in love with Miriam, she kisses him fervently and tells him he must live for his art and never let any woman trap him into marriage and prevent him from making something of himself.

Through Miriam, Paul meets Clara Dawes, a beautiful, buxom suffragette five years his senior, separated from her blacksmith husband, Baxter Dawes. Clara is just the opposite of Miriam. Where Miriam is spiritual, fearing any physical contact with men, Clara is sensual and earthy. Before long, she becomes Paul's mistress. Miriam knows of this but is sure that her loftier, platonic love will win out in the end. Clara, however, refuses to divorce her estranged husband. Paul is, in a sense, relieved for he does not really want to marry anyone. No woman, he has been brought up to believe, is as worthy as his long-suffering mother.

Paul's paintings have met with some local acclaim. Annie, after studying to be a teacher, marries; and Arthur, after a brief stretch in the army, marries too, after his fiancée has become pregnant. Mr. Morel suffers a leg injury in a mine accident and, no longer able to get around as he used to, begins to age rapidly. Paul takes his place as breadwinner and tries to buy his mother all the things her husband's irresponsibility has deprived her of.

Sensing that Clara represents less of a threat to her dominance over Paul than Miriam, Mrs. Morel lets her son know she approves of his mistress. But after Clara's husband, the

powerful blacksmith, hears of the affair and gives Paul a bad
beating, Paul stops seeing Clara for a time.

Paul returns to Miriam and finally possesses her, but without joy, because he realizes she has given him nothing but her
body. Meanwhile, Mrs. Morel has come close to death. Visiting
her in the hospital one day, Paul meets Baxter Dawes again.
He is recuperating from typhoid fever, and, oddly, the two
rivals become close friends. But Mrs. Morel's disease grows
more painful and hopeless. She is brought home to die. Unable
to watch her suffering any longer, Paul gives his mother a
lethal dose of morphine. She is found dead the next morning.

Now Paul is depressed and confused. He has broken off with
Miriam because of her loathing for sex. Clara has gone back
to Baxter Dawes. Paul and his father, who have never understood one another, are unable to live together now that Mrs.
Morel is dead, and they take separate lodgings. For a long
time Paul wanders about purposelessly, occasionally thinking
of studying art abroad and at other times longing to be
united with his mother in death.

Slowly Paul's painting begins to find acceptance among art
critics, and he feels now that his mother would have wanted
him to continue with it. He has one final meeting with Miriam
in Nottingham and finally realizes that she is capable only of
sacrificing herself to him, never of loving him. They only
torment each other when they are together. Leaving Miriam,
Paul determines somehow to make his way in life on his own,
without his mother to guide or impede him.

Critical Opinion

Sons and Lovers, Lawrence's first really mature novel, remains his most widely respected. It was written before ill
health, poverty, and critical misunderstanding had made Lawrence an embittered prophet. Most significant, although it is a
classic study of the oedipal relationship between mother and
son, it was written before Lawrence had ever read Freud,
with whom, as a matter of fact, he later disagreed violently.

The material of *Sons and Lovers* is almost purely autobiographical. Paul Morel is Lawrence. Miriam is actually
Jessie Chambers, who knew Lawrence, encouraged him to
write, and left a curious book of her own (*D. H. Lawrence*:

A Personal Record) in which she tells "her side" of the relationship so painfully dissected in the novel.

As an autobiographical novel, *Sons and Lovers* ranks with
Joyce's *Portrait of the Artist as a Young Man*, Maugham's
Of Human Bondage, and Bennett's *Clayhanger*. What makes it
unique is not only its piercing psychological insights into the
highly complex relationships between mother and son and
between son and other women, but Lawrence's passionate
involvement with the characters and even the landscapes of
the novel—an involvement that underlies every page of its
richly lyrical prose.

The fault that mars some of Lawrence's later books—a
tendency to forget the story in order to harangue his readers
—is fortunately missing from *Sons and Lovers*, in which all
the ideas are rendered symbolically or in pure fiction.

The sexual ideas for which Lawrence became notorious are
presented in full in *Sons and Lovers*. Briefly, he felt that because of the rationalism of the eighteenth century and the
industrialism of the nineteenth, a vital force—the individual
relationship between man and woman—had been submerged
and all but crushed. Social convention, disembodied spirituality, and worship of the machine were Lawrence's enemies.
They are embodied in the ghastly coal mine and in Miriam, a
crippled being who loves Paul but cannot give herself to him.
At the same time, Lawrence disapproved of Clara's promiscuity as he saw sex as an essentially religious function.

Before Paul can fulfill himself as man or artist he must come
to grips with the "dark forces" Lawrence worshiped: understand the hold his mother has over him, free himself from the
destructive inhibitions of Miriam, and even come to appreciate
the animal vitality of his father. By the end of the novel he
is on the brink of manhood because he has succeeded in
mastering these forces in himself and understanding them in
others.

The Author

Like his hero, Paul Morel, *David Herbert Lawrence* was the
son of a collier, born in the mining village of Eastwood, Nottinghamshire, on September 11, 1885. His mother, a schoolteacher, was, like Mrs. Morel, determined that her children

should rise above the poverty into which they were born.
A sickly youth, Lawrence was encouraged by his mother to
study. He entered Nottingham High School on a scholarship,
later training to be a teacher at University College, Nottingham.

His career as a teacher was short-lived. Encouraged by
the prototype of Miriam, he began to write. Ironically, Lawrence's first novel, *The White Peacock,* appeared in 1911, a
month after his mother's death. Lawrence then fell in love
with Frieda von Richthofen, an aristocrat, married and the
mother of three children. He persuaded Frieda to leave her
husband and join him in his travels through Europe. Frieda
was the sister of the famous German air ace, Baron von
Richthofen. When war came, Lawrence and Frieda went to
England where they were under constant suspicion as spies.

Suffering from poverty and tuberculosis, Lawrence nevertheless wrote steadily throughout the war. *Sons and Lovers*
appeared in 1913, followed by *The Rainbow* in 1915. This
novel, with its outspoken views on sex, caused a furor in the
press and a whole edition was destroyed by the police.
Lawrence did not help matters by his caustic scorn for his
critics and his passionate—often absurd—involvements in the
literary world of London. Quick to make friends, Lawrence
jealously expected absolute loyalty and would reject friends
the instant their views failed to coincide with his.

The Rainbow was followed by a sequel, *Women in Love,*
in 1920, and by a variety of splendid travel books recounting
Lawrence's experiences in his search of health. His travels
took him to Australia, Sardinia, Mexico, and the southwestern part of the United States. Among the most notable
of these travel accounts are *Twilight in Italy* (1916), *Sea and
Sardinia* (1921), and *Mornings in Mexico* (1927). In addition, Lawrence was a talented if eccentric painter, a fine poet,
and a first-rate short-story writer.

Recognition came very slowly to the ruthlessly puritanical,
bearded prophet of sex. In all his writing, Lawrence combined a painter's eye for natural scenery with fierce polemic
about modern man whom he saw as surrendering his natural
instincts and functions to an emasculating rationalism and
industrialization.

Desperately ill, Lawrence came to Italy for the last time in
1926, after completing his novel about Mexico, *The Plumed*

Serpent. Embittered by his struggles with censorship and public misunderstanding, Lawrence in his last years wrote *Lady Chatterley's Lover* (1928), the most notorious if not the best work of his fiery career. He died of tuberculosis in a sanatorium at Vence, France, on March 2, 1930. The controversies he and his works aroused have continued unabated to the present day.

By the Same Author

The Rainbow: Confiscated by the police when it first appeared, *The Rainbow* is a vast novel about three generations of farmers (the Brangwens) and their sexual and social conflicts, from the tempestuous marriage of Tom Brangwen and a Polish widow, Lydia, to the wedding of his foster child, Anna, and his cousin Will Brangwen on to the third ·generation. These darkly passionate men of the English soil find themselves locked in combat with their women who, like Mrs. Morel, try to "civilize" them or, like Miriam, withhold themselves in the hope of crushing the occasionally brutal but essentially healthy masculine spirit.

Women in Love: A sequel to *The Rainbow, Women in Love* centers around two sisters, Ursula and Gudrun Brangwen, and their men, Gerald and Birkin. Fiercely individualistic and intent upon primacy in any sexual relationship, the characters torment one another in a series of often bizarre scenes. Lawrence's underrated gift for satire appears here, too, as he describes Birkin's adventures in pseudosophisticated London society. Lawrence's favorite among his own novels, *Women in Love* is the most fully developed example of his penetrating psychological exploration of the war between the sexes and the ills of modern society.

Of Human Bondage

by

W. SOMERSET MAUGHAM (1874–1965)

Main Characters

Philip Carey—A highly sensitive man, orphaned very young. He has a clubfoot.

William Carey—Philip's clergyman uncle, a narrow, cold man with an inflated sense of his own position.

Louisa Carey—Philip's kindly aunt who longs for a child of her own.

Miss Emily Wilkinson—Twice Philip's age and far more sophisticated, his first love.

Cronshaw—An egocentric hack poet and amateur diabolist who influences Philip in Paris.

Fanny Price—An untalented woman trying to become an artist in Paris.

Mildred Rogers—Utterly unattractive and self-seeking, yet she is able to enslave the infatuated Philip.

Thorpe Athelny—An eccentric who befriends Philip during a wretched period in his life.

Sally Athelny—A direct and warm-hearted girl.

The Story

Philip Carey is only nine years old in 1885 when his mother dies and he goes to live with his Uncle William and Aunt

Louisa in the vicarage of Blackstable, not far from London. The highly sensitive orphan suffers agonies of self-consciousness and embarrassment about the clubfoot he was born with. His uncle is a "close" man with money and emotion, a self-righteous and smug domestic tyrant. Philip's childless Aunt Louisa gives him the only warmth and affection he knows as a boy.

Philip's schooldays are made wretched by his affliction. Unable to participate in sports and constantly mocked by his callous schoolfellows, Philip learns to retreat into himself and becomes a lonely but independent boy. His uncle is a great collector, if not reader, of books, and soon Philip devours all the books of romance and adventure he can find in the vicarage library.

At the King's School in Tercanbury, where Philip is eventually enrolled, he is forced to show his deformed foot to the other boys, who cruelly imitate his peculiar gait. This horrible experience drives him even further into himself. When a religious revival sweeps the school, Philip, the nephew of a low churchman, takes to reading the Bible avidly. When he learns that faith can move mountains, he decides to try an experiment. One night he prays fervently to God to heal his clubfoot. When he awakens the next morning as deformed as ever, Philip loses whatever faith he may have had and becomes an agnostic for the rest of his life.

At eighteen, Philip persuades his uncle to let him use some of his own inheritance to study in Germany instead of at Oxford. He spends a year at the home of Professor Erlin in Heidelberg where he comes under the intellectual influence of the famous university town. Philip studies German and philosophy and becomes hardened in his agnosticism. The year in Germany is a happy one for Philip. Here he begins to appreciate the great world outside Blackstable.

On his return to England, Philip falls in love with Miss Emily Wilkinson, daughter of a clergyman, who is staying at the vicarage. She is twice his age, but gay and high-spirited, and has little difficulty in seducing the innocent Philip who, at twenty, shyly feels that he ought to have an affair. When she returns to Germany as a governess, however, Philip quickly recovers and settles in London to become an apprentice to a firm of chartered accountants.

Lonely and bored with his job, Philip decides that he must

go to Paris to study art. His uncle strongly disapproves and refuses to subsidize him. But Aunt Louisa gives Philip her savings of £100, and he is launched on the bohemian life of a poor art student.

In Paris he comes under the influence of Cronshaw, an untalented writer but a magnetic speaker with heady ideas about diabolism that intrigue Philip for a while. Although he works hard at painting, Philip learns from his frank instructor that he has no real talent. Affected by the tragic fate of Fanny Price, a fellow art student who killed herself when she discovered she had no talent, Philip decides to return to England and begin life anew as a medical student.

With his uncle's approval, he enrolls in St. Luke's Hospital and studies hard. But he is still lonely. He meets Mildred Rogers, a waitress, pale and consumptive-looking, vulgar and utterly selfish, and becomes obsessed with the desire to possess her. She is coy with him, however. In his frustrated and humiliating preoccupation with her, Philip fails his examinations. Then Mildred tells him she is going to marry a rich German named Miller.

Philip is crushed, but he is consoled by a young widow named Norah. Their love affair is hearty and direct, but Norah cannot take his mind off Mildred. When Mildred reappears, she tells Philip that Miller was already married and poorer than he pretended to be. He has deserted her, and she is pregnant with his child.

Unable to let Mildred fend for herself, Philip pays her medical bills; and when a baby girl is born, he takes mother and daughter into his rooms to live with him. He comes to love the little girl, but Mildred still despises him and taunts him about his clubfoot. She soon leaves him for a lecherous friend of his named Griffiths. The degraded Philip has even paid for one of Mildred's outings with her lover.

Meanwhile Philip has repeated the course he failed in medical school and has become a popular intern. An operation is performed on his clubfoot, and his limp improves considerably. He meets an eccentric patient named Thorpe Athelny, who at forty-eight has a wife and nine children, but little money to support them. When Athelny leaves the hospital, he invites the lonely young doctor to visit his home. Philip is delighted by the happy family life he sees there—so different from the grim atmosphere in which he spent his childhood. He becomes a frequent visitor at the carefree Athelny cottage.

Late one evening Philip meets Mildred again on the streets of London. Deserted by Griffiths, she has become a prostitute. Once again Philip feels he must shelter her, although by now he has gotten over his early infatuation. Mildred, seemingly a sadder and wiser woman, consents to live with Philip as his housekeeper. But now it is she who desires Philip. She is outraged when he refuses to have anything to do with her, and one day in his absence she rips up his furniture and paintings. Philip returns to find his apartment wrecked and Mildred gone.

He takes lodgings across the street and, on the advice of a Scottish friend who works for an investment firm, begins investing the rest of his inheritance in the stock market. At first he is successful, but then the Boer War knocks the bottom out of the market, and Philip loses his inheritance. Again he must quit medical school. For a period he faces starvation. Thorpe Athelny gets him a job in the linen draper's shop where he is employed, but Philip hates being a floorwalker. Eventually things improve a bit as he puts his artistic training to use designing posters and dresses.

Left £500 at his uncle's death, Philip is able to resume his medical studies. Eventually he gets an assistantship with a physician in Dorsetshire. The old doctor wants Philip to become his full partner, but Philip, now thirty, is filled with wanderlust and wants to become a ship's doctor.

Before signing aboard a vessel, however, Philip goes on a holiday to the Athelnys' cottage. There he notices for the first time that the Athelny daughter, Sally, whom he had always thought of as a little girl, has matured into an attractive woman. They walk in the country together, and Philip makes love to her.

A few weeks later, Sally tells Philip that she is pregnant. Philip sees that the only honorable thing to do is to abandon his plans for travel and marry the girl for whose plight he is responsible. But when Sally later tells him that she was mistaken, Philip, far from being relieved, feels disappointed. He realizes that what he really wants in life is not aimless travel as a lonely bachelor but a happy, secure home life with the sympathetic Sally Athelny. Accordingly they are married, and Philip, settling down as a country doctor, is finally released

from the bondage of his hopeless love for Mildred Rogers and
his lack of faith in himself.

Critical Opinion

In the tradition of *David Copperfield*, *The Way of All Flesh*,
and *Sons and Lovers*, *Of Human Bondage* is concerned with
the growing pains—emotional, intellectual, and spiritual—of
a youth on the way to maturity. It is a highly autobiographical
record not only of the young Maugham's life and loves but of
his intellectual development as well, ranging from the joyless
religious upbringing in his uncle's vicarage through the
heady philosophic freedom of Heidelberg, the bohemian life
in Paris with all its absurdities and tragedies, and finally the
coming to grips with the meaning of life in London and in the
kindly, sensible home of the Athelny family.

The title, taken from Spinoza's *Ethics*, is a clue to the
theme of the work which differentiates it from other autobiographical novels. To Spinoza, human bondage consisted of
centering one's being on an inadequate object, that is to
say on something transient rather than on something permanent. Freedom came only when one was able to control the
lusts of the flesh and the weakness of the spirit and attach
oneself to some permanent good.

This is the course that Philip Carey must follow in his
youth. He falls into a hideously degrading bondage to Mildred, knowing all the time that she is a vulgar slut. He is,
however, too weak-willed to free himself from his passion for
her until he has suffered greatly. Mildred nearly wrecks his
life on several occasions, but gradually Philip's soul is purged
of her influence, and he gains control of his passions. His love
for Sally Athelny at the end of the book is perhaps less
passionate than his love for Mildred, but it is a saner and
healthier emotion, one that will allow him to build a good
life rather than destroy himself.

Thus *Of Human Bondage* is essentially a success story in
which the hero, after many trials and tribulations, usually
self-imposed, emerges happy and in general unscathed. The
ideas that have influenced Philip finally evolve into an urbane,
reasonable skepticism about life and human motives. From
each of his love affairs, beginning with Miss Wilkinson and

ending in marriage to Sally, Philip learns something—mostly how to endure the torture of being in love with someone who despises or at best ignores him and how to free himself eventually from the shackles of such love.

If *Of Human Bondage* is psychologically less penetrating than *Sons and Lovers,* or technically less exciting and venturesome than Joyce's *Portrait of the Artist as a Young Man,* it is nevertheless a surely written, well-balanced, and frequently perceptive treatment of the great theme of youth's awakening. In the fifty years since its publication it has been widely and consistently popular.

The Author

William Somerset Maugham, one of the best-loved English storytellers, was born in Paris on January 25, 1874, son of the solicitor to the British Embassy there. A happy boy, he grew up speaking French before he learned English. By the time he was ten, however, he was orphaned, like Philip Carey, and sent to live in his uncle's home in Whitstable.

Maugham's youth was very similar to Philip's. He studied at King's School, Canterbury, and went to Heidelberg instead of the more traditional Oxford. A pronounced stammer produced the psychological effect on Maugham that Philip's clubfoot had on him. Shy and lonely and suffering from incipient tuberculosis, Maugham spent a troubled youth searching for his vocation.

Like Philip, Maugham became a qualified physician, but he always yearned to write. His first book, *Liza of Lambeth* (1897), was a drab but expertly told story of life in a London slum as Maugham had come to know it while interning at St. Thomas' Hospital. Narrated in the then fashionable vein of French realism, *Liza of Lambeth* was not highly successful although it was respectfully received by the critics.

Maugham persisted in writing and for ten years almost starved in Paris until the production in 1907 of his first successful play, *Lady Frederick.* From that point on, Maugham became an immensely popular playwright and novelist. His royalties permitted him to indulge his passion for travel and art collecting. On his voyages around the world Maugham collected the material for his many stories, of which "Rain" became the most famous.

During World War I, Maugham enlisted with an ambulance unit but was soon shifted to the Intelligence Department, where he gained the espionage experience that he used in his tales about the British agent, *Ashenden* (1928). It was the story of his own troubled youth, however, to which Maugham turned for his finest novel, *Of Human Bondage*. Its publication in 1915 was a great success. Maugham followed this with *The Moon and Sixpence* (1919) and *Cakes and Ale* (1930) as well as numerous other novels, stories, and essays. His career as a playwright extended from well before the war right through the 1920's. Such sparkling plays as *The Circle* (1921), *Our Betters* (1923), and *The Constant Wife* (1927) made Maugham the toast of the English stage.

In the early 1930's Maugham settled in the famous Villa Mauresque at Cap Ferrat, in the south of France, where he remained—except for occasional voyages—until his death in 1965.

By the Same Author

The Moon and Sixpence: Based on the life of the great French painter Gauguin, *The Moon and Sixpence* is Maugham's interpretation of the selfishness and single-mindedness that go into the making of a great artist. His hero, Charles Strickland, is a stockbroker with a wife and two children, who becomes possessed by the desire to paint. He abandons his job and family and settles down to an amoral, poverty-stricken life in Paris where he ruthlessly pursues his art. In the process he drives the wife of his friend and admirer Dirk Stroeve to suicide and emigrates to Tahiti where he eventually goes blind and dies, leaving the walls of his primitive hut covered with paintings of great splendor.

A Portrait of the Artist as a Young Man

by

JAMES JOYCE (1882–1941)

Main Characters

Stephen Dedalus—The young Irish artist-hero who struggles against poverty and lack of understanding to find his life's vocation.

Simon Dedalus—Stephen's sentimental, good-natured father, a minor civil servant, fond of drinking and arguing about politics with his friends.

Dante Riordan—Stephen's pious but argumentative aunt, bitterly opposed politically to Simon Dedalus.

Cranly—Stephen's college friend, a sounding board for Stephen's ideas about art and religion.

Father Dolan—The stern prefect of studies at Stephen's school, ever on the lookout for lazy students.

Mr. Tate—Stephen's English teacher who accuses him of committing heresy.

Emma—Stephen's fickle girl friend who also accuses him of being a heretic.

The Story

We first meet Stephen Dedalus, a sensitive Dublin boy, listening to nursery songs and nonsense verses at his mother's knee.

Before long he is enrolled in the Clongowes Wood School, run by strict Jesuit teachers. Young Stephen suffers immensely from his shyness, his nearsightedness, and his strange, un-Irish last name. The other boys also bully him unmercifully because his father is a humble civil servant. One of them, Wells, even shoulders him into a ditch of cold, filthy water crawling with rats, because Stephen will not trade him a valuable little snuffbox for a marble.

As a result of this ducking, Stephen becomes sick and spends some time in the school infirmary. Filled with self-pity, he dreams about how sorry everyone would feel if he were to die. While Stephen is in the infirmary, the great Irish patriot and leader Parnell dies. The wailing of the people outside fixes this date, October 6, 1891, forever in the boy's memory.

Home for Christmas, Stephen finds that the death of Parnell has aroused intense antagonisms in his family. His father, Simon Dedalus, staunchly defends the dead leader, while his aunt, Dante Riordan, attacks Parnell as a heretic who betrayed both the Catholic Church and Ireland by having an adulterous affair with Kitty O'Shea, another man's wife. Simon Dedalus protests bitterly that the church and country for which Parnell fought all his life hounded him to death for one moral slip.

This fierce dispute ruins the first Christmas dinner that Stephen remembers. He feels that he is already being forced to take sides in religious and political disputes that do not really concern him. He sees them dividing his family as they have divided all Ireland.

More misfortunes await Stephen when he returns to school after the holiday. A student on a bicycle collides with him while Stephen is walking on a cinder path, and breaks his glasses. Stephen is excused from work until his father can send him a new pair, but Father Dolan, the prefect of studies, prowling up and down Father Arnall's Latin class looking for lazy and mischievous boys, spots Stephen not doing his lesson. Without waiting for an explanation, Father Dolan accuses Stephen of having broken his glasses intentionally and beats Stephen's hand furiously with a "pandybat." As he fights back his tears, his classmates, even "Nasty Roche," seem to sympathize with him for the first time. Craving excitement, they egg Stephen on to complain to the rector of the school about the unjust punishment. The rector sympathizes with him and promises to tell Father Dolan to excuse Stephen until his glasses arrive. His courage in speaking to the rector makes Stephen a sort of hero to his classmates, and they carry him about the campus in their arms. Later Stephen finds out that the rector and Father Dolan had enjoyed a good laugh over the incident.

As Stephen grows older, he becomes better able to handle bullies. At one point, Mr. Tate, the English teacher, accuses Stephen of inserting a heretical statement into one of his compositions. Stephen immediately apologizes and changes the essay, but later a group of the boys attack him for being a heretic and for liking the "immoral" poet Byron. Stephen sticks to his guns, however, and tells them that a poet's greatness has nothing to do with his private morality. The boys gang up on him and beat him with a cane. It is his first encounter with the bigotry and narrow-mindedness of his schoolfellows, but Stephen does not flinch from their jeers and abuse.

Family embarrassments hound Stephen at this time, too. His father, a shallow, easygoing man, given to sentimental talk about his own youth, takes Stephen on a trip to Cork where he embarrasses his rigorously honest son by treating everyone he meets to sentimental harangues over glasses of beer. From this point on, the fortunes of Simon Dedalus decline, and the family keeps moving to cheaper and drearier quarters.

Stephen is able to improve their financial lot temporarily by winning some prizes at the end of the term. Filled with ambition to live a less grimy life, he buys all sorts of delicacies, decorates his room, and even establishes a family loan service. The money soon runs out, however, and the Dedalus family is plunged again into genteel poverty. With the last of his prize money, Stephen wanders into Dublin's red-light district and, at the age of sixteen, has his first, unsatisfactory experience with sex.

This experience torments him when he is back at school where a religious retreat is being held. During the retreat, Stephen, almost constantly in chapel, hears a priest describe the torments of hell in lurid terms. Stephen is thoroughly frightened and believes that his experience with the prostitute will send him to endless damnation. He has nightmares every night, and yet feels he cannot confess at school. Instead he goes to a Dublin church where nobody knows him. There a kindly, wise old priest hears his confession and directs him on the road to penitence.

Stephen is so relieved by the old priest's comforting words that he studies very hard and resolves to lead a life free of all sensual temptations. He tries to imitate the monks and saints by mortifying his flesh, seeking out disagreeable experiences in order to rise above them. He tries not to dream about girls and plunges into the study of Aristotle, St. Augustine, and St. Thomas Aquinas.

Stephen is so successful at his studies and in his new regimen that the director of the college tries to persuade him to enter the priesthood. The director thinks that Stephen, with his intelligence and will power, must have a vocation. Stephen is flattered by the director's attention. He soon begins to see himself in the role of a priest. In his egoism he enjoys the idea of having all the power of the Catholic Church behind him.

As Stephen grows older, however, religious doubts begin to plague him. The more he doubts the more he studies, and the more he studies the more he becomes confused about the Church and its dogma. He finds some measure of intellectual companionship with his friends, Davin, Lynch, and Cranly, although they cannot match his intelligence. He gives up a girl, Emma, because he thinks he saw her flirting with a priest.

Stephen's friendships are not very successful. Most of his classmates are involved in the Church or in the Irish nationalist movement, now gaining momentum. Many of them are studying Gaelic, hoping it will eventually replace the hated English. But Stephen admires English poetry too much to throw the language overboard. He begins to have his doubts about the wisdom of the Church, and insultingly calls Ireland "the old sow that eats her farrow." He has not forgotten the Christmas dinner discussion of how Parnell was betrayed by his own people. When his fellow students ask Stephen to sign a petition calling for world peace, he rejects it on the grounds that the movement is headed by the Russian czar. Also, he tells them, he has determined to become a writer, and an artist cannot waste his time with politics.

When Stephen meets Emma again, she asks him why he has been staying away from her. He answers that he intends to become a monk. She replies that she thought he was setting out to become a heretic. This finally convinces him that the priestly life is not for him. He must cut himself off from friends, family, church, and country in order to make his own way as a lonely but independent artist. When his friends try to bring him back to the Church, Stephen merely questions them about their ideas of beauty, which is all that now concerns him. To him beauty is largely a matter of "art for art's sake" and has nothing to do with conventional morality. Even if it means breaking his religious mother's heart, he must leave Ireland, where the Church, he feels, has destroyed beauty. He must go in search of his artistic destiny.

As the novel ends, Stephen is about to leave Ireland, certain at last that he has found his true vocation, that of the artist. "Welcome, O life!" he writes in his diary. "I go to encounter for the millionth time the reality of experience and to forge in the smithy of my soul the uncreated conscience of my race."

Critical Opinion

A Portrait of the Artist as a Young Man was Joyce's first novel. Originally he wrote a very long draft of it called *Stephen Hero,* most of which he later destroyed. Then he rewrote the book, intensifying the experiences and selecting those that dealt with Stephen's emotional and spiritual development. A deeply autobiographical book, *A Portrait of the Artist as a Young Man* is in some ways like any number of novels written between 1890 and World War I about the growing up of an artistic young man in an insensitive family and a hostile environment. What distinguishes it, however, from such novels as Butler's *The Way of All Flesh* or Maugham's *Of Human Bondage* is the originality of the style.

Since every incident is filtered through Stephen's sensibility, the prose at the beginning of the book is almost baby talk. As Stephen matures, however, the writing grows more and more complex, keeping pace with the growth of his mind.

Although Joyce seems to be writing from within Stephen's mind, he also manages to comment obliquely to the reader about his hero who often acts foolishly or pompously. This double vision keeps the novel from becoming just another story about a sensitive young man. Above all, Joyce is coolly objective about both his hero and the environment against which the hero is struggling. Throughout the novel Joyce is detached; he never comments or moralizes. The result is a classic of fictional method as well as an intense and exciting account of the development—against all odds—of the artistic mind and soul.

The Author

James Joyce was born into a lower-middle-class family in Dublin on February 2, 1882. There was no hint in his background that he would become one of the most significant writers of his time. His father was an undistinguished civil servant more interested in drinking and arguing about politics than in reading literature. His mother, although more artistically inclined, had, unlike her son, a conventional mind.

Young Joyce got a thorough Jesuit education at Clongowes Wood School and later at Belvedere College and University College in Dublin. While in school, he thought he might become a priest or an opera singer (he had a fine tenor voice), but upon graduation in 1902 he turned his back, like his hero, Stephen Dedalus, on home, religion, and country. He eloped with a simple girl, Nora Barnacle, and went into voluntary, lifelong "exile" on the Continent, determined to become a writer.

Forced to support his wife and two children, Joyce nevertheless refused to write to suit the popular taste of his time. Instead he struggled for a living in Paris, Trieste, and Zurich by doing translations and reviews and by tutoring students in English. The originality of his style and his realistic, antiromantic view of Irish life, made it difficult for Joyce to get his work published.

Although he completed his volume of short stories, *Dubliners*, in 1905, it was not published until 1914. *A Portrait of the Artist as a Young Man*, which he had worked on from the beginning of his writing career, was finally published in 1916. *Ulysses*, Joyce's crowning achievement in the novel, was published only through the intervention of friends in 1922. For many years it was banned in England and the United States for its alleged obscenity. Joyce's most startlingly original work, *Finnegans Wake*, appeared in book form in 1939, although parts of it had been printed in the "little magazines" throughout the twenties and thirties. Because the increasing complexity of his style attracted only sophisticated readers, Joyce was never able to support himself and his family by his writing.

Joyce was a fantastically erudite man who was never pedantic in company, a heavy drinker who never allowed alcoholism to interfere with his regular work habits, and a professional writer totally indifferent to personal notoriety or popular success.

A highly sensitive man, Joyce was forced to endure a series of extremely painful eye operations, none of which was entirely successful. Although his last years brought him some measure of fame among his more literate contemporaries, they were clouded by his increasing blindness, concern for his mentally ill daughter, and the approach of World War II. Joyce died in Zurich on January 13, 1941, while fleeing from the Nazis.

By the Same Author

Ulysses: Ulysses is an immense and stylistically complex sequel to *Portrait of the Artist as a Young Man.* All the action of the novel takes place in Dublin on June 16, 1904. Stephen is living in a tower on the beach with a medical-student friend, Buck Mulligan. His mother has died tragically after Stephen, in his atheistic pride, has refused to give her benediction. His father, Simon Dedalus, has become a hopeless drunkard.

Closely paralleling Homer's *Odyssey,* the novel concerns itself with Stephen's search for an adequate father, just as Homer's Telemachus searches for his father, Odysseus. Stephen ultimately finds a father in Leopold Bloom, a middle-aged Dublin Jew who also wanders through Dublin trying to sell newspaper advertisements. Bloom and his sensual wife, Molly, represent a modern Odysseus and Penelope who undergo a series of erotic and comic misadventures culminating in Molly's famous long, unpunctuated monologue as she is lying in bed after midnight mulling over the events of the day.

Ulysses is even more of a technical tour de force than *A Portrait of the Artist as a Young Man.* In addition to the close parallels to Homer's *Odyssey* which govern the action of the book, *Ulysses* represents the full flowering of Joyce's stream of consciousness technique. The point of view is restricted to what is seen, thought, and remembered by the three main characters, Stephen Dedalus and Leopold and Molly

Bloom. Since everything is seen through their eyes, the reader must figure out what specific sight or memory is eliciting any particular thought. Flashbacks are used with great virtuosity, necessarily, since the "action" of the book is restricted to a single day. Finally, the novel abounds in puns and word play and alludes to actual Dublin "characters" of the period whom Joyce knew or had heard about but who are largely forgotten today.

Finnegans Wake: Even more complex than *Ulysses* in its mythological framework and verbal experimentation, Joyce's last novel follows the dreams of a single character, the Dublin public-house keeper, Humphrey Chimpden Earwicker, through a single night. The logic of the book is as difficult to follow as that of a dream. Symbolism, free association, and puns in nearly all languages make *Finnegans Wake* the most puzzling as well as the most ambitious of British novels. Earwicker, whose initials also stand for Here Comes Everybody, represents all humanity, and his dream encompasses all human history, myth, and, ultimately, experience.

South Wind

by

NORMAN DOUGLAS (1868–1952)

Main Characters

Thomas Heard—The Church of England bishop of Bompopo who unbends somewhat under the softening influence of Nepenthe's famous south wind.

Mrs. Meadows—The Bishop's cousin, living in mysterious seclusion on Nepenthe and beloved by the natives.

Mr. Muhlen—Alias Retlow, a blackmailing scoundrel come to haunt Mrs. Meadows.

Don Francesco—A fat, jolly, pleasure-loving Catholic priest.

Cornelius Van Koppen—An American millionaire who travels around the world on a yacht filled with beautiful young girls.

Sir Herbert Street—Van Koppen's pompous art expert and adviser.

Freddy Parker—The corrupt proprietor of the Alpha and Omega Club.

Mr. Keith—A rational Scotsman who enjoys the civilized pleasures of Nepenthe.

Ernest Eames—An elderly scholar-recluse who lives only to work on a new edition of Perrelli's *Antiquities*, a quaint old history of Nepenthe.

Count Caloveglia—A poor but aristocratic lover of the good things in life, especially sculpture.

Signor Malipizzo—The anticlerical, corrupt chief magistrate
of Nepenthe.
Denis Phipps—A moody young English poet, in love with
Angelina, a local serving maid.
Edgar Marten—Denis' chief rival for Angelina, a joyless,
unimaginative young geologist.
Commendatore Giustino Morena—Otherwise known as "the
assassin," a widely feared lawyer and member of the Black
Hand.

The Story

Returning to England after his largely unsuccessful efforts to
convert the heathens of Africa, Thomas Heard, the Bishop of
Bompopo, stops en route at the idyllic Mediterranean island of
Nepenthe. There he plans to pick up his cousin, Mrs.
Meadows, whose husband is in India, and take her and her
child back to England with him. On the boat the bishop meets
Mr. Muhlen, a rather mysterious and disagreeable man, and
Don Francesco, a jovial, easygoing Catholic priest who con-
firms Mr. Heard in his prejudices against Rome and Medi-
terranean frivolity.

It is Don Francesco, however, who introduces Mr. Heard
to local society, which includes a variety of eccentrics ranging
from the American Duchess of San Martino, at the top, to the
Little White Cows, a group of harmless Russian religious
fanatics led by the mystic Bazhakuloff, at, or near, the bottom.
Mr. Heard finds that not even his years spent among the
happy-go-lucky natives of Bompopo have adequately prepared him for such Nepentheans as Miss Wilberforce, an
English lady given to strong drink and undressing in public;
Ernest Eames, a hermit scholar devoting his life to producing
a new edition of a book of Nepenthean lore; Mr. Keith, the
urbane man of pleasure; and Freddy Parker who serves
atrociously adulterated liquor to the patrons of his notorious
Alpha and Omega Club.

The first days of Mr. Heard's visit are spent calling on his
elusive cousin who gives him a chilly welcome, and watching
with dismay the pagan celebration of the Festival of Saint
Dodekanus, the somewhat bogus patron saint of Nepenthe.
The even tenor of life on Nepenthe is soon disturbed, how-

ever, by a series of omens, beginning with the drying up of the famous medicinal wells and culminating in a thick, suffocating snowfall of ashes from a nearby volcano. Usually, all the Nepentheans have to contend with from the elements is the enervating south wind, or sirocco, which constantly blows from Africa. But the shower of ashes is more than anyone can bear, least of all Freddy Parker. His stepsister, a malicious old gossip, has just died, but she cannot be buried until the fall of ashes stops. To add to Freddy's troubles, he learns that the Nicaraguan minister, who gave him a sinecure as finance commissioner for Nepenthe, has been thrown out of office. Freddy may now have to look for some new source of graft.

Freddy gets the brilliant idea of enlisting the Church in behalf of his negotiations with Nicaragua. Hinting to the local parish priest, a puritanical enemy of Don Francesco, that he might be willing to become a convert to Catholicism, Freddy suggests that the priest organize a religious procession to implore Saint Dodekanus to stop the fall of volcanic ash. The priest agrees, and miraculously the ashes stop falling and are washed away by a rainstorm.

New excitement comes to Nepenthe with the arrival by yacht of Cornelius Van Koppen, a lecherous American millionaire. Van Koppen's annual visits to Nepenthe are eagerly anticipated because nearly everyone manages to extract some money from him. The parish priest always gets a contribution for unnecessary church repairs, and other Nepenthean causes are liberally financed by the shrewd and benevolent magnate. One such charity broached to Van Koppen is the founding of a rest home for Miss Wilberforce who was last seen undressing in public (contrary to her custom, in *daylight*, albeit the false daylight of the ash fall). Van Koppen, amused at the hypocritical busybodies who hope to make some dishonest money out of the rest home, replies that he will gladly give a vast sum if they can get even a tiny sum of money from Mr. Keith. He knows that his hedonistic friend will react violently to any suggestion that Miss Wilberforce's freedom be curtailed. Van Koppen is right. On the morning of Freddy Parker's step-sister's funeral, a delegation interrupts Mr. Keith at his leisurely breakfast and is sent about its business with a stern lecture on puritanical hypocrisy.

Another scheme to get at Van Koppen's money is more successful, however. Count Caloveglia, a kindly, decayed aristocrat who has but two passions in life (his daughter, Matilda, and sculpture), has not enough money for Matilda's dowry. He tells Van Koppen that he has found a rare antique statue of a faun buried in his estate on the mainland, has smuggled it past the Italian authorities, and is willing to part with it—for a price—to enhance the millionaire's art collection. Van Koppen summons his art expert, Sir Herbert Street, who pronounces the faun a genuine masterpiece of classical art. Although Van Koppen knows Count Caloveglia has sculpted the faun himself and then buried it, he is so amused at Sir Herbert's gullibility and at the count's ingenious story that he buys the piece anyway, thus providing a handsome dowry for Matilda.

Practically the only unhappy islander is young Denis Phipps, a frustrated English college student and poet who is losing out in competition for the favors of Angelina, the duchess' shapely maid. His rival, Edgar Marten, is a sour geologist, more aggressive with women than Denis is. One day Denis calls on Mr. Heard to go mountain climbing with him. Mr. Keith has told him he will get in touch with "elemental powers" atop the cliffs of Nepenthe which will give him a vision of the future, at present somewhat murky. In the blinding midday heat the two men trek up the mountain to a spot near Mrs. Meadows' villa. When they sit down to rest, Mr. Heard sees his cousin in the distance strolling along the cliffside with Mr. Muhlen.

He cannot imagine what she sees in this questionable character whose real name, it is rumored, is Retlow and who is reputed to make his living in shady ways. Suddenly the bishop is appalled to see Mrs. Meadows shove Muhlen off the cliff to his death. He later realizes that Retlow was the name of his cousin's first husband. Retlow was apparently blackmailing Mrs. Meadows because her second marriage is illegal and her child illegitimate. The bishop finds himself in a moral quandary: should he tell the authorities that he has witnessed a murder committed by his own cousin?

Formerly his course would have been clear. Duty would have come first. But the pervasive south wind of Nepenthe has had its effect on him. Now he is no longer so sure that morality is a matter of black and white. Retlow deserved to die. Mrs. Meadows deserves to live happily with her second husband and child. The bishop decides to keep silent.

When Retlow is missed, everyone assumes that he has simply sneaked off to avoid paying his bills. One day, however, a coin belonging to the departed blackmailer is found in the possession of a young cousin of the parish priest. Seeing his opportunity to harass this old enemy, Signor Malipizzo, the anticlerical Freemason chief magistrate of Nepenthe, arrests the boy and doctors the "evidence" against him.

Immediately the parish priest swings into action. He enlists the aid of the powerful Commendatore Morena, a lawyer and political bigwig who is a power both in Church politics and in the much-feared Black Hand Society. Known to his many victims as "the assassin," the great commendatore arrives at Nepenthe to defend the accused murderer. Terrified by his reputation, Signor Malipizzo immediately arrests most of the Little White Cows, too, to show that he was not prejudiced in bringing charges against the priest's cousin. His gesture of impartiality fails, however. Roused by the commendatore's highly emotional eloquence, the jury acquits the boy and everybody tacitly agrees to forget about the murder of Mr. Retlow who was, after all, only a foreigner and a Protestant at that. Justice—after the Nepenthe fashion—has been done, and Mrs. Meadows, now a free and happy woman, will never be accused of the murder she committed.

As he prepares to leave Nepenthe with his cousin, the bishop realizes that he has learned a good deal about civilized life during his two-week stay. Although the local religion is almost pagan, it keeps the natives happy—happier, in fact, than most English people. Although affairs of church and state are handled in a wildly corrupt manner, a kind of rough justice does seem to prevail. The bishop learns that people are made happy not by being harangued into feeling guilty for their pleasures all the time but by being left alone to enjoy their lives as chaotically as they choose.

Critical Opinion

South Wind is both a backward glance at Europe before World War I and a prophetic novel of the breakdown of organized religion and traditional, puritanical morality that took place in the 1920's. In form it is a series of interrelated anecdotes about Nepenthe's ancient history and current pop-

ulation of eccentrics, both local and foreign. Imitating the
early nineteenth-century novels of Thomas Love Peacock,
Douglas sets his oddly assorted characters in action, or, more
often, conversation, and sits back to watch the intellectual
sparks fly. In its technique *South Wind* also looks forward
to the iconoclastic, witty novels of Aldous Huxley.

A serious vision of life emerges, however, from the absurd
behavior of the natives and expatriates on Nepenthe. While
Douglas modeled his island on Capri, it must be remembered
that "nepenthe" is the name of a drug used by the ancients
to dull pain and bring on oblivion. In this sense, *South Wind*
is about a utopia where nobody needs to work hard or worry
much, where the climate is gentle, and where men can cultivate their leisure in a variety of urbane pursuits. The brunt
of Douglas' usually gentle satire falls on those, like Marten,
who disregard the physical beauty of life for a humorlessly
dogmatic career.

Thus Catholicism in the hands of the jovial, high-living Don
Francesco is a fine religion. It becomes odious, however, when
practiced by bluenoses like the parish priest. Agnosticism is
equally fine to Douglas when expressed in witty conversation
by Mr. Keith. In the heavy hands of the aggressive, doctrinaire
priest-baiter, Signor Malipizzo, it becomes life-denying and
absurd.

If Douglas has a central character in his gallery of eccentrics, it is Bishop Heard who learns the lesson of Nepenthe:
to be easygoing, tolerant of one another's foibles, and to enjoy
life both sensually and intellectually in the manner of the
best pagans of the past. Those who create trouble, like Mr.
Muhlen, deserve to reap trouble for their pains. Although
some of the conversations in the book are slow and outdated
in their schoolboyish irreverence, *South Wind's* wise, tolerant
vision of human eccentricity and sensuous yet witty evocation
of the best in Mediterranean culture have never been surpassed.

The Author

Norman Douglas was well equipped by temperament and
education to write a witty, erudite, and iconoclastic novel like
South Wind. Born in an ancestral castle in Scotland on Decem-

ber 8, 1868, Douglas studied languages and science in Karls-
ruhe, Germany, for a few years and then entered the British
foreign service, in which he served for three years in Russia.
Primarily interested in science—especially zoology and arche-
ology—he left the foreign service to settle with his wife and
family on the island of Capri, the model for Nepenthe. There
he wrote learned papers on science, eventually departing from
this pattern in 1911 with what was meant to be a "popular"
book, *Siren Land*. Undismayed by its lack of success, Douglas
labored on *South Wind* for several years, finishing it in 1917.
The book was highly successful, providing as it did a nostalgic
look at prewar life at its most sophisticated.

Like Mr. Keith in the novel, Douglas was a man of wide
culture and many interests. He lived the life of an English
gentleman in Capri, producing few works but indulging to
the utmost his cultivated tastes for fine wine, witty conversation, music, and the Mediterranean way of life. One of his
most engaging books is *Old Calabria* (1928), ostensibly a
travel book but actually a compendium of the Italian folklore and customs that so appealed to the author. Other typical
productions of his are his memoirs, *Looking Back* (1933),
and a posthumously published cookbook of allegedly aphro-
disiac recipes called *Love in the Kitchen*.

The only thing Norman Douglas hated was the spirit of
fanaticism, whether religious or political. Christianity and
Communism were almost equally abhorrent to him. He
managed to live as a more or less virtuous pagan, untouched
in his island paradise by the ideological strife of the twentieth
century. Douglas died on February 9, 1952, an Edwardian
gentleman to the last and a delightful anachronism in his own
time.

A Passage to India

by

E. M. FORSTER (1879–   )

Main Characters

Dr. Aziz—A sensitive, intelligent young Moslem surgeon attached to the hospital at Chandrapore.

Dr. Callendar—Aziz' coldly condescending superior.

Ronnie Heaslop—The unimaginative but decent young city magistrate of Chandrapore.

Mrs. Moore—Heaslop's mother, an open-minded Englishwoman seeing India for the first time.

Adela Quested—A plain, well-intentioned girl, engaged to Heaslop who has come to India with Mrs. Moore.

Cyril Fielding—The forty-five-year-old principal of Government College, highly suspect among the British colony for his friendliness to Indians.

Professor Narayan Godbole—A high-caste, mystical Hindu teaching at Government College.

The Story

Dining one evening with his friends, young Dr. Aziz, a lonely widower with three children, is interrupted by a summons to the hospital where he serves under the arrogant Dr. Callendar. Aziz regretfully leaves his friends and arrives by cab at the hospital, only to find that Dr. Callendar has departed without leaving him a message. To add insult to injury, just as Aziz is about to leave, his cab is requisitioned by two Englishwomen who do not even bother to thank him.

Upset at this typical treatment at the hands of the English, Aziz drops into a mosque for a moment of peace. Seeing an Englishwoman there, he shouts at her, assuming she has neglected to remove her shoes. But the Englishwoman, Mrs. Moore, is sensitive to Moslem custom, and has entered the mosque barefooted. This pleases Dr. Aziz so much that he starts a conversation with Mrs. Moore who has recently arrived in India and wants to see as much of it as possible. Dr. Aziz is pleased to find that Mrs. Moore shares his low estimate of Mrs. Callendar, the doctor's wife.

A woman in late middle age, Mrs. Moore has come to the dusty, undistinguished town of Chandrapore in order to see her son, Ronnie Heaslop, the city magistrate. She has brought with her Ronnie's rather plain friend, Adela Quested, who is determined to see the "real India," not the superficial India known to most of the British colony. To satisfy what he considers an eccentric and misguided whim, one of the club members suggests to Adela that they hold a bridge party— not to play cards, but to "bridge the gap," so to speak, between East and West.

The bridge party is a dismal failure because, with the exception of Adela, most of the English condescend haughtily to their Indian guests who are not even allowed inside the club house. Instead, the Indians stand, deeply embarrassed, on the lawn, as some of the Anglo-Indian matrons make small talk with them. Dr. Aziz refuses to attend. At the party Adela meets Mr. Fielding, principal of Government College and one of the few Englishmen in Chandrapore genuinely sympathetic to the Indians.

Fielding invites Adela and Mrs. Moore to have tea at his house. He also invites some genuine Indians, Dr. Aziz, a Moslem, and Professor Godbole, a Hindu. Fielding and Dr. Aziz take to one another immediately, and everything seems to be going well until Heaslop shows up to escort the ladies to a polo match. He disapproves of social contact between English and Indians for, although Heaslop is basically a good and sympathetic young man, his experience in meting out justice to Indians has soured him. He curtly interrupts a Hindu song

Professor Godbole is singing and takes Adela and Mrs. Moore away with him.

Adela is annoyed with Heaslop's rude behavior at the tea party and tells him she can never become engaged to him. Ronnie takes the announcement in stride and proposes an automobile ride in the car of the wealthy Nawab Bahadur. In the dark the car runs over an animal. The accident draws Ronnie and Adela together again, and they decide to become engaged after all.

Meanwhile, ignoring Ronnie's stern injunction to have no social contacts with the natives, Adela has accepted an invitation extended to her and Mrs. Moore by Dr. Aziz to visit the celebrated Marabar Caves. Aziz himself has never seen these caves but is eager to show off India to Mrs. Moore. The caves are the most interesting spot near Chandrapore.

Disaster plagues the expedition from the start. First Fielding and Professor Godbole, who were supposed to come along, miss their train because of the professor's extensive morning prayer. The day is very hot, and after seeing one cave, Mrs. Moore begins to feel ill and decides not to see any more. She is disturbed by the number of native servants hired for the occasion who crowd into the cave with her and by the hollow, meaningless echo that seems to mock her.

While Mrs. Moore sits on a rock outside, Adela and Aziz visit the other caves. They become separated for a moment. When next he sees Adela she is racing hysterically down the hill to join a friend, Miss Derek, in a motorcar. Fielding, who had arrived with Miss Derek, returns to Chandrapore with Mrs. Moore and Aziz.

When Aziz arrives at the train station, he is placed under arrest. Adela has charged that he attacked her in the cave, breaking her field glasses. Indeed, Aziz had seen the broken glasses lying on the ground, had picked them up, and is found with them in his possession. Although Fielding insists the charge is nonsense, Aziz is put into jail. The English colony is up in arms at the alleged affront to their visitor who is now suffering a nervous breakdown.

The trial sharpens the animosity between English and Indians as ranks draw together behind Adela and behind Dr. Aziz. When Mrs. Moore tells her son that she is sure Aziz would never have attacked Adela, she is shipped off to England to visit her two younger children. Ever since her experience at the caves, Mrs. Moore is a changed woman. She takes no more interest in the doings of her son or of anyone, but broods about the nothingness of existence as symbolized by the meaningless echo she heard in the cave.

When Fielding supports Dr. Aziz, he is ostracized by the English community and excluded from the English club. Because Ronnie is so personally involved, the case is presided over by his subordinate, a capable but timorous Indian justice, Mr. Das. The English colony crowds the steamy courtroom and tries to intimidate Mr. Das. When the Indians learn that Mrs. Moore has suddenly left India, despite the terrible heat in the Indian Ocean, they assume she has been spirited away because she would have testified for Dr. Aziz. A strange, semi-religious chant is heard outside the courtroom as the Indians transmute Mrs. Moore's name into that of a goddess, "Esmiss Esmoor," over and over again.

When Adela is finally put on the witness stand, she breaks down. She is by no means sure that it was Dr. Aziz who followed her into the cave; in fact she is not sure that the whole dreadful experience was not just a nightmare. The trial, of course, ends abruptly. The English colony is furious. Dr. Aziz' lawyer, a violent Anglophobe, demands heavy damages from Adela. In the victory celebration among the Indians after the trial, Fielding is separated from Aziz and thrown together with Adela, to whom he gives sanctuary at his college.

Only after the trial is it learned that Mrs. Moore has died aboard ship, embittered and disillusioned. Adela then leaves for home, her engagement to Ronnie terminated. Fielding succeeds in convincing the now bitterly anti-English Dr. Aziz not to sue Adela for damages.

Two years later, Aziz has left the British state of Chandrapore for an independent Hindu state where he is court physician to an aged rajah. Fielding has returned to England and has written frequently to his old friend, but Dr. Aziz is furious with him because he assumes Fielding has returned home in order to marry Adela on the money that was rightfully Aziz'. Professor Godbole, who in his spiritual indifference to worldly matters refused to take sides during the trial, has poisoned Aziz' mind against Fielding, telling him that the schoolmaster has married Adela when in fact he has married Mrs. Moore's daughter, Stella.

One night during a Hindu religious celebration, Fielding comes to visit Aziz accompanied by Stella and her brother Ralph. Aziz is cold to him even when he learns the truth about Fielding's marriage.

But after the festival, during which Aziz' potentate dies, the doctor and Fielding take a ride together through country-side strange to both of them—to Fielding as an Englishman and to Aziz as a Moslem. They become reconciled to each other although Aziz realizes that their friendship is doomed by India herself. For Fielding, by his marriage, is now committed to the English colony he once despised, and Aziz has become increasingly Indian as a result of his experience during the trial. The friends part, never to see each other again.

Critical Opinion

The title *A Passage to India* comes from Walt Whitman's exuberantly optimistic poem of that name. In a sense, the novel is a wry, ironic commentary on the American poet's hopeful nineteenth-century vision of a world unified by technical progress. Hailing the passage to India made possible by the building of the Suez Canal, Whitman had bravely intoned:

"Nature and Man shall be disjoin'd and diffused no more,
The true son of God shall absolutely fuse them."

And earlier in the poem, Whitman prophesied:

"All affection shall be fully responded to. . . ."

Early in the novel these sentiments are adopted by the liberal Cyril Fielding, who believes that the world "is a globe of men who are trying to reach one another and can best do so by the help of good will plus culture and intelligence." But it is a creed, Forster comments, "ill suited to Chandrapore." The tragedy of the novel lies in the breakdown of communication, both between races and between individuals.

"Only connect!" was Forster's plea in his earlier novel *Howards End*. But more connections are severed than made between the people in Forster's essentially pessimistic work.

The trouble is not merely a basic antipathy and misunderstanding between races, however, because there are also failures to connect among the English and among the Indians. Ronnie Heaslop does not understand his mother's bleak view of the world; Fielding is cut off from his own countrymen because of his humane view of the Indians; and Professor Godbole, a Hindu mystic, refuses to aid Dr. Aziz, the Moslem rationalist. Everywhere Forster sees division between people as well as between races and cultures. Tenuous friendships, like that between Fielding and Aziz, break down under the pressure exerted on both sides.

The center of the novel is in the mysterious caves at Marabar, those uncharted jests of nature that divide people and return only a hollow, echoing laugh to whatever man tries to communicate. To the sensitive Mrs. Moore who has tried to love and understand people, the caves' echo seems to say: "Pathos, piety, courage—they exist, but are identical, and so is filth. Everything exists, nothing has value."

Whatever one says in the caves, the answer is the same: the meaningless "ou-boum" of the echo. Man, Mrs. Moore realizes, is alone in an uncaring universe. All he has for comfort is his fellow man. When Mrs. Moore realizes that the divisions between people cannot be bridged, she dies.

Thus for all its sparkling wit and satiric observation of the social mores of Englishmen and Indians, *A Passage to India* is profoundly pessimistic about the inability of man to communicate with or understand his fellows.

The Author

One of the famous "Bloomsbury Group" of Cambridge-oriented intellectuals which included Virginia Woolf, Lytton Strachey, and T. S. Eliot, *Edward Morgan Forster* was born in 1879 and attended the Tonbridge School and King's College, Cambridge. After college, he went to Italy, which provided the background for two of his early novels, *Where Angels Fear to Tread* (1905) and *A Room with a View* (1908). Quietly effective, with moments of high comedy, these novels deal with the cultural barrier between Englishmen and Italians, just as *A Passage to India* later dealt with misunderstandings between Englishmen and Indians.

In 1907 Forster returned to England, which was the scene for two other novels, *The Longest Journey* (1907) and *Howards End* (1910), his most important work up to that time. Four years after his return to England, Forster set out for India with a Cambridge preceptor and friend, Goldsworthy Lowes Dickinson, whose biography Forster later wrote. A second visit, in 1921, strengthened the impression India had made on Forster. In 1924, after a lapse of fourteen years, he wrote *A Passage to India,* the last novel he published.

Untroubled by financial problems, Forster has published only these five novels in his long lifetime. The meticulous craftsmanship that went into them has made them all modern classics, especially the rich and haunting *A Passage to India,* which stands with *Kim* as Britain's finest perception of the subcontinent she once ruled.

But if Forster's production of novels has been comparatively slight, he has been a prolific essayist. In 1927 he was invited to deliver the annual Clark lectures at Cambridge. These he later turned into his remarkable treatise on fiction, *Aspects of the Novel.* Two collections of essays and reviews, *Abinger Harvest* and *Two Cheers for Democracy,* have also appeared over the years.

An honorary Fellow of King's College, Forster has spent most of his later years residing at his alma mater. Except for occasional lectures and conferences, he has not officially taught there. Ever since his early days in the heady intellectual atmosphere of Bloomsbury, Forster has aligned himself with liberal causes. An outspoken enemy of fascism, he delivered valuable radio talks to India during World War II, enlisting his former friends behind the British cause.

By the Same Author

Where Angels Fear to Tread: Forster's first novel announces most of his future themes. The conflict between English and Italians is represented by the ghastly Mrs. Herriton and her silly, widowed, daughter-in-law, Lilia, on one side, and by the handsome, charming, but unconventional (by English standards) son of an Italian dentist, Gino, on the other. Gino and Lilia marry and have a child, but Lilia's life with her Italian husband is miserable. Mrs. Herriton's son, Philip, is sent to investigate. When Lilia dies in childbirth, the Herritons descend on Italy en masse, in order to "rescue" the baby from Gino. The novel reaches a tragic climax as the baby is killed in an accident while being kidnapped by Mrs. Herriton's odious, small-minded daughter, Harriet.

Howards End: Howards End is the country home near London of the Wilcox family, whose lives become intertwined with those of two intellectual girls, Helen and Margaret Schlegel. Mrs. Wilcox dies, leaving Howards End to Margaret Schlegel, but the family does not acknowledge the bequest and disapproves when the widowed Mr. Wilcox eventually marries Margaret. Finally, after a family tragedy involving the death of Helen Schlegel's lover, a social inferior named Leonard Bast, Margaret gets the mansion, as had been originally intended. *Howards End* is chiefly concerned with class differences in prewar England and with the snobbery and unintentional cruelty these differences produce.

Mrs. Dalloway

by

VIRGINIA WOOLF (1882–1941)

Main Characters

Clarissa Dalloway—A sensitive, imaginative, middle-aged London society woman.

Richard Dalloway—Her husband, a semi-successful member of Parliament.

Peter Walsh—Mrs. Dalloway's former suitor, recently returned after five years in India.

Elizabeth—Mrs. Dalloway's impressionable seventeen-year-old daughter.

Doris Kilman—Elizabeth's embittered, ugly tutor, a religious zealot.

Sally Seton—Mrs. Dalloway's former friend, once full of life and high spirits but now quite matronly.

Septimus Warren Smith—A shell-shocked war veteran haunted by his inability to feel emotion.

Lucrezia—Smith's troubled, affectionate Italian wife.

Sir William Bradshaw—A fashionable psychiatrist, pompous and overbearing.

The Story

One fine, hot June morning Clarissa Dalloway emerges from her handsome home in Westminster to go shopping. She is giving an important dinner party that night. On the street she meets an old friend, Hugh Whitbread, now grown fat and rather pompous. Hugh is in town, Mrs. Dalloway knows, to consult a doctor about his constantly ailing wife, Evelyn. Clarissa wonders what sort of present would be appropriate to take to Evelyn in the nursing home. But first she must buy some flowers for her party.

While she is ordering flowers, Mrs. Dalloway sees a grand limousine pull up to the curb. Its drawn curtains arouse the curiosity of passers-by. Is the Queen inside or an important cabinet minister—perhaps even the Prime Minister? Mrs. Dalloway's husband is a member of Parliament, but for some reason his career has never advanced as it should have. He will never be a member of the cabinet. He is a good man, but rather stuffy and unimaginative. When the limousine pulls into Buckingham Palace, Mrs. Dalloway is sure the Queen is inside.

A plane flies overhead skywriting an advertisement for some toffee. Skywriting is still a novelty in the twenties, and Mrs. Dalloway feels at one with all the Londoners craning to see the marvel.

The bustle and spectacle of London remind her of her past. She was a well-bred girl whose father's house in the country was always filled with guests. Among these, Clarissa's favorite was Sally Seton, a lively, iconoclastic girl on whom Clarissa had a schoolgirl crush. Sally was careless and mischievous. When she made fun of the stuffy Richard Dalloway, with whom Clarissa had fallen in love one evening, the friendship cooled. Now the Dalloways have an almost grown-up daughter, Elizabeth, whose schoolgirl crush on Doris Kilman, an odious, embittered, religious fanatic, worries Mrs. Dalloway.

Before she married Richard Dalloway, Clarissa had been in love with handsome, brilliant Peter Walsh, but he always mocked her family's pretensions and sided with Sally Seton against Richard Dalloway. Then he had left for India, and Clarissa had heard he had gotten married en route. All these memories of the past bring a warm feeling of nostalgia to Clarissa as she is enjoying her shopping, the fine weather, and the thought of the party she is to give.

But another soul wandering the streets of London is not so happy. Septimus Warren Smith is a shell-shocked war veteran with an Italian wife, Lucrezia. Smith is haunted by the memory of Evans, his great friend and commanding officer in the war. Shortly before the armistice, Evans had been killed, and Smith is shocked to realize that he really did not feel one way or another about his closest friend's death.

He himself, idealistically enlisting early in the war, showed valor in action, fighting, as he believed, for the England of Shakespeare. Now he is obsessed with the vileness of human beings and is haunted by the dead Evans. His wife, Lucrezia, lost in foreign London, does not know what to do. Smith, who married her soon after the war, refuses to have any children. Instead, he broods about life and death. The bluff, hearty Dr. Holmes, who is treating him, has warned Lucrezia that at all costs he must avoid shock and excitement. Septimus loathes the insensitive, dull doctor and refuses to see him.

Meanwhile, Clarissa Dalloway has returned home with her flowers to learn that her husband has been invited—without her—to have lunch with Millicent Bruton, a clever, ruthless woman. Mrs. Dalloway is hurt at not being invited (Lady Bruton's luncheons are reputed to be so very entertaining) but she realizes that Lady Bruton cannot abide the wives of her men friends, especially if she thinks they have held their husbands back politically.

While she is sewing up her dress, Mrs. Dalloway receives a surprise visit from Peter Walsh, just back after five years in India. He has not changed at all: he still makes fun of Clarissa for being so caught up with society. He tells her that he has fallen in love with Daisy, a married woman in India, and is in London to consult with lawyers about her divorce. He has been divorced, his career is a shambles, and he hopes that Hugh Whitbread will help find him a job in London to support Daisy and her two children.

When Clarissa introduces Peter to her daughter, Elizabeth, Peter realizes what he has missed in life. But when Clarissa reminds him not to forget her dinner party, Peter Walsh suddenly sees her life, so filled with social events, as empty and trivial.

At Lady Bruton's luncheon, meanwhile, Richard Dalloway and Hugh Whitbread help their hostess compose a letter to the *Times* about some petty matter. Lady Bruton is all for political "causes," but she is too scatterbrained even to write a letter to a newspaper. Hugh Whitbread composes an appropriately pompous and cliché-ridden letter for her.

Meanwhile Lucrezia is deeply worried about her husband. Because he has refused to see the jovial Dr. Holmes, Lucrezia has engaged the services of the wealthy, impressive Harley Street psychiatrist, Sir William Bradshaw; but even the innocent Lucrezia can see that Bradshaw is a selfish, unsympathetic man. Sir William suggests that, to avoid the possibility of suicide, Septimus may have to go to a rest home in the country—where Lucrezia cannot join him—as long as his fits of depression persist.

Late that afternoon, when Dr. Holmes blunders his way upstairs to see Smith in his apartment, the haunted veteran leaps out of the window, impaling himself on the rusty grating outside, and dies. Dr. Holmes cannot understand why a young man with a beautiful wife and a brilliant future should do such a rash, unnatural thing. Lucrezia is completely crushed by her husband's suicide.

During the same afternoon, Doris Kilman comes to take Elizabeth shopping. Mrs. Dalloway cannot help hating the woman Richard hired as a tutor for their daughter. Miss Kilman is a poor woman who despises and envies the Dalloways for their wealth and easy life. A highly intelligent but unprepossessing student of modern history, she had lost her post in a school during the war because of her German ancestry and sympathies. Ugly and lonely, Miss Kilman has turned to religion for consolation. The liberal, easygoing Mrs. Dalloway is shocked to find that Miss Kilman is indoctrinating Elizabeth in church ritual. "Love and religion!" Mrs. Dalloway muses. "How detestable they are!" Why cannot people leave others alone, lead their own lives, and not impose their wills on others? Knowing she is wrong to hate anyone, Mrs. Dalloway nevertheless finds herself loathing the unfortunate Doris Kilman.

By now the hour for the party has arrived. After some initial awkwardness, it proves a great success. The Prime Minister's arrival causes quite a stir. Everyone agrees that Clarissa Dalloway is a remarkable hostess.

Only Peter Walsh is unhappy. An overwhelming sense of age comes over him when he meets Sally Seton, now Lady Rossetter and the mother of five sons. The once vivacious, iconoclastic Sally has become selfish and class-conscious. She still despises Clarissa for marrying the socially acceptable but unromantic Richard Dalloway. Peter, who had reveled in his return to civilized London, begins to wonder if he can bear society again.

In the midst of the party, Sir William Bradshaw and his wife arrive. They are late, he explains, because one of his patients, a war veteran, has just committed suicide. Perhaps, he suggests to Richard Dalloway, Parliament ought to take up the matter of veterans suffering from delayed shell-shock.

Wealthy and self-assured, Sir William has no personal sympathy for the dead Septimus Smith; but when Clarissa hears the story, she feels a sudden sense of identification with the haunted youth although she had never known him. Her life, too, she perceives in an instant, has been a failure; she completely understands any suicide. But after most of the guests have gone, Peter Walsh comes to her and senses the excitement in her presence that he had felt long before, realizing that he is still in love with the aging but still beautiful Clarissa Dalloway.

Critical Opinion

Like Joyce's *Ulysses, Mrs. Dalloway* takes place in a single day and is narrated by means of the so-called "stream of consciousness" of several individual characters. The principal interior monologues are those of Clarissa Dalloway herself, sensitive, questioning, in love with life but aware of failure; and the haunted Septimus Warren Smith whom Clarissa doesn't know and never meets, except in the callous description given by Sir William Bradshaw at her party.

Of all the people in London, it is, nevertheless, to the young veteran that Mrs. Dalloway feels herself closest in spirit. In a sense both are searching for some clue to the meaning of life, something to carry them from moment to moment. Both fail in this quest. Septimus cannot communicate his feeling of guilt and emptiness to his sympathetic but foreign wife; Mrs. Dalloway cannot convey her intense, lonely perceptions of the world around her to her good-natured, practical husband.

Aligned against these two lonely people who never meet are the crass, deformed spirits of Sir William Bradshaw and

Doris Kilman. Although they, too, never meet, they are soul-destroyers for Septimus and Mrs. Dalloway. Both are egoists who seek to impose their wills on others: Sir William on his unfortunate patients and Miss Kilman on the naïve, adolescent Elizabeth Dalloway.

Various technical devices of great brilliance and ingenuity tie together the monologues and destinies of the different characters. The chimes of Big Ben tolling each hour of the day, for instance, are heard by all—each in his isolation. (Virginia Woolf's original title for the book was *The Hours*.) The various characters stop to look at the royal limousine and at the skywriting plane, and these symbolic events also help tie them together. At one point Peter Walsh sees a little girl run crying to Lucrezia Smith; he doesn't know who Lucrezia is, but he can sense her suffering. These devices are not merely mechanical. They serve to stress a major theme of the novel: the paradox that, although we seem utterly alone, a common destiny binds us together. The best people are those who are most keenly aware of their links with the rest of humanity, however much suffering this awareness may entail. The only "villains" in life are the egoists who, like Sir William Bradshaw, are oblivious and think themselves superior to their fellow men.

The Author

Virginia Woolf was born in London in 1882, the daughter of the celebrated Sir Leslie Stephen, a scholar and critic who edited the *Cornhill Magazine* and the vast *Dictionary of National Biography*. The American poet James Russell Lowell was her godfather. In her father's home she knew Hardy, Ruskin, Stevenson, and Meredith.

A frail, shy girl, Virginia educated herself in her father's massive library. In 1912 she married Leonard Woolf, a brilliant journalist who had just returned from Ceylon after seven years in the civil service. Five years later, the Woolfs, who were part of the artistic coterie of Bloomsbury, set up their own hand printing press dedicated to publishing in beautiful format the works of promising, unknown writers. This later became one of the most important of English publishing companies, introducing Freud, among other luminaries, to the English reader.

Mrs. Woolf's own career began in 1915 with *The Voyage Out,* a novel considerably influenced by her friend E. M. Forster. This was followed in 1919 by *Night and Day* and in 1922 by *Jacob's Room,* her first really characteristic novel.

The 1920's were her most productive years. *Mrs. Dalloway* (1925), *To the Lighthouse* (1927), and the strange, esoteric fantasy *Orlando* (1928) brought her fame and prestige among sophisticated readers. Her later novel *The Waves* (1931), her most experimental work, was followed by the more traditional *The Years* (1937), a novel about an English middle-class family somewhat in the tradition of Galsworthy.

Mrs. Woolf was also an ardent feminist, as *A Room of One's Own* (1929) and *Three Guineas* (1938) demonstrate. A prolific and sensitive critic, she contributed frequently to the *Times Literary Supplement.* Some of her best literary criticism appeared in *The Common Reader* (1925). She conceived of herself as a spokesman for her generation and was outspoken in her derision of such Edwardian forebears as Bennett, Galsworthy, and Wells.

Always sensitive and high-strung, Mrs. Woolf suffered a severe nervous breakdown in her youth. When World War II came, her nerves snapped again. Fearing a second breakdown and unable to accept the carnage of another war, Virginia Woolf drowned herself in a river near her country home in Sussex on March 28, 1941.

By the Same Author

To the Lighthouse: One of Mrs. Woolf's most psychologically and technically complex novels, *To the Lighthouse* tells of the Ramsay family, who spend their summers on a remote island in the Hebrides. The novel is divided into three parts. The first and longest is a detailed account of the happenings of a single summer; the second is a highly impressionistic rendering of the passage of time, during which Mrs. Ramsay dies; and the third is the story of a meeting years later of the principal characters. The lighthouse is the symbolic point about which the novel revolves. At the beginning, young James Ramsay longs to go there on an expedition but is frustrated by his egocentric father, who (like Sir Leslie Stephen) is a famous scholar. By the end of the book young James, now more compassionate and understanding of his father, finally makes the passage across the choppy water to the lighthouse, and symbolically achieves maturity through his understanding of his oedipal relationship with his parents.

Orlando: Orlando is at once one of the most baffling and one of the most delightful of Mrs. Woolf's novels. Based on the family heritage of her friend, Vita Sackville-West, *Orlando* is the fantastic tale of a sixteen-year-old Elizabethan boy who lives through the centuries, is transformed into a girl during the Victorian period, and finally, as a woman of thirty-six, glimpses a plane in the sky in 1928. Essentially, the tale of *Orlando* is an imaginative chronicle of English literary and social history filtered through the sensibilities of a poetic youth. The change in sex, for instance, symbolically represents the effeminate character of Victorian literature as opposed to the rugged masculinity of the seventeenth and eighteenth centuries. *Orlando* is a unique work—part novel, part poetic fantasy, part astute literary criticism.

Point Counter Point

by

ALDOUS HUXLEY (1894–1963)

Main Characters

Philip Quarles—A coldly intellectual "novelist of ideas."

Elinor Quarles—Philip's dissatisfied wife.

Little Phil—The Quarles' artistically precocious son.

John Bidlake—Elinor's father, a great but selfish painter, a cantankerous and lascivious man.

Walter Bidlake—Elinor's brother, the weakly romantic staff member of a pretentious magazine, *The Literary World*.

Marjorie Carling—Walter's self-pitying mistress.

Lucy Tantamount—Walter Bidlake's beautiful and amoral mistress.

Mark Rampion—Artist and writer, he sees himself as the natural man unfettered by convention.

Denis Burlap—The sanctimonious, lecherous editor of *The Literary World*.

Beatrice Gilray—A rich, repressed woman in love with Burlap.

Maurice Spandrell—A melodramatic cynic and wastrel who has never forgiven his mother for her second marriage.

Illidge—An ugly Communist biologist who aids Lucy's father in his research.

Everard Webley—The leader of a neo-fascist movement, the Brotherhood of British Freemen.

The Story

Walter Bidlake, son of the great old painter John Bidlake by his third marriage, is bored and unhappy with his pregnant mistress, Marjorie Carling. Walter stole Marjorie from her religious fanatic husband, but now, disillusioned with her self-pitying pseudo-culture, he has fallen madly in love with Lucy Tantamount, a rich, beautiful nymphomaniac. Despite Marjorie's pleadings, Walter leaves her to go to a party at Tantamount House.

There he meets his father, who despises him as a weakling, and his pious, penny-pinching employer, Denis Burlap, editor of *The Literary World*. Lucy's father, an absent-minded scientist, makes a brief and ludicrous appearance with his assistant, Illidge, while the guests are listening to Bach's *B Minor Suite for Flute and Strings*.

Bored by the pretentious party conversation, Walter pries Lucy away from the other guests and spirits her off to Sbisa's, a fashionable Soho restaurant where the intellectuals and bohemians congregate nightly. Walter wants desperately to have Lucy for himself, but she flirtatiously insists on staying at Sbisa's with the group which includes the unhappy cynic Spandrell and some worthless hangers-on in the world of art. Miserable, Walter goes home to Marjorie who nags him about giving up Lucy and trying to get a raise in salary from Burlap.

Meanwhile Walter's sister, Elinor, is in India with her husband, Philip Quarles. Their little son, Phil, is staying in England with his grandmother and a nurse, Miss Fulkes. The Quarleses are preparing to leave India. Elinor once again tries to get her husband to pay her some attention, but he is engrossed with a notebook he is keeping in preparation for writing a novel very much like *Point Counter Point*.

Although Walter fails to get a raise from Burlap who is more interested in seducing the rich Beatrice Gilray than in being honest with his employees, he does make Lucy his mistress. Their affair is short-lived. Lucy goes off to Paris in search of more piquant amorous adventures, leaving Walter with the ever-whining Marjorie.

Philip and Elinor Quarles return to England to find their son a precocious, artistically gifted young boy. He evidently takes after his maternal grandfather, John Bidlake. The return home is marred, however, because Philip's father, Sidney Quarles (a pompous, stuffy failure who has been pretending to work on a giant history of democracy), has really been using his visits to the British Museum as a cover for an affair with a cheap little cockney girl named Gladys. One day Gladys appears at the Quarles estate and announces that she is pregnant. Philip is given the unpleasant task of placating her since his father has retreated from his responsibility into a morass of self-pity. Philip, who cannot bear any emotional contact with other people, least of all his social inferiors, delegates the problem to his lawyer.

On her return to England, Elinor's life is complicated, too. Despairing of ever getting her husband interested in her, she begins to see Everard Webley, the magnetic, egocentric leader of the Brotherhood of British Freemen, a neo-fascistic organization devoted to suppressing the working class. In the past, Elinor has always rejected Webley's advances. Now she finds herself more and more fascinated by this dynamic, aggressive man of power and action, the complete opposite of her abstracted, intellectual husband.

The only people in the London literary and social set who seem happy are Mark and Mary Rampion. Mark was a talented lower-class boy when he fell in love with the aristocratic Mary. Their marriage has been a success, despite all predictions, and Mark has become a well-known painter and writer. Contemptuous of the superficiality of London life, Rampion believes in going back to nature. He believes real civilization will come when the instincts are given equal rein with the mind. He continually baits Burlap who conceals his lechery behind high spiritual talk. Burlap, indeed, is writing a popular book on St. Francis while endeavoring to seduce the skittish, repressed Beatrice.

A friend of Mark Rampion's, Maurice Spandrell, is perhaps the most desperately unhappy frequenter of Sbisa's restaurant. Plunged into melodramatic adolescent despair when his doting mother married a gruff, insensitive military man, Spandrell is totally cynical and nihilistic. Sponging off his mother, he lives in squalor, does nothing, and delights only in puncturing his friends' illusions and in subjecting innocent working girls to obscene rites.

One evening Elinor is preparing for a tryst with Everard Webley at her London flat. She receives a telegram telling her that little Phil is sick, and rushes back to the country, asking Spandrell to phone Webley that their appointment is off. Spandrell instead calls Illidge, a poor, unprepossessing biologist, a Communist who has been a bitter foe of Webley ever since he was roughed up by some of Webley's green-uniformed followers.

When Webley arrives at Elinor's flat, he is bludgeoned to death by Spandrell and Illidge, who then hide the body in the trunk of Webley's car and park it in a busy section of London. Elinor, meanwhile, on returning home, is shocked to find that little Phil is suffering horribly from meningitis. Eventually she is joined in her bedside vigil by her husband who resents having been called away from his intellectual society in London. Also staying with the Quarleses is old John Bidlake. Suffering from cancer, the painter has come home to die, though he has seen his wife, Elinor's mother, only intermittently through the years. Old Bidlake superstitiously pins his hopes for his own health on his grandson's recovery.

After days and nights of agony, little Phil dies. His guilt-ridden parents decide to travel abroad again. The news that Webley had been killed on his way to meet her, fills Elinor with more guilt and remorse. Her brother Walter is also unhappy. After inviting him to meet her in Madrid, Lucy has written a cruel letter from Paris informing him that she will stay there with her muscular Italian lover. She vividly describes their lovemaking to the wretched Walter who finally goes with Marjorie to Philip's mother's house where the elder Mrs. Quarles preaches religious resignation to Marjorie.

The police have been unable to solve Webley's murder. But one day Spandrell, disgusted with life, writes an anonymous letter to Webley's organization, informing them that the murderer of their leader can be found the following afternoon at his address. Then he buys a phonograph and a recording of Beethoven's *A Minor String Quartet,* which he insists on playing for the Rampions as a proof of the existence of God. Mark Rampion is unimpressed by the spiritual music. While they are listening, there is a knock on the door. Spandrell answers it and is mowed down by the guns of the British Freemen.

Spandrell's death is ironically counterbalanced by Burlap's ultimate success in seducing Beatrice. The editor's joy reaches its apex as he and his rich mistress take their bath together like little children.

Critical Opinion

"Novel of ideas," Philip Quarles writes in his notebook. "The character of each personage must be implied, as far as possible, in the ideas of which he is the mouthpiece. . . . The great defect of the novel of ideas is that it's a made-up affair. . . . Living with monsters becomes rather tiresome in the long run."

Like Gide's *The Counterfeiters, Point Counter Point* is a kaleidoscopic novel much like the one Philip is thinking of writing. And like *The Counterfeiters,* Huxley's work is constructed as a novel within a novel. In fact, it is a novel about a novelist writing a novel about a novelist—as involuted as a series of Chinese boxes. Huxley moves rapidly from one set of characters to another, all of whose lives at some point impinge on each other. And in the process, he applies the contrapuntal techniques of music, especially the theme and variations form, to fiction. The theme is sexual desire and unfulfillment. The variations are played by the different characters.

Thus Walter loves Lucy hopelessly, just as Marjorie loves him hopelessly. Elinor loves her husband but is willing to be seduced by Webley who really loves only his own power. Spandrell's love for his mother has soured into general hatred of women, political nihilism, and self-destructiveness. Burlap tries to conceal his lust with piety; Lucy's father has sublimated sex into science; and old John Bidlake is openly promiscuous but cannot face death. Only Mark Rampion, whose character and ideas are based on those of Huxley's friend D. H. Lawrence, gives sex its proper place in life.

Speaking through the characters as they interact with each

other, Huxley gives the reader a panoramic view of the ideas and mores of the London sophisticates in the years just following World War I. Rootless and overcivilized, their lives consist of a series of usually sordid or ludicrous erotic adventures which generally end unhappily.

For all its nihilistic wit, erudition, and satiric puncturing of society's hypocrisies and superficialities, *Point Counter Point* attains a genuine emotional power rare in satire. Although most of the characters are indeed the "monsters" Philip Quarles predicted they would have to be, they are fascinating monsters. The play of wit and ideas in this immensely learned novel is constantly beguiling to the alert, sophisticated reader.

Brave New World

by

ALDOUS HUXLEY

Main Characters

Bernard Marx—A highly intelligent misfit in the Brave New World, shy with girls and bullied by his fellow workers.

Lenina Crowne—Promiscuous and "pneumatic" worker in the London Hatchery and Conditioning Center.

Fanny Crowne—Not related to Lenina, but a friend and confidante.

Henry Foster—An enthusiastic scientist working in the Hatchery.

The Director—A pompous man of power in the Brave New World.

Mustapha Mond—Urbane and sophisticated, a former physicist who is now one of the ten World Controllers.

John—A Shakespeare-quoting "savage" discovered on a New Mexico reservation.

Linda—John's vulgar mother.

Popé—Linda's Indian lover.

Helmholtz Watson—A poet friend of Bernard's and John's.

The Story

Proudly the pompous Director of the Central London Hatchery and Conditioning Center is showing the plant to a group of avid young students. The year is 632 After Ford, for time in the Brave New World is measured from the epoch-making discovery of the Model T Ford and mass-production assembly methods. In the hatchery, people are being mass-produced by artificial insemination and chemically conditioned to fit into the rigidly ordered hierarchy that society has become.

The Director explains that if society is to achieve its goals—Community, Identity, and Stability—there is no room for individual differences. From the fetal stage on, people are to take their predestined places in a society that ranges from Alpha Plus, the highly intelligent leaders, to Epsilon Minus Morons, the ill-shaped, ape-like goons who do the dirty work.

One of the great inventions that has made this ultra-scientific planning possible, the Director points out, is the Bokanovsky Process by means of which up to ninety-six identical twins can be produced from a single fertilized egg, thus ensuring maximum conformity. As the students assiduously take notes, the Director, now joined by his eager protegé, Henry Foster, and by one of the ten all-powerful World Controllers, the brilliant Mustapha Mond, takes them on a tour of the Conditioning Center. Here, from earliest infancy, babies are taught to keep their places in society and to repress their individualistic instincts.

Mustapha Mond lectures the students on the advantages of a totally controlled society in which such individual passions as love have given way to communal spirit and casual promiscuity. The dirtiest words in the Brave New World are "mother" and "father" because, Mond explains, in the bad old days before artificial insemination and conditioned, communal childhood, there was actually intense, private love between individuals, which kept society in a chaotic state. Now that everything is planned and ordered, he boasts, people are much happier.

One person who is not happier is Bernard Marx, a brilliant but intensely shy and misanthropic scientist. The popular theory is that too much alcohol was accidentally put into Bernard's blood-surrogate when he was a fetus. So instead of being as handsome, outgoing, and casually sensual as all the other Alphas, Bernard is morose, introverted, and dwarf-like. Because he is so peculiar, he attracts the attention of Lenina Crowne, a superficial, "pneumatically" fleshy girl who has been having an affair with Mr. Foster, one of the scientists working in the hatchery. Lenina's chum, Fanny, cautions her that remaining faithful to one man is frowned upon. Promiscuity is the order of the day in the Brave New World.

Since he occupies a high position in the intellectual ranks, Bernard has access to one of the few reservations left in the world where people are allowed to live as savages, untouched by the hypercivilization of Europe. His offer to take Lenina to New Mexico on a weekend visit to such a reservation intrigues her. Off they go to Malpais, a forbidding mesa in the desert where the Indians live in the squalid chaos they have always known.

At first, Lenina is horrified by the absence of creature comforts. There are no feelies (an especially titillating kind of movie), no cleanliness, and no great consumption of products, as in England. When a garment develops holes, it is mended instead of thrown away. Worst of all, she has forgotten her supply of soma, the universally popular tranquilizer that has taken the place of alcohol and drugs.

Watching the Indians do a wild and exotic rain dance, Bernard and Lenina meet a young man named John who speaks beautiful but rather stilted English and is always quoting Shakespeare. John is the son of Linda, a blowzy, middle-aged woman, brought to New Mexico years before by the Director of Hatcheries. As a result of a momentary lapse in contraception she bore his son. Deserted by the Director, Linda was adopted by the reservation where she took a succession of lovers, including Popé, a wild-eyed, passionate Indian keenly resented by her son.

John's position on the reservation is ambiguous. Born to white, highly civilized parents, he has been brought up part a savage, part an intelligent, if self-taught, being. He immediately falls in love with Lenina, but because of his puritanical, "savage" morality, he fails to do anything about it. Bernard, whose job is always in jeopardy because the Director dislikes him, sees in John a perfect opportunity to get even with his boss and at the same time to conduct a fascinating experiment. He gets permission from Mustapha Mond to bring John and Linda back to England with him.

There the Director is jeered at by his students when they learn that he was actually at one time a father. About to exile Bernard to Iceland, the Director himself is exiled instead.

The Savage, as John is called, becomes a great social success. All the jaded sophisticates of London want to meet him and are even willing to put up with Bernard in order to do so. Lenina, too, finds herself greatly attracted to this natural young man and does her best to seduce him. But although he lusts after her, John sternly rejects her because she is representative of the loose morality of civilization. Linda, hardly a social asset in London, is kept happy in seclusion on overdoses of soma.

John is appalled by the hedonism of civilized society and yearns to return to the stricter, more meaningful morality of the primitive life. One day, as Bernard is about to show him off to some dignitaries, including the Arch-Community-Songster of Canterbury (a great religious leader in this materialistic world), John refuses point-blank. Bernard is again in disgrace.

A sudden phone call summons John to the hospital where his mother is dying of an overdose of soma. There he is disgusted to see a group of children cavorting about the beds of the dying in order to be conditioned against the fear of death. Guilt-ridden because of his mother's death, John goes berserk and tries to destroy the soma rations that are being doled out to the hospital workers. He harangues the incensed Deltas, trying to get them to see how reliance on soma is making them less than human. They mob him and nearly kill him before a police squad arrives and quells the riot with water pistols that shoot tranquilizers.

Bernard, John, and a frustrated poet friend, Helmholtz Watson, are all arrested after the melee and brought before Mustapha Mond. The urbane World Controller exiles Bernard and Helmholtz to the Falkland Islands and then settles down to a long philosophical argument with John. Mond explains that the Brave New World has no room for art (it prefers feelies to Shakespeare), science (it fosters gadgetry, not abstract speculative science), or religion because these are disruptive forces that require social instability and occasional misery in order to thrive. No one who was completely happy or well-adjusted could have written *Othello,* Mond contends, or could undergo religious martyrdom. Since happiness is equated with sensual pleasure, and since every desire must be requited at the moment of its inception, the Brave New World has no room for the visionaries, cranks, and egoists who were the great culture heroes of the past.

Eloquent as Mond is, the Savage remains unconvinced. He still feels that Shakespeare, suffering, motherhood, and God are important values, and he decides to become a hermit in a lighthouse on the coast of Surrey. There he goes, determined to be self-sufficient and independent of the gadgets and creature comforts for which everyone else exists.

He fashions his own bows and arrows for hunting, plants a garden, and occasionally whips himself when he thinks of his lust for Lenina. But soon word of John's eccentric behavior gets around, and a sensation-seeking mob descends on him in helicopters. Reporters come to interview him. John kicks them out. But eventually the mob (which now includes Lenina) becomes too much for him. They want to make his whippings a mere spectacle. Enraged, John applies the whip to Lenina instead, killing her in his furious passion.

When the mob comes looking for him the next day, they find he has hanged himself in the lighthouse, unable to bear the burden of human emotions in the Brave New World.

Critical Opinion

"O brave new world that has such people in it!" exclaims Miranda on the enchanted island that is the world of Shakespeare's *The Tempest.* With characteristic cynicism, Aldous Huxley takes her words for the title of a novel that describes a future that is anything but brave. Unable to face realistically such facts of life as pain, grief, and death, protected against anything disagreeable by the ever-present soma, living for the sensation of the moment, the people of Huxley's brave new world are a grotesque projection of "civilized" life in the 1920's.

Like all utopian books from Plato's *Republic* to Orwell's *1984, Brave New World* merely projects into the future the tendencies of the present. Those which fascinated and repelled Huxley most were scientific gadgetry (hence Henry Ford is the God of his society); promiscuous sensuality divorced from any concept of love, sacrifice, or honor; and an increasing antiseptic sterility (exemplified by the proudly displayed motto of one famous contemporary chain of snack bars, "Human hands never touch our food").

While utopias from Plato to Sir Thomas More tended to project an idealized vision of what society could be like if human reason were employed to its utmost, more recent utopias, of which *Brave New World* has been the most influential, are a nightmare vision of the future. In Huxley's projection, civilization has been drained of love, vitality, and irrational excess. Everything is machine-made, mass-produced, and sterile. But where people should be seeking happiness through stability, they find themselves hedonistically searching for one superficial pleasure after another, immersing themselves in Community Sings (which have replaced religious services), feelies (hypersensual movies), and heavy doses of soma.

Into this twilight world Huxley injects two malcontents: Bernard Marx, who is unable to get along with his somatized fellow human beings, and the Savage, victim of a civilized heredity at war with a primitive environment. By exiling Bernard and driving the Savage to murder and suicide, Huxley seems to be saying, as H. G. Wells did in *The Time Machine,* that the world will someday be divided sharply between the ultra-civilized and the ultra-primitive. It will be impossible for an individual caught between these extremes to find a sane, satisfactory life. In *Brave New World,* neither the sterile, loveless world of Europe nor the squalid, bestial life of the Indians in New Mexico offers a satisfactory alternative for man.

The Author

Aldous Huxley was born in Surrey on July 26, 1894, into one of the most distinguished families in English intellectual life. His grandfather was Thomas Henry Huxley, an important disciple of Darwin and popularizer of science in Victorian England. His great-uncle was Matthew Arnold, one of the finest Victorian poets and essayists, and his brother, Sir Julian

Huxley, is a distinguished biologist and writer on scientific subjects.

It seemed destined that the lanky, avidly curious youth should make a name for himself in science or letters or both. That he did so was a triumph, however, over at least one great obstacle. When Huxley was seventeen and embarking on a study of medicine, he fell victim to an inflammation of the cornea that nearly blinded him. After two years of treatment, Huxley was able to read again, using a magnifying glass. After his education at Oxford, in 1919, he joined the staff of the *Athenaeum*, a London literary magazine. Although he regretted not having a scientific training (it was impossible for him to look through a microscope), he once ironically said that the affliction had fortunately prevented him "from becoming a complete public-school English gentleman."

Huxley's extraordinarily prolific career as a novelist, essayist, and philosopher began with the novels *Crome Yellow* (1921) and *Antic Hay* (1923). Both were literary sensations. The reading public was immediately caught by their irreverent wit, wild inventiveness, and scorching satire on the mores of the "Bright Young Things" who flitted about Mayfair society in the 1920's. *Point Counter Point*, published in 1928, reveals Huxley at his best as a mordant observer of the social scene and as a novelist of ideas. With *Brave New World* (1932) and *Eyeless in Gaza* (1936) Huxley's writing began to lose its satiric flash and became more serious, verging on mysticism. When he moved to California in 1937, his interests turned to philosophy, history, and mystical experiences. His later novels suffered as a result.

A friend once described Huxley as looking "like a willow that swayed and bent, not ungracefully, in the middle." Over six feet tall and very thin, Huxley's gentleness surprised people who expected only bitter sarcasm from the author of *Point Counter Point*. Later in his life, as a result of rigorous exercises described in *The Art of Seeing* (1942), Huxley regained some measure of his eyesight. He became interested in such Indian hallucinogens as peyote and mescalin which he had earlier described in *Brave New World*. He wrote a controversial book on his visionary experiences with these drugs, *The Doors of Perception*.

Married twice (his first wife died in 1955), Huxley died of cancer in Hollywood on the day of President Kennedy's assassination, November 22, 1963. Although he had often been mentioned for the Nobel prize, he never received it, perhaps because of the vitriolic nihilism of his early novels.

By the Same Author

Crome Yellow: For his first novel Huxley resorted to the technique (used by Thomas Love Peacock and Norman Douglas) of gathering a group of eccentrics in a country house and letting them act and react upon one another. A shy young poet named Denis (who resembles his namesake in *South Wind* and Bernard Marx in *Brave New World*) comes to Crome, the country house of the Wimbushes. There Denis meets Mr. Scrogan, a diabolical rationalist who tries to rid him of his romantic preconceptions; Ivor Lombard, who paints ghosts; and Anne Wimbush, with whom he falls in love. In a series of brilliantly witty conversational scenes Huxley shows how Denis tortures himself over his inability to conquer Anne, makes a complete ass of himself, and finally leaves Crome a sadder but wiser poet.

Antic Hay: Fuller and more original than his first novel, *Antic Hay* is a corrosive satire of literary, artistic, and social poseurs in London in the 1920's. The hero is a young dilettante named Theodore Gumbril who makes his unsure-footed way through London's bohemia, meeting such odd figures as Shearwater, an absent-minded scientist, and Casimir Lypiatt, a self-styled genius. A less richly developed novel than *Point Counter Point, Antic Hay* is nevertheless uproariously funny; it set the style for such later social satirists as Evelyn Waugh and Anthony Powell. Huxley expresses his urbanely nihilistic point of view as he dissects and caustically discards the intellectual frauds around him.

Decline and Fall

by

EVELYN WAUGH (1903–)

Main Characters

Paul Pennyfeather—A serious-minded, unassuming young Oxford divinity student with a talent for getting into trouble.

Sir Alastair Digby-Vane-Trumpington—A pleasure-loving young aristocrat at Oxford, member in good standing of the exclusive Bollinger Club.

Arthur Potts—Paul's high-minded friend doing confidential work for the League of Nations.

Dr. Augustus Fagan—The harried headmaster of the dreadful Llanabba School in Wales.

Peter Beste-Chetwynde—The one civilized boy at Llanabba, who soon becomes Paul's friend.

Margot Beste-Chetwynde—Peter's beautiful, unconventional mother, a luminary in Mayfair society.

Captain Grimes—A teacher at Llanabba who depends on his being a public-school man to get him out of his frequent scrapes with society and the law.

Mr. Prendergast—Another member of the Llanabba staff, a clergyman until he began to doubt.

Solomon Philbrick—A confidence man and swindler temporarily employed as butler at Llanabba Castle.

Sir Wilfred Lucas-Dockery—Governor of Blackstone Gaol and a crackpot about prison reform.

Sir Humphrey Maltravers—A political bigwig who later becomes the influential Lord Metroland.

Otto Silenus—The mad, insomniac architect responsible for Margot Beste-Chetwynde's hideous mansion, King's Thursday.

The Story

Paul Pennyfeather, a shy young divinity student at Scone College, Oxford, is minding his own business one evening when he is attacked by members of the Bollinger Club, a group of aristocratic students celebrating their annual dinner by getting roaring drunk and going berserk. Before he knows what has happened, Paul has been stripped of his trousers and has to make his way across campus in his shorts. The next day the Bollinger Club is fined £230 (which hardly puts a dent in their limitless funds), but Paul is dismissed for unseemly conduct.

Paul's guardian informs him that under the provisions of his father's will the legacy can be withheld from him if he behaves badly. Not caring to hear Paul's side of the story, his guardian cuts off his allowance, using the money to provide a husband for his daughter.

Paul must look for a job, and so he consults with Mr. Levy of Church and Gargoyle, a sleazy teacher employment agency, to help him to find a teaching post. The only school low enough to accept someone sent down from Oxford for indecent behavior, Mr. Levy tells Paul, is Llanabba School in the depths of Wales. Dr. Fagan, its headmaster, hires Paul at slave wages, telling him he should feel honored to teach at an institution boasting such aristocratic students as little Lord Tangent, son of the Earl of Circumference. Dr. Fagan is a consummate snob and hypocrite who refuses to acknowledge that the school he is running is tenth-rate at best and that his daughters, Flossie and Diana, are vulgar, penny-pinching young shrews out to catch any husband they can.

At Llanabba, Paul meets the other masters—a sorry lot. One of them, Mr. Prendergast, is terrified of the tough, semi-literate students. Mr. Prendergast had been a clergyman until he realized that he had serious doubts about his religion. Instead of concealing his doubts, he gave up his post and came to Llanabba where he now lives a penurious, miserable existence. Paul's other colleague, Captain Grimes, is a raffish man who is constantly getting into trouble but always manages to escape his just punishment because he went to a good public school. Grimes has become engaged to Flossie Fagan as insurance against losing his job at the Llanabba School. He loathes his job.

Assigned to the fifth form, Paul finds his students a noisy, squabbling group of little monsters. The first day he teaches, they try to unnerve him by all claiming to be named Tangent. Paul outwits them, however. He offers a half crown prize to whichever student can write the longest essay, regardless of merit. This keeps them all busy writing and leaves Paul in peace. He becomes the envy of Mr. Prendergast who is constantly being taunted by his students for wearing a wig.

The only decent pupil Paul has is Peter Beste-Chetwynde, a precociously alcoholic young aristocrat. Paul finds himself assigned to teach young Peter the organ, which Paul doesn't know how to play and which Peter doesn't want to learn. Instead they spend the practice hour gossiping about the school and its peculiar inhabitants.

One day Paul gets a letter from his old school friend Arthur Potts, telling him that Sir Alastair Digby-Vane-Trumpington, a member of the Bollinger Club, has offered to send Paul £20 as remuneration for his being thrown out of Scone College. Paul debates with himself whether it would be right to accept this money, but the problem is settled for him by Captain Grimes who telegraphs an acceptance in Paul's name. The hard-pressed masters use the money for a rare festive treat.

Dr. Fagan decides to hold a lawn party and sports competition in order to get some more money out of the few aristocratic parents who have sent their children to his school. The party, like everything else at Llanabba, is a ghastly failure. First, Philbrick, the butler, strenuously objects to the extra duties involved. In confidence he tells Paul that actually he is a well-known underworld figure who came to Llanabba to kidnap little Lord Tangent but under the benign influence of Diana Fagan he has reformed. He tells totally different and conflicting stories to Mr. Prendergast and Captain Grimes. Lady Circumference, Lord Tangent's mother, manages to insult everybody to whom she hands out prizes. The sports meets are either rigged or mismanaged. Mr. Prendergast, who is supposed to signal the start of races by firing a pistol, accidentally shoots Lord Tangent in the heel. Lady Circumference is beside herself with rage. The boy subsequently dies of his wound.

But the biggest sensation is caused by the arrival of Peter's mother, Margot Beste-Chetwynde, accompanied by a Negro gigolo whom she has adopted. Despite her bizarre antics, Margot fascinates Paul who promptly falls in love with her. He is hired by her to tutor Peter during vacation, and he goes to her country house, King's Thursday.

This extraordinary mansion was once one of the stately homes of England, but Margot had hired Otto Silenus, an eccentric architect, to rebuild it into a hideously modernistic affair of glass, concrete, and aluminum. Silenus cannot stand people. He lies awake nights thinking up designs for factories to house his real love—machinery.

Paul learns that he has a rival for Margot's hand in Sir Humphrey Maltravers, Minister of Transport and a political power. But Margot, seeing that her son genuinely likes Paul, tells him she will marry him, impoverished though he is. She insists that he not return to Llanabba after vacation. Instead, Paul becomes involved in Margot's mysterious business activities, which seem to be concerned with supplying show girls to South American night clubs. Paul's friend, Arthur Potts, now working for the League of Nations, also shows an interest in Margot's affairs.

Shortly before he is to be married to Margot, Paul is sent by his fiancée to Marseilles to expedite the emigration of some girls to South America. He unwittingly bribes some officials and returns to England successful. On the morning he is to marry Margot, he is drinking champagne with Alastair Trumpington when a Scotland Yard inspector breaks in on the party and arrests him. Paul learns that in all innocence he has been helping Margot Beste-Chetwynde conduct a thriving white-slave trade.

Abandoned by Margot at his trial, Paul finds the chief witness against him is Potts who has been investigating the operation for the League of Nations. Paul is convicted and sentenced to seven years in prison. He is taken to Blackstone Gaol, where he is reunited with Philbrick, a fellow prisoner, and Mr. Prendergast, the prison chaplain. Prendergast is murdered by a religious fanatic prisoner because the governor of the prison, Sir Wilfred Lucas-Dockery, is too interested in abstract, nonsensical prison reform to notice what is actually going on in his own prison.

After the murder, Paul is transferred to Egdon Heath Penal Settlement where he finds Captain Grimes a fellow prisoner. Grimes had married Flossie Fagan and, not being able to stand it, had escaped; he had presumably drowned. Once again he disappears—slipping away from a work gang into the fog—and is never seen or heard from thereafter.

Paul is visited by Margot who informs him that she is about to marry his former rival, Sir Humphrey Maltravers, now advanced to the rank of Home Secretary and to the position of Lord Metroland. However, taking pity on Paul, Margot arranges for his escape from prison. With Lord Metroland's connivance, Paul is removed to a nursing home for a fake appendicitis operation. The home is run by Dr. Fagan who has given up his career in education for one in medicine. A drunken doctor is persuaded to sign a death warrant stating that Paul died under the knife, and Paul is spirited off in a yacht to Margot's home in Corfu where he takes a much-needed rest.

After a few months, Paul unobtrusively slips back into England, and, sporting a moustache, re-enters Scone College as a sadder and wiser divinity student.

Critical Opinion

Although Waugh has claimed that he is not a genuine satirist because satire implies a fixed set of social values which he has not found in his world, his novels are most frequently discussed as satires of particularly mordant and vitriolic wit. They are not, indeed, about a stable society but about one which is crumbling before Waugh's amused, if horrified, eyes.

Decline and Fall is not merely a comedy about the decline and fall of Paul Pennyfeather's fortunes. It chronicles, by strong implication, the destruction of traditional English values in the chaotic postwar world. Thus Margot's stately Tudor home, King's Thursday, has been "modernized" into a dwelling more suitable for machines than for civilized human beings. Captain Grimes has deliberately exploited the

English tradition of the "old school tie" for criminal ends. The young aristocrats in the novel are either callous dilettantes like Alastair Trumpington or nice boys like Peter Beste-Chetwynde given to drink too early in life. The social mobility that Waugh abhors is symbolized by Margot's appearance at the Llanabba *fête* accompanied by a Negro gigolo.

Decline and Fall is not a traditional satire. Such satire implies the author's belief in the possibility of some kind of improvement in conditions as he sees them. No such implication can be found in Waugh's early novels. Life is unfair to Paul Pennyfeather; the world is grotesque and chaotic, but nothing can be done about it. For all its wit, *Decline and Fall* is essentially pessimistic—a black comedy of a kind rare in English fiction. Waugh simply laughs hollowly at the curious doings of the world about him. His ingenious and outrageous incidents and examples of human depravity force us to laugh with him. In a way, *Decline and Fall* is the counterpart in fiction of T. S. Eliot's *The Waste Land*. Both are precisely observed pictures of a world bereft of traditional values, searching—not very hard or successfully—for something to replace them.

The Author

Evelyn Waugh, the man Edmund Wilson called "the only first-rate comic genius that has appeared in England since Bernard Shaw," was born in October, 1903, into a literary family. His father, Arthur Waugh, was a famous critic and publisher; his younger brother, Alec, is a popular novelist and author of travel books. Evelyn Waugh studied modern history at Hertford College, Oxford, and art at Heatherly's Art School in London.

Like Paul Pennyfeather, he was briefly a master at a private school. He then worked as a society reporter for the *Daily Express* where he acquired valuable training as an observer of the brittle Mayfair society which later furnished the material for many of his novels.

In 1929 Waugh launched his writing career in fiction with the successful *Decline and Fall*. This was followed by a brilliant series of satiric novels including *Vile Bodies* (1930), *Black Mischief* (1932), *Scoop* (1938), and *Put Out More*

Flags (1942). In 1930 Waugh was received into the Roman Catholic Church. Since then he has enthusiastically propagated its doctrines in such diverse works as *Edmund Campion* (1935), a biography of the Elizabethan Jesuit martyr; *Brideshead Revisited* (1945), a nostalgic study of English Catholic life, and *Helena* (1950), a fictionalized biography of the mother of Constantine the Great.

In World War II Waugh joined the Royal Marines, became a commando in the Middle East, parachuted into Yugoslavia on a British military mission to Marshal Tito in 1944, and was nearly killed in the crash of a transport plane. His war experiences provided the background for his most recent major work, the trilogy, *Men at Arms*.

A postwar visit to the United States produced one of Waugh's most savage satires, *The Loved One* (1948), about the gaudy funeral practices of Southern California. It anticipated by several years the recent attacks on the funeral industry. With the exception of *The Loved One*, however, Waugh's recent books have tended to be less extravagantly comic than his earlier novels. The trend toward more serious novels started with *A Handful of Dust* (1934) and reached a culmination in *Brideshead Revisited* (1945).

Married in 1937 and the father of a large family, Waugh has an almost cherubic personal manner that belies the ferocious wit of his novels. An arch-conservative in most matters from politics to dress, he is a collector of books on early English architecture and art and lives as best he can the life of an English country gentleman in an age in which that special breed is fast becoming an anomaly.

By the Same Author

Vile Bodies: In a sense a sequel to *Decline and Fall* (Lady Margot Metroland appears in both novels), *Vile Bodies* chronicles the further doings of the "bright young things" of Mayfair in the postwar world. Waugh's hapless hero in this novel is Adam Fenwick-Symes, an innocent young writer whose autobiography in manuscript is seized by customs when he returns to England, and destroyed as pornography. This loss forces Adam to all sorts of bizarre expedients to earn enough money to marry Nina Blount, the daughter of an eccentric country squire. In his adventures Adam meets Mrs. Melrose Ape, a sordid female evangelist, and such "bright young people" as Miles Malpractice and Agatha Runcible (who cracks up in a racing car and dies). Very brief episodes are juxtaposed for an even more surrealistic comic effect than any achieved in *Decline and Fall*. The mixture, as before, is one of hilarity and despair. Waugh fiddles a jazz tune as English civilization burns.

A Handful of Dust: More somber in tone than Waugh's earlier novels, *A Handful of Dust* deals with the unhappy marriage of Tony and Brenda Last. Bored with life in magnificent Hetton Abbey and unable to see why her husband Tony delights in this relic of the past, Brenda establishes herself as an enlightened modern woman by having an adulterous fling with John Beaver, a young social climber. The accidental death of her son, John, instead of bringing the parents together, merely widens the breach. Brenda sues for divorce, demanding fantastic alimony. To escape his sick world, Tony joins an expedition to the jungles of South America, but finds jungle life no more appealing than life in England. He falls into the hands of a mad trader named Todd who keeps him prisoner in his hut, demanding that Tony read to him daily from the works of Dickens.

In this novel Waugh's conservative outrage at modern vulgarity and loose morality is at its most intense. Here, the joke of the "bright young things," with their casual, amorous escapades and hedonistic selfishness, has suddenly gone sour. A return to the old values is unlikely, Waugh seems to be saying, yet people without values are merely a handful of dust.

Lost Horizon

by

JAMES HILTON (1900–1954)

Main Characters

Hugh Conway—A British consul in the East whose daring
exploits have won him the nickname "Glory" Conway,
brilliant, handsome, and disillusioned with Western civilization.

Charles Mallinson—Conway's hero-worshiping subordinate,
totally impervious to the charm, wisdom, and mystery of
the East.

Rutherford—A novelist friend to whom Conway first tells
the story of Shangri-La.

Henry Barnard—Alias Chalmers Bryant, an American embezzler escaping from the law.

Roberta Brinklow—An English missionary who wants to convert everyone to Christianity.

Chang—The mysterious, highly civilized Chinese lama at
Shangri-La, who tries to help Westerners adapt to the ways
of the lamasery.

Father Perrault—A French Capuchin missionary who has
become the High Lama of Shangri-La.

Lo-Tsen—A beautiful, musically gifted Chinese girl living
at Shangri-La.

The Story

Hugh Conway had been one of the most promising and charming young men at Oxford when Rutherford, the novelist, knew him there. During the ten years in which Conway wandered from post to post as a British consul in the East, Rutherford lost track of him.

One day in a Catholic mission hospital in Chung-Kiang, Rutherford sees his old friend again. The exhausted Conway, weak and somewhat disoriented, tells him an extraordinary story:

At thirty-seven, Conway is consul in Baskul, which, in May 1931, is torn by revolution. With heroic effort, Conway manages to evacuate the white population and to destroy secret documents. Then he boards a special plane lent by an Indian maharajah and piloted by a capable English aviator named Fenner. With Conway on the plane are Charles Mallinson, his high-strung young subordinate, Henry Barnard, a talkative but suspicious American, and Miss Brinklow, an English missionary.

After about an hour in the air, Mallinson senses that the plane is not keeping on course and that the pilot is not Fenner. Conway soon realizes, too, that they are flying over peculiar terrain—the rugged mountain ranges of Tibet. They catch a glimpse of the pilot. He is Chinese!

Gradually the pilot, making an almost impossible landing, noses the plane down into a mountain valley. Natives carrying guns hurry to meet the plane and replenish its dwindling supply of fuel. The passengers assume they have been kidnapped and will be held for ransom. But as soon as the plane is refueled, it takes off again without a word of explanation from the Chinese pilot.

Hours later, the pilot makes a forced landing high on a plateau west of the Himalaya mountains. When the dazed passengers emerge from the plane into the freezing air, they discover that the pilot is seriously injured. He tells them that they can find refuge in a nearby lamasery called Shangri-La, and then he dies. The travelers are debating whether to head for the lamasery or try to get back to civilization on their own when a group of men from the lamasery approaches.

One of them, a Chinese named Chang, introduces himself in flawless English to the bewildered travelers and insists that they accompany his men to the lamasery. Despite Mallinson's misgivings about trusting any non-European, the group have no choice but to make the tortuous journey to Shangri-La. When they arrive, they find in the midst of a forbidding mountain range a pleasant and fertile tract of land, unexplored and unmapped by any Westerner. The lamasery building is centrally heated and luxuriously furnished in a style the travelers are accustomed to associate only with Western progress.

Although they are given comfortable rooms and fine food, the travelers—especially Mallinson—immediately ask Chang when they can return to India. Chang evasively replies that since Shangri-La is so isolated they will have to wait until a band of porters arrives over the mountains. This will not be for another few weeks, and so they may as well make themselves comfortable. He tells them that the lamasery is run by a High Lama whom they will not be allowed to meet. Conway suspects from Chang's manner that they have been brought deliberately to Shangri-La and will never be allowed to leave.

After some time Chang informs Conway that he will be permitted to meet the High Lama. Mallinson sees this as an opportunity for Conway to insist on their immediate passage home. Among other things, Mallinson wants the High Lama's help in turning over to the authorities the American, Henry Barnard, who has been unmasked as Chalmers Bryant, an embezzler and confidence man traveling incognito.

When Conway is ushered into his presence, the High Lama tells him the extraordinary tale of the founding of Shangri-La. In 1734 Father Perrault, a traveling French Capuchin friar in his early fifties, found sanctuary in a Buddhist lamasery. Gradually he was won over by the serene life there and stopped trying to convert the people to Christianity. His ties with his own church severed by time and distance, Father Perrault stayed on, gradually achieving a merger of the best elements of Christianity and Buddhism.

In 1789 Father Perrault thought he was dying. However, the pure air of the place combined with some miraculous drugs known to the local inhabitants preserved his life. Workmen built the present lamasery of Shangri-La where Father

Perrault lived a life of serene contemplation and scholarship
with the other lamas. Occasionally a wanderer would accidentally find his way to Shangri-La, where men lived and
worked in harmony, free from the conflicts and problems of
the world outside. From this utopia, however, no one was
ever allowed to depart. The few who tried to escape were
never heard from again.

Conway learns that he and his party have been brought
to Shangri-La in order to restock the lamasery. Since the High
Lama feels that a new war is about to engulf civilization,
he is eager to gather enough people in Shangri-La to preserve
culture and to begin civilization anew. The High Lama also
tells the astounded Conway that he himself is Father Perrault, now 250 years old and nearing the end of his days.

Conway is now faced with the problem of breaking the
news to his fellow travelers. Weary of the conflicts of Western
civilization, he is quite content to remain in Shangri-La for
the rest of his life. But he knows that Mallinson wants to
return to England and is counting on the porters to lead him
back through the mountain passes. Conway learns, however,
that Miss Brinklow is willing to remain in Shangri-La because
she still hopes to convert everyone there to Christianity.
Barnard, of course, does not want to return home to certain
capture and imprisonment.

Conway spends his time pleasantly and profitably in the
lamasery. He makes good use of the amazingly well-stocked
library and he becomes friends with two musicians—Briac,
who was a pupil of Chopin and can play works never published by the master, and Lo-Tsen, an exquisite Chinese girl
with whom Conway falls in love. He is shocked when he
learns that Lo-Tsen is actually sixty-five years old. The serene
life at Shangri-La has kept her from aging. Conway with-
holds this information from Mallinson when he finds that
Mallinson, too, has fallen in love with her.

After several more meetings, the High Lama tells Conway
that death will soon overtake him and that he wants Conway
to lead the lamasery when that time comes. He has faith
that Conway will preserve the great culture of Shangri-La
after war has destroyed the rest of the world.

One evening, after a long discussion with Father Perrault,
Conway sees him slump in his chair and realizes the end has
finally come. Profoundly moved, Conway goes out into the

garden. Mallinson breaks in on his reflections about the future to tell him that the porters have arrived. Mallinson has lost no time in paying the porters to take Conway, Lo-Tsen, and himself away from Shangri-La, leaving Miss Brinklow and Barnard behind. Conway tries to tell Mallinson that Lo-Tsen is really an old woman, miraculously preserved by the climate of Shangri-La, who will suddenly age and die in the outside world. Conway doesn't want to leave but succumbs to Mallinson's pleas that he help them on the long, arduous journey. He realizes that he is leaving the only place on earth untouched by human fears and anxieties.

This is the last that Rutherford hears of Conway's story until he meets him in the mission hospital. A doctor tells him that Conway was brought to the hospital by an ancient Chinese woman who must have been Lo-Tsen. When last heard from, Conway has recovered and is headed once again for the high Himalayas, hoping to find the peace and serenity of Shangri-La.

Critical Opinion

It is easy to understand the appeal *Lost Horizon* had for its readers when it first appeared in the grim year of 1933. Sick of war and fearing a new one, searching for enduring values in the chaotic world of the 1920's and finding instead the bleak depression, people saw in the easy philosophy of *Lost Horizon* a fantasy fulfillment of their deepest hopes and dreams. The peaceful, tolerant, wise world of Shangri-La—alluring, if unattainable—seemed an answer to the troubled thirties.

Essentially, *Lost Horizon* is one in a long line of utopian romances. Like most utopias, Shangri-La is physically difficult to reach and therefore has escaped contamination by the self-destructive world outside. Like most utopias, too, it is a better if a duller world than the real one. But Shangri-La can make its appeal only to those who are willing to give themselves to it. Young Mallinson, for instance, can never be happy anywhere but in the struggle of the real world and is totally unready for the timeless wisdom of the lamasery. His failure is the result of his assumption that only the values of Western "civilization" count. In her Christian ardor,

Miss Brinklow, too, cannot accept the serene, humanistic religion of the lamasery. But Conway has seen enough of the "real" world to understand its limitations and to appreciate a life of peaceful contemplation of the eternal.

The Author

James Hilton, one of the most prolific producers of best sellers in the 1930's, was the quiet, reserved son of a London schoolmaster, the model for Mr. Chips. He was born on September 9, 1900, in Lancashire.

Like Hugh Conway, Hilton was a brilliant student, winning his Cambridge degree with honors in 1921. His first article was accepted by the *Manchester Guardian* when he was seventeen, and his first novel, *Catherine Herself,* was published in 1920 when he was still an undergraduate. Leaving college during the postwar slump, he struggled for ten years as a free-lance journalist and book reviewer. His big chance came when the *British Weekly* asked him to write a Christmas story in two weeks. Hilton found himself unable to think of one until one day, taking a bicycle ride, he got the idea for *Goodbye, Mr. Chips.* Always a rapid writer, he set the story down in four days. It was published in the United States in the *Atlantic Monthly* and became a best seller in 1934 when Alexander Woollcott, the American critic, praised it on his radio program.

The success of *Goodbye, Mr. Chips* led to the republication of *Lost Horizon* which had won the highly coveted Hawthornden Prize in 1933 but had not attracted much general attention. Now, however, it, too, became immensely successful, and the name Shangri-La became a household word. President Roosevelt even named his summer retreat after the utopia in the Tibetan fastness.

From 1935 on Hilton spent much of his time in Hollywood, adapting for the screen many of his own novels, including *We Are Not Alone* (1937), *Random Harvest* (1941), and *So Well Remembered* (1945), in addition to *Goodbye, Mr. Chips.*

Unlike many other authors, Hilton felt at ease in Hollywood and never chafed at the difficulties of writing for the movies. His quiet, unassuming manner endeared him to many who heard him talk on the radio. Although he never again achieved the success of *Lost Horizon* or *Goodbye, Mr. Chips,* Hilton continued to write highly popular novels. He died in Hollywood on December 20, 1954.

By the Same Author

Goodbye, Mr. Chips: This novel is a delicate tribute to Hilton's schoolmaster father. It dwells gently on the past of Mr. Chipping, beloved by generations of schoolboys at Brookfield, a minor English public school. Sitting before his fire at the age of eighty-five, Mr. Chips, as the boys have dubbed him, realizes that his outwardly uneventful life has not been wasted. Never very brilliant, he has taught Latin in an undistinguished school. But he loved and married the beautiful Katherine Bridges, who died tragically in childbirth only a few years later. He survived the war years, giving boys the courage to face a world wholly unlike Brookfield. Grown crusty and eccentric in his late years, he has nevertheless maintained a tradition of gentle humanism and decency in the old school, and this has given value to his life. Written as a Christmas story, *Goodbye, Mr. Chips* is a nostalgic, sentimental evocation of all that is good and enduring in the English tradition.

The Power and the Glory

by

GRAHAM GREENE (1904–)

Main Characters

The priest—Guilt-ridden and tormented by his weaknesses and sinfulness, he finally comes upon the true meaning of grace and salvation. He sometimes assumes the name of Montez.

The lieutenant—Single-minded and determined on principle to rid Mexico of all priests.

The chief of police—The lieutenant's boss, more concerned with his toothache than with pursuing priests.

María—Mother of the priest's child.

Brigida—The priest's young daughter, already wise in the ways of sin and corruption.

Father José—A priest who has knuckled under to the anti-clerical regime and renounced his religion.

The mestizo—A crafty, half-caste police informer.

Coral Fellows—A brave, lonely young English girl living on her father's remote banana plantation.

Mr. Lehr—A Protestant plantation owner who gives the priest temporary sanctuary.

The Story

Under an anti-clerical, communistic government in Mexico in the 1930's, all priests in certain provinces have been killed, banished, or forced to abandon their vocation. One of them is Father José who has become a laughing stock by marrying a shrewish wife. The government even gives him a pension because he brings ridicule on the Catholic Church.

But news comes from the governor's office that another priest has remained in the province and is secretly administering the sacraments, hearing confessions, and saying masses. The police lieutenant, an ardent revolutionary, is determined to rid the province of its last functioning priest.

The priest, knowing he is in mortal danger, and afraid of death, tries to slip aboard a boat headed for the safe city of Vera Cruz. At the last minute, however, a little boy pleads with him to administer last rites to his dying mother. The priest goes by mule to the boy's house.

Meanwhile the lieutenant has tacked two pictures to his wall in the police station: one of the priest in earlier, happier days, and another of an American murderer who is in hiding somewhere in Mexico. Of the two, the lieutenant is more concerned with catching the priest because he believes that only when Mexico is rid of the clergy will the poor people have a chance to improve their lot. He gets permission from the corrupt chief of police to take hostages from any town in which the priest has found shelter, and, if necessary, to shoot them.

The priest, who is an alcoholic, finds temporary refuge in a remote banana warehouse run by Captain Fellows, an unhappy English exile. The captain's daughter, Coral, who tells the priest she lost her faith when she was ten, hides him against her parents' wishes and brings him beer to drink. Determined not to make trouble for the girl, the priest painfully makes his way by mule into the interior, always on guard against the Red Shirts who will kill any priest on sight.

He eventually comes back to the tiny village where his former mistress, María, lives with their daughter, Brigida. The priest had known María in only one moment of sin and desperate loneliness. Though she is completely estranged, María gives him shelter for the night. Brigida, who does not know her own father, shocks him by her savagery. Comparing her with Coral, he realizes it will not be long before she is old in the ways of sin. Before dawn he conducts a secret mass for the villagers. In the midst of the ceremony the police arrive.

María pretends the priest is her husband, and Brigida identifies him as her father. Furthermore, he has changed so much from the plump, complacent young seminarian of the police photograph that he is unrecognizable, even to the lieutenant. Although the police take a hostage from the village, no one informs on the priest. He learns to his horror, however, that another hostage from his former parish of Concepcion has been shot, and he volunteers unsuccessfully to take this hostage's place. The villagers refuse and beg him to leave.

Once again he wearily mounts his mule and plods off in search of a safe province. But soon he is accosted by a wheedling, wretched mestizo (half-caste) who travels with him to the nearby village of Carmen. Although the mestizo swears he is a good Catholic, the priest knows that eventually he will betray him to the police for the seven-hundred-peso reward. The priest does not judge him, for his poverty is extreme.

Temporarily eluding the mestizo, the priest comes to a fairly large town where he desperately goes looking for wine. He buys some contraband brandy from a corrupt official, but is soon caught by the Red Shirts with the bottle in his pocket and is arrested. Alcohol, like religion, has been officially banned in the puritanically communistic state.

Thrown into a vile jail, the priest is forced to clean up the cells in order to pay his fine. Although his fellow captives know he is a priest, they will not betray him. He sees the mestizo who as an informer is a "guest" of the police. But the mestizo refuses to betray him, for fear of not collecting his full seven-hundred-peso reward since the priest is already a captive.

Brought before the lieutenant, who does not recognize him, the priest is released, and the lieutenant gives him five pesos to ease his journey.

On the road again, the priest comes across a poverty-stricken Indian woman whose child is dying of bullet wounds. The priest learns that the child was shot while being held as a hostage by the American gangster in a gun duel with the police.

He buries the child and proceeds painfully through forbidding, uninhabited country. At last a German-American Lutheran, Mr. Lehr, gives the priest sanctuary on his plantation but clearly shows his disapproval of Catholicism and of its whiskey-sodden representative. In a few days the priest has recovered and hopes to make his way to the safe territory of Las Casas.

Just as he is about to resume his journey, the mestizo finds him, bringing news that the American gangster, a Catholic, has been mortally wounded and desires last rites. Knowing it is a trap, the priest nevertheless changes his plans and goes back with the mestizo on the dangerous journey.

When they arrive at the hut where the killer is dying, the priest offers to hear his confession; but the bandit, still seething with hate, insists only that the priest take his revolver, for he knows the police are waiting just outside. When the bandit dies, the lieutenant enters the hut and places the priest under arrest. Together they make their way to the capital of the state where the priest is placed in jail to await execution.

During the tortuous journey, the lieutenant is impressed with the priest's humility and sincerity, and grants him his illicit request to receive communion from Father José before being shot. When the lieutenant goes to fetch Father José, the old man refuses to come, fearful of losing his government pension.

The priest is tried *in absentia* for treason against the state and condemned to be shot the next morning. On his last night, terrified of death and damnation, he tries to reconcile himself to his fate. He goes to his execution convinced he has been a total failure as priest and man.

However, the evening after the priest is shot, another priest slips secretly into the town and is welcomed by a boy, once cynical about the clergy, who was impressed with the stoicism of the whiskey priest. The priest's whole wretched life has not been in vain. From his sin and corruption the power and the glory of God have been mysteriously vindicated.

Critical Opinion

François Mauriac has accurately described Graham Greene's novels as being about "the utilization of sin by Grace." Like Dostoyevski, Greene sees God's grace being bestowed on the insulted and the injured, on the wretched of the world who are close to despair but who somehow keep the faith.

Thus the hero of *The Power and the Glory* is a miserable, sodden, whiskey priest, haunted by his sins of commission and omission (he fathered a child, then abandoned her to sin), and barely believing in the possibility of his redemption. As the priest makes his painful way on mule-back, accompanied by the Judas-like mestizo, the identification with Christ on his way to Calvary, which on the suface may seem blasphemous, becomes increasingly apparent.

The priest, once a callow young man, the pudgy-cheeked innocent of the photograph in the police station, becomes ennobled through suffering. The more wretched people are, the more saint-like, Greene seems to be saying; even if they are guilty of adultery, fornication, drunkenness, and blasphemy. Those who will never achieve grace are the complacently pious, like the woman the priest meets in prison who clings to her conventional, snobbish faith, unable to recognize true holiness in the suffering wretches around her.

The priest is significantly pitted against the lieutenant who in some ways is the true tragic hero of the novel. (In Greene's own words, the film version failed because the director "gave the integrity to the priest and the corruption to the lieutenant," the reverse of what Greene had intended.) The lieutenant is a kindly man and an incorruptible idealist. He truly believes that the village children, whom he loves so much, will lead a better life than he did if the clergy are destroyed. Like the priest, the lieutenant is isolated; his chief of police is corrupt and self-centered, carrying out orders that he does not understand or believe in.

The lieutenant's tragedy, then, is that he must hound to death a man as worthy as himself. Though he executes the priest, he fails to prevail over him.

Throughout the novel a boy, Luis, is seen listening cynically to his mother's reading of a sanctimonious tale. The boy is far more impressed with the lieutenant's shining revolver and holster, and it would seem that the future belongs to the secular state. However, when the priest is executed, Luis changes sides and welcomes with a reverent kiss on the hand the new fugitive priest who comes to town. The hunted whiskey priest who, for his venial weaknesses, considered himself a failure, has triumphed in death.

The Author

Graham Greene, England's foremost Catholic novelist, is (like Evelyn Waugh) a convert to the faith. He was born on October 2, 1904, in Hertfordshire where his father was headmaster of the Berkhampstead School. Educated there and at Balliol College, Oxford, Greene became a sub-editor for *The Times* of London and later film critic for the *Spectator.*

Greene was married in 1927 to Vivien Dayrell-Browning. Before the war he traveled a good deal in the United States and Mexico (where he gathered the material for *The Power and the Glory*), and when war broke out he worked with the Foreign Office on special duty in West Africa, the scene of *The Heart of the Matter.* In 1954 he covered the Indo-Chinese War for *The New Republic,* and his experiences in the East supplied the background for one of his most controversial novels, *The Quiet American* (1955).

Always a tormented man, Greene had toyed with the idea of suicide in his youth. Later he became a Communist for a brief period. A convert to Catholicism, he is one of the most distinguished Catholic laymen in the English-speaking world. In 1952 he applied for a visa to the United States to receive the Catholic Literary Award, but ran into trouble with the McCarran Act because of his early Communist affiliation. In 1954, granted a visa, he scornfully rejected it and has been a sharp critic of American policy ever since.

Admitting to two great influences on his writing, the Scottish suspense writer John Buchan (author of *The Thirty-Nine Steps*) and the French Catholic novelist François Mauriac, Greene has himself divided his prolific literary production into "entertainments" and serious novels. The entertainments, fast-moving psychological spy and suspense yarns, include *The Man Within* (1929), *The Orient Express* (1932), *This Gun for Hire* (1936), and *The Third Man* (1950), all of which have been made into successful films.

The serious novels began with *Brighton Rock* (1938). *The Power and the Glory* (first published, unsuccessfully, in the United States as *The Labyrinthine Way*), *The Heart of the Matter* (1948), and *The End of the Affair* (1951) are the finest of these.

The interesting point about this arbitrary distinction between "entertainments" and novels is that the technique and point of view are pretty much the same in both the thrillers and in the novels which seriously explore Catholic dogma. As in Francis Thompson's famous poem, "The Hound of Heaven," God pursues man relentlessly through all of Greene's fiction. Greene's fictional forte has always been a mastery of swift pacing and a depth of psychological penetration and religious meaning recalling the novels of Dostoyevski. These gifts have been lavished equally on the pure suspense stories and the richer, more serious novels.

By the Same Author

The Heart of the Matter: Like *The Power and the Glory,* this novel, set in a steaming colony in British West Africa, deals with sin and salvation, grace and damnation. The hero is Major Scobie, for fifteen years a police chief famed for his scrupulous honesty but isolated from his fellow Europeans by his alcoholism and his difficult temperament. Scobie commits adultery with a refugee girl and shares complicity in a murder. Ultimately he commits the supreme sin of suicide by faking a heart attack so that his wife can inherit his insurance. Like the priest in *The Power and the Glory,* Scobie is guilty of every sin that would traditionally lead him to damnation, but because of the intensity of his suffering (the book implies) God's mercy will be extended to him.

1984

by

GEORGE ORWELL (1903–1950)

Main Characters

Winston Smith—An average, intelligent man, a minor employee in the Ministry of Truth, Oceania's propaganda mill.
Julia—A beautiful, rebellious young mechanic in the Fiction Department of the Ministry of Truth.
O'Brien—Ugly, highly intelligent, and a member of the Inner Party.
Mr. Charrington—The old proprietor of a London junk shop filled with charming relics of the past.
Big Brother—The all-seeing, all-powerful ruler of Oceania whose magnetic eyes stare out from every billboard.
Emmanuel Goldstein—The semi-mythical arch-enemy of Oceania.

The Story

At lunchtime on April 4, 1984, Winston Smith takes time off from his job at the Ministry of Truth to go home and begin a secret journal. He has a lovely old notebook bought at Mr. Charrington's junk shop a few days before, a dangerous act in 1984, when secret thoughts and relics from the past are forbidden.

Winston Smith lives in London, now the principal city of

Airstrip One, part of Oceania which comprises Britain and
North and South America. Like the two other massive power
blocs of the world, Eurasia and Eastasia, Oceania is a completely totalitarian police state, rigidly adhering to the principles of Ingsoc, or English Socialism.

The majority of the population are called Proles; they are
considered too stupid to matter. To ensure the complete loyalty of its members, the Party has placed a two-way telescreen
in every room. Winston, a minor white-collar worker in the
Outer Party, has a room so peculiarly shaped that he can hide
in a corner from the ever-watchful telescreen. And he hides
as he opens his journal and several times writes the highly
treasonous statement, "Down with Big Brother." Big Brother,
whose heavy, moustachioed face glares down from every billboard, is the mysterious leader of Oceania in its endless wars
with Eastasia and Eurasia. No one has ever seen him, but in
the torture rooms and dungeons of the Ministry of Love, his
power is made clear to anyone defying the State.

Returning to the Ministry of Truth, Winston settles down
to his job, which consists of falsifying back numbers of the
Times in order to keep them in line with present policy in
Oceania. History is a plaything of the Party. Objective truth
no longer exists. Winston is an expert at his job, but he
loathes it and most of his zealous fellow workers who are
compiling a new edition of the Dictionary of Newspeak, the
official language of Oceania.

Winston's dreary, soul-destroying work is briefly interrupted
by the Two Minutes Hate session which all workers must
attend. In a large hall they watch movies of Eurasian war
atrocities. The climax is reached with the picture of Emmanuel
Goldstein, the almost legendary enemy of the Party, an alleged
counter-revolutionary and scapegoat for all the military, social,
and economic failings of the Party. As the pictures appear on
the screen, the audience works itself up into a frenzy. Anyone
who fails to scream curses at the screen is immediately reported to the Thought Police and is afterward "vaporized."

At the Two Minutes Hate session, Winston sees Julia, a
lovely, cool, dark-haired girl who he thinks has been following him, probably because she is a member of the dreaded
Thought Police. Dressed in regulation overalls (she repairs
the machines that churn out cheap fiction for the Proles),
with the banner of the Anti-Sex League draped around her,

Julia secretly slips Winston a note reading "I love you." Winston and Julia arrange a rendezvous in a secluded nook in the country, far from any telescreen.

Winston was married once; his wife was an ardent Party worker and member of the Anti-Sex League who looked on sex in the orthodox Party way, as a disagreeable duty to perform for the good of the State. When Winston failed to give her any children, she left him. The only love Winston ever knew was his mother's and she had disappeared many years ago—probably to be vaporized.

In the country, Julia and Winston become lovers and spend an idyllic afternoon exchanging confidences. Julia tells him that she is a member of the Anti-Sex League and a seemingly loyal Party worker only for security reasons. Actually she is promiscuous, loves life, and despises the Party. Like Winston, she is fond of exploring the black markets run by the Proles, where Party members are never supposed to venture. There she can sometimes get real coffee and chocolate instead of the synthetic "Victory" substitutes that Outer Party members are supposed to consume.

Winston is fascinated by Mr. Charrington's junk shop. He returns there again and again, searching for clues to the past which he feels must have been a happier time than the present and which could not have been as dreadful as the Party history books would have it. On one of these furtive visits, Mr. Charington shows Winston a secret upstairs bedroom, preserved just as it was before the Ingsoc revolution.

The room is seedy but comfortable, and, best of all, has not been equipped with a telescreen. In a moment of folly, Winston rents it from Mr. Charrington, and it becomes an occasional haven for the lovers.

Bolstered by their love for each other, Winston and Julia feel there must be other secret rebels against the stifling State of 1984. If only they could make contact! Winston remembers in particular a man named O'Brien, a member of the Inner Party on whose ugly, intelligent face he thinks he has seen an ironical gleam of contempt for the Party. Winston and Julia go to O'Brien's plush apartment and ask him if there is really a counter-revolutionary conspiracy. O'Brien answers *yes* and enlists the lovers in its ranks, but warns them they will probably be killed long before their ideals are realized. He tells them that Emmanuel Goldstein exists and is the author of a heretical book which O'Brien lends Winston.

Before Winston can read Goldstein's book, however, he is engulfed in preparations for Hate Week. Oceania has suddenly and unaccountably switched sides in the war. Now Eurasia is the ally and Eastasia the enemy. All documents to the contrary must be immediately altered.

Relaxing with Julia after Hate Week, Winston is reading Goldstein's book which points out the infinite cruelties, lies, and deceptions of the State, when a voice seeming to come from nowhere orders Winston's and Julia's arrest. To his horror, Winston realizes that a telescreen has been in his secret room all along and that Mr. Charrington is a member of the Thought Police. Guards invade the sanctuary. One of them kicks Julia in the stomach. Winston is hustled off to a stinking dungeon in the Ministry of Love.

There he is kicked, clubbed, and bludgeoned for days until he no longer knows what or where he is. Then he is subjected to weeks of "conferences" with O'Brien, during which he is given electric shocks and kept barely alive so he can confess the error of his rebellion. O'Brien, however, wants more than a confession. He insists that Winston realize in the depths of his soul that Big Brother is all-powerful and all-good, that individuals have no right to private ideas, and that if the Party says two plus two equals five, that is correct. He tells Winston that he himself wrote Goldstein's book as a trap for rebels.

Through his tortures and O'Brien's inquisition, Winston clings to one small reason for pride: his love for Julia. Nothing, he thinks, can conquer that, even though he no longer knows whether she is alive or dead. But one of the techniques of the Thought Police is to find out what its victims are most terrified of. O'Brien knows that Winston cannot bear the thought of rodents. A large cage of ravenous rats is placed right next to him, and O'Brien threatens to open the door. In a moment of unreasoning panic, Winston begs him to set the rats on Julia instead; then he knows that he has nothing left worth living for.

After this great betrayal, Winston is set free. He is a shambles, physically, mentally, and spiritually. His teeth have been knocked out, his hair is gone. He is not considered worth vaporizing and is given a very minor job that leaves him plenty of time to sit in a café, alone and despised, drinking

Victory gin. One day he sees Julia who is equally beaten and dulled by her ordeal. The two have nothing to say to one another after they confess that both had betrayed their love.

One day Winston hears over the telescreen that Oceania has won a great victory in Africa. Formerly Winston would have been skeptical but now he believes it. The brainwashing and shock treatments have succeeded. In the depths of his soul, Winston knows he truly loves Big Brother.

Critical Opinion

Like Huxley's *Brave New World, 1984* is a reverse utopia— a vision of the future as nightmare rather than paradise. Significantly, when Huxley wrote his book he cast his utopia six hundred years into the future. Orwell, writing seventeen years after Huxley, saw the dangers of brainwashing, rigid social control, and political bestiality as far more imminent, and placed his nightmare state only thirty-five years into the future.

Another difference between these superficially similar books is that while Huxley concentrates on scientific "advances," Orwell is preoccupied with politics. The ideals of Huxley's state are "Community, Identity, Stability." These are taken for granted in *1984* but are made far more sinister by political absolutism. The slogans of Orwell's state are "War is Peace," "Freedom is Slavery" and "Ignorance is Strength." Huxley's world of the future is unconcerned with war; the dreariness of social predestination and of scientific gadgetry and material- ism are the greatest plagues of his Brave New World. His tone, too, is wittily satiric. Orwell's is grim and bitter.

Much of the difference between these two twentieth-cen- tury visions of the future can be explained by the events be- tween 1932, the date of Huxley's book, and 1949, the date of Orwell's. These seventeen years saw the Moscow purge trials, the Spanish Civil War, the rise of the dictators, the universal holocaust of World War II with its genocide, its promis- cuous slaughter of soldiers and civilians alike, and the be- ginning of the cold war. Thus, life in Oceania is not merely drab and joyless; it is truly terrifying.

Primarily an essayist and polemicist, Orwell succeeds best

in *1984* when he is describing the mechanisms and techniques of the police state. His coinages "thoughtcrime," "newspeak," "Big Brother" and "doublethink" have become part of the English language. They are based on his keen perception and analysis of tendencies existing in his own time, not merely in Nazi Germany and Soviet Russia but, in a milder if no less insidious form, in the nations of the "free world." This book is both a prophecy and a warning of what life might be if individuals allow themselves to be coerced into conformity by the state.

The Author

George Orwell's real name was Eric Blair. Born in India in 1903, he became a poor "scholarship boy" in a snobbish, ill-run English prep school. The horrors of his schooldays live in a bitter essay, "Such, Such Were the Joys." He did, however, win a scholarship to Eton.

Unwilling to face university life and further snobbery, Orwell went to Burma in 1921, where he spent five years as a policeman and wrote his first novel, *Burmese Days*. Disgusted by his first-hand glimpse of imperialism, Orwell quit and lived in Paris and London, subsisting on infrequent, squalid jobs in restaurant kitchens. His experiences led him to the writing of his first great book, *Down and Out in Paris and London* (1933).

From then on Orwell struggled to earn a living as a journalist and author. He became involved in various left-wing causes during the depression but always remained suspicious of any political doctrine when it violated the basic human rights of the individual. Political idealism led him to fight on the Loyalist side in the Spanish Civil War, in which he was wounded. Returning to England, he wrote *Homage to Catalonia*, an impassioned attack on the betrayal of the Spanish Loyalists by the Communists. Orwell's blistering contempt for the police states he saw growing in Spain, Italy, Germany, and Russia, combined with his warnings to England of the coming conflict between democracy and totalitarianism, appeared in his many masterful essays, which were disregarded or attacked by Left and Right alike.

Although he had always suffered from weak lungs, Orwell

exposed himself during World War II to exhaustion and privation, serving as an air-raid warden when he was rejected by the army. A mortally ill man by the end of the war, he wrote his two masterpieces, *Animal Farm* (1945) and *1984*, before his death on January 23, 1950. Ironically, his only real popular success came after his death with *1984* which has remained his most widely read book.

By the Same Author

Animal Farm: Animal Farm is a brilliant fable of the success, betrayal, and ultimate failure of the Russian Revolution. Under the brutal regime of Farmer Jones, the animals are miserable. They revolt, rout Jones from his farm, and try to run things themselves. Soon, however, a new hierarchy emerges, with the cunning, selfish pigs lording it over the more docile and less assertive animals. The high ideals of animal equality and sovereignty proclaimed at the beginning of the revolution are quietly dropped. Under the oppressive rule of the scheming, power-hungry pig Napoleon, the lot of the other animals becomes as wretched as it had been under Farmer Jones. Although it is less exhaustive a treatment of totalitarianism than *1984*, *Animal Farm* is a brief, pungent tour de force in the very difficult, rarely explored genre of the political fable.

Lord of the Flies

by

WILLIAM GOLDING (1911–)

Main Characters

Ralph—The sensible, good-natured leader of the stranded boys.

Piggy—Ralph's fat, intelligent, asthmatic, and bespectacled sidekick.

Jack Merridew—Leader of the choir boys, carrot-haired and given to violent emotion.

Simon—A short boy, quiet and imaginative.

"Samneric"—The inseparable twins, Sam and Eric.

The Story

While being evacuated from an atomic war, a group of school-boys aged six through twelve are ejected from their doomed plane and land on an uninhabited island somewhere in the Pacific. The first two to make contact are Ralph, a handsome, good-natured lad, and Piggy, fat and lower class, who has always been the butt of schoolboy jokes. Piggy can barely see without his glasses, and he suffers from asthmatic attacks brought on by any exertion.

Together the boys find a large, beautiful conch shell in a lagoon, and Ralph learns to blow on it. He is sure that eventually his father, a commander in the Royal Navy, will rescue them, but first he will call a meeting of all the other boys stranded on the island, using the blast of the conch to summon them. Piggy begs Ralph not to let the other boys know his humiliating name.

The trumpeting of the conch brings the scattered boys together at a central meeting place. Among them is a group of choir boys led by Jack Merridew. They are still perspiring fiercely under their heavy black cassocks. The meeting is called to order, while the frightened younger boys, called "littluns," whimper for their parents. Ralph tells the group that apparently there are no grownups on the island, but if they organize their little society well they will surely be rescued soon. To Jack's dismay, Ralph is elected chief. Jack, as choir leader, fancies that position for himself. But Ralph has the conch shell, symbol of authority and leadership.

The boys' first action is to send a scouting party, including Ralph, Jack, and a small but intelligent boy, Simon, to explore the island. Piggy wants to go along, but he is rudely rejected by Jack after Ralph inadvertently gives away his name. Once again the unhappy Piggy is made the butt of all jokes; even the littluns laugh at him.

As Ralph, Jack, and Simon explore the island that first day, their spirits are high. Fruit grows in abundance, there are many glorious swimming places, and, above all, there are no adults to tell the boys what to do. They skip exuberantly around the island, locating a huge mountain at one end and a fortress-like rock formation which they call Castle Rock at the other. Returning to report their findings, the three youths are pleased with themselves and with their adventure.

Ralph calls another meeting to decide what to do until they are rescued. The boys agree that whoever holds the conch may speak while the others must listen. All is very democratic and parliamentary. Ralph decides that the most important thing to do is keep a smoky fire going on the mountain top so that any ship passing can spot and rescue them. Before he can outline his other plans, the boys chase off to light their fire. Their only difficulty is that they have no matches. Ralph has an idea: use Piggy's glasses to concentrate the sun's rays and thus get the fire started. This works well. But soon the whole top of the mountain is ablaze, and one of the littluns disappears, presumably burned to death.

This disaster convinces Ralph that, if the boys are to survive until they are rescued, law and order must prevail. He finds it difficult, however, to keep the boys' attention concentrated on any one project. They wander off to swim or eat fruit. Only Simon and the twins, Sam and Eric, called Samneric because they are always together, help Ralph build necessary shelters. Piggy, because of his asthma, which the boys cruelly call "ass-mar," cannot do manual work, but as he is the most intelligent boy on the island, he makes invaluable suggestions.

The boys suffer at night from bad dreams because some of the littluns claim they have spotted what they call a "beastie," a hideous, snake-like monster, somewhere on the island. At first the older boys laugh at this story, but at night everyone is rather frightened, and the littluns cling together for protection.

Soon Jack, chafing at his subordinate position under the elected leader, Ralph, decides to organize his choir boys as hunters. He is tired of the steady fruit diet and of the unglamorous labors of building shelters and tending the fire. Jack has noticed there are wild pigs on the island, and determines to kill some for food. Camouflaging his face with black and red streaks of clay until he looks like a savage, he becomes an adept and ruthless hunter.

During his first successful hunt, however, Jack allows his choir boys to neglect the fire they were supposed to tend. Ralph sees a ship on the horizon, but looking up to the mountain, sees no smoke to signal it. Furious, he confronts Jack with his negligence, but Jack laughs it off, saying that if the boys want to eat meat he needs all the hunters he can get. He hints that Ralph is concerned with such mundane things as shelters and fires because he is useless as a hunter.

Ralph calls a special evening meeting to lecture the boys about their various lapses from discipline. It is obvious, he tells them, that the most important thing they can do is to keep the smoky fire lit or else they will never be rescued. They must also build sturdy shelters against the rainy season. But by now Jack is obsessed with his hunting—he has tasted blood and wants more of it. He despises the peaceable, practical Ralph and his hopelessly fat and inactive friend, Piggy. He tries to wrest the leadership from Ralph, but the other boys are too cowed and apathetic to change. Furious and frustrated, Jack leaves the meeting with his loyal band of hunters in tow.

Meanwhile the boys are still terrified of the "beastie" on the island. During a temporary truce, Jack and Ralph join forces to investigate. First they go to Castle Rock, the only unexplored part of the island, where Jack wants to remain and build a fortress. Eventually they get back to the mountain, however, where they see a hideous, ape-like creature suspended, as if asleep, in the trees. Terrified, they return to the other boys, who decide that they can no longer use the mountain for their fire but will have to be content with a less visible fire on the shore.

Jack and his hunters, who are now staying at Castle Rock, kill a huge sow while it is nursing its piglets and cut off its head to place on a pole as an offering to the monster. But Simon, by now terrified by the proceedings on the island, investigates and sees what the monster really is. A flier whose plane was apparently downed off the island had parachuted to his death. His parachute was caught in the treetops. The monster is his decayed, hideous body, still caught in the parachute and waving back and forth in the wind.

When Simon runs to tell the other boys what he has discovered, they are celebrating their latest kill with a wild, savage dance. By now their hair has grown long, they are filthy with war paint, and they are no longer interested in listening to Ralph. When they see Simon, they all leap on him as if he were a sacrificial pig and kill him.

Morose and disillusioned at what has happened to his little civilization, Ralph is left with only the twins and Piggy whose glasses have meanwhile been broken. They are too few to keep the fire lit. One night a band of marauders from Castle Rock descends on them and, in the melee, makes off with Piggy's broken glasses to light their own fire.

Ralph goes to plead with Jack to return the glasses to Piggy, promising him that he can borrow flame for his hunters to cook pig with any time he wants. But Jack answers him contemptuously from the fortress he has built. Roger, one of the boys who has gone over to Jack's side, catapults a huge boulder at Piggy, sending the unfortunate boy careening to his death in the sea below. Sam and Eric, the twins, are forcibly brought over to Jack's side. Now Ralph is all alone. He is told by the twins that Jack intends to kill him, and he flees for safety. He is pursued all over the island by the hunters who even set fire to the island in order to smoke him out.

Ironically, this smoke attracts a passing vessel, and, just as Ralph thinks he is going to be murdered by the other boys, the whole group is rescued by an English cruiser. When the sailors land, they are appalled to find that good English school-boys have become the savages now infesting the island. The boys are rescued, however, and "in the middle of them, with filthy body, matted hair, and unwiped nose, Ralph wept for the end of innocence, the darkness of man's heart, and the fall through the air of the true, wise friend called Piggy."

Critical Opinion

The theme of *Lord of the Flies*, according to Golding, "is an attempt to trace the defects of society back to the defects of human nature. The moral is that the shape of a society must depend on the ethical nature of the individual and not on any political system however apparently logical or respectable."

Rejecting as unreal and sentimental the myth of the "noble savage," Golding shows how the removal of civilized restraints results not in the creation of a more innocent, healthier society, but in a complete regression to savagery and brutality, the seeds of which are lodged deep in every human heart.

In a sense, then, *Lord of the Flies* is a parable much like *Heart of Darkness* (the last lines of the novel even paraphrase Conrad's title), in which the boys who, somewhat like Kurtz, start off with high hopes of creating their own utopian society free from all adult restrictions, gradually become murderous brutes, rescued from themselves just in the nick of time.

But the rescue is ambivalent and ironic. The men who take the boys off the island are sailors whose own cruiser is com-mitted to murder and destruction during an unnamed atomic war, and, as Golding notes, "Who will rescue the adult and his cruiser?" This pessimism about the adult world is fore-shadowed when Ralph cries, earlier in the book, "If only they could get a message to us. If only they could send us some-thing grown-up . . . a sign or something." What "they," the adults, send is the hideous, decaying corpse of a parachutist. The adult world, then, is no better, only more sophisticated in its savagery, than the world the boys have built on the island.

"Lord of the Flies" is a translation of the Hebrew word,

Ba'alzevuv (Beelzebub in Greek), a name for the devil, who is ultimately the central figure in the novel. When Jack's hunters slay the harmless sow and cut her head off as propitiation to the "beastie," the head, decaying on a stake in the hot sun, seems to tell Simon that "everything was a bad business." But when Simon tries to communicate this idea, he is murdered in a savage ritual dance.

Lord of the Flies is thus a parable, like one of the first English novels, *The Pilgrim's Progress.* The intervening centuries, however, have changed the religious message from hope for salvation to fear of damnation and knowledge of original sin.

The Author

William Golding, one of the most challenging British novelists to emerge since World War II, was born in Cornwall in 1911, descended from a long line of schoolmasters. Destined to be a scientist, he changed his course after two years at Oxford and studied English literature instead, specializing in Anglo-Saxon poetry. He published a book of poems in 1934 and wrote three unpublished novels.

Appropriately enough for the author of a book about the savagery inherent in boys, Golding earned his living as a schoolmaster and was not very happy in that profession. The outbreak of World War II was a turning point in his career. Golding joined the Royal Navy, and, except for six months in New York on special assignment under Lord Cherwell, he saw active duty throughout the war, ending as a lieutenant in command of a rocket craft on D day. "The war produced one notable effect on me," Golding is quoted as having said. "It scared me stiff."

It did that in more ways than one. "It was the turning point for me," Golding has commented. "I began to see what people were capable of doing. Where did the Second World War come from? Was it made by something inhuman and alien—or was it made by chaps with eyes and legs and hearts?"

The vision of evil inherent in the human heart that Golding found in the war was the basis of his first published novel, *Lord of the Flies.* Its publication in 1954 was hailed by discerning critics on both sides of the Atlantic, but its first American edition sold only 2500 copies. It was not until 1959, when it was published in paperback, that the novel became immensely popular, especially among high school and college students.

In 1955 Golding published *The Inheritors,* a strange tale about man's ancestors on earth, the peaceful "people" who were ruthlessly supplanted by *homo sapiens.* This was followed in 1956 by *Pincher Martin* and in 1959 by *Free Fall.* Golding's most recent novel, *The Spire* (1964), is again about guilt and redemption, a story of the building of a mighty but flawed English cathedral during the Middle Ages.

Scraggly-bearded and shy, Golding is married and has two children. In view of his bleak vision of children in *Lord of the Flies,* he has said, "I try to treat my family with affection and I suppose if that added up all around, we might have a better society." Recently Golding taught for a year at Hollins College in Virginia. He lists his favorite occupations as music, sailing, chess, archaeology—and thinking.

By the Same Author

Pincher Martin: When Christopher Martin is blown off his ship by a submarine attack in mid-Atlantic, he manages to make his way to a jutting rock where he tries by all rational means to survive. But he is constantly plagued by guilt for his past sins. He has always been a "pincher," a stealer of everything, including love. He loses his battle for physical and spiritual salvation. Eventually his body is washed ashore where a naval officer notices from the condition of the corpse that Martin could not have suffered for long. We are given to understand that the self-questionings and desperate struggle for survival in the novel occurred in only a split second in Martin's mind.

Free Fall: Less of a parable than Golding's other novels, *Free Fall* describes in realistic terms the rise from the slums of Sammy Mountjoy, an egocentric artist obsessed with desire for Beatrice, the model for his only successful picture. In his relentless pursuit of Beatrice, he loses his own freedom of action, ultimately deserts her, and sends her to an insane asylum, where the doctor tells him he may or may not have been immediately responsible for plunging her into incurable madness. The degree of his guilt is something he will have to decide in his own Faustian soul.

Appendix

50 British Novels, arranged by date of publication

The Pilgrim's Progress 1678
Robinson Crusoe 1719
Gulliver's Travels 1726
Tom Jones 1749
The Vicar of Wakefield 1766
Tristram Shandy 1767
Humphry Clinker 1771
Pride and Prejudice 1813
Ivanhoe 1819
The Last Days of Pompeii 1834
The Pickwick Papers 1836
David Copperfield 1850
A Tale of Two Cities 1859
Great Expectations 1861
Jane Eyre 1847
Wuthering Heights 1848
Vanity Fair 1848
Barchester Towers 1857
Adam Bede 1859
The Ordeal of Richard Feverel 1859
Alice in Wonderland 1865
Erewhon 1872
The Way of All Flesh 1903
The Return of the Native 1878
The Mayor of Casterbridge 1886
Jude the Obscure 1896
Treasure Island 1883
The Picture of Dorian Gray 1891
The Time Machine 1895
Tono-Bungay 1909
Lord Jim 1900
Kim 1901
Heart of Darkness 1902
Green Mansions 1904

The Man of Property   1906
The Old Wives' Tale   1908
The Crock of Gold   1912
Sons and Lovers   1913
Of Human Bondage   1915
A Portrait of the Artist as a Young Man   1916
South Wind   1916
A Passage to India   1924
Mrs. Dalloway   1925
Point Counter Point   1928
Brave New World   1932
Decline and Fall   1928
Lost Horizon   1933
The Power and the Glory   1940
1984   1949
Lord of the Flies   1954

Bibliography

1. Allen, Walter. *The English Novel: A Short Critical History.* New York: E.P. Dutton & Co., 1955.
2. Church, Richard. *The Growth of the English Novel.* New York: Barnes & Noble, 1961.
3. Drew, Elizabeth. *The Novel: A Modern Guide to Fifteen English Masterpieces.* New York: Dell Publishing Co., 1963.
4. Forster, E.M. *Aspects of the Novel.* New York: Harvest Books, Harcourt, Brace & World, 1956.
5. Kettle, Arnold. *An Introduction to the English Novel.* 2 vols. New York: Torchbooks, Harper & Row, 1961.
6. Lubbock, Percy. *The Craft of Fiction.* New York: Compass Books, The Viking Press, 1957.
7. Neill, S.D. *A Short History of the English Novel.* New York: The Macmillan Company, 1952.
8. Pritchett, V.S. *The Living Novel and Later Appreciations.* New York: Random House, 1964.
9. Schorer, Mark (ed.). *Modern British Fiction: Essays in Criticism.* New York: Oxford University Press, 1961.
10. Trilling, Lionel. *The Liberal Imagination.* New York: Anchor Books, Doubleday & Co., 1953.
11. Van Ghent, Dorothy. *The English Novel: Form and Function.* New York: Torchbooks, Harper & Row, 1961.
12. Wagenknecht, Edward. *Cavalcade of the English Novel.* New York: Holt, Rinehart and Winston, 1954.

Index